Yearbook 2025
Global Governance,
Compliance & Integrity

Bartosz Makowicz (ed.)

Global Governance, Compliance & Integrity

Yearbook 2025

Authors

Shujath Bin Ali, Kalapurakkal Suresh Aravind, Ruben Bahamonde, Meric Bloch, Jeanine Bretti Rainalter, Piotr Chmiel, Ana Lucia de Melo Custódio, Meriem Debbih, Antonio Giuseppe Di Pietro, Adam Domagała, Carlos Lelo Filipe, Susanne Friedrich, Maria Eugenia Gil, Marcela Greggo, Christian Hauser, Marc Herkenrath, Martin Hilti, Anna Hlebicka-Józefowicz, Eduard Ivanov, Bethany Jackson, Piotr Janecki, Nada Kakabadse, Andrew Kakabadse, Andrejs Klisans, Claus Köhler, Jeannine Lemker, Alexander Leonhardt, Mariola Lisewska, Bartosz Makowicz, Akif Mert, Christian Miege, Joan Meyer, Juan Gregorio Nazar de Boulin, Ana Cristina Perdomo Gomez, Alex Sander Pires, Anita Punwani, Matthew Ridings, Mickaël Roumegoux Rouvelle, Ramona Stampfli, Stanisław Zygmunt Strejmer, Simina Suciu, Andrew Samuels, Yasmine Sadek, Rajeev Thykatt, Anna Tomiczek, Pedro Trovão Do Rosário, Nicole Vossius, Nick John Weir, Patrick Wellens, Gniewomir Wycichowski-Kuchta

PETER LANG

Berlin · Bruxelles · Chennai · Lausanne · New York · Oxford

Bibliographic Information published by the Deutsche Nationalbibliothek
The Deutsche Nationalbibliothek lists this publication in the Deutsche Nationalbibliografie; detailed bibliographic data is available in the internet at http://dnb.d-nb.de.

Library of Congress Cataloging- in- Publication Control Number
LCCN: 2025016786

A CIP catalog record for this book has been applied for at the Library of Congress.

Cover Image © Bartosz Makowicz
Cover Design by Peter Lang Group AG

ISBN 978-3-631-93753-2 (Print)
ISBN 978-3-631-93798-3 (E-PDF)
ISBN 978-3-631-93799-0 (E-PUB)
DOI 10.3726/b22905

Published by Peter Lang GmbH, Berlin (Germany)
info@peterlang.com

www.peterlang.com

Contents

Preface

A lot has happened in the last two years (2023-2024), during which the articles for the 2025 edition of this Yearbook were submitted. After all, organizations, including in particular companies, are still facing significant challenges with regard to their governance and compliance, which can have a direct impact on the integrity of their members. As always, in this work that was initiated with the first volume in 2018, we are trying jointly with fifty authors from around the world, to cover these effects from different angles.

The organizations have not yet really recovered from the many changes brought about by the Covid-19 pandemic, so Russia's invasion of Ukraine, as well as some national aspirations and market conditions, have given a decisive impetus to the change in geo-politics and geo-economics relations. Naive would be those who think that these developments will not affect the governance and compliance of organizations. Equally naive are those who assume that the development of AI and digitization will bypass the previous governance and compliance models. Because the opposite is the case. All together fundamental changes started on various levels concerning governance and compliance.

This work covers several of these developments and we strive not only to show the challenges that lie ahead for organizations in terms of governance and compliance, but also the modern tools that can be used to effectively address them. This Yearbook starts with a chapter dealing with various governance developments enclosed in the ESG concept, closely followed by the second chapter, which looks at trends in Compliance Management.

Chapter three focuses on latest trends and tools in the area of Integrity and Ethics and chapter four delivers a great update on AI Compliance and Financial Compliance. In chapter fife we focus, again, on still challenging anti-corruption to touch upon sustainability, supply chain compliance and sanctions in chapter six. In the closing chapter seven we present you some modern insights on whistleblowing and internal investigations.

It is both a pleasure and an honor for me that we have been able to continue publishing this Yearbook despite all the turbulence. Nevertheless, as changes in the area of governance and compliance are taking place rapidly and the integrated approach is increasingly coming to the fore, the title of the yearbook will be changed from "Ethics, Compliance & Integrity" to "Governance, Compliance & Integrity" starting with this issue.

At this point, I would like to express my sincere thanks to everyone who has contributed to the creation of this book. These include but is not limited the highly effective Teams at the Viadrina Compliance Centers and at Peter Lang Publishing House, as well as the KBA NotaSys Fund, which is kindly supporting this publication for the last time. Above all, however, I would like to thank to the numerous world-leading expert authors of this edition, whose excellent expertise and knowledge are the reason for what you hold in your hands today. Thank you very much for your efforts!

I wish you happy and fruitful reading!

Berlin, February 2025 *Prof. Dr. Bartosz Makowicz*

Introduction: Integrated Governance & Compliance Approach – This is the Way Forward!

Bartosz Makowicz

There is hardly a management area that has developed as dynamically in recent years as compliance management, an area which is related strictly to organizational governance. On the one hand, the regulatory activities are constantly increasing, which resulted in more and more tasks being assigned to the compliance departments, such as new due diligence obligations in the supply chain or the implementation of ESG obligations. This is associated with increased management and governance effort for companies. On the other hand, there are hardly any binding guidelines on how the various new regulations are to be implemented by companies and how should they ensure compliance with them. Developments have been taking place at several levels simultaneously, in an uncoordinated manner and in various directions. In this article, an attempt is made to briefly outline the development of compliance with its relations to governance to date and to show why it makes sense to continue with an Integrated Approach.

1. The Starting Point

The development of compliance is quite straightforward from the perspective of organizations. First there were some regal regulations and the expectation of the legislator and society that organizations, which make up a fundamental part of social systems, would comply to these rules laid down by the legislator. If we go further, this expectation is a result of democracy, as the regulations mentioned are ultimately set by our representatives in the democratically elected constitutional bodies (e.g. national parliaments). However, this legal-political postulate of compliance to rules on the one hand clashes with the principle of neoliberal economics pursued in most countries on the other. According to this principle, companies should be free to decide how they achieve this postulate, i.e. how they organize their internal procedures, processes and structures. This results in two defining concepts: following the rules and regulations, which is nowadays understood as "compliance", and the implementation of this activity with the means of well thought-out procedures and structures, which is nowadays described as a compliance management system (CMS for short). A similar vacuum of organizational guidelines exists also with regard to the higher organizational level (more on this in a moment), namely governance, which is about the purpose, accountability and control of organizations.

This mixed situation must be clearly understood in order to have a clear view of the development trends in governance and compliance. To date, hardly any legislator has dared to provide companies with clear statutory rules as to which CMS model should be pursued or even which specific measures should be implemented within such a system. On the other hand, as the many advantages of CMS have been recognized both by companies and the legislator, various incentives have been put in place to motivate companies to introduce a CMS. As a rule, these take the form of sanction discounts or exemption from liability within the framework of so-called compliance defense.

The wide scope that still existed in the area of organizational governance and compliance management meant that companies took the initiative themselves and implemented structures and processes as required, usually in response to compliance cases that had occurred and in relation to a specific risk (reactive), such as corruption, in order to get a better grip on these specific risks. In addition, there were the challenges of several developments taking place at the same time and finding their way to the national and global level in a highly uncoordinated manner.

2. Heterogeneous Design of CMS

As a result of these developments, governance and CMS structures vary from country to country, from culture to culture. What's more, they sometimes vary within a single country, depending on the sector or industry in which the companies concerned operate.

This starts with the basic orientation and primary function of a CMS: for some companies, a CMS should only have a preventive effect, i.e. prevent possible violations from within the company (preventive function). For other companies the focus should be on the repressive effect, i.e. detecting non-compliance cases as early as possible and clarifying them by means of internal investigations (restrictive function). In turn, there are other companies in which both functions should have a cumulative effect (mixed function).

The ideas about which management models should be pursued in order to achieve the aforementioned objectives also differ widely in some cases, mainly when it comes to the focus of these systems. For example, some companies pursue the so-called prevent-detect-react approach, which covers both preventive and repressive functions, but where the focus is on potential non-compliance case; the aim is to prevent them as far as possible and, once they have occurred, to detect them and react adequately. Some focus on the CMS as a management system and pursue the so-called PDCA (Plan, Do, Check, Act) approach for its continuous improvement. According to this approach, systems and the measures taken within their framework are first planned, then implemented, evaluated and, if necessary, improved, which should not only lead to an increase in effectiveness, but also to a reduction in costs, i.e. efficiency. The latest trends, on the other hand, focus on people and the question associated with their undesirable behavior as to why people are inclined to break rules under certain circumstances and what measures can be taken to prevent this. These efforts are usually described using the Integrity Approach,[1] which is justified by the fact that the focus should not be on processes and potential non-compliance cases, but on the individuals who could be accountable for these non-compliance. In some cases the Integrity Approach is described even as Behavioral Compliance, where some methods from behavioral science are being adopted.[2]

The differences become even more visible when comparing various CMS from the perspective of compliance risks. For example, there are still companies for which compliance is synonymous with anti-corruption and a CMS is limited to developing guidelines for accepting invitations or gifts and organizing training on this. Some go further and add competition rules. Most, on the other hand, do not want to see areas such as tax or export risks alocated in the compliance department at all. Many companies implement parallel management systems with identical tools that are used to assess different compliance risks, thereby driving themselves into an invisible and highly counterproductive bureaucratic madness. It results in the existence of several stand-alone management systems having in focus different compliance risks.

3. Fragmentary Reaction of the Legislators

As if the heterogeneity of CMS models that already exists in the companies were not enough reasons for confusion, legislators in many countries have put it even on higher level in recent years. A defragmented picture is emerging, in which one thing at least is visible: The partial break with the previous status quo, which was characterized by the aforementioned relationship between democracy and the neoliberal economy and in which it were companies to decide on the shape of its one Governance and Compliance Management. This break can be observed, at least from the European perspective, on two levels: the national level and that of the European Union.

3.1 National Level

With a few exceptions (such as the German Supply Chain Due Diligence Act, DE-SCDDA for short),[3] legislators at national level are hesitant when it comes to regulating CMS, sometimes taking isolated measures and sometimes appearing to have no plan at all.

A certain direction, however, can be seen in the laws on corruption prevention in the USA (the Foreign Corrupt Practices Act, FCPA for short)[4] and in the UK with the UK Bribery ACT (UKBA for short),[5] as both laws are applicable extraterritorially (more on this below). However, the weak points of both are, first, that they have become completely detached from the reality of CMS and are limited to just one compliance risk (and thus encourage companies not to pursue the Integrative Approach). Secondly, as far as the specific guidance on the design of CMS is concerned, both laws exhaust themselves in a brief comment that these should be "adequate procedures".

In doing so, they actually only bring the aforementioned discretion of companies to the point (with limitations however, see below). In Europe, there have been isolated attempts in some countries, such as the so-called SAPIN II[6] in France or the failed attempt at central regulation with the so-called Association Sanctions Act in Germany.[7] However, these laws or their drafts also followed the US American and British restrictive models.

3.2 European Union Level

The Member States of the European Union (EU), or rather their legislative bodies, are chronically resistant to regulating the remarkably advanced development of CMS. In view of this, it is no wonder that the EU legislator has taken the initiative where it can only do so on the basis of the principle of limited competencies. Since then, more and more areas of compliance have been regulated either by regulation (e.g. General Data Protection Regulation)[8] or directive (e.g. protection of whistleblowers).[9] In addition to the examples mentioned above, there are now a number of entire compliance areas in which the EU has adopted comprehensive regulations, from regularly updated Anti-Money-Laundering (AML) packages[10] to an area that the EU was reluctant to tackle for a long time, namely the prevention of corruption. A directive is also planned here.[11]

It should be noted that EU legal acts do not always achieve a sufficiently harmonizing effect. Although this does not apply to regulations, which are directly legally binding in all member states and in all their parts, the harmonization effects fails partially in the case of directives, which are only binding for the Member States and only with regard to the objectives specified therein. They first have to be transposed into national law, and Member States sometimes have considerable free discretion for implementation. This became very clear, for example, with the directive on the protection of whistleblowers, which was implemented differently regarding several regulations by Member States, with the result that not only the level of protection of the whistleblowers in the Member States differs,[12] but also the requirements for whistleblowing systems, which makes day-to-day life more difficult for companies that are active in more than one country of the European Common Market at the same time.

3.3 Mixed Situation

But the situation is becoming even more complex. The area of supply chain compliance has strikingly demonstrated how uncoordinated and, as a result, harmful it is only for the users, i.e. the companies implementing it. Apart from the fundamental dogmatic questions of whether the protection of human rights within the supply chains can be the accountability of companies (and not states) and whether they are actually in a position to increase human rights standards in the countries of origin, the EU has long had its sights set on legally obliging companies in this area. This should send a signal that something is being done to prevent the global North from enriching itself from the deplorable working conditions, including child labor, in the global South. A regulation of due diligence in supply chains was firmly programmed into the implementation of the European Green Deal[13] and work on the corresponding regulation (Corporate Social Due Diligence Directive, CSDDD for short) was well advanced when, at the same time, the German legislator decided to enact a similar law at national level as the so-called German Supply Chain Due Diligence Act, which has since come into force bevore the EU directive was enacted. Ultimately, the mixed situation led to such a chaotic implementation that not only the BAFA, authority responsible in Germany for supervision of companies in regards to supply chains, had doubts about the validity of the deadlines,[14] but some politicians surprisingly even called for the law to be "suspended".[15]

3.4 Game Changer in CMS Regulation

Leaving aside the uncoordinated action and its serious consequences, it remains to be said that the EU Member States have been presented with at least two European regulations that can be described as the Game Changer in the area of so far restriced CMS regulation. Whether this was a calculation by the European Commission or a coincidental side effect remains to be seen. In both cases, we are talking about the aforementioned Whistleblower Protection Directive and the CSDDD, the latter has yet to be implemented in the Member States.

Both acts are representative of the fact that EU legislator have now shown the courage to implement a paradigm shift in the development of compliance and governance regulation. In both cases, not only are certain duties to act set out as postulates and companies are called upon to implement them accordingly on the basis of their previously so highly praised entrepreneurial discretion. No. This time, the laws specify in astonishing detail how a management system in regards to the protection of whistleblowers should be designed in the first case and how a risk management system focusing on the protection of human rights and the environment with all its facets should be designed in the company in the case of the CSDDD. Goodbye neoliberalism? A taboo has been broken and the relationship of the legislator to the establishment of rules (compliance) on the one hand and rules for their practical implementation (CMS) on the other, as discussed here in the introduction, has demonstrably gone off the rails. But this time, too, it is only fragmentary and not really well thought out. However, it might be the beginning of something.

But the bottom line is that the EU's efforts are positive and the trend is to be welcomed. The fact that harmonization cannot always be achieved perfectly (the aforementioned example of a directive as an instrument for action) must be seen in the EU's weak constellation, which is still programmed in, and which the EU Member States should quickly abandon in favor of a centrally strengthened structure if they still want to play a role in the newly forming geopolitical and geo-economic relationships. This can only succeed if a single voice is spoken and this must be reflected in uniform regulations.

4. Attempts at Harmonization (Incentive Models)

The brief analysis above showed how important it is to consider national, EU and geopolitical trends for the development of compliance. While the focus so far has been on the development of compliance and CMS and the position of legislators in this regard, we are moving now the question who and what efforts have been made to harmonize the design of CMS among various companies. However, as most countries in the world lack a cross-industry legal obligation for companies to introduce CMS, it can be difficult for national legislators to specify the details of such systems in a legal act. A different idea has therefore been proposed, which could be described as harmonization through loopholes and which is directly linked to the incentive models mentioned earlier.

4.1 Hard Coded Incentive Models with Soft Coded Guidelines

The constellation works quite simply and could be described as bypassing democratic legislative processes (more on this later). Good examples of this are the FCPA and UKBA, which have already been mentioned in another context. These provide that in the event of a non-compliance, the amount of sanctions can be reduced if the company has introduced "adequate procedures" to prevent such a case. However, the law continues to search in vain for what is to be understood as "adequate" and what is not, in other words, how a CMS aimed at preventing corruption should be designed. In order not to leave companies completely mired in legal uncertainty, the relevant authorities / ministries, i.e. parts of the executive power, have become active and issued guidelines to close the intended legislative gap.[16] In this way, executive bodies are taking the place of not only the companies themselves at a not insignificant point - after all, it is about the internal organization of companies - and are thus calling into question the neoliberal approach mentioned at the beginning, but also the legislators, who, as representatives of the citizens, would be called upon to issue such regulations, if that is what is wanted by them. After all, such guidelines have a de facto binding effect. One could come up with the idea of not following the guidelines because they are not binding, but if it is later checked whether the CMS was "adequate" (in order to claim it as a sanction-reducing measure), a company would be badly advised not to comply with them. One can even go further and say that their non-compliance is sanctioned since then the sanction is higher. The term "harmonization through a bypass" or soft regulation should now become clearer.

4.2 Incentives Without any Guidelines

But even apart from this side effect, there are some countries, such as Germany, where the situation with regard to compliance incentives is even worse from the company's point of view. Let's take Germany as an example. The incentive model is now firmly recognized in Germany. Not least, even the Federal Cartel Office (FCO) joined the same ranks and confirmed the incentive model in contrast to its previous position, which it had insisted on for years. It argued that if a non-compliance occurred despite the existence of a CMS, then the company should be sanctioned even more severely as the system was clearly not working. In the meantime, the FCO has moved away from this conviction and rewards a CMS itself.[17] The incentive model has also now been confirmed by the Federal Supreme Court.[18] However, unlike in the USA and the UK, there is a lack of generally recognized guidance in Germany on what an adequate system or what a country-specific CMS known as "suitable precautions" (ger. *geeignete Vorkehrungen*) should look like in practice, leaving companies completely mired in legal uncertainty.

As the situation is similar in many other countries, it will be interesting to see in the coming years to what extent the legal requirements for a CMS already introduced in Germany with the GE-CSDD, which have found their home in national laws in other countries with the implementation of the CSDDD, will have a spillover effect on other legal areas where "adeuqate procedures" are demanded. Although these detailed recommendations on CMS relate to the supply chain sector, most countries maintain the generally applicable principle of uniformity of the legal system, which means that once legal requirements have been made in relation to one area, they could have an impact on other areas of law if similar requirements are made there. This should at least be taken into considerations when interpreting the laws. There are detailed regulations relating to compliance risk assessment, a code of conduct, whistleblower protection systems and much more; all measures that are also de facto used in the area of anti-trust compliance, anti-corruption compliance etc., but are not legally foreseen.

4.3 Global Impact of the Incentive Models (Compliance Monitors)

It remains to be seen whether the side effect of this quasi-harmonization through incentive models at the global level was intentional or coincidental. To a certain extent, however, it has taken place via the extraterritorial application of the laws (especially the FCPA) and partly via the so-called compliance monitors, which will be discussed briefly. Several European companies have been involved in various non-compliance cases in the USA, with the result that the so-called monitor was imposed as a form of sanction. In Germany, this applies, among others, to the two biggest economic scandals to date, which have also contributed significantly to the development of compliance in the country, which are the Siemens scandal relating to corruption and, more recently, the so-called diesel gate with Volkswagen in the leading role. Both companies had the deal with a very costly US compliance monitor. Such a monitor can be described as an educational measure for compliance purposes, obliging companies to introduce certain optimization measures in relation to the existing or to be implemented CMS – under supervision of external experts. As the sanctions originate from the USA and their implementation is overseen by US compliance experts, they are naturally shaped by the understanding that is widespread there (and based on the aforementioned guidelines). The USA thus created its new export product and contributed in its own way to the global but one-sided and imposed harmonization of compliance development.[19]

4.4 Hard Codification as an Alternative?

Hypothetically spoken, would it have been better to take the route of a hard codification of CMS requirements from the very beginning? One could argue, which is a very valid argument, that CMS must be adapted to the specific risk portfolio of the respective company in order to be effective, so a hard codification of CMS requirements is at odds with this fundamental principle of CMS design. However, the incentive model results to the same, because in order to benefit from the reduction in sanctions, the requirements set out in a guideline must be implemented. The same logic can be used to the argument that a hard codification would affect SMEs in particular. This is because even with incentive models, SMEs have to implement the same guidelines as large companies.

Codification would certainly have been cleaner in terms of legal doctrine, and the legislator would not even have had to go into as much detail as in the case of the over mentioned supply chain regulations. Overall requirements, which are already considered as the best practice of a CMS in all expert circles worldwide, would be sufficient. These could be made subject to the principle of adequacy in order to take account of the need for flexibility in CMS. The rest would be left to the practice - and the judiciary, of course, which now has to come up with completely new models and approaches without any statutory approach.

5. Standardization

The uncontrolled development of various CMS approaches in different companies, deviations in national legislation, the use of compliance incentives supplemented by guidelines and the confusion caused by fragmentary regulatory approaches on the one hand and the urgent need for global uniformity on the other created a book-like starting position for the "intervention" of the International Organization for Standardization (ISO). The advantage over all the approaches described above is that ISO standards are developed by practitioners for practitioners, i.e. they create very needs-oriented management tools that can be implemented flexibly and appropriately in different legislative environments thanks to their characteristics.

But here, too, the beginnings were difficult. ISO became successful through the publication of industry standards, but it only achieved its breakthrough in the field of management systems standards in the mid-1990s. The breakthrough was made with ISO 9001 Quality Management Systems, which set a global quality standard, completely bypassing national legislators and other international players. From today's perspective, with well over 1 million certifications, this can be stated without hesitation. Despite ISO's rather expansive standardization policy, however, the other management system standards were less successful due to various factors. Many ISO standards have not really been able to establish themselves to this day.

The start for standardization in the governance and compliance sector was neither easy, nor quick. In any case, it was the Australian Standards Institute that took the initiative that led to the first globally uniform CMS standard (ISO 19600, now replaced by ISO 37301). In the meantime, ISO has set up the Technical Committee 309 "Governance of Organizations",[20] which has published a number of standards at both the governance and management levels. These include the so-called "parent standards", such as ISO 37000 Governance of Organizations, with their respective plug-ins for measuring effectiveness, for example, or the aforementioned ISO 37301 Compliance Management Systems. A number of other plug-ins for specific compliance risks (e.g. ISO 37001 Anti-Bribery Management Systems) or specific tools (e.g. ISO 37002 Whistleblowing Management Systems) are gradually rounding off the standards portfolio. However, even in the area of standardization of governance and compliance management, the hoped-for global recognition has yet to materialize.

6. Interim Conclusions

Some interim conclusions can be drawn from the development described above. Firstly, the development has gone in different directions: On the one hand, the intensity of regulation regarding companies' due diligence obligations to be followed (compliance) is increasing rapidly in various areas. On the other hand, various legislators are demanding that companies implement them without, however, showing which structures and processes can be used to achieve this (CMS). Secondly, this has led to the implementation of various solutions and models. Thirdly, various players at national and international level have attempted to close these gaps and to harmonize different soultions through extraterritorial laws or incentive models and, last but not least, the ISO has also become active with various worldwide uniform standards.

The overall picture is not a good one. In the meantime, companies are moving forward, business partners are being screened, due diligence obligations are being implemented in supply chains and codes of conduct are being adapted. The internsity of regulation is not stopping growing, some legislators are only just warming up, if you look at the amount of EU regulations that have already been passed as part of the implementation of the Green Deal and what else is planned.[21] With regard to the implementation of regulations, i.e. the adoption of rules concerning the CMS, it is not foreseeable that more legal certainty will be provided at national, EU or global level, apart from the ISO standards. What should companies do now?

7. Integrated Approach

Although, as already mentioned, various approaches and models are being pursued in order to meet the fragmented requirements found in different areas, a certain trend is emerging in many companies,[22] for which quite good reasons can be given: Where possible, the merging of structures and processes, which overall can be described as an Integrated Approach (INTAP). If an organization goes for this approach, it makes sense to implement it using globally recognized tools, such as those found in the various ISO standards.

The development of concepts and measures to date, which has been driven by companies but has always been accompanied and shaped by compliance associations, research institutions, authorities and consultants, has provided the initial findings that can be reduced to a common denominator and implemented in the organizations in a uniform and, above all, integrated manner. In this respect, the development stage was also mature enough for the establishment of globally recognized ISO standards in order to bundle the globally prevailing know-how and thus develop universally applicable tools. ISO standards, which are revised at least every four years, also take account of the dynamic development of compliance. Furthermore, as is often misunderstood, they are not intended to replace national rules and regulations, but rather to support organizations with implementation tools.

Finally, ISO standards also take the Integrated Approach into account when it is noted that all so-called Management System Standards (MSS) are subject to the uniform superordinate structure, the so-called Harmonized Structure (HS for short). The standard's uniform structure therefore already suggests where there is certain potential for integration in terms of structures and processes.

7.1 Governance and Management

However, before going into the details of potential integration, the fundamental differences between governance and management are briefly explained, which is the basis for the implementation of the integrated approach.

Governance is the highest level of organizational leading and controlling and the accountability for it. Another crucial element of governance is the so-called organizational purpose and the way it is embedded in all processes and structures in order to build up the quality of the organization and have a clear view on its development. The governance level thus primarily concerns the leading level of the organizations, i.e., the persons or bodies who give the essential thrust to the organization, who shape its purpose and provide the framework for its achievement. In doing so, however, they are still setting something important: Namely, the behavior that may be followed by further staff. The tone from the top will therefore play an important role on the management level as well just to suggest the first possibility of interrelations (integration). Let us now descend hierarchically one level lower. At this level, we speak of management, which should certainly be closely and skillfully synchronized with governance on the one hand and among itself - with other management systems - on the other. Responsibilities can and are usually transferred to this executive level, while accountability usually remains with the leadership.

So how does governance differ from management? The question cannot be answered unequivocally. For sure, governance is one level higher than management, but for sure, the boundaries can often be barely visible. This will especially be the case if both systems are well integrated with each other. On the other hand, for reasons of accountability and responsibility alone, a clear formal distinction must always be made between them.

7.2 Integration Directions

If we take a clear theoretical look at where the lines between governance and management run and map this in the structure and processes of the organization as well as the distribution of corresponding responsibilities, we can use this as a basis for thinking about potential integration. In principle, it can run in two directions.

7.2.1 Vertical Integration

The first direction of integration is vertical, i.e. between governance and management systems. This involves meaningful and mindful integration between individual measures and elements of leading, controlling and being accountable for an organization on the one hand and their operational implementation on the other.

To explain this further, here are a few examples based on the four fundamental elements of governance: Purpose, Leadership, Risk and Control. The purpose of the organization is the reason for its existence. The organization's strategy should be derived from its purpose, which should be carefully embedded in all subsequent structures and processes, including at management level. In the modern sense, the purpose of an organization should not be only focused on making profit, but should take into account the modern principles of sustainable social and environmental development, inclusion of stakeholders and diversity just to mention few. The second element is the leading of the organization and the corresponding accountability, sustainable and responsible leadership, from which the so-called tone from the top emanates, which radiates into all other areas of management. The third element is the risk approach, which is the operational heart of every organization, beating in the middle between governance and management systems. There is hardly a management system without the risk approach at its center, assessing not only the risks but also the opportunities. This is where immense vertical and horizontal integration potential arise. After all, governance also means appropriate control of organizations. This should be precisely designed within the framework of governance and implemented as part of various measures at management level, including reviews, internal control, auditing and ongoing evaluation.

7.2.2 Horizontal Integration

With horizontal integration, a further distinction must be made as to whether one management system is merged with another (e.g. environmental management and quality management) or whether various functions are fulfilled within one management system (e.g. fulfillment of tax and data protection obligations as part of an integrated CMS). Let's touch upon these two cases.

Horizontal integration between different management systems is widely practiced in companies, but with varying degrees of success. Companies are often not even aware of this. However, it is not about cooperation between departments, which is a matter of course, for example when the HR department asks the Legal department for advice on a possible dismissal of employees or the Sales department asks the Compliance department about the extent to which gifts can be accepted. Rather, this version of horizontal integration is about using the elements available in different management systems for various purposes. If, for example, both the environmental management system and the compliance management system start with a risk assessment, the results of which are incorporated into a code of conduct and communicated accordingly, the integrated approach can consider using a uniform risk assessment tool for this purpose, combining the results in a uniform code of conduct with various areas and explaining this as part of a uniform communication strategy. The same idea can apply to a uniform non-financial reporting if there are reporting obligations regarding different areas.

If, on the other hand, we only move within a specific management system whose elements are to be used for different purposes, we are dealing with the second of the two cases of horizontal integration mentioned above. This can best be explained in the case of the compliance management system itself. Whether in the area of anti-money laundering, anti-trust, anti-corruption, data protection or supply chains - for all risk areas, various national and international frameworks require at least the establishment of risk management systems and the corresponding addressing of identified risks, which can be done in different ways. If the integrated approach is pursued, the company concerned will not develop five isolated management systems for the risk areas mentioned, but will identify, evaluate and manage all five risks as part of a uniform risk assessment and address them accordingly with uniform measures, structures and processes.

7.3 Profits of the Integrated Approach

The implementation of an integrated approach is associated with various benefits for the organization itself, its staff and thus for the societies and states in and for which they exist. Just a few of them are worth mentioning.

Firstly, the merging of structures and processes reduces complexity, which on the one hand leads to a reduction in costs and less bureaucracy, but on the other hand allows us to act faster from an operational perspective. In view of the rapidly changing circumstances, speed is more important than ever. Secondly, the bundling of structures and processes can prevent conflicts of competency from arising. Although this increases the risk of conflicts of interest, this can also be significantly reduced/eliminated with clear rules and high level of transparency. Thirdly, integration automatically promotes the necessary acceptance of the systems by the personnel and thus increases the willingness to use them accordingly. The less complex structures and processes are, and they become less complex with integration, the more comprehensible and transparent they are and therefore the greater the willingness of staff to accept them. A further consequence is, fifthly, the promotion of general transparency and thus the creation of further advantages both internally and externally. Last but not least, integration leads to an increase in effectiveness and efficiency. Effectiveness means that the measures implemented have a practical effect, i.e. that non-compliance cases are prevented or detected and dealt with using a compliance management system, for example. Efficiency, on the other hand, means that the same objectives are achieved with less cost-intensive measures.

If the integrated approach based on the ISO standards is also implemented, organizations are not only demonstrating that they are using the prevailing global best practice. At the same time, they are opting for "one language" that has been developed worldwide as the standard for governance or management areas and is immediately understood by other organizations that do the same. The security this can provide and the savings it can bring to business relationships are obvious.

8. Conclusion

The times in which organizations operate are not easy. The intensity of regulation is constantly increasing, geopolitical and economic conditions are changing, and established national economies are being put to the test. In response to the increasing complexity of the world, national legislators are reacting with ever new and more complicated regulations that organizations must comply with. In fulfilling these obligations it is up to them to decide which path they take, driven slightly by the indirect routes provided by the incentive models with their supplementary guidelines. Navigating on this difficult terrain, often with a lack of clarity and motivation, is not an easy task and creates further risks. The Integrated Approach based on globally recognized uniform tools can provide a good remedy. If a company is guided by the ISO standards, it can navigate forward unerringly in uncertain waters without losing sight of the big picture and losing scope for action. Time and practice will tell whether the Integrated Approach will be the natural evolution of compliance and CMS concepts. There are already many good reasons for this. In my humble opinion this is the way forward.

Notes

1 For more see: *A. Pollmann*, Integrität, Bielefeld 2018.

2 For more see: *M. Jüttner*, Die Kunst erfolgreicher Compliance, Frankfurt am Main 2023.

3 The German Act in Englisch: https://www.csr-in-deutschland.de/SharedDocs/Downloads/EN/act-corporate-due-diligence-obligations-supply-chains.pdf?__blob=publicationFile.

4 Full text: https://www.justice.gov/criminal/criminal-fraud/foreign-corrupt-practices-act.

5 Full text: https://www.legislation.gov.uk/ukpga/2010/23/contents.

6 Full text: https://www.legifrance.gouv.fr/loda/id/JORFTEXT000033558528?init=true&page=1&query=2016-1691+du+9+decembre&searchField=ALL&tab_selection=all.

7 The draft act in German: https://dip.bundestag.de/vorgang/gesetz-zur-st%C3%A4rkung-der-integrit%C3%A4t-in-der-wirtschaft/265689.

8 Full text: https://eur-lex.europa.eu/eli/reg/2016/679/oj/eng.

9 Full text: https://eur-lex.europa.eu/legal-content/en/TXT/?uri=CELEX%3A32019L1937.

10 For latest AML package see: https://www.consilium.europa.eu/en/press/press-releases/2024/05/30/anti-money-laundering-council-adopts-package-of-rules/.

11 Draft proposal: https://eur-lex.europa.eu/legal-content/EN/TXT/?uri=celex:52023PC0234.

12 To compare directly the differences, go to: www.EuroWhistle.eu

13 More on Green Deal here: https://commission.europa.eu/strategy-and-policy/priorities-2019-2024/european-green-deal_en.

14 See press note in German: https://www.bafa.de/DE/Lieferketten/Berichtspflicht/berichtspflicht_node.html.

15 See for more details: https://www.reuters.com/world/europe/german-government-considers-pausing-supply-chain-law-two-years-says-minister-2024-06-07/.

16 See for UK Bribery Act: https://assets.publishing.service.gov.uk/media/5d80cfc3ed915d51e9aff85a/bribery-act-2010-guidance.pdf.

[17] See Guidance of the German Federal Anti-Trust Office on Assessing Sanctions in Anti-Trust Offences: https://www.bundeskartellamt.de/SharedDocs/Publikation/DE/Leitlinien/Bu%C3%9Fgeldleitlinien_Oktober2021.pdf?__blob=publicationFile&v=7

[18] Judgment of the German Federal Supreme Court (Bundesgerichtshof) 09.05.2017 - 1 StR 265/16.

[19] The temporary suspension of FCPA enforcement has been ordered by Donald Trump after the manuscript was completed and is not reflected here.

[20] For more go to the webpage of the ISO/TC309: https://www.iso.org/committee/6266703.html

[21] Details on EU Green Deal here: https://www.consilium.europa.eu/en/policies/green-deal/.

[22] For Novartis AG see *K. Moosmayer*, Ethics and Integrated Assurance: The Challenge of Building Trust, in: Risk & Compliance, April 2024.

Chapter 1

Trends and Challenges in Sustainable Governance

Exploring the Future of Global ESG – Disclosures and Reporting Requirements

Meriem Debbih, Jeannine Lemker, Mariola Lisewska

"A Challenge, a Chance and a New Source of Risk for Organizations."

1. Introduction

ESG issues and regulations rapidly move – at times, in different directions. To better appreciate the real world and regulatory impact of modern ESG, the Global Business Law Institute brought together experts from multinational corporations, the International Standards Organization, the Japan Research Institute, leading outside counsel, and academia to discuss the landscape of ESG in Greater Asia, the European Union, and United States. Following is a commentary on the wisdom and emerging trends discussed by these practitioners and researchers in regulations and standards, policy and political tailwinds (and headwinds), and how corporations are adapting and thriving in the midst of it all. This article also discusses in more depth the regulatory landscape across the globe and reporting requirements affecting wide array of organizations.

2. Doing Good: Not Just "Smart Business" Anymore – European Union Perspective

The European Union set ambitious goals to remedy climate change,[1] advance human rights protections,[2] and enact mandatory auditing and reporting requirements[3] for much (if not soon to be most) of corporate ESG programs. Much like its push for privacy, the EU's ESG regulations are derived from its longstanding policies that seek to save the planet and protect individuals from uninformed investment decisions.[4] In doing so, the EU firmly established itself as the "tip of the spear" in moving from voluntary ESG frameworks to regulation. Its policies are now widely considered the bellwether for a coming global regulatory landscape – cementing itself (and its continuously expanding policies) as a leader in advancing responsible business.

In the EU, ESG has become a "layered cake" in which companies must continue to advance longstanding practices such as human right due diligence (previously accomplished under the UN Guiding Principles on Business and Human Rights[5]) or monitoring climate impact *and* build layers of mandatory reporting pursuant to law.[6]

> In the area of "S" we are seeing requirements for companies now to have to conduct mandatory human rights due diligence in their supply chains and business operations. We are seeing the hardening of soft law, in particular the hardening of rules based on the UN Guiding Principles on Business and Human Rights.
>
> - *Anita Ramasastry*[7]

Emerging from this "hardening" is an intersection of – and need to rely on – corporate compliance strategy and programs. To ensure repeatability, accuracy, and consistency, corporations are looking to their existing operational and compliance infrastructure, applying longstanding methodologies of monitoring and OKRs / KPIs to ESG programs. While many began this journey as companies waded into public statements about their "aspire to" climate goals or human rights impacts, the EU's mandatory auditing requirements are "hardening" these programs into corporate DNA to ensure accuracy and avoid material omissions, much like financial reporting.

2.1 Triad of regulations CSRD, SFRD and EU Taxonomy

Anchoring the EU's regulatory landscape are three seminal ESG compliance regulations: Sustainable Finance Disclosure Regulation (SFDR);[8] Corporate Sustainability Reporting Directive (CSRD);[9] and the EU Taxonomy (an EU-wide classification system for sustainable activities).[10] In short:

- CSRD, effective 2023, requires companies to report on (and audit) the impact of their products, services, and operations on the environment and society. It applies to companies listed in an EU-regulated market, EU companies (or subsidiaries of multinational companies) of a certain size (regardless of whether they are listed), multinational subsidiaries whose parent exceeds the same preset size, and non-EU multinationals who exceed revenue thresholds in the EU and maintain a physical EU presence.

- SFDR, enacted in 2021 several years before CSRD, applies to financial market participants offering investment products and financial advisers. It contains guidelines and requirements for sustainable investing applicable mainly to investors, including disclosure of sustainability risks and adverse impacts.
- The EU Taxonomy provides a classification system for sustainable economic activities. Both CSRD and SFRD require reporting using the EU Taxonomy.

The above triad create broad reporting duties for organizations – and bring downstream impact to supply chains and smaller partners who now are accountable for enabling larger corporations to comply. As a consequence, while large multinational and European businesses are building compliance infrastructure, supply chain partners who likewise set up initiatives may gain a competitive advantage and reap the benefits of sustainable business practices.

Arguably CSRD's two most innovative components are its double materiality standard and expanded scope which begin to codify "conscious capitalism" for the largest group of corporations (estimated to be nearly 50,000).[11] Under double materiality, corporations must build strategies – and report – on the impact to people and the environment (impact materiality) and mandatory assurance for all reported sustainability initiatives (financial materiality).

2.2 Corporate due diligence directive and supply chain regulation

Recently, Corporate Due Diligence Directive ("CSDDD") was adopted by the Council of the European Union. CSDDD fosters sustainable and responsible corporate behavior in companies' operations and across their global value chains imposing a corporate due diligence duty.[12] "The core elements of this duty are identifying and addressing potential and actual adverse human rights and environmental impacts in the company's own operations, their subsidiaries and, where related to their value chain(s), those of their business partners."[13] Shortly, we expect CSDDD to be transposed into the legislation in European Countries, affecting many organizations across the globe doing business in Europe.

2.3 A Country-By-Country Patchwork

Beyond the EU framework, multinational companies are faced with a tapestry of emerging regulations throughout Europe designed to foster sustainable investment and protect human rights. Countries such as Germany (with the Supply Chain Due Diligence Act[14]) and Norway (with the Supply Chain Transparency Act[15]) among others have domestic laws that affect multinational businesses operating in those countries. On the near horizon, we expect to see similar country-by-country legislation in France, the United Kingdom, Switzerland, and possibly beyond. Against a similar backdrop, the General Data Protection Regulation (GDPR) emerged and became the global leader in privacy regulations, serving as a global catalyst for renewed consumer focus, quickly followed by increased corporate investments in privacy protections. While still unfolding, all signals point to the EU's framework driving a similar path to a European-anchored global framework for ESG.

While arguably more burdensome than its sister geographies (so far), the EU's ESG compliance framework is intended to address pivotal policy issues such as global climate change, environment (the EU Green Deal[16]) and human rights protections.[17] The benefits to organizations and society at large are irrefutable as ESG compliance opens up the potential for better informed decisions of the organization and stakeholders, and elevated transparency around non-financial risk factors or programs that are now more important to investment decisions. It remains to be seen whether the downstream impact will have a net positive effect the world and bring about lasting change.

3. Regulatory ESG updates in key Asian financial markets and liability concerns for businesses operating in Asia.

The Asian market is gigantic – as expected, so is its regulatory landscape. Like its sister geographies, Asian ESG regulation develops at a galloping pace. We observe four main areas of focus of the regulators in APAC (Asia-Pacific) (1) liability for greenwashing; (2) reaching carbon neutrality; (3) sustainability reporting obligations; (4) and ESG due diligence. Interestingly, industry response across APAC countries varies. Japan multinationals not only need but want to engage in sustainable business practices. On the other hand, Hong Kong, Singapore and China follow the latest ESG trends but may advance unclear obligations to remain compliant. Here we analyze several financial hubs that tend to drive the APAC economy:

3.1 Japan's approach to ESG

Japanese businesses support laws stimulating sustainable investment and companies are eager to disclose their practices.[18] Somewhat different from its EU counterpart, Japan's movement into ESG centers on the belief that pushing corporations to advance climate programs, human rights, and other initiatives will have a direct and positive impact on the economy.

To advance sustainable investment, Japan has, among other actions: (1) adopted the recommendations issued by the Task Force on Climate-Related Financial Disclosures;[19] (2) revised the Corporate Governance Code;[20] (3) adopted the concept of responsible investment by the Government Pension Investment Fund;[21] (4) formed the Sustainability Standards Board of Japan;[22] (5) and passed GX (Green Transformation) Promotion Act.[23]

With these actions, the Japanese government has multiple objectives. The Japanese government aims to improve ratings of Japanese companies for overseas investors, asset managers and financial institutions.[24] Also, Japan aims to balance the amount of greenhouse gases emitted with an equivalent number of emissions removed from the atmosphere and achieve carbon neutrality by 2050. The GX initiative's ultimate objective is to shift Japanese industrial structure from being significantly dependent on fossil fuels to green energy dependence. Twenty-two industrial sectors are expected to transform to meet carbon neutrality. The Basic Policy for the Realization of GX[25] has two parts (1) energy oriented addressing energy efficiency, renewable sources of energy, nuclear, and other energy sources;[26] (2) and pricing schemes as incentives to green investment.[27] However, GX is controversial in Japan as some dispute whether GX sufficiently addresses what needs to be done to achieve key climate targets and some are concerned with the ramifications of overregulating as it could prevent businesses from flourishing[28]. With that in mind, a principle-based approach seems to work better for Japan than a rule based one.

3.2 Hong Kong, Singapore and China regulatory disclosures landscape

3.2.1 Hong Kong

Hong Kong Stock Exchange (HKEX) currently imposes both mandatory and "comply or explain" provisions in relation to ESG reporting.[29] 2024 brings enhanced reporting obligations (based of International Sustainability Standards Board (ISSB)) applicable to issuers for financial years commencing on or after January 1, 2025, with the exception of Large Cap Issuers which will be required to make mandatory disclosures on the New Climate Requirements for financial years commencing on or after January 1, 2026. The ESG Guide will be renamed Environmental, Social and Governance Code, suggesting a stiffening of the rules. HKEX also issued the Implementation Guidance[30] setting out examples and workflows for listed companies. Interestingly, HKEX' approach allows issuers to adopt international ESG reporting guidance, such as the ISSB Standards, so long as they provide for comparable disclosures to those required by the ESG Code.[31] Also, those issuers must clearly indicate where the disclosures required under ESG Code are incorporated.

Materiality is at the center of ESG reporting as it decides whether certain events require reporting. Firstly, the ISSB Standards require disclosure of material information about sustainability related risks and opportunities that could reasonably affect the entity's cash flows, its access to finance or cost of capital over the short, medium or long term. Therefore, if the risk in question does not affect the financial situation of an entity, the entity is not required to report on it.[32] The ESG Code defines "materiality" more broadly, encompassing a range of materiality considerations, including but not limited to financial materiality. "Materiality" is defined as the threshold at which ESG issues determined by the board are sufficiently important to investors and other stakeholders that they should be reported.[33] The issuers are also allowed to use "double materiality" applied by the European Union to provide additional disclosures. Notably, there is a clear shift away from the current "comply or explain" approach, as climate related disclosures will eventually become mandatory for most companies according to the phased approach.

The Cross-Agency Steering Group[34] in Hong Kong promotes green and sustainable finance and support the Government's climate strategies. From the advisory perspective there are no robust local disclosure/reporting standards applicable to all businesses; and ESG reporting is delegated to accountants.[35] Accounting does play a huge role and will in ESG as most of the regulations worldwide require filing ESG reports as non-financial information attached to the yearly financial statements. However, accountants shouldn't be responsible for ESG reporting. Instead, this task should be assigned to a specialized department and dedicated professionals. This way we can address the vast issues that don't only show numbers, statistics but improve the culture of the organization. The culture of the organization plays a crucial role especially within the scope of the "S" and "G" of the ESG compliance. Currently it appears that not listed companies who provide robust ESG disclosures are unfortunately rather in minority in Hong Kong, says the voice from practice.[36] Fortunately, the 2023 ESG Reporting Study shows that "the level of disclosure completeness in listed companies' ESG reports has been increasing." Given the evolving regulations, we can expect a growing need for listed companies to create specialized departments exclusively addressing ESG reporting requirements.

3.2.2 Singapore

Since 2016, Singapore Exchange (SGX) has been requiring publicly listed companies to disclose and publish annual sustainability reports. Similarly to Hong Kong, Singapore started with a "comply or explain" sustainability reporting approach before moving to mandatory climate related disclosures.[37] For example, while only selected industries will be affected in 2024, by 2025 all listed companies will be affected and required to report Scope 1 and 2 greenhouse gas emissions, and Scope 3 starting from 2026.[38] Even large non-listed companies with annual revenue of at least S$1 billion will be required to report Scope 1 and 2 by 2027.[39] The entities must align their reporting according to the International Financing Reporting Standards and International Sustainability Standard Board guidelines and make sure they also follow the local rules.

3.2.3 China

As one of the world's largest economies, China does not yet impose mandatory disclosures. Early this year China has published draft ESG reporting guidelines for public consultation and finalized them in April.[40] The guidelines are in effect since May 1, 2024. Large companies are required to issue sustainability reports by 2026. This is a pivotal shift in China's policy. The Guidelines tend to align with the Global Reporting Initiative (GRI), the ISBB and the Task Force on Climate-Related Financial Disclosures (TCFD). Interestingly, China decided to move away from the "materiality" principle as outlined by ISSB and to introduce a "double materiality" principle which may suggest that China is leaning toward the EU's approach to ESG disclosures.[41]

Businesses operating in key Asian financial markets must stay abreast of evolving ESG regulations. Already, most large companies must proactively manage risks associated with sustainability. This includes principally ensuring regulatory compliance, avoiding greenwashing, addressing supply chain issues, protecting fundamental human rights, and mitigating climate change liabilities. Naturally, Asia is looking toward the United States to see how the market giant will address Environmental, Social and Governance compliance needs and issues.

4. A Tale of Two Voices: Rising controversies around ESG strategy in the United States.

The intersection of – or collision between - Compliance and ESG programs is gaining additional momentum. Unlike anywhere else around the globe, there is a unique schism across the United States. While the majority of the States support ESG initiatives, many States proposed anti-ESG bills, and a large number moved forward with legislation that prohibits application of ESG factors while making investment decisions related to state funds use.[42]

4.1 Federal ESG regulation landscape in the United States

The United States has no national law (or framework) that directly governs ESG or requires reporting comparable to what we see in the EU. As with US privacy legislation, there are many state-by-state laws and pending ESG legislation.

The closest the US has to a federal ESG requirement can be found in the materiality standards defined in federal securities laws and regulations that apply to public companies. These standards are primarily found in the Dodd-Frank Wall Street Reform and Consumer Protection Act (Dodd-Frank

Act)[43] and the rules promulgated by the Securities and Exchange Commission (SEC). These laws and regulations impose several disclosure requirements. The required disclosures encompass topics such as: conflict minerals in a company's products and supply chain diligence related to these minerals;[44] ratio between a company's median annual compensation of all employees and the CEO's annual compensation;[45] payments to the US federal government or foreign governments, if the company's business is centered around certain natural resources;[46] board diversity; human capital resources; cybersecurity risk management, strategy, governance, and material incidents.

Further, there is the Foreign Corrupt Practices Act[47] that prohibits US companies and individuals from bribing foreign government officials to obtain or retain business and the forced labor prohibition regulation introduced in the Smoot-Hawley Tariff Act.[48]

Lastly, the Federal Trade Commission (FTC) outlined principles for green marketing claims in its Green Guides (part of the FTC's effort to prevent greenwashing, i.e., misleading consumers regarding company's environmental practices).[49]

4.2 SEC climate-related disclosure rules

And yet on March 6, 2024, the SEC adopted rules to enhance and standardize climate-related disclosures by public companies and in public offerings.[50] This regulation requires registrants (public companies) to provide certain climate-related information in their registration statements and annual reports.[51] According to the new rules, a company is required to disclose climate-related risks that either have materially impacted, or are reasonably likely to have a material impact on the company's business strategy, results of operations, or financial condition.[52] Interestingly, the SEC does not use a double materiality standard, which would require disclosure of how the company impacts climate change in addition to disclosing how climate change impacts the company (which the rules require).[53] As expected, the rules were challenged in courts almost immediately after the SEC adopted them. The SEC exercised its discretion and decided to stay its new climate disclosure rules, pending judicial review.[54] Nevertheless, the SEC's climate change proposal is the closest step to a federal framework the US has seen to date.

4.3 Regulation that encourages sustainable investment

The United States also introduced regulations that encourage – but do not require - sustainable investment. The Inflation Reduction Act (IRA) is boosting the energy sector and encouraging sustainable investment. The Helpful Incentives to Produce Semiconductors Act (CHIPS) provides funding to support the development and adoption of secure and trusted telecommunications technologies, secure semiconductors, secure semiconductors supply chains, and other emerging technologies. Businesses already enjoy the benefits of those regulations, especially IRA, that in some cases can bring 30% to 70% return rate from the sustainable investment in hydrogen technology, biofuels, solar energy etc. – as long as all the requirements from the IRA are met.[55]

4.4 State legislation requiring climate-related disclosures.

California has three acts that will require climate-related disclosures and reporting today: (1) the Climate Corporate Data Accountability Act (Senate Bill (SB) 253) which applies to entities with 1 billion dollar annual revenue and mandates reporting of their Scope 1, Scope 2 and Scope 3 emissions, and to obtain assurance for their reported emissions; (2) Greenhouse Gasses: Climate-Related Financial Risk Act (SB 261), which requires business entities with more than $500 million in total annual revenues to disclose their climate-related financial risks that align with TCFD biennially starting on or before January 1, 2026; and finally (3) the Voluntary Carbon Market Disclosure Act (California A.B. 1305), which requires disclosures for business entities that participate in carbon offset markets or that make claims about achieving net zero.[56]

There is also a multitude of other state laws that pivot to ESG compliance. For example, the California Supply Chains Act addresses supply chain compliance and requires certain companies that meet thresholds to combat human trafficking and slavery.[57] Finally, in certain states (e.g., California, Washington) regulations require board diversity.

5. How Boards of Directors Interpret "E", "S" and "G"

There are diverse opinions what *"E", "S" and "G"* stand for and how they should be interpreted. Most commonly we hear: (1) "environmental" addresses climate change, greenhouse gas emissions, emissions to air, water and land, pollution and waste; biodiversity, deforestation and land use, energy efficiency, resource depletion (including water);[58] (2) "social" encompasses human rights (including modern slavery and forced labor), health and safety, diversity, equity and inclusion (DEI), conflict zones and conflict minerals, community engagement;[59] (3) "governance" is the executive pay an board independence and structure, conflicts of interest, anti-money laundering, bribery and corruption, responsible tax strategy, stakeholder engagement.[60] However, many question whether Governance is properly defined as it does not seem viable to say governance is analogous with corporate governance. In fact, voices from multinational businesses opine that: "'G' is how companies manage the ESG, not how they manage the company generally, which would be the corporate governance portion of 'G' in the ESG context."[61] To be more specific, "the "G" is about how do we make sure that for the "E" and "S" actions we have the appropriate oversight, metrics and risk management in place, and if it matches the rigor we do business in any other way."[62]

While the "E" and "S" appear to be less controversial in interpretation, the "G" factor has emerged – somewhat unexpectedly – as the most complex and forever evolving. "G" certainly is more than just corporate governance or board diversity as it must motivate the organization to make sure the ESG strategy aligns with business goals and objectives while assuring ESG compliance. "G" cannot be simply quantitative but is ephemeral and changes as the organization changes.

6. Conclusion

ESG compliance is ubiquitous. The past decade or more has shown that the world is calling on corporations to step in and help solve large scale global problems (climate, human rights and dignity, equality, etc.) often previously left to governments and diplomacy. In answering this call, corporations are now experiencing an all too familiar ramification: when corporate investments change the nature of the way people invest their money, quick to follow are regulations intended to protect people's money and prevent corporate abuse.

As we watch the world's ESG regulations unfold, there is a common ground and major differences. Some regulations remain vague, still searching for the transparency needed to assure policy objectives are met. There is a myriad of issues related to reporting and materiality standards, including a lack of agreement on the standards to be met in disclosure and diverse auditing and monitoring requirements.

Businesses across the globe certainly can expect continued growth of applicable regulations addressing all components of "E", "S" and "G" – the question will be how corporations that are multifaceted, multinational, and represent vastly different industries prepare for what is to come. And, whether global regulators will start to coalesce around a global framework (as we have seen with anti-bribery legislation) that will aid corporations in their efforts to both do good in the world and advance the global economy. Whatever the regulatory future holds, the future of corporate global ESG will be characterized by deeper integration into business strategies, greater accountability, and a stronger emphasis on sustainability and social responsibility.

Notes

1 *See e.g.*, Corporate Sustainability Reporting Directive, Directive (EU) 2022/2464 of the European Parliament and of the Council of 14 December 2022 amending Regulation (EU) No 537/2014, Directive 2004/109/EC, Directive 2006/43/EC and Directive 2013/34/EU, as regards corporate sustainability reporting. https://eur-lex.europa.eu/legal-content/EN/TXT/?uri=CELEX:32022L2464.

2 *See e.g.*, Corporate Sustainability Due Diligence Directive. https://commission.europa.eu/business-economy-euro/doing-business-eu/corporate-sustainability-due-diligence_en.

3 *Supra fn. 1;* and *see also* Sustainable Finance Disclosure Regulation. Regulation (EU) 2019/2088 of the European Parliament and of the Council of 27 November 2019 on sustainability-related disclosures in the financial services sector. https://eur-lex.europa.eu/legal-content/EN/TXT/?uri=CELEX:32019R2088.

4 *See*, What the EU is doing and why SFDR. https://finance.ec.europa.eu/sustainable-finance/disclosures/sustainability-related-disclosure-financial-services-sector_en; What the EU is doing and why CSRD. https://finance.ec.europa.eu/capital-markets-union-and-financial-markets/company-reporting-and-auditing/company-reporting/corporate-sustainability-reporting_en; What the EU is doing and why EU Taxonomy. https://finance.ec.europa.eu/sustainable-finance/tools-and-standards/eu-taxonomy-sustainable-activities_en; What are the benefits of the new CSDDD rules. https://commission.europa.eu/business-economy-euro/doing-business-eu/corporate-sustainability-due-diligence_en.

5 The United Nations' Guiding Principles on Business and Human Rights. https://www.ohchr.org/sites/default/files/documents/publications/guidingprinciplesbusinesshr_en.pdf.

6 *Supra fn. 3.*

7 Anita Ramasastry, Director of the Sustainable International Development Graduate Program, Professor at the University of Washington, and advisor to many governments, international institutions and organizations. Ramasastry is an advisor to the European Parliament's Working Group on Responsible Business Conduct and assisted in drafting the EU's Corporate Sustainability Due Diligence Directive addressing environmental and human rights protection through due diligence in the global supply chain.

8 *See supra fn. 3.*

9 *See supra fn. 1.*

10 The EU taxonomy of sustainable activities. *https://finance.ec.europa.eu/sustainable-finance/tools-and-standards/eu-taxonomy-sustainable-activities_en*.

11 "The term 'conscious capitalism' refers to a socially responsible economic and political philosophy. The premise behind conscious capitalism is that businesses should operate ethically while they pursue profits. This means that they should consider serving all stakeholders, including their employees, humanity, and the environment. They shouldn't limit the impact of their achievements to just their management teams and shareholders. The idea of conscious capital was created by Whole Foods co-founder John Mackey and author and marketing professor Raj Sisodia." Will Kenton (author), Michale Boyle (reviewer), Suzanne Kvilhaug (fact checker), Investopedia. https://www.investopedia.com/terms/c/conscious-capitalism.asp

12 *See supra* at *fn.* 2.

13 *Id.*

14 The Supply Chain Act. Act on Corporate Due Diligence Obligations in Supply Chains (Gesetz über die unternehmerischen Sorgfaltspflichten in Lieferketten). https://www.csr-in-deutschland.de/EN/Business-Human-Rights/Supply-Chain-Act/supply-chain-act.html

15 The Transparency Act - Forbrukertilsynet. https://www.forbrukertilsynet.no/vi-jobber-med/apenhetsloven/the-transparency-act.

16 *See* The European Green Deal. https://commission.europa.eu/strategy-and-policy/priorities-2019-2024/european-green-deal_en.

17 *See* https://european-union.europa.eu/priorities-and-actions/actions-topic/human-rights-and-democracy_en#:~:text=Human%20rights%20are%20at%20the,torture%2C%20human%20trafficking%20and%20discrimination

18 Mr. Eiichiro Adachi, Senior Counsel, Head of ESG Research Center at the Japan Research Institute.

19 *See* https://www.fsb-tcfd.org "Concurrent with the release of its 2023 status report on October 12, 2023, the TCFD has fulfilled its remit and disbanded. The FSB has asked the IFRS Foundation to take over the monitoring of the progress of companies' climate-related disclosures."

20 *See* https://www.jpx.co.jp/english/news/1020/b5b4pj0000046kxj-att/b5b4pj0000046l0c.pdf

21 *See* https://www.gpif.go.jp/en/investment/esg/

22 *See* https://www.ssb-j.jp/en/exposure_drafts/y2024/2024-0329.html.

23 *See* https://www.eu-japan.eu/sites/default/files/imce/2024.4.18%20METI.pdf

[24] Mr. Eiichiro Adachi, Senior Counsel, Head of ESG Research Center at the Japan Research Institute

[25] The Basic Policy for the Realization of GX was compiled on December 22, 2022, depicting a roadmap for energy and environmental policies covering the next 10 years. *See* https://www.enecho.meti.go.jp/en/category/special/article/detail_178.html

[26] *Id.*

[27] *Id.*

[28] Mr. Eiichiro Adachi, Senior Counsel, Head of ESG Research Center at the Japan Research Institute.

[29] Carolyn Sng, Partner at K&L Gates, Hong Kong, primarily focused on capital markets, mergers and acquisitions, and financial services regulatory matters. Also see Appendix C2 of the Main Board Listing Rules of HKEX: Environmental, Social and Governance Reporting Guide. https://en-rules.hkex.com.hk/rulebook/appendix-c2-environmental-social-and-governance-reporting-guide-0

[30] *See* Implementation Guidance for Climate Disclosures under HKEX ESG reporting framework. https://www.hkex.com.hk/-/media/HKEX-Market/Listing/Rules-and-Guidance/Environmental-Social-and-Governance/Exchanges-guidance-materials-on-ESG/guidance_enhanced_climate_dis.pdf; and https://www.hkex.com.hk/-/media/HKEX-Market/News/Market-Consultations/2016-Present/April-2023-Climate-related-Disclosures/Conclusions-Apr-2024/cp202304cc.pdf

[31] The Environmental, Social and Governance Reporting Guide (to be renamed as the Environmental, Social and Governance Reporting Code with effect from 1 January 2025) set out in Appendix C2 to the Main Board Listing Rules or Appendix C2 to the GEM Listing Rules; https://en-rules.hkex.com.hk/rulebook/appendix-c2-environmental-social-and-governance-reporting-guide-0

[32] "A company is asked to disclose material information about sustainability-related risks and opportunities that could reasonably be expected to affect its prospects. The definitione of material information is aligned with that used in IFRS Accounting Standards—that is, information is material if omitting, obscuring or misstating it could be reasonably expected to influence investor decisions."ISSB: Frequently Asked Questions. https://www.ifrs.org/groups/international-sustainability-standards-board/issb-frequently-asked-questions/

[33] See paragraph 11(1) of Appendix C2 of the Main Board Listing Rules.

[34] The Green and Sustainable Finance Cross-Agency Steering Group was established in May 2020 and is co-chaired by the Hong Kong Monetary Authority and the SFC. Members include the Environment Bureau, the Financial Services and the Treasury Bureau, the Accounting and Financial Reporting Council, HKEX, the Insurance Authority and the Mandatory Provident Fund Schemes Authority. The Steering Group aims to co-ordinate the management of climate and environmental risks to the financial sector, accelerate the growth of green and sustainable finance in Hong Kong and support the Government's climate strategies.

[35] Carolyn Sng, Partner at K&L Gates, Hong Kong, primarily focuses on capital markets, mergers and acquisitions, and financial services regulatory matters.

[36] *Id.*

37 *See* Rules 711A and 711B of the SGX Rulebooks, added on July 20, 2016 for the "complain or explain" approach; https://greenco-esg.com/sgx-sustainability-reporting-guide/ and https://www.acga-asia.org/advocacy-detail.php?date2=2016&id=64; https://rulebook.sgx.com/sites/default/files/net_file_store/SGX_Mainboard_Chapter_7_July_20_2016.pdf. Also see updated rules from January 2022 and https://rulebook.sgx.com/sites/default/files/net_file_store/SGX_Mainboard_Chapter_7_July_20_2016.pdf; https://www.acga-asia.org/advocacy-detail.php?date2=2016&id=64 and https://greenco-esg.com/sgx-sustainability-reporting-guide/

38 "Recognising the demand for such information, Singapore Exchange Regulation (SGX RegCo) in
2021 introduced a phased approach to mandatory climate reporting for listed issuers based on the
recommendations of the TCFD." *See* https://api2.sgx.com/sites/default/files/2023-11/SGX%20Sustainability%20Reporting%20Review%202023_FA_Optimised.pdf; https://api2.sgx.com/sites/default/files/2023-11/SGX%20Sustainability%20Reporting%20Review%202023_FA_Optimised.pdf

39 *Id.*

40 *See* https://www.china-briefing.com/news/china-releases-esg-reporting-standards-for-businesses/

41 The climate and sustainability disclosure guidelines introduced by the Shanghai and Shenzhen stock exchanges mandate that "companies report on the impact their activities have on the environment as well as the risks and effects of environmental factors on their business, the so-called double materiality." https://www.scmp.com/business/china-business/article/3264437/climate-change-china-aims-introduce-nationwide-corporate-esg-disclosure-standards-2030.

42 Environmental, Social, and Governance (ESG) Risk (US): Compliance Roadmap by Practical Law Commercial Transactions (Westlaw)

43 Dodd-Frank Wall Street Reform and Consumer Protection Act, Pub. L. 111-203, H.R. 4173 (July 2010) (the "Dodd-Frank Act"). https://www.congress.gov/bill/111th-congress/house-bill/4173/text

44 Section 1502 of the Dodd Frank Act. See e.g., https://www.globalwitness.org/en/campaigns/conflict-minerals/dodd-frank-act-section-1502/

45 Section 953(b) of the Dodd-Frank Act. See e.g., https://www.sec.gov/newsroom/speeches-statements/statement-open-meeting-pay-ratio-aguilar.

46 See e.g., Section 1594 of the Dodd-Frank Act. https://www.arnoldporter.com/-/media/files/perspectives/publications/2010/08/doddfrank-csr-provisions-mandate-disclosure-of-o__/files/newsletter-item/fileattachment/advisorynew_corporate_social_responsibility_requ__.pdf?rev=c919ef589de047578edc78728759ac1e&sc_lang=en&hash=1D319709DF77D2A34B607FE972275C77

47 The Foreign Corrupt Practices Act of 1977, as amended, 15 U.S.C. §§ 78dd-1, et seq. ("FCPA"). https://www.justice.gov/jm/jm-9-47000-foreign-corrupt-practices-act-1977

48 19 U.S.C. 1307. https://www.govinfo.gov/content/pkg/USCODE-2021-title19/html/USCODE-2021-title19-chap4-subtitleII-partI-sec1307.html; *see also* https://www.cbp.gov/trade/forced-labor

[49] https://www.ftc.gov/news-events/topics/truth-advertising/green-guides
[50] https://www.sec.gov/news/press-release/2024-31
[51] https://www.sec.gov/files/rules/final/2024/33-11275.pdf
[52] https://www.sec.gov/files/rules/final/2024/33-11275.pdf
[53] *See e.g.,* https://blogs.law.columbia.edu/climatechange/2024/03/11/the-secs-final-climate-disclosure-rule-key-requirements-and-the-materiality-threshold/; and a discussion of double materiality at https://www2.deloitte.com/cn/en/pages/hot-topics/topics/climate-and-sustainability/dcca/thought-leadership/the-challenge-of-double-materiality.html
[54] https://www.whitecase.com/insight-alert/sec-voluntarily-stays-its-climate-rules-pending-judicial-review
[55] Ankur Tohan, Partner at K&L Gates, Seattle, practice group coordinator for the firm's global Environment, Land, and Natural Resources practice group. His practice focuses on energy infrastructure and natural resource development, compliance counseling, and defense of governmental and citizen enforcement actions.
[56] https://leginfo.legislature.ca.gov/faces/billTextClient.xhtml?bill_id=202320240AB1305
[57] https://oag.ca.gov/SB657
[58] Environmental, Social, and Governance (ESG) Risk (US): Compliance Roadmap by Practical Law Commercial Transactions (Westlaw)
[59] Environmental, Social, and Governance (ESG) Risk (US): Compliance Roadmap by Practical Law Commercial Transactions (Westlaw)
[60] Environmental, Social, and Governance (ESG) Risk (US): Compliance Roadmap by Practical Law Commercial Transactions (Westlaw)
[61] Amanda Gardiner, Head of ESG at Meta, leading the company's ESG strategy, governance, engagement and reporting. Previously, she spent three years at the United Nations leading the Business Call to Action, an initiative of 300+ corporations innovating to achieve the UN Sustainable Development Goals.
[62] *Id.*

ESG in a Global Context

Bethany Jackson, Anita Punwani

1. Introduction

Much of the discourse on Environmental, Social and Governance (ESG) in both the public and epistemic spheres is organisation centric. To deal with the nature of the global challenges we face, ESG should be viewed in a wider context. The United Nations' (UN) principles are founded on organisations taking their social as well as environmental responsibilities seriously, including in managing the risks to vulnerable members of society, notably those at risk of modern slavery. Such language is reflected in the business facing UN documentation – the UN Guiding Principles on Business and Human Rights – which considers environmental and social impacts through a human rights framing (UN OHCHR 2011). This chapter presents the view that organisations should be framing their environmental and social responsibilities in this context by ensuring that leaders make a formal commitment to achieve all the United Nations Sustainable Development Goals (UN SDGs) (UN 2015); the reason for the modern organisation to take such a perspective is illustrated by studying the local impacts of modern slavery risks in Bangladesh and India posed by the climate and ecological crisis.

2. Environmental Crises and Modern Slavery

"We are at the beginning of a rapidly escalating climate and ecological crisis. A sustainability crisis" states the prominent climate activist Greta Thunberg, who also asks "[h]ow can we talk about an existential human crisis created by inequality, the exploitation of workers and nature, land theft, genocide and overconsumption without any mention of morality?" (Thunberg 2024: p.41-42).

Thunberg – who has become a powerful actor on the world stage in raising the issue of climate change – in this statement recognizes the complex nature of the issue and the need for moral principles in handling the crises we face. She has raised public awareness of the climate crisis by cutting through rhetoric to hold to account those in power for their actions, as well as inaction. This has compounded the pressure on organisations across the world to ensure the climate is firmly on-board the agenda and to report on their activities in relation to limiting carbon dioxide (CO_2) emissions, increasingly in expressing terms which align with UN global targets and 'net zero' framing. Acting on climate change is often discussed in relation to reporting requirements to key actors such as regulators and funders. This framing, indeed discourse, in relation to ESG more widely, is inclined to focus on 'E', 'S' and 'G' separately instead of the interconnected, and often clashing, nature of environmental and social matters (Walk Free 2023a; Gözlügöl 2022).

Consensus on climate change has been noted globally (Myers et al. 2021), and the reality is, both the high-income countries (HIC) as well as low- and middle-income countries (LMIC) are now facing a climate crisis.[1] Yet, the experience of these impacts is vastly unequal. Current action fails to acknowledge the unequal nature of climate change and the impact it is having on social conditions. For example, Parsons (2023) highlights the 'outsourcing' of the climate crisis from HICs toward those who are bearing the brunt of the climate crisis and feeding directly into perpetuating issues of labour exploitation and inequality. McGuire (2014) further identifies how some countries are at a disadvantage compared to others in their ability to respond – through adaptation or mitigation – to climate change. He notes that the rapid nature of climate change means highly vulnerable countries in Asia, Africa and other areas of the world are limited in their response options; and that rising populations, falling incomes, and increased pollution will further expose communities to global environmental and social hazards. More recent analysis has highlighted how responses to climate change vary depending on the nature of the hazard being slow-onset or rapid-onset (Bharadwaj et al. 2021) which affects the levels of preparedness and ability to set in motion interventions and responses where needed. Further, researchers have highlighted the need to integrate responses to intersectional risks into national climate action plans and global climate finance response mechanisms in the context of labour risks (Bharadwaj et al. 2021; Jackson 2023; Jackson et al. 2024).

The inequity in the burden of exploitation reflects the nature of climate change upon many LMIC geographies. This is shown in both the services and support that are available; for example, lower adaptive capacities in LMICs and access to infrastructure are linked to poorer health, lost productivity, and migration (Sharpe and Davison 2021; Saeed et al. 2023). Such risks from climate change can be compounded when combined with extreme forms of exploitation. For example, climate change in the context of modern slavery is viewed as a 'stress multiplier' (Bharadwaj et al. 2022) exacerbating a range of social, cultural, and economic issues to either *push* or *pull* persons into exploitative working conditions (Jackson et al. 2024). Furthermore, recent global reports have highlighted the risks of climate change (US Department of State 2023; Nakate 2023) to vulnerable communities, and others towards development opportunities for tackling exploitative labour linked to the SDGs (Cockayne 2021).

Modern slavery is defined as the "the status or condition of a person over whom any or all of the powers attaching the right of ownership are exercised" with such control including the deprivation of liberty, withholding of documentation, intent of exploitation for profit, movement, of disposal of an individual (Bellagio-Harvard Guidelines 2012). Those subjected to modern slavery are controlled, face violence, threats, are forced into inescapable debt, have their passport taken away and are threatened with deportation. Exploitation of this sort has been linked to multiple sectors including garment manufacturing (Walk Free 2023b), hospitality (Robinson 2013; Bullock et al. 2024), care work (Unseen 2023), construction (Gutierrez-Huerter O et al. 2023), and agricultural production (LeBaron and Gore 2020; Palumbo and Sciurba 2015; Weir et al. 2024) amongst others. Globally, almost 50 million people are estimated to be subjected to modern slavery (both through forced labour and cases of forced marriage) (ILO 2022); and the vast majority of those subjected to modern slavery in LMICs are from LMICs themselves. According to the ILO (2022), 94% of those subjected to modern slavery globally are exploited within similar economic regions, suggesting global economic factors play as large a role in poor working conditions being perpetuated as climate change.

3. Global Economic Factors

Such a global economic landscape that feeds into labour dynamics and risks is part of broader economic trends. As defined by Anthony Giddens, globalization is "the intensification of worldwide social relations which link distant localities in such a way that local happenings are shaped by events occurring many miles away and vice versa" (Steger 2013: p.13). Globalization itself is a core framing of the way modern slavery can be presented (Landman and Silverman 2019) within economic and governance systems. Actions to respond to such combined risks are being considered at the policy level (Jackson et al. 2024; Anti-Slavery International 2021; Gonzalez De Aguinaga 2024), for example through the recently adopted European Union Corporate Sustainability and Due Diligence Directive (CSDDD) despite the initial ambitions being watered-down (McGowan 2024; Foley 2024) that feed into a global governance approach on national and regional scales. As with the environment, it has predominantly been community action through civil society organisations (CSOs) that have brought pressure in relation to regulation and reporting on modern slavery within these governance contexts, reflecting the push for reframing the climate crisis and response. Yet activities through ESG at an organisational context have often been pushed to frame action through a 'net zero' lens and focused on the domestic policies of HIC (Koonce 2023) with the perspective of tackling issues of climate change and human rights risks in other 'outsourced' localities becoming lost (Parsons 2023). This further creates disparities in response and burdens supply chains, communities, and countries who are facing the dual impacts of climate change and modern slavery. Some organisations are beginning to use the framing of the 'climate transition' in their planning and activities instead to better align intersectional ESG issues to mitigate against these disparities in addressing problems (see Sokolowski et al. 2023).

There is a need to focus on actions to recenter the responsibility for those who are driving the causes of climate change and labour exploitation through a globalized economy (Parsons 2023) and addressing the climate and human rights response to one that is, as climate activist Vanessa Nakate states, "about the people… the people who are being impacted right now" (UN 2022). In refocusing on the role of globalization as a form of localized community governance, we here assess the dual risks of modern slavery and climate change through two studies illustrating the duality of how these risks are impacting vulnerable communities in Bangladesh and India.

4. Case Study I – Bangladesh

Bangladesh is considered one of the higher risk countries facing the effects of anthropogenic climate change; with risks of rainfall, drought, cyclones, sea level rise, salinity and heat all being identified as climate-related hazards (Ahmed and Khan 2022). Such climate effects have been linked to concerns of migration and human trafficking (Jackson 2023). There is a relationship between international and internal migration, modern slavery and the higher risk of being forced into labour and trafficked on migration journeys (Punwani 2023a, p.92-94; Jackson 2023).

Risks in Bangladesh may also come from the actions in place nationally to mitigate the health and climate impacts from polluting industries. For example, the brick manufacturing sector is being encouraged to alter its manufacturing processes to be more environmentally sustainable (Siddique 2024) but there are concerns about the impact that may have on working opportunities; particularly as seasonal migrant labour making working choices linked to climate change responses are shifting into informal labour in this sector (Jackson 2023). Some projects implemented in Bangladesh – such as the Bangladesh Environmental Sustainability and Transformation (BEST) Project (World Bank 2024) and the Supporting Effective Jobs Lending at Scale (SEJLS) (Divanbeigi and Saliola 2022) – are working toward transitioning kiln technologies whilst also supporting more stable and consistent job generation for informal and often vulnerable workers (Divanbeigi et al. 2023).Yet, globally there is a lack of consultation with workers with regards to climate change and the impact that policy measures have on both their ability to work and opportunities for adaptation (Harrisberg and Tripathi 2023). These risks are also evident in Bangladesh with youth advocates and workers being limited in their inclusion around climate responses (Zami 2023).

Efforts to tackle climate change – and the intersection with other social and economic concerns – have been led primarily through community-based resilience measures. Many of these measures are focused on climate resilience through agricultural activities (e.g., USAID n.d.) and have been centered in many communities through the training and empowerment of women within communities (Bloxham 2023) reflecting the nature of seasonal migration and community dynamics required as livelihoods change as a results of climate variables (Jackson 2023). As a result, it is suggested that the achievement of the

UN SDGs may be compromised by the resulting pressures of climate change (Ahmed 2018; Ahmed and Eklund 2021). Only a governance perspective that accounts for communities in assisting to lead the implementation of the UN SDGs is likely to be successful.

5. Case Study II - India

Over recent years India has experienced huge amounts of excessive heat which have led to concerns that in several states the achievement of decent working conditions is likely to be difficult. Debnath et al. (2023) highlight West Bengal, Odisha and Arunachal Pradesh are particularly at risk of not achieving UN SDG 8 and with all three states facing extreme danger, or danger from heat. These impacts will have detrimental impacts on the globalized supply chains reliant upon resources and products from India. Despite this, the current overview of SDGs within some businesses and supply chain compliance mechanisms has been noted as lacking in India (Srivastava et al. 2024). It is this disconnect which demonstrates the need for a more accessible approach aligning the UN SDGs as a global governance framework.

Nationally, the economic toll climate change is predicted to lower the overarching Gross Domestic Product (GDP) of India (Piciariello et al. 2021), yet it is also expected to impact those most vulnerable in Indian society – potentially increasing their risks of exposure to more extreme forms of exploitation (Jackson 2023; Bharadwaj et al. 2021, 2022). There are limited resources for communities to locally respond to extreme climatic variabilities (Bharadwaj et al. 2021). Social mobilization has been leading climate justice action within India to address the climate crisis and push for governmental policy and reform (Kashwan 2022), which is echoed in the movement to support bonded labourers working in poor conditions by CSOs and coalitions – such as the National Coalition for Abolition of Bonded Labour (NCABL) – who work towards eradicating exploitative working practices and improving working conditions for all in India (NCABL 2016). Improved worker welfare and conditions in these cases should also include reasonable redress of climate change impacts moving forward too.

6. Global Governance

These cases illustrate how the climate crisis is facing some of the most vulnerable communities in the world, with social and environmental dynamics intertwined. The case studies illustrate why there is a need for taking a global perspective – together with a focus placed on collaborative community action – and a need to address all not just one of the UN SDGs to be mirrored at global, national and community scales. This is reflected in literature which frames modern slavery links between environmental degradation and climate change as a driving and resulting factor have been linked by several actors (see Coelho 2016; Brown et al. 2021; O'Connell 2021; Jackson et al. 2021); and notions of combined governance action have been identified as having positive influences in most cases, with some risks continuing to be observed (Decker Sparks et al. 2021).

Governance at all levels must account for the trade-offs in both supporting economic development whilst also ensuring fair and decent working conditions, in mitigating or reversing the impacts of the climate crisis. This is the essence of what the 'just transition' should look like – but it is those directly impacted by these concerns that should be leading the efforts to design and lead community-based resilience. Effected voices must be heard.

The definition of globalization, as previously defined, reflects the economic forces which have linked often distant localities in such a way that local impacts are shaped by boards of organisations, often many miles away, without adequate regard for the human beings working in the global supply chains. Steger terms "[h]umane forms of globalization" as "more attuned to what are shaping up to be two most daunting tasks facing us in the 21st century: the reduction of global disparities in wealth and wellbeing and preservation of our wonderous planet" (Steger 2013: preface, xiii). This distance and complexity of supply chains within the current globalized economic structures creates barriers to addressing risks and (Simpson et al. 2021) and require novel supply chain management activities (Gold et al. 2015). When addressing these complexities Andrew Wallis[2] states that the "[o]verarching is a structural and systemic problem that cannot be ignored. Namely procurement is entirely predicated on an extractive or dare I say exploitative profit model. This pushes inevitable pressure down the supply chain that has an inevitability – forced labour due to the insatiable demand it creates for cheap labour, services and goods and profit margin" (Punwani 2023b). Issues of procurement linked to modern slavery and climate change responses are beginning to be explored and recommendations provided in some cases (see Rogerson et al. 2024). Yet this raises questions around worker voice integration and leadership at scale, particularly as Wallis notes, that social audit frameworks currently favoured by many businesses have many failings (Punwani 2023b) in their reach, inclusion of worker-voice, and lack of access (Savill 2022).

Handling the social and environmental dimensions of the climate crisis need recognition that it is a complex matter and not only an environmental one but one affecting society including in terms of the risks posed by modern slavery, notably vulnerable communities in the LMIC. In understanding the issue, multiple factors need to be viewed alongside the changing climate, including the need to address the co-occurrence and monitoring of environmentally degrading sectors/activities associated with exploitative working conditions. In this regard, UN SDG target 8.3 highlights the innovation required to promote community-resilience – supporting both climate and improvements to working conditions through economic access. The target states that countries should "promote development-oriented policies that support productive activities, decent job creation, entrepreneurship, creativity and innovation, and encourage the formalization and growth of micro-, small- and medium-sized enterprises, including through access to financial services" (UN 2015).

Within the SDGs there are two main goals targeting the dual risks of modern slavery and climate change. Target 8.7 within Goal 8 (Decent Work and Economic Growth) refers to "immediate and effective measures to eradicate forced labour, end modern slavery and human trafficking and secure the prohibition and elimination of the worst forms of child labour, including recruitment and use of child soldiers, and by 2025 end child labour in all its forms" (UN 2015).[3] This is in contrast with the targets contained in SDG 13 (Climate Action) which are more well-defined and tied to direct action and financing. Further, target 13.4 refers to the need to "implement the commitment undertaken by developed-country parties to the United Nations Framework Convention on Climate Change to a goal of mobilizing jointly USD$100 billion annually by 2020 from all sources to address the needs of developing countries in the context of meaningful mitigation actions and transparency on implementation and fully operationalize the Green Climate Fund through its capitalization as soon as possible" (UN 2015).

However, present examples of providing such support noted in target 8.3 can have detrimental impacts – for example several articles focused on

Cambodia note that in response to climate change, community members acquired loans to support their businesses but have since had to migration to more insecure employment in sectors that are tied to environmentally degrading practices and poor or exploitative working conditions (Brickell et al. 2018; Natarajan et al. 2021a, 2021b). Yet they can also have several benefits particularly where informality creates barriers to economic development and security which can have consequences to both workers and the broader economy. Across multiple African countries, informal trade – often linked to the work of women – is seen as vulnerability indicator with the UN highlighting how the development of a deeper-integrated regional governance strategy can reduce employment vulnerabilities for women and youth populations, strengthen supply chains, and reduce the informal trade and business transactions (UNCTAD 2019) – yet the risks of climate change in driving these risks is limited in scope. Furthermore, in responding to climate change migration is often an option chosen (or forced upon) impacted communities depending on circumstances (McLeman 2019; Marotzke et al. 2020) in addition to economic migration that already occurs. Yet precarity and a changing climate in destination countries can still lead to climate and working vulnerabilities, as has been noted in the United Arab Emirates with migrant workers from Bangladesh and other South Asian nations exposed to extreme heat and poor working conditions (HRW 2023). As such it is clear a holistic and integrated approach to addressing the social, economic and environmental drivers of vulnerability are needed, to which the SDG framework in the ESG context can support.

It should be noted that whilst all the SDGs should be considered in an interconnected manner, the availability of data and scale of resources can be barriers to effective combined action – this is something which has been highlighted when addressing modern slavery and climate change (Jackson et al. 2021). This is also fueling the limited understanding and action that governance mechanisms in ESG can undertake at scale. By developing worker-led and focused actions that align with the SDGs there are opportunities to enact social-ecological change for the benefit of workers, businesses and the planet moving forward.

Leaders unwilling to change their perspectives or unable at present to proactively address the complex dual challenges of modern slavery and climate change should consider the following: in an ever-increasing globalized world combined action is necessary for complex issues. Integration of the SDGs into ESG framing for organisations is an established framework that can be an avenue to addressing global concerns. As Parosha Chandran[4] summarizes "[i]t is important that every organisation has a clear understanding of the nature of the way in which it is procuring goods and services through due diligence and ensuring transparency of operations across its supply chains" but adds "[t]he need to address modern slavery through civil and criminal corporate liability is gaining momentum across the world" (Punwani 2023b).

7. Conclusion

The moral principles enshrined in the UN principles and goals provide a basis for organisations to take their environmental and social responsibilities seriously including in eradicating the risks of modern slavery for vulnerable communities such as those in Bangladesh and India. The interconnected way in which this issue is being exacerbated by the climate and ecological crises illustrates why a principled, global perspective is needed. Further, the need for greater global efforts in understanding the complex nature of this discussion – including the critiques of the UN SDGs – should be accepted and welcomed to enable a more inclusive and community-focused agenda, led by those most affected by climate change, in achieving all the UN SDGs through ESG obligations.

Notes

1 References to high-income (HIC), and low- and middle-income countries (LMIC) are made following the publication of suggested guidance on language around "development" see Mahler et al. (2024).

2 CEO of Unseen (a UK NGO working in the anti-slavery sector) contributed expertise to the development of the 2015 UK Modern Slavery Act.

3 To note, the consideration of indicators and tangible actions tied to SDG target 8.7 are limited.

4 Professor of Modern Slavery Law at King's College London, human rights barrister at One Pump Court Chambers, and parliamentary advisor.

Bibliography

Ahmed, S. (2018). Climate-induced poverty in coastal Bangladesh: Policy implications. Poverty Brief, 43, 1-4.

Ahmed, S., and Eklund, E. (2021). Climate change impacts in coastal Bangladesh: Migration, gender and environmental injustice. Asian Affairs, 52(1), 155-174.

Ahmed, S., and Khan, M.A. (2022). Spatial overview of climate change impacts in Bangladesh: a systematic review. Climate and Development, 15(2), 132-147.

Anti-Slavery International. (2021). EU law. Global Impact. A report considering the potential impact of human rights due diligence laws on labour exploitation and forced labour. London UK.

Bellagio-Harvard Guidelines. (2012). The Bellagio-Harvard Guidelines on the Legal Parameters of Slavery. Yale University, New Haven CT. Available: https://glc.yale.edu/sites/default/files/pdf/the_bellagio-_harvard_guidelines_on_the_legal_parameters_of_slavery.pdf

Bharadwaj, R., Bishop, D., Hazra, S., Pufaa, E., and Kofi Annan, J. (2021). Climate-induced migration and modern slavery. IIED and Anti-Slavery International, London UK.

Bharadwaj, R., Chakravarti, D., Karthikeyan, N., Hazra, S., Daniel, U., Topno, J., and Abhilashi, R. (2022). Climate change, migration and vulnerability to trafficking. IIED, London UK.

Bloxham, L. (2023). The female farmers tackling climate change in Bangladesh. Concern Worldwide. Retrieved 10 May 2024, from https://www.concern.org.uk/news/female-farmers-tackling-climate-change-bangladesh

Brickell, K., Parsons, L., Natarajan, N., and Chann, S. (2018). Blood Bricks: Untold Stories of Modern Slavery and Climate Change from Cambodia. Royal Holloway, University of London UK.

Brown, D., Boyd, D.S., Brickell, K., Ives, C.D., Natarajan, N., and Parsons, L. (2021). Modern slavery, environmental degradation and climate change: Fisheries, field, forests and factories. Environment and Planning E: Nature and Space, 4(2), 191-207.

Bullock, K., Di Domenico, M., Miller, G., Shirgholami, Z., and Wong, Y. (2024). Under the radar? Modern slavery and labour exploitation risks for the hotel industry. Tourism Management, 102, 104857.

Cockayne, J. (Ed.). (2021). Developing Freedom: The Sustainable Development Case for Ending Modern Slavery, Forced Labourm Human Trafficking. United Nations University, New York NY.

Coelho, S. (2016). The Climate Change-Human Trafficking Nexus. IOM, Bangkok.

Debnath, R., Bardhan, R., and Bell, M.L. (2023). Lethal heatwaves are challenging India's sustainable development. PLOS Climate, 2(4), e0000156.

Decker Sparks, J.L., Boyd, D.S., Jackson, B., Ives, C.D., and Bales, K. (2021). Growing evidence of the interconnections between modern slavery, environmental degradation, and climate change. One Earth, 4(2), 181-191.

Divanbeigi, R., and Saliola, F. (2022). Mobilizing development lending to create more and better jobs. World Bank Blogs. Retrieved 23 May 2024, from https://blogs.worldbank.org/en/jobs/mobilizing-development-lending-create-more-and-better-jobs

Divanbeigi, R., Li, Y., Ru, J., and Yoshijima, S. (2023). Greening Bangladesh's brick sector: A win-win for workers and the planet. Jobs & Development Partnerships World Bank Group. Retrieved 23 May 2024, from https://www.jobsanddevelopment.org/11-greening-bangladeshs-brick-sector-a-win-win-for-workers-and-the-planet/

Foley, M. (2024). Beware: The Scaled-Down CSDDD Regulation Still Has Bite. Forbes. Retrieved 23 May 2024, from https://www.forbes.com/sites/maryfoley/2024/03/27/beware-the-scaled-down-csddd-regulation-still-has-bite

Gold, S., Trautrims, A., and Trodd, Z. (2015). Modern slavery challenges to supply chain management. Supply Chain Management: An International Journal, 20(5), 485-494.

Gonzalez De Aguinaga, S. (2024). Effectiveness of mandatory human rights and environmental due diligence legislation in addressing modern slavery in business value chains (updated). Human Rights Policy & Evidence Centre, London UK.

Gonzalez De Aguinaga, S. (2024). Effectiveness of mandatory human rights and environmental due diligence legislation in addressing modern slavery in business value chains. Modern Slavery Policy & Evidence Centre, London UK.

Gözlügöl, A.A. (2022). The clash of 'E' and 'S' of ESG: just transition on the path to net zero and the implications for sustainable corporate governance and finance. The Journal of World Energy Law & Business, 15(1), 1-21.

Gutierrez-Huerter O, G., Gold, S., and Trautrims, A. (2023). Change in Rhetoric but not in Action? Framing of the Ethical Issue of Modern Slavery in a UK Sector at High Risk of Labor Exploitation. Journal of Business Ethics, 182, 35-58.

Harrisberg, K., and Tripathi, B. (2023). 'Invisible' informal workers rally for a role in green movement. Context. Retrieved 10 May 2024, from https://www.context.news/just-transition/invisible-informal-workers-rally-for-a-role-in-green-movement

HRW. (2023). UAE: Migrant Worker Abuses Linked to Broader Climate Harms. Human Rights Watch. Retrieved 23 May 2024, from https://www.hrw.org/news/2023/11/21/uae-migrant-worker-abuses-linked-broader-climate-harms

ILO. (2022). Global Estimates of Modern Slavery: Forced Labour and Forced Marriage. International Labour Organization, Geneva CH.

Jackson, B. (2023). Climate change, migration and human trafficking: Assessing the impact of climate change, migration and human trafficking risks for populations in the Bangladesh and India Sundarbans. Rights Lab, University of Nottingham.

Jackson, B., Brotherton, V., Blackstone, N.T., and Decker Sparks, J.L. (2021). Modern slavery, environmental degradation and climate change: present and future pathways for addressing the nexus. Rights Lab, University of Nottingham UK.

Jackson, B., Weir, E., Mead, J., DiPreta, A., Tucker, M., Sebastian, M., Hutchison, K., Olatunbosun, J., Bengtsen, P., Brotherton, V., Boyd, D.S., and Alexander, M. (2024). Integrating policies addressing modern slavery and climate change: Realigning modern slavery and climate change policies for equitable governance and action. Modern Slavery Policy & Evidence Centre, London UK.

Kashwan, P. (2022). Social Mobilizations for Climate Action and Climate Justice in India (p. 140-161). In Kashwan, P. (Ed.) Climate Justice in India (Vol. 1). Cambridge University Press, Cambridge UK.

Koonce, K. (2023). The Race to Net Zero: How ESG Investors Are Driving Corporations to Ethically Lower Greenhouse Gas Emissions. Environs: Environmental Law and Policy Journal, 46(2), 111-134.

Landman, T., and Silverman, B.W. (2019). Globalization and Modern Slavery. Politics and Governance, 7(4), 275-290.

LeBaron, G., and Gore, E. (2020). Gender and Forced Labour: Understanding the Links in Global Cocoa Supply Chains. The Journal of Development Studies, 56(6), 1095-1117.

Mahler, D.G., Holla, A., and Serajuddin, U. (2024). Time to stop referring to the "developing world". World Bank Blogs. Retrieved 1 May 2024, from https://blogs.worldbank.org/en/opendata/time-stop-referring-developing-world

Marotzke, J., Semmann, D., and Milinski, M. (2020). The economic interaction between climate change mitigation, climate migration and poverty. Nature Climate Change, 10, 518-525.

McGowan, J. (2024). European Parliament Approves Corporate Sustainability Diligence Law. Forbes. Retrieved 23 May 2024, from https://www.forbes.com/sites/jonmcgowan/2024/04/24/european-parliament-approves-corporate-sustainability-due-diligence-law

McGuire, B. (2014). Global Catastrophes: A Very Short Introduction (2nd Edition). Oxford University Press, Oxford UK.

McLeman, R. (2019). International migration and climate adaptation in an era of hardening borders. Nature Climate Change, 9, 911-918.

Myers, K.F., Doran, P.T., Cook, J., Kotcher, J.E., and Myers, T.A. (2021). Consensus revisited: quantifying scientific agreement on climate change and climate expertise among Earth scientists 10 years later. Environmental Research Letters, 16(10), 104030.

Nakate, V. (2023). Climate change and human rights: The inextricable link (p. 14-15). In Walk Free (Ed.) The Global Slavery Index 2023. Minderoo Foundation, Perth WA.

Natarajan, N., Brickell, K., and Parsons, L. (2021a). Diffuse Drivers of Modern Slavery: From Microfinance to Unfree Labour in Cambodia. Development and Change, 52(2), 241-264.

Natarajan, N., Brickell, K., Guermond, V., Lawreniuk, S., and Parsons, L. (2021b). Challenging the financial inclusion-decent work nexus: evidence

from Cambodia's over-indebted internal migrants. Global Public Policy and Governance, 1, 361-381.
NCABL. (2016). Joint stakeholders' report on situation of bonded labour in India for submission to United Nations Universal Periodic Review III. National Coalition for Abolition of Bonded Labour, Odisha IN.
O'Connell, C. (2021). From a vicious to a virtuous circle: Addressing climate change, environmental destruction and contemporary slavery. Anti-Slavery International, London.
Palumbo, L., and Sciurba, A. (2015). Vulnerability to Forced Labour and Trafficking: The case of Romanian women in the agricultural sector in Sicily. Anti-Trafficking Review, 5, 1-10.
Parsons, L. (2023). Carbon Colonialism: How rich countries export climate breakdown. Manchester University Press, Manchester UK.
Piciariello, A., Colenbrander, S., Bazaz, A., and Roy, R. (2021). The costs of climate change in India: A review of the climate-related risks facing India, and their economic and social costs. ODI, London.
Punwani, A. (2023a). 'Unmasking modern slavery in global migration'. Crisis Response Journal, 18(4), p 92-94.
Punwani, A. (2023b). Stamping out slavery. Enterprise Risk Magazine, IRM. Retrieved 23 May 2024, from https://issuu.com/irmglobal/docs/enterprise-risk-autumn-2023/s/32949312
Robinson, R.N.S. (2013). Darker still: Present-day slavery in hospitality and tourism services. Hospitality & Society, 3(2), 93-110.
Rogerson, M., Grosvold, J., and Alves, K. (2024). Climate change and modern slavery in public procurement. Modern Slavery Policy & Evidence Centre, London UK.
Saeed, S., Makhdum, M.S.A., Anwar, S., and Yaseen, M.R. (2023). Climate change vulnerability, adaptation, and feedback hypothesis: A comparison of lower-middle, upper-middle, and high-income countries. Sustainability, 15(5), 4145.
Savill, E. (2022). The inadequacies of social auditing: why we need worker-led solutions. Anti-Slavery International. Retrieved 23 May 2024, from https://www.antislavery.org/latest/social-auditing-inadequate-why-we-need-worker-led-solutions

Sharpe, I., and Davison, C.M. (2021). Climate change, climate-related disasters and mental disorder in low- and middle-income countries: a scoping review. BMJ Open, 11, e051908.

Siddique, A. (2024). Expediting environmental policy: Interview with Bangladesh minister Saber Hossain Chowdhury. Mongabay. Retrieved 10 May 2024, from https://news.mongabay.com/2024/03/expediting-environmental-policy-interview-with-bangladesh-minister-saber-hossain-chowdhury/

Simpson, D., Segrave, M., Quarshie, A., Kach, A., Handfield, R., Panas, G., and Moore, H. (2021). The role of psychological distance in organizational responses to modern slavery risk in supply chains. Journal of Operations Management, 67(8), 917-1016.

Sokolowski, A., Boldyreva, T., Jenkins-Long, E., Bamkole, S., and Twigg, S. (2023). Are companies developing credible climate transition plans? Disclosure to key climate transition-focused indicators in CDP's 2022 Climate Change Questionnaire. CDP, London UK.

Srivastava, A., Vyas, V., and Gurtu, A. (2024). Relationship between Socially Sustainable Supply Chains and United Nations Sustainable Development Goals: A Perspective from the Indian Auto Ancillary Industry. Global Business Review. DOI: 10.1177/09721509241240522

Steger, M.B. (2013). Globalization: A Very Short Introduction (3rd Edition). Oxford University Press, Oxford UK.

Thunberg, G. (Ed.). (2024). The Climate Book. Penguin Random House, London UK.

UN OHCHR. (2011). Guiding Principles on Business and Human Rights: Implementing the United Nations "Protect, Respect and Remedy" Framework. United Nations, New York NY.

UN. (2015). Transforming our world: The 2030 Agenda for Sustainable Development. United Nations, New York NY.

UN. (2022). Vanessa Nakate: Climate change is about the people. Voices of Change. Retrieved 9 May 2024, from https://www.un.org/en/climatechange/vanessa-nakate-climate-change-is-about-people

UNCTAD. (2019). Economic development in Africa report 2019: Made in Africa – rules of origin for enhanced intra-African trade. United Nations Conference on Trade and Development, Geneva CH.

Unseen. (2023). Who cares? A review of reports of exploitation in the care sector. Bristol.

US Department of State. (2023). Trafficking in Persons Report June 2023. Office to Monitor and Combat Trafficking in Persons, Washington DC.

USAID. (n.d.). Environment, Energy, and Climate Resilience. Retrieved 10 May 2024, from https://www.usaid.gov/bangladesh/environment-energy-climate-resilience

Walk Free. (2023a). Bridging ESG silos: The intersection of climate change and modern slavery. Minderoo Foundation, Perth WA.

Walk Free. (2023b). Spotlight on the garment sector: Stitched with slavery in the seams (p. 176-181). In The Global Slavery Index 2023. Minderoo Foundation, Perth WA.

Weir, E., Trautrims, A., and Smyth, D. (2024). Agriculture and Modern Slavery Act Reporting. Rights Lab, University of Nottingham UK.

World Bank. (2024). Bangladesh Environmental Sustainability and Transformation Project. Retrieved 23 May 2024, from https://projects.worldbank.org/en/projects-operations/project-detail/P172817

Zami, M.T. (2023). Young Bangladeshis push for climate action but workers left out. Context. Retrieved 10 May 2024, from https://www.context.news/just-transition/young-bangladeshis-push-for-climate-action-but-workers-left-out

Not only must have but natural evolution - why well organized ESG should be treated as a next level of mature GRC system in a production company

Piotr Janecki

1. Introduction

This study will not be a detailed analysis of the issue of sustainable development and the tasks related to it as defined by the acronym ESG. However, according to the author's assumptions, it will be a practical analysis demonstrating the validity of the thesis stated in the title that in order to effectively implement ESG, it is necessary - in the author's opinion - to establish clear rules for correlating ESG with the risk management system implemented in a production organisation[1] and the CMS system[2] .

2 Basic definitions - what are we talking about?

2.1 Need to act formal requirements as well as a natural business need

The CMS and GRC models taking into account ESG is not only an organizational decision, but in the author's opinion a challenge facing each organization that has decided to implement a central risk management approach. While in the area of soft compliance, where the starting point is the declaration made by the company, one can limit oneself to preventive and informative measures, in the area of ESG, measures need to be taken that are structured and organized in a more professional and structured way. It should be remembered that manufacturing companies, to a large extent, are entities that carry out their activities generating profit from the production and sale of products, which at the same time, irrespective of the adopted internal codes or commitments made to external stakeholders[3] , are subject to ESG regulations, and thus sanctions and obligations resulting from them. Thus, irrespective of the strategies adopted or the more or less successful attempts - to develop a business strategy that takes into account ESG assumptions - effectiveness in this respect will, over the years, be the responsibility of the entities subject to the relevant ESG reporting regulations. What these obligations are and how this requirement relates to properly implemented GRC standards - the author will briefly discuss this later in this paper.

2.2 GRC models

Governance Risk and Compliance further GRC[4] is a strategy resulting in the implementation of an organizational model and structure that ensures the organization's safety and compliance in the areas of work organization, centralized risk management as well as the examination of compliance in the broadest sense. This compliance with the adopted and required standard is organized within the CMS. GRC itself, according to the author, is an accepted model and an element of organizational culture. Without clearly defined principles, methodologies to control them as well as support in building awareness of them, the implementation of a highly effective GRC model will simply not be possible. Risk management is also about building an organizational culture that rewards appropriate behavior and implementing methodologies for machine-based (e.g. transaction control) as well as *event-driven (ICS)* catching of irregularities. The model of a successfully implemented GRC is also a structure and strategy that safeguards the organization. Actions are taken in the triangle of Governance, Compliance and Risk Management. Within which actions are taken to identify, as Appropriate:

a) Clear rules (internal *soft compliance rules of the* legal regulations applying to the company within the defined major compliance risks *hard compliance rules*) and risk appetite
b) Pragmatist in the GRC area (for process, risk and compliance management)
c) Organizational structures and components so that the assumptions defined in a and b can be enforced, and
d) Targets and planned activities - e.g. effectively supervised CMS and non-financial KPI's against which both the organization and the GRC structure itself will be held accountable

As a starting point, most GRC solutions as originally defined do not actually perform any of the activities required by the organization to achieve ESG goals, except of course for the benefits that for the designed ESG activities arise from the process-based order and governance put in place as part of the GRC implementation. In addition to monitoring and reporting, GRC solutions can facilitate information flows in processes that support ESG goals. These specific process flows can manage some of the more transactional elements of ESG as the author will discuss in the next section[5] .

2.3 ESG brief overview

It is not the intention of the author to carry out a detailed analysis in this paper as a comprehensive presentation of the assumptions of modern ESG systems. The key point, however, is to indicate the assumptions that should be a *must have for* any large manufacturing organization with plans to implement a unified system to ensure standardization and oversight of the ESG system already in place (whether as a voluntary decision of the entrepreneur or due to a legal obligation) . This *modus operandi* is also characteristic of the implementation of GRC systems. However, before the author goes on to discuss common mechanisms, it is necessary to point out the components and recommended actions in the area of ESG definition and implementation. E-which stands for environmental aspects means the necessary declaration and assumptions to be made in order to reduce negative impacts on the environment. In the case of manufacturing companies, it means managing resources within a closed loop and implementing a number of initiatives relating to CO2 neutrality as well as recycling and the product life cycle. The life cycle is to be understood in a broad sense, as it is also about ensuring transparency in this regard in the supply and distribution chain. E-label issues are also about quality and service requirements - the standard is a standard for extending the 'life' of a product. Durability is therefore not only a technical parameter, but also a mandatory element of product compliance, touching on product design, development and quality testing procedures. Another issue is defined as S in the acronym. S stands for social, which means nurturing respect, diversity, non-discrimination and inclusiveness in the workplace. It also means respect for workers' rights and human rights - as in the case of the previously discussed *E* both within the organization and in relations with suppliers and customers (social responsibility), and as in the case of soft and hard compliance rules, it means adopting a standard of appropriate codes of conduct, which will have to become an immanent part of purchasing and commercial contracts. In addition to the previously derived definition of Governance, i.e. G, *it* should be reiterated that, similarly to the assumptions of GRC, it is about the obligation to conduct business in accordance with the law and to comply with and implement increasingly better business practices and internal processes, as well as a more stringent obligation to report data in ESG areas that were not previously recorded non-financial indicators.

3. Development of the ESG model in the organization in conjunction with the GRC model

With regard to ESG, it is worthwhile, in the context of defining terms, to look at the differences that doctrine notes in defining the subject area that is identical for both definitions -*Governance*. Here, the author is referring, among other things, to the definition of *Governance* adopted for the study created by the German Compliance Institute, hereinafter *DICO*. The ESG study defines *Governance in* two ways: *" G of ESG means certain sustainability-related tasks or topics related to corporate governance, such as corporate governance principles, remuneration, diversity, lobbying, risk management and anti-corruption. The list of topics is based on the relevant EFRAG 'G1' standard. ESG governance, on the other hand, refers to the governance or regulatory framework, i.e. the overall control and monitoring system to establish sustainability goals as a whole, ensure their implementation and report on them*[6] . The author pays particular attention to the second part of this definition. Based on his own experience, both scientific and managerial, he points out that, just as the original definition of compliance objectives should not have been limited to a single standard, in the case of ESG, the 'managerial' part of the definition should be understood as an opportunity to integrate governance, risk and compliance into a modern environmental, social and governance model. As noted by some doctrine, GRC provides a standardized framework for governance, risk and compliance management. By integrating GRC with ESG, companies can coordinate efforts more effectively and ensure that relevant stakeholders receive relevant information quickly[7].

3.1 So what needs to be done and how to take advantage of the models developed under the previously implemented GRC when implementing ESG

In order to indicate the basic obligations arising from the implementation of an ESG system, it is worth using the individual ESG elements already briefly indicated above as a starting point. An analysis of the activities recommended in the author's opinion for the implementation of the standard will also indicate a number of similarities with GRC implementation projects. This, in turn, will serve for further analysis in the next section.

Starting with E- defining the indicators in this area for the production company, it is necessary to review the common - statements of goals and objectives- included in the organization's Code of Ethics. This code[8] is a starting point and a declaration, but the ESG objectives themselves should be included in a document that refers to the code but clearly defines the scope and subject matter of the sustainability policy adopted by the organization. Such a document can also be a health and safety policy and environmental management regulations, which are linked to the general declaration. Here, a first similarity can be seen to GRC and CMS, where the main compliance risks also need to be specified in internal regulations. In these documents, as well as in the source regulations for clearly defined compliance risks, reference should also be made to issues in the scope and S *social*. In addition to the sources mentioned above, an employee relations policy - such as an anti-bribery policy or a general policy regulating standards for formal management aspects of Human Resources - could complement the catalogue of sources. Social obligations and standards should also be derived from purchasing and sales policies, to which relevant codes of *conduct* should be annexed. The company should also implement and monitor a standard on human rights and environmental requirements. The natural direction taken by many in the manufacturing industry is to expand the areas responsible for implementing ISO systems, which, in the author's opinion, seems like a good idea. Management also needs to update its policies and implemented management pragmatics with regard to the requirements of defined ESG - just as the GRC standardizes risk management - ESG should naturally become an example for the next implementation of an effective internal corporate procedure. It is important to anchor the new regulations clearly and comprehensibly in a catalogue of internally applicable internal standards. Such an approach will also allow GRC elements to be used to test the effectiveness of ESG implementation. For example, within the ICS framework, it is possible to define controls based on existing internal procedures.

3.2 What practical examples and benefits can the implementation of an integrated GRC and ESG system bring to a manufacturing company

Implementing GRC processes can lead to cost savings by eliminating duplicated efforts and improving overall process efficiency. Improve the quality of information collected in ERP and ICS Systems on non-financial indicators. GRC helps organizations provide reliable and accurate data and, in addition, by incorporating GRC practices into ESG reporting, companies can provide high quality information to stakeholders, increasing the transparency of reported data.

Specific examples of the integration of governance, risk and compliance (GRC) practices with environmental, social and governance (ESG) frameworks, could also be the integration of ESG risks into the company's overall risk assessment process. For example, assessing environmental risks related to climate change, resource scarcity or pollution and integrating them into the risk management framework.

On supervisory matters, the ESG policy plugged into the GRC standard ensures that the board actively oversees ESG issues. This includes setting ESG targets, monitoring progress and integrating ESG issues into strategic decision-making.

Turning to compliance reporting, it should be noted that aligning ESG reporting with existing compliance processes allows ESG indicators to be integrated into regular financial or sustainability reporting.

A clearly manifested and repeatable ESG process allows stakeholders such as investors, employees, customers and communities to be involved in ESG issues promoted by the company. This allows GRC mechanisms to be used to manage stakeholder views, address issues and incorporate their perspective into ESG initiatives.

In the area of internal controls (as previously ICS), these can be supplemented with controls specific to ESG factors. For example, establishing controls related to data accuracy, ethical behavior and environmental impact.

Audit and verification here you can, under the 3 lines of support, initiate independent audits or verification of ESG disclosures. As with GRC audits, this can be used to determine that ESG information is accurate, reliable and consistent.

As with GRC policies (as discussed above), the integration of ESG policies into the company's overall governance framework is another similarity to the GRC area. This includes policies related to diversity and inclusion, environmental protection and social responsibility.

It is important to remember that effective integration of GRC and ESG requires a holistic approach that includes cross-departmental collaboration and clear communication with stakeholders.

When GRC is effectively integrated with ESG, companies can better address environmental, social and corporate governance aspects, contributing to long-term sustainability goals.

In summary, GRC plays a key role in achieving ESG objectives by ensuring effective governance, risk management and compliance practices, but it is important to remember that integrating governance, risk and compliance (GRC) practices with environmental, social and governance (ESG) frameworks can be challenging due to several factors:

- Complexity and interdependencies, ESG covers a wide range of factors, including environmental impact, social responsibility and corporate governance. Integrating GRC practices requires understanding the interdependencies between these areas and developing a coherent approach
- availability and quality of data, collecting reliable data for ESG reporting can be difficult. Companies need to collect relevant information on environmental performance, social initiatives and corporate governance practices. Ensuring data accuracy and consistency is critical
- Stakeholder expectations, Stakeholders (investors, customers, employees, regulators) have different expectations regarding ESG performance. Balancing these expectations while complying with compliance requirements can be challenging.
- Regulatory landscape, ESG regulations are evolving rapidly. Companies need to stay informed of new requirements and adapt their practices accordingly. Compliance with different regulations in different regions adds to the complexity of the

- Integrating with existing processes, aligning GRC practices with ESG initiatives often requires modification of existing processes. This can disrupt established workflows and require change management efforts
- Risk assessment, identification and evaluation of ESG risks (such as climate risks, supply chain vulnerabilities or social controversies) requires specialist knowledge. Companies need to assess these risks alongside traditional financial risks
- Board engagement, integrating GRC with ESG relies on board-level engagement. Ensuring that board members prioritize ESG and allocate resources accordingly can be challenging
- Cultural change, successful integration of GRC and ESG requires a cultural change within the organization. Employees need to accept ESG principles and understand their impact on business decisions
- The complexity of reporting, ESG reporting involves multiple stakeholders and different metrics. Companies need to navigate reporting frameworks (such as SASB, GRI or TCFD[9])) and communicate effectively with investors and the public
- Long-term perspective, ESG goals often go beyond short-term financial returns. Balancing long-term sustainability with immediate business needs can be challenging

Despite these challenges, companies that successfully integrate GRC and ESG can improve their reputation, attract responsible investors and contribute to a more sustainable future. So what are the best practices for implementing ESG referring to and anchored in previously implemented GRC ? It is imperative to obtain support from senior management and ensure that the board and management actively support ESG integration and allocate the necessary resources additionally by design the benefit calculus of effective implementation should be clearly demonstrated, do not promise too much or propose phantom initiatives or in extreme cases generate *greenwashing* risks.

Use a holistic approach, i.e. see ESG as an integral part of business strategy rather than a separate function. Aligning ESG objectives with overall corporate objectives, and here citing the obvious gains and potential losses from non-implementation will help. It is natural to perform an up-to-date materiality assessment. Identify material ESG issues relevant to the industry in which we operate and the broadly defined (looks above) stakeholders. Prioritize actions based on their impact and importance.

Metrics and reporting is another task, not only to parameterize the ESG assumptions themselves, but also the ICS, which is worth using as a proven tool in terms of control and supervision. The development of clear ESG metrics and reporting frameworks is, by the way, a *must have* and fits in with the overall principles of GRC. Use recognized standards (e.g. SASB, GRI and communicate transparently with investors and stakeholders.

In the author's opinion, the introduction of new ESG issues into an existing process standard is worth defining specific tasks resulting from the above-mentioned challenges; these are tasks for those wishing to remodel existing GRC systems in the necessary context, i.e:

- Integrating ESG risks into existing risk management processes. Assessment of climate risk, supply chain vulnerability and social impact
- Engaging with investors, employees, customers and communities. Understanding their expectations and taking their opinions into account
- Educate employees on ESG principles. Fostering a culture of responsibility and sustainability
- Use of technology for data collection, analysis and reporting. Use of GRC tools to manage ESG risks
- Balance short-term financial goals with long-term sustainability. Avoid prioritizing immediate profits over ESG goals
- Regularly review and adjust ESG practices. Monitor progress, learn from challenges and refine strategies, a PDCA cycle familiar to anyone who has developed GRC implementation principles

4. Implementation options - which method to adopt

As in the case of GRC and CMS implementation, so in the case of ESG (this is another similarity for both challenges) one can speak of a tailor-made system implementation design. Using design nomenclature, it is up to the project sponsor and the internally implemented regulations and external needs/obligations to decide which ESG implementation modality to adopt. A valuable source in this respect, already indicated above, is the comprehensive comparison of possible options presented in the DICO study[10] . The models described therein depend on the assumptions and needs of the organization, but it is important to note that irrespective of the choice of the options presented therein, such as the "pillar model - small solution", the "multifunctional model" - which according to the authors of this study is an intermediate solution, or the "overall control model", each of these solutions has clear tasks for the compliance organization and must be changed or adapted to the needs of reality with a clearly defined ESG policy.

Based on his observations and practical experience over the last several years of managing compliance topics and building an organizational culture conducive to effective prevention, detection and continuous improvement cms, the author is of the opinion that only integrating the implementation of ESG with the GRC already in place in the organization will give the desired effect and effectiveness required for this type of project. This seems a natural conclusion after the analysis shown in the previous section of this paper.

5. Summary

Today, no one needs to be convinced anymore that a process-based and interdisciplinary approach to CMS is the only way to develop an effective compliance risk management system. Just as the very definition of compliance has evolved from an internal control system to GRC, the ESG assumptions are now the benchmark for modern systems based on a strong foundation of Governance Risk and Compliance.

The author points out the etymology and logic of GRC systems, drawing on the practically presented assumptions of Compliance by default and Compliance by design to show the similarities with the assumptions of ESG systems. The analysis of small, medium and full-scale implementation solutions already commented on in the literature is enriched by the results of the author's insights on an interdisciplinary approach to the topic of implementing compliance management systems, as well as defining the right stakeholders for compliance policies. This activity will be described in order to create a plan for the initial assessment and scope of the implementation of a GRC system compliant with a parallel ESG standard, or to create a plan for the broad implementation of a system of which an effective GRC will be part, defining compliance risks, including a product compliance policy, as well as an ESG standard for a manufacturing organization. The scope of compliance risks is evolving, the methodology for managing them is evolving - such a necessary evolution we describe in this publication. Heraclitus said that the only certainty in life is change, and just as this Greek philosopher was contrasted with Parmenides, who advocated the doctrine of unchanging being, proponents and opponents of including ESG processes in GRC processes are trying to argue the point. Certainly, as the analysis by DICO, for example, shows, it is possible to adopt a methodology of broad or narrow integration of the two systems, but certainly, in the author's opinion, the question of integrating ESG assumptions into the organizational dogma of GRC, or at least adopting a similar methodology for the successful implementation of ESG in a manufacturing organization, is inevitable in the long term. Certainly, there are already a number of interesting studies on the market indicating possible ways to integrate or incorporate ESG issues into the GRC standards already adopted. The indicated DICO study is one of them. However, it is certainly indisputable to recognize the desirability of treating the implementation of the processes defined by the ESG project as a continuation of an already implemented GRC system. This is due to the similarities outlined above as well as the undeniable benefits of such a solution.

Notes

1 After all, the original definition of compliance meant enforcing controls internally to detect irregularities and potential fraud, from a declaration of acting in accordance with the law and accepted standards, compliance management systems have evolved to a systematic control of internal processes and check and follow up activities in line *with the assumptions of* the Deming cycle *Plan to check and act*

2 On the definition of CMS and its 7 elements, as well as the interdisciplinary approach to successful CMS implementation, more extensively: P, Janecki *Interdisciplinary compliance approach as a response of entrepreneurs to the IoT reality and the challenges of the VUCA Times, in Global Ethics, Compliance & Integrity Yearbook 2021, ed: B. Makowicz, pp. 452 and the literature cited therein;* The rapid development of this field of supervisory control and standardisation is also accompanied by the development of certification systems, watot in the context of CMS mention The general standard ISO 37301 'Compliance management systems - Requirements with guidance for use' has been published and replaces ISO 19600, more on this topic: ISO 37301:2021 - Compliance management systems - Requirements with guidance for use (accessed:10.06.2024)

3 On the broad definition of stakeholders of a company's activities see, inter alia, P. Janecki....page 460.

[4] The acronym GRC was created by the OCEG (originally called the Open Compliance and Ethics Group) as a shorthand reference to the critical capabilities that must work together to achieve Principled Performance - capabilities that integrate the governance, management and assurance of performance, risk and compliance activities, cited: What is GRC (Governance, Risk, and Compliance)? - OCEG, accessed: 10.06.2024;

[5] https://cential.co/how-to-use-grc-to-manage-and-accomplish-esg-goals/

[6] For more information on Szerej see: https://www.dico-ev.de/2023/06/29/veroeffentlichung-des-dico-positionspapiers-esg/, p. 8

[7] https://www.esgenterprise.com/esg-reporting/importance-grc-esg/ and https://ditchcarbon.com/blog/how-grc-can-support-companies-esg-goals-the-ultimate-guide/ as well as https://cential.co/how-to-use-grc-to-manage-and-accomplish-esg-goals/ accessed 11.06.2024

[8] For how to effectively implement and frame such a code and compliance objectives, among others, see: P. Janecki in: "How to develop a compliance culture within an international organisation".

- a few practical remarks," Deutsch-Polnische Juristen-Zeitschrift 3&4(2015); 29–36; http://www.dpjz.de/dpjz-32015-dpjz-42015/

[9] On this topic see: https://help.sasb.org/hc/en-us/articles/360052463951-How-do-GRI-and-SASB-Standards-work-together-Do-companies-report-on-both-sets-of-standards; accessed 11.06.2024

[10] https://www.dico-ev.de/2023/06/29/veroeffentlichung-des-dico-positionspapiers-esg, pp. 2 ff; accessed: 12.06.2024

Sustainable Reporting in the Digital Age: Examining Global ESG Evolution, Non-Financial reporting landscape and the Empowering Role of AI

Shujath Bin Ali, Kalapurakkal Suresh Aravind

1. Introduction

The demand for Environment Social Governance (ESG) disclosure around the World has been increasing day by day. Compared to last decade, ESG based investing has grown which has also resulted in expansion of the data considered by investors.[1] The accountability of businesses have increased due to pressure from the government, consumers, and investors as more and more focus is being drawn to various environmental and social issues. ESG necessitates a business not only to excel in its financial performance but also their environmental, social and governance practices. It prompts organizations to consider its impact on the planet, communities, and stakeholders beyond profit margins, fostering a more conscientious and accountable business landscape. This can be achieved only through sustainable operation of business, responsible community engagement and effective corporate governance.

ESG Reporting involves the systematic and transparent disclosure of information about a company's sustainability efforts and their impacts on various stakeholders. It provides a comprehensive, realistic, and balanced view, aiming to encourage long-term value creation. ESG evaluates environmental factors such as greenhouse gas emissions, waste management, renewable energy use, and pollutants released into air, land, and water. It assesses social aspects, including employee management practices, labor conditions, training, safety standards, diversity, equality, inclusion, and corporate social responsibility. Additionally, it examines governance elements like decision-making and accountability systems, board independence, executive compensation, ethical behavior, shareholder rights, risk management, stakeholder engagement, and regulatory compliance.

As of now, various guidelines and reporting standards are present which can be used by businesses to formulate their ESG strategy and reporting, these include sustainability standard by the Global Reporting Initiative, Task Force on Climate-related Financial Disclosures, SASB Standards and the recent IFRS disclosures etc. Countries around the world also have been implementing their own disclosure standards through rules and regulation to ensure company transparency as well to achieve various commitment made under international treaties. Due to these increase in regulations, the ESG compliance has become mandatory for companies.

Companies' ESG standing is assesed through data disclosed. Stakeholders use these reports to understand and compare various businesses. For this reporting, it is essential to collect relevant data that will be then interpreted by various stakeholders like rating agencies, investors as well as company itself for decision making. Due to the sheer volume of data available, it is time consuming and difficult to identify the relevant data with traditional methods. Moreover, the quality and accuracy of data interpreted is also important. This is where the role of Artificial Intelligence comes, which can collect vast amount of data and process in shorter time.

This paper provides an understanding of the development of International ESG Disclosures and emphasizes in ESG disclosures across regions like European Union, United States, South Africa and India to get an overview about the developing ESG disclosure trend. The paper further looks at the benefit of Non-Financial Disclosures and how Artificial Intelligence can play a role in assisting companies with their ESG disclosures.

2. ESG Disclosures

2.1 International Framework

The evolution of ESG can be traced back to 1970 when environmental challenges began to be identified. The United Nations Environment Programme was established to coordinate world environmental efforts and brought a significant contribution to bringing environmental awareness. Further in 1983, The United Nations established the Brundtland Commission with the aim of tackling the dual challenges of economic development and environmental protection. The commission published its landmark report, "Our Common Future," which played a pivotal role in popularizing the concept of "sustainable development."

The focus on ESG issues was significantly boosted with the introduction of the Global Reporting Initiative as it emphasized on both corporate social responsibility and the broader impact of ESG issues. In 1999, The United Nations Principles for Responsible Investment (UNPRI) was formed by a group of institutional investors. This consists of six principles facilitating the integration of ESG factors into investment strategies. The Paris Agreement of 2015 was a significant step of commitment for participating nations to mitigate the effects of climate change. Further, in 2017 Task Force on Climate Related Financial Disclosure was developed which became a widely accepted standard for accessing climate-related ESG Metrics.

Non-Financial ESG Disclosures cover those factors that do not have direct impact on the financial of the company but have an impact on the reputation and performance of a company as it shows the way the company operates. This includes welfare policies, impact on environment etc. Non-financial ESG disclosure plays a crucial role in corporate transparency by offering stakeholders a holistic perspective of a company's endeavors and effects that extend beyond financial metrics. The same can be also seen enshrined in the Guiding Principle 21 of UN Guiding Principles on Business and Human Rights which states businesses should uphold human right and implement policies that demonstrate the same. Sustainable Development Goal 12, urges companies to embrace sustainable practices and incorporate sustainability information into their reporting cycles.

The existence of numerous standards has caused confusion and uneven disclosure.[2] As such, several initiatives were taken to standardise the same, which resulted in the formation of the Sustainable Disclosure Standards, by International Financial Reporting Standard (IFRS), issued in June 2023.[3] The two disclosures are the General requirement for Disclosure of Sustainability-related Financial Information (IFRS-S1) and Climate-related Disclosure (IFRS-2).[4]

Climate-related disclosures, similar to IFRS S1, includes a wide range of important elements needed to understand the entity's climate risk position and mitigation strategies. Some of them comprise the classification of climate-related risks into physical risks, those that are directly impacted by climate change and transition risk. Moreover, entities will need to describe how they intend to achieve the climate-related targets and any current or expected changes in business models and strategies that are needed for addressing climate change risks and opportunities. In addition, it is important to provide insights about transition plans toward a more carbon economy, and assess the climate resilience which evaluates the entity's ability to prepare for and recover from climate change effects.

In addition, these disclosures are supported by a broader framework under IFRS S2 which contains metrics across the following categories: greenhouse gas emissions, transition and physical risks, climate opportunities, capital allocation, internal carbon pricing and remuneration. Additionally, regarding emissions, entities shall separately identify the Scope 1 and 2 emissions (including those of joint ventures and associates) while specifying the Scope 3 emissions. Together, these disclosures enable stakeholders to understand an entity's climate-related risks and how the organization will adapt to and mitigate them, as well as how an organization is contributing and prepared fora transition toward a sustainable future.

2.2 European Union

Europe is one of the nations that has made clear guidelines concerning ESG reporting by enacting specific legislations and rules for the same. This includes ESG: the Taxonomy Regulation, the Non-Financial Reporting Directive (NFRD), the Corporate Sustainability Reporting Directive (CSRD), the Sustainable Finance Disclosure Regulation (SFDR), and the Corporate Sustainability Due Diligence Directive (CSDDD).[5]

Certain large EU firms are required by the NFRD to provide diversity and non-financial information in their annual reports, which addresses various aspects of their ESG responsibilities. It aims to make it easier for investors, customers, politicians, civil society groups, and other interested parties to evaluate the non-financial performance of major corporations. Its objective is to persuade these businesses to use responsible business practices.[6] More sizable EU-listed businesses are impacted by the CSRD, which updates and replaces the NFRD. Additional reporting obligations under ESG factors are also covered by this. The CSRD came into effect on January 5, 2023. Businesses that must comply with the CSRD must submit reports using the European Sustainability Reporting Standards. [7]

The directive extends to all large companies with over 250 employees, more than €50 million in turnover, or over €25 million in total assets. It encompasses listed companies across all EU member states, excluding micro-enterprises, thereby covering a significant portion of the EU market.[8] It is also applicable to Non-EU company with a net turnover of € 150 million in EU at a consolidated level, conducting "significant activities" in EU. It introduces requirements such as clarifying double materiality (identifying both ESG impacts on business and business impacts on people and planet), more detailed reporting aligned with the EU Taxonomy and European Sustainability Reporting Standards, integrating ESG disclosures into financial and management reporting, externally auditing the reported information, and digitally tagging reported information for a central database.[9]

The European Sustainability Reporting Standards arose from the European Green Deal and were formulated to meet the reporting requirement under CSRD and SFDR, which requires a company to report on how they impact ESG factors and financial risk and opportunities arising from the same. In the ESRS, there are general requirement & disclosures. Environment Standards has five standards, which are Climate Change, Pollution, Water and Marine Resources, Biodiversity, and Circular Economy. It can be seen that this is complimentary to the above-discussed IFRS disclosure standards though it is not as broad as the same. The Social category is divided into Workforce, Workforce in the value chain, Communities impacted, Consumers, and end-users. Governance has Business conduct.[10]

Disclosure obligations based on materiality are mandatory, not discretionary. If the information is considered material, it has to be revealed, and the determination of materiality needs to be confirmed by a third party. Organizations must report all pertinent sustainability-related data and complete a materiality review in order to achieve the target and standards of the Accounting Directive. A corporation must give a detailed explanation of its materiality assessment results regarding climate change if it decides that a parameter isn't a significant issue and doesn't report on it in accordance with the standard.[11] The ESRS offers a significant step toward streamlined sustainability reporting. ESRS aligns closely with the ISSB for climate change disclosures, minimizing redundancy for companies complying with both frameworks

The European Parliament adopted the Corporate Sustainability Due Diligence Directive on April 24, 2024,[12] which sets out detailed human rights and environmental obligations for EU and non-EU companies that exceed certain thresholds of turnover, starting in 2027. It requires businesses to exercise due diligence by identifying, assessing, preventing, mitigating, and bringing to the lowest possible level the negative human rights and environmental effects within their operations, subsidiaries, and business relationships. The company is further obliged to design an efficient climate change mitigation transition plan in accordance with the objective under the Paris Agreement of keeping global warming within the threshold of 1.5 °C. The Directive contains stiff penalties and a liability regime for failure in compliance. The main provisions apply to EU companies with more than 1,000 employees and a net turnover above EUR 450 million, and non-EU companies whose aggregate turnover in the Union exceeds EUR 450 million. The application will be progressive, starting with the larger companies in 2027.[13]

On February 5, 2024, the EU released a draft proposal[14] to regulate ESG ratings, which sought to address transparency and risk to investors concerns that were flagged by European Securities and Markets Authority. The proposal requires all ESG rating providers in the European Economic Area be registered and regulated by ESMA, detailing companies' impacts on ESG factors, such as human rights, be thoroughly assessed and recorded. It also stipulates clear distinctions and defined weightings for environmental, social, and governance categories in ratings, with deviations needing explicit justification.[15]

2.3 USA

The Securities and Exchange Commission (SEC),[16]holds significant influence in ESG and non-financial reporting through its mandate for publicly traded firms to divulge pertinent ESG-related data crucial for investment evaluations. While traditionally emphasizing financial risks, the SEC is transitioning towards broader ESG disclosures, encompassing climate risks and human capital management, acknowledging their significance in a company's performance and enduring value.

On March 6, 2024, the SEC implemented fresh climate disclosure regulations. These regulations mandate companies to release information detailing climate-related risks anticipated to materially affect their business or consolidated financial statements. The introduction of these regulations signals a substantial shift in the type and scope of disclosures expected from US companies regarding the repercussions of climate change. Compliance with these additional disclosures may necessitate significant alterations to a registrant's systems, processes, and oversight mechanisms.[17] Businesses may be required to reveal a number of broad climate risk-related elements, such as the management and control of these risks, their possible short-, medium-, and long-term effects on corporate value, and how they affect the company's outlook, strategy, and business model. In addition, they have to explain how they identify, evaluate, and manage climate risks as well as how these procedures fit into their larger risk management strategies. Companies should also disclose how transactions and events connected to climate change have affected financial line items. They must also disclose greenhouse gas (GHG) emissions, which include Scope 1 and 2 emissions in terms of absolute and intensity-based metrics, as well as aggregate and disaggregated emissions. If the emissions from Scope 3 are significant or pertinent to the company's emissions objectives, these must be reported as well.[18]

With respect to Social aspect, In 2021, NASDAQ rule change that requires NASDAQ-listed corporations to have at least two diverse members on their boards or offer an explanation if they don't was authorized by the SEC. Companies must also provide the voluntarily self-identified gender, racial characteristics, and LGBTQ+ status of their board members in accordance with the new NASDAQ regulations.[19] There was a lawsuit contesting the legislative validity and legality and in December 2024 the same was quashed in Alliance for Fair Board Recruitment v. SEC, (Case: 21-60626) the US Court of Appeals for the Fifth Circuit.[20]

2.4 South Africa

While South Africa does not have specific ESG disclosure mandates, It is enshrined in its legislation as seen in South African Constitution that includes Socio-Economic Rights as well as right to healthy environment and other guidance note such as guidance on Regulation 28 by Financial Sector Conduct Authority which takes into consideration of ESG factors integral to evaluating the sustainability of an asset.[21]

Even though South Africa does not have specific disclosure mandate, companies listed on the Johannesburg Stock Exchange(JSE),[22] are bound by broad ongoing disclosure obligations outlined in the JSE Listings Requirement, this also include following non-financial disclosures under GRI, IIRC. The JSE has developed optional guidelines for JSE-listed firms to improve their reporting on sustainability and climate change, known as the Sustainability Disclosure Guidance and Climate Disclosure Guidance. These recommendations make use of well-established worldwide frameworks while being specifically suited to the South African environment. A twofold materiality approach, evaluating effect relevance in addition to financial significance is applied. These rules describe material information as data that potentially affect the way finance providers make judgments about the organization's ability to create long-term value and how other stakeholders perceive the organization's effects on the economy, the environment, and society.[23]

The King IV Report on Corporate Governance for South Africa 2016 emphasize ethical responsible leadership and a well-balanced board of directors committed to independent decision-making for benefit of all parties involved.

2.5 India

In India, the Business Responsibility and Sustainability Report (BRSR) covers the ESG Disclosure. Under the BRSR, listed companies needs to make performance based reporting as well as on management and proceedings. It also allows a company to report using internationally recognized reporting framework and then cross reference it to the mandatory disclosures under the BRSR.

With the introduction of BRSR Core, SEBI created a regulatory framework for ESG disclosures, ratings, and investments in mutual funds in July 2023. This framework mandates large listed companies to disclose some Key Performance Indicators (KPIs) under nine ESG categories: waste management, employee safety and well-being, gender diversity, inclusive development, fair engagement with suppliers and customers, GHG footprint, water footprint, energy footprint, and business transparency. Starting in FY 2023-2024, the updated BRSR format requires the top 1000 listed firms by market capitalization to report and obtain assurance for value chain operations in their annual reports. They must publish value chain KPIs based on interactions with partners, either individually or in aggregate. For the top 250 listed companies, value chain ESG disclosure will be mandatory on a comply-or-explain basis beginning in FY 2024-2025 and continuing through 500 for FY 2025-2026 and 1000 for FY 2026-27.[24]

The Reserve Bank of India issued a draft regulation titled "Draft Disclosure Framework on Climate-related Financial Risks, 2024" after its 2022 Discussion Paper on Climate Risk and Sustainable Finance on February 28, 2024.[25] Following the TCFD recommendations on climate-related financial risks to Indian financial stability, the framework tries to make them assessed and managed, inform their proper disclosure to facilitate better decision-making, and ensure consistency and comparability in climate-related financial disclosure. It will apply to Scheduled Commercial Banks (excluding Local Area Banks and Payments Banks), Regional Rural Banks, Tier-IV Primary Urban Co-operative Banks, All-India Financial Institutions, Top and Upper Layer Non-Banking Financial Companies, and foreign banks operating in India, while other entities will be encouraged to follow it. Regulated Entities will have to make disclosure of their process for assessing and managing the risk under the Governance, Strategy, Risk Management, and Metrics & Targets pillars.

2.6 Understanding importance of Non – Financial Disclosure:

Investors around the World are increasingly looking at the Non –Financial Disclosures of Companies they are investing in. According to various research following benefits were identified.[26]

- **Reduction in Information Asymmetry:** By providing additional non-financial information voluntarily, companies reduce information asymmetry, leading to decreased risk for investors considering investing in the reporting company. This reduction in risk enhances the liquidity of the company's shares.
- **Improvement in Investment Decision Making:** With reduced information asymmetry and improved liquidity of shares, investors can make more efficient investment decisions, potentially resulting in better allocation of capital.
- **Enhanced Reliability:** Financial analysts are more positive about the accuracy of the mandatorily disclosed information when the companies also provide voluntary information. This may indicate that the voluntary disclosure is supplementary to the mandated disclosure, thus making it more credible.

- **Reputation:** By reporting ESG, Company shows their stakeholders that they are transparent hence boosting confidence of the stakeholders like investors and customers.
- **Improved Company Decision Making:** With the data collected from ESG metrics, the companies can further improve their decision making by choosing those areas that will increase their performance while mitigating risk.
- **Risk Mitigation:** ESG reporting especially non-financial disclosures can help companies identify the area that can be potential risk. For example, if a company realises their pollution emission is high, they can work to reduce the same as otherwise it can bring sanction or affect reputation

It can be seen that ESG-related compliance is increasingly becoming mandatory, with regulations being implemented in a phased manner. This trend requires companies to start integrating and adhering to comprehensive environmental, social, and governance standards. Directives such as the CSDDD and BRSR exemplify this shift, mandating companies to conduct thorough due diligence and implement measures to address human rights and environmental impacts, along with climate change mitigation strategies. This gradual but firm approach ensures that companies systematically adapt to the evolving regulatory landscape, enhancing their sustainability practices and accountability.

3. Artificial Intelligence and ESG Disclosure

3.1 What is AI?

In the recent decade, the term Artificial Intelligence (AI) and its applicability has become a topic of discussion in our society. AI was first coined by John McCarthy as a branch of computer science that dealt with creating computers that behaved like humans. It is the science and engineering of making intelligent machines, especially intelligent computer programs. While providing an exact definition of AI is difficult it is broadly characterized as the study of computations that allow for perception, reason and action.[27]

There are various types of Artificial Intelligence Methods, let's see two examples. Machine Learning is where the applications of AI allow machines to learn and improve based on experience without explicit programming. Deep

Learning, an area of Machine Learning, uses artificial neural networks to undertake predictive analysis. Unsupervised Learning is one form of machine learning that deals with uncategorized data with no guidance; supervised learning is another area that deals with training data comprising input/output pairs, while reinforcement learning involves the choice of the best action for the machine to maximize rewards. Automation is another example where burden of mundane and routine work is shifted to machines, helps increase productivity and can deliver cost-effective, efficient results. Organizations use machine learning, neural networks, and graphs to automate. This can reduce fraud in online financial transactions using techniques such as CAPTCHA. Robotic process automation is designed to manage high volume, repetitive tasks and adapt to changing circumstances.[28]

The Traditional methods of data processing has its limitation especially when large volume of data has to be processed. The traditional methods like document review, survey, interview etc but the same are time consuming as well as susceptible to human error which affects the overall efficiency. Owing to the same, Industries are increasingly using AI in their operations for processing data faster hence making overall system efficient.

3.2 How AI can assist with ESG Disclosure

With the quantity of data that is available it has become difficult to identify and streamline the process of data collection. Earlier, the data used to be sourced from reports, statistics but now more sources of information exist in internet. One of the common issues that is faced during data collection for ESG is the information asymmetry. Stakeholders face different challenges during data collection. ESG rating providers use their own unique method and tools to analyze companies, leading to different conclusions due to varying definitions, measurements, and weightings of ESG indicators. This inconsistency creates significant issues for investors. The varied interpretations of data by rating companies leaves investors uncertain about which rating aligns with their investment criteria or goals. The issue also arises with the fact that the rating is done relying on the information provided by the business itself which can create information bias. The Companies may only disclose information that is favourable to the them inturn helping them get favourable scores. These stand as an uncertainty for the investors and other stakeholder who evaluate the data to compare the organisation. [29]

The issues with ESG ratings would be best addressed by consistently collecting qualitative data to support quantitative data. AI can assist in the same by having inputs that helps them identify the qualitative information. AI can also analyse across the internet or provided data to convert them in a structured manner to mitigate information asymmetry. [30] Along with this, AI can also identify the reporting trends and collect the data accordingly which can help with respect to decision making of the companies.

With respect to internal application, by analysing the company's data the AI will be able to identify the business's exposure to ESG risk like environmental impact, labour practices that can help the company mitigate the same. This can be done by training AI to track the emission, social metric like gender diversity for example, checking how many female board members are there based on records and see if it fits the ESG requirement. AI can make compliance tasks automated, thereby bringing down costs and improving efficiency.[31] This integration aids companies in understanding and complying with evolving ESG policies and reporting requirements specific to countries, sectors, and organizations.[32]

AI may be trained on the accepted reporting standards and which data should be mapped under various ESG reporting specification. By using Machine Learning, AI can train on these data and then start automatically mapping these points to the relevant fields. It can also highlight if information has been mapped under the wrong head as well. AI may be further trained for real time tracking for example, continuously tracking the emissions and alerting when it goes higher than the industry standard or other standard that has been inputed. This makes it easier to monitor and analyze data continuously, making it possible to spot deviations or abnormalities in a timely manner.

One of the main challenge in implementing AI for data collection is data bias. If the data in which the AI is trained on is biased towards the company then the findings of AI will also be the same. AI may only identify those data that is favourable to the company while ignoring the others resulting in ESG data favourable to the company. The other challenge that can be faced is if AI create "Hallucinations" i.e. false information which the AI believe it to be true. The use of AI also poses concerns about privacy, data security, and responsible technology use. Ethical practices and ensuring that AI solutions align with societal and environmental goals should be there to maintain trust in the ESG investing ecosystem.

These challenges may make it difficult for the stakeholders to rely on the AI assessed data hence, it is important for companies those implement AI to disclose regarding how the AI tool is implemented. This also necessitates a need for standard for governing implementation of AI tools. Once the standards are put in place the potential of using AI for ESG data collection and reporting will be significant.[33]

3.3 Way Forward

When it comes to ESG disclosures, the major challenges faced by the organization is the absence of a uniform reporting frame work, lack of ESG experts and ensuring data reliability and correction. As seen by IFRS, global efforts are being put to make the a uniform disclosure framework. Countries have to ensure that when making regulations, they are compatible with international frameworks so that companies have the option to follow a unified standard when disclosing, thereby avoiding the complexity of adhering to multiple standards.

While the benefit of adopting AI for ESG disclosure will help in streamlining the process by helping in data collection, automated mapping and real time checking, it is essential that a company exercise caution when implementing the AI tool to ensure responsible usage to address the inherent risk. Firstly, The company should have clear AI integration strategy, where it is clearly determined for which ESG aspects the AI will be used, this can be determined by having a holistic assessment to understand which area will have most significant impact, usage and possibility to have data accuracy when using AI. Companies should ensure that the same is implemented in a manner where human judgment should be taken before AI makes decision or reports the data. This directly ties to the Second aspect which is ethics and accountability, Companies should disclose if they are integrating AI tools as well as have a team to oversee the AI, this shall ensure accountability in reporting and data collected. Companies should ensure that the data in which the AI is trained on is without bias and should be ready to disclose how the

AI is trained to endure fairness and transparency. Companies should also be able to provide clarity on how the decisions are being made by AI. Thirdly, Companies should ensure it takes safeguard to protect its own data and as well as any data it collected is not affected by AI tools ie. To ensure better cybersecurity protocol to protect data breaches from happening. Vulnerability test should also be done on the AI tool before implementing the same to assess the potential risk. Fourthly, With AI related regulatiosn constantly being developed as well as new laws being implemented, Companies should monitor the same as well as be prepared for any future regulations to ensure that they are compliant.

By adopting a clear and transparent structure for AI implementation along with balancing human judgment with AI insight a company can have more robust and informed ESG disclosure system.

4. Summary

The global landscape of Environmental, Social, and Governance (ESG) disclosures is rapidly evolving, driven by a series of regulatory initiatives across various regions. International Financial Reporting Standards (IFRS) introduced sustainability and climate-related disclosure standards (IFRS-S1 and IFRS-S2) in June 2023, being a new step towards harmonization of ESG related disclousre. In the European Union, comprehensive regulations such as the NFRD, CSRD, SFDR, and the new ESRS, effective January 2024, mandate extensive ESG reporting. In the United States, the Securities and Exchange Commission (SEC) has implemented climate disclosure rules as of 2024, requiring detailed reporting on climate-related risks and greenhouse gas emissions. South Africa follows suit with guidelines under the Johannesburg Stock Exchange (JSE) and the King IV Report on Corporate Governance, emphasizing sustainability and responsible corporate governance. India, through SEBI's BRSR Core, mandates extensive ESG disclosuresreflecting a global commitment to standardized ESG reporting.

These disclosures are of utmost importance since they offer a holistic transparent view of the corporation, giving insights into the environmental, social, and governance practices of a company beyond the traditional metrics of finance. It decreases information asymmetry and increases investor confidence in a firm, which also helps to increase the liquidity of shares. Other important benefits include enhanced investment decisions, as the enhanced transparency allows investors to make more informed choices, resulting in better capital allocation. In addition, the reliability and credibility of corporate reports are enhanced when voluntary ESG disclosures complement the mandatory ones. This aspect of transparency not only raises the investors' confidence and customers but also is instrumental in enhancing the corporate reputation. Such disclosure also assists in better corporate decision-making and mitigation of risks through identifying and acting on such potential risks for the improvement of overall performance and sustainability.

One of the hurdles faced by corporations are the plethora of disclosures standards that are present, hence harmonization of the ESG disclosure is required for a consistent and comparable reporting. This will make it easier for stakeholders to evaluate various companies as well as compared to when companies have different disclosures.

Artificial intelligence reduces information asymmetry by effectively gathering, processing, and analyzing massive amounts of data, which simplifies ESG disclosure.AI facilitates real-time tracking of ESG metrics, standardizes data, assures consistency, and spots trends that guide strategic choices. By matching data to legal requirements and highlighting inconsistencies, it improves compliance. Data bias and ethical issues are obstacles that call for strong governance and transparent AI use. The rise of global requirements for ESG disclosure has led to a demand for AI integration as a means of improving data quality and procedures. Companies may promote sustainable development and long-term wealth generation by strengthening their ESG policies and utilizing AI in conjunction with a solid governance structure and ethical standards.

Notes

1 David A. Cifrino, McDermott Will & Emery LLP, *Rise of international ESG Disclosure Standards,* Harvard Law School Forum on Corporate Governance, June 29 2023. URL: https://corpgov.law.harvard.edu/2023/06/29/the-rise-of-international-esg-disclosure-standards/

2 Jennifer Laidlaw, *New global sustainability board aims to cut through disclosure confusion*, S&P Global, 2021, URL:https://www.spglobal.com/esg/insights/new-global-sustainability-board-aims-to-cut-through-disclosure-confusion

3 IFRS, *ISSB issues inaugural global sustainability disclosure standards*, 26 June 2023, URL:https://www.ifrs.org/news-and-events/news/2023/06/issb-issues-ifrs-s1-ifrs-s2/

[4] IFRS S2, *Climate-related Disclosures*, June 2023, URL: https://www.ifrs.org/issued-standards/ifrs-sustainability-standards-navigator/ifrs-s2-climate-related-disclosures/

[5] .Andreas Fillmann, Hannah Kendrick,*Update: ESG Laws across the World*, Squire Patton Boggs, October 2023. URL: https://www.squirepattonboggs.com/-/media/files/insights /publications/2023/07/esg-laws-across-the-world/esg-laws-across-the-world.pdf?rev=d07 530018eb946a0859825094c85c565

[6] Plan A, *What is the Non-Financial Reporting Directive (NFRD)*?,

[7] United Nation Environment Programme Finance Initiative, *European Sustainability Reporting Standards (ESRS)*, 3 April 2024. URL:https://www.unepfi.org/impact/interoperability/european-sustainability-reporting-standardsesrs/#:~:text=3%20April%20 2024%3A%20UNEP%20FI,UNEP%20FI%20Holistic%20Impact%20Methodology.

[8] Tara Bernoville, *All 2024 ESG and non-financial reporting regulations in the EU*, Plan A, March 14 2024, https://plana.earth/academy/eu-esg-regulations .

[9] Ibid.

[10] European Commission, *Questions and Answers on the Adoption of European Sustainability Reporting Standards*, 31 July 2023, URL: https://ec.europa.eu/commission/presscorner/ detail/en/qanda_23_4043

[11] Ibid.

[12] European Parliament, *Due diligence: MEPs adopt rules for firms on human rights and environment,* Press Release, April 24 2024

[13] Selina Sagayam, Susy Bullock, et.al, Landmark EU *"Corporate Sustainability Due Diligence Directive" Imposing Human Rights and Environmental Due Diligence Obligations on EU and Non-EU Companies Approved by European Parliamen*t, Gibson Dunn, April 30 2024

[14] Council of the EU, *Environmental, social and governance (ESG) ratings: Council and Parliament reach agreement,* Press release, 5 February 2024, updated on 14 February 2024. URL: https://www.consilium.europa.eu/en/press/press-releases/2024/02/05/environmental-social-and-governance-esg-ratings-council-and-parliament-reach-agreement/

[15] Andreas Fillmann, Hannah Kendrick,*Update: ESG Laws across the World*, Squire Patton Boggs, May 2024. URL: https://www.squirepattonboggs.com/-/media/files/insights/ publications/2024/05/update-2-esg-laws-across-the-world/update-2-esg-laws-across-the -world.pdf?rev=a28dd602ab7643eab8b92076a1f288fc

[16] US Securities & Exchange Commision, https://www.sec.gov

[17] US Securities & Exchange Commission, *SEC Adopts Rules to Enhance and Standardize Climate-Related Disclosures for Investors*, 6 March 2024. URL: https://www.sec.gov/news /press-release/2024-31

[18] Sustain Life, Understanding the SEC's climate risk disclosure rule, March 13 2024. URL: https://www.sustain.life/blog/understanding-sec-climate-risk-disclosure-rule

[19] US Securities & Exchange Commission, *Statement on Nasdaq's Diversity Proposals – A Positive First Step for Investors*, August 6 2021, URL: https://www.sec.gov/news/public -statement/statement-nasdaq-diversity-080621

[20] Jessica, Allison, *Fifth Circuit Will Reconsider Challenges to Nasdaq Board Diversity Rule, Holland & Knight SECond Opinions Blog*, March 4 2024. https://www.hklaw.com/en/ insights/publications/2024/03/fifth-circuit-will-reconsider-challenges-to-nasdaq

21 Ezra Davids, Ryan Kitcat, Charles Douglas, *ESG: South Africa*, ICLG, 17.01.2024. URL: https://iclg.com/practice-areas/environmental-social-and-governance-law/south-africa

22 Johannesburg Stock Exchange, https://www.jse.co.za

23 Ibid

24 Taxmann, *Guide to ESG in India – Features | Principles | Reporting Requirements*, 6 March 2024, https://www.taxmann.com/post/blog/guide-to-esg-in-india

25 Reserve Bank of India, *Draft Disclosure framework on Climate-related Financial Risks*, 2024, Press Releases, https://www.rbi.org.in/Scripts/bs_viewcontent.aspx?Id=4393

26 Reza Malek-Yonan , Mahmoud Bakhtiar and Milad Rafsanjani, *Analytical study on the importance of non-financial information in company reporting*, International Journal of Management and Business Studies ISSN 2167-0439 Vol. 6 (3), pp. 251-255, March, 2016 URL: https://www.internationalscholarsjournals.com/articles/analytical-study-on-the-importance-of-nonfinancial-information-in-company-reporting.pdf

27 N.H.Patil,S.H.Patel,S.D.Lawand, *Research Paper On Artificial Intelligence And It's Applications*, Journal of Advanced Zoology ISSN: 0253-7214 Volume 44 Issue S-8 Year 2023 Page 229 -238

28 Ibid.

29 Terence Tse, *AI-powered ESG: Our chance to make a real difference?*,ESCP Business School, ESCP Impact Paper No.2021-06-EN

30 Ibid.

31 Gihan Hyde, *Power of AI for ESG*, Fintech Futures, 21st June 2023, Url: https://www.fintechfutures.com/2023/06/the-power-of-ai-for-esg/

32 Alexy Thomas, *How Generative AI can build an organization's ESG roadmap*, Ernst & Young, 24 July 2023. https://www.ey.com/en_in/ai/how-generative-ai-can-build-an-organization-s-esg-roadmap

33 Natalie Runyon and Zach Warren, *From hallucinations to clarity? The potential – and pitfalls – of using AI in ESG reporting*, Thomson Reuters, January 8 2024. Url: https://www.reuters.com/sustainability/sustainable-finance-reporting/hallucinations-clarity-potential-pitfalls-using-ai-esg-reporting-2024-01-08/

Bibliography

Alexy Thomas, *How Generative AI can build an organization's ESG roadmap*, Ernst & Young, 24 July 2023

Andreas Fillmann, Hannah Kendrick, *Update: ESG Laws across the World*, Squire Patton Boggs, May 2024.

Andreas Fillmann, Hannah Kendrick, *Update: ESG Laws across the World*, Squire Patton Boggs, October 2023

Council of the EU, *Environmental, social and governance (ESG) ratings: Council and Parliament reach agreement*, Press release, 5 February 2024, updated on 14 February 2024.

David A. Cifrino, McDermott Will & Emery LLP, *Rise of international ESG Disclosure Standards*, Harvard Law School Forum on Corporate Governance, June 29 2023.

European Commission, *Questions and Answers on the Adoption of European Sustainability Reporting Standards*, 31 July 2023,

European Parliament, *Due diligence: MEPs adopt rules for firms on human rights and environment*, Press Release

Ezra Davids, Ryan Kitcat, Charles Douglas, *ESG: South Africa*, ICLG, 17.01.2024

Gihan Hyde, *Power of AI for ESG*, Fintech Futures, 21st June 2023

IFRS S2, *Climate-related Disclosures*, June 2023,

IFRS, *ISSB issues inaugural global sustainability disclosure standards*, 26 June 2023

Jennifer Laidlaw, *New global sustainability board aims to cut through disclosure confusion*, S&P Global, 2021

Jessica, Allison, *Fifth Circuit Will Reconsider Challenges to Nasdaq Board Diversity Rule, Holland & Knight SECond Opinions Blog*, March 4 2024

Natalie Runyon and Zach Warren, *From hallucinations to clarity? The potential – and pitfalls – of using AI in ESG reporting*, Thomson Reuters, January 8 2024

N.H.Patil,S.H.Patel,S.D.Lawand, *Research Paper On Artificial Intelligence And It's Applications*, Journal of Advanced Zoology ISSN: 0253-7214 Volume 44 Issue S-8 Year 2023 Page 229 -238

Plan A, *What is the Non-Financial Reporting Directive (NFRD)?*,

Reserve Bank of India, *Draft Disclosure framework on Climate-related Financial Risks*, 2024, Press Releases

Reza Malek-Yonan , Mahmoud Bakhtiar and Milad Rafsanjani, *Analytical study on the importance of non-financial information in company reporting*, International Journal of Management and Business Studies ISSN 2167-0439 Vol. 6 (3), pp. 251-255, March, 2016

Selina Sagayam, Susy Bullock, et.al, Landmark EU *"Corporate Sustainability Due Diligence Directive" Imposing Human Rights and Environmental Due Diligence Obligations on EU and Non-EU Companies Approved by European Parliamen*t, Gibson Dunn, April 30 2024

Sustain Life, Understanding the SEC's climate risk disclosure rule, March 13 2024

Tara Bernoville, *All 2024 ESG and non-financial reporting regulations in the EU*, Plan A, March 14 2024

Taxmann, *Guide to ESG in India – Features | Principles | Reporting Requirements*, 6 March 2024

Terence Tse, *AI-powered ESG: Our chance to make a real difference?*,ESCP Business School, ESCP Impact Paper No.2021-06-EN

United Nation Environment Programme Finance Initiative, *European Sustainability Reporting Standards (ESRS)*, 3 April 2024

US Securities & Exchange Commission, *SEC Adopts Rules to Enhance and Standardize Climate-Related Disclosures for Investors*, 6 March 2024.

US Securities & Exchange Commission, *Statement on Nasdaq's Diversity Proposals – A Positive First Step for Investors*, August 6 2021

Chapter 2

Compliance Management from Organizational and Global Perspective

The Compliance Conundrum: Winning Hearts or Forcing Hands?

Nick John Weir

1. Introduction

What does your staff think of your compliance program? Do they associate your policies and procedures with upholding safety, precision, quality, and privacy? Or do they see your framework as imposing draconian rules—or worse yet, as a performative program that they never read or follow?

If this last question resonates, it's likely that your compliance program has gone adrift. You're certainly not alone. Many programs impose rules that are disregarded because they "get in the way" of the work your teams want to focus on. When teams fail to understand the value of the controls in place, they are more likely to foster resentment and are less likely to internalize and follow those controls. Just as importantly, when we fail to understand the context our teams are working in, the controls we define may be ignored or circumvented.

Compliance programs that work are only as large as they have to be and no larger. In my experience, it is possible to build a framework of policies that consistently creates value for your entire organization without feeling burdensome, bureaucratic, or performative. The key is knowing which controls to not implement and which controls do not need to be strictly followed. When you succeed in this, you'll be well on your way to creating a self-correcting compliance system, which ultimately simplifies the work of your Governance, Risk and Compliance (GRC) team.

2. The Must-Haves

I'm not suggesting a laissez faire approach or turning a blind eye to non-compliance. Compliance programs exist for good reason. They ensure your organization upholds its principles and honors your customer agreements. They serve to mitigate the risk of violating laws or the political fallout of a data breach or privacy violation. When implemented well, your compliance program can represent your organization as disciplined, safe, and trustworthy—traits you can and should use to instill trust and sell your products and services.

Some standards are simply too important not to fully enforce. These establish the foundation of your program. My organization manages vast amounts of US health data—millions of patient records. Regardless of laws, contracts, privacy standards, or any other requirements, every individual deserves the right to have their data protected following the strictest standards. It's simply the right thing to do. More importantly, data corruption, omissions, or even delays in delivering accurate content can interfere with the quality of care given to a patient. Issues impacting patient safety require immediate escalation and rapid resolution to ensure no harm comes to your patients if software problems arise.

You could say the same of people's financial information and many other forms of data. Although the requirements set the minimum bar, self-imposed standards set around these data sets serve the greater good. These internally defined standards have the added benefit of reducing the risk of financial consequences as well as building trust in your organization and the industry as a whole.

3. Strategic Deviations

Looking beyond these essential compliance requirements, I propose a controversial idea: Tolerate deviations from your defined rules and allow your organization to "color outside the lines," at least on a temporary, case-by-case basis. Most certifications require you to meet a certain minimum score in order to pass, so complete adherence is neither realistic nor cost effective. My team's edict is "deliver great work, at pace, with acceptable risk." To maintain the pace of our business, we must take calculated risks for the sake of continuing to move forward. Sometimes that comes at the cost of strict adherence to written policies.

Naturally, we don't tell our staff that they can ignore our policies. When we discover deviations, we have discussions with the people involved and analyze the potential harm it could cause. We consider the cost to remedy the issue, and we explore the available options which include choosing to not fix it immediately—or possibly ever. In all cases, we document our knowledge of the problem, the analysis we conducted, and the plan to resolve (or not). For issues we choose not to fix—that is, ones we risk accept—we reevaluate them on a yearly basis to account for changes to our calculations, risk exposure, or newly available solutions.

How do you know which issues must be fixed and on what timeframe those fixes must be applied? As the security adage goes, "Don't build a million dollar fence to secure a thousand-dollar asset." In the case of policy deviations, the "fence" is the cost it takes to remedy them. Sometimes you must simply acknowledge that you have chosen to depart from your set policies. If a good solution is forthcoming, oftentimes it is more cost-effective to allow the exception to remain until a better solution is in place rather than apply a temporary fix.

Sometimes the loss expectancy of the infraction (the likelihood multiplied by the average expense incurred if the event occurs) amounts to less than the cost to mitigate. In other words, building a better fence exceeds the calculated damage to your asset. This is an argument for long-term risk acceptance. Cost calculations such as this one are complicated and often imprecise, though even fuzzy risk management projections can still offer useful direction to inform mitigation prioritization and timing.

4. Staff Rapport is Paramount

It's folly to expect to reduce all risk to zero or to ensure that no policies are ever violated. It is in your best interest to detect and track most policy violations, but resist the temptation to sniff out every possible issue in your environment, and certainly refrain from forcing all of them to be resolved immediately. Aside from escalating costs for diminishing returns, such an effort will rapidly build staff resentment and encourage more secrecy. This can manifest as the use of shadow IT or an adversarial relationship between your compliance team and the rest of your company. Employee trust in your program is essential to graceful policy implementation.

Bear in mind that your entire compliance program hinges on the actions of your staff. Although you can perform audits and even embed automatic notifications and monitoring on some controls, the stability of your framework relies on your staff to understand and follow all the rules. The better situation is when your staff genuinely want to follow the rules and report and work to resolve anomalies once they detect those anomalies.

Fear of punishment for reporting issues does far more harm than good. Rarely does my company reprimand our staff for failing to adhere to our policies. Outside of flagrant disregard for guidelines, we assume good intent and approach these moments as growth opportunities. If the root cause is a lack of awareness or diligence, my team adjusts our training and advocacy efforts rather than criticizing those individuals for their lack of familiarity with the material. This approach builds goodwill with the people you rely on to maintain compliance.

Is it realistic to expect your staff to be so invested in your compliance program that they genuinely want to follow those rules and work with you to manage exceptions? In my experience, folks who have been coached to understand the reasoning behind the controls are more likely to choose to support analysis and adjustments to them. The key here is to inspire your team to participate in achieving the goals of your compliance program. Your staff must believe in the value of your compliance program. They must trust that you have built the program with the right principles in mind. In doing so, you shift some of the burden of administering your program to the teams that are directly impacted by those controls.

This can often be achieved by aligning to your common goals, such as achieving your corporate mission. In the healthcare industry you must maintain clear, structured processes to respond to issues impacting patient safety. If your staff doesn't consistently respond to patient safety issues with urgent escalation invoking these protocols, you should become a passionate advocate for the value of those procedures. Convey the urgency of protecting the health and well-being of all patients whose care may be impacted by your environment. In other words, inspire your team to save patients' lives. Instead of reacting with the thought "I'm required to escalate," they should think "this issue is too important to solve this alone" and naturally invoke emergency protocols.

This goes beyond patient safety, and arguably applies to all components of your compliance program. If your staff believes that the compliance program is built with the necessary components to fulfill your commitments and make your organization successful, then they will respond similarly to any compliance violation. If they associate flaws in your security framework with jeopardizing sales, impacting your reputation, or leading to lawsuits, then they are more likely to understand the financial impact of the flaw and work to correct it.

You cannot be the sole champion for your program, but you're the key evangelist. To develop a system your staff believes in, they must participate in the development of those rules. Your subject matter experts (SMEs) play critical roles in developing your policies and standards. Those same SMEs become your key advocates to communicate and reinforce the value of the controls they develop. You can then focus your efforts on inspiring those SMEs, and in turn supporting their efforts to inspire their own teams to follow the policies.

5. More Controls May Cause Less Control

To build rules that inspire rather than demand adherence, resist the urge to overprescribe. The best set of policies are the minimal set of rules that achieve the necessary results you desire. Be wary of introducing any non-essential controls until you have achieved complete buy-in on all essential ones. Well-intentioned efforts to implement aspirational policies often undermine otherwise sensible policies.

Just as bad as having too many controls is setting rules that don't make sense for your organization. You may be tempted to broadly enforce "best practice" recommendations, but these will not be right-sized to your organization. Because best practices are designed to guide any organization regardless of size or industry, they fail to account for the nuances of your specific context. This also risks causing your staff to view your team as being out of touch, which often leads to poor adherence. Although many best practice recommendations offer wise and prudent guidelines, you should trust your teams to implement only those which add tangible benefit. When they no longer serve the organization, your teams should have the flexibility to modify or deviate from those recommendations. If agility is a priority to your organization, consider whether your company needs your governance team to set those standards at all versus allowing your teams to guide themselves.

Staff education is also important for inspiring adherence and promoting good will. To compliance and security teams, education is a key intervention in preventing numerous threats ranging from phishing, insider threats, and intellectual property theft. Let's be honest: most compliance education is boring and easily ignored, though it doesn't have to be. Training should ensure your staff exhibits certain behaviors. The staff who already understands and complies with your policies deserves your trust; they should be allowed to expedite portions of their training by demonstrating their understanding. Those who don't show comprehension should be compelled to truly learn the material. Focus on those groups and develop courses that are engaging and memorable. Micro-learning lessons have been shown to be particularly effective–my company uses ones created by a comedy troupe and have achieved consistently high completion and retention rates as a result.

6. Summary

Your compliance program is only as effective as the willingness of your staff to understand the policies, comply with the procedures, and report any issues when they identify problems. By developing a lean set of procedures in collaboration with SMEs—and leveraging them to advocate for the value of those guidelines—you transform your program into a self-correcting system. Engaging, memorable, targeted training communicates to your teams that the program exists to serve their needs. When your workforce believes in the goals of the program and trusts that you have designed it to allow teams to work independently and efficiently, you will have truly created a system that serves, supports, and will remain stable into the future.

Law Practice and Compliance Officer practice

Pedro Trovão Do Rosário

1. Introduction

Compliance, from the English verb "to comply", defines a function intended to control compliance with the regulatory, legal and regulatory framework to which different institutions are subject, from preventing money laundering and terrorist financing to Data Protection Officer (DPO) in organisations dealing with personal or sensitive data. DPOs are under the regime provided for in Articles 37, 38 and 39 of the General Data Protection Regulation GDPR, being subject to the duty of confidentiality and the duty of incompatibility and may not exercise any functions and responsibilities resulting from a conflict of interest for the performance of functions.

Compliance programs serve as a shield, aiming to protect essential legal assets. They span from preventing money laundering and financing terrorism and corruption to safeguarding privacy, image, personality development, and freedom...

The importance and development of Compliance programs have taken particular emphasis thanks to the financial crises arising from or enhanced by the banking sector and new forms of impairment of citizens 'fundamental rights, such as computerised personal data. Compliance programs are increasingly essential to institutions' development of their activities, promoting the transparency of their modus operandi and functioning as a fundamental line in their performance. They imply forms of action and ethical principles that become essential to pursuing several national interests, European and international.

Thus, the role of the Compliance Officer has become crucial, with a central responsibility in monitoring applicable standards (international, European, and national). This role has been developed and implemented to enhance the transparency of operations, foster better relations between institutions, prevent acts of corruption and fraud, and safeguard fundamental rights. The Compliance Officer's role is integral to institutions' integrity and success.

2. Compliance Officer

At the heart of Compliance, regardless of its form in each institution, lies the role of Compliance Officers. Their function is rooted in impartiality and independence, ensuring the absence of potential conflicts of interest. They uphold transparency by following national, European, and international regulations, avoiding situations that compromise the objectives of Compliance Programmes.

2.1 Position of Compliance Officer

The increasing complexity of issues related to the "figure" of Compliance has increased regulatory requirements and, consequently, the risk of non-compliance with the current rules and regulations. This implies the growing importance of developing compliance programs with rules of conduct intended to prevent potential conflicts of interest.

In addition, employees are subject to new conduct duties, creating a standard for Compliance Officers, surpassing the "general regime" applicable to other workers and imposing a specific regime regarding codes of conduct, to which all are bound. Thus, there are consequences to the practice of certain acts, under penalty of a potential conflict of interests that jeopardises the compliance of the institution's performance, such as situations in which the performance of the employee, due to prior relations, increases the risk of non-compliance and the objectives associated with the Compliance program. These restrictions, even if they conflict with employees' rights, freedoms, and guarantees, are vital to protecting other fundamental legal assets. These assets are required to safeguard the Compliance program and, in some cases, to comply with other specific incompatible regimes.

Such a function may(?) be assigned to a Lawyer, who will act preventatively, avoiding lawsuits. This professional will ensure that the institution (public or private) never exceeds the limits of the law (international, European, or national).

2.2 Remarks under Portuguese jurisdiction on the lawyer status

In the Portuguese case, Article 99 of Law no. 145/2015, of September 09, with the Statute of the Bar Association (E.O.A.), under the epigraph "Conflict of Interest", lays down that

1. The lawyer must refuse to act on an issue in which he or she has already intervened in any other quality or is connected with another in which he or she represents or has represented the other party.
2. The lawyer must refuse to act against whom, in another pending cause, he or she has represented.
3. The lawyer may not advise, represent, or act on behalf of two or more clients in the same matter or a related matter if there is a conflict between their interests.
4. If a conflict of interest arises between two or more clients, if there is a risk of breach of professional secrecy or decreased independence, the lawyer shall cease to act on behalf of all clients within the framework of this conflict.
5. The lawyer must refrain from accepting a new client if this puts at risk the fulfilment of the duty to keep professional secrecy regarding the affairs of a previous client or if knowledge of these matters results in illegitimate or unjustified advantages for the new client.
6. Where the lawyer performs his or her activity in association, in the form of a company or not, the provisions of the preceding paragraphs shall apply either to the association or each of its members.

However, an essential service of the compliance lawyer is to understand the company's behaviour that may lead to noncompliance with the law and define the necessary measures to reduce losses. Defining and managing compliance risk situations integrates the concept of preventive advocacy, in which the lawyer fights against any cause of infringement.

On the other hand, in compliance with regulatory provisions, the lawyer's role is increasingly vital in prior-verifying compliance of third parties that contract with the institution with which the lawyer collaborates. In this field, the lawyer prepares and follows due diligence for each case to verify compliance with all standards.

The Compliance Lawyer should previously define the legal duties of the institution with which he or she collaborates and the best internal procedures for complying with them. Since these legal provisions are constantly altered, the lawyer should inform the institution of any normative alterations.

Thus, as a general rule (Article 99 of the E.O.A.), the lawyer must "refuse to act on an issue in which he has already intervened in any other quality", refraining, for example, from actions that result from non-compliance with rules for which the lawyer has or should have alerted the institution with which they collaborate.

2.3 Data Protection Officer

There are also other specific situations whose analysis requires greater care and relevance, considering their greater complexity and the existence of a particular normative regime. This is the case of the Data Protection Officer ("DPO"). Regulation (EU) 2016/679 of the European Parliament and of the Council /f 27 April 2016 on the protection of individuals about the processing of personal data and the free movement of such data led to the creation of the "DPO" (most common designation, even in Portugal). This will be the one who, within an organisation, independently promotes compliance with the rules on personal data protection and ensures respect for the rights of the holders of personal data *(see* 37 to 39 GDPR). The existence of a DPO within each institution dealing with personal data is always recommended and even, in some cases, mandatory (Article 37(1) GDPR). Under Art. 37(5) GDPR, the DPO" *is chosen based on professional qualities and, in particular, expertise in law and data protection practices, as well as in their ability to perform the functions*". The DPO should "*properly and in good time be involved in all matters related to personal data protection*"(cf . Article 38(1) GDPR). According to Art. 39 (1) GDPR, the DPO "*has at least the following functions*:

(a) *inform and advise the controller or processor, as well as the workers who process the data, regarding their obligations under this Regulation and other data protection provisions of the Union or the Member States;*
(b) *monitor compliance with this Regulation, with other Union or Member State data protection legal provisions and with the policies of the controller or processor relating to the protection of personal data (…);*
(c) *provide advice (…) on the impact assessment on data protection and monitor its implementation (…);*
(d) *Cooperate with the supervisory authority;*
And

(e) *be the supervisory authority's contact point on data processing matters*".

The DPO may be contacted (Art. 38/4 GDPR) by the "*data subjects (…) on all issues related to the processing of personal data and the exercise of the rights conferred by the*" GDPR.

The DPO may be a worker of the organisation "*or perform his or her duties based on a contract for the provision of services*" (Art. 37/6 GDPR), and "whether or not they are employees of the controller, they should be able to perform their duties independently" (under § 97 of the GDPR). Article 38/6 of the GDPR lays down that the DPO may perform other functions and duties in the organisation provided that these duties do not result in a conflict of interest with those inherent to the DPO, i.e., compromise the DPO's ability to be impartial or the DPO's reputability.

Article 81(1) and (2) of the aforementioned Statute of the Bar Association (EOA) states that *the lawyer exercises the defence of rights and interests entrusted to him always with full technical autonomy and in an exempt manner, independent and responsible* and that *the practice of law is irreconcilable with any position, function or activity that may affect the exemption, independence and dignity of the profession.*"

The lawyer *must immediately suspend the profession and request, within a maximum period of 30 days, the suspension of registration in the Bar Association when there is a supervenient incompatibility* (Article 91/ d) of the EOA) and, from the outset," *Those in a situation of incompatibility may not be registered (…)*" (Art. 188/1/d) of the EOA). Thus, the lawyer is prevented from exercising the profession whenever there is a situation of incompatibility.

Besides these incompatibilities, there are also impediments to exercising law practice (Article 83/1 and 2 of the EOA), *which constitute relative incompatibilities of the forensic mandate and legal consultation* in a specific context (often individual or unique) given a particular relationship with the client, with the subjects concerned or irreconcilable availability for the profession. "

In addition to the conflict of interests already mentioned (Article 99/1 of the EOA), the lawyer must refuse to assist on an issue in which he has already intervened in any other quality or is connected with another in which he represents or has represented the opposite party.

The General Council of the Portuguese Bar Association, in its Opinion N.º14/PP/2018-G, established that "the statutory incompatibilities provided for in Article 82(1) of the Statute of the Bar Association are merely an example, so the mere fact that the duties of the DPO are not listed is not sufficient to remove the possibility of incompatibility. (...). "Considering the type and nature of the DPO's duties, and essentially the fact that such duties are provided to one or more clients, we may affirm that the exercise of such activity is not incompatible with law practice. It is also clear that an impediment decreases the extent of the practice of law and constitutes a relative incompatibility (...) given a relationship with a client for whom the lawyer is or was the DPO. (...) The lawyer shall consider himself to be prevented from acting for clients for whom he or she has acted as DPO, as this may cause specific incompatibility if those acts conflict, as expected, with the deontological rules that regulate law practice. "

Thus, the General Council of the Bar Association decided on the impediment, provided that the lawyer is—or has been—the client's DPO.

Situations of conflict of interest (Art. 99/ 1 of EOA) may arise when the lawyer should act in the scope of legal advice and/or legal assistance on matters in which he or she acted as DPO. When this occurs due to failure in the system established and monitored by the DPO/lawyer, the lawyer may be able to favour his position to the detriment of the best defence of the client's interests.

In the opinion of the General Council, it is also stated, "(...) It could be argued that the impediment should only exist if the forensic mandate or legal consultation respected the subject that had, in some way, to do with the DPO's activity. I believe such a distinction should not be made as it would be misleading. What the lawyer knows in the scope of the DPO duties could always deontologically poison his or her performance both in the exercise of the forensic mandate and in the legal consultation (...)", thus realising that the lawyer should not advise the client institution or take the sponsorship regarding the performance as DPO or in matters in which the lawyer has acted in a way capable of causing a conflict of interests.

3. Conclusion

Thus, the lawyer may exercise law practice (including naturally the forensic mandate and legal consultation) for entities for whom they still exercise or have exercised the duties of DPO; however, they must refrain from doing so in cases of current or potential conflict of interests between the exercise of those duties and the interests of the client, or in which they may call into question the professional secrecy to which they are admitted as Lawyers, for – let us not forget – the DPO may be contacted (Art. 38/4 GDPR) by the "data subjects (…) on all issues related to the processing of personal data and the exercise of the rights conferred on them " GDPR. Verifying technical competencies will be the most sensitive situation, as it transcends the domain of the Bar Association, which can (Article 3 of its Statutes) (...). c) award the professional title of lawyer and certify the status of trainee lawyer, as well as regulate the access and exercise of the profession; (...) (g) regulate access to the profession through the recognition of professional qualifications and professional internship and regulate the access and exercise of the profession in terms of ethics; (...) (j) contribute to the development of legal culture and improvement of drafting the law.

Bibliography

Barton, T. D. E Cooper, J. M. (2000). Preventive Law and Creative Problem Solving: Multi-Dimensional Lawyering. California: NCPL.

Carneiro, Claudio e Junior, Milton de Castro Santos "Compliance e Boa Governança - Pública e Privada" – ISBN 978853628387-6, Coleção FGV Direito Rio – 2018.

Rodrigues, André Alfar – "Manual teórico-prático de compliance" – ISBN 978-989-40-0116-4, Edições Almedina – Coimbra, 2022.

Rosário, Pedro Trovão do - "O Compliance e os Estados Europeus" in "Compliance – Perspectivas e novas dinâmicas" – ISBN 978-972-40-8268-4 Edições Almedina - Coimbra, Dezembro 2019.

Managing Compliance Risks in Overseas Subsidiaries and Affiliated Companies

Joan Meyer, Matthew Ridings

1. Introduction

On the bustling campus of GlobalCorp's world headquarters, a complex tale of risk and compliance unfolds. The company, a significant player in the computing and technology industry, operates across continents, working in each country with its own set of financial laws and accounting practices. At the heart of this intricate web sits the compliance officer, Alex.

Alex's days are consumed by the labyrinthine task of weaving together the disparate accounting systems of GlobalCorp's international offices. In Europe, the accounting is meticulous, every transaction recorded with precision. But those practices are not uniform. GlobalCorp recently acquired a Brazilian subsidiary, bringing the challenge of integrating a new company that operates under different financial regulations and reporting standards into the fold, all against a backdrop of Latin customs and practices. The challenge for Alex is not merely technical. Each system speaks a different language, not just in terms of code but in the principles that underpin them. What is considered an asset under the laws of one country might be a liability in another. The regulations are a puzzle, and Alex occupies one of the key roles tasked with fitting it all into a coherent picture that adheres to the strictest of global compliance standards.

As Alex's day progresses, she finds herself on a video conference call with one of GlobalCorp's Asian offices. The language barrier and cultural differences make the call difficult, especially since the call involves a concern that some of GlobalCorp's technology and code relating to artificial intelligence – potentially having military applications – has been leaked to a foreign government by a former mid-level manager at GlobalCorp. Alex, along with trusted counsel and experts, spends hours combing through digital trails and communication logs, employing computer forensics to trace the pathway of the leaked information. After consulting with GlobalCorp's head of IT about addressing vulnerabilities in GlobalCorp's security measures, Alex approves the decision to disclose the leak to federal authorities in the United States where the company is headquartered. She works in partnership with the Asia office and legal counsel to manage the scope of the investigation. She knows that no matter the result of the investigation, the allegations will become public through a regulatory disclosure and send ripples through the company, shaking the trust of GlobalCorp's board, employees, and business partners. She also knows that this will mean new protocols and procedures – rebuilding the network security component of the compliance program will be critical to rebuilding trust within the organization.

But that is not all Alex has to grapple with even if that presently takes up most of her working days. As GlobalCorp expands with additional acquisitions, so does the complexity of Alex's task. New markets mean new rules, new expectations, and new risks. These risks can be mundane, such as the integration of a subsidiary's accounting system, or more sinister, such as the compromise of confidential information or misconduct by a foreign manager, whether inadvertent or deliberate. Alex's work is not a matter of plug and play; it's a delicate dance of negotiation, interpretation, and adaptation. She must be vigilant, always on the lookout for changes in regulations that could ripple through the company's operations. A new tax law in Asia, a change in financial reporting standards in the United States, or a shift in diplomatic relations between countries – each has the potential to unravel the work she has done in crafting GlobalCorp's compliance program. Alex knows that it will be impossible to eliminate compliance risks at GlobalCorp, but by learning from case studies and applying those lessons to GlobalCorp, she can position the company to best avoid the catastrophic risks that can come in the absence of an effective compliance program.

Over the last decade, managing compliance risks associated with subsidiaries has become paramount for multinational corporations. Along with this new emphasis, the compliance challenges for global companies have increased exponentially during the same period. A compliance officer's attention and resources are simultaneously pulled in different directions requiring frequent shifts in priorities and resources. However, four challenges have consistently emerged as common root failures in managing risk in subsidiary or affiliated companies operating overseas: working with decentralized accounting systems, structuring the compliance program to include centralized and on-the-ground monitoring, managing data security and trade secret risks, and closing the vulnerability gap created by autonomous mid-level managers at foreign subsidiaries. In this chapter, we will discuss these risks from the perspective of Alex, our fictional Chief Compliance Officer at GlobalCorp, a hypothetical multi-national company, by using real-world examples and case studies to highlight the challenges that compliance officers such as Alex often face – and recommending the solutions that compliance officers such as Alex may implement.

2. Diverse Accounting Systems as a Compliance Risk

One of the most significant challenges for compliance in any international organization is managing the accounting system, particularly where the accounting is decentralized. At GlobalCorp, Alex knows this all too well. Her daily routine involves working with GlobalCorp's audit and accounting team to navigate through the complexities of multiple accounting systems in order to monitor red flag transactions, a task made more difficult by GlobalCorp's decision not to integrate the different accounting systems after a series of mergers. GlobalCorp's rationale was that it needed to maintain separate systems in order to meet localized business needs and regulatory requirements, but this decision, while currying favor with local operations resistant to change, creates hurdles for maintaining consistent and transparent financial reporting across all of GlobalCorp. More nefariously, it also may contribute to a subsidiary's success in concealing misconduct from headquarters.

2.1 Regulatory Challenges to a Decentralized Accounting System

Attempting to manage a compliant decentralized accounting system in a multinational company comes with significant compliance challenges, not just because of the size and scope of the challenge, but also because the organization must navigate the varied and diverse waters of the global regulatory environment:

- *Accounting Standards*: There are a number of different accounting standards around the world, most of them designed using the concepts in the International Financial Reporting Standards (IFRS) and Generally Accepted Accounting Principles (GAAP). Even within these two frameworks, countries have local accounting standards that may operate alongside these standards. Ensuring that the financial statements comply with the relevant standards for each jurisdiction is a cumbersome and time-consuming task, especially since the rules are dynamic and continuously evolving. Within the compliance function, compliance officers should form a strong working relationship with the finance and audit teams, because they will need to work together to ensure that the organization monitors changes in their regulatory environments, adopts accounting changes to comply with regulatory revisions, and also makes appropriate revisions to monitoring and auditing processes to reflect these changes.

- *Taxation*: Every country has its own tax law with different rates, deductions, credits, and filing requirements. Adequate reporting and payment of tax are required in each jurisdiction and the company will need to have a good understanding and management of this issue. Further, most countries enforce specific rules for transfer pricing to avoid base erosion and profit sharing to ensure the right amount of profits are properly taxed and to ensure all transactions between subsidiaries are at arm's length. Compliance with these rules requires detailed documentation and analysis, and likewise places Alex in the position of relying on assistance from her accounting and finance teams to ensure that the tax risk is adequately assessed and managed within GlobalCorp.
- *Financial Reporting*: Different jurisdictions impose various requirements on the format and amount of time when the financial reports should be submitted. This makes careful planning and performance necessary to meet these varied requirements. The level of detail and types of disclosures expected in financial statements also vary, and therefore all relevant information must be accurately and fully disclosed in reports prepared for each jurisdiction.
- *Business Licensing*: A company may be operating in countries that require serial business licensing and renewals, each with certain regulatory requirements. Some industries have sector-specific regulatory requirements—in banking, insurance, or pharmaceuticals, for instance. Participating in these industry sectors requires compliance with industry-specific regulations

which differ between countries. This means that the compliance officer needs to master – and apply – different rules in each jurisdiction.

- *Data Privacy*: Privacy laws vary widely from country to country, with examples like the EU's General Data Protection Regulation's (GDPR) regime that imposes strict requirements for handling personal data, and that may conflict with regulations in other jurisdictions, such as the United States. China's enactment of the Data Security Law in 2021 has increased tensions with other countries seeing to protect their intellectual property and to promote their own trading interests, but it may conflict with the data privacy regimes of other countries. To meet the data privacy requirements of every country in which a company is operating may be next to impossible, particularly considering the varying restrictions on cross-border data transfer, but substantial compliance requires an organization to have its own data protection measures and a process by which ever-evolving global rules related to data privacy are constantly monitored.
- *Anti-Bribery & AML Compliance*: Different countries have distinct AML regulations, and ensuring compliance involves extensive due diligence, reporting, and monitoring. Moreover, disparate accounting systems can pose a challenge in the monitoring and detection of bribery in foreign countries where the practice is common. Alex is well aware of these obstacles, as she has studied examples, including Wal-Mart's delegation of accounting responsibilities to local managers in Mexico, which allowed them to make unauthorized payments and inhibited Wal-Mart's ability to detect them earlier.
- *Regulatory Audits:* Organizations may be subject to audits and inspections by local regulatory authorities. Preparing for and managing these audits requires detailed knowledge of local laws and regulations, and protocols in place in the event that authorities are conducting pretextual audits, *e.g.* to obtain confidential information or force a company to make an improper payment. Ensuring consistent and accurate responses to audits and inspections across multiple jurisdictions is challenging, especially when regulatory expectations differ, and Alex must work with closely with the finance, legal, and internal audit team to ensure that the audits provide GlobalCorp with useful information in designing changes to its compliance procedures.

2.2 Strategies to Overcome Regulatory Challenges

Overcoming regulatory challenges, particularly within the confines of a limited compliance budget, can be overwhelming for any compliance officer. Alex has been tasked with upgrading GlobalCorp's compliance department, and that will require innovative solutions. To do this, she spearheaded the transition to a technologically advanced compliance framework, blending regulatory technology, or RegTech, and cloud-based accounting systems to streamline operations and enhance the department's effectiveness.

2.2.1 The Adoption of Regulatory Technology and Cloud-Based Accounting

Alex's strategic decision to adopt RegTech was driven by the need to overcome the limitations of traditional compliance processes. She recognized that manual, time-consuming, and error-prone methods could no longer keep up with the complexity and speed of global business operations. RegTech is viewed by regulators and businesses as a cost-effective solution to the problems posed by traditional compliance methods because it encompasses two main functions: automated data reporting and real-time monitoring.

The primary advantage of RegTech is its ability to process vast amounts of data.[1] AI and machine-learning algorithms can collect and analyze data from different sources within the organization to ensure a more comprehensive report and analysis of GlobalCorp's operations and compliance status. Alex leverages these technologies to identify trends and risks that human compliance officers might miss over a comparable period – a shift that the industry coined as "Compliance 2.0." Today, GlobalCorp is at the forefront of "Compliance 3.0," using even more advanced technology for data and behavior analysis, which enables proactive, rather than reactive, compliance.[2]

Global financial regulators have already zeroed in on the importance of RegTech, which is common in banking and other highly-regulated industries. Because of the compliance benefits that are otherwise impossible to obtain using traditional methods, it is only a matter of time until RegTech becomes a universal requirement for an effective compliance program. Within the last five years, regulators around the world have emphasized the importance of RegTech as part of a well-functioning risk management program, including in the European Banking Authority, EBA Analysis of RegTech in the EU

Financial Sector (2021); Financial Conduct Authority (UK) AI Update (2023); Monetary Authority of Singapore Guidelines on Outsourcing (2018); Office of the Comptroller of the Currency OCC Bulletin 2018-9 (2018); and the Hong Kong Monetary Authority RegTech Adoption Practice Guide (2021).

In addition to RegTech, Alex has also pushed GlobalCorp to invest in cloud-based accounting software to revolutionize the way the compliance team operates. By centralizing financial data, cloud platforms make it significantly easier to standardize and reconcile information from different locations. This centralized approach ensures that all financial data is stored in a single, accessible repository, reducing inconsistencies and discrepancies that often arise from using multiple, isolated systems. Once the data is centrally stored, GlobalCorp can apply data standardization protocols to ensure that that financial data from different sources is comparable and accurate and adheres to a uniform set of standards and formats. This standardization is essential for meaningful data analysis, as it allows for seamless integration of data from various units, making consolidated financial information reliable and consistent. By combining cloud-based accounting software with RegTech data analysis, compliance officers and their internal audit counterparts are better able to gain real-time insights not only to an organization's financial performance, but also its compliance status. This allows for the identification and elevation of potential compliance concerns before they become a significant problem for the organization.

2.2.2 Structuring an Effective Compliance Department

The decision on how to structure the compliance team within an organization can be an important one, both from a substantive and cost-management perspective. Mid-level management in foreign subsidiaries must be folded into the team. Alex at GlobalCorp, navigates this challenge by implementing a hybrid approach that combines a centralized compliance team with local employees assigned compliance responsibilities. This strategy significantly enhances GlobalCorp's ability to navigate ever-changing regulatory landscapes, ensuring both consistency and adaptability in compliance efforts.

This two-pronged approach works. The centralized compliance team ensures uniformity in the interpretation and implementation of regulatory policies across the organization. By having a single, cohesive unit responsible for compliance, the organization can develop standardized processes, protocols, and training programs. This consistency helps in maintaining an unvaried compliance culture, reducing the risk of divergent practices and ensuring that all business units adhere to the same high standards. Further, it allows for an efficient allocation of resources -- the central team can oversee the distribution of tasks to direct resources towards the most critical areas. This structure also prevents the duplication of efforts, as the centralized team coordinates activities, shares best practices, and leverages common tools and systems, such as the RegTech tools Alex has championed.

At the same time, using local expertise in a given country or region allows for flexibility that does not otherwise exist in a purely centralized system. The central team develops and enforces broad, global-scale compliance policies, while localized employee assets can tailor policies to address local law or customs. In addition to regional regulatory knowledge, properly trained local employees can bring cultural insights, improve communications with local regulators, and better align with local business strategies, making it more likely that the local organization will support the organization's compliance goals.

Alex's leadership and strategic vision are evident in the way she has structured GlobalCorp's compliance team. She understands that a centralized team alone cannot address the diverse and dynamic regulatory environments in which GlobalCorp operates. By integrating local expertise, Alex ensures that GlobalCorp's compliance program is both robust and adaptable, capable of responding to regional regulatory changes while maintaining global standards.

Alex also prioritizes continuous training and development for her team. She regularly organizes workshops and training sessions to keep both the centralized team and local compliance officers updated on the latest regulatory developments and best practices. This commitment to ongoing education fosters the development of a knowledgeable and agile compliance team.

Likewise, Alex's innovative use of technology, such as RegTech and cloud-based accounting systems, further strengthens GlobalCorp's compliance framework. The centralized team uses these tools to streamline processes and enhance data analysis to monitor transactions while local compliance officers investigate on the ground and provide context-specific insights to block problematic practices before they spread. The effective interplay between centralized oversight and localized knowledge creates an efficient monitoring system at the core of every global compliance program. Although RegTech allows companies better insight into their data, it is not a magical talisman that wards off compliance failures. From the data that RegTech generates, however, compliance officers such as Alex may be in a better position to identify areas of risk that may not be readily apparent without the benefit of the data analysis that RegTech solutions provide. Ultimately, companies must use this data to identify and understand the sources of risk and then implement the appropriate controls to reduce that risk.

- A Comprehensive Compliance Framework and the Toshiba Accounting Scandal[3]

In American football, blocking and tackling may be unglamorous tasks, but they are crucial to a team's success. Similarly, training, controls, and effective communication are the essential building blocks of an effective compliance program. While these elements might not be exciting or glamorous, they are vital for the program's success, and this is especially true for an international organization. As demonstrated below in the Toshiba case study, the organization's basic failures in training, communication, and internal controls, augmented by a decentralized accounting system, created a billion-dollar scandal for Toshiba that not only exposed significant flaws in Toshiba's financial reporting practices but also highlighted the challenges of maintaining the same compliance standards across a large and diverse organization.

Internal controls typically involve multiple layers of oversight to ensure that no single individual or group has unchecked authority over certain areas of financial reporting. At Toshiba, senior executives wielded considerable influence over accounting decisions with insufficient oversight from independent board members or external auditors. This lack of oversight enabled executives to pressure subordinates into inflating profits without fear of detection or repercussions. Relatedly, Toshiba's system of checks and balances within the reporting process was insufficient because it did not require a segregation of duties, which meant that the same executives who pressured subordinates into manipulating the accounting data could also override the standard accounting procedures and approve the manipulated financial results.[4]

Further compounding the problem, the internal audit mechanism at Toshiba was flawed. Internal audits are designed to provide an independent assessment of an organization's financial practices, but poor documentation and record-keeping practices were prevalent at Toshiba. This meant that it was very difficult for auditors to trace and verify financial data, and therefore, Toshiba's internal audits were either insufficient or their findings were ignored by the organization, allowing improper accounting practices to continue.[5]

Toshiba also lacked a clear "tone at the top." In an organization with a strong tone at the top, there is a visible commitment to ethical behavior, integrity, and adherence to policies. At Toshiba, however, the dominant environment was one of fear and obedience. Employees felt pressured to meet unrealistic financial targets set by senior management, leading them to participate in, or turn a blind eye to, unethical accounting practices. This culture discouraged employees from reporting irregularities or challenging dubious instructions, further eroding the company's internal controls.[6]

Because these deficient practices continued for years at Toshiba, the fallout from the scandal was significant. To restore credibility, Toshiba revamped its accounting practices, including the adoption of a unified accounting framework that ensured consistency and transparency in financial reporting. It also revamped internal control systems by implementing stricter oversight and monitoring mechanisms to prevent the recurrence of similar issues. Most important, Toshiba recalibrated its tone at the top messaging. It established a new audit committee at the board of directors level, improved the quality of its audit oversight, and made changes to its organizational culture to emphasize the importance of ethical behavior, transparency, and accountability, including a newly-invigorated reporting protocol so that employees could report unethical practices without fear of retaliation.

Alex learned from these case studies. Taking notice of the lessons from Toshiba's compliance failures, Alex is determined not to permit GlobalCorp to repeat Toshiba's mistakes. She has implemented a unified accounting framework that ensures consistency and transparency in financial reporting, adopted strengthened internal control systems with multiple layers of oversight and worked with internal audit to develop specific audit protocols for various subject matter areas, *e.g.* anti-bribery and AML. She also implemented a quarterly training program for management to recalibrate the tone at the top and establishes a management messaging blog on the intra-company compliance portal, which helps to foster a better ethics environment at GlobalCorp. With these changes, Alex believes that GlobalCorp is well-positioned to navigate the accounting and regulatory challenges of an international company.

3. Data Security and Trade Secret Compliance Challenges in Foreign Subsidiaries

The accounting systems are not the only challenge that Alex faces in her role as Chief Compliance Officer. Alex is acutely aware of the significant compliance challenges posed by the diversity in data handling requirements across different jurisdictions. Diversity in data handling can create significant compliance challenges for multinational corporations, as they must ensure their policies and practices align with local requirements while maintaining a consistent global approach. For example, the GDPR implemented by the European Union imposes strict data protection requirements on companies operating within its jurisdiction. However, these requirements can conflict with local laws in other countries, such as the United States, which has a more fragmented approach to data privacy.

Data privacy presents a particularly difficult challenge for international organizations. There are over a dozen countries with data privacy laws that have an international or global impact, including the GDPR, China's Personal Information Protection Law (PIPL), Brazil's General Data Protection Law, and the California Consumer Privacy Act (CCPA), to name only a few. Although these laws are all based on the same principles of consent, purpose limitation, data minimization, and individual rights, the application of these laws in practice can be extraordinarily challenging. Particularly within the compliance function, data privacy laws can create tensions that the compliance officer, along with her colleagues in the legal department, must navigate. For example, it is not uncommon for an organization to have a cross-border internal investigation that may implicate data privacy laws on multiple continents, along with multiple countries' labor and employment law, whistleblower protections, and criminal law. It may not be possible to simultaneously comply with each of these laws, and the legal and compliance departments must then determine how best to prioritize the company's objectives in such a situation. This is always a case-by-case determination, but an important consideration is taking care to design the data privacy policy to be adaptable, allowing it to meet local legal requirements while maintaining a consistent approach to data security across all of GlobalCorp's subsidiaries. Alex understands that flexibility is crucial, as it enables the company to reduce risk arising from the various regional regulations without compromising the integrity of its overall data protection framework. This approach dovetails with GlobalCorp's decision to establish local compliance teams in its key jurisdictions, which can also provide valuable insights into the specific legal landscape, enforcement regime, and cultural nuances of each region. This can be particularly valuable in assessing the permissive uses of the data under local law in the event of an internal investigation and how local enforcers may view data transfers done to facilitate an investigation. A flexible global framework can never solve all data privacy challenges, but it is a good first step.

3.1 Cybersecurity Threats

Constantly evolving cybersecurity threats increase the challenge of safeguarding sensitive information in the organization. Foreign subsidiaries may face additional risks due to varying levels of technological infrastructure and expertise and increasing threats from sophisticated state actors that use computer hacking as a geopolitical weapon. In the last decade, cyberattacks have become damaging and disruptive for companies, and in many instances, these attacks can be politically motivated. Alex closely monitors high-profile cyberattacks, learning from each incident, to strengthen GlobalCorp's defenses. Some well-known attacks include the 2014 Sony Pictures attack that appears to have been supported by the North Korean government,[7] the Solar Winds breach that is believed to have been executed by state-sponsored hackers affiliated with the Russian government,[8] and the 2023 MGM cyberattack. This last attack is notable because the way that entry was gained was not through a code vulnerability, but through social engineering whereby the hackers specifically targeted certain MGM Resorts employees, called the MGM IT help desk to request assistance logging into the account and, as a result, obtained administrative privileges to MGM's cyber environments.[9]

To counter such sophisticated threats, Alex has implemented a multi-layered cybersecurity strategy at GlobalCorp.[10] This includes advanced encryption protocols, multi-factor authentication, and continuous monitoring of the company's IT infrastructure. Alex also emphasizes the importance of employee training to recognize and prevent the type of social engineering attacks that were pivotal in the MGM cyberattack.

Alex's strategy also involves conducting regular security audits, penetration testing, and thorough risk assessments. Security audits provide a comprehensive review of GlobalCorp's security policies, procedures, and infrastructure to ensure they meet industry standards. Alex collaborates with the internal audit team to review documentation, interview key personnel, and examine technical controls to test the effectiveness of the organization's security framework.

Penetration testing, also known as "white hat" hacking, is another critical component of Alex's strategy. Working with the GlobalCorp's Information Security department, she oversees simulations of cyberattacks on GlobalCorp's systems, networks, or applications to identify security weaknesses and implement controls and policies designed to reduce the risk of a cyber-attack. This proactive approach helps GlobalCorp stay ahead of potential threats by addressing vulnerabilities before they can be exploited by malicious actors. During these tests, Alex ensures that testers mimic the tactics of real attackers, including breaching network defenses, exploiting software vulnerabilities, and gaining unauthorized access to sensitive data.

Security issues in compliance go beyond cybersecurity and hacking. Compliance officers must also address the challenges in securing the organization's trade secrets, even from its own employees. Alex understands the gravity of this task and has put robust measures in place to protect GlobalCorp's intellectual property.

One recent incident that Alex has studied is Micron Technology. Three Micron employees resigned to join a competitor, United Microelectronics Corporation (UMC), and allegedly stole certain computer technology as they left the company.[11] The United States eventually brought criminal charges against two of the employees and UMC, alleging that the People's Republic of China, unable to develop technologically advanced production capabilities, facilitated the theft of technology from Micron in order to provide the technology to a company controlled by the PRC government; UMC ultimately entered a guilty plea to charges brought by the United States.

To prevent similar incidents at GlobalCorp, Alex has implemented stringent access controls and conducts regular risk assessments for GlobalCorp's technology. These controls, physical and electronic, ensure that only employees with a legitimate need to use trade secret information can access it, and Alex regularly reviews and updates these controls as employees change roles within the company.[12]

4. Mid-Level Management Vulnerability

4.1 Managing Mid-Level Risk in Decentralized Subsidiaries

Alex must be constantly on guard against known areas of vulnerability, and one of the most significant vulnerabilities in any compliance program is the role of mid-level managers in foreign subsidiaries. In a company with decentralized management and accounting systems, mid-level managers are frequently allowed to operate autonomously as long as their business units are operating at a profit. Many of the compliance issues – embezzlement, financial frauds, bribery – arise when these managers are not properly trained and operate subsidiaries as stand-alone entities that can take advantage of disreputable local customs and practices to generate business. Many anti-bribery cases brought by law enforcement authorities, costing companies millions of dollars in penalties per year, have had their origin in an errant mid-level manager eager to perform for his superiors.

4.2 Walmart Case Study

The Walmart Mexico bribery scandal, which surfaced in 2012, is an instructive case study in both how compliance must engage with cultural differences across organizations, but also the role of foreign mid-level managers in promoting compliance within the organization. The Walmart case involved the activities of its Mexican subsidiary, Wal-Mart de México, which was alleged to have engaged in a widespread bribery scheme to obtain construction permits and gain market dominance. The scandal originated from a report by The New York Times, which revealed that Walmart executives had been aware of these activities since 2005 but failed to take appropriate action.[13] Instead of conducting a thorough investigation, the company's executives reportedly shut down the inquiry and did not inform law enforcement authorities. The allegations further detailed how Walmart de México paid millions of dollars in bribes to local officials to accelerate the approval process for new store locations, which allowed the company to expand rapidly across Mexico. These illicit payments were made to facilitate zoning approvals, environmental permits, and other regulatory requirements, bypassing normal legal procedures.

Walmart promoted a corporate culture of rapid expansion and aggressive growth, and outside of the United States, the corporate culture weighed heavily on the management in Mexico, who were expected to achieve high-growth targets. This pressure led employees to psy bribes to obtain construction and land use permits faster than normal governmental administrative processes would have allowed. Like Toshiba, reports of bribery and corruption within the company were inadequately addressed, allowing bribery to proliferate in Mexico. These activities were facilitated by the corrupt business environment in Mexico where improper payments to local government clerks and minor government officials are seen as a customary part of doing business. Since the bureaucratic processes in Mexico can be slow and cumbersome, they created an incentive for businesses to use bribes to expedite permits and approvals. This environment made it easier for Walmart's local management to justify their actions, rationalizing bribery as a necessary evil to achieve business objectives in a competitive market.

In considering the placement and training of overseas personnel, Alex recognizes the critical challenge of identifying the proper role and responsibilities for foreign mid-level management in the compliance process. These managers play a pivotal role in implementing compliance policies and ensuring adherence to them at the local level. At Walmart de México, mid-level managers were the key to implementing the corrupt scheme. These managers were responsible for identifying and negotiating with local officials to expedite the permit process. They arranged and facilitated the payments, ensuring that the bribes were delivered to the appropriate officials in exchange for favorable treatment. The bribes were used to circumvent legal and regulatory hurdles, allowing Walmart to build stores in prime locations without the usual delays associated with obtaining zoning approvals, environmental permits, and satisfying other regulatory requirements. Moreover, these managers actively concealed the bribery schemes from higher authorities within the organization and from the company's external auditors by manipulating records and creating false documentation to hide the illicit payments.

To avoid the same mistakes as Walmart de México, GlobalCorp implements several key strategies. First, Alex knew that her compliance team needed to consider how cultural differences impact the company's compliance policies. Corruption has been a persistent issue in Mexico and is commonly seen as a way to navigate bureaucratic red tape and expedite business processes; moreover, the complexity and inefficiency of the regulatory and permitting processes in Mexico created strong incentives for the business to seek shortcuts. Alex recognized that these cultural and regulatory issues create pressure points for a compliance program, and to combat this, she introduced cultural sensitivity training for both local employees and corporate managers to help bridge the gap and ensure a unified approach to compliance. Training reduces risk in the organization by focusing on understanding and respecting local customs while reinforcing the importance of adhering to the company's ethical standards.

Effective communication is essential for implementing compliance policies, especially in foreign markets, yet language barriers and differing communication styles can hinder this process. In many multinational corporations. Subsidiaries operate in different languages, which can create misunderstandings and misinterpretations of compliance policies. The culture of the headquarters home country may have no meaning to employees in a far-flung subsidiary. Alex has established clear communication channels and provided translation services where necessary. This involves using bilingual staff, translating key documents, and ensuring that local managers have a clear understanding of compliance requirements. Regular meetings and updates help ensure that mid-level managers are aligned with corporate compliance goals. These meetings provide an opportunity to clarify any ambiguities, address concerns, and reinforce the importance of compliance.

Last, Alex believes in empowering mid-level managers to take ownership of compliance within their subsidiaries. This requires providing them with the necessary resources, support, and authority to enforce compliance policies. At the same time, Alex has established accountability mechanisms to ensure that these managers are held responsible for any compliance breaches. This includes regular performance reviews, audits, and clear consequences for non-compliance, each of which targets a weak point in any compliance program – the individual employees who have their own motivations and incentives that may not always been in alignment with the organization's code of ethics.

5. Conclusion

The journey of Alex, our fictional Chief Compliance Officer at GlobalCorp, illustrates the challenges that today's compliance officer faces, along with some strategies that may be implemented to manage compliance risks in a multinational corporation. Although it is impossible to eliminate all risk within a company, and there are no magic cure-alls, the organization can take steps to meaningfully reduce the risk that it faces in an international environment. A critical part of this risk reduction exercise for a compliance officer is adaptation. Alex must continually adapt GlobalCorp's compliance strategy to respond to changes in accounting standards or regulatory environments, introduction of new technology or new methods that fraudsters and hackers may use to scam the company, or changes in corporate culture, either through expansion or acquisition.

The lessons that Alex learned from high-profile cases like Walmart and Toshiba underscore the primary need for a strong ethical culture within the organization. From that foundation, the compliance officer can build a system of robust internal controls, effective communication, and a hybrid compliance team to combine centralized oversight with localized expertise in the regions in which it operates.

Ultimately, an effective compliance officer must thoroughly understand the risks faced by the organization, including structural risks, and be prepared to devise a plan to mitigate those risks. Ensuring compliance works in a global context is not just about avoiding legal repercussions; it is about fostering trust and integrity within the organization and with its stakeholders. As the business landscape continues to evolve, compliance officers and legal professionals must remain vigilant, adaptable, and proactive in addressing the ever-changing challenges of international compliance. Through strategic planning, leveraging local resources, employing advanced technologies, and fostering a top-down culture of transparency and responsiveness, organizations can navigate the complexities of international regulations and build a robust compliance infrastructure that safeguards their operations and reputation worldwide.

Notes

1 Johansson, E.; Sutinene, K.; Lassila, J.; Lang., V. (2019). RegTech – A necessary tool to keep up with compliance and regulatory changes? *ACRN Journal of Finance and Risk Perspectives* 8, 71-85. https://www.acrn-journals.eu/resources/SI08_2019f.pdf.

2 Vernier, N. (2024). *The next frontier of compliance: Compliance 3.0 and the era of automated testing.* Cable. https://community.cable.tech/the-next-frontier-of-compliance-compliance-3-0-and-the-era-of-automated-testing/

3 See Independent Investigation Committee for Toshiba Corporation, *Investigation Report*, July 20, 2015, *available at:*
https://www.global.toshiba/content/dam/toshiba/migration/corp/irAssets/about/ir/en/news/20151208_2.pdf?utm_source=www&utm_medium=web&utm_campaign=since202203CorpIr
(last accessed May 31, 2024).

4 *Id*. at p. 307.

5 *Id*. at p. 313-315.

6 *Id*. at p. 309-310.

7 *See United States of America v. Park Jin Hyok*, Case No. 18-1479, Criminal Complaint, at §6 (C.D. Cal. June 8, 2018).

8 United States of America Government Accountability Office (2022). *Federal response to Solarwinds and Microsoft Exchange incidents*. https://www.gao.gov/assets/gao-22-104746.pdf.

9 Kagan, S. (2023). *Unmasking the ALPHV-MGM Saga: A masterclass in cybersecurity missteps and ethical conundrums*. The Final Hop. https://www.thefinalhop.com/unmasking-the-alphv-mgm-saga-a-masterclass-in-cybersecurity-missteps-and-ethical-conundrums/

10 Baig, A. (2024). *Insider threats: Best practices to counter them*. United States Cybersecurity Magazine. https://www.uscybersecurity.net/insider-threats-best-practices-to-counter-them/.

11 *See United States of America v. United Microelectronics Corporation, et al.*, Case No. 18-0465, Indictment, at 2-3 (N.D. Cal. Sept. 27, 2018).

12 Dibernardo, I; Sobel, J.; Strong, M., *Trade Secret Protection in Corporations: Best Practices* (2022). Reuters. https://www.reuters.com/legal/legalindustry/trade-secret-protection-corporations-best-practices-2022-04-15/.

13 Barstow, D. (2012). *Wal-Mart Hushed Up a Vast Mexican Bribery Case*. The New York Times. https://www.nytimes.com/2012/04/22/business/at-wal-mart-in-mexico-a-bribe-inquiry-silenced.html.

Bibliographical References

Baig, A. (2024). *Insider threats: Best practices to counter them*. United States Cybersecurity Magazine. https://www.uscybersecurity.net/insider-threats-best-practices-to-counter-them/.

Barstow, D. (2012). *Wal-Mart Hushed Up a Vast Mexican Bribery Case*. The New York Times. https://www.nytimes.com/2012/04/22/business/at-wal-mart-in-mexico-a-bribe-inquiry-silenced.html.

Dibernardo, I; Sobel, J.; Strong, M., *Trade Secret Protection in Corporations: Best Practices* (2022). Reuters. https://www.reuters.com/legal/legalindustry/trade-secret-protection-corporations-best-practices-2022-04-15/.

European Central Bank, EBA Analysis of RegTech in the EU Financial Sector (2021), *available at:* https://www.eba.europa.eu/sites/default/files/document_library/Publications/Reports/2021/1015484/EBA%20analysis%20of%20RegTech%20in%20the%20EU%20financial%20sector.pdf

Financial Conduct Authority, AI Update (2023), *available at:* https://www.fca.org.uk/publication/corporate/ai-update.pdf

Hong Kong Monetary Authority, Regtech Adoption Practice Guide, Issue 4 (2021), *available at:* https://brdr.hkma.gov.hk/eng/doc-ldg/docId/getPdf/20211126-2-EN/20211126-2-EN.pdf

Independent Investigation Committee for Toshiba Corporation, *Investigation Report*, July 20, 2015, *available at:*

https://www.global.toshiba/content/dam/toshiba/migration/corp/irAssets/about/ir/en/news/20151208_2.pdf?utm_source=www&utm_medium=web&utm_campaign=since202203CorpIr (last accessed May 31, 2024).

Kagan, S. (2023). *Unmasking the ALPHV-MGM Saga: A masterclass in cybersecurity missteps and ethical conundrums*. The Final Hop. https://www.thefinalhop.com/unmasking-the-alphv-mgm-saga-a-masterclass-in-cybersecurity-missteps-and-ethical-conundrums/

Johansson, E.; Sutinene, K.; Lassila, J.; Lang., V. (2019). RegTech – A necessary tool to keep up with compliance and regulatory changes? *ACRN Journal of Finance and Risk Perspectives 8*, 71-85. https://www.acrn-journals.eu/resources/SI08_2019f.pdf.

Task Force on Artificial Intelligence: Hearing Before the House Comm. on Financial Services, 117th Cong. (2022) (statement of Kevin Greenfield, Deputy Comptroller for Operational Risk Policy, Office of the Comptroller of the Currency), *available at* https://www.occ.gov/news-issuances/congressional-testimony/2022/ct-occ-2022-52-written.pdf.

Vernier, N. (2024). *The next frontier of compliance: Compliance 3.0 and the era of automated testing*. Cable. https://community.cable.tech/the-next-frontier-of-compliance-compliance-3-0-and-the-era-of-automated-testing/

Navigating EU Product Safety and Product Liability Law Reform

Claus Köhler, Nicole Vossius

1. Introduction

In 2024, the European Union (**"EU"**) is implementing a comprehensive reform in product safety and liability regulations by addressing the challenges posed by digitization in distribution with the newly adopted General Product Safety Regulation (EU Regulation 2023/988; **"GPSR"**), the impending ratification of the Cyber Resilience Act; (2022/0272(COD); **"CRA"**) and the Product Liability Directive; (2022/0302(COD); **"PLD"**). The GPSR exacerbates information, notification and cooperation obligations to economic operators distributing products in the EU and the EEA and extends product responsibility to online marketplace providers. Designated to improve cybersecurity, the CRA introduces mandatory conformity procedures for digital elements. Complementary to the regulatory changes by the GSPR and the CRA, the PLD governs product liability for all economic operators assigned responsibility for product safety under the GPSR and CRA. Moreover, the PLD aims to restrict liability exemptions previously provided, particularly concerning software-related defects occurring after the product's release, emphasizing the manufacturer's responsibility for ongoing safety updates and cybersecurity measures. Against this background of regulatory revision, this legal overhaul delves into the implications and objectives of the respective regulatory frameworks, aiming to provide an analysis of the potential impact on businesses and regulatory compliance both in the EU and the EEA.

2. Overview of Contents of GPSR, CRA and PLD

2.1 GPSR

2.1.1 Background

With the EU's GPSR coming into effect on December 13, 2024, the European Commission has not only taken charge of product compliance regulation through the instrument of regulation itself but has also comprehensively reformed and modernized product safety law in light of the challenges posed by the digitization of distribution, extended product safety responsibilities to all so-called economic operators (Art. 3 (13) GSPR) and other participants in the distribution chain such as providers of online marketplaces who are now included in the responsibility for product conformity. The GPSR, which came into effect on June 12, 2023, largely replaces the German Product Safety Act (ProdSG) of 2021, which implemented the so-called New Legislative Framework of 2008 (NLF) and Directive 2001/95/EC on general product safety. The GPSR, initially proposed by the European Commission as a directive in fall 2022, reflects an increased tendency towards harmonizing the EU's internal market law, as already pursued with the Market Surveillance Regulation 2019/1020 ("**MSR**"). The future German ProdSG will essentially only require national regulation for the provisions of the GPSR concerning safety marks and sanctions under administrative and criminal law, for which Member States are responsible according to Art. 44 para. 1 GPSR.

2.1.2 Scope of Application

2.1.2.1 Subject Matter

The GPSR applies to products as defined in Art. 2 GPSR that are placed on the EU market or made available on the EU market (Art. 3 (6) and (7) GPSR). Excluded from this are, among other products, for example human and veterinary medicinal products, food and transport vehicles (Art. 2 para. 2 (a), (b), and (g) GPSR). The definitions of placing a product on the market pursuant to Art. 3 (7) GPSR and making products available on the market according to Art. 3 (6) GPSR are identical to those in Art. 3 MSR. What is new is the so-called remote sales provision in Art. 3 (7) GPSR in conjunction with Art. 4 GPSR.[1] This provision stipulates that all products offered on the World Wide Web fall under the GPSR's scope if the offer is directed at consumers in the EU, as stated in Art. 4 sentence 2 GPSR.

2.1.2.2 Personal Scope

The GPSR addresses, as already stipulated in the ProdSG, all economic operators based in the EU (Art. 3 (13) GPSR), i.e. manufacturers, importers, distributors and authorized representatives. Additionally, fulfillment service providers have been included as economic operators (Art. 3 (12) GPSR). Fulfillment service providers are, however, not subject to direct obligations under the GPSR but are nevertheless subject to the obligations provided by Section 6 para. 6 ProdSG. Additionally, there is an inclusion of online retailers under Art. 4 GPSR; the GPSR applies due to the remote sales provision in Art. 4 GPSR, also to online retailers who are not required to be based in the EU. Furthermore, the GPSR introduces a responsibility to an actor sui generis with the so-called provider of an online marketplace (Art. 3 (14) GPSR), which operates an "online interface" as a platform through which entrepreneurs can offer products for sale to consumers.[2] The characteristic feature of providers of online marketplaces is that they do not act as contractual partners vis-à-vis consumers.[3] However, if a provider of an online marketplace decides to sell products on a platform, the liabilities of such provider evolve to those of a distributor under the GPSR with respect to the sale of the distributed product.[4]

2.1.3 Catalogue of Compliance Requirements under the GPSR

The GPSR adopts a tiered system of duties, assigning the primary responsibility for product compliance to manufacturers and importers.[5] This principle is consistent with the NLF and the European Commission's so called "Blue Guide".[6]

Both manufacturers under Art. 9 para. 1 GPSR and importers under Art. 11 para. 1 GPSR are required to ensure general product safety pursuant to Art. 5 GPSR. All economic operators pursuant to Art. 3 (13) GSPR have comprehensive information, notification and cooperation obligations according to their role in the distribution chain and their ability to manage risks.[7] As part of their extensive information obligations, economic operators shall include their contact details on products to facilitate traceability and communication with product safety authorities for consumers. Moreover, all economic operators shall ensure that complaints are processed in an internal reporting system of the manufacturer or importer to ensure traceability of safety risks.[8] Additionally, the GPSR provides an external reporting system called Safe-Gateway as a RAPEX 2.0 system in its Chapter IV.[9] Three different portals are provided for rapid alert systems for market surveillance authorities, businesses, the public, and the Commission.[10] The Safe-Gateway portals mandate reporting of safety concerns for manufacturers, importers, and distributors.[11]

Moreover, a mutual monitoring of compliance obligations among economic operators is stipulated.[12] Manufacturers, responsible for setting essential safety standards based on internal risk analysis (Art. 9 para. 2 GPSR) and for developing internal procedures to ensure product conformity (Art. 9 para. 4 GPSR), are required, among other duties outlined in Art. 9 paras. 2, 3, and 7 GPSR, to continuously provide updated technical documentation, user manuals, and safety information for a period of ten years, as well as to appropriately label their products (Art. 9 para. 5 GPSR). Importers (Art. 11 paras. 1 and 5 GPSR) and distributors (Art. 12 paras. 1 and 2 GPSR) shall ensure that manufacturers have fulfilled their obligations and complied with safety requirements within their scope of responsibility. Alongside mutual monitoring within the distribution chain, internal monitoring through a "product compliance process" is stipulated pursuant to Art. 14 GPSR which does not set forth the details but requires fitness to comply with the relevant requirements of this regulation. Unlike the provisions set out in Art. 29 of the Digital Services Act (EU Directive 2022/2065; "**DSA**"), a comprehensive regulation to ensure the accountability on online platforms and to protect users from illegal online content that came into effect in February 2024, the GPSR's internal conformity procedures do not provide for exemptions for small businesses (<50 employees) or microenterprises (<10 employees) who solely bear the responsibility for internal conformity procedures.

The product safety responsibilities of an online marketplace provider pursuant to Art. 3 (13) GPSR differ from the responsibilities of the economic operators. The online marketplace provider's responsibilities do not pertain to product manufacturing or provisioning but to maintaining a platform, on which economic operators distribute compliant products under their own responsibility and surveillance (Art. 22 para. 3 GPSR). The online marketplace provider shall monitor violations with the duty to temporarily suspend non-compliant products from sale on their platform for a reasonable period of time after a prior warning (Art. 22 para. 11 GPSR).[13] However, the beforementioned obligation to monitor product non-compliance does not extend to an obligation to actively investigate the non-compliance of products as provided by Art. 8 DSA.[14] Complimentary to the information obligations of manufacturers and importers, online marketplace providers are required under Art. 22 paras. 9 and 12 GPSR to provide said information on the "online interface." Online marketplace providers are additionally required under Art. 22 para. 8 GPSR to inform consumers about product safety issues in cooperation with market surveillance authorities and other economic operators under Art. 22 paras. 4, 5, and 12 GPSR. [15]

2.2 CRA

2.2.1 Background

On March 12, 2024, the CRA was approved by the EU parliament. Unlike previous EU legislation regarding cybersecurity, which focused solely on ensuring individual vertical, sector-specific regulations (e.g. the NIS2 Directive for the protection of network and information systems), this landmark initiative underscores the pressing need to fortify the cybersecurity of digital products amidst escalating cyber threats spanning borders and industries. Yet again relying on the instrument of regulation to establish a cohesive legal standard across the EU, the CRA seeks to foster the development of secure digital products, mandating manufacturers to prioritize cybersecurity throughout a product's lifecycle besides its general product safety in accordance with the GPSR[16], thus following principles such as "cybersecurity by design" and fostering synergies with existing frameworks like GDPR for robust data protection.[17] In connection with other cybersecurity legislation, the CRA is believed to be a cornerstone of EU cybersecurity legislation, stipulating the most comprehensive compliance obligations in the history of cybersecurity law.[18] Upon approval by the EU Council and ratification of the CRA, the CRA will apply 24 months after its date of entry into force (Art. 57 CRA).

2.2.2 Scope of Application

2.2.2.1 Subject Matter

The CRA applies to products featuring digital elements that are either explicitly designed for or could reasonably foreseeably involve a direct or indirect logical or physical data connection to a device or network (Art. 2 para. 1 CRA).

While the term "product with digital elements" may seem reminiscent of the language used in the implementation of the Digital Content and Digital Services Directive in Sections 327 onwards of the German Civil Code

("**BGB**"), it is worth noting that the meaning of "products with digital elements" as defined in CRA extends beyond mere software (see Section 327 para. 1 BGB). It encompasses "any software or hardware product and its remote data processing solutions, including software or hardware components intended for separate market placement" (Art. 3 para. 1 CRA), although not including software as a service ("**SaaS**") that is generally subject to the NIS2 Directive. However, the CRA is applicable to digital services in the sense of "remote data processing" (Art. 3 para. 2 CRA) with the requirement that a distinction is made based on whether the data processing is integral to the product. The reason is that unlike SaaS, data processing solutions developed under the responsibility of the product manufacturer are essential for the full functionality of products with digital elements, therefore providing for an inherent necessity of data processing for product usage.[19]

In spite of its designation to serve as a vertical regulation spanning different sectors, the scope of application of products with digital elements pursuant to the CRA does not extend to certain products with specific cybersecurity requirements (e.g. medical devices as stated in Art. 2 para. 2 CRA as well as matters regarding national security as stated in Art. 2 para. 5 CRA). Moreover, software not intended for commercial use, specifically open-source software, falls outside the scope of the CRA to prevent exacerbating the challenges associated with providing open-source software, particularly concerning liability risks.[20] Regarding the CRA's relation to other EU harmonization legislation and the GPSR, the CRA is superseded by regulations concerning product safety requirements pursuant to Art. 7 CRA.

2.2.2.2 Personal Scope

Following the principle set out by the GPSR, the CRA also provides for a graduated tiered system of obligations and liabilities for economic operators as defined in Art. 3 (17) CRA. However, unlike Art. 3 (13) GPSR, Art. 3 (17) CRA does not specifically name fulfillment service providers and online retailers, assigning responsibility to manufacturers, authorized representatives, "importers, distributors," or any other individual or legal entity who is subject to obligations under the CRA.

Following the principle "cybersecurity by design", manufacturers – meaning any individual or legal entity developing or manufacturing products with digital elements or having products with digital elements designed, developed, or manufactured, and marketing them under the individual's or legal entity's name or trademark, whether for payment or free of charge (Art. 3 (18) CRA) – are primarily responsible for the cybersecurity of their products. Manufacturers shall ensure that before placing products on the market, they meet the essential requirements outlined in Section 1 of Annex I to the CRA (Art. 10 para. 1 CRA). This includes ensuring that products are only placed on the market without any (known) exploitable vulnerabilities and with a secure default configuration, safeguarding the confidentiality and integrity of all processed data. The general cybersecurity warranty also applies to importers who place products with digital elements on the EU market (Art. 13 para. 1 CRA).

However, the extensive obligations of manufacturers also apply to other economic operators if they assume a role comparable to that of the manufacturer. This pertains to e.g. the authorized representative (Art. 12 CRA), who takes on the obligations of the manufacturer within its designated authority, subject to any specified limitations. Moreover, certain responsibilities assigned to manufacturers extend to importers (after the manufacturer has already placed a product onto the EU market) and distributors (Art. 15 CRA) if they introduce the product to the market under their own name or trademark, therefore communicating their direct responsibility for product conformity to the market, or if they make substantial modifications a product containing digital components that has already been introduced to the market. [21]

The delegation of product conformity responsibilities by so-called substantial modifications, meaning changes to products with digital elements following its placing on the market, cause a reevaluation of the issue of compliance of the product with digital elements or its intended use with the essential requirements set out in Section 1 of Annex I (Art. 3 (31) CRA), reflects the significant influence importers and distributors wield in the reassessment of product compliance.[22] Yet, the delegation of responsibility of manufacturers under the CRA to importers and distributors applies solely to the part of the product influenced by the significant alteration, unless the material change affects the cybersecurity of the entire product, in which case importers and distributors assume responsibility for the entire product.[23]

2.2.3 Catalogue of Compliance Requirements under the CRA

2.2.3.1 Compliance Requirements for Manufacturers

2.2.3.1.1 Compliance Requirements Prior to Placing Products onto the Market

Prior to placing products onto the market, manufacturers shall perform a risk assessment of their product with digital elements as to its compliance to the essential requirements set out in Annex I to the CRA. Such risk assessment has to be technically documented (Art. 10 paras. 2 and 7 and Art. 23 CRA). The technical documentation of the risk assessment shall provide all relevant data to ensure that the product is compliant with the (i) essential requirements set out in Annex I to the CRA pursuant to Art. 23 para. 1 CRA, (ii) with its minimum requirements listed in Annex V that range from the requirement for basic information on the product such as the intended purpose of the product and user information, to proprietary information such as the specifications of the production and monitoring processes of the product (iii) as well as with the complete information on the design and development of the product with digital elements. Such extensive documentation requirements may conflict with the issue of the protection of trade secrets.

Upon completion of the risk assessment, the manufacturer shall perform a conformity assessment and sign a conformity declaration that can, however, be carried out by an authorized representative (Art. 10 para. 7, Art. 20 and 24 CRA). The requirements for the relevant conformity assessment procedure (Art. 24 CRA and Annex VI) are based on the respective classification of the product. Critical products, which are divided into two classes according to Annex III, are intended to reflect the degree of cybersecurity risk associated with them. Criteria for the classification of the products in class I including password managers and in class II products including operating systems and industrial firewalls that are subject to a higher cybersecurity threat level are primarily their functionality and their intended use.[24] Manufacturers are permitted to conduct conformity assessments independently for critical class I products by adhering to joint specifications and certification systems (Art. 24 para. 2 and Art. 19 CRA). Conversely, for critical class II products, which undergo an EU-type examination procedure or comprehensive quality assurance (outlined in Annexes VI and VIII), assessment shall be performed by a third party (Art. 24 para. 3 CRA in conjunction with Annex VI and VIII).

2.2.3.1.2 *Compliance Requirements for Products already on the Market*

After the product has been introduced to the market, the manufacturer is primarily responsible for meeting update requirements to guarantee compliance with the essential cybersecurity standards outlined in the CRA throughout its lifespan, but at least for up to five years following its market introduction (Art. 10 para. 12 CRA). This obligation extends to the update of its technical documentation (Art. 23 para. 2 CRA) as well as its conformity declaration (Art. 20 para. 2 CRA). As per Art. 10 para. 6 CRA, robust vulnerability management entails implementing policies and procedures facilitating the coordinated disclosure of vulnerabilities. This approach aims to promptly address and resolve potential vulnerabilities in digital products, as reported by internal or external sources. Emphasis should be placed on ensuring that such reports on the digital products are received before third parties who could exploit them maliciously. Therefore, manufacturers should consider implementing recognition and reward systems ("bug bounty programs") to encourage vulnerability reporting.[25] In the event of an "actively exploited vulnerability" (see Art. 3 para. 39 CRA) or any event giving concern to the cybersecurity of the product in question, the manufacturer shall inform the European Union Agency for Cybersecurity (ENISA) within 24 hours at the latest (Art. 11 paras. 1 and 2 CRA). Unlike other provisions of the CRA, manufacturers shall conform to Art. 11 CRA as early as twelve months after its date of entry into force. Furthermore, even without the requirement of a concrete cybersecurity threat, the CRA provides for extensive cooperation obligations for all economic operators with the market surveillance authorities (Art. 17 and 42 CRA).

2.2.3.2 *Compliance Requirements for Importers and Distributors*

Importers and distributors shall generally ensure that the manufacturer has provided the product with digital elements with all relevant information as well as the relevant instructions to ensure safe use (Art. 13 para. 5 and Art. 14 para. 2 CRA). Other than that, they are essentially subject to reporting obligations. They shall report vulnerabilities to the manufacturer and, if there are significant cybersecurity risks, also to market surveillance authorities (Art. 13 para. 6 and Art. 14 para. 4 CRA). If the manufacturer cannot ensure compliance of its products, importers, and distributors may need to inform users or launch a product recall (Art. 13 para. 6 and Art. 14 para. 4 CRA).

2.3. PLD

2.3.1. Background

Finalizing its quest for a comprehensive reform of product safety and liability law, the PLD was also approved on March 12, 2024 by the European Parliament. The new PLD is intended to revoke and replace the current Directive 85/374/EEC from 1985, enhancing consumer safeguards amidst the complexities brought by digitalization and global supply chains such as the possibility of direct online purchases from economic operators outside the EU and EEA.[26] The main objective of the PLD is to ensure the legal tangibility of both a respondent and a responsible party within the EU, while also enhancing consumer protection by lowering the requirements necessary for successfully asserting damage claims.[27] Additionally, the PLD seeks to synchronize the updated regulations of product safety law with those of product liability law, thus ensuring legal clarity by defining its scope of application more clearly than its previous EEC legislation from 1985. As the PLD was enacted as a directive, its direct application is generally only effected in a Member State after its provisions have been implemented by such EU's Member State. Member States will therefore have after the impending ratification of the PLD until mid-2026 to enact the directive, adhering to the 24-month implementation deadline from the PLD's effective date (Art. 18 para. 1 PLD).

2.3.2 General Liability Provisions

An important innovation is enacted through Art. 4 para. 1 PLD, extending the definition of "product" to all movable items, even if they are integrated into another movable or immovable item and therefore including electricity, digital construction documents, and software, i.e. operating systems, firmware, computer programs, applications, and AI systems, conclusively settling the legal debate whether or not SaaS or software as an intangible object falls within the scope of application of Section 2 of the German Product Liability Act (“**ProdHaftG**”) through the explicit inclusion of software. Similar to the CRA's approach in not impeding innovation and research within coding any more than deemed necessary, the PLD provides for a specific exemption in its scope of application for free and open-source software. Moreover, Art. 4 para. 6 (c) PLD expands the scope of compensable damages by recognizing the significant importance of data as assets and deeming them particularly worthy of protection by clarifying that the loss and falsification of data, even when not exclusively used for professional purposes, can be considered as damage.

2.3.3 Specific Liability Provisions

Art. 5 PLD establishes the legal basis for claims and specifies who is entitled to claim damages. Individuals who have suffered damage caused by a defective product or individuals to whom the beforementioned damage claim has been legally or contractually transferred as well as authorized individuals acting on behalf of the injured parties are potential claimants (Art. 5 PLD). Art. 6 PLD defines the defectiveness required for product liability claims. Per its definition, a product is in principle defective if it does not offer the level of safety that the general public may expect, taking into account all the circumstances.

In particular, the following aspects have been renewed compared to the previous legislation from 1985 on product liability issues. Firstly, under Art. 6 (1) (a) PLD, the product's defectiveness can arise from its presentation, which includes instructions for installation, use and maintenance. Consequently, software updates shall also be considered in this context. Secondly, Art. 6 (1) (c) PLD states that in assessing defectiveness, consideration must be given to the effects of a product such as AI systems' ability of continued learning. Therefore, product defects also encompass pursuant to Art. 6 (1) (c) PLD issues caused by self-learning functions and the impacts on other products that can reasonably be expected to be used with the product in question.[28] However, the lack of a precise definition of "learning" could pose challenges since it is unclear if the test of product defects of a product under Art. 6 (1) (c) PLD only comprises defectiveness arising from the product itself, but also arising as a consequence of its algorithm's self-learning functions.[29] When employing such techniques, companies shall therefore monitor the results of the learning process and evaluate potential interactions with other products before placing them on the market.[30] Thirdly, under Art. 6 (1) (d) PLD the effects on other products of the product in question will have to be considered since product defects may also arise as part of an interaction with other products that are likely to be used together.[31] Consequently, companies utilizing such technologies will have to assess the possible interactions with other products prior to market placement.

Lastly, Art. 6 (1) (f) and (h) PLD determine defectiveness based on the legitimate safety expectations of consumers and product safety requirements, including cybersecurity. When assessing the safety expectations of the general public, it is important to consider the intended purpose, objective characteristics, and properties, of the product, along with the specific requirements of the intended user group.[32] This may present challenges for economic operators, particularly in determining responsibility for intentional unlawful interference with the software by an external third party. To determine defectiveness of a product, it will have to be to differentiated (i) if the attack was able to occur even though the product itself or the software not meeting the prevailing state-of-the-art standards at the time of market launch or at the time of the attack or (ii) if the attack was facilitated because proper security measures were not initially taken.[33]

2.4 Examples of Compliance Risks

2.4.1 GPSR and CRA

The compelling case for implementing compliance measures lies in the looming threat of potential violations. The imposition of sanctions for violations against the CRA as well as the GPSR are delegated to the EU Member States and therefore may vary from one Member State to another (Art. 44 para. 1 GPSR and Art. 53 para. 1 sentence 1 CRA). However, those measures need to be effective, proportionate, and dissuasive (Art. 44 para. 1 GPSR, 53 para. 1 sentence 2 CRA). The significance of this triad and the severity of corresponding sanctions have been well known since the enactment of Art. 83 GDPR.

While the GPSR does not provide for a minimum penalty for incompliance, the CRA regulates a penalty for incompliance for all addresses under its scope of application, requiring fines up to EUR 10 million or 2% of their worldwide annual turnover for the proceeding financial year, depending on whichever figure is higher (Art. 53 para. 4 CRA). Violation of obligations set out in Art. 10 CRA (Obligations of Manufacturers) and Art. 11 CRA (Reporting Violations of Manufacturers or other Economic Operators Assuming Responsibility for Cybersecurity Conformity), i.e. being non-compliant with the essential cybersecurity requirements laid down in Annex

I, may cause fines up to EUR 15 million or 2.5% of their worldwide annual turnover for the proceeding financial year, depending on whichever figure is higher (Art. 53 para. 3 CRA).

Furthermore, there is a significant concern surrounding the legal ambiguity regarding how economic operators can adequately meet the precise compliance standards outlined in the CRA and the GPSR. Even though guidelines have been announced (not yet published) to explain the fulfillment of the catalog of obligations for economic operators pursuant to Art. 17 para. 2 sentence 2 GPSR, the specific requirements for the internal product compliance process in accordance with Art. 14 GPSR have not yet been sufficiently clarified.

With regard to the CRA's compliance requirements there remains considerable uncertainty regarding compliance to ensure adequate compliance to the cybersecurity requirements under Annex I to CRA, due to the lack of standardized procedures for cybersecurity requirements as there are simply no relevant technical standards on cybersecurity compliance which provide de facto assistance to economic operator. Such technical standards are essential to determine a minimum standard to assess the necessary state of the art relevant to product liability law. To address this issue, the EU has introduced a new proposal on April 4, 2024, elucidating the available standardization outputs on the cybersecurity of products under the CRA carried out by the European Standardization Organization as well as international Standards Development Organizations and comparing the existing cybersecurity standards against the essential requirements listed in Annex I of the CRA proposal as well as conducting a gap analysis between the mapped standards and the requirements pursuant to Annex I of the CRA.[34]

2.4.2 PLD

The provisions of the PLD also entail significant liability risks in the event of non-compliance with the compliance regulations and errors in the compliance process. These include inter alia the non-effectiveness of liability limits, such as the liability cap for personal injury claims (see Section 10 ProdHaftG), of a deductible for property damage (Section 11 ProdHaftG) and the exclusion of liability for products manufactured outside of professional activity for non-commercial purposes (Section 1 para. 2 (3) ProdHaftG).

Additionally, the PLD expands responsibility for defective software beyond the initial market release, deviating from the typical exemption of liability in the event that the defect likely did not exist when the product entered the market, the reason for this being that manufacturers are able to maintain control over their product's flawless operation, i.e. through software updates post-release beyond its initial release; the manufacturers therefore shall assume responsibility beyond the initial release of their products (see Art. 6 para. 1 and Art. 10 para. 2 PLD).[35]

Moreover, it will be easier to overcome the burden of proof in product liability proceedings because defectiveness and causality between the defective product and the damage occurred can be (albeit rebuttably) assumed in case a violation of product safety regulation can be asserted (Art. 9 para. 2 (b) PLD).[36] The new evidence disclosure requirement pursuant to Art. 8 PLD is of substantial significance, since this process causes the risk that the fact, which proves that the defect is accountable to the respondent, i.e. the respondent is in non-compliance with product safety law, may be revealed. The novelty of the provisions set out in Art. 8 PLD exists in the fact that the EU has traditionally refrained from intervening extensively in the procedural laws of the Member States regarding product liability. Disclosure, although found in common law legal systems, it is not the usual approach to taking evidence in Member States with codified civil law systems, i.e. in the procedural laws of such Member States (see for example the German Code of Civil Procedure ("ZPO")).

The ZPO for example stipulates an obligation for disclosure for documents subject to certain requirements (Section 142 ZPO), provides for disclosure duties in exceptional cases like in the areas of antitrust law, intellectual and individual property law and trade secrets; furthermore there are procedural case law rules (i) on a secondary duty of the respondent to establish facts in case of a lack of knowledge of the claimant of such facts and after the claimant has fully established the facts which could be known by the claimant and (ii) on a rebuttable prima facie evidence and (iii) on an actual rebuttable presumption, with the effect of a shift of the burden of proof. Still, such procedural rules in their entirety, although the common law system and the codified law systems could be characterized as converging to some extent, are by far not as far-reaching as the disclosure in the common law systems.

Although courts are tasked with restricting the disclosure obligation to what is essential and reasonable, the thorough fulfillment of this obligation still sparks apprehension regarding the safeguarding of trade secrets. However, failing to comply with this disclosure obligation will result in the (rebuttable) assumption of product defectiveness and subsequent liability (Art. 9 para. 2 (a) PLD). Since the parameters and extent of the new disclosure requirement remain inadequately defined in the PLD, it falls upon the Member States to institute suitable safeguards for trade secrets.

3. Conclusion

The comprehensive reform of product regulation through the introduction of the GPSR, the CRA and the PLD illustrates the EU's efforts to meet the evolving challenges of the digital age aiming to improve product safety, strengthen cybersecurity and clarifying liability for defective products. Furthermore, it elucidates the EU legislative's aim to generally heighten compliance obligations and repercussions for non-compliance among economic operators in the EU and EEA. This aligns with a series of additional compliance requirements recently introduced by the EU, including, but not limited to, those outlined in the GDPR, DSA and the EU Supply Chain Directive[37] and future legislation pertaining to AI and sustainability. Such legislation might also have a direct or an indirect impact on product safety and product liability legislation, e.g. on the admissibility and on the conformity with the legal requirements of products, which would have to be further investigated in detail in a separate analysis.

Moreover, the recent legislation clearly demonstrates the EU's intention to establish comprehensive accountability for product safety, customized based on the level of control and oversight feasible for each economic actor. The fundamental notion of overall responsibility for a product is not unfamiliar to jurisprudence either, as demonstrated by the European Court of Justice ruling in 2018 on the joint responsibility of Facebook and fan page operators on Facebook for the proper data processing of their users (European Court of Justice (ECJ), Judgment of 5 June 2018, Case C-210/16).

However, by introducing such a tiered system of obligations and responsibilities for all economic operators and emphasizing principles such as "cybersecurity by design", the EU marks an important step towards a safe and resilient digital marketplace strengthening consumer's reliance in product safety and ultimately product quality while also harmonizing and modernizing EU product safety legislation. Manufacturers are strongly challenged by the wide range of extensive product safety and product conformity regulations stipulated by the GPSR and the CRA and ultimately by the PLD. This will in the first instance put manufacturers' compliance management systems considerably to the test. Therefore, even though the GPSR, CRA, and PLD will come into force at the end of 2024 (GPSR) or mid-2026 (CRA and PLD), all economic operators are already advised to familiarize themselves with the before mentioned regulations by taking their own internal compliance systems into review and conducting the necessary adaptations. It will, however, subsequently have to be considered after having gained experience with the advantages of the new product safety and product liability regime for the consumer whether the costs to be incurred by the manufacturers and the other responsible individuals or legal entities to be finally borne by the consumers will be outweighed by such advantages or whether corrections of the compliance standards will be required to achieve a reasonable ratio between advantages and costs.

Notes

1 Schucht, GewArch, 2022, 394, 396.
2 Spiegel, ZVertriebsR 2023, 72.
3 Spiegel, ZVertriebsR 2023, 72.
4 See Recital 46 zu GPSR.
5 Guidelines for the Implementation of EU Product Regulations 2022 ("**Blue Guide**"), ABl. 2022 C247, 1 no. 3.1. and no. 7.4.2.1.
6 Blue Guide, ABl. 2022 C247, 1 Nr. 3.1. und Nr. 7.4.2.1; Klindt, ZRP 2023, 108, 109.
7 See Recital 32 to GPSR
8 See Recital 40 to GPSR.
9 See Recital 68 to GPSR; Implementing Decision (EU) 2019/41.
10 See Recital 68 to GPSR; Implementing Decision (EU) 2019/41.
11 See Art. 9 para. 8 (c) GPSR; Art. 10 para. 2 (c) GPSR; Art. 11 para. 8 (d) GPSR; Art. 12 para. 4 (c) GPSR.
12 See Art. 9 para. 10 GPSR, Art. 12 paras. 2, 9 GPSR; Art. 12 paras. 3, 4 GPSR, Art. 20 GPSR.
13 Spiegel, ZVertriebsR 2023, 73.
14 See Recital 56 to GPSR.
15 See Recital 36, 37 to GPSR.
16 Explanatory Memorandum, Context of the Proposal, page 1, Recital 28 to CRA.

17 Recital 4 to CRA.
18 Dittrich/Heinelt, RDi 2023, 309,310.
19 Recital 4 to CRA.
20 Recital 9 to CRA, Dittrich/Heinelt, RDi 2023, 309, 311.
21 Dittrich/Heinelt, RDi 2023, 309, 312.
22 Dittrich/Heinelt, RDi 2023, 309, 312.
23 Dittrich/Heinelt, RDi 2023, 309, 312.
24 Recital 26 to CRA, Voigt/Falk, MMR, 2023, 88, 90.
25 Recital 36 to CRA; Dittrich/Heinelt, RDi 2023, 309, 315.
26 See Recitals 3 and 5 to PLD.
27 See Recitals 3, 8, 13 to 16 to PLD.
28 Reusch, RDi 2023, 152, 158.
29 Reusch, RDi 2023, 152, 158.
30 See Recital 23 to PLD.
31 Reusch, RDi 2023, 152, 158.
32 See Recital 22 to PLD.
33 Reusch, RDi 2023, 152, 158.
34 See Hernandez Ramos, J.L., Karopoulos, G., Nai Fovino, I., Spigolon, R., Sportiello L., Steri, G., Gorniak, S., Magnabosco, P., Atoui, R., Crippa Martinez, C., Cyber Resilence Act Requirements Standards Mapping, Publication Office of the European Union, 2024, https://data.europa.eu/doi/10.2760/905934, JRC137340.
35 See Recitals 15 and 37 sq. to PLD.
36 See Recital 33 to PLD.
37 The EU Supply Chain Directive that has been approved by EU council at the end of May 2024 aims to set forth human rights and environmental standards across supply chains. It requires companies to ensure that their operations, as well as those of their subsidiaries and affiliates, do not cause or contribute to adverse impacts on human rights and the environment.

EU Law on companies' liability and the role of compliance

Anna Hlebicka-Józefowicz, Gniewomir Wycichowski-Kuchta

"Did you ever expect a corporation to have a conscience, when it has no soul to be damned, and no body to be kicked?... (and, by God, it ought to have both)."
Edward, First Baron Thurlow 1731-1806

1. Introduction

Although the EU's power to harmonise the criminal law of the Member States is considered peripheral and unusual, criminal law is one of the areas that has developed most dynamically in recent years – from substantive law directives,[1] through procedural acts[2] to new institutional developments.[3] It is expanding into new fields and is, in particular, playing an increasingly important role in protecting the EU's single market. At the same time, the growing influence of corporations in the EU economy, sometimes at the expense of the EU's and other common European interests, has over the years prompted the Union to establish a system of protection.[4] In this system, although the direct liability of legal persons plays a significant role, the decision on the exact nature of this liability and its enforcement is left to the Member States. Given this regulatory landscape, the potential criminal nature of sanctions imposed on legal persons is becoming an increasingly pressing matter and is, at the same time, puzzling from a legal perspective. On the one hand, more and more EU legislative acts mention the potential criminal liability of corporations. On the other, not all Member States provide for such liability in their domestic legal systems,[5] though the majority of them do – either with "classical" criminal liability[6] or "para-criminal" liability[7] (Mongillo, 2012a).

This pluralism of regimes at the national level and the rather permissive approach taken by the EU to criminal sanctions imposed on legal entities raise a great many practical questions and issues. Firstly, it can lead to "forum shopping", where litigants shop around among different legal systems offer varying levels of protection and sanctions. This can allow potential perpetrators to select a jurisdiction with less stringent laws regarding corporate crime and endanger potential victims of corporations' harmful conduct (Selvagi, 2014). Secondly, the diversity in laws and regulations among EU Member States poses challenges to cooperation and mutual recognition of sentences for offences committed by legal entities (Adam, Vermeulen, & De Bondt, 2008). In the absence of a framework for the criminal liability of legal entities, some sentences may be difficult to enforce. The Court of Justice of the European Union (CJEU) has addressed this issue, but has taken a rather conservative stance on the matter, stating that national courts are obligated to interpret national law in accordance with EU law to the broadest extent possible. However, due to the limits of pro-European interpretation, they cannot act *contra legem*, that is, against their national law, so they cannot enforce such penalties issued in another Member State if there is no legal basis in their national legal system allowing them to do so.[8] Thirdly, in its recommendations, the Committee of Ministers of the Council of Europe urged its members to introduce such liability for legal entities,[9] setting the international standard higher than the EU, while international NGOs have also urged countries to introduce such a regime to their legal systems.[10]

Due to this fragmentation, it needs to be clarified whether and in what form Member States are obliged to introduce such a legal regime to their domestic legal systems. It is an important issue, since, as Ester Herlin-Karnell aptly noted, due to the EU's increasing involvement in criminal law, although it is true that the CJEU has been reluctant to explicitly lay down the obligation to introduce criminal liability for legal persons,

> it remains less certain whether in practice, Member States have much choice when asked to comply with effective sanctions. This poses potential difficulties for Member States that do not recognise criminal liability for legal persons.[11]

In this paper, we first reconstruct the legal situation as it emerges from EU legislation and CJEU case law on the criminal liability of legal persons. We then move on to consider how this issue could be comprehensively regulated in EU law in light of the theoretical models of such liability in the Member States. Finally, we highlight internal compliance procedures as a critical element of collective entities' liability and ponder whether an internal compliance system may become a public, obligatory requirement for businesses.

2. Current status – what does EU law say about the criminal liability of collective entities?

EU criminal law, which includes the Treaties, the Charter of Fundamental Rights, directives, regulations, framework decisions, and CJEU jurisprudence, has a general part that outlines the principles of criminal responsibility and criminalisation (Klip, 2021) (Blomsma & Peristeridou, 2013). This is further supported by the constitutional traditions of the Member States (Articles 4(2) and 6(3) TEU). Within this framework, the concept of the criminal liability of collective entities emerges from individual regulations in a specific form (Satzger, 2018).

When examining the history of the criminal liability of legal persons in EU legislative acts, it is crucial to consider the Second Protocol to the Convention on the protection of the European Communities' financial interests. This Protocol was a turning point, as EU legislators first directly required Member States to enact provisions ensuring that a legal person can be penalised with effective, proportionate and dissuasive sanctions, including criminal or non-criminal fines. Importantly, it was in this context that the idea of "functional equivalence" (Selvagi, 2014) was introduced. This concept has been carried forward in the new legislative acts of the post-Lisbon era; it presumes that, regardless of the labelling (administrative or criminal) at the domestic level, the liability should be severe enough to promote the achievement of directive goals. New legislative acts, utilising the EU's new post-Lisbon authority to harmonise the substantive criminal law of the Member States (Article 83 TFEU), continue to apply this approach (Peers, 2016). However, these new directives have provided a new scope of a legal entity's liability regarding the attributability of the sanction (Fiorella, 2012). From an analysis of directives adopted in 2024[12] (which are typical examples of the EU's approach), two bases for liability can be observed, corresponding to two different models of corporate "guilt" (these models are discussed in more detail in Section III). They indicate the circle of individuals for which a legal person is responsible under the threat of criminal liability – basically a "corporate liability trigger" (Pieth & Ivory, 2011) (Valenzano, 2012). Although they indicate different scopes of agents, they share a common principle – the connection between the offence and the legal entity should involve the "benefit" of the "guilty" entity.[13] Therefore, the initial step in connecting a specific entity and an offence is the *cui bono* principle. However, as Selvagi astutely points out, it is important not to overstate this principle:

> The notion of 'benefit' itself should not be accepted as the sole basis for corporate criminal liability, since it is, at best, an evidential, rather than an operative, fact.[14]

The first type of "triggers" are persons "in charge" of the entity. The provisions of EU laws indicate three types of actor, namely those with the power:

- to represent the legal person;
- to make decisions on behalf of the legal person;
- to exercise control within the legal person.

In contrast to the paradigm described above, EU laws introduce another basis for criminal corporate liability. This mechanism is grounded in the private law principles of guilt in choice/surveillance or control. It operates on the basis of negligence, where the failure to act or inappropriate action by those in charge leads to the offence, even if it was committed by a regular employee or a third-party vendor. The core tenet of this mechanism is that the legal person's liability is established by a "causal nexus", a direct link between the offence and failure of supervision.

This paradigm has a long tradition in CJEU case law. One of the most prominent judgments in which the CJEU tackled the issue of domestic sanctions for breaches of EU law was the famous "Greek Maize" case,[15] in which the CJEU addressed the Greek scandal involving Greek officials who exported two shipments of maize from Greece to Belgium in May 1986. These shipments actually contained Yugoslavian maize, but the Greek authorities falsely declared it as Greek. Consequently, neither Belgium nor Greece collected the agricultural levy owed to the Community, as the maize was considered to be Greek rather than from a non-EU country. The Greek authorities refused to take any criminal or disciplinary action against the officials involved in the incident. The CJEU (then known as the ECJ) emphasised the duty of loyalty of the Member States, which requires them to impose sanctions for violations of EU law:

> It should be observed that where Community legislation does not specifically provide any penalty for an infringement or refers for that purpose to national laws, regulations and administrative provisions, Article 5 of the Treaty [now: Article 4(3) TEU] requires the Member States to take all measures necessary to guarantee the application and effectiveness of Community law. For that purpose, whilst the choice of penalties remains within their discretion, they must ensure in particular that infringements of Community law are penalised under conditions, both procedural and substantive, which are analogous to those applicable to infringements of national law of a similar nature and importance and which, in any event, make the penalty effective, proportionate and dissuasive.

This approach settled the Member States' general competence to choose the measures which they consider appropriate, including sanctions which may be criminal in nature.[16] The very same approach was adopted regarding the criminal nature of legal persons' liability under EU law – in the *Vandevenne* and *Giovanardi* cases the CJEU stated that it required a Member State to introduce into its national law a specific system of criminal liability, such as the criminal liability of legal persons,[17] but it is important to note that this notion was not of a general nature, but based on specific EU laws (the road transport directive and the victims' rights directive, respectively). The CJEU has not to date delivered a judgment that clearly and generally addresses the Member States' obligation to hold collective entities criminally liable. The CJEU's first encounter with the issue of criminal liability of legal persons in a Member State was particularly intriguing due to the complexity of the Danish legal system, which was subject to the CJEU's assessment. Despite introducing a system of strict criminal liability – the most severe type of corporate liability – the CJEU deemed it compatible with the EU framework, thereby highlighting the freedom of Member States in selecting their sanctioning regime[18] (see Section III). Thus, based on the CJEU case law mentioned above, it seems that this is a decision that is left to the discretion of the Member States.

However, upon a close examination of CJEU case law, scenarios can be found in which Member States might be required to incorporate in their domestic legal systems a regime of criminal liability for legal entities, despite the EU's general reluctance to impose this obligation on the Member States. Firstly, it is evident that, under the equivalence principle, which was first established in the Greek Maize case, where the Member States envisage criminal liability of legal persons for breaches of national provisions of a particular nature, they are also obliged to provide similar sanctions for breaches of EU law of a similar kind ("similar nature and importance"). Secondly, there are some areas of EU law where the protection of common interests is of such importance that the CJEU stated that it was necessary to introduce criminal sanctions for them to be "effective, proportionate and dissuasive".[19] This is primarily the case with the protection of the financial interests of the EU, where the responsibilities of the Member States are enshrined in the Treaty, namely in Article 325 TFEU. According to this provision, Member States shall counter fraud and any other illegal activities affecting the financial interests of the Union through measures to be taken in accordance with this provision, which shall act as a deterrent and be such as to afford effective protection in the Member States, and in all the Union's institutions, bodies, offices and agencies. In several cases, the CJEU suggested (without stating it explicitly) that, as regards the protection of the final interests of the Union (understood broadly, e.g. covering VAT fraud), only criminal penalties would be considered proportionate due to the gravity of those offences:

> Although the Member States have freedom to choose the applicable penalties — which may take the form of administrative penalties, criminal penalties or a combination of the two — in order to ensure that all VAT revenue is collected and, in so doing, that the financial interests of the European Union are protected in accordance with the provisions of Directive 2006/112 and Article 325 TFEU (…), *criminal penalties may nevertheless be essential to combat certain serious cases of VAT evasion in an effective and dissuasive manner.*[20]

A similar conclusion can be reached on the grounds of CJEU case law on penalties for violating fishing quotas (although in its conclusion, the CJEU left the Member States some wiggle room between criminal *sensu stricto* and administrative sanctions).[21] Thus, it can be presumed that where a criminal sanction at the domestic level is the only adequate reaction for a particular breach, it should not be limited only to natural persons, but it should also apply to collective entities.[22] Thirdly, a situation where some form of criminal sanctions that may also be applied to legal persons is required is where an international agreement to which the EU is a signatory demands it. This was the case with the TRIPS Agreement and the sanctioning of the infringement of trademarks, where the CJEU stated that when Member States perform their obligations resulting from an international agreement entered into by the European Union, which forms an integral part of EU law from its entry into force, they must be considered to be implementing EU law.[23] In the case of TRIPS, Article 61 lays down the obligation to provide for criminal procedures that are, at the very least in cases of wilful trademark counterfeiting or copyright piracy on a commercial scale, capable of resulting in effective, deterrent and proportionate penalties and that are binding on each Member of the WTO, including the European Union and its Member States. The fact that the obligation is laid down in an international agreement entered into by the European Union and not in internal EU legislation is, in that regard, irrelevant. The CJEU underlined that:

> it must be borne in mind that, while leaving the choice and detailed rules of the criminal procedures and the applicable penalties to the discretion of the members of the WTO, Article 61 of the TRIPS Agreement requires those members to impose criminal sanctions on at least some infringements of intellectual property rights, such as wilful trademark counterfeiting on a commercial scale.

In consequence, there are some atypical scenarios where Member States must seriously consider introducing criminal liability for legal persons in order to meet obligations stemming from EU law. Thus, implementation would not be at the complete discretion of the domestic legislator – it would have to abide by all the fundamental principles that are related to criminal liability. The CJEU has confirmed that most basic principles of the EU fundamental rights system, such as *ne bis in idem*[24] or the presumption of innocence, apply to legal persons.[25] However, not all principles and rules are easily transferable to the realm of corporate crime since they were developed with natural persons in mind. For example, this is the issue with the right to remain silent. In *Consob*,[26] the CJEU provided a straightforward answer to the situation of the natural person in administrative proceedings that was deemed "criminal" in nature in the light of the Engel criteria,[27] but in its reasoning, the Court referred to case law on legal persons' right to remain silent under EU competition law (the sanctions for which are considered "criminal" under EU law and therefore criminal law safeguards apply), which states that a legal person in such proceedings cannot be compelled to admit unlawful anti-competitive conduct but can be compelled to provide all necessary information or to disclose documents that are in their possession, even if the latter may be used to establish the existence of anti-competitive conduct. This raises the question of whether this line of thought may be leveraged to obtain more robust protection for companies in some instances, such as market abuse cases where both natural and legal persons may be involved under different criminal and quasi-criminal liability regimes. One intellectually stimulating argument that can be raised is *a fortiori* reasoning, which states that *a minori ad maius* if such safeguards apply in competition cases (which are "criminal" only *sensu largo*), similar guarantees would have to apply in criminal proceedings *sensu stricto*, based on the logical progression of the argument. Another significant challenge from the perspective of EU law standards is the subjective aspect of crime, i.e. *mens rea*. It is often considered as a "fault" element of crime, it encompasses the subjective elements of a crime, like intention, as well as the doctrines that govern its application (Blomsma, 2012). It is especially important for collective entities since this component may deemed absent for legal persons (see Section III on issues related to this matter). Nevertheless, as Advocate General Lenz stated:

> the connection between the conduct contrary to Community law and the objective national prohibition of holding treated animals in stock is established through the subjective element of knowledge regarding the circumstances of acquisition. Only in the absence of this subjective element does the national measure catch a situation which does not reveal a direct connection with the Community law prohibition. Imputability of conduct, however, is normally a precondition of criminal liability. The general principle of law nulla poena sine culpa makes it clear that personal fault is a prerequisite for criminal liability.[28]

So, the subjective element is, as a matter of principle, required from the perspective of EU law. EU instruments are usually focused on "direct intent" or "serious negligence". For example, Council Regulation (EC) No 423/2007 of 19 April 2007 stated that it

> shall not give rise to liability of any kind on the part of the natural or legal persons or entities concerned, if they did not know, and had no reasonable cause to suspect, that their actions would infringe these prohibitions – it can be seen as declaratory for most EU instruments.[29]

On the other hand, in some areas, especially environmental law, negligence of the perpetrator is also criminalised – in a *ship-source pollution* case the CJEU defined autonomously the concept of "serious negligence", stating that it referred to an unintentional act or omission by which the person responsible commits a patent breach of the duty of care which he should have and could have complied with in view of his attributes, knowledge, abilities and individual situation.[30] Thus, a subjective element, either intentional or non-intentional,[31] is treated as default in the EU system when it comes to punitive sanctions. Strict criminal liability, which requires only criminal conduct to punish the perpetrator, his *mens rea* being irrelevant, would require specific and robust justification to be put in place instead of "classical" criminal liability with a subjective component. On several occasions, the CJEU has indicated that, although such a strict liability system does not *per se* violate EU law, it should be treated with suspicion and closely scrutinised from the perspective of the proportionality principle. It is important, since subjective elements of crime are associated by the CJEU with proportionality:

> the determination of factors constituting an infringement and the determination of the rules concerning the severity of fines, but also as regards the assessment of the factors which may be taken into account in the fixing of a fine.[32]

In this respect, CJEU jurisprudence strongly favours the classical form of criminal liability, which considers the subjective element of the offence, over an objectivised strict liability. This is not irrelevant to the possible regulation of the criminal liability of legal persons, as it indicates that, from the perspective of EU regulations, a subjective element in the form of culpability would generally be required (more on this in Section III).

Thus, as regards legal entities, EU legislative acts set relatively permissive standards – they generally require Member States to implement measures to establish direct responsibility, regardless of the type of liability. That the penalties are effective, dissuasive, and proportionate is more important than their specific legal classification. In this context, EU law defines liability as holding an entity accountable for the consequences (criminal, administrative, or civil) resulting directly from a criminal offence carried out by a perpetrator acting in the entity's name or supervised by the entity. However, given the current status of the EU legal framework, there are a few instances in which criminal corporate liability may be at least implicitly demanded by the EU. Furthermore, if a Member State establishes a (para)criminal liability system while implementing obligations under EU law, it must comply with substantive and procedural safeguards based on CJEU case law, which concern the most fundamental rights of the prosecuted person.

3. What could the EU-wide liability model look like?

After delving into the challenges that emerge from the diversity of approaches to corporate crime among the Member States and the potential for an implicit obligation to introduce the criminal liability of legal persons, it is crucial to analyse the potential EU-wide harmonisation of this issue. Drawing on existing models of such liability, potential EU policy regarding corporate criminal liability could foster equal competitiveness among the legal persons that operate in different Member States. However, constructing a uniform model in such a diverse legal landscape is a formidable task. This topic is the subject of extensive discussion in literature, where different regimes and theoretical doctrines are under scrutiny. Notably, despite minor terminological differences, scholars have reached a consensus on the typology of the criminal liability of legal persons, identifying three main models: vicarious liability model, direct liability model, and aggregation model (Mongillo, 2012a) (Laufer, 2006) (Gobert & Punch, 2003) (Adam, Vermeulen, & De Bondt, 2008) (Lederman, 2000).

The first model mentioned, the vicarious liability model, is based on the private law assumption that an agent entrusting specific actions to others bears liability for their acts. In this model, the collective entity is responsible for the actions of all those who act on its behalf within the framework of the tasks entrusted to them, including the acts of these persons unlawfully undertaken against the supervising entity's will and even expressly by that person forbidden (Sepinwall, 2012). Therefore, this concept assumes that a collective entity bears objective responsibility for a crime, the elements of which it did not carry out. Consequently, it is one of the types of objective responsibility, so-called strict or absolute liability. It means, in practice, holding criminally liable a person whose act does not fulfil the criteria for a prohibited act and who cannot also raise a plea of culpability. That person therefore bears vicarious liability, though it is of an accessory nature in relation to the liability of the immediate perpetrator. It permits a crime being assigned to the latter by a collective entity being held accountable. In some countries, the concept discussed is referred to as "acting for someone else". This model functions in England and Canada, where it has been applied to crimes in the so-called strict liability group. As regards EU standards for the criminal liability of legal persons, as discussed in Section II, there is a preference for models based on guilt, and such an objective legal regime can be used within the realm of criminal law only in exceptions, where there is robust justification for them and the requirements of the proportionality principle are met.

The direct liability model envisages the liability of collective entities according to the so-called directing mind (corporate bodies) theory, which identifies the acts of a group of persons forming part of the structure of a collective entity with the entity itself and its activity. It means that the acts of people in the structure of a corporation are recognised as acts of the corporation itself (Lederman, 2000). A physical person identified with an enterprise in the laws of most countries is a body of the enterprise, its representative, who acts on behalf and for the benefit of a collective entity (the scope of their authority and on behalf of the corporate body). Thus, the model in question is based on the fact that the bodies of a collective entity constitute its "brain", represent it and express its will, thus constituting the "ego" of the collective entity. Thus, by recognising that the bodies of a collective entity constitute its "brain", their actions and faults are attributed directly to the collective entity. In this approach, it should be stated that the collective entity is responsible for its own, not for other people's, actions. However, calling this type of liability "direct liability of legal persons" is not entirely accurate, as the collective entity cannot be held liable if it is impossible to identify the natural person responsible for committing a prohibited act. This model is partially present in EU law since, as described in Section II, the bodies of those legal persons are considered classical "liability triggers" in accordance with this doctrine.

The last model of liability, the so-called aggregation doctrine, a model of direct criminal liability *sensu stricto*, accepts that a collective entity acts independently on the economic market, and thus, social reality. It broadens the range of agents acting in the name and on behalf of a collective entity, including regular members of such an organisation (Mongillo, 2012b). Thus, a legal fiction is assumed, whereby the behaviour of individual persons belonging to a collective entity is combined in a single entity – behaviour constituting the basis for the liability of a legal person. In practice, this makes it possible for a collective entity to be held accountable not only when the behaviour of individual members constitutes separate crimes but also when each behaviour does not constitute a crime, but their sum is of such nature. Therefore, it is the responsibility of the collective entity for its own actions (Villani, 2012). Adopting this concept is attractive as it allows the collective entity to be held accountable when it is impossible to identify the direct perpetrator. Nevertheless, this model is a complete departure from the canons of criminal law and has given rise to the current discussion about the existence of the so-called guilt of collective entities. It is worth noting that a specific model of the criminal liability of collective entities is provided in the Criminal Code of Finland, which includes the concept of so-called anonymous guilt and direct response. This concept refers to the entity's guilt being "anonymous", as it is not attributed to any specific individual, and the entity's "direct response" to the crime, which can include measures to prevent future crimes and compensate for the damage caused (Korkka-Knuts, 2022). For example, a corporation may implement stricter internal controls or provide restitution to victims. In this model, corporations can only exculpate themselves from this guilt if they have taken all necessary and reasonable measures to prevent their employees committing corporation-related crimes. These necessary and reasonable measures include effective compliance programmes and corporate codes of conduct or ethics. Furthermore, giving relevance to an "organisational fault" could help to develop an element such as that in traditional criminal law which corresponds to the psychological (or moral) element of the offence, thus addressing the theoretical, constitutional and policy objections according to which the liability of a legal entity is strict. As is known, these objections are traditionally raised by arguing that a collective entity cannot bear guilt (have a "guilty mind") and would lead to the culpable agent being identified with the (implicitly, collective) entity (Laufer, 2006). On the other hand, a system aimed at giving relevance to the general attitude of a legal entity particularly in terms of organisation, policy, and culture, could play a pivotal role in shaping a culture that better ensures the prevention of crimes typically associated with collective actors, especially entrepreneurial crimes, given the typical complex structure of such entities: by exonerating collective entities from liability, corporations are encouraged to set up controls over their own activities and organisations and to adopt procedures in order to prevent crime. This model is also partially present in EU laws, which indicate a broader scope of "liability triggers" than only the people in charge of an entity. It is also considered one of the most popular among the Member States (Mongillo, 2012b) and fits the requirements of EU principles as it provides the subjective element of the crime by ensuring the possibility of exculpation.

4. Towards a compliance-orientated approach in EU law?

The introduction of organisational guilt as an imputation criterion has raised a problem in the various legal systems regarding when organisational failure may exist. In this regard, several different solutions have been put forward, which also include the importance of compliance programmes as a point of reference to establish the idea of the culpability of a legal entity. The stress on internal procedures structuring some aspects of a legal person's conduct is vital in EU law. The latest developments, i.e. the Whistleblowers Directive[33] and the newest AML Regulation[34], oblige businesses to introduce internal procedures that structure the organisation's process and limit the risks of violating EU law. Thus, the rising importance of compliance programmes can be clearly seen. However, it is not yet public "criminal compliance"; for now, EU law does not allow exculpation from a crime based solely on due diligence and internal procedures. However, the organisational guilt model is becoming increasingly prominent and may become an essential reference for future EU criminal policy.

The approach described above sets the stage for a compliance system to be a legal requirement and obligation. The most fundamental purpose of a compliance system is to incentivise corporations to self-police, thereby shifting the regulatory burden of crime deterrence from the authorities. This shift in deterrence from criminal law to internal governance underscores the crucial role of corporations in maintaining compliance. An "effective" compliance programme, a key player in this shift, is an internal mechanism that companies implement to detect and prevent criminal conduct within the corporation. The programme operates throughout the corporation, providing a robust shield against potential criminal activities. It has twofold importance: pragmatic, since an effective compliance programme may be used as proof of due diligence (and in extreme cases, as a criminal defence), and symbolic, putting forward values and transparency, and thus fostering a positive corporate culture. Compliance operates mainly in a prospective manner with its rules, standards, and mechanisms. This is a significant departure from the reactive nature of economic or tax crime law. The prospective nature of compliance is closely tied to the anticipation of potential criminal responsibility and liability. It involves foreseeing the criminal implications of actions (or lack thereof) in a business activity. This anticipation is not just a theoretical exercise. It is a practical necessity for designing and implementing rules, standards, and mechanisms that ensure compliance with the applicable law. It has much to do with ethos, structure, policy, and corporate culture. Regardless, compliance programmes provide a benchmark for assessing whether corporate wrongful conduct has occurred. This is consistent with how the state wants corporations to control risks, given that the government lacks the resources and the knowledge to deal effectively with these problems.

To develop a standard EU corporate liability model, it should be agreed that if there is agreement on the idea of imputation criteria to refine the analysis of the entity's attitude towards wrongdoings, it would undoubtedly be desirable to opt for an indication of practical criteria, such as the presence of a robust compliance programme, regular training for employees, and a culture of ethical conduct, to test the existence of organisational guilt, which refers to the collective responsibility of the organisation for the actions of its members, possibly through a reference to the compliance programmes or preferably to organisational measures that shall in any case result from the organisation set up within the entity. In the same perspective, as regards the analysis of the entity's attitude, some statutory indications for due diligence certainly appear appropriate, as they are applicable in relevant cases (see the Whistleblowers Directive or AML regulations and their requirements for internal procedures).

Moreover, following American examples, compliance programmes can play a substantial role in ascribing liability and the sentencing phase of a criminal prosecution against a company. For example, such a programme may even provide a reduced sentence for the corporation, even if the corporation's compliance programme failed to prevent the commission of the crime (Teichmann, Wittmann, & Boticiu, 2023). Additionally, as in the US, the order to introduce or improve internal compliance systems could be introduced as an element of the sentencing of the legal person (Wellner, 2005). Therefore, all of this may provide an incentive for organisations to implement an effective compliance programme and limit potential fraudulent activities, which would not only benefit the corporation but also contribute to the stability and growth of the entire EU single market.

5. Conclusions

Based on the analysis above, there is a strong case for creating a consistent framework for holding legal entities accountable for criminal acts. This would help ensure better cooperation and enforcement of penalties across the EU, ultimately promoting fair competition in the single market. It seems beneficial to have more harmonization standardization in this area.

Compliance is crucial in this context. Currently, without a unified approach to criminal liability for corporate entities operating in the EU, companies must navigate various legal frameworks and comply with differing requirements in each Member State. Given that multiple EU legal acts require the establishment of internal control systems and due diligence procedures, the role of compliance within EU law is becoming increasingly significant. Moreover, the establishment of the European Public Prosecutor's Office and the Directive on combating fraud against the Union's financial interests through criminal law reflect the EU's commitment to addressing corporate crimes and safeguarding the single market. Companies should proactively engage with these developments to ensure their compliance efforts align with the evolving legal landscape. If the EU were to embrace a model of criminal liability for collective entities, compliance systems and internal efforts of due care undertaken by a professional operating in the market would be absolutely crucial in ascribing liability and attributing blame to a specific entity.

The complexities surrounding the criminal liability of legal entities in the EU underscore the importance of strong compliance measures for companies operating in the region. As of now, by staying informed about regulatory developments and implementing effective compliance strategies, businesses can navigate legal complexities, and uphold ethical standards in their operations, however, in the not-too-distant future compliance system may be key to avoiding severe criminal penalties.

Notes

1 In 2004, the EU adopted two completely new directives which broaden the substantive scope of EU criminal law: Directive 2024/1226 of 24 April 2024 on the definition of

criminal offences and penalties for the violation of Union restrictive measures and amending Directive (EU) 2018/1673, and Directive (EU) 2024/1385 of the European Parliament and of the Council of 14 May 2024 on combating violence against women and domestic violence. There was also a revision of a pre-existing legislative act, Directive (EU) 2024/1203 of the European Parliament and of the Council of 11 April 2024 on the protection of the environment through criminal law and replacing Directives 2008/99/EC and 2009/123/EC.

2 In late 2023, political agreement was reached on the Directive on asset recovery and confiscation.

3 The most important being the establishment of the European Public Prosecutor's Office.

4 Directive (EU) 2017/1371 of the European Parliament and of the Council of 5 July 2017 on the fight against fraud to the Union's financial interests by means of criminal law.

5 E.g. the German legal systems do not provide for such criminal liability, and German scholars reject this as a "logical impossibility" (Dubber & Hörnle, 2014).

6 E.g. Finland (chapter 9 of the Criminal Code), Slovenia (Article 42 of the Criminal Code), Estonia (§ 14 and § 37 of the Criminal Code) and Lithuania (Article 20 of the Criminal Code).

7 E.g. Poland (*Ustawa o odpowiedzialności podmiotów zbiorowych za czyny zabronione pod groźbą kary*) and Austria (*Verbandsverantwortlichkeitsgesetz*).

8 Judgment of 4 March 2020, *Bank BGŻ BNP Paribas S.A.*, C-183/18, ECLI:EU:C:2020:153.

9 Recommendation No. R (88) 18.

10 Transparency International Switzerland (2020) "Corporate Criminal Liability: Incomplete Legislation, Inadequate Enforcement, Serious Lack of Transparency", https://transparency.ch/wp-content/uploads/2021/02/Corporate_Criminal_Liability_Report.pdf access: 18.05.2024.

11 Herlin-Karnell, 2012, pp. 182-183.

12 See Article 6 of Directive 2024/1226 of 24 April 2024 on the definition of criminal offences and penalties for the violation of Union restrictive measures and amending Directive (EU) 2018/1673; Article 6 of Directive 2024/1203 of 11 April 2024 on the protection of the environment through criminal law and replacing Directives 2008/99/EC and 2009/123/EC.

13 The concept of "benefit" or "gain" is especially prominent in economic theories of corporate punishment (Cohen, 2020).

14 Selvagi, 2014, p. 53.

15 Judgment of 21 September 1989, *Commission vs Hellenic Republic*, Case 68/88, ECLI:EU:C:1989:339.

16 Judgment of 2 February 1977, *Amsterdam Bulb BV v Produktschap voor Siergewassen*, Case 50-76, ECLI:EU:C:1977:13.

17 Judgment of 2 October 1991, *Vandevenne*, C-7/90 ECLI:EU:C:1991:363 and Judgment of 12 July 2012, *Giovanardi*, C-79/11, ECLI:EU:C:2012:448.

18 Judgment of 10 July 1990, *Hansen & Son*, C-326/88, ECLI:EU:C:1990:291.

19 This idea emerged as early as 1990 in the Order of the Court of 13 July 1990, *J. J. Zwartveld and others*, C-2/88 Imm, ECLI:EU:C:1990:315, where it was stated that: "*In that community subject to the rule of law, relations between the Member States and the*

Community institutions are governed, according to Article 5 of the EEC Treaty, by a principle of sincere cooperation. That principle not only requires the Member States to take all the measures necessary to guarantee the application and effectiveness of Community law, if necessary by instituting criminal proceedings (...)".

20 Judgment of 8 September 2015, *Taricco*, C-105/14, ECLI:EU:C:2015:555 and Judgment of 26 February 2013 *Åkerberg Fransson*, C-617/10, EU:C:2013:105.

21 Judgment of 1 February 2001, *Commission vs France*, C-333/99, ECLI:EU:C:2001:73.

22 See similar discussion (Adam, Vermeulen, & De Bondt, 2008, pp. 395-396).

23 Judgment of 19 October 2023, *G. ST. T.*, C-655/21, ECLI:EU:C:2023:791.

24 See Judgment of 14 September 2023, *Volkswagen*, C-27/22, ECLI:EU:C:2023:663.

25 Judgment of 23 March 2023, *Dual Prod SRL*, C-412/21, ECLI:EU:C:2023:234.

26 Judgment of 2 February 2021, *Consob*, C-481/19, ECLI:EU:C:2021:84.

27 The Engel criteria involve the application of three tests to the case under scrutiny: 1) the legal classification of the offence in domestic law; 2) the nature of the offence; 3) the degree of severity of the possible sanction, see Judgment of the ECHR of 8 June 1976, *Engel and Others v. The Netherlands* (CE:ECHR:1976:0608JUD000510071), § 82.

28 Opinion of Mr Advocate General Lenz delivered on 11 June 1992, C-143/91, ECLI:EU:C:1992:260.

29 See e.g. Judgment of 21 December 2011, *Criminal Proceedings against Mohsen Afrasiabi and Others*, C-72/11 in which the CJEU stated that "the terms 'knowingly' and 'intentionally' imply cumulative requirements of knowledge and intent, which are met where the person participating in an activity having such an object or such an effect deliberately seeks that object or effect or is at least aware that his participation may have that object or that effect and he accepts that possibility".

30 Judgment of 3 June 2008, *Intertanko*, C-308/06, ECLI:EU:C:2008:312.

31 This division, which is of utmost relevance to our analysis, can be found in the Judgment of 26 May 1981, *Rinkau*, C-157/80, ECLI:EU:C:1981:89, a case that has set a significant legal precedent in this area.

32 Judgment of 22 March 2017, *Euro-Team Kft*, C-497/15 and C-498/15, ECLI:EU:C:2017:229.

33 Directive (EU) 2019/1937 of the European Parliament and of the Council of 23 October 2019 on the protection of persons who report breaches of Union law.

34 Regulation (EU) 2024/1624 of the European Parliament and of the Council of 31 May 2024 on the prevention of the use of the financial system for the purposes of money laundering or terrorist financing.

Bibliography

Adam, S., Vermeulen, G., & De Bondt, W. (2008). Corporate criminal liability and the EC/EU: bridging sovereignty paradigms for the sake of an area of freedom, security and justice. In S. Adam, Colette-Basecqz, Nathalie, & M. Nihoul (eds.), *La responsabilité pénale des personnes morales en Europe - Corporate Criminal Liability in Europe* (pp. 373-432). La Charte/Die Keure.

Blomsma, J. (2012). *Mens rea and defences in European criminal law.* Intersentia.

Blomsma, J., & Peristeridou, C. (2013). The way forward: A general part of European criminal law. In F. Galli, & A. Weyembergh, *Approximation of Substantive Criminal Law in the EU : the Way Forward* (pp. 117-138). Editions de l'Université de Bruxelles.

Cohen, M. (2020). Punishing Corporations. In M. Rorie (ed.), *The Handbook of White-Collar Crime* . Wiley.

Dubber, M., & Hörnle, T. (2014). *The Oxford Handbook of Criminal Law (1st ed).* Oxford University Press.

Fiorella, A. (2012). From 'macro-anthropos' to 'multi-person organisation'. Logic and structure of compliance programs in the corporate criminal liability. In A. Fiorella (ed.), *Corporate Criminal Liability and Compliance Programs, II. Towards a Common Model in the European Union.* Jovene.

Gobert, J. J., & Punch, M. (2003). *Rethinking corporate crime.* Butterworth's.

Herlin-Karnell, E. (2012). *The constitutional dimension of European criminal law.* Hart Publishing.

Klip, A. (2021). *European Criminal Law. An Integrative Approach (4th edition).* Intersentia.

Korkka-Knuts, H. (2022). Behaviourally informed approach to corporate criminal law: Ethicality as efficiency. *Bergen Journal of Criminal Law and Criminal Justice*, pp. 27-56.

Laufer, W. (2006). *Corporate Bodies and Guilty Minds.* University of Chicago Press.

Lederman, E. (2000). Models for Imposing Corporate Criminal Liability: From Adaptation and Imitation Toward Aggregation and the Search for Self-Identity. *Buffalo Criminal Law Review*, pp. 641-708.

Mongillo, V. (2012b). The Nature of Corporate Liability for Criminal Offences: Theoretical Models and EU Member State Laws. In A. Fiorella (ed.), *Corporate Criminal Liability and Compliance Programs, Vol. II, Towards a Common Model in the European Union* (pp. 55-120). Jovene.

Mongillo, V. (2012a). The Allocation of Responsibility for Criminal Offences Between Individuals and Legal Entities in Europe. In A. Fiorella (ed.), *Corporate criminal liability and compliance programs. Vol II. Towards a Common Model in the European Union.* Jovene.

Peers, S. (2016). *EU Justice and Home Affairs Law: Volume II: EU Criminal Law, Policing, and Civil Law.* Oxford University Press.

Pieth, M., & Ivory, R. (2011). Emergence and Convergence: Corporate Criminal Liability Principles in Overview. In M. Pieth, & R. Ivory (eds.), *Corporate Criminal Liability: Emergence, Convergence and Risk.* Springer.

Satzger, H. (2018). *International and European Criminal Law (2nd ed.).* C.H. Beck.

Selvagi, N. (2014). Ex crimine liability of legal persons in EU legislation. *European Criminal Law Review*, pp. 46-58.

Sepinwall, A. (2012). Guilty by Proxy: Expanding the Boundaries of Responsibility in the Face of Corporate Crime. *Hastings Law Journal*, pp. 411-454.

Teichmann, F., Wittmann, C. & Boticiu, S. (2023). Compliance as a form of defense against corporate criminal liability.*Journal of Economic Criminology*, pp. 1-3.

Valenzano, A. (2012). 'Triggering Persons': the role of the offender in 'ex crimine' liability of legal entities. In A. Fiorella (ed.), *Corporate criminal liability and compliance programs. Vol II. Towards a common model in the European Union.* Jovene.

Villani, E. (2012). Compliance programs and 'organisational fault' in Europe. In A. Fiorella (ed.), *Towards a Common Model in the European Union. Vol. II. Corporate criminal liability and compliance programs* (pp. 249-282). Jovene.

Wellner, P. (2005). Effective compliance programs and corporate criminal prosecutions. *Cardozo Law Review*, pp. 497-528.11.(Herlin-Karnell, 2012, pp. 182-183)

14. (Selvagi, 2014, p. 53)11.(Herlin-Karnell, 2012, pp. 182-183)

14. (Selvagi, 2014, p. 53)

Regulatory Compliance under Australian Financial Services License Obligations

Akif Mert

1. Introduction

The regulatory landscape in Australia affecting the banking and financial services industry has undergone significant reforms and changes in the recent years in order to focus on introducing more consumer protecting practices as well as improving the service and integrity culture of financial services in the Australian market.

These reforms are directly linked to the outcome of the investigation of the *Royal Commission into Misconduct in the Banking, Superannuation and Financial Services Industry (Royal Commission)*, which was established by the Australian Government in December 2017, including their findings, which were published in February 2019[1].

This article will provide an overview of the new and partially revised key obligations and requirements under the Australian Financial Services Licence (AFSL) regime imposed by Australia's financial markets conduct regulator *Australian Securities and Investment Commission (ASIC)*.

2. Australian Financial Services Licence Obligations

What is the significance of an AFSL for financial services providers in Australia? An AFSL authorises the financial service provider as a licensee[2] to, among others:

- provide financial product advice to customers;
- deal in a financial product;
- make a market for a financial product;
- operate a registered scheme;
- provide a custodial or depository service; or
- provide traditional trustee company services.

As an AFSL holder there are several obligations which the licensee needs to adhere to. These requirements are outlined in the Corporations Act[3], section 912A(1) and comprise the following key obligations:

a) do all things necessary to ensure that the financial services covered by the AFS licence are provided efficiently, honestly and fairly (see section 912A(1)(a));
b) have adequate arrangements in place for managing conflicts of interest (see section 912A(1)(aa));
c) comply with the conditions on the AFS licence (see section 912A(1)(b));
d) comply with the key financial services laws (see section 912A(1)(c));
e) take reasonable steps to ensure that representatives comply with the financial services laws (see section 912A(1)(ca));
f) have adequate financial, technological and human resources to provide the financial services covered by the AFS licence and to carry out supervisory arrangements (see section 912A(1)(d));
g) ensure that representatives are adequately trained and competent to provide the financial services covered by the AFS licence (see section 912A(1)(f));
h) have a dispute resolution system if financial services are provided to retail clients (see section 912A(1)(g));
i) establish and maintain adequate risk management systems (see section 912A(1)(h)), and;
j) meet certain knowledge and competence standards (see section 912A(1 (e)).

In order to govern and administer these obligations apart from the legal provisions in the Corporations or ASIC Act[4], ASIC issues dedicated regulatory guides for the majority of the obligations. These papers are designed to provide guidance to regulated entities by[5]

- explaining when and how ASIC will exercise specific powers under the legislation (in most cases this refers to obligations outlined in the Corporations Act);
- explaining how ASIC interprets the law;

- describing the principles underlying ASIC's approach;
- giving practical guidance.

Guidance on how to introduce measures and procedures to comply with the general obligations under section 912A(1) of the Corporations Act[6], can be found in the regulatory guide "*RG 104 – AFS licensing: Meeting the general obligations*".

3. Compliance Management Obligations

The key obligations a), c) and d) mentioned above are considered as the broad compliance obligations. Although there are no specific prescribed "governance" requirements, it is recommended to implement at least the following key compliance/governance elements or measures to comply with these obligations[7]. When introducing the relevant governance elements or measures, the organization`s individual circumstances as well as the nature, size and complexity of both, the particular business and organisation, needs to be considered.

3.1 Compliance Framework

The compliance framework serves as an overarching governance guideline that sets out the strategies and procedures for complying with applicable laws and regulations. It comprises of the key standards, policies and functional rules which create the required governance relating to the AFS license obligations. In addition, corporate compliance obligations can also be included in order to manage local legal, regulatory and corporate (usually internal) compliance requirements within a single framework.

The compliance framework is to be documented in a central depository (e.g., in the corporate rules book), regularly reviewed and approved by the relevant governing body which is usually the legal entity's Board of Directors. With regard to the regular review cycle, it is to be noted that each individual standard, policy or functional requirement that is part of the compliance framework has to be reviewed according to the prescribed individual review cycle of the relevant document. However, the overarching framework should be reviewed at least every two years for completeness and appropriate coverage.

3.2 Compliance Function

From a regulatory perspective, a standalone and independent Compliance Function or Department (or at least a nominated Compliance Manager) is to be established with clear reporting lines to the Executive Management and/or the Board of Directors. ASIC emphasizes strongly on the suitability ("fitness") and propriety of the individuals working in the Compliance Function. This requires appropriate and regular training of each employee responsible for compliance. In addition to the requirement of independence, the Compliance Function should also have unrestricted access to the information required to perform their compliance responsibilities.

When introducing the compliance framework, the "three-lines-of-defence concept" should be considered to highlight the role and responsibilities of the compliance function as key second line function[8].

3.3 Compliance Communication & Awareness

Regular communication and awareness for compliance requirements is a key element of a successful compliance management system. This goes beyond the management's commitment from a tone-from-the-top perspective or providing training to relevant employees. Rather, a communication plan is required that includes regular communication and awareness-raising activities to promote an open culture of compliance within the organisation and the right level of accountability. Regular compliance trainings usually form the basis, supplemented by a series of additional occasional activities and initiatives to familiarise employees with compliance requirements. In particular, when new compliance measures are introduced as part of new regulations, the compliance function should consider specific communication and awareness-raising activities for relevant employees.

3.4 Responding to compliance failures

AFS licensees have to establish end-to-end processes to identify, investigate and remedy and rectify compliance failures and breaches of the regulation, respectively. In particular, the identification of potential issues and incidents is closely linked to the organisation`s compliance culture. Only if the corporate culture allows for open communication without fear of retaliation, employees can speak up and report issues to the Compliance Function.

A central overview or register of all failures or incident is to be kept to enable a range of data analyses throughout the year. Such a register helps to identify trends, but also to determine potential systemic issues or deficiencies that the organisation needs to address as a top priority.

3.5 Breach reporting

The obligation to report breaches is one of the most important regulatory reporting requirements. This obligation requires licensees to self-report specified matters to ASIC within prescribed timelines and formats. ASIC has issued a separate regulatory guide[9] to provide licensees practical guidance on how to comply with the breach reporting requirements. Please see chapter 7 for more details.

3.6 Record keeping

The obligation to retain records relates to the minimum statutory requirements for the retention of certain business, accounting and compliance records. The Corporations Act defines a minimum of seven years for the majority of business-related documents[10]. This includes the documentation of disclosure documents as well as documents relating to financial advice to customers. The same seven-year retention period is also prescribed by the Anti-Money Laundering and Counter-Terrorism Financing (AML-CTF) Act[11] for all Know-Your-Customer-(KYC)- or transaction-related documentation.

ASIC mentions the documentation and retention obligations several times in its regulatory guides. Therefore, the organisation should at least introduce a record retention policy or checklist which outlines the record-retention obligations for relevant documents. It is also recommended to maintain a basic document management system to flag and track the documents that fall within the scope. If necessary, tool-based solutions are also advisable in order to manage the obligations in a structured and compliant manner.

3.7 Conduct and disclosure obligations

An AFS licensee which provides financial product advice to retail customers is required to adhere to certain conduct and disclosure obligations. These obligations have been introduced by ASIC to provide retail customers with all the necessary information and quality advice on the financial product in order to support their decision making.

In practice, there are three main disclosure documents that a retail customer must receive:

- Financial services guide (FSG) that describes the service the customer is getting;
- Specific statement of advice (SOA) in case the customer is receiving a personal advice by a financial advisor;
- Product disclosure statement (PDS) that explains the main characteristics of the product the customer intends to purchase.

3.7.1 Financial services guide and statement of advice

The requirement to prepare and provide a FSG depends on whether the AFSL holder or its authorized representative provide advice to the customer[12]. When the advice is of personal nature (in contrast to general advice), a separate SOA must also be issued to the customer[13]

General advice does not consider any personal details or circumstances of the individual's financial situation or objectives. However, the advice or recommendation becomes personal once the individual's objectives, financial situation, risk tolerance and needs have been taken into account[14].

Both FSG- and SOA-related obligations are explained in the regulatory guide "*RG 175- Licensing: Financial product advisers - Conduct and disclosure*" which includes minimum content and procedural requirements when preparing and providing these documents[15]. With regards to the FSG, the guide contains a list of minimum requirements for the design, distribution and content that a FSG must include[16].

The requirement to also provide a SOA is triggered by the individual advice given to the customer. In these circumstances the SOA summarises the advice given to the customer including the information provided by the customer which was used to determine the advice. From a transparency perspective the SOA also needs to include detailed information about the remuneration, commissions, or any other benefits that the licensee or another person (e.g., an authorized representative) has received or will receive[17]. Finally, when preparing the SOA (or the advice itself), the adviser must fulfil the duty to safeguard the 'best interest for the customer' which includes providing complete and accurate advice that puts the customer's needs and interests first[18].

Licensees need to take all reasonable steps to ensure that their representatives comply with that obligation; non-compliance with this requirement can result in a civil penalty against the AFS licensee or authorised representative including additional punitive measures for breaching this duty[19], and causing (financial) detriment to the customer. Given the importance of this obligation, ASIC has outlined its expectations in a dedicated section of the regulatory guide RG 175 which provides guidance for licensees on how to best comply with the best interests duty[20].

3.7.2. Product disclosure statement

The obligations relating to product disclosure statements (PDS) are published in the regulatory guide "*RG 168 - Disclosure: Product Disclosure Statements (and other disclosure obligations)*". This guide specifically includes good disclosure principles[21] which should be considered when creating disclosure documents that are intended for customers. These principles include:

- Timeliness;
- Relevance and completeness;
- Promoting the understanding of the product;
- Promoting the comparability with other products;
- Highlighting important information;
- Considering the needs of the customer.

The regulatory guide provides a separate section[22] with detailed guidance for each principle including key considerations when drafting and implementing a product disclosure statement.

4. Risk Management Obligations

ASIC expects an adequate risk management system[23] which includes processes for identifying, evaluating, and managing risks. As part of the risk management system, a dedicated framework can serve as the overarching governance guideline to describe the processes and responsibilities within the organisation.

4.1 Risk management framework

The risk management framework captures the key risks as well as risk-related policies and functional rules. Based on the organisation's business model, a standalone risk strategy or risk appetite statement can be created to define the level of residual risk that the organisation is willing to accept. For most financial institutions holding a AFS license the following risk categories can be considered[24]:

- Market risks;
- Credit risks;
- Underwriting risks;
- Business risks;
- Operational risks;
- Reputation risks;
- Liquidity risks;
- Strategic risks;

Based on the business model, the organisation then must define a set of risk appetite statements including risk alert and risk limit levels. The following distinction can be considered for each appetite statement:

- No appetite;
- Limited appetite;
- Balanced appetite;
- High appetite.

When introducing the framework, the Risk Management Function as key second line function should be integrated into the three-lines-of-defence concept.

4.2 Risk Communication & Awareness

Similar to the compliance communication and awareness activities, a specific risk related communication plan is to be established to promote the risk culture and awareness within the organisation. A close alignment with the Compliance Function is advised to jointly plan and execute various communication and awareness activities throughout the year. For example, a tone-from-the-top communication from the senior management can include a combined message on risk and compliance topics. Training sessions and town hall presentations can have a more meaningful impact when executed jointly. Senior Managers must act as role models and should not only demonstrate awareness but also accountability for managing risks according to the company's risk appetite.

4.3 Risk Identification, Evaluation and Mitigation

The established risk management system includes at least policies and processes to identify risks related to the business model of the organisation. In particular, the risks relating to non-compliance with the obligations of the Corporations Act should be considered, focussing on the specific risks that may impact the consumer and market integrity.

The identification measures should be based on the risk categories of the risk appetite and be consistent with the operating business model. A risk profiling exercise could be helpful in the initial assessment of the organisation`s risk areas. Such profiling can be carried out together with relevant line 2 functions such as the Compliance or Legal department, and also involving stakeholders from across the organisation.

5. People Obligations

Under the people obligations (see key obligation under 2.e)[25]), ASIC requires licensees to take steps to monitor and supervise their representatives to ensure that they comply with financial services laws. These obligations also outline the training and competence requirements for fulfilling the key license obligation 2.g)[26].

The guide RG 104 defines[27] "representatives" being employees, directors, selected third-party service provides and authorised representatives[28] such as agents.

5.1 Monitoring and Supervision

Given the broad definition of representatives, it is advised to establish a monitoring and supervision framework to manage this obligation in a structured manner. The measures for each representative may be different, for example, based on the role or responsibilities of the particular representative or specific areas of risk. However, there are also specific requirements prescribed by ASIC when appointing representatives to act as financial advisors[29]. An initial risk assessment can support the identification of areas and functions with increased risk exposures.

Monitoring and supervision activities can include a broad range of activities based on the organisation`s business model. At the very least, licensees need to demonstrate that they understand the various roles and responsibilities of their representatives and ensure that they perform their duties within the defined job description. In addition, representatives need to understand and adhere to the applicable compliance requirements such as controls and standard operating procedures. In the event of violations or failures (both intentional or by negligence), the representatives must comply with a reporting procedure that also provides for remedial or corrective measures.

Screening requirements for all representatives, especially during the recruiting or onboarding phase, may include background and reference checks as well as integrity and due diligence checks for third parties and intermediaries.

5.2 Training and Competence

The training and competency requirements in the people section of the guide limits its scope to representatives who provide financial services[30]. However, this does not mean that representatives who are not directly involved in the provision of financial services, such as back-office staff, directors and third parties, are exempt from any training requirements. The general obligation to provide training to all employees and third parties is part of the broader compliance obligation, which is ideally embedded in the compliance framework and managed, for example, by the human resources function (see 6.1 human resources obligations). Not every representative is required to take all available training, but there should be a minimum training plan for all representatives to be completed, such as the conduct of conduct training. For certain roles and functions that are exposed to certain risk areas, additional training modules should be introduced to provide the necessary knowledge and skills to perform their duties.

ASIC has introduced specific training and competency requirements for representatives advising retail customers on financial products. These additional requirements are outlined in a separate regulatory guide and require representatives who fall within the scope to undertake additional training to ensure they have a minimum level of knowledge and skills to advise customers[31]. A very common training is the "RG 146 accreditation tiers", which is organised by the Australian New Zealand Institute of Insurance and Finance (ANZIIF)[32].

Given the size and the complexity of the organisation, a tool-based training and learning management solution or system can help to manage the training and competency obligations in a structured and documented manner.

6. Resource Obligations

A rather unique obligation (key obligation f), see section 912A(1)(d)) is described in the final section of the regulatory guide RG 104, which relates to adequate resources (financial, technological and human resources). The guide emphasises that adequate resources must be available to demonstrate that the organisation fully complies with applicable laws and regulations.

Adequateness is understandably not directly defined and there is no one-size-fits-all approach. However, the regulatory guide states that licensees are supposed to consider the nature, scale and complexity of their organisation. To determine the adequateness, the guide refers to the relevant section[33], which lists a number of factors that could be considered.

6.1 Human Resources

While the people obligation focuses on the monitoring, supervision and training of representatives, the human resources (HR) obligations require organisations to implement the following minimum measures:

- HR strategy including workforce and succession planning;
- Staff recruitment, retrenchment and redundancy processes;
- Induction programs for new employees;
- Training framework including a training plan, needs analysis and refresher cycles;
- Performance management systems.

In practice, a dedicated HR department or function can be established, which is responsible for introducing and managing the HR related measures. The HR strategy including the adequateness needs to be reviewed regularly. The guide also provides examples of key indicators or early warning indicators for monitoring the adequacy of the organisations' human resources, such as customer complaints, the ratio of compliance staff to total staff/representatives or too many vacant positions[34].

6.2 Technological Resources

Similar to the human resources considerations, the guide outlines minimum requirements to fulfill the technological resources obligation. In particular, organisations need to have the following elements:

- Information technology (IT) framework;
- IT strategy to manage the current and future operational requirements;
- Trained and qualified IT staff to provide or manage the delivery of IT services;
- Disaster recovery and back-up plan;
- IT security measures to protect sensitive and confidential information;
- IT systems to maintain customer records and data integrity.

In most financial institutions, a dedicated IT department or function is assigned with these obligations, including the creating of an IT framework and strategy with reporting to relevant stakeholders, such as Senior Management or Committees, and regular reviews to ensure ongoing adequacy.

7. Deep Dive - Compliance incident and breach reporting regime

One of the most important new obligations for ASFL holders following the Royal Commission`s findings is the so-called "reportable situations" regime which came into effect on 1 October 2021[35]. This obligation requires licensees to self-report certain breaches of law to ASIC within prescribed timelines and formats. With this obligation, ASIC expects to be in a better position to detect violations of their licensees earlier and take regulatory action where appropriate[36]. At time of commencement, ASIC has thoroughly revised the dedicated regulatory guide for this obligation, namely *'Regulatory Guide 78 - Breach reporting by AFS licensees and credit licensees'*.

7.1 Reportable situations

The reportable situations rules require AFS licensees to lodge a report with ASIC if there are reasonable grounds to believe that a reportable situation has been identified. Although there is no specific threshold, the following situations are considered reportable:

- Breaches, or likely breaches, of core obligations that are significant:
  - Either deemed significant (Corporations Act section 912D(4)); or
  - Require an objective determination of significance;
- Investigations into breaches, or likely breaches, of core obligations that are significant:
  - Investigations that continue for more than 30 days; and
  - The outcome of such an investigation that continued for more than 30 days;
- Additional reportable situations:
  - Conduct that constitutes gross negligence; or
  - Conduct that constitutes serious fraud.

7.2 Core obligations

The core obligations of AFS licensees can be found in sections 912A and 912B of the Corporations Act[37]. Whilst section 912A mainly relates to the key obligations set out in chapter 2 above, the obligations in section 912B require licensees that are also providing financial services to retail customers, to maintain arrangements for compensating those customers for any loss or damage arising from breaches of the relevant obligations by the licensee or its representatives[38]. This requirement is largely met by having adequate professional indemnity insurance which is in line with the regulatory expectations as set out in ASIC's regulatory guide *"RG 126 - Compensation and insurance arrangements for AFS licensees"*[39].

7.3 Significant breaches

Compared to the historical approach[40], the assessment of the significance of a (likely) breach is now linked to specific situations that automatically classify a breach as significant. These deemed significant breaches can include[41]:

- offences under any law (including the Corporations Act) that is punishable by conviction of 12 months or more (three months if the offence involves dishonesty); or
- breaches of a prescribed civil penalty provision under any law (including the Corporations Act); or
- misleading or deceptive conduct pursuant to section 1042H of the Corporations Act; or
- breaches that result, or are likely to result, in material financial loss or detriment to customers.

In addition to the above list, a breach or likely breach of a core obligation needs to be assessed considering certain factors or criteria set out in section 912D(5) of the Corporations Act[42]. These factors include:

- the number and frequency of similar breaches;
- the impact of the breach or likely breach on the license holder's ability to provide financial services;
- the breach indicates that the licensee's compliance processes and procedures are inadequate.

The regulatory guide provides a number of examples and potential scenario descriptions to support license holders in assessing a (potential) reportable situation[43].

7.4 Reportable investigations

ASIC expects that investigations into whether there has been a significant breach or likely significant breach of a core obligation must be reported, if the investigation continues for more than 30 days[44]. However, if the entire investigation is considered complete within 30 days and there are no reasonable grounds to believe that a reportable situation has occurred, licensees will have no further reporting obligations. Obviously, organisations are regularly looking into compliance issues or reviewing certain processes and procedures. The fact, that organisations regularly deal with compliance issues or review certain process and procedures, might create some uncertainty in determining whether an investigative activity qualifies as an investigation under the Corporations Act and therefore requires a formal report to ASIC. The term "investigation" is not legally defined, but the regulatory guide RG 78 contains some examples of scenarios which are not required to be reported, such as[45]:

- initial inquiries into or analyses of customer complaints, whistleblowing reports or regulatory requests which the organization has received;
- regular scheduled reviews, audits or any other planned assurance activities as part of a wider annual plan.

These detective measures and control activities may, based on the content received, trigger a separate investigation into a potential issue or breach of a core obligation which then becomes a reportable investigation.

7.5 Other key reporting obligations

For completeness, AFS licensees also take into account a number of other regulatory reporting requirements that they may be required to comply with. The following reporting obligations may affect most financial institutions:

- Data breach reporting (Privacy Act): when an organisation has reasonable grounds to believe that an eligible data breach has occurred, it must promptly notify the Office of the Australian Information Commissioner (OAIC) and any individual at risk of serious harm[46];
- Reporting of significant dealings related to product design and distribution obligations (Corporations Act): product distributors must notify issuers of certain matters, and issuers must notify ASIC of "significant dealings" that are inconsistent with a product's target market determination[47];
- Reporting of breaches of specific industry codes (e.g. General Insurance Code Governance Committee (CGC)): the CGC is the independent association that monitors and enforces insurers' compliance with the general insurance code of practice (GICOP)[48]. The code specifies that the

organisation that has subscribed to the code, must report a significant breach to the CGC within 10 business days of discovering the breach[49].

- Reporting of suspicious transactions that may be linked to a crime: the Australian Transaction Reports and Analysis Centre (AUSTRAC), which is the regulatory body monitoring obligated organisations` compliance with the AML/CTF Act, requires reporting companies to lodge a suspicious matter report if they have reasonable grounds to believe that a transaction may be related to money laundering, terrorism financing, tax evasion, proceeds of crime or any other serious crimes under Australian law [50].
- Reporting of suspicious market activity: ASIC is also responsible for overseeing and supervising the licensed financial markets in Australia and has established specific market integrity rules for market operators and participants[51]. These rules also require organisations to promptly lodge a suspicious activity report, e.g., if they become aware of insider trading.

7.6 Organisational set-up

Overall responsibility for reporting breaches is typically assigned to the Compliance Function that is also in charge of formally submitting the report to ASIC. For the formal submission of reportable situations, ASIC maintains a web-based regulatory portal[52] accessible to registered users of the organisation. However, when establishing an end-to-end incident management process, a number of other key stakeholders need to be included in the process, such as the Legal and Risk Management function. The Legal function typically assesses or supports the legal assessments of incidents while the Risk Management Team is involved to monitor compliance incidents from an operational risk event perspective.

8. Summary

Following the findings of the Royal Commission, the regulatory landscape for AFSL holders has changed significantly with the introduction of new as well as updated, more stringent compliance obligations under the financial services laws. Affected licensees are required to establish robust risk and compliance management frameworks and systems that are not only in line with the general obligations imposed by ASIC but also been continuously updated to reflect the current risk environment as well as changing regulatory regimes. Additionally, the focus areas communicated by the regulator are to be incorporated into the risk and compliance plans to prepare the organisation for (potentially) future areas of enforcement. A good source of reference is ASIC`s annual analyses and insight reports on specific regulatory obligations[53]. These reports can help organisations to assess their compliance and adherence to their license obligations as part of an industry-wide analysis.

Notes

1 A Royal Commission is an independent public inquiry appointed by the Australian Governor General and is considered the highest form of inquiry on matters of public importance. For more details, please refer to: https://www.royalcommission.gov.au/banking.

2 A full list of authorised financial services can be found on ASIC's website: https://asic.gov.au/for-finance-professionals/afs-licensees/do-you-need-an-afs-licence/what-is-an-afs-licence/.

3 https://www.legislation.gov.au/C2004A00818/latest/text/4

4 https://www.legislation.gov.au/C2004A00819/latest/text.

5 https://asic.gov.au/regulatory-resources/find-a-document/regulatory-guides/.

6 See ASIC RG 104, published on ASIC's homepage: https://download.asic.gov.au/media/zboexfrp/rg104-published-23-june-2022.pdf.

7 The suggested list of minimum requirements consists of the author's recommendations and may not fully reflect all regulatory requirements under the AFS licensing obligations.

8 The "three-lines-of-defence concept" differentiates the responsibilities between the business management (first line), risk and compliance functions (second line) as well as internal audit (third line); see ASIC's *"Report 298 - Adequacy of risk management systems of responsible entities"*, paragraph 46, available of ASIC's homepage: https://download.asic.gov.au/media/1343990/rep298-published-10-September-2012.pdf.

9 refer to *"Regulatory Guide 78 - Breach reporting by AFS licensees and credit licensees"*, published on ASIC's homepage: https://download.asic.gov.au/media/phtcg0as/rg78-published-19-december-2023.pdf.

10 Corporations Act, section 286.

11 See Part 10 of the AML/CTF Act, https://www.legislation.gov.au/C2006A00169/latest/text.

12 Corporations Act, section 941A.

13 Corporations Act, section 946A.

14 Corporations Act, section 766B(1)(3).

15 Published on ASIC's homepage: https://download.asic.gov.au/media/bbjdpjjc/rg175-published-15-june-2021-20231103.pdf.

16 See RG 175.110 for the minimum content; RG 175.137 refers to the requirement on how the FSG can be distributed to the customer.

17 See RG 175.183 which lists the full list of minimum content requirement of the SOA.

[18] See RG 175.171; Corporations Act, section 961B.
[19] Corporations Act, sections 961K and 961Q; see also RG 175.237.
[20] See section E of RG 175.
[21] Published on ASIC's homepage: https://download.asic.gov.au/media/b1gpxbuq/rg168-published-06-july-2022.pdf.
[22] See section C of RG 168.
[23] See ASIC RG 104.59; Corporations Act, section 912A(1)(h).
[24] In no particular order.
[25] Corporations Act, section 912A(1)(ca).
[26] Corporations Act, section 912A(1)(f).
[27] See ASIC RG 104.72.
[28] AFS licensees can appoint 'authorised representatives' to provide specified financial services on its behalf.
[29] See reference to ASIC RG 146 under 5.2. Training and Competence
[30] See ASIC RG 104.81.
[31] For more details refer to "*Regulatory Guide 146 – Licensing: Training of financial product advisers*", published on ASIC's homepage https://download.asic.gov.au/media/1240766/rg146-published-26-september-2012.pdf.
[32] ANZIIF offers a range of ASIC RG 146 training solutions for financial services professionals, for more details: https://anziif.com/professional-development/compliance.
[33] See ASIC RG 104.22.
[34] An overview of other "red flag" indicators can be found in human resources section of the guide, see ASIC RG 104.96.
[35] Prior to October 2021, ASIC expected licensees to self-report certain matters as well. However, the revised breach reporting obligations have significantly lowered the reporting threshold.
[36] See ASIC RG 78.3.
[37] See Corporations Act, section 912D(3).
[38] See Corporations Act, section 912B.
[39] https://download.asic.gov.au/media/niddj53n/rg126-published-06-july-2022.pdf.
[40] The reportable situations regime before October 2021 allowed license holders to subjectively assess if the breach is significant.
[41] See ASIC RG 78.34.
[42] See ASIC RG 78.45.
[43] See ASIC RG 78, pages 17-21 (Table 2 and 3).
[44] See Corporations Act, section 912D(1)(c).
[45] See ASIC RG 78.55.
[46] The OAIC defines an eligible data breach as follows: There is a disclosure or unauthorized access of personal information which is likely to result in serious harm to any of the individuals to whom the information relates and the organisation has been unable to prevent the likely risk of serious harm with remedial action; see https://www.oaic.gov.au/privacy/notifiable-data-breaches/report-a-data-breach.
[47] Corporations Act, section 995G. The significant dealing notification requirement does not replace reportable situations obligations under RG78, but requires a notification to

ASIC within 10 business days. ASIC has issued a separate regulatory guide for design and distribution obligations, RG274 (https://download.asic.gov.au/media/dlpccdof/rg274-published-11-december-2020-20220628.pdf).

48 https://insurancecode.org.au/.

49 See guidance note no. 2 which covers the significant breach obligations under the GICOP: https://insurancecode.org.au/resources/guidance-note-no-2-significant-breach-obligation/.

50 See Section 41 of the AML/CTF Act.

51 For more information, please refer to ASIC's regulatory guide 265, https://download.asic.gov.au/media/vylbcvwt/rg265-published-2-august-2022.pdf.

52 https://asic.gov.au/online-services.

53 For example, in October 2024 ASIC published a report on reportable situations regime for the time period July 2023 to June 2024. This report includes insights into the trends observed in reports lodged by licensees under the RG 78 regime, see https://download.asic.gov.au/media/vw0pjzow/rep-800-published-31-october-2024.pdf.

Chapter 3

Shaping Corporate Culture based on Integrity and Business Ethics

Cross Sectoral Challenges for Integrity and Compliance, typical cultural clashes among silos cultured areas in multinational corporations

Maria Eugenia Gil, Juan Gregorio Nazar de Boulin

1. Introduction

In the globalized and increasingly interconnected environment in which multinational corporations operate, integrity and compliance are no longer mere regulatory issues but have become fundamental pillars of business strategy. However, this new context poses complex cross-cutting challenges that must be addressed with rigor and long-term vision.

This article explores some of the main challenges that multinational corporations face when trying to maintain integrity and compliance in such a diverse and dynamic landscape. From combating corruption, to adapting to disparate environmental standards and labor practices, to protecting data privacy and overcoming internal bureaucracies, each challenge requires a specific strategic approach.

In addition, the interaction between different cultures, potential conflicts of interest in Ethics Committees, and the tension between business urges and compliance risks highlight the need for ethics management that is both global and local.

This article not only addresses these issues in detail, but also discusses tools and strategies that can help organizations navigate these challenges, ensuring that integrity becomes a culture and remains at the core of their operations anywhere in the world.

2. Cross-sectoral challenges for integrity and compliance

2.1. Bribery and corruption:

In international business, bribery and corruption present one of the greatest challenges for multinational corporations, both (i) in their relations with the local public sector where they operate, (ii) internally in their subsidiaries, (iii) and in their business relations with competitors. While in many cultures, practices related to "accepting" gifts to accept, facilitate, accelerate or directly enable processes may be considered part of the norm, international laws such as the U.S. FCPA and the UK Bribery Act do not make concessions for such customs, do not naturalize them, do not legitimize them. Otherwise, they create a virtuous international standard towards which the most advanced state and parastatal standards and groups, such as the OECD, converge. In the case of Argentina, Law 27401 on Criminal Liability of Legal Entities is forceful in establishing the liability of legal entities for acts of bribery and corruption, among other of the five crimes it typifies, in their relations with the public sector, following by far the example of the FCPA, which is much earlier.

However, nations and/or companies that deliberately choose to operate outside this convergent and virtuous international standard, in cultures of high tolerance to corruption, immediately become an unfair competitor to those that do comply. And a competitor with an irresistible comparative advantage for officials of corrupt governments and cultures.

This creates a conflict when a company's global policies, designed to comply with these strict laws, in the framework of cultures whose enforcement is effective, must be applied in contexts where local practices contrary to such enforcement may be culturally deeply rooted, so much so as to be impossible to apply, and leave the "right" ones at a clear disadvantage against the "wrong" ones. The remarkable thing is that this can happen not only within the same culture: it can happen within the same organization, even within two areas of the same subsidiary, in the same territory.

Multinationals must design compliance programs that are not only robust and compliant with the international regulations of their headquarters, but that are also culturally sensitive to the geographies and cultures where they intend to operate and/or be applied.

The great challenge for corporations is precisely not to download the policy package to each region, as a "canned program", but to adapt it to the reality and culture of each region in which they develop their business and/or activities, without such adaptation implying an excessive flexibility of fundamental ethical framework criteria, such that they are distorted or taken below an acceptable standard of compliance.

At the last OECD - GACIF Forum in Paris, the Compliance Officer of a multinational company explained specifically how policies must be adapted to the local culture, and that it is precisely not the same to apply the same policy to the reality of South America as it is to the reality of Denmark. This goes hand in hand with considering the social aspects of each company linked to the reality of each country.

This implies educating and training local employees on the importance of following international standards, while recognizing and respecting cultural sensitivities, emphasizing the right balance between the two, the common ground that always exists: we do not cease to share a nature, the human one, which is above all cultures.

But integrity implies behaviors, and compliance is made up of people who have different behaviors. What would be desirable is that those behaviors are always ethical; then education and training must provide the necessary tools to make them so.

And it is more than that, it is to educate by transmitting the culture of integrity, of doing things right because it is the only acceptable way to do them. Expanding the culture of integrity means transmitting to the value chain how the organization wants its business to develop and what principles and values it wants them to follow in order to be part of its work ecosystem. Cultural transformation does not happen overnight; it requires effort, dedication, commitment and resources. And a value chain that is integrated and acts ethically becomes more sustainable and healthy.

How is it transmitted? With training, communication, education, so that it is long term; including all actors and all areas of the company. Fundamentally, it is a matter of bringing the values down to reality and to day-to-day operations. And that these values are then reproduced in decision making and in life outside the company.

This generates a better reputation and therefore more trust, not only from suppliers, but also from customers, employees and the society in which the organization develops its business. This will generate greater business opportunities and market expansion and attract more investors.

And extending this culture of integrity to the society in which the corporation develops its activities is the first step to build a sustainable and reliable business. And it should be the first link of any ESG policy: the impact of bringing a culture of ethics and rational compliance to a given geography, society, culture, is invaluable for its future development, insertion in the world, etc.

However, this task is not easy. Lack of understanding or respect for local cultural practices can lead to resentment or even passive resistance, which in turn can hinder the effective implementation of compliance policies.

A proactive approach could involve creating integrity policies that incorporate aspects of local cultures, as long as these do not conflict with international standards. Including local leaders in the development and communication of these policies can facilitate greater acceptance and adaptation to global standards, without compromising corporate integrity.

2.2 Labor practices: Balancing cultural differences while upholding ethical-global labor practices

Labor practices, from the number of working hours to employee benefits and rights, can vary drastically between different regions. What is considered exploitative in one country may be perceived as an acceptable norm in another. However, multinational companies must ensure that, despite these differences, global standards of work ethics, which are aligned with international agreements and treaties on human and labor rights, are maintained.

We return here to the previous point of different cultures and different social realities. The same organization may have subsidiaries in different countries around the world, which respond to different international standards and regulations, making the application of a uniform labor policy to the entire structure a major challenge in practice.

To address this challenge, companies should adopt a two-pronged approach. First, they must ensure that their global labor policies respect and adhere to international labor rights laws and regulations. Second, they must be flexible, in order to comply with local regulations and also be willing to adapt certain practices to accommodate local customs and expectations, as long as these do not contradict fundamental labor rights principles.

For example, if a corporation operates in a country where working hours are traditionally longer than the global standard, the company could look for ways to compensate local employees fairly, such as through additional benefits or paid time off, while working with local authorities to advocate for reforms that align more closely with international standards.

2.3 Environmental standards: varying global versus local environmental conservation standards

Expectations around environmental conservation can vary considerably globally. While in some regions, environmental regulations may be stringent and strongly enforced, in others, laws may be more lax or not properly enforced.

Examples of this can be found today in the European CSRD: Sustainability Reporting Directive - EU or the recent CSDDDD: Corporate Sustainability Due diligence - EU, the German Due Diligence Act or the US SEC (Security Exchange Commission) regulations, such as Regulation SK, among others.

This creates a dilemma for multinational corporations that wish to operate responsibly, but must also compete with local companies that may not be subject to the same restrictions.

A multinational company committed to environmental sustainability must overcome these disparities by implementing its own internal standards that meet or exceed local regulations, regardless of their laxity. This not only protects the company from legal and reputational risks, but also reinforces its commitment to global sustainability.

We believe it is extremely important to consider the concept of Sustainable Integrity, promoted by the Global Compact in Argentina[1], a proposal for responsible business integrity work, structured on the basis of the relationship between the fight against corruption, sustainability and in accordance with SDG 16 "Peace, Justice and Sound Institutions". This work mentions that SDG 16 is crossed by four thematic axes, which are: Anti-Corruption,

Environment, Human Rights and Labor Standards. These four axes cannot be worked on in isolation, but rather in a joint and integrated manner. Therefore, the environment is part of any integrity program, and must contain a clear policy that determines the organization's commitment to care for and respect and preservation of the environment. As an essential part of the ecosystem in which organizations carry out their activities, companies should have a preventive approach, promote greater environmental responsibility and develop technologies that favor environmental protection.

In addition, corporations can play an active role in promoting better environmental practices in the countries in which they operate, working in partnership with local governments, non-governmental organizations and communities to raise local standards. This not only improves local environmental sustainability, but also helps to level the competitive playing field.

One challenge we face at this point, which we must consider, is the case of SMEs, small and medium-sized enterprises. Almost 80% of the global economy is represented by the work and activities of small and medium-sized enterprises, which play a fundamental role in societies, providing employment and mobilizing the local and often international circular economy. In some (many) cases, these organizations do not have the capacity to manage all the risks, and often do not have the capacity to have specific and independent areas; instead, the same person performs several functions; and much less do they have the possibility of having a structured compliance program, either due to lack of resources or lack of knowledge on the subject.

What happens with these companies, how are they trained to comply with local and international environmental regulations, within their capabilities and volume? And what role does the local government play in incentivizing and supporting small businesses so that they can comply at the same levels as a multinational corporation.

2.4 Data privacy: Multinational corporations must navigate strict versus relaxed culturally grounded regulatory differences towards privacy laws

Data privacy laws vary dramatically around the world. In regions such as the European Union, regulations such as GDPR impose strict rules on how companies can collect, store and handle personal data. However, in other countries, laws can be much less stringent, presenting a challenge for multinationals that must balance compliance with local laws and international standards.

To manage these regulatory differences, multinationals must adopt a compliance approach that, by default, adheres to the highest possible standards. This means that even in regions with less stringent regulations, the company still applies the same robust data privacy policies that it would use in countries with stricter laws.

Implementing a global standard for data privacy not only protects the company from potential legal penalties, but also strengthens customers' trust in the brand, regardless of where they operate. Companies should also invest in ongoing training for their employees in all regions to ensure clear understanding and strict compliance with data privacy policies.

2.5 Internal cross-border bureaucracy:

2.5.1 Risk analysis for client registrations: Criteria vary greatly from country to regions

Client registration and risk analysis vary considerably from one region to another, which can lead to conflicts within a multinational corporation. Lack of unified criteria and internal bureaucracy can result in accusations of bad faith or favoritism, especially when it comes to operating in regions with more flexible regulatory standards

To avoid these conflicts, multinationals should establish clear and uniform criteria for risk analysis and client registration that are applicable in all regions. This includes the creation of a global governance structure that oversees these processes, ensuring that integrity is maintained in all operations.

In addition, internal communication must be transparent and effective to prevent misunderstandings and suspicions. The creation of committees or task forces with members from different regions can help ensure that all cultural and regulatory perspectives are considered and respected in decision-making processes.

The great challenge that a multinational company faces today is to reconcile its own bureaucratic issues when performing due diligence with the operational part of business development. Many times, corporations "*fall in love*" with their own processes, which leads to delays in the organization's time in providing the service or delivering the goods, in compliance with processes that are often not one hundred percent efficient.

2.5.2 Internal allegations of bad faith and good, when different religions and cultures collide

Cultural differences can generate tensions and conflicts within the ethics committees of a multinational corporation, especially when these differences influence the interpretation of ethical principles. In addition, the involvement of certain areas, such as Human Resources, in these committees can lead to conflicts of interest.

To manage these challenges, companies should structure their ethics committees to reflect the cultural diversity of the organization, ensuring that no one culture or perspective dominates discussions and decisions. This may involve the inclusion of external advisors or the regular rotation of committee members to avoid the formation of factions.

With regard to conflicts of interest, it is crucial that companies clearly define the roles and responsibilities of each area within the ethics committee, ensuring that any potential conflicts are identified and addressed in a transparent and effective manner.

Within this topic, we cannot fail to mention the participation of HR as a member of the Ethics Committee's eventual conflicts of interest.

The participation of the Human Resources (HR) area in ethics committees may result in conflicts of interest, especially when HR is responsible for both the implementation of policies and the supervision of their compliance. These conflicts can arise when committee decisions directly impact HR policies or personnel management, compromising the committee's impartiality and effectiveness.

To address this challenge, corporations should establish safeguards to mitigate potential conflicts of interest. One effective measure can be the appointment of independent or external members to ethics committees, who can provide an unbiased perspective and ensure that decisions are made objectively.

Another strategy is to clearly define the roles of HR within the ethics committee, limiting their influence on decisions that could directly affect their functions. In addition, it is important that the ethics committee has procedures in place to identify and manage potential conflicts of interest, ensuring that decisions are made in a fair and transparent manner.

And once again, we return to the issue of training, coaching and education of people who occupy positions of relevance and at the same time are in charge of defining a sensitive, confidential and strategic issue, based on strong ethical knowledge and convictions. It is essential that both the members of the Ethics Committees and the persons responsible for private investigation processes are trained and educated to be able to conduct an internal investigation following the rules of due criminal process, respecting the constitutional guarantees of the persons involved, knowing how to conduct an investigation process without bias, without finding guilty beforehand, without predetermined opinions. The Code of Ethics and the policies on investigations of any company play a fundamental role in this regard, which serve as a guide and a guideline for the investigation processes, including as a control measure to avoid possible cultural and personal biases that may hinder the processes.

2.5.3 Procurement, sales and marketing areas' urgencies against compliance risk & regulatory global 3rd parties enrollment

The purchasing, sales and marketing areas in a multinational corporation often operate under intense pressure to meet business objectives, which can sometimes conflict with compliance requirements and global regulations in the registration and handling of third parties. The urgency to close contracts, the drive to meet commercial and incentive goals such as bonuses, and to secure supplies or launch campaigns can lead to omitting or minimizing due diligence processes and controls necessary to ensure that partners and suppliers comply with regulations and ethical standards.

In fact, according to ACFE (Association of Fraud Examiners) Report to the Nations 2024[2], the five most sensitive areas of a company are: Accounting, Operations, Sales, Senior Management and Customer Service. These five departments, together with Finance and Purchasing, account for the internal fraud that occurs in a company. It has also been proven that these are the departments where employees are most often associated in a pernicious way to commit fraud against organizations.

Dealing with the consequences of these situations can and usually does have a much higher cost than putting in place risk prevention mechanisms.

To mitigate these risks, it is crucial that compliance areas work closely with purchasing, sales and marketing, integrating risk assessment and due diligence into the selection and management of third parties. This includes the implementation of clear policies that require thorough verification of suppliers and partners before formalizing agreements, ensuring that they comply with international regulations and the company's ethical standards.

It also includes the implementation of control measures, such as, for example, the management of a whistleblower hotline that allows for the anonymous, non-retaliatory, secure, impartial and independent reporting of acts contrary to the policies or the Code of Ethics.

In addition, companies should establish mechanisms that balance the need for business agility with rigorous compliance. This could include ongoing training of procurement, sales and marketing personnel on compliance issues, the creation of cross-functional teams for third-party risk assessment, and the use of technology tools that facilitate the global third-party enrollment and verification process.

For example, the use of technology in value chain management today is a necessary tool that every compliance program should have.

The value chain is managed not only to comply with international and local regulations, but also to prevent associated risks.

Managing the value chain within an integrity program not only protects companies from risk, but also boosts their ability to build a more sustainable and ethical future. The culture of integrity is not only a matter of legal compliance, but of establishing a culture that permeates every area of the organization.

Finally, among the benefits of managing the value chain, we can mention: firstly, the transmission of the culture of integrity; it is essential to foster a corporate culture where compliance is not seen as an obstacle, but as an essential component of long-term success. Secondly, operational efficiency, as a way of early identification of problems, allowing agile responses to avoid interruptions in production and operational processes. If only a company works with individuals or companies it knows, and knows how they will behave, the business will be well taken care of. Thirdly, it enhances reputation, since complying with international standards strengthens the company's image with customers, investors and the public. Transparent and ethical companies are perceived as trustworthy, attracting better business opportunities.

This facilitates access to international markets and strengthens business relationships: Companies that manage their value chain under these principles are better perceived by investors, customers and regulators, generating trust and attracting growth opportunities. Fourthly, we mention risk reduction, since due diligence and preventive processes not only mitigate risks, but also improve operational efficiency by optimizing relationships with suppliers and strengthening transparency. It minimizes legal sanctions, fines and protects the brand from reputational damage, avoiding the loss of trust by consumers and investors. Finally, and as a fifth benefit, we consider the loyalty of customers and collaborators, since the commitment to ethics and sustainability generates loyalty among customers and employees. This has a positive impact on both the retention of talent and key customers. The commitment to integrity has a direct impact on the profitability and reputation of the company, reinforcing its position in a global market that increasingly values ethics and sustainability. Building trust and good relations with society is a key point. Integrity is built by people, so it is a collaborative effort. And those people have behaviors, so that they are ethical and have integrity, we must constantly train them.

2.5.4 Legal and compliance areas separated, as mandated by local Stock Exchange market rules

In some jurisdictions, the rules imposed by local stock exchanges require that Legal and Compliance areas be kept separate. Some legislation even considers that Audit and Compliance areas must also work separately, as a way of maintaining impartiality, independence and direct access to the Board, necessary for any exercise of compliance. As is the case, for example, with the Corporate Governance Code of the CNV (National Securities Commission) of Argentina. This mandate can create challenges in the coordination and alignment of compliance policies, especially in multinational corporations where the integration between Legal and Compliance is essential to manage risks and ensure compliance with regulations. The mandatory separation of these two areas can lead to communication problems and a lack of coherence in the implementation of compliance policies. Companies must develop strategies to ensure that, despite the structural separation, there is effective collaboration between Legal and Compliance. This may include creating joint committees, clearly defining roles and responsibilities, and establishing robust communication channels.

It is essential that both areas have regular and regular communication regarding contracts and/or contractual clauses, compliance with local and international regulations and standards. In addition, it is essential that both areas work with a shared vision of risks and legal obligations, using compliance management systems that allow joint monitoring and supervision of legal and regulatory matters. This approach helps to minimize the risk of duplication of efforts or gaps in compliance.

2.5.5 Silo cultures and global/local matrices

The existence of silo cultures within different areas of a multinational corporation can hinder the effective implementation of integrity and compliance programs. These internal barriers can result in a lack of coordination and communication between local units and headquarters, making it difficult to align global objectives with local needs. To overcome these challenges, companies must foster a culture of collaboration and open communication. This can be achieved by creating multidisciplinary teams that include representatives from different regions and areas of the company, with the aim of aligning global strategies with local practices.

In addition, technology can play a crucial role in integrating global and local operations. Internal communication platforms, such as corporate intranets and online collaboration tools, can help break down silo barriers and facilitate the sharing of information and best practices across the organization.

At this point, it is necessary to emphasize the need to transmit the culture of integrity as a guiding principle in the development of the organization's activities, whether public or private. The culture of integrity must be closely linked to the business. And it must be established as the internal and external regulatory framework of the organization, so that activities are developed only within that framework and contrary behavior is not allowed. The role of senior management in this transmission is fundamental. Leadership plays a fundamental role. The tone at the top, so often mentioned in compliance, is a key piece. The values of the organization will determine its daily operation and decision-making. That is why leaders must act with integrity and ethics, as those responsible for shaping behavior within that regulatory framework of integrity. And they must act ethically, in a transparent and upright manner, both inside and outside the company, convinced that it is the only way to do it, functioning as an example for the entire organization and the society in which they operate. But what happens in public institutions or organizations, where the replacement of authorities or leaders is frequent? Policies must be built for the long term. They must be designed with such magnitude that they ensure that their implementation lasts over time, regardless of the length of the position of the person who implemented and developed them. And this long-term vision requires collaborative work, with constant monitoring of the actions implemented, with a leader who pushes but with a multi-stakeholder team that helps to provide long-term sustainability. Think of the integrity program not as regulatory compliance or out of fear of sanctions, but as part of a culture of integrity.

3. Summary

Navigating cross-sectorial challenges for integrity and compliance in multinational corporations implies setting clear limits, hence requiring a prior, deep understanding of cultural norms and expectations in each country of operation, confronted with global/Headquarters cultural criteria. Such understanding should lead the internal global rules to local alignments, and not vice versa, for the sake of efficiency rather than cultural respect, while upholding ethical standards and compliance with international laws, when global ethical criteria is not negotiable (e.g. as in those from Human Rights UN Conventions).

In conclusion, multinational corporations face an increasingly complex and challenging environment in their quest to maintain integrity and compliance in a globalized world. Cultural diversity, regulatory differences, and operational pressures require companies to adopt a comprehensive and adaptable approach that combines ethical responsibility with operational effectiveness. Challenges related to bribery and corruption, labor practices, environmental standards, and data privacy are just some of the areas where meticulous and proactive management is required. Likewise, cross-border internal bureaucracy, risk analyses in customer registration, and clashes between different cultures underscore the need for inclusive policies and transparent decision-making processes. Conflicts of interest within ethics committees and the tension between business urgency and compliance risks reinforce the importance of a strategic vision that not only protects organizations, but also promotes sustainable and ethical practices across their value chain. By addressing these challenges with determination and using the right technological tools, companies can not only meet regulatory demands but also strengthen their reputation and create a positive impact globally. Ultimately, the key to navigating this complex landscape lies in integrity management that is as global as it is local, ensuring that ethical principles guide every decision, regardless of context or region, as an extension of a sustainable integrity culture.

Notes

1 https://pactoglobal.org.ar/wp-content/uploads/2023/08/eBook-Integridad-Sostenible-2023_V6.pdf

2 https://www.acfe.com/-/media/files/acfe/pdfs/rttn/2024/2024-report-to-the-nations.pdf

Practical implementation of business ethics in Compliance Management Systems

Piotr Chmiel

1. Introduction

Business ethics is the application of moral reasoning to matters that arise in corporate life[1]. It takes into account the actions of individuals as well as actions taken by companies. Another name that is used to describe it is *business integrity* (or, much older, *merchant's integrity*). Expectation of ethical conduct by businesses is, *par excellence*, applied to all big, multinational companies operating in personal customer space. Customers (and other stakeholders) are very vocal about what they understand (or rather *believe*) as ethical business and related behavior, though both definitions shift based on circumstances. Such shifts in understanding what is business ethics may result in public outrage and protests, having a short-lived impact on a company's reputation[2]. Usually, though, companies that were perceived as ethical will remain so, and others will have a hard time in building such a reputation. Moreover, quite often topic of *business ethics* is limited to perception of the company from the outside. So-called "brand safety" is treated very seriously and companies ask their media agencies to even restrict where their brand will be placed (for instance, avoiding connections to conspiracy theories). Obviously, that is not enough and may even bring forward accusations of manipulation by the company.

The situation is not much better when asking Compliance professionals about what is business ethics, as one often gets some variation of "we should be good and respect the interests of stakeholders" answer. In general, it sounds right but doesn't answer how a company is expected to implement it within its Compliance Management System (CMS). There are some other options[3] for introducing ethical requirements to processes within a company, but by far the most common is linking business ethics with Compliance activities. It can be said that there are two basic tasks that need to be done — defining ethical rules in internal documents and implementing these in daily processes (which means making these rules practical and applicable).

Ethical rules may not be negotiable, but how a company decides to implement these is. This dependency is linked to a person given this task, whom usually is a Compliance Officer. And her or his character will have strong impact on how company will approach business ethics and how it will in future enforce its rules.

2. What needs to be added to CMS

First, let's discuss changes that need to be done to the existing Compliance Management System, so a company could show that ethical rules are in place and operating effectively. I'll use a simplified model of CMS, based on three areas:

1. Awareness, including training, communication, and policy management
2. Advisory, covering point of contact for employees' questions and support in operational processes
3. Enforcement, including contact point for whistleblowers and managing internal investigations

In all of the above described elements of CMS ethical rules can and should be included, improving the culture of compliance within the company and making sure that subjective elements, which strongly depend on the Compliance Officer's character aspects, are limited and well controlled. One of the most important ideas to keep in mind would be *integrity*, since it can (and should) be applied both to the rules at the company and to personal traits of the CO. Implementing consistent rules that would be enforceable with minimal subjectivity is the key aim here.

2.1 Awareness

Initial and crucial building block of an effective Compliance Management System. Here companies set the rules, by defining them in internal policies and procedures, telling their employees what is allowed (or more often, what is forbidden, as in most cases a model of "all is allowed unless it is forbidden" is adopted). This usually includes a some sort of *code of ethics* or *code of conduct* document, describing ethical elements that the company sees as significant and applicable to their business area. And here is the first point where we should look at the practical element of adding business ethics. If we follow general expectations of what *should* be included in such a document, we'll end up with a rather bland and generic result where all proper topics are included (human rights, caring for stakeholders, environment and making sure that there is no discrimination or bias, to just name some)[4] but where there are no links to actual daily activities and challenges. So the first order of the day would be to identify areas where ethical issues may arise, based on business activities and current experiences. Then these areas should be translated into examples that would be understandable to all employees and included in the document, of course, along with standard, market accepted (and expected) elements. This way, the key document will be at the same time compliant with the best practices, will include ethical rules and will present practical adoption of these rules. The same process should be applied to all policies supporting the *code of ethics*, extending the examples to more detailed topics and even more specific situations. The last level of internal documents that should see such treatment, though without examples, is the group of operational procedures, which tell employees how particular activities need to be performed. Still, steps described there must be in line with higher level documents, so there is no contradiction between expectations and actual behavior. It's worth remembering that it is not possible to cover all situations, and that's why ethical rules adopted by the company need to allow for subjective assessment and have to provide guidance on how to act in case of situation not covered in internal documents.

After the formal adoption, *code of ethics* and policies[5] have to be communicated to all employees and also here ethical element should be applied — the most important is a show of commitment from the top management. Obviously, this will be based on words, as actions will come later, but if possible, some reference to past decisions made with ethics in mind should be included in the communication. And similar to translation of ethical rules from the *code* to policies, communication by managers to their direct units should address their particular issues or experiences — again, to ground the expectations in business reality and translate them into everyday behavior. Such communication needs to be regularly repeated, enhancing proper behavior and maintaining a solid level of awareness. To be effective in repeating of the communication, the Compliance Officer should identify employees who are agents of change within the company. They don't usually come from management (in fact almost never do) but typically are senior people, long employed by the company, with significant experience and knowledge and are deeply trusted by the employees. The aim is to convince these people (one could call them *Compliance influencers*) that the addition of ethics to daily operations of the company is serious and will be beneficial to all. If their support can be won, other employees will follow and compliance culture at the company will be healthy. Otherwise, no effort from the management will convince employees to behave in accordance with ethical rules.

Another part of maintaining awareness is continuous learning — both in terms of updating guiding documents when the company identifies topics that need to be redefined or clarified and in terms of ensuring that this knowledge is shared with new employees (and even business partners). Learning needs to be applied to all levels of hierarchy, especially including management. Experience shows that the use of so-called *ethical dilemmas* as examples and basic topics in learning materials is extremely effective, since it involves actual decision-making and puts participants in situations that may arise in daily business situations.

2.2 Advisory

Having set proper rules and communicated them, another part of the Compliance Management System needs to be updated with ethical elements. Effective CMS requires companies to set up a point of contact, where employees can ask questions regarding unclear regulations or uncertain business situations. Such contact points can be managed internally or can be outsourced and quite often are called "ethical contact lines", suggesting that ethical rules are already implemented there and are a part of managed topics. Unfortunately, that is rather frequently not the case and may be seen by employees as misleading, undermining efforts to build a compliance culture based on ethics.

So it is very important for the company to make sure that ethical questions, which usually go beyond the simple interpretation of written rules (even if these rules are already created with ethical issues in mind), are answered and managed. This can be achieved by assigning well trained Compliance staff to these positions and supplying them with necessary access to information, such as strategic plans of the company (so questions regarding plans and actions having impact on stakeholders can be correctly addressed, without making too much of them public), reactions to potentially publicly communicated issues (for instance Public Relations communiqués on topics discussed in public or company's position on difficult topics, such as politics) or upcoming critical public communication by the company on actual or upcoming topics of high importance. In other words, Compliance staff responsible for giving answers to employees needs to be well-informed about significant issues arising at the company and how these may be interpreted from an ethical point of view. Other employees in the company should be made aware that Compliance may ask for data or explanations needed to provide answers. It should be part of trainings, as well as informing all employees that some of their inquiries may be responded with a "trust us" type of answer if giving more details would be at that time harmful to the company or its business. However, if possible, a more detailed answer should be sent when confidentiality is no longer required. In general, trust and openness have to be part of the communication rules when answering employees' ethical questions. It is also important because such an approach is sometimes rejected based on the need to keep information secret, even when measured, followed later, communication would have build positive relations with the employees. Obviously, it is essential to make sure that all of this information is kept internal, not used for other purposes than answering the question (so limiting details given) and that all employees understand their duty to protect the company. Compliance staff should have dedicated confidentiality clauses in their contracts as well.

The other part of the *advisory* function of the CMS is direct support in business processes. By that, it is understood that Compliance units can be involved in operational processes in the company, as long as the overall responsibility for the process remains with its business owner and not Compliance. Examples include business partner and supplier evaluation, control activities within the sponsorship process or involvement in design of new products or services. And again, in all of such activities, Compliance should bring ethical elements, embedding them within processes. It should be explained, as to avoid discussions about "making simple things too complicated" but shouldn't be negotiable (perhaps leaving only space for process improvement).

For instance, when performing business partner check, Compliance would include all standard elements (registration data, finance data, sanctions check) and add ethical analysis based on market type they operate in, opinions on the web, their public communication. One of the important things to remember here is that results of ethics evaluation should be treated with similar weight as business ones — showing that the company is seriously applying ethics to everyday business — otherwise that would be perceived as window dressing activity only.

2.3 Enforcement

Last but not least, all of the rules, including ethical ones, implemented in codes and policies, communicated to employees and used in daily processes must be enforced in the company. The first level is making sure (by trainings and direct feedback from Compliance) that the management is "walking the talk", actually behaving as expected and not only telling employees how they should behave. In other words, managers must lead by example. This requirement should also be included in the employee evaluation process, with different expectations set for managers and for employees without managerial responsibilities. Both groups need to be assessed on whether they behave in accordance with ethical rules, with managers being given additional responsibility of leading with ethics in mind. That would be obviously responsibility of the HR area with support from Compliance.

However, there will be situations where someone will not behave in a desired way. In order to detect such cases, Compliance needs to implement and operate a contact point for whistleblowers. Regardless of technology used, all solutions must be managed with ethics in mind — personal information of whistleblowers should be protected, their messages have to be treated seriously even if the language used is simple or incoherent, every signal should be verified and if deemed probable, investigated. If communication with the whistleblower is possible, it should be kind and open as it builds trust and may help in obtaining additional information. That's also an ethical requirement to treat whistleblowers with respect, given the risks they take.

This leads to another process within CMS — performing internal investigations. Again, regardless whether it is done with in-house resources or is outsourced to a special company or legal firm, the same ethical requirements apply. All investigations should start as efforts to identify what and why happened, not focusing on finding who could be responsible for a situation. From the company point of view, it is more important to identify the situation and initiate protective measures than to look for a person who did it. Of course, identifying perpetrators and disciplining them is essential but should never be a main aim of the investigation. During the casework all individuals involved should be approached initially as witnesses and only in final steps any potential disciplinary action should be evaluated and potentially recommended. This is also an ethical element in this process — ensuring equal treatment and limiting bias during the investigation. Another one is to resist pressure that may be coming from people suspected of misbehavior to identify the whistleblower, regardless whether contact was anonymous or not. While this is a duty of Compliance Officer, this is also an ethical requirement, critical in building and maintaining trust among employees that they can safely signal potential issues in the company.

When the investigation is finished, there is time to decide on any necessary measures or disciplinary consequences. It needs to be ensured that decisions made are in the best interest of the company but also take into account the actual situation, not management's perception of it. There are situations when identified and confirmed issue is not as serious as reaction to it (the most typical scenario is reaction to pornography, which may be offensive to some but in general is deemed legal) and Compliance Officer must be able to control and evaluate proposed measures, so these reflect actual case and confirmed facts. From the ethical standpoint it is to again ensure fair and equal treatment, regardless of personal opinion. Internal investigations shouldn't be treated as a sort of "hit list" activity too. Compliance unit (or other units in the company or outside) are not *mercenaries* waiting to be hired when someone doesn't like someone else in the company and wants that person removed (in other words, Compliance mustn't accept requests based on "here is the person, find a paragraph"). The need to remain an independent function also means that it must apply the highest ethical standards to its operations.

3. Compliance Officer's character

It can be seen from the presented examples that introducing ethics to the Compliance Management System is a challenging task, one that needs focus and strong support from the management. And there also lies one of the crucial risks of transposing business ethics to CMS — some of the actions will be based on the character traits of the Compliance Officer responsible for it. So any good and bad parts of her or his personality could be multiplied by the size of the company and have oversized effect on business processes (for instance CO who is too strict on imposing rules regarding business partners may limit company's ability to enter innovative markets or cooperation).

Compliance Officers (COs), who are responsible for effective CMS' need to have specific character traits. First of such would be *integrity*, meaning being honest, transparent and adhering to ethical principles. High integrity in making difficult decisions sets a strong example for the employees and assures fair and consistent treatment. Next, *empathy*, which means showing understanding of other points of view, considering others' perspectives and their feelings. Empathetic CO is able to define rules that take into account the needs of employees, set fair expectations and allow for trustful cooperation even when issues arise. Lastly, a Compliance Officer needs *courage* to act ethically even when faced with pressure or adversity from others. Being courageous means being able to address unethical behavior regardless of where it is detected in the company and uphold the company's ethical standards. Of course, being a leader able to inspire and motivate others with a clear vision regarding the company's ethical goals is also expected from the CO, but these *can* be learned. However, courage, empathy, and integrity are elements of one's character and either person has them or not. There are no trainings that would teach these traits to a Compliance Officer, so a dedicated recruitment process is necessary, one that checks for these qualities.

As mentioned in the **Advisory** section above, there will be situations when existing rules will not be enough. That's why internal regulations should allow for some degree of subjectivity in treating such situations, with Compliance as an arbiter (if necessary). Here is the first potential pitfall related to the Compliance Officer's character, because of the subjective element. The person in this position needs to be able to understand circumstances present around decision time and only then make an assessment whether it was really in line with rules and ethics.

A similar situation arises during evaluation of results of internal investigation. It is important to keep a balanced and objective view, so the integrity and empathy of the CO come into play. Consistency is also critical when deciding what kind of disciplinary action should be taken and again character of the Compliance Officer needs to be considered, as a person who is easily influenced by other's opinions or follows their temporary mood could take decisions that are not in line with those made previously in cases with similar circumstances.

4. Summary

It can be seen that making ethics part of the compliance culture and of the Compliance Management System requires trust from the employees towards Compliance unit and top management but also a similar level of trust the other way around. Open, though controlled, communication is the basis for building trust. Integrating ethical decision-making into CMS enhances a company's ability to navigate complex ethical dilemmas and maintain high standards of conduct. By embedding ethical requirements into policy development, training, decision-making processes, monitoring, and leadership practices, companies can foster a stron compliance culture of integrity and ethical behavior.

Just as important is having a Compliance Officer who shows key character traits of integrity, empathy, and courage as their decisions and actions have significant impact on how CMS is perceived within the company and often decide whether employees want to respect the rules or reject them.

We should also be working towards creating a more standardized definition of business ethics, that can be adopted by a wide range of businesses. Replacing ethical requirements with *ESG*[6] and *DEI*[7] frameworks is not enough because ethical rules must apply to all stakeholders in all circumstances. So there needs to be a continuous work toward creating, defining and promoting business integrity that is easy to understand both by businesses and customers and to translate into Compliance Management Systems.

The good news is that an ethics-based CMS is not much different than a standard Compliance Management System. It *just* needs definition of rules defining business ethics (fitting the company but not deviating from general understanding of the term), that are later translated into policies regulating daily business and operational procedures. It is very important not to go too much into philosophy (as ethics sometimes is perceived) and making these rules simple, easy to understand and apply. Furthermore, they need to be easy to enforce. Communication of the above to employees would be important as well, building trust in company's compliance culture.

Notes

1 https://www.scu.edu/ethics/focus-areas/business-ethics/resources/what-is-business-ethics/

2 There are many examples confirming that, especially noted during early months of Russian war in Ukraine, where there were numerous call for boycott of specific companies operating in Russia.

3 For instance by introducing *ethical councils* or *ethic advisors*, but which, without proper links to internal processes won't be able to effectively enforce implemented rules.

4 That's not to discourage companies from creating and adopting *codes of ethics*, however doing so only to check off a requirement from the Compliance list is not what is really expected from ethical company.

5 This requirement doesn't necessarily apply to operational procedures, because of their nature — giving direct steps that need to be performed. It's good though to include short information about these documents in overall communication, stating that activities described there are in line with ethical rules and expectations.

6 Environment, Social and Governance

7 Diversity, Equity and Inclusion

Business Ethics: It's Employee Management, Not Philosophy

Meric Bloch

1. Introduction

Managers and employees require useful guidance on ethics.[1] Most compliance officers are not meeting this need.

A common misconception is that people acquire their own sense of ethical conduct when they are young, and that business ethics are useless to teach once an employee joins the workforce. When an employee commits misconduct, some say that they are just a "bad apple" and should be fired. They think the company is powerless to stop misconduct. This is not true.

Ethics in a business context should mean how rules and standards guide decision making. More specifically, how ethics are applied to business decisions where the main objective is to achieve a profit and increase shareholder value. Compliance officers should be focused on the application of rules and standards to decisions that determine how the company is perceived by its stakeholders[2] and its ability to maintain stable growth."[3]

The typical corporate ethics resources are suited for academics, philosophers, and compliance specialists. Businesspeople do not find them valuable. Compounding the problem is sensationalized accounts of companies that have "gone bad" and exhortations to "do the right thing" in corporate ethics training. These resources take a simplistic approach to ethical dilemmas, like "Should Jacob steal from the company?" and "Should Daniel accept a kickback from a vendor?" The workplace is more complicated, and this training is not helpful.

Philosophical ethics discussions regarding business decisions are falling on deaf ears. Consider the Code of Conduct for Booking Holdings, Inc., a publicly traded, multinational travel company. Their code states that "Achieving results through . . . unethical means is unacceptable." The company also claims a core value of "Absolute Integrity: We will always strive to do the right thing and achieve success with integrity and accountability."[4] All fine and good, but where is the guidance regarding how to apply those obligations when making business decisions on the company's behalf? It is not enough to follow simple rules like "Don't lie," and "Don't cheat."[5]

If the business of a company is business, compliance officers must appreciate what motivates an employee's decision making.[6] Most managers want their employees to be ethical, productive, and able to provide high-quality goods and services while also treating clients well. Business ethics enter the picture here. The proper application of ethics closes the gap between required conduct and business realities. Despite all the talk about a company's "culture," the reality is that culture is just an aggregation of leaders', managers', and employees' ethical conducts and values.[7]

2. Why Isn't the Typical Compliance Program Enough?

A corporate compliance program succeeds when employees are trained to identify actual or suspected violations of workplace rules and are motivated to report them. The "success" of ethics training is not determined by the absence of infractions. There might be instances where employees stop doing something improper because they just realized it was wrong. That is the exception. Employees who participate in prohibited activities are often aware that they are prohibited, but they continue. The number of employees who report unethical conduct by others may be a better indicator of effective compliance training.

Compliance officers write codes of conduct. But a code of conduct can only do so much. A code will never be enough to establish an ethical business. Employees are unlikely to read a lengthy code.[8] On the other hand, shorter codes give generalized aspirational guidance. The impact of a code of conduct is limited either way.[9]

Programs for ethics can be divided into two categories: compliance-based and values-based. The legal terminology, instruction, code of conduct, and sanctions for noncompliance are all part of the compliance-based system. Instead of using coercion, the value-based system depends on motivation and self-policing. The regulations of the compliance-based system are based on ethics. Ethics is a tool that the value-based system employs to make decisions.

Codes of conduct do not make companies more ethical. Better organizational performance arises from the application of a core set of organizational values to business decision-making.

Traditional ethics training is also inadequate and makes employees cynical. Although these programs bring ethical issues to light, the training content indirectly suggests that the company is not addressing the actual challenges that employees face. Off-the-shelf ethics training focuses on superficial, formulaic recommendations. Furthermore, the world's best customized program would be compromised if a company leader deviated from those guidelines. Consequently, generic training content does little to guide employees to act ethically.

Business ethics training does not need to be academic or philosophical. Business ethics is about recognizing, anticipating, and modifying employee conduct. Compliance officers, collaborating with managers, are essential to foster the development of business ethics. Codes of conduct and ethics training are just part of the story.

And how are compliance officers responding to this challenge? By treating ethical lapses as an academic discussion of what is going wrong and not focusing on root causes and practical guidance. The compliance officer uses one or more of these techniques:[10]

- Turn another company's scandal into a moral tale about how employees should not do the same bad thing in their company.
- Show survey data whose results make some high-level point, such as how employees feel work pressure to compromise standards.
- Make an obvious statement like "ethical failure is not cheap"[11] without further elaboration.
- Tell scary stories about huge scandals which, however spectacular and harmful, are unlikely to occur to this company.[12]
- Cite internal data on various ethics and compliance topics that show correlation but not causation.
- State why ethics is important as if it's obvious but then give no guidance to apply it to daily business decisions.
- Offer admonitions that something must be done, but delegate that responsibility to another department in the company.

- State that the company would benefit from something like ethics ambassadors but with no business case to justify the use of resources or data to show that it would make a meaningful difference.

Compliance officers should instead teach ethical decision making to help their colleagues make sound choices when confronted with ethical dilemmas.[13]

3. Developing Bad Ethical Habits

People are perceptive and observe their surroundings. Employees quickly learn what aligns with their company's culture and how ethically aware the company is—or is not. Employees are acting rationally in the workplace setting the company creates. Their decisions are based on what they believe helps them the most.

Unethical business practices grow in a company for several reasons. Compliance officers need to assess their surroundings. They should use their institutional knowledge to understand their company's culture and then ask these questions:

- Are the leaders in my company trusted by the employees?[14]
- What is my company's reputation among external stakeholders?[15]
- Does my company give too much weight to individual and corporate sales performance?
- Is maximizing profit my company's only goal?
- Does my company follow the letter rather than the spirit of the Code of Conduct and our other business conduct standards?
- Do we have ethical "window-dressing" policies that are perceived as little more than virtue signaling? [16]
- Does my company have sufficient internal controls in place to assure ethical conduct?
- Does my company prioritize speed over other crucial factors when it comes to the sales process?
- Do my colleagues focus on limited options when making business decisions and only consider an idea or two?
- Do my colleagues favor their short-term gains to the exclusion of longer-term issues?

- Do my colleagues assume that the decision they make will be the best decision for all the stakeholders? Do they even think about it?

Company reward programs have an impact on employee conduct as well.[17] Rewarding conduct simply encourages more of it. Employees are always watching for cues from their leaders about rewards and penalties, particularly if expectations like ethical conduct are not stated clearly.

The answers to these questions provide the compliance officer with a realistic picture of the dynamics at work as well as focus areas to make their guidance count. If company norms contradict codes of conduct and other company policies, employees will follow the norms.[18]

4. Correcting Misperceptions about Business Ethics

Compliance officers should then calculate the true value of their current ethics training. Polite messages of support from company leadership are not an indicator. Leaders who say they support these programs may do so more as a sign of being a "team player" or because their role obligates them to say it. The truth lies beneath that polite veneer.

Ethics has traditionally been an area covered by academics, social scientists, and philosophers. Ethical considerations are explained with case studies, philosophical stances, and criticisms of social responsibility. Discussing ethics with a real-world connection left managers underserved.

Managers feel that there are many ethical "gray areas" in business transactions. From their perspective, the realities of the marketplace may force them to choose between options that are partially ethical and partially unethical. They do not benefit from the presentation of business ethics issues as some kind of ethical absolutism, presented by staff functions with no revenue-generating responsibilities.

External factors have not helped. Scandals in business, politics, sports, and education characterize ethics violations as some technical error about a particular act rather than viewing ethics as a principled approach to making decisions. Naturally, the next scandal reinforces a cynical view that ethics may be nothing more than a ruse employed by an accused person to project a false sense of moral innocence.

5. A Better Consideration of Business Ethics

Scrap the morality tales. Compliance officers would do better to convey to employees that business ethics means setting expectations about how to conduct business properly and making sure that employee conduct aligns with the expectations.

Bear in mind that morals and ethics are not the same thing. Morals are the rules about what is right and wrong. Ethics is the framework that helps us act consistent with those values. Ethics must be integrated into decision making. Ethical considerations make employees more aware of their own responsibilities.

We need a practical understanding of ethics. Let's first identify what ethics is not:

- Ethics does not care about feelings. Many people feel good about themselves even when they do something wrong. Some people feel bad when they make a mistake. Feelings are not good ethical indicators.
- Ethics is more than just following the law. While ethical principles are incorporated into a sound legal system, the law occasionally deviates from what many people would consider ethical conduct.
- Ethics is more than following socially accepted norms. Some cultures may seem ethical, while others get corrupted or lose sight of ethical issues (like slavery or segregation).
- Ethics is not science. Natural and social sciences offer useful information to support sound decision-making. However, science cannot make decisions for us. Ethics offers justifications for appropriate human conduct.

A compliance officer cannot simply categorize those who act unethically as "bad people." Examining unethical conduct includes reviewing the company procedures involved and identifying the contributing factors that enabled the unethical conduct. The company can then redefine appropriate and inappropriate conduct and reduce pressure on employees to act unethically. Stated differently, when unethical conduct occurs, a compliance officer should look for ways to reduce the opportunities for future unethical conduct.

6. Ethical Dynamics within a Company

Ethical conduct does not occur in a vacuum. It is based on human interaction. Thinking about ethical matters necessitates having a basic grasp of the interpersonal dynamics that exist within a company. Each company has a unique culture and corresponding expectations for colleague interactions. Many ethical problems that arise in a business are foreseeable. Think about these typical situations:

- An employee uses company time to browse the Internet and shop for personal items.
- Despite knowing that a part's quality issue prevents the part from functioning properly, a plant manager chooses to ship the product to a client because he believes the client will not notice the defect.
- Even though a sale is uncertain, a salesperson marks parts as "sold" in the company database, preventing others from selling the parts.
- A retailer makes false claims about the features or quality of a product that is on sale.
- An employee stocks their home office with supplies they bring from work.
- A finance officer provides dubious explanations for expenditures and purchases.
- When an accountant knows they have not written a check, they tell a supplier that their "check is in the mail."

Good companies try to hire good people. But good character on its own does not give colleagues the skills needed to resolve ethical dilemmas. Ethical conduct is influenced by the "locus of control." This is a person's perception of how much they can control life's circumstances. This perception does not occur naturally but evolves over time through interactions with other people and their surroundings. People with a high internal locus of control better understand the connection between their actions and the results of those actions than people who believe that external factors, like peer pressure, control their circumstances. Compliance officers must understand where employee groups fall on this spectrum.

One of the external factors is the proffered excuse that "everyone does it." People are more inclined to act unethically if they believe that others are doing the same thing. This offers both a legitimate explanation and justification for their actions which releases them from accountability. A group might also come up with other justifications for unethical actions. For instance, inflating costs could be justified to compensate for the additional time spent away from home or as a means of covering a cost not covered by the company's travel policy. The manager, who either initiates the conduct or suggests it, may support the justification.

Compliance officers should remember that the "everyone does it" defense is not only a way to justify a particular action; it also shows the effect of peer pressure. Reluctant people are encouraged by the argument. Employees might follow the rules if left on their own. However, they feel compelled to follow the group, or at the very least to keep quiet about what other employees are doing.

Another external factor is the willingness of some employees to follow instructions without question. A company has an authority structure that necessitates, among other things, a certain amount of obedience from employees. Employees also anticipate receiving instructions from their managers. They also think they should fulfill their obligations. Companies run efficiently as a result.

Employees typically believe they have a duty to be loyal to the company and their manager, which increases the pressure to conform to the company's expectations. Therefore, when people in positions of company authority behave unethically, they undermine the value of ethics and implicitly encourage others to do the same.

People in higher management positions at work must delegate responsibility to others. The employee receiving the delegations is merely told not to worry; someone else will manage an issue or choice. The colleague may soon feel that they simply have no obligation to watch out for actual or suspected unethical conduct, and they might stop alerting their managers to issues. If employees believe they are accountable for the results of their choices and actions, they may be more likely to act ethically.

Employees must feel accountable for the results of their actions to see a connection between their actions and what they believe to be right. Compliance officers must admit the existence of these internal forces. Employees who believe they are accountable for the consequences of their choices and deeds are far more likely to behave ethically. An employee's sense of accountability for the results of any decisions or actions that affect other members of the company is increased when individual responsibility is emphasized in terms of information sharing, problem-solving, and ownership of group decisions.

This creates an opportunity for a compliance officer to contribute significantly to the company's business success.

7. What Does an Ethical Company Do Now?

What steps must a company take—or not take—to act ethically toward its clients, employees, the community, and shareholders, given that the company, and not individual employees, sets ethical standards? The golden rule enters the picture.

Companies that uphold ethics treat people how they want to be treated. When partners, clients, and employees receive ethical treatment, they are likely to reciprocate. Sustained success depends on ethical conduct.

Compliance officers who wish to contribute meaningfully must tailor their guidance accordingly:

7.1. Core Principles.

Ethics typically follow a company's core values. These values are often described as the foundation of the company's compliance and ethics program.

Are the leaders perceived as trustworthy? If so, then all ethical concerns will fall into place. Mission statements, codes of conduct, and everything else are useless if the leaders do not seem trustworthy. Employees also evaluate a leader's ethics based on how they manage small decisions. Small things do matter.

By establishing unambiguous standards, upholding them, actively communicating them, and demanding that everyone follow them, an ethical company gains the trust of its employees and other stakeholders.

7.2 Awareness.

Do colleagues know that some business decisions may present ethical dilemmas? The process of making ethical decisions begins with awareness. A certain circumstance or problem may present ethical questions and need to be considered accordingly. Employees may be unaware of the ethical implications of the problem with which they are dealing.

7.3 Honestly.

Does the company value honesty in decision making? When a company behaves honestly, it does not mislead people. This includes everything from employee relations to accounting to making claims about products doing things for which they were never intended. No one can fairly disagree that an ethical company must treat its employees and other stakeholders honestly. But companies still act dishonestly. For example, managers manipulate financial reports to portray them positively before sending them up to higher managers. Because their figures have been positively manipulated on so many successive levels the information has little connection to reality.

7.4 Openly.

Are business decisions made transparently so colleagues will accept the decision as credible, appropriate, and well considered? Ethical companies are transparent about their actions and motivations. Acting ethically includes not withholding information that someone might be interested in knowing and that would not be harmful to the company. It also means that information that could influence a shareholder, employee, client, or member of the community to act differently toward the company should not be unreasonably withheld.

7.5 Consistency.

A company that behaves consistently doesn't alter its practices over time unless there is a good reason to do so. When a company does not care enough about someone or a group of people to take the time to respond thoughtfully to a request or action, inconsistency results. This suggests that the company doesn't care. Employee perceptions of policy violations or accepted disregarding for some policies creates an ethical dilemma when it comes to inconsistent application. Clearly communicating what people can expect from you is the best way to guarantee that you won't be asked to compromise your values.

7.6 Discipline.

How does the company manage the employee discipline function? Sanctions must be meted out consistently. Employees can distinguish between fair and unfair penalties. Employees will anticipate punishment when they disobey the rules if punishment is applied consistently to enforce them. Ethical application of discipline demands that the penalty is commensurate with the offense and in line with prior treatment.

7.7 Fairly.

Are company decisions viewed as fair or capricious? The other aspect of consistency is fairness. It means treating every individual in a group equally. To be fair, not everyone must receive the same treatment; rather, differences in treatment must be justified by legitimate, objective factors.

7.8 Best Interest of Others.

Does the company value whatever generates revenue? Or are the interests of its employees, clients, community, and shareholders actively promoted? An ethical company strives for the success of its employees, clients, community, and investors. The difficult part is determining what acts are best for others (as opposed to short-term gain at the expense of long-term harm) and how to strike a balance between the conflicting interests of various groups. Shareholders, for instance, want the company to increase the value of their stock. Although there may be a short-term gain for shareholders because of an unethical act, this hurts future shareholders who bought the stock at high prices by limiting their gains, and it does not help shareholders who do not sell their stock while it is high. In general, it is always preferable for the company to give the shareholders a strong return over the long run, either through dividends or steady growth, and to endeavor to make sure that the stock price is fairly aligned with the underlying value of the company.

7.9 Living up to Commitments.

Does the company do what it says, rather than just virtue signal? An ethical value system revolves around commitment. When there is a problem, commitment is crucial to how someone views the ethical company practices of a company. Building dependable connections and trust requires commitment.

Good managers consider carefully what their standards are, communicate with them, and actively enforce them because they know that their subordinates want to know what the rules are. Managers possess the ability to establish an ethical atmosphere if they establish high expectations, promote effective communication, and set an example for others. They are less likely to do so if they see others in the company rising through the ranks by trolling others, lying to clients, and fabricating reports.

7.10 Ask for Advice or Clarification.

Does the company encourage discussion and creative conflict? Codes of conduct usually include guidance for ethical conduct. These codes cannot address every scenario an employee may encounter. In other cases, when the code is ambiguous, an employee might view the ethical dilemma as one of interpretation. An ethical company recognizes the existence of ethically ambiguous situations and tries to find solutions. Unethical conduct may not be intentional. It could be the result of employees failing to sufficiently weigh the risks involved in acting in the "gray area" of acceptable conduct. Compliance officers should ensure that employees do not risk the company's reputation or their own career goals because an employee mistakenly decided than an unethical decision was appropriate. Gaining approval has the added benefit of providing that manager with a "safe harbor." The manager can avoid major issues by citing the earlier approval as an ethical justification if the act is criticized later.

7.11 Job Competence

Are employees competent for their roles? Ethical problems arise from ignorance and incompetence rather than deliberate wrongdoing. An ethical company commits to hiring the best candidates, assessing their work, reprimanding subpar employees, and even firing them. Job competence includes making ethical decisions.

8. What Does the Compliance Officer Do?

Compliance officers can raise the collective awareness of the perceived conflict and can plan accordingly. There are specific steps to make the consideration of ethics a practical and relevant part of business decision making:

8.1 Guide managers to offer the right incentives.

Draconian sales targets or the threat of firing employees for missing them does not encourage ethical decision making. Positive incentives are used to inspire employees. Bonuses are offered for respectable sales growth, and providing honest, responsible client service is emphasized as a requirement for internal promotion. A good manager does not hire unethical employees, and it is uncommon for employees to be more ethical than their manager. Use your role to help managers set clear boundaries for acceptable and unacceptable conduct, then hold employees accountable for their actions. This is how ethical parameters are created. If a manager discovers unethical activity, they should receive some sort of reward. Reward systems set the standard for acceptable conduct.

8.2 Reputation rules.

Remind managers that the company's reputation in the marketplace can be ruined by unethical practices. Treating clients and suppliers with honesty is a necessary component of ethical sales. Honesty should extend to company rivals as well. The long-term loyalty and referrals that result is known to accomplish more by ethical managers than fighting.

8.3 Salespeople are ambassadors.

Salespeople should receive targeted training to identify and resolve ethical dilemmas. Salespeople are company representatives, and others will assume that they are speaking on behalf of the company. The company suffers if a salesperson violates company policy or engages in unethical conduct with a client, such as making unrealistic promises. Sometimes, a client's only interaction with the company is through the salesperson. The client cannot trust the company if they do not trust the salesperson.

8.4 Repeat clients are a bargain.

Leverage the value of ethical business practices. Ethical business dealings serve as cheap advertising in addition to improving a company's reputation. Long-term gains are practically assured for a company that has a reputation for ethical business conduct.

8.5 Retaining employees.

Ethical employees usually stay with ethical companies. What should employees do when they see unethical conduct by higher-level managers? At most, they become disengaged from the company or quit. Worst case scenario, they soon believe that lying is the secret to success and mimic that conduct.

Go beyond generalizations like "integrity is important here." Encourage managers to make more specific declarations like "I expect sales representatives to be absolutely honest with our customers about such things as the characteristics of our products and our ability to deliver by a certain date."

Lastly, the manager bears the same responsibility for encouraging ethical behavior and discouraging unethical behavior in the workplace as they do for managing for productivity or quality.[19]

9. Compliance Officers Should Guide Colleagues to Resolve Ethical Dilemmas

The compliance officer's objective should be to create a culture where ethical decision-making as a standard is the ultimate objective. Developing a practical decision-making process is the first step towards achieving this goal.

But every ethical dilemma can be foreseen and resolved beforehand. Employees face ethical decisions with no established rules. It takes awareness of ethical issues and a process to consider its ethical implications to make ethical decisions.

9.1 Decision-making framework

Consequently, compliance officers should offer a decision-making framework to managers and employees for resolving ethical dilemmas. The framework could incorporate these questions:

9.1.1 Has the problem been clarified?

Many people make snap decisions before fully understanding the situation. Many ethical decisions are challenging due to the uncertainty involved. Even if you are aware of information gaps, acknowledging these constraints will assist you in compiling the available data. Most people overestimate their level of factual knowledge.

Which facts are pertinent? Which details are not known? Are you knowledgeable enough to decide?

9.1.2 What is the precise ethical issue?

Do not leap to solutions before determining the ethical dilemmas. Do not stop at the first ethical dilemma that occurs to you either. It is possible that you overlooked some others.

9.1.3 What is the true price of the decision?

Even though you can't foresee every outcome, you should try to identify potential outcomes. Consider the costs not only for the bottom line but also for integrity and reputation. Any action's symbolic effects are something you should also consider. All decisions and actions have a message to convey.

9.1.4 How does the problem look from another person's perspective?

When a salesperson becomes other focused, they make good decisions. Stated differently, would you object if someone subjected you to this? Seeing things from other people's perspectives is an essential reasoning ability.

9.1.5 Who does the decision affect?

A decision not only impacts the bottom line but also the kind of relationship you are developing with the client and how you plan to conduct business going forward. After stakeholders have been identified, the effects can be viewed from each of their various angles.[20]

9.1.6 What is the intention in making this decision?

Are you acting in this way just to get away with it? Analyzing a decision's immediate and long-term effects helps you make the best choices.[21]

9.1.7 How does this intention compare with the probable results?

Put differently, even assuming you have the best of intentions, will the company benefit from the outcome?

9.1.8 Will the current position hold up over time?

People frequently make unethical mistakes because they are only thinking about their immediate needs. If the issue is serious, though, its consequences will not go away even after the quarterly reports are forgotten. Making ethically sound decisions has long-term and short-term benefits.

9.1.9 What are the obligations to others?

You need to determine what responsibilities you currently have or will have to others because of your choice. The responsibilities depend on the circumstances. They include openness and truthfulness.[22]

9.1.10 Are there alternatives?

Do not put yourself in a difficult situation. Verify that you haven't overlooked any additional workable answers. Use your imagination. Ask whether the decision involves a choice between a good and bad alternative.

9.1.11 How does the dilemma seem from a distance?

In addition to using reason in your assessment, trust your instincts. A valuable resource for ethical decision-making in business could be intuition. Consider it carefully and make use of it when making decisions.

9.1.12 Take The New York Times test

Would you feel comfortable if your actions were printed on the front page of *The New York Times*? [23]

Once the advantages and drawbacks of each choice have been weighed, the ethical values can be identified easily. Variables including general good, honesty, transparency, equality and justice, rights, and duty are valued in ethical decisions.

9.2 Prompt Decision-Making in Critical Situations

Employees should plan sufficient time for evaluation, thought, and information gathering regarding the matter at hand. But in cases where a prompt choice is required:

- Never undervalue the significance of using your "gut feeling" to determine whether you are in an ethical bind. Take your intuition as a warning sign if it tells you something is off. [24]
- Request some time to consider it. Most rash choices do not have to be made in that manner.
- As soon as possible, ascertain whether the decision is subject to any applicable company policies.
- Consult your peers or manager for guidance. Never be afraid to seek a second opinion.
- Take *The New York Times* test. Do not do it if reading about the decision in the newspaper makes you feel ashamed.

These steps will help employees make informed choices about ethical decisions in business.

10. Conclusion: Putting it all Together

The goal of a compliance and ethics program is to achieve desired workplace behaviors. The compliance officer's preferred behaviors are the most important outcome, as with any management practice. Even the greatest ethical principles and intentions are useless if they do not lead to just and fair workplace practices. Because of this, programs that produce codes of ethics or lists of ethical values also need to produce the policies, guidelines, and training necessary to convert those values into actual appropriate conduct.

Combine the management of ethics with other management techniques. Incorporate the ethical values that are preferred in the workplace when creating the values statement during the strategic planning phase. Consider the ethical principles that leaders want to see most prevalent in the company culture when creating personnel policies, and then create policies that encourage these kinds of actions.

Compliance officers should make employees aware of the value of ethics. Managers should operationalize these principles. Company leaders should establish an environment that encourages ethical business conduct by combining a discipline that guarantees marketing accuracy, managers who are prepared to foresee and identify ethical issues, and a willingness to sanction those who transgress ethical standards.

The compliance officer and management are partnered for success when ethics are incorporated into business decision making. Although the compliance officer is part of a staff function, facilitating the integration of ethics into business decision making can be a tangible contribution to the company.

Notes

1 Ethics is defined as "the principles of conduct governing an individual or a profession." (Merriam Webster, "Ethics")

2 A stakeholder is any group or individual who can impact or may be impacted by a company strategy, its key business decisions, or other business activities. (Bright, 2019, p. 150)

3 (Elgood, 2014, p. 2)

4 *Booking Holdings Code of Conduct*. Core values need to be integrated into corporate strategy and decision making.

5 (Gutterman, 2023)

6 This paraphrases the quote attributed to US President Calvin Coolidge in the 1920's. President Coolidge stated that "The business of the American people is business."

[7] In a sense, all business decisions are ethical decisions of some kind.

[8] Enron, the company whose 2001 scandal made them the exemplar of unethical conduct, had a 64-page extensive code of ethics.

[9] Preventing ethical dilemmas from arising in the first place is the best approach to resolving them. This is the reason it's crucial to follow procedures like creating codes of conduct and ethics. Through their development, employees become more aware of ethical issues and reduce the likelihood that unethical behavior will occur in the first place.

[10] (Owili, 2017)

[11] (Owili, 2017)

[12] For example, an online travel company's ethics training is not necessarily enhanced by learning how a pharmaceutical company responsibly dealt with reports of product tampering on supermarket shelves.

[13] Ethical dilemmas include situations where there is no clear "right" or "wrong" answer, time-sensitive situations that require quick decision making, and dealing with suspected conflicts of interest.

[14] The degree to which leaders are trusted depends on four characteristics: (i) the leader's ability to do their job; (ii) the leaders concern for others beyond their own needs; (iii) the leader's integrity; and (iv) the predictability of the leader's behavior. (Elgood, 2014, p. 7).

[15] Reputation means "the manifestation of the regard with which the company is held." (Elgood, 2014, p. 8).

[16] This organization focused on communicating their standards but not ensuring the standards were implemented when making business decisions.

[17] People do what is rewarded. The rewards do not need to be explicit. For example, a sales compensation plan that focuses on goals and does not mention the acceptable means to accomplish those goals. The compliance officer must think about the behavioral outcomes and the potential unintended consequences.

[18] (Watts, 2021, p. 7).

[19] (Trevino, 2017, p. 258).

[20] This is a practical application of the commonly found corporate core value of respect.

[21] This aligns with the value of excellence.

[22] This aligns with the value of complying with the spirit of applicable laws, regulations, and company policies.

[23] This applies the commonly found corporate core value of responsibility and accountability.

[24] "Even if you are sure the decision is reasonable and that you could defend it to others, does your gut instinct tell you it is the wrong thing to do?" (Gutterman, 2023, p. 29).

Bibliography

(2022, April 11). *Ethical Decision-Making Process: How to Make Ethical Decisions*. MasterClass. Retrieved May 1, 2024, from https://www.masterclass.com/article/ethical-decision-making-process.

Bazerman, M. (2011, April 1). *Ethical Breakdowns*. Harvard Business Review. Retrieved May 3, 2024, from https://www.hbr.org/2011/04/ethical-breakdowns.

Booking Holdings Code of Conduct. Booking Holdings. Retrieved May 3, 2024, from https://www.bookingholdings.com/code-of-conduct/.

Boyles, M. (2023, July 27). *What Are Business Ethics and Why Are They Important?* Business Insights Blog. Retrieved May 3, 2024, from https://online.hbs.edu/blog/post/businessethics.

Bright, D. (2019). *Principles of Management* (pp. 128-165). OpenStax. https://openstax.org/details/books/principles-management.

Elgood, C. (2014, August 1). *Ethics in Business Decision-Making*. Retrieved May 3, 2024, from https://www.chris-elgood.com/wp-content/uploads/2017/07/n10-Ethics-in-Business-Decision-Making-c1.0.pdf.

"Ethics." Merriam-Webster.com Legal Dictionary, Merriam-Webster, https://www.merriam-webster.com/legal/ethics. Accessed 3 May 2024.

Gutterman, A. (2023, November 11). *Ethical Management*. SSRN. Retrieved May 3, 2024, from https://ssrn.com/abstract=3833970.

Jamnik, A. (2011). The Challenges of Business Ethics-Management and the Question of Ethics. *Tourism and Hospitality Management*, *17*(1), 171. https://doi.org/https://ssrn.com/abstract=2062389.

Martinez, C. (2020). Managing Organizational Ethics: How Ethics Becomes Pervasive within Organizations. *Business Horizons*, *64*(1), 83-92. https://doi.org/https;//doi.org/10.1016/j.bushor.2020.09.008.

Minkes, A. L. (1999). Leadership and Business Ethics: Does it Matter? Implications for Management. *Journal of Business Ethics*, *20*, 327-335. https://doi.org/10.1023/A:100574152800.

Owili, G. (2017, January 1). Ethical Decisions in Business. *Australian Corporate Lawyer*, *27*(2), 24-25. https://www.acc.com/sites/default/files/resources/upload/Ethical%20Decisions%20in%20Business.pdf.

Paine, L. (1994, March 1). *Managing for Organizational Integrity*. Harvard Business Review. Retrieved May 3, 2024, from https://hbr.org/1994/03/managing-for-organizational-integrity.

Santa Clara University (2023, January 9). *Ethical Decision Making: Navigating Tough Choices with Confidence*. Leavey School of Business. Retrieved May

3, 2024, from https://onlinedegrees.scu.edu/media/blog/ethical-decision-making-navigating-tough-choices-with-confidence.

Santa Clara University (2021, November 8). *A Framework for Ethical Decision Making.* Retrieved May 3, 2024, from https://www.scu.edu/ethics/ethics-resources/a-framework-for-ethical-decisionmaking.

Stark, A. (1993, May 1). *What's the Matter with Ethics?* Harvard Business Review. Retrieved May 3, 2024, from https://www.hbr.org/1993/05/whats-the-matter-with-business-ethics.

Trevino, L. (2017). *Managing Business Ethics* (7th ed.). Wiley & Sons.

Trevino, L. (n.d.). *Managing to Be Ethical: Debunking Five Business Ethics Myths.* The Academy of Management Executive. Retrieved May 3, 2024, from https://www.jstor.org/stable/4166063.

Watts, L. L. (2021). *Ethics Training for Managers: Best Practices and Techniques* (pp. 1-11). Rutledge.

Webster, J. (2023, February 14). *How Ethical Business Tactics Can Improve Profitability.* Forbes.com. Retrieved May 3, 2024, from https://www.forbes.com/sites/forbesfinancecouncil/2023/02/14/how-ethical-business-tactics-can-improve-profitability.

Ethics and leadership practice in Financial Institutions in a time of changing regulatory landscape

Yasmine Sadek

1. Introduction

The banking industry operates within a highly sensitive sector of the economy, where it plays a pivotal role as an agent within a system where the savings of one individual become the investments of another, creating a web of interdependency among all economic agents. This interdependency underscores the critical importance of the banking sector in maintaining economic stability.

This delicate balance is governed by a framework of laws and regulations designed to ensure the integrity of the financial system despite multiple crisis. In "The Apology of Socrates," Meletus argues that it is the laws that educate people by imposing the measure they inherently lack. While Socrates acknowledges a kernel of truth in this, he contends that true education comes not from the mere imposition of laws, but from adherence to carefully reasoned principles. Socrates champions the authority of these principles over the absolute authority of the city or its laws.

This philosophical debate has practical implications in the modern financial sector. In recent years, the landscape of financial regulation has undergone significant changes due to global economic shifts, technological advancements, evolving societal expectations, and major financial crises. These changes have highlighted the need for ethical leadership within financial institutions. Leaders are now expected not only to comply with these regulations but to proactively incorporate ethical considerations into their strategic decision-making processes.

Financial regulation involves a complex set of rules and laws designed to maintain the integrity of the financial system, safeguard investor confidence, prevent financial crimes, and ensure economic stability. The challenge lies in balancing the adherence to these regulations with the ethical imperatives that guide decision-making, echoing the tension between the authority of laws and the principles of reasoned ethics.

The effects of financial regulation on the global economy can be analysed from two perspectives: the referees' (public good) view and the risk-takers' (private good) view[1]..

A bank leader's ethical strategy can affect the direction, success, operations, and profits of banks impacting the whole Society.

This paper examines how financial institutions' leadership incorporates ethics when adapting to key regulatory changes (1) such as anti-corruption laws and Environmental, Social, and Governance (ESG) regulations. This analysis aims to offer insights into the practices that define ethical leadership (2) in the modern financial sector and explore how these practices impact both local and global regulatory compliance and organizational culture. It includes a broad meaning relating to rules and morals, rights and duties which includes law and morality in ethics. This meaning is suggested by Kant at the beginning of the Metaphysics of Morals, when he states that: The doctrine of law, as the first part of ethics, is what one could call the metaphysics of law, such as it is required as a system emanating from reason. In this overly broad sense, the doctrine of virtue will constitute the second part of ethics, following a first part entitled doctrine of law[2.]

2. The ever changing Regulatory Landscape

The financial regulatory environment is continually evolving, shaped by economic challenges (1.1), technological advancements (1.2), and heightened societal expectations (1.3). This section outlines the current trends in financial regulations and their implications for leadership practices within the sector. Michel Aglietta[3] often discusses the necessity of adapting financial regulation in response to economic instability and the evolving macroeconomic landscape[4].

Indeed, the landscape of financial regulation has undergone substantial transformations driven by a confluence of factors. These include global economic shifts, such as the fluctuating dynamics of trade relationships and market dependencies, which have compelled regulatory bodies to rethink their strategies to maintain financial stability and prevent systemic risks. Advancements in technology have also played a pivotal role, as innovations like blockchain, cryptocurrencies, and fintech solutions challenge traditional regulatory frameworks, necessitating updates to accommodate new business models and mitigate associated risks. Additionally, evolving societal expectations have pushed for greater transparency and accountability, prompting regulators to enhance consumer protection and enforce stricter compliance measures.

Furthermore, major crises, including the global financial crisis of 2008 and the more recent economic disruptions caused by the COVID-19 pandemic, have exposed vulnerabilities in financial systems worldwide, leading to a surge in regulatory changes aimed at strengthening the financial sector's resilience and integrity. Collectively, these factors have reshaped the regulatory production and priorities, making it increasingly complex and integral to the functioning of global financial markets.

Financial Institution need to prioritize both event-driven and existing regulations to create value and remain competitive whilst safeguarding the market integrity and consumers interests.

Some authors describe in recent publications like "La Banque: Comment Goldman Sachs dirige le monde" by Marc Roche (2021) and "Le Capitalisme à l'agonie[5]?" critically examine the ethical responsibilities of financial institutions in this new regulatory environment. These works argue that beyond compliance with regulations, banks must embrace ethical leadership that integrates broader societal values into their strategic decision-making processes.

2.1. Economic Challenges

Economic downturns and crises have necessitated a profound reevaluation of financial risk management and compliance frameworks, this has served as a significant case study within the broader European context. The French examples reflects that local authorities have been proactive in enhancing regulatory measures to strengthen the financial system's resilience. This approach aligns closely with broader European Union strategies, which aim for harmonization and stringent oversight across member states.

Moreover, it worth noting that uncertainty is not risk. Under uncertainty economic agents ignore the true model of the economy. The rationality of Markets being bounded, market participants rely on heuristic patterns that select and integrate the knowledge relevant with their type of activity (Akerlof and Shiller, 2009). However they are aware of the limits of their knowledge. They are thus induced to enlarge it in taking care of the opinions of others that they presume might have better information. Because others are on the same footing, strategic complementarities arise.

Economic downturns and crises have necessitated a profound reevaluation of financial risk management and compliance frameworks, providing fertile ground for case studies within the broader European context. The French experience, particularly in the wake of the 2008 financial crisis and the more recent economic challenges posed by the COVID-19 pandemic, underscores the proactive role of local authorities in enhancing regulatory measures to fortify the resilience of the financial system.

This regulatory evolution in France aligns closely with broader European Union strategies, which emphasize harmonization and stringent oversight across member states. For instance, the works of scholars such as Jean-Pierre Jouyet and Philippe Dessertine, notably in "La Crise des Subprimes: Comprendre pour en tirer des leçons" (2009), delve into how the 2008 crisis served as a catalyst for overhauling financial regulations in Europe. They highlight how France, through laws such as the "Loi de séparation et de régulation des activités bancaires" (2013) and the "Pacte Law" (2019), has aimed to create a more resilient financial sector by separating speculative activities from essential banking functions and promoting corporate responsibility. Customer protection became then a target and a purpose of the financial industry.

Further, the increasing convergence of regulatory frameworks across Europe, driven by the EU's commitment to financial stability and risk mitigation. France's regulatory advancements are not only aligned with but also influential in shaping broader EU financial strategies.

In "Regulating Finance: Balancing Freedom and Risk" by Tommaso Padoa-Schioppa[6], the critical role that national initiatives play in the European context highlits how this aims to strike a balance between financial innovation and systemic risk.

In France, the adaptation of EU directives into national law, such as the EU's Markets in Financial Instruments Directive (MiFID II) and the Capital Requirements Directive IV (CRD IV), has fundamentally reshaped the compliance requirements and risk management strategies of French financial institutions. These directives, emphasizing transparency and the mitigation of systemic risks, have led to increased knowledge and scrutiny through a more robust regulatory framework.

Some French scholars have advocated for these changes, emphasizing the need for regulatory frameworks that are both resilient and adaptable to the complexities of modern financial markets.

Looking at the broader European perspective, authors such as Anil Kashyap have examined how regulatory policies in major economies are interconnected with those in other European countries. Kashyap's analysis often highlights the necessity for international coordination in financial regulation, pointing out how interconnected the European financial markets are and how regulatory changes in one nation often have ripple effects across the region.

In terms of case law, the French judiciary's role in interpreting and enforcing these regulations is crucial. The case of "Société Générale v. Jérôme Kerviel" serves as a stark reminder of the importance of internal controls and risk management. The repercussions of this case resonated across Europe, prompting financial institutions to bolster their compliance and oversight mechanisms.

Moreover, European Court cases, like those adjudicated by the European Court of Justice (ECJ), also reflect this trend. For example, cases dealing with the enforcement of CRD IV directives have underscored the importance of strict adherence to risk management procedures stipulated by European law, which impacts member states.

This integrated approach—whereby French legal reforms and scholarly discussion are framed within the broader context of European financial regulation—illustrates a concerted effort to fortify financial systems against future crises. The emphasis on robust, adaptable regulatory frameworks across Europe, informed by both legal and academic perspectives, underscores a commitment to maintaining financial stability and protecting the economic interests of the broader European community.

Leaders in financial institutions now face the challenge of navigating these complex and often stringent new regulations to ensure stability and restore public trust. The importance of regulatory responses tailored to address the financial system's vulnerabilities is regularly exposed and increasing during crises[7].

the European Central Bank (ECB), acting as the supervisory authority under the Single Supervisory Mechanism (SSM), imposed significant requirements to adjust its capital structure and liquidity management practices to align with CRD IV standards. The case exemplifies how supervisory actions, rather than traditional court cases, play a crucial role in enforcing regulatory standards like those outlined in CRD IV.

Collectively, a national proactive regulatory approach, which closely mirrors broader European Union efforts, may become a significant case study in understanding the dynamics of financial regulation in a post-crisis Europe. This convergence aims to enhance the financial system's resilience, promote investor confidence, and ensure that financial institutions across Europe operate under a stringent and harmonized regulatory framework.

However, the increasing burden of regulatory costs is escalating, putting an extreme upward pressure on operating costs in addition to the emerging technological challenges.

2.2. Technological Advancements

From risk management in retail banking to investment banking, digitalization and artificial intelligence have a transformative effect on the finance industry. But this change – both in financial services and regulation – is announcing a new era of more efficient and fast services despite its complexities.

The impact of technological advancements on ethical considerations has prompted experts to delve into the challenges and opportunities presented by digitalization, fintech, and blockchain technologies, as highlighted in recent publications[8]examines the ethical dilemmas posed by algorithmic decision-making and the need for adaptive regulatory frameworks. Similarly, "Blockchain and the Law[9]," explores the ethical implications of blockchain technology, particularly in terms of transparency, privacy, and regulatory compliance. These publications underscore the necessity for a nuanced regulatory approach that addresses the ethical complexities arising from these technological innovations.

In fact, innovations such as blockchain, artificial intelligence, and data analytics are transforming the financial industry with increased efficiency and new business models but also pose unique regulatory challenges. How to Regulate and to what extend regulating. It also unveils the complexity of the market competition. Binance case is the ideal example underlying that the technology progress remains a risk. Ethical leadership in this context involves ensuring that technology adoption does not outpace the institution's ability to manage risks ethically and comply with regulatory expectations. Technological innovation necessitates changes in regulatory approaches to ensure market stability and consumer protection[10].

Also innovations such as blockchain, artificial intelligence (AI) offer paths to increased operational efficiency and the creation of innovative business models, these technologies introduce a spectrum of regulatory challenges that necessitate astute oversight. French legal scholars. Thierry Bonneau, for example, emphasizes the importance of updating regulatory frameworks to keep pace with technological advancements to ensure market stability.

The trajectory towards a fully algorithmic finance industry, where multiple operations like trading, valuation and textual analysis will become automated and highly efficient, appears unstoppable. This raises pressing questions about the future orientation of financial regulations and leadership role to set the appropriate level of control and ethical conduct.

The application of blockchain in financial transactions and record-keeping introduces questions about security, data integrity, and privacy that are yet to be fully addressed by existing financial regulations. In the context of AI, issues arise around algorithmic transparency, decision-making accountability, and the prevention of bias, which can have significant implications for both consumer rights and the systemic risk profile of financial institutions. Data analytics, while beneficial for risk assessment and management, raises concerns about data protection and the ethical use of consumer information.

For example, machine learning algorithms can assist in identifying irregularities or discrepancies in financial transactions. These could be indicative of non-compliance, fraud or other illicit activities[11].

Professor Bonneau argues that the rapid adoption of these technologies could outstrip current regulatory frameworks unless these frameworks are adapted promptly[12]. He suggests that ethical leadership within financial institutions should play a proactive role in shaping the development of these technologies. This involves engaging with regulators to ensure that technology adoption is balanced with comprehensive risk management strategies that are ethical and compliant with existing and forthcoming regulations.

Further contributing to the discourse, Professor Marie-Anne Frison-Roche, specializing in regulatory and compliance issues at Sciences Po, has advocated for a regulatory environment that encourages innovation while enforcing strict adherence to ethical standards and consumer protection. In her works, she highlights the dual role of regulators in promoting innovation and safeguarding the public interest. Frison-Roche points out the necessity for "smart regulation" that is both flexible enough to adapt to new technologies and robust enough to prevent financial abuses and protect stakeholders[13].

These perspectives underscore a broader consensus among French legal academics that while technological innovations offer substantial benefits to the financial sector, they also require an evolved regulatory approach. This approach should not only address the risks associated with these technologies but also ensure that their deployment aligns with overarching ethical standards and public policy objectives. Thus, the challenge for ethical leadership in financial institutions is to navigate these innovations not just from a technological standpoint but also from a regulatory and ethical perspective, ensuring that advancements enhance rather than compromise the stability and integrity of the financial system.

2.3. Societal Expectations

There is a growing demand from consumers, investors, and regulators for greater transparency and accountability from financial institutions. This shift is reflected in the strengthening of regulations around consumer protection, anti-money laundering (AML), and corporate governance. Ethical leaders must ensure their organizations not only meet these legal requirements but also engage with stakeholders in a transparent and responsible manner.

The evolution of regulatory frameworks in Europe, particularly with the implementation of the General Data Protection Regulation (GDPR), reflects an increased legislative focus on transparency and accountability[14] and studies examined how these regulations not only mandate stricter compliance but also drive institutions towards greater transparency in their data processing and operational practices, thereby enhancing the protection of individual rights and fostering greater public trust.

A similar trend is observed in the evolving requirements for Environmental, Social, and Governance (ESG) reporting, as outlined in the Non-Financial

Reporting Directive (NFRD) and the Corporate Sustainability Reporting Directive (CSRD). These transparency requirements are designed to protect investors by providing them with reliable, comparable information on the sustainability practices of companies. This regulatory push towards greater transparency not only strengthens investor protection but also enhances the overall integrity of financial markets by holding corporations accountable for their environmental and social impacts.

On the same trends, more on the social perspective, several European Union texts on financial matters have required Member States to put in place specific systems for the protection of persons reporting breaches. In addition, the EU Directive 2019/1937 on the protection of persons who report breaches of EU law has set up general provisions to protect whistleblowers, imposing on companies with fifty or more employees the requirement to implement a whistleblowing procedure as well as a requirement on member states to put in place external reporting channels to public authorities. French law also has general provisions regarding whistleblowers included in the so-called Sapin II Law of 9 December 2016 as amended (the "General Regime"), as well as specific provisions applicable to the financial sector included in the French Monetary and Financial Code (the "Specific Regime"), both recently amended by the Law no. 2022-401 of 21 March 2022 in order to implement the EU Directive 2019/1937 aimed at reinforcing the whistleblowers' protection, the so-called "Waserman Law". The financial industry adopted the whistblowing regime long time ago, most of the famous cases did not report ethical misconduct from its social aspect but definitely serious breaches have been brought to light such as Danske case; a $230 billion money laundering scheme —that moved rubles out of Russia, converted them to dollars at the Estonian branch of Danske Bank, and then moved the dollars to New York with the assistance of three correspondent banks.

The ethical tone set by an organization's leadership indeed plays a crucial role in shaping its culture and operational integrity. This principle is particularly evident in the context of whistleblowing rules in Europe, which have been strengthened significantly by the EU Whistleblower Protection Directive that came into effect in December 2019. This directive mandates that all EU member states must provide comprehensive legal protections for whistleblowers, creating a more uniform framework across Europe. Here's how leadership's ethical tone aligns with these rules to foster an environment of integrity and accountability:

By encouraging a profession to be organized in open communication and enabling sound escalation mechanisms in the financial industry[15], Leaders who establish a strong ethical tone make it clear that honesty and transparency are valued within the organization. This approach is crucial in the context of whistleblowing because it encourages employees to speak up about unethical practices without fear of retaliation. When leaders openly support whistleblowing, they signal that the organization prioritizes ethical behavior over concealing misconduct. This can lead to more proactive identification and resolution of issues that could otherwise escalate into serious legal or reputational risks.

Moreover, effective leadership involves the development and implementation of clear policies that support whistleblowing. These policies should not only comply with the EU Whistleblower Protection Directive but should also be tailored to the specific needs and risks of the organization. Leaders setting an ethical tone will ensure these policies are well communicated and accessible to all employees, reinforcing the organization's commitment to ethical practices and legal compliance.

One clearly defined, a policy cannot live without embedment, reason why Leadership influences culture by ensuring that all members of the organization understand their rights and responsibilities regarding whistleblowing. This includes providing training on how to recognize unethical behavior and how to report it. Furthermore, resources should be available to support employees throughout the whistleblowing process. This training and resource provision reflect the organization's commitment to uphold ethical standards and protect those who expose wrongdoing.

A key aspect of the EU directive is the protection of whistleblowers from retaliation. Leaders who set a strong ethical tone will go beyond mere compliance by actively promoting and facilitating a safe mechanism for anonymous reporting. By doing so, they protect individuals who might otherwise be hesitant to come forward. Ensuring these protections are not only in place but also actively endorsed by top management is crucial for maintaining trust and integrity within the organization.

When whistleblowing leads to the exposure of misconduct, the response by leadership is telling of the organization's true ethical stance. Leaders who act swiftly and decisively in addressing the issues reported, applying appropriate sanctions and remedial actions, reinforce a culture of accountability. Conversely, a lackadaisical or defensive response can undermine the ethical tone, leading to a culture of skepticism and fear.

Entities also need to clearly state what can be reported - it is important to stress that it is not a channel for complaints. Instead, the purpose is to detect or ideally prevent crimes and persons can report any violation or omission which is illegal. So, opposed to existing regulations, reporting is not limited to money laundering or internal governance, although this is clearly included. Now, reports can for instance contain information about theft, harassment, bodily harm and all types of fraud or financial crime.

Finally, ethical leadership in the context of whistleblowing rules means committing to continuous improvement. This involves regularly reviewing and updating whistleblowing policies and practices to ensure they remain effective and reflect the latest legal requirements and best practices. Leaders should actively seek feedback on the effectiveness of these measures and be willing to make changes to enhance protections and procedures.

In sum, the ethical tone set by leadership is instrumental in cultivating a culture that embraces transparency, protects whistleblowers, and adheres to high standards of integrity and accountability. This culture is not only vital for compliance with European whistleblowing regulations but also for fostering an environment where ethical behavior is the norm, and misconduct can be addressed openly and effectively.

Out of EU, similar trends have taken a strong commitment towards ethics. In May 2023, the FCA published a report setting out the findings of a qualitative assessment of its own handling of whistleblowers who directly reported to the FCA, which was explored in a briefing note of 15 May 2023. The FCA's findings were concerning and reflected deficiencies in the current processes and practices related to whistleblower management in UK Financial Industry. This admission of shortcomings could imply that the mechanisms for protecting and supporting whistleblowers may be inadequate or ineffective, potentially undermining the confidence of individuals who might consider reporting misconduct. The acknowledgment of these issues might lead to legal and regulatory implications, including the need for reform to ensure that whistleblower protections are strengthened and that the regulatory authorities frame the adequate obligations to effectively address and act on the information provided by whistleblowers.

3. Ethical Leadership in Practice

The regulatory landscape is not the only rationale of how ethical leadership is operationalized within financial institutions amidst these regulatory changes. For financial institutions, effective leadership translates into setting a clear vision for growth, fostering innovation, and steering the organization through market turbulence.

However, it remains crucial that new regulatory requirements examine how leaders can foster a culture of integrity and transparency, particularly when embracing regulatory changes. One can discuss the role of leadership in not just adhering to regulations but also in exceeding them to build trust and long-term stability.

As the financial industry plays a pivotal role in global economic systems, the need for stringent ethical standards becomes increasingly apparent[16]. This encompasses various dimensions of ethical considerations, ranging from corporate governance and risk management to customer relations and social responsibility.

Furthermore, the governance framework of any regulated financial institution must evaluate the role of its leadership and organizational culture in setting the tone from the top (2.1) and fostering ethical behavior within the structure specifically during crisis[17]. It examines case studies of ethical lapses and their repercussions, shedding light on the importance of accountability and transparency in maintaining public trust and sanctioning breaches (2.2). The ethical implications of financial decision-making spreads at all levels considering issues such as fair lending practices, responsible investing, and the ethical dimensions of risk assessment. Therefore, the corporate governance has the obligation to scrutinize the role of financial education in promoting ethical awareness among stakeholders and addresses the ethical considerations associated with emerging financial products and services through an accountability mechanism (2.3). This review synthesizes key insights into the ethical practices within banking and finance, offering a holistic perspective on the challenges and opportunities faced by the industry. By understanding and addressing ethical concerns, financial institutions can contribute to the development of a sustainable and responsible financial ecosystem that benefits both the industry and society at large.

3.1. Setting the Tone from the Top

The ethical tone set by an organization's leadership is crucial in shaping its overall culture and operational integrity. Leaders must demonstrate a commitment to compliance at the higher level of the Governance body and through their actions and decisions, creating a culture of integrity that permeates all levels of the organization[18].

This covers strategies for implementing robust ethical frameworks that align with regulatory requirements, including the development of internal controls and the promotion of ethical behavior at all levels. The adoption of a Code of conduct may seem as a must but the words must be preceded by cultural believe embedded into the way regulations are designed, implemented and regularly assessed.

A sound ethical framework is something which can lay the foundations for, and strengthen, both the culture and conduct of an organisation. Meanwhile, whether an institution operates in accordance with its core values and principles needs to be examined by reference to its culture and conduct on a day-to-day basis. Issues of ethics, culture and conduct are, accordingly, intertwined.

The revised "Decree of 3 November 2014" concerning banking control in France, which provides a detailed framework for internal control systems within banking institutions, can be directly linked to the concept of "Setting the Tone from the Top" in terms of ethical leadership. This Decree emphasizes the importance of governance and internal controls, which are key elements where leadership can demonstrate their commitment to ethical practices. Here's how this link can be established:

The Decree published ten years ago and revised in 2021 requires that banks establish rigorous internal control mechanisms. This includes risk evaluation, compliance checks, and audit functions that align with regulatory standards. Leadership's role in this context is critical—they must ensure these controls are not only in place but are also part of the bank's daily operations and long-term strategy. By actively supporting these processes, leaders set an ethical tone that underscores the importance of compliance and risk management throughout the institution.

Leadership and Compliance Culture set the foundation of one of the key provisions of the Decree is the requirement for banks to have clear organizational structures with well-defined, transparent responsibilities. Leaders must demonstrate ethical governance by establishing a compliance culture that values transparency and accountability. This means making decisive actions and policies public and understandable to all employees, ensuring that the ethical standards are communicated clearly and are reflected in every decision made by the top executives.

The Decree supports the idea that internal controls should not just function as compliance checks but should actively promote ethical behavior across all levels. Leaders are responsible for embedding ethical considerations into the fabric of the organization. This includes training programs that educate and encourage employees to act ethically, systems that reward ethical behavior, and mechanisms that allow for the safe reporting of unethical activities. Leaders must champion these initiatives to foster an environment where ethics guide decision-making processes.

According to the Decree, the effectiveness of internal controls must be regularly assessed and adjusted as necessary. This dynamic approach to compliance and ethics management reflects the leadership's commitment to continuous improvement. By regularly reviewing and refining the control processes, leaders can adapt to new challenges and ensure that the organization remains on the cutting edge of ethical banking practices.

Finally, the Decree underscores the necessity for senior management to lead by example. The ethical tone set at the top has a trickle-down effect on all employees. If leaders are visibly committed to upholding and enhancing internal controls and ethical standards, it is more likely that employees will also adhere to these standards. The actions and behavior of senior leaders serve as a model for the rest of the organization, illustrating the practical application of the ethical frameworks laid out by a risk appetite that is now a must in every Financial Institutions with in more and more instance zero risk appetite to regulatory or unethical misconduct.

Linking the provisions of the "Decree of 3 novembre 2014 on Banking Control" to the concept of setting the ethical tone from the top illustrates how regulatory frameworks and leadership ethics are intertwined. Effective leadership involves more than compliance; it requires a commitment to creating a culture of integrity that influences every aspect of the organization's operations. This has taken more than decades to come into concrete actions and the increasing amount of regulatory fines has helped paving the way; the most illustrative example is the amount of fines in the Libor scandal.

3.2. Handling of Ethical Breaches

Effective leadership involves not only preventing ethical breaches but also managing them decisively when they occur. This includes establishing clear protocols for investigation and sanctions of unethical behaviors, ensuring that these measures are applied consistently and transparently.

A sound ethical framework is something which can lay the foundations for, and strengthen, both the culture and conduct of an organisation. Meanwhile, whether an institution operates in accordance with its core values and principles needs to be examined by reference to its culture and conduct on a day-to-day basis.

By analogy to the Banking industry, The French Duty of Care, introduced in 2017, provides an excellent framework for understanding how legal mechanisms can enhance effective leadership within companies, especially in preventing and managing ethical breaches. This law is specifically designed to ensure that large corporations monitor and prevent human rights abuses and environmental damage throughout their supply chains, which includes both direct operations and the operations of subcontractors and suppliers. Here's how this law can help leaders in effectively managing ethical standards:

The Duty of Care Law requires large companies Establishing Clear Protocols for Care: They must create, publish, and implement a Vigilance plan. This plan must outline the measures the company will take to identify risks and prevent severe impacts on human rights and fundamental freedoms, human health and safety, and the environment resulting from the company's activities and those of the companies it controls, directly or indirectly. For leadership, this means establishing clear and actionable protocols for monitoring these risks across all operations. These protocols help in setting a concrete framework within which potential ethical breaches can be identified and addressed promptly.

Effective leadership under the Duty of Care Law involves conducting regular and systematic risk assessments to identify areas where the company's activities may lead to ethical breaches or violations. These assessments are crucial in anticipating potential issues before they arise and setting in place preemptive measures to avoid such outcomes. By institutionalizing this approach, leaders ensure that the company not only reacts to problems but actively works to prevent them.

A key component of the law is the requirement for transparency. Companies must publicly report on their Care measures, which include the results of their risk assessments and the actions taken as part of their Care plan. This requirement pushes leaders to maintain high standards of accountability, ensuring that all actions are documented and made available for scrutiny by stakeholders, including shareholders, customers, and regulatory bodies. Transparency in these processes also builds trust and reinforces the company's commitment to ethical practices.

The law also emphasizes the importance of stakeholder engagement in developing and implementing the Vigilance plan. Effective leadership, in this context, means actively involving various stakeholders, including NGOs, unions, and local communities, in the Care processes. This involvement can provide diverse perspectives and expertise, which enhance the effectiveness of the measures implemented and ensure broader oversight and accountability.

When breaches occur, the Duty of Care Law mandates that companies must not only address these breaches effectively but also take steps to remediate any harm caused. For leaders, this means having in place robust mechanisms for dealing with violations, which include as mentioned above clear procedures for investigation, immediate response actions, and, critically, measures for rectifying the damage done. Ensuring these measures are applied consistently and transparently is vital for upholding the law and maintaining ethical standards.

In summary, the Duty of Care Law provides a structured and legally backed approach to enhancing ethical leadership within companies. By mandating systematic prevention, continuous monitoring, transparent reporting, and active stakeholder engagement, the law not only guides leaders in managing ethical risks effectively but also sets a standard for corporate responsibility that can inspire similar regulations globally.

3.3. Accountability Mechanisms

Accountability mechanisms are essential for enforcing ethical standards within an institution. These may include regular audits, compliance training programs, and the establishment of an independent ethics committee to oversee the institution's ethical practices. Gorton analyzes how financial crises reveal critical weaknesses in financial regulatory practices, urging for reforms to improve system resilience[19].

In the context of ethics, the Kreps (1990) approach would say that it is virtually impossible (or exorbitantly costly) to write down every future contingency in which an employee could choose between an ethical decision and a multitude of possible unethical decisions involving varying degrees of transgression the bank behaves in a manner that complies not only with the law but also with the spirit of regulation. Indeed, the trust game sets the behavioral measure of choice in social science investigations of trust. This measure is often used uncritically to compare levels of trust across people and cultures even though those levels may be affected by people's attitudes to risk.

Nonetheless, the substantial fines paid by banks since the financial crisis paint a somewhat troublesome picture about ethics in banking and risk aversion.

Financial services regulators view ESG as a priority, conscious that climate change and ESG factors can threaten financial stability via physical and transition risks. Globally, the regulatory approach to ESG appears to be fairly fragmented which presents a particular problem for those financial services firms operating across borders. Regulatory reform is on the horizon in certain jurisdictions with new rules on sustainable disclosures expected[20].

4. Conclusion

The increasing complexity and volume of ESG related legal and regulatory change presents a compliance challenge and the risk of potential enforcement action from regulators.

The need for improved corporate governance structures within financial institutions is critical in ensuring accountability and facilitating transparency. For instance, Professor Klaus J. Hopt, has extensively discussed the need for boards of directors to play a more active role in overseeing management and ensuring compliance with ethical standards and regulations. His works often cite the need for directors to have access to information and the necessary tools to challenge and oversee management effectively. This is more and more considered nowadays and has been reflected in multiple regulatory changes in the recent years specifically where in many jurisdiction and string regulated markets some Topics must directly sit with the Board such as Compliance matters or more specifically Financial Crime issues.

Could a proposal of new architecture of regulatory supervision of Banks in western Europe create synergies in the EU and generate additional clarity to the system, perhaps the new Public Prosecution Office[21] along with the new AML package may bring a more centric, standardized, and harmonized approach to the Financial Industry.

Notes

1 "The Future of Central Banking under Post-crisis Mandates" in Lucerne, Switzerland on 24-25, June 2010.

2 Chifflot, Martine. « Éthique et droit », *L'Enseignement philosophique*, vol. 64a, no. 4, 2014, pp. 4-18.

3 Régulation et crises du capitalisme, L'expérience des États-Unis - Michel Aglietta Calmann-Lévy, 1982.

4 Michel Aguilietta Regulation and Crises: A New Comparative Political Economy

5 Paul Jorion, le Capitalisme à l'agonie, Fayard. 2011.

6 Padoa-Schioppa, Tommaso. Regulating Finance: Balancing Freedom and Risk. OUP Oxford, 2004.

7 Charles Goodhart, The Regulatory Response to the Financial Crisis.

8 Buckley RP, Arner DW, Zetzsche DA. Digital Transformation of Finance and Regulation. In: FinTech: Finance, Technology and Regulation. Cambridge University Press.

9 De Filippi, P., & Wright, A. (2018). Blockchain and the Law: The Rule of Code. Harvard University Press.

10 AWREY, Dan. Complexity, innovation, and the regulation of modern financial markets. Harv. Bus. L. Rev., 2012, vol. 2, p. 235.

11 Banks and FINANCIAL MARKETS, BARRY QUINN, FEARGHAL KEARNEY, ABHISHEK PRAMANICK - How will artificial intelligence affect financial regulation? 2023.

12 Thierry Bonneau, Innovation and Development in Business Law Contributions to the 10th International Conference Perspectives of Business Law in the Third Millennium.

13 The contribution of Compliance Law to the Governance of Internet ", report of M.A. Frison-Roche (July 2019).

14 Herke Kranenborg, O. Lynskey, *The Foundations of EU Data Protection Law, International Data Privacy Law*, Volume 6, Issue 4, November 2016, Pages 324–326.

15 McGrath, J. and Walker, C. (2023), Regulating ethics in financial services: Engaging industry to achieve regulatory objectives. Regulation & Governance, 17: 791-809.

16 Adaga, Ejuma & Egieya, Zainab & Ewuga, Sarah & Abdul, Adekunle & Abrahams, Temitayo. (2024). A COMPREHENSIVE REVIEW OF ETHICAL PRACTICES IN BANKING AND FINANCE. Finance & Accounting Research Journal.

17 JEFFERS Esther; ABIDI Asma, « La gouvernance des banques à l'épreuve de la crise : comment concilier intérêt général et intérêts des parties prenantes ? », Revue d'économie financière, 2018 / 2 (N° 130), p.277-287.

18 Marie-Anne Frison-Roche, Pour une Europe de la compliance, Dalloz, May 2019 ; Le droit de la compliance au-delà du droit de la régulation, Recueil Dalloz 2018 p.1561; Droit de la concurrence et droit de la compliance, Revue Concurrences n° 4-2018, November 2018.

19 Gary B. Gordon, "Slapped by the Invisible Hand: The Panic of 2007" – Oxford University Press.

20 Sarra, Janis, 'Regulatory Oversight of Climate Governance of Companies and Institutional Investors', *From Ideas to Action: Governance Paths to Net Zero* (Oxford, 2020; online edn, Oxford Academic, 17 Dec. 2020).

21 Smith, D. (2024). Supervision & Regulation; Investigation & Prosecution. In: Money Laundering, Terrorist Financing and Virtual Assets. Contributions to Finance and Accounting. Springer, Cham.

Bibliography

Ethical Leadership in Financial Services" by David Beim

Finance Ethics: Critical Issues in Theory and Practice" edited by John R. Boatright

The Ethical Banker: Navigating Challenges in the Financial Sector" by Brian Griffiths

Banking and Regulation: Post-Crisis Challenges and Perspectives" by Rosa Lastra

Devine, Jeannette, "Exploring the Ethical Leadership of Bank Managers" (2019). *Walden Dissertations and Doctoral Studies*. 7377.

McGrath, J. and Walker, C. (2023), Regulating ethics in financial services: Engaging industry to achieve regulatory objectivees. Regulation & Governance, 17: 791-809

de Bruin, Boudewijn, 'Ethics Management in Banking and Finance', in Nicholas Morris, and David Vines (eds), *Capital Failure: Rebuilding Trust in Financial Services* (Oxford, 2014; online edn, Oxford Academic, 23 Oct. 2014).

. "The Gordon Gekko Effect: The Role of Culture in the Financial Industry." Economic Policy Review (Federal Reserve Bank of New York) 22 (1): 17–42. Lopez-Espinosa, G., S. Mayordomo,

Bruno B. Deffains, Thomas Perroud. La régulation. Le droit économique au 21e siècle, inPress. ffhal-02515216f

L. Boy, « La fonction de régulation de l'Autorité de régulation des télécommunications (réflexions contributives à la notion de régulation) », in Rapport intermédiaire au GIP « Droit et Justice » du Ministère de la justice, Juillet 1999 ;

L. Boy, « Réflexions sur « le droit de la régulation » (à propos du texte de M.-A. FrisonRoche) », Recueil Dalloz, 2001, Chron., p. 3031 ;

M.-A. Frison-Roche, « Le droit de la régulation », D. 2001, chron., p. 613 ;

M.-A. Frison-Roche, « Définition du droit de la régulation économique », D. 2004, p. 126 ;

G. Marcou, « La notion juridique de régulation », AJDA 2006 p. 347 suiv. ;

G. Marcou, « Régulation et service public – Les enseignements du droit comparé », in Droit de la régulation, service public et intégration régionale, tome 1, Comparaisons et commentaires, p. 60.

Danny Busch, 'A Bank's Duty of Care: Perspectives from European and Comparative Law – Part II', (2019), 30, European Business Law Review, Issue 3, pp. 367-415

La Banque: Comment Goldman Sachs dirige le monde" by Marc Roche (2021)

Le Capitalisme à l'agonie? by Jean-Michel Naulot (2022)

Managing a corporate ethics program: development, risk management and evaluation

Stanisław Zygmunt Strejmer

1. Introduction – ethics management in modern business

Ethics management is an essential part of the organization, and its importance is bound to exponentially grow within the following years, as both the regulatory environment (e.g., ESG legislation or the EU proposal for an anti-corruption directive) and the stakeholders' focus become more integrity-centered, shifting towards ethical aspects of corporate governance[1].

Although many corporations recognize the importance of integrity, their understanding of the issue is often intuitive. This intuitiveness is reflected in the approach to ethics management, which often lacks constancy, applied to other management (sub)systems. This results in significant limitations in ethical risk identification, risk management and integrity-based decision making.

The purpose of the article is to present certain aspects of ethics program management, utilizing both theory and practice as basis for introduced considerations. The article focuses on the most elusive aspects of corporate ethics – assessing integrity risks and evaluating the effectiveness of corporate endeavors, undertaken to strengthen company's value-oriented processes.

1.1 Corporate ethics program – rationale and goals

An ethics program is a structured element of the broader management system, which is aimed at assuring, that the organization acts with integrity and achieves its ethical objectives. It consists of 'tangible and explicit measures and instruments organizations adopt to manage ethics' (Kaptein 2014, p. 420).

The ethics program is sometimes considered a formal element of the organizational ethical context, the other, informal one, comprising the ethical climate and culture (Huhtala et al., 2022; Roy et al., 2024)[2]. Considering, that both aspects heavily overlap, this formal character of an ethics program must be considered broadly, including structured, 'systemic' elements and practices, creating the organization's 'ethical infrastructure' (Tenbrunsel et al., 2003).

The main purpose of an ethics program is to:

- create a coherent and comprehensible framework for ethical behavior;
- reasonably reduce the likelihood of unethical behavior by internalizing and reinforcing ethics, trust and transparency;
- establish, protect, and improve the company's reputation as an ethical enterprise;
- influence and improve the ethical culture, climate and overall performance of the organization (Roy et al. 2024).

1.2 Integrity vs. (?) Compliance

One of often discussed topics is the relation between integrity and compliance and whether an ethics program should be considered an element of the compliance management system (CMS). The basic standard relating to CMS, ISO 37301:2021, while underlining the importance of integrity in compliance management, does not resolve the abovementioned issue definitively.

The author believes that ethics could be considered a part of a broader compliance framework, and obligations based on values and standards of conduct, can be treated as compliance obligations. There are at least three arguments which justify such interpretation:

- ISO 37301:2021 confirms that obligations related to values constitute basic means towards safeguarding compliance and constitute a significant element of the organization's CMS;
- the abovementioned obligations are consistent with the standard's definition of requirement, as a need or expectation that is stated (e.g., Code of conduct), obligatory (e.g., laws against corruption) or generally implied (e.g., external stakeholders' expectations to conduct business ethically, or internal interested parties' expectation for an ethical workplace[3]);
- at least some of the obligations related to company values and standard practices fulfill the examples of requirements provided in Annex A of the standard, as they may arise from law and regulations (e.g. preventing

employee harassment), organizational requirements (policies and procedures) or relevant organizational and industry standards.

This leads to a conclusion, that adopting and improving an ethics program should be integrated with the CMS, and the organization may successfully utilize strategies and elements used in compliance management.

However, an effective ethics program cannot rely solely on a compliance-based approach and requires adopting a strategy and measures to improve the organization's overall ethical culture.

The presented considerations position the ethics program as either an element of the CMS or a standalone management (sub)system. For this reason, Maesschalk et al. (2024) have rightly proposed to use the term 'Integrity Management System'[4].

1.3 Scope of the ethics program

The argument for considering the ethics program a part of a CMS or a standalone management (sub)system is further reinforced when considering typical elements of a well-developed program.

- **Engagement and commitment in 'practicing' integrity on all levels of organization** – the top management should provide resources, set goals for the ethics program and act as an example for the organization ('tone at the top'[5]). The middle management oversees ethical conduct, implements the values into practice and management systems, and sets an example for their subordinates ('tone at the middle'). And finally, the company's values and integrity-related objectives and risks are considered in the decision-making process, project planning, by everyone and at their every step ('integrity at the core').
- **Established and documented values and integrity-related expectations** – to foster ethical culture and expect the interested parties to abide by the organization's values, the company should determine, document, and clearly communicate these values, including their daily-life application. Also, other elements of the ethics program should be documented for the purpose of communication, risk management and evaluation[6].

- **Obligations and appointing an ethics function** – the organization should clearly define the obligations related to the ethics program. Also, it is advised to appoint an ethics office(r) responsible for developing and communicating the ethics program and advising the company on matters related to business ethics[7]. The function, similar to the compliance function, should have appropriate knowledge, experience, authority and standing within the company structure.
- **Ethics risk management** – to maintain compliance with values and standards, the organization should adopt a risk management system, including risk assessment and planning (see section 3).
- **Training and communication** – the company should provide a comprehensive training system, which allows all levels of organization to develop a deepened understanding of the company's ethics program and its practical application. Both values and relevant documented information should be clearly communicated to interested parties. This includes also demonstrating good practices and engaging in promoting ethical behavior outside the organization.
- **Whistleblowing systems, internal investigations, and whistleblower protection** – the organization should encourage and facilitate providing information on actual/potential unethical conduct and risks, as well as protect the whistleblowers.
- **Assessment, assurance, and improvement** – the established ethics program requires constant assessment to determine, whether its goals are met, and identify risks/opportunities (see section 4).
- **Accountability policies, including non-discriminatory enforcement** – unethical behavior should be met with adequate response, regardless of the perpetrator's position, the value generated by the individual and other factors that are irrelevant to the misconduct. Also, proper incentives for ethical behavior should be established and applied.

Like other management systems, the practical application of the abovementioned elements should be adjusted to the company's strategy, goals, available resources, and other relevant factors.

The abovementioned elements bear strong resemblance to other management systems, including CMS, responding to the High-Level Structure, adopted by the International Organization for Standardization. This further reinforces the position, that the ethics program can be considered either a part of a broader (e.g., compliance) management system or a standalone management (sub)system.

2. Developing an ethics program

As a general, practical observation, it is possible to indicate the following steps of ethics program development and organizations' maturity in its approach towards integrity:

- the organization demonstrates no interest in business ethics;
- the ethics program, values and principles are embodied in the owner and its position towards particular aspect of the enterprise, but mostly on an intuitive level. The values and standards of conduct are applied without any formal framework, and often without consistency;
- the organization develops a basic understanding of the necessity to manage ethics, which results in drafting an ethics code or other relevant, documented framework. The framework, however, is often not fully applied in practice and lacks the necessary uniformity (for example, highly achieving individuals may avoid punishment in case of misconduct);
- the organization begins to implement other elements of ethics management, including training, specifying expected behaviors and attitudes, adopting whistleblowing procedures, and conducting internal investigations;
- the organization develops and manages a complex ethics program, based on predetermined values, goals, strategy, metrics, and ethics risk management. The ethics program is constantly evaluated and improved.

The presented breakdown is a basic description of the ethics program maturity levels, though it will be usually reflected in more complex depictions (see, for example, Ethics and Compliance Initiative, 2018).

Planning and adopting an ethics program should consist of:

- defining the organization's goals related to integrity;
- defining the internal and external context of the organization, in particular regarding ethical (compliance) obligations, risks, industry practices;

- appointing a dedicated function and providing adequate resources for the ethics program;
- establishing an ethics risk management and ethics program assessment framework;
- documenting and communicating the abovementioned elements;
- conducting training and further communication
- introducing incentive policies[8].

When implementing the abovementioned strategy, I advise to take into consideration the following:

- when defining the company's goals and values and documenting them, it is important to include, and, more importantly, actively engage, all the relevant stakeholders. This may be conducted by inviting different stakeholders to participate in discussion meetings, consulting documents, decision-making;
- training and communication related to the ethics program should be designed as an ongoing process, utilizing every means that are at the organization's disposal. The training should be function-specific and should differ between managers, 'regular' employees, high-risk areas, etc.

After the ethics program has been established it is important to monitor ethical risks and assess the program's effectiveness, constantly improving it, according, for example, to the Deming cycle (Maesschalk et al., 2024).

3. Ethical risk management

ethics risk is the effect of uncertainty on the organization's integrity objectives (see 1.1.).

Ethics risk management can be (and often, at least in some capacity, is) included in the compliance risk management processes or at least constitute a possibly formalized risk management framework[9].

However, even a superficial examination of the issue shows that ethical risk relates to highly diversified types of misconduct and may, at least partly, diverge from what is typically considered a compliance risk. Not all of behaviors that would amount to an ethical risk, constitute a violation of law and would be subject to legal sanctions, which is often the focus of CMS. This diversity influences the methods of managing specific integrity risk scenarios.

Therefore, in practice, a typical compliance risk assessment (and, further – risk management) within a company may not fully include integrity-specific risk scenarios and risk treatment measures (particularly if they are not reflected in the regulatory context).

That does not, of course, mean that ethical risk is not usually somehow managed in an organization. Even risk control measures utilized through other segments of the broader management system (e.g., CMS) lead often to successful deterrence of misconduct. However, applying these measures may usually lack adequate awareness, constancy, and appropriate risk treatment planning.

3.1 Ethical risk

Defining what constitutes an ethical risk (or particularly – unethical behavior that amounts to such risk) is difficult due to a number of reasons.

In public discourse the understanding of ethical risks tends to be based on a general, intuitive comprehension of the issue. We 'simply' assume, that at least some of the expected attitudes are shared within our social frame of reference, and that deviation from them will be adequately punished.

Secondly, ascertaining, whether a behavior is considered unethical or not, relies often heavily on the regulatory context. Within different legal systems, some types of misconduct may constitute a violation of law, or not. Some, on the other hand, may be only 'included' in the legal system in a limited scope (e.g., conflict of interest).

Regardless of these difficulties, for the purpose of corporate risk management, considering integrity risk management requires at least a basic recognition of potential behaviors, which can be regarded integrity violations and pose an ethical risk.

3.1.1 Current research

Researchers have identified and proposed different approaches towards distinguishing what constitutes an ethical risk for the purpose of corporate risk management.

D. Collins and P. Kanashiro (2022) presented an extensive overview of ethical risks, based on research conducted by various organizations. The authors indicate, for example:

· misuse of company time
· abusive behavior
· employee theft
· lying to employees
· violating company internet policies
· conflict of interest
· violations of health and/or safety regulations
· corruption
· discrimination
· sexual harassment

Huberts and Lasthuizen (2019, pp. 57-58) have even proposed a typology of integrity violations, which includes:

· bribery
· favoritism
· fraud and theft of resources
· conflict of interest through 'gifts'
· conflict of interest through 'sideline activities'
· improper use of authority
· misuse and manipulation of information
· indecent treatment of colleagues (…) or customers
· waste and abuse of organizational resources
· misconduct in private time

It is clear, that the list of risks scenario examples constitutes an amalgamation of vastly diverse types of integrity violations, of which:

· some are reflected in the current regulatory (legal) context, whilst other are not;

- some are easier to define and specify by indicating examples of such unethical behavior (e.g., employee theft), whilst other may prove difficult to delimit (e.g., misuse of company time);
- for some types of risks the methods of prevention and treatment will significantly differ, than those usually applied to particular compliance risks (e.g. a different approach is required when analyzing employee theft, than abusive behavior).

Also, management of these risks, based on their diversity, will usually be dispersed (or rather – shared) within an organization, as it involves different topics, such as corruption (which is usually dealt with by a compliance department or a dedicated anti-corruption function), harassment (which is usually administered by HR) or fraud (which is often handled cross-functionally).

3.1.2 Further considerations

The diversity and reliance on regulatory and social context lead to difficulty in specifying ethical risk, including risk scenarios. There is, however, a more general observation to be made, which leads to outlining at least three types of ethical risks.

First group of ethics risks refers to a group of behaviors that are explicitly included in the regulatory context and constitute specific, usually well recognized compliance risks (e.g., corruption, discrimination). This type of risk is often encompassed in management systems, including determining particular risk scenarios. What characterizes this group (from the risk management perspective) is that risk scenarios, consequences and methods of deterrence are generally known, as they have been considered an element of the compliance risk management framework.

The second group consists of ethics risks related to obligations which are included in the regulatory context, though are not explicitly stated, as they arise from a regulatory reference to a more general clause, referencing certain social systems, such as the 'principles of community coexistence' included in the Polish Labour Code (Jamroży, 2019). What characterizes this group is that, regardless of their legal significance, they are usually considered in risk management only as long as they can be related to another, more specific type of obligation (one from the first group, described above). For example, infringement of the abovementioned 'principles of community co-existence' would be taken into consideration usually when it is connected to another, 'obvious' violation of employee rights (e.g., harassment). This may lead to these risks being omitted.

The third and last type of ethics risks relates to sets of behaviors and attitudes which are considered unethical but lack 'legal reinforcement'. What characterizes this group of ethics risks is that:

- they are often based on mostly intuitive understanding and the precise definition of what they constitute may be quite elusive;
- these types of risks usually have the potential to evolve into the abovementioned categories (for example, a conflict of interest if not properly managed, may lead to corruption);
- the consequences of materialization are vaguer that the abovementioned groups, and usually strike the organizational culture (the 'internal context') or company reputation, rather than other, more 'tangible' aspects of the enterprise. This in turn leads to difficulty in a precise assessment of the consequences of such misconduct and planning treatment measures.

The difficulties are one of the reasons, why it is advised to adopt codes of conduct and/or employee handbooks, which specify certain expected attitudes and undesired behaviors. It allows this type of integrity risk to resemble the first or second category (depending on the way they are described). However, considering these risks only as a violation of a code of conduct would be a significant oversimplification on the side of the organization.

As mentioned before, risk typology may differ based on the regulatory context, even within a particular legal system. A notable example is the conflict of interest. In Polish law there is no general, legal definition of conflict of interest, nor the legal regulations define any general approach towards the issue. The duty to responsibly manage/avoid conflict of interest is included only in specific regulations (e.g., ones regarding attorneys-at-law, corporate management, public servants). Therefore, there are no specific requirements, which would be directed at all companies and interested parties. This, in turn, means, that the same type of unethical behavior (finding oneself, or rather acting while, in conflict) will require different approach, based on the individual and organization affected by this conflict. At the same time, there is no doubt, that conflict of interest should be effectively managed and included in the ethics/compliance risk framework.

3.2 Ethical risk management – general remarks

For effective ethics program management, all the identified integrity violations should be included (at least in some capacity) in the ethical risk management process, regardless of their type and perceived severity.

Risk management, as always, will be influenced by the organization's risk appetite and available resources – both in terms of choosing, which risks to 'actively' treat, and what resources should be allocated to managing the identified risks, according to the risk-tailored resource allocation rule (U.S. Department of Justice, 2023).

It is important to note, however, that even integrity risks that at first seem to pose a lesser significance to the organization, may influence other, more severe ones. Consider a company-wide practice of gossip – at first it may seem a trivial matter, but, if not correctly managed, it can significantly hinder whistleblowing procedures, obstructing maintaining confidentiality and distorting internal investigations.

From a practical perspective, it may not always be necessary (or even possible) to manage certain integrity risks using a highly formalized risk management framework, but a thorough assessment of risks and appropriate treatment is necessary to mitigate its negative impact on the company's objectives[10].

3.3 Ethical risk assessment

A typical risk assessment comprises risk identification (recognizing and describing the risks / risk scenarios), analysis (i.e., determining the possible outcomes) and evaluation (i.e., comparing the results of various risk analyses with its risk criteria and then prioritizing particular risks).

As mentioned before, it is advised to identify a possibly broad scope of integrity risk types and scenarios. Risk identification requires a thorough understanding of risk context, and a careful consideration of events triggered by the risk, the potential causes, consequences, and impact (ISO 31022:2020)[11].

The analysis of integrity risks also must take into account their distinctiveness and may require consideration of specific outcomes of each risk (e.g., eroding organizational culture, hinderance to internal investigations and information safety, employee dissatisfaction and leaves). Of course, some potential outcomes will be shared between integrity risks and other types of risk (e.g., employees leaving, breach of confidentiality, distortion of business continuity).

Evaluation of ethics risk should result in prioritizing particular risks and developing a risk treatment plan, according, for example, to company stakeholders and their expectations, its values, objectives, strategy, and the risk profile of the organization (the maturity of its risk management system).

3.4 Ethics risk treatment and planning

When approaching identified integrity risks, not all the typically applied risk treatment strategies (retention, transfer, mitigation, and avoidance) may be adequate (Rotta, 2010).

Bearing in mind the potential significant impact of integrity risk (both legal, in case of the first two types of integrity risks, reputational and internal, for all types of risk), retention seems an unlikely form of treatment and is not advised.

Transferring the risk also does not usually constitute a viable strategy. As C. P. Rotta (2010, p. 67) indicates, 'transferring particularly delicate and fraud-prone processes does not offer any advantage'. Not only such transfer does not actually affect reputational risks (a misconduct would be treated as if committed by the outsourcing company itself) but also diminishes the organization's control over the risk.

Mitigation is a potentially viable strategy for integrity risk management (at least for some types of risk). Implementation of this treatment, however, would rely significantly on detective measures. These measures, though, may not be effective enough in case of fraudulent behavior. Also, the intention to mitigate the risk may not be sufficient in case of a sudden materialization of risk (Rotta, 2010)[12].

Having that in mind, in most cases avoidance will be the most viable risk treatment plan (Rotta, 2010). Implementing prevention measures to avoid the risk usually includes:

- proper screening (e.g., recruited or promoted employees, business partners);
- staff training – to provide proper knowledge on requirements, company values, culture, expected behaviors, as well as risk detection and whistle-blowing procedures);
- specifying the abovementioned values, expected attitudes and behaviors, for example by adopting a Code of conduct, rules for suppliers, standard operating practices etc.
- including particular requirements, attitudes, or issues in the assessment process.

As previously stated, this may not be applicable to all types of integrity risks. For example, in case of conflict of interest, avoidance is usually not considered a viable strategy. This is due to a number of reasons, e.g.:

- conflict of interest is a 'naturally occurring phenomenon' and its occurrence is near impossible to completely avoid;
- from a practical point of view, avoidance of risk in case of conflict of interest, may not necessarily be the best business strategy and applying mitigating measures is usually enough to reduce the risk level. In some instances, complete avoidance of conflict of interest may also lead to an increase of risk of diverse types of misconduct[13].

Therefore, in case of conflict of interest, avoidance is not a usually adopted strategy, and is replaced by its conflict management (mitigation), or, sometimes, even acceptance.

Awareness of viable strategies for integrity risk management heavily influences further planning. For example, if treatment of fraudulent behavior is prioritized (mostly because of identified, high probability of occurrence), then the organization would shift its focus and resources towards detective controls (e.g., additional IT measures, increasing compliance or other types of audits). If, on the other hand, the organization considers abusive behavior as a significant risk, the preventative measures would be focused on staff screening, training, organizational changes (e.g., strengthening the role of HR business partners).

From a practical perspective, ethics risk treatment requires implementing two important strategies.

Firstly, it requires a cross-functional approach and cooperation of different units within the organization. Secondly, to effectively implement these measures, the responsibility for particular risk treatment actions should be precisely assigned and enforced.

Risk treatment measures should be subject to further assessment and development, in accordance with established key risk indicators.

3.5 Ethics risk management – conclusion

Integrity risk management is a complex process, mostly because integrity risk types significantly vary, in terms of their source, potential severity and outcomes, as well as mitigation strategies.

Therefore, the process may often elude a particular risk management framework. Simultaneously, the potential consequences of integrity risks to the ethics program and company objectives (even if those risks are often considered less 'substantial' than other legal and compliance risks) may be significant.

This complexity, diversity, and potential impact of integrity risk on the organization must be reflected in the risk management system.

The presented analysis leads to the following, basic conclusions regarding the ethics risk management system:

- the system should encompass all relevant types of ethics risks, both those included in the regulatory context and ones not specified by law[14];
- to facilitate risk assessment and treatment, particular behaviors and attitudes, which may constitute integrity violations, should be specified, if possible, by company policies, code of conduct, standard operating practices and training;
- the system should be integrated as broadly as possible with existing risk management framework, even though the diversity of ethics risks may necessitate a more specific approach;
- the demonstrated complexity of the topic requires that a company adequately plans risk treatment measures, focusing on prevention. This, however, may not be applicable to all types of ethics risk, and requires a tailored approach.

Developing a proper risk management system also requires building and improving the organization's risk culture, which 'encourages the reporting and communication of new and emerging risks and ensures that every person in the organization understands their risk management responsibility' (ISO 37000:2021).

4. Evaluating the effectiveness of a corporate ethics program

Like other types of management systems, also the ethics program requires regular evaluation, to assess its effectiveness, gaps, and potential for further improvement.

There are certain factors that must be taken into consideration when evaluating the ethics program:

- it is important that the top management is convinced of the need to evaluate the ethics program and prepared to utilize the information obtained through evaluation;
- measuring certain aspects of ethical culture will require a cross-examination of sources;
- repeated evaluation requires retention of at least some basic metrics to ensure a proper 'point of reference'[15].

4.1 Purpose and scope of evaluation

The general purpose of the ethics program evaluation is assessing the state of the organization's ethical climate, culture and the effectiveness of its strategies, tactics, communications, and other processes in achieving the desired level of compliance (The Institute of Internal Auditors, 2012, p. 1). It is a deepened assessment of the organization's ethical objectives and their fulfillment, aimed at providing the organization with comprehensive knowledge about the ethical (and, other) risks, the state of organizational culture, and potential for further improvement.

The scope of evaluation should consider the following aspects of the ethics program:

- assessing the maturity of the ethics program – its fulfilment of the adopted and/or relevant standards and its readiness for further improvement;
- determining whether the employees (and, if needed, other interested parties) identify themselves with (have internalized) the company's values;

- measuring both perceived and actual effectiveness of the program, its elements, and related functions (e.g., compliance function, ethics advisor);
- identifying, assessing, and deepening the company's understanding of ethics risks, risk controls and treatment plans;
- reviewing the 'formal and informal processes within the organization that could potentially create pressures and biases that would undermine the ethical culture' (The Institute of Internal Auditors, 2012, p. 4).

4.2 Methods of evaluation

4.2.1 General remarks

The methods and scope of evaluation presented in the article relate to a comprehensive, entity-wide process, aimed at a holistic assessment of the ethics program.

Such evaluation does not directly relate to other assurance-oriented tasks, including internal or external audit, compliance audits and analyses, which are related to particular processes or other aspects of the organization[16], though often such forms of examination will utilize some or even most of the proposed instruments and methods of evaluation.

Regardless of the function chosen to perform the evaluation and the potential overlap of the abovementioned functions and assurance processes, I strongly advise that the results of each assessment are shared and taken into consideration as broadly as possible while planning the further development of an ethics program.

4.2.2 Survey

A survey is a direct method of obtaining a significant amount of information from the company employees or other stakeholders.

When utilizing surveys in the evaluation process, is important to note that (The Institute of Internal Auditors, 2012):

- ethical issues are rarely answerable in a 'yes/no' manner. Therefore, a usual questionnaire should include open questions and ones that are answered using a Likert scale;
- it is important to provide the participants with full confidentiality of the disclosed data and answers. However, as explained below, there is a sound

reason to allow the participants to fill the survey both disclosing their personal data and remaining completely anonymous;
- a proper stratification of answers (e.g., management, 'regular' staff, age, unit) is important for obtaining different perspectives, assessing potential discrepancies, which may in turn indicate a particular level of organization, on which the issues occur;
- it is important to use plain language, as well as meticulously plan the questions, according to general standards of survey development.

One of the most important aspects of evaluation based on employee survey is measuring the trust in the organization's ethics program, values, and the company's integrity. For this purpose, evaluation systems often refer to one, basic metric, which is the number (or percent) of employees which participated in the evaluation.

There is, however, another important metric, which is sometimes referred to as 'net ethics'. It is the percent of participants who decided to disclose their personal data, in relation to the overall number of participants. The metric is a potential indicator of the overall trust in the organization, its transparency and the employees' willingness to actively participate in the discussion about integrity and the ethics program[17].

Questions included in the survey may relate to particular aspects of the enterprise (e.g., communication, managerial attitude towards ethics, fair competition, relationship with customers, etc.).

4.2.3 Walkthroughs, workshops, and tabletop exercises

Walkthroughs, workshops, and tabletop exercises relate to meetings and other activities, during which ethical issues are discussed with a selected group, often guided by a trained professional (Collins & Kanashiro, 2022).

Such activities can have multiple purposes:

- risk identification, treatment and evaluating control measures;
- testing and discussing responses to a hypothetical situation (e.g., risk materialization, business continuity threats);
- obtaining interested parties' opinion on important topics;

- providing employees with deepened understanding of particular (e.g., ethical) issues and the means to resolve them.

It is important to note, that walkthroughs, workshops, and tabletop exercises are not only useful whilst evaluating the ethics program, but as a constant element of the company culture (Collins & Kanashiro, 2022).

In ethics program evaluation, these activities are specifically useful for obtaining a deepened understanding of the issues previously assessed in the surveys.

Some of the topics, which can be covered, are:

- the employees' understanding and practical application of the company values and standards of conduct;
- the employees' perception of internal and external communication;
- managerial engagement ('tone at the top' and 'tone at the middle');
- the employee's understanding of abusive behavior and instances of such;
- the employees' perception regarding the enterprise and its corporate social responsibility.

The latter is particularly interesting and is helpful in determining whether the employees are 'on board' with the company's activities and a possible indication of a general view by the public. This may be particularly useful for organizations that:

- are currently (re)formulating their reputation management and communication plans;
- operate in specific industries, which significantly affect the society and are highly dependent on the public perception (e.g., VLOPE, VLOSE, alcohol, tobacco and other legal stimulants, gambling, arms manufacturing and distribution, pharmaceutical trials etc.);
- struggle with reputational risks.

4.2.4 Reviewing documents and good practices

Another essential element of the ethics program evaluation is reviewing the organization's documents regarding ethics and compliance and comparing the actual state of compliance and integrity management systems to available standards and good practices and frameworks adopted by various external interested parties.

Reviewing own documents is important in assessing, whether the organization actually utilizes them and whether these document cover topics and requirements relevant from the company objectives' and values' perspective. It also facilitates the identification of compliance risks and/or inaccuracies.

Comparing the organizations documents and practices to external standards allows for the assessment of maturity of the ethics program and identification of potential gaps and opportunities for improvement.

The evaluation results should reflect the comparison and indicate significant discrepancies, and/or potential for improvement.

4.2.5 Case and risk analyses

The evaluation also requires an analysis of identified risk, treatment measures, possible misconduct, near-misses, and gaps.

The sources of such information usually include:

- audits;
- risk assessment;
- whistleblower cases;
- legal and compliance opinions.

The purpose of this part of evaluation is to determine whether there are ethics risk, which are not appropriately managed, examine potential tendencies or recurrence regarding unethical conduct, identify potential gaps and weak points.

4.3 Effective utilization of the evaluation results

The evaluation provides the organization with valuable information on several ethics-sensitive topics, such as the state of ethical culture, the effectiveness of the ethics program, potential risks, gaps, and pressure points.

The results of the evaluation therefore should be thoroughly disseminated, broadly discussed, and presented (at least) to the top management, to adopt a strategy for improvement, process adjustment and reaction to risk and/or misconduct. It is advised to indicate clearly, which unit is responsible for taking the required actions.

At least some of the relevant results should be disclosed to the employees and other participants, as a statement that the company acts with transparency, recognizes potential issues and is willing to further discuss and correct them.

In case the evaluation has determined instances of misconduct (e.g., indicated in the survey), even if available information is vague and/or scarce, they should be further examined, instead of disregarding them as a token of employees' misguided dissatisfaction.

5. Summary

Managing corporate ethics, though often performed intuitively, requires a complex approach, similar to other subtypes of management systems. It can be considered a part of a CMS, or a separate (sub)system and many solutions implemented for the purpose of compliance management (including good practices based on industry standards) can and should be adopted while managing corporate ethics.

Creating an effective ethics program requires combining a structured, consistent approach towards ethics risk management with significant focus on proper communication, training and other practices aimed at promoting values and desired behaviors, as well as directing the organizational culture towards ethical conduct.

Like other management systems (or even more so), the ethics program and related values should not only be established and communicated, but actively demonstrated in every aspect of the enterprise, such as decision making, project planning, developing company strategy, communication, and PR policy (integrity by design).

It is important that the organization is aware of the interdependence of various risk management subsystems and the necessity to integrate them. The complexity of ethical risks requires that they be managed using a systemic approach. At the same time, ethical risk incorporates a highly diversified group of integrity violations and requires a specific, creative, and cross-functional approach to assessment and treatment.

This cross-functionality is crucial to effective ethics risk management and ethics program assessment, as this type of risks requires proper allocation of duties and resources and cooperation between different parts of the organization, such as the compliance function, HR (including HR business partners), internal and external communication, risk management functions, internal and/or external audit.

It is important to remember, that the consequences of ignoring ethics, though not always easily quantifiable, may be extremely severe, exceeding reputational loss, violation of law and potential fines, or other consequences usually associated with compliance risks.

Business ethics is a matter of creating an ethical organizational culture in which everyone can find and share a sense of purpose; a chance to positively impact the surrounding business environment and good practices, creating a lasting corporate legacy and, more important, raise one's own integrity awareness.

Notes

1 Having in mind, that both ethical risk and integrity risk may relate to conformity with a set of moral values and principles, both terms are used interchangeably.

2 The ethical climate includes 'perceptions among organisational members about what constitutes (un)ethical behaviour' (Roy et al., 2024), while ethical culture relates to the organizations' capacity to 'stimulate ethical conduct of employees' (Huhtala et al., 2022). Somewhat simplifying, ethical climate is about 'what it means to act ethically and according to (company) values', while ethical culture regards whether 'is it encouraged to act in that specified manner and what stimulates/hinders such behavior'.

3 It is worth noting, that another standard, ISO 37001:2021, expressly includes 'ethical or moral conventions' as sources of corporate responsibility.

4 While I fully concur with using this term, and look forward to its further popularization, as it relates to the 'systems' perspective', for the purpose of this article I decided to remain within the seemingly more popular naming convention and refer to 'ethics programs'.

5 Both standards (e.g. ISO 37301:2021) and scientific research (e.g. Hambrick, Mason 1984) underline the senior management's prevalent influence on the organization's and employees' outcomes.

6 When considering and communicating the relationship between the organization's values and its Code of ethics and/or other documents, I recommend adopting an approach, according to which the documented information "confirms' the values adopted by the company, instead of "establishing' them. The values should come from the organization's firm belief in specific principles, attitudes, its mission, and vision, regardless of their recording.

7 Often compliance officers are appointed ethics-related duties. It is a reasonable approach (having in mind the relationship between the CMS and ethics program). However, given that the compliance function often is provided with limited resources, this may lead to insufficient focus on ethical matters.

8 Based on study, M. Kaptein (2014, p. 416) suggested, that the optimal sequence for adopting the abovementioned elements is: a code of ethics, ethics training and communication, accountability policies, monitoring and auditing, investigation and correction policies, an ethics office(r), ethics report line, and incentive policies.

9 An interesting relation between legal and compliance risk management and integrity is included in ISO 37022:2021. Though the standard does not directly relate to the issue of integrity risk management, it aptly states, that the internal context of risk management includes the 'value structures of the organization', stressing out that 'establishing the principles of equity guides the management of legal risk and includes managing conflicts of interest and provides an unbiased, independent voice in decisions and support due diligence and fairness for the best interests of an organization'. Also, the standard indicates, that the organization may identify legal risks related to ethics structures.

10 It important, however, to avoid 'integritism' (Huberts, 2024), i.e. oversimplifying the issue of integrity and 'overstepping' in considering particular acts as integrity violations.

11 An interesting perspective on analyzing weak points has been presented by Stark & Morbach (2024).

12 Also, an approach based predominantly on investigation and corrective policies has been found to be less effective than the preventive and value-based one (Kaptein 2014 p. 434).

13 Consider an example: an employee, pressured by a difficult financial situation, asks his employer for permission to start a business. The other work does not interfere in any way with the employee's duties, nor does it pose any significant risks for the employer. Regardless, the employer refuses, telling the employee that the company policy forbids any type of conflict of interest. This outcome, considering, for example, the fraud triangle, may increase both pressure (the employee is 'deprived' of means to remedy his situation) and, more important, rationalization (the employer can be considered as "forcing the employee's hand' with his unfair refusal).

14 ISO 37000:2021 states explicitly, that the organization should adapt a holistic view, which includes all types of relevant risks.

15 For more considerations see, e.g., The Institute of Internal Auditors (2012) and Jurkiewicz (2024).

16 Of course, unless these functions have been expressly tasked with performing the entity-wide evaluation.

17 Of course, the willingness to disclose such information may also depend on other factors/variables, such as individual traits, e.g., "corporate civic responsibility,' openness, conscientiousness, or, on the other hand, a notion of "having nothing to lose,' when facing a (perceived) unethical corporate environment.

Bibliography

Collins, D., & Kanashiro, P. (2022). Business ethics. Best practices for designing and managing ethical organizations (3rd ed.). CQ Press

Ethics and Compliance Initiative (2018). High-Quality Ethics and Compliance Program Measurement Framework, www.ethics.org/wp-content/uploads/2018-ECI-HQP-Measurement-Framework.pdf

Hambrick, D. C., & Mason, P. A. (1984). Upper echelons: The organization as a reflection of its top managers. Academy of management review, 9(2), 193-206.

Huberts, L. (2024), Integrity, integrity violations and integritism, in Kaptein M. (ed.), Research handbook for organizational integrity (pp. 62-65). Edward Elgar Publishing. doi:doi.org/10.4337/9781803927930.00043

Huberts, L., & Lasthuizen, K. M. (2019). Corruption in context: What goes wrong in governance. In M. Powell, D. Wafa, & T. A. Mau (Eds.), Corruption in a Global Context: Restoring Public Trust, Integrity, and Accountability (pp. 44-67). (Routledge corruption and anti-corruption studies). Routledge. https://doi.org/10.4324/9780367822125-3

Huhtala, M., Kaptein, M., Muotka, J., & Feldt, T. (2022). Longitudinal patterns of ethical organisational culture as a context for leaders' well-being: Cumulative effects over 6 years. Journal of Business Ethics, 1-22.

International Organization for Standardization. (2021). Compliance management systems — Requirements with guidance for use (ISO Standard No. 37301:2021). www.iso.org/standard/75080.html

International Organization for Standardization. (2021). Governance of organizations — Guidance (ISO Standard No. 37000:2021). www.iso.org/standard/65036.html

International Organization for Standardization. (2020). Risk management — Guidelines for the management of legal risk (ISO Standard No. 31022:2020). www.iso.org/standard/69295.html

International Organization for Standardization. (2018). Risk management — Guidelines (ISO Standard No. 31000:2018). https://www.iso.org/standard/65694.html

Jamroży, A. (2019). Kodeks pracy. The Labour Code. Beck

Jurkiewicz, C. L. (2024). Contemporary research into organizational integrity, in Kaptein M. (ed.), Research handbook for organizational integrity (pp. 542-557). Edward Elgar Publishing. doi:doi.org/10.4337/9781803927930.00043

Kaptein, M. (2008). Developing and testing a measure for the ethical culture of organizations: The corporate ethical virtues model. Journal of Organizational Behavior: The International Journal of Industrial, Occupational and Organizational Psychology and Behavior, 29(7), 923-947.

Kaptein, M. (2014). The Effectiveness of Ethics Programs: The Role of Scope, Composition, and Sequence. Journal of Business Ethics, 132(2), 415-431.

Maesschalk, J., Hoekstra, A., & van Monfort, A. (2024) Integrity management systems, in Kaptein M. (ed.), Research handbook for organizational integrity (pp. 542-557). Edward Elgar Publishing. doi:doi.org/10.4337/9781803927930.00043

Morbach, Y., & Stark, C. (2024). The weak point analysis as a method for measuring and improving organizational integrity, in Kaptein M. (ed.), Research handbook for organizational integrity (pp. 542-557). Edward Elgar Publishing. doi:doi.org/10.4337/9781803927930.00043

The Institute of Internal Auditors. (2012). Evaluating ethics-related programs and activities, www.theiia.org

Rotta, C.P. (2010). A short guide to ethical risk. Gower Publishing

Roy, A., Newman, A., Round, H., & Bhattacharya, S. (2024). Ethical Culture in Organizations: A Review and Agenda for Future Research. Business Ethics Quarterly, 34(1), 97–138. doi:10.1017/beq.2022.44

Tenbrunsel, A. E., Smith-Crowe, K., & Umphress, E. E. (2003). Building houses on rocks: The role of the ethical infrastructure in organizations. Social justice research, 16, 285-307.

U.S. Department of Justice (2023). Evaluation of Corporate Compliance Programs. www.justice.gov/criminal/criminal-fraud/page/file/937501/dl

Corporate Integrity in Brazil: An Analysis of Ethos Indicators

Marcela Greggo, Ana Lucia de Melo Custódio

1. Introduction

In the ever-evolving landscape of corporate responsibility, the Ethos Institute, a Brazilian institute, stands out as a beacon of commitment, actively shaping the agenda of Integrity, Transparency, and Anti-Corruption over the past 25 years. From influencing significant legislative milestones to leading pioneering initiatives such as the Business Pact for Integrity and Against Corruption, the Ethos Institute has continuously demonstrated its dedication to promoting a business environment characterized by ethical conduct and sustainability.

Founded in 1998, the Ethos Institute has been at the forefront of advocating for responsible business practices in the Brazilian context. Its active involvement in crucial legal frameworks, including the "Clean Record Law" (Complementary Law No. 135 of2010), "Access to Information law" (12.527/2011) and the Brazilian anti-corruption law (12.846/2013) reflects an unwavering commitment to shaping the ethical landscape of corporate entities in Brazil. The launch of the Business Pact for Integrity and Against Corruption in 2006 highlighted the proactive stance of the Institute, establishing the foundation for a coalition of over a thousand companies committed to fostering a market characterized by integrity, transparency, and resilience against corruption.

One of the Ethos Institute's significant contributions to the field of corporate integrity is the development of Ethos Indicators, a structured set of criteria and metrics encompassing various aspects of social and environmental impact. These indicators have become instrumental in guiding Brazilian organizations toward sustainable and ethical business practices. In 2015, the Institute took a decisive step forward by launching the Thematic Guide: Integrity, Prevention, and Combating Corruption[1], a strategic tool designed to deepen the understanding and implementation of ethical principles within Brazilian organizations.

In the pursuit of fostering corporate integrity, the Private Integrity Management Guide, generously sponsored by the KBA-NotaSys Integrity Fund, emerges as a significant milestone in the Brazilian context. This guide, informed by the principles and indicators established by Ethos, represents a collaborative effort to provide Brazilian organizations with a robust framework for evaluating, planning, and enhancing their integrity management capabilities.

By juxtaposing the Ethos Institute's enduring commitment with the current state of corporate integrity in Brazil, this article seeks to provide a concise analysis of corporate integrity within the Brazilian context, particularly following the enactment of the Brazilian Anti-Corruption Law. We will examine the impact of these indicators as an essential tool for diagnosing, planning, and enhancing integrity management capabilities, thereby promoting integrity, transparency, and combating corruption over the past 19 years.

2. Integrity and Anti-Corruption Efforts in Brazil: A Retrospective Analysis from the Business Pact for Integrity and Against Corruption to the Present Day

The Business Pact for Integrity and Against Corruption was launched on June 22, 2006, through the initiative of the Ethos Institute of Business and Social Responsibility, UniEthos - Training and Development for Socially Responsible Management, Patri Government Relations & Public Policies, the United Nations Development Programme (UNDP), the United Nations Office on Drugs and Crime (UNODC), and the Brazilian Committee of the Global Compact. During its development process, the Business Pact also received support from the Brazilian Association of Advertising Agencies (Abap) and the Ford Foundation.

Based on two international seminars held in São Paulo and Rio de Janeiro in 2005, which included the participation of representatives from dozens of companies to discuss aspects of the relationships between the private sector and public entities and agents, inputs were gathered for drafting the first version of the Pact. This version was subjected to a 90-day public consultation, during which suggestions were received from various companies, entities, and citizens.

The final text contains a set of guidelines and procedures to be adopted by the signatory companies and entities in their interactions with public authorities. These guidelines will be widely disseminated to be used by the market as a reference in dealings with companies. Its principles are based on the Charter of Social Responsibility Principles, the UN Convention Against Corruption, the 10th principle of the Global Compact, and the OECD guidelines.

The main commitments expressed in the text of the Pact can be summarized as follows:

- Information on Legislation: Laws must be internally known to ensure full compliance;
- Dissemination, Guidance, and Responses: Providing information on legal principles applicable to their activities;
- Prohibition of Bribery: Strictly forbidding bribery in all forms;
- Promotion of the Pact's Principles: Spreading the principles of the Pact among their stakeholders;
- Open and Transparent Investigations: Ensuring investigations are conducted openly and transparently;
- Engagement with the Supply Chain: Actively working with the entire supply chain to uphold these standards.

By becoming signatories of the Pact, companies commit to disseminating Brazilian anti-corruption legislation to their employees and stakeholders, ensuring full compliance. Additionally, they pledge to prohibit any form of bribery, advocate for legality, prioritize transparency of information, and cooperate in investigations when necessary.

Signatory companies of the Pact also commit annually to completing the Indicators of the Thematic Guide on Integrity, Prevention, and Anti-Corruption of the Ethos Institute. This serves to assess their progress in the integrity and anti-corruption agenda, and as a diagnostic tool for policies that may need improvement. It is through these data that an analysis of the situation of Brazilian companies regarding the Integrity and Anti-Corruption agenda in Brazil can be conducted. This tool manages corporate integrity practices, providing not only implicit recommendations but also serving as an instrument to evaluate the maturity level of companies in terms of integrity and transparency.

Companies can—and should—play a crucial role in combating corruption by working to foster a more ethical and integrous market. This is the aim of the Business Pact for Integrity and Against Corruption: to unite companies in the pursuit of creating a more ethical and integrous market, and to eradicate bribery and corruption.

The commitments made by signatories of the Pact are monitored annually to enhance visibility and transparency in corporate practices and strengthen the Pact itself, providing insights for company planning. This integration is also beneficial for companies not yet signatories of the Pact, as they can use the document as a thematic deepening guide.

Another significant initiative aimed at promoting corporate integrity and combating corruption in Brazil is the. On December 9, 2010, during the International Anti-Corruption Day celebrations, the Ethos Institute, in partnership with the Brazilian Office of the Comptroller General (CGU), launched the Pro-Ethics, a pioneering initiative in Latin America. Created with the purpose of promoting the voluntary adoption of integrity measures and corruption prevention in the business sector, this partnership has been crucial in fostering a more integrous, ethical, and transparent corporate environment.

Subsequently, important federal laws emerged such as the Clean Record Act, the Access to Information Act, the Conflict of Interest Act, and the Anti-Corruption Act (or Clean Company Act).

In recent years, Brazil has made significant progress in the transparency and anti-corruption agenda, and the role of companies as political actors has been crucial in these advancements. It is imperative that companies incorporate ethical and transparent practices into their management, aligned with the principles of social responsibility. In addition to fostering a more integrous business environment, these practices promote sustainability and strengthen the integrity of the business sector.

Therefore, it is essential to reflect on the main challenges for the development of effective corporate governance, including the implementation of risk management and compliance, the establishment of integrity policies and practices, and the adoption of best transparency practices such as integrated reporting. It was with this objective in mind that the Private Integrity Management Guide emerged, sponsored by the KBA-NotaSys Integrity Fund.

Good management in these areas presupposes constant monitoring of the economic, social, and environmental assets and liabilities of the company and its value chain, where responsibility for issues may fall on the company. It is important to remember that today, more than shareholders and the government, it is society that is increasingly interested in monitoring companies' actions, operations, treatment of employees, sourcing of production inputs, and so on.

3. The Use of Data from the Indicators of the Thematic Guide on Integrity, Prevention, and Anti-Corruption in the Construction of the Private Integrity Management Guide

The starting point for the development of the Private Integrity Management Guide was an analysis of the regulatory landscape in which Brazilian companies currently operate. Considering the latest legislative innovations, the guide aimed to present the set of international and domestic standards applicable to national companies.

In light of the guide's overarching objectives, these legal references were foundational for the analyses and recommendations provided. However, the advancement of integrity and transparency within the private sector hinges on commitments, policies, and practices that transcend mere compliance with legal mandates. These encompass genuine efforts to mitigate irregularity risks and foster corporate social and environmental responsibility.

In this regard, guidance from public agencies, international organizations, NGOs, research centers, and other institutions, although not legally binding, holds particular significance due to its quality and legitimacy. Internationally, bodies such as the United Nations Office on Drugs and Crime (UNODC), the Organization for Economic Co-operation and Development (OECD), the World Economic Forum, the World Bank, and Transparency International were among the key institutions consulted. Within Brazil, besides the Comptroller General's Office (CGU), the Brazilian Institute of Corporate Governance and the UN Global Compact Network Brazil were frequently referenced institutions.

The Brazilian Anti-Corruption Law, which celebrated its tenth anniversary in 2023, marked the inception of many integrity policies and programs. In this context, an analysis was conducted on the results of the Ethos Indicators in the dimension of Integrity, Prevention, and Anti-Corruption. Companies voluntarily complete a form each year where they indicate whether they comply with certain criteria. Apart from binary questions with yes or no answers, companies also provide quantitative data detailing their level of compliance with the indicators. The completion process is managed by the companies themselves through a digital system, and there is no validation or verification process for the information provided. These data are confidential, and the information presented in both the Private Integrity Management Guide and this article consists only of aggregated data without any identification of the responding companies. The total number of responding companies varies from year to year but has generally increased. In 2018, there were 437 companies; in 2019, 531 companies; in 2020, 514 companies; and in 2021, 708 companies participated.

It is important to highlight that the database used for analysis in the Private Integrity Management Guide and in this article does not represent a random sample of the Brazilian private sector. Rather, it consists of companies committed to annually seeking improvement in this agenda through the completion of the indicators. In this regard, companies familiar with and voluntarily participating in this self-assessment process are already at an advanced level of awareness and structuring of their integrity programs. The fact that the results indicate nearly complete compliance with some indicators should therefore be tempered by these considerations. Similarly, the low compliance with other indicators, even among companies at the forefront of the anti-corruption movement in Brazil, signals systemic and persistent deficiencies that need to be addressed. This underscores why work on the integrity and anti-corruption agenda is ongoing and continuously evolving.

4. Results: Analysis of Companies in the Integrity and Anti-Corruption Agenda in Brazil

The Brazilian Anti-Corruption Law, which reached its ten-year mark in 2023, is relatively recent and has brought about significant changes in the Brazilian business sector. Prior to this law, only individuals involved in acts of corruption could be punished. However, Law 12.846/2013 introduced administrative penalties for companies engaged in corrupt activities as well.

In this scenario, the universe analyzed by the Private Integrity Management Guide, using Ethos Indicators, demonstrates that 99.4% of companies have adopted an ethical code of conduct, with over 98% stating that their respective Codes of Conduct comply with the Brazilian Anti-Corruption Law 12,846/13 (Private Integrity Management Guide, 2023).

The Ethos Indicators assess various elements directly related to the structure of the integrity area within companies. Initially, they verify whether the company has a department, committee, or group of employees responsible for compliance activities and the integrity program. Subsequently, they implicitly recommend that companies define in their bylaws or articles of incorporation the area responsible for these activities, as this would signal a permanent commitment of the company to maintaining the integrity program (INT 2.5.2). The progress regarding the first criterion, which already shows near-universal compliance among evaluated companies, does not translate to the second criterion, where only slightly more than half of the companies have taken this additional step.

The indicators also assess whether this area has the necessary independence and autonomy to carry out its responsibilities effectively and whether it influences internal decision-making processes (INT 2.3.1). More specifically, they inquire whether this area has access to documents and data from various departments within the company, a power necessary for it to perform its functions adequately (INT 2.3.4). Regarding both indicators, it is noteworthy that only 1 in 20 companies do not comply with them:

	2018	**2019**	**2022**	**2021**
The company has a department, committee, or person responsible for compliance activities/integrity program (INT. 2.2.1).	87,13%	97,92%	97,28%	98,59%
The company has established in its bylaws/articles of incorporation a department responsible for compliance/integrity program activities, demonstrating ongoing commitment to maintaining this program (INT. 2.5.2).	49,31%	52,17%	54,28%	54,87%

	2018	2019	2022	2021
The department, committee, or person responsible for implementing and maintaining compliance/integrity program activities has the necessary independence and autonomy to carry out its responsibilities and influence decision-making processes (INT. 2.3.1).	83,26%	94,52%	95,14%	95.63%
The department, committee, or person responsible for compliance/integrity program activities has access to documents and data from different departments/areas of the company (INT 2.3.4).	86,01%	96,98%	94,94%	96,47%

The practice of subjecting the integrity program to independent external evaluation processes has remained limited to just over half of the participating companies in the recent assessment cycles of the Ethos Indicators (INT 2.4.4). Similarly, there is relatively lower adherence to third-party audits of company policies and procedures (INT 5.4.5).

	2018	2019	2020	2021
The company submits the integrity program to independent external evaluation processes (INT. 2.4.4).	57,11%	53,31%	58,17%	61,07%
The company ensures the participation of at least 20% independent directors on the board of directors (INT. 5.4.5).	58,94%	60,23%	62,06%	59,68%

The commitment of senior management to the integrity program of companies is assessed through various criteria, particularly in the section on Promoting a Culture of Integrity. For example, it is verified whether senior management periodically reinforces its commitment to the integrity program (INT 3.1.2) and whether actions supporting and promoting integrity are disseminated internally and externally (INT 3.1.3). Regarding training, it is expected that senior management supports and encourages employee participation in training on the integrity program (INT 3.2.3) and monitors the progress of training and communication actions (INT 3.2.4). Since 2018, more than 90% of participating companies have responded affirmatively to these criteria.

Senior management should also be knowledgeable about the main corruption risks and take actions to prioritize the improvement of controls and mitigation of these risks (INT 3.3.3). Additionally, they should strive to be perceived, in evaluations with internal stakeholders, as receptive to ethical concerns raised by employees (INT 3.3.5) and capable of prioritizing integrity over short-term business objectives (INT 3.3.6). Similarly, these items also appear to have widespread adherence among companies, with affirmative response rates exceeding 90%.

	2018	**2019**	**2020**	**2021**
The senior management periodically reinforces its commitment to the integrity program with its employees and other stakeholders (INT. 3.1.2).	93,81%	94,13%	96,69%	35,35%
The senior management's actions supporting and promoting integrity are disclosed internally and externally (INT. 3.1.3).	90,14%	88,83%	92,59%	89,94%
The senior management supports and encourages employees' participation in training on the integrity program and related issues (INT. 3.2.3).	94,72%	95,45%	97,08%	97,74%
The senior management monitors the training and communication actions of the integrity program (INT. 3.2.4).	90,37%	95,45%	92,98%	95,91%
The company's senior management is aware of the main corruption risks and prioritizes actions to improve controls and mitigate these risks (INT. 3.3.3).	93,35%	34,51%	95,52%	94,78%
In evaluations conducted with the internal audience, such as organizational climate surveys, the company's senior management is perceived as receptive to employees' ethical concerns or acting equally in cases of misconduct, regardless of the employee's hierarchical level (INT. 3.3.5).	91,28%	91,10%	92,98%	90,41%
In these same evaluations, the company's senior management is perceived as prioritizing integrity over short-term business objectives (INT. 3.3.6).	88,76%	90,53%	92,40%	90,97%

Efforts were also made to verify whether companies establish compliance objectives for the entire senior management (INT 3.4.2). In this case, the indicator assesses whether "the company's variable compensation and recognition programs consider qualitative aspects of adherence to the integrity program" (INT 3.4.4). However, adherence to these criteria is substantially lower compared to previous indicators. Compliance objectives are present in a growing number of companies participating in the Ethos Indicators, reaching 78.21% of companies in 2018, 82.39% in 2019, and 84.6% in 2020. As for INT 3.4.4, even in 2021, slightly less than half of the companies (45.98%) included integrity-related issues in the variable compensation program for senior management.

	2018	**2019**	**2020**	**2021**
The company sets compliance objectives for the entire senior management (INT 3.4.2).	78,21%	82,39%	84,60%	85,19%
The company's variable remuneration and recognition programs consider quantitative aspects of adherence to the integrity program (INT. 3.4.4).	42,43%	54,20%	54,55%	45,98%

The commitment of senior leadership was a high indicator in 2018 and remains high until the period analyzed for the development of the Private Integrity Management Guide. More than 90% of companies stated that in internal assessments, such as organizational climate surveys, the company's senior management is perceived as responsive to ethical concerns of its employees or acts consistently in cases of employee misconduct, regardless of the hierarchical level of the professional involved (Private Integrity Management Guide, 2023). In these same evaluations, senior management is perceived as prioritizing integrity over short-term business objectives (Private Integrity Management Guide, 2023).

In this scenario, over 92% of these companies conduct a preliminary analysis of their business units/areas to determine which ones are more exposed to corruption and bribery practices (Private Integrity Management Guide, 2023). In this regard, more than 94% of companies state that senior management is aware of the primary corruption risks and prioritizes actions to enhance controls and mitigate these risks (Private Integrity Management Guide, 2023).

Reports of irregularities are essential for detecting not only cases of corruption and violations of internal codes of conduct and policies, but also for identifying and addressing human rights violations, environmental damage, moral or sexual harassment, discriminatory conduct, and threats to democratic institutions. Therefore, whistleblower mechanisms and the protections afforded to whistleblowers should encompass reports not only of corruption, but more broadly, of irregularities or illegalities.[2]

Indicators point to the significant relevance of whistleblower channels in Brazil. A survey on integrity programs conducted by Deloitte, based on responses from 113 Brazilian companies, highlighted that internal reports (69%) and external reports (31%) are among the top three methods for detecting fraud and irregularities. Similarly, investigations stemming from anonymous reports (55%) were the primary means of identifying risks.[3]

In Brazil, both the Anti-Corruption Law (article 7, VIII) and its regulatory decree (article 41) include the encouragement of reporting irregularities as a central element of any effective integrity program. Decree No. 11,129 of 2022 goes further by specifying that channels for reporting irregularities must be open and widely promoted to employees and third parties. It also emphasizes the importance of mechanisms for handling reports and protecting whistleblowers acting in good faith (article 57, X).

The Ethos Indicators assess various aspects related to the existence and operation of mechanisms for whistleblowing (INT 6). In this regard, it is noted that almost all participating companies claim to have a whistleblowing channel directed at their employees (INT 6.1.1) and encourage them to report violations of norms, the code of conduct, or integrity policies (INT 6.2.1). Similarly, the vast majority of companies affirm having procedures for investigating received reports and for imposing penalties when violations are substantiated (INT 6.4.9). They also state that they forward suspicions or reports of fraud, misconduct, and corruption to the competent authorities (INT 6.5.1).

	2018	**2019**	**2020**	**2021**
The company has a whistleblowing channel directed towards its employees for legal and ethical issues (INT. 6.1.1).	95,88%	96,02%	97,65%	98,59%

	2018	2019	2020	2021
The company encourages its employees to report violations of norms, the code of conduct, or integrity-related policies (INT. 6.2.1)	96,34%	97,16%	97,85%	98,45%
The company has a procedure for investigating complaints and imposing sanctions in case of proven occurrences (INT. 6.4.9).	83,75%	92,61%	94,72%	94,92%
Suspicions or reports of fraud, misconduct, and corruption, when applicable, are forwarded to the appropriate authorities (INT. 6.5.1).	92,24%	92,33%	94,58%	97,42%

With regard to the effectiveness of whistleblowing mechanisms, there are several additional recommendations, the implementation of which is verified by Ethos Indicators. For instance, it is recommended that the whistleblowing channel be operated by an independent ombudsman to ensure confidentiality and protect whistleblowers (INT 6.4.1). Regarding this indicator, there has been a slow evolution in corporate practices since 2018, with nearly a quarter of participants, however, stating they do not comply with this recommendation. Other recommendations include conducting third-party audits of whistleblowing mechanisms to assess the efficiency of investigating reports and allegations (INT 6.4.4). Approximately half of the companies reported not adhering to this recommendation, even in the most recent assessment. Lastly, it is recommended that data from whistleblowing channels be used to enhance training, communication efforts, and to improve internal processes and controls within companies (INT 6.4.11). In this case, however, nearly all companies indicated compliance with this Ethos Institute recommendation, as demonstrated by the data below:

	2018	2019	2020	2021
The company's whistleblowing channel is operated by an independent ombudsman, ensuring confidentiality and protection for whistleblowers (INT. 6.4.1).	72,31%	74,43%	76,32%	81,36%
The company's whistleblowing channels are audited by a third party to verify the effectiveness of the investigation of facts and reports received (INT. 6.4.4).	46,45%	46,78%	51,47%	57,69%

	2018	2019	2020	2021
The company uses indicators from the whistleblowing channel for feedback on training and communication, as well as for improving its internal processes and controls (INT. 6.4.1).	85,58%	87,31%	92,37%	93,93%

Elements of the remediation process are considered and evaluated in various ways by the Ethos Indicators. Initially, the focus is on verifying whether companies' integrity policies include and enforce disciplinary measures, sanctions, and penalties for violations of the code of conduct in proportion to the severity of the acts committed, applicable to all employees, including leaders and governance members (INT 1.3.4). For this purpose, it is necessary for the company to have a procedure to investigate reports and impose penalties in cases of proven occurrences (INT 6.4.10).

Furthermore, it is verified whether the company's integrity policy includes promptly ceasing any irregularities detected and applying appropriate solutions to address the damages caused (INT 1.3.7). It is also recommended that companies disclose, as part of their compliance activities' outcomes, information regarding identified cases of corruption, being accountable for the corrective measures taken and ongoing processes (INT 2.5.3). Regarding this particular point, there is still observed low adherence among participating companies. Additionally, concerning the application of sanctions, the evaluation seeks to determine whether companies anticipate formal sanctions or penalties and enforce them in case of code of conduct violations by their suppliers or business partners (INT 1.4.5).

	2018	2019	2020	2021
The policy includes and applies disciplinary measures, sanctions, and penalties for violations of the code of conduct and integrity program proportionate to the severity of the acts committed, applicable to all employees, including leadership and governance members (INT. 1.3.4).	83,75%	88,51%	88,52%	96,47%

	2018	2019	2020	2021
The company has a formal procedure that identifies and prevents possible retaliation against whistleblowers who report in good faith (INT. 6.4.10).	76,46%	77,84%	82,19%	87,69%
The policy includes and applies disciplinary measures, sanctions, and penalties for violations of the code of conduct and integrity program proportionate to the severity of the acts committed, applicable to all employees, including leadership and governance members (INT. 1.3.7).	87,41%	87,10%	89,11%	88,72%
The company discloses the results of its compliance/integrity program activities even when cases of corruption are identified, reporting on corrective measures taken and ongoing processes (INT. 2.5.3).	56,09%	62,95%	64,98%	66,29%
The company has formal sanctions or penalties and applies them in case of code of conduct violations by its suppliers or business partners (INT. 1.4.5).	88,33%	87,01%	92,22%	91,68%

The interaction between companies and governments is a central element of public life. In countries like Brazil, where the state has a vast presence in the economy and significant capacity to impact the performance of private enterprises, this interaction gains even more relevance. However, many aspects of these interactions remain poorly regulated or inadequately regulated by Brazilian legislation, underscoring the importance of companies adopting voluntary policies and practices aimed at ensuring integrity and transparency in these relationships.

Among these aspects, political engagement stands out, which refers to the involvement of companies in public-policy activities, including political and electoral donations, as well as lobbying. Corporate political engagement is a legitimate activity when conducted responsibly and ethically. Companies possess specific and in-depth knowledge of their fields of operation and can contribute to public discourse by presenting relevant information and enabling a better understanding of the impacts of public policies[4].

The Ethos Indicators evaluate, for example, whether the company's code of conduct includes explicit rules regarding relationships with public officials (INT 1.1.5.3) and whether the integrity policy provides specific guidelines for meetings and activities with public servants or employees (INT 1.3.6.2). According to the data below, there has been progress among responding companies in recent years for both indicators. The indicators also include an entire section (Section 14) to assess the company's involvement in public policy development. Within this scope, it is questioned whether companies maintain records of all employees responsible for engagement with the public sector and document their participation in public policy development (14.3.1). Specifically, regarding documentation, it is recommended that companies document and formalize their interactions with the public sector, including agendas, main deliberations, and participant lists published in minutes or similar documents (14.3.3), and that these minutes are published on the company's websites (14.3.4.3). Regarding this last point, only 1 out of 10 companies adopt this transparency practice regarding their interactions with the government. In recent years, these are the proportions of participating companies in the Ethos Indicators that responded positively to the respective questions:

	2018	**2019**	**2020**	**2021**
Explicit rules on relationships with public officials (INT. 1.5.3).	91,97%	93,79%	95,72%	93,51%
Conducting meetings and activities with public servants or employees aimed at preventing fraud and illicit acts, such as favoritism or bribery payments to avoid scrutiny or expedite the obtaining of authorizations, licenses, permits, and certificates (INT. 1.3.6.2)"	74,37%	79,28%	81,52%	79,27%
The company maintains a record of all employees responsible for engagement with the public sector and keeps records of their participation in the development of public policies (INT. 14.3.1)	51,88%	50,83%	47,93%	52,56%

	2018	2019	2020	2021
The company documents and formalizes its interactions with public authorities to ensure that all meetings and hearings with public officials have agendas and identified participants published in an official schedule, recording the main deliberations in minutes or a similar document (INT. 14.3.4.3)	48,87%	57,92%	55,60%	54,97%
The minutes or similar documents are published on its website (INT. 14.3.4.3).	7,27%	10,21%	9,13%	9,94%

Lastly, there is a wide range of information whose disclosure is not necessarily required by law but is suggested by international recommendations and endorsed by best practices, as seen above. The Ethos Indicators evaluate, for example, whether the company annually discloses and makes available on its public corporate website, even if not legally required, all legal entities within its corporate group, their holdings, and the list of countries where they are incorporated and operate (9.5.3). Additionally, they verify whether the company publishes its corporate organizational chart showing the aforementioned legal entities and those that control the company, aimed at identifying the ultimate corporate beneficiary (9.5.4). Including information about contracts with the government in sustainability reports is also considered relevant (9.5.7). It is recommended as well to publish the related party transaction policy (5.5.5). Furthermore, the evaluation assesses whether companies publish reports on their Environmental, Social, and Governance (ESG) performance (8.4.2).

	2018	2019	2020	2021
The company annually discloses, even if not required by law, and makes available on its public corporate website all legal entities within the corporate group, their holdings, and the list of countries where they are incorporated and operate (INT. 9.5.3).	41,92%	64,82%	69,81%	50,93%
The company discloses a corporate organizational chart showing the aforementioned legal entities and those that control the company, aiming to identify the ultimate corporate beneficiary (INT. 9.5.4).	43,79%	63,47%	72,73%	54,70%

	2018	2019	2020	2021
The company discloses in its sustainability reports or on its website the names of its main shareholders or owners, its organizational chart, its financial statements and other accounting data, as well as information about financial contracts entered into with the government (INT. 9.5.7).	51,52%	48,57%	56,47%	52,71%
The company has and discloses its Related Party Transaction Policy (INT. 5.5.5).	85,71%	85,39%	91,67%	88,72%
The company discloses reports on its Environmental, Social, and Governance (ESG) performance (INT. 8.4.2).	62,07%	62,81%	64,71%	75,64%

5. Conclusion

To conclude, the development of the Private Integrity Management Guide, sponsored by the KBA-NotaSys Integrity Fund, was based on a thorough analysis of the regulatory landscape of Brazilian companies and recent legislative innovations. The starting point for this guide was the incorporation of Ethos Indicators, which serve as an essential tool for diagnosing and planning integrity policies. While legal frameworks provide a solid foundation, the effective implementation of integrity and transparency practices in the private sector requires commitments that go beyond legal obligations, fostering a culture of socio-environmental responsibility.

The analysis of data from the Ethos Indicators, particularly in the dimension of Integrity, Prevention, and Anti-Corruption efforts, reveals significant progress while also highlighting areas that require greater attention. The increasing participation in filling out the indicators demonstrates a commitment from companies to the integrity agenda. However, the variability in implementing certain practices, such as external audits of integrity programs, disclosure of interactions with the government, and the inclusion of compliance objectives in variable compensation programs, indicates that there is room for improvement.

The Brazilian Office of the Comptroller General (CGU) has played a crucial role in promoting private integrity in Brazil through initiatives such as the Pro-Ethics and the recently launched Brazil Pact, which includes a self-assessment component. These initiatives not only encourage companies to adopt integrity practices but also provide a framework for assessment and continuous improvement. Pro-Ethics has been pivotal in promoting a more ethical and accountable corporate environment, while Brazil Pact reinforces companies' commitment to transparency and responsibility. It offers a self-assessment tool that facilitates identifying strengths and areas for improvement in integrity practices.

The constant evolution and improvement of these practices are essential to strengthen the culture of integrity and to effectively face the challenges associated with corruption in Brazil.

Notes

1 https://www.ethos.org.br/cedoc/indicadores-ethos-guia-tematico-integridade/
2 GOVERNMENT ACCOUNTA - BILITY PROJECT. International best practices for whistleblo - wer policies. Washington, 2013.
3 DELOITTE. Corporate integrity in Brazil: evolution of compliance and good business practices in recent years. São Paulo, 2022.
4 TRANSPARÊNCIA INTERNACIONAL REINO UNIDO. Open Business: principles and guidance for anti-corruption corporate transparency. 2020.

Bibliography

Controladoria-Geral da União (CGU). Empresa Pró-Ética. Available at: https://www.gov.br/cgu/pt-br/assuntos/integridade-privada/avaliacao-e-promocao-da-integridade-privada/empresa-pro-etica. Accessed on 20 May 2024.

Controladoria-Geral da União (CGU). Pacto Brasil. Available at: https://www.gov.br/cgu/pt-br/assuntos/integridade-privada/pacto-brasil. Accessed on 18 May 2024.

Deloitte. Corporate Integrity in Brazil: Evolution of Compliance and Best Business Practices in Recent Years. São Paulo, 2022.

Empresa Limpa. Available at: http://www.empresalimpa.org.br/. Accessed on 20 May 2024.

Ethos Institute. Ethos Indicators: Integrity Thematic Guide. Available at: https://www.ethos.org.br/cedoc/indicadores-ethos-guia-tematico-integridade/. Accessed on 20 May 2024.

Government Accountability Project. International Best Practices for Whistleblower Policies. Washington, 2013. Available at: https://whistleblower.

org/wp-content/uploads/2018/12/Best_Practices_Document_for_website_revised_April_12_2013.pdf. Accessed on 22 May 2024.

Private Integrity Management Guide, 2023, Ethos Institute. Available at: https://www.ethos.org.br/cedoc/guia-de-gestao-de-integridade-privada-ggip/

International Transparency United Kingdom. Open Business: principles and guidance for anti-corruption corporate transparency. 2020. Available at: <https://www.transparency.org.uk/sites/default/files/pdf/publications/TIUK_OpenBusiness_WEB4.pdf. Accessed on 22 May 2024.

Chapter 4

AI Compliance and Financial Compliance

Governance of AI: Compliance, Ethics, and Standardisation are but a Distant Dream

Nada Kakabadse, Andrew Kakabadse

1. Introduction

Despite the many different forms of AI, it remains critically predisposed to simulate human intelligence (Mintz and Brodie, 2019). AI is reshaping industries and societies, through offering unprecedented opportunities and challenges.

AI advances, however, raise ethical, legal, and social concerns (Bélisle-Pipon et al., 2021). It is no surprise that questions surrounding AI compliance and the nature of the ethical standards to meet through robust regulation have become increasingly prominent. Ethical concerns are at least alluded to in the work of the grandfather of AI, Alan Turing (1950: 455), who contemplated the problem of the 'margin of safety' and how 'to find out how to programme these machines to play the game'. The debate concerning the ethical implications of AI took hold in the 1960s (Samuel 1960) and that intensified by the early 1980s. Mason (1986: 12), for example, identified the four ethical issues of the information age: privacy, accuracy, property, and accessibility, adding the moral imperative to 'ensure that information technology, and the information it handles, are used to enhance the dignity of mankind'. Currently, the intensity of the debate among scholars, policymakers, and, to some extent, practitioners has reached levels comparable to the technological innovations in genetics and nuclear power (Prem, 2023).

Algorithmic systems are now being deployed for high-stakes applications such as law enforcement and automated decision-making. These tools have the potential to increase bias, injustice, and misuse at an alarming scale. As AI technology rapidly advances, it is accompanied by a growing presence of uncertainty and unease alongside the conveniences it offers. The consequences of new AI often only become apparent after the technology gains momentum, leaving people with a sense of limited control due to them only reacting to established trajectories. When the demand for new technology intensifies, the “dilemma of technology control”, also known as the “Collingridge dilemma” (Collingridge, 1980) takes a grip. Collingridge (1980) perceives control technology for a social good as problematic, mainly due to inadequate ‘governance’ of science, technology, and innovation.

Enhancement in decision-making processes due to AI innovation poses unique challenges for governance oversight due to the technologies inherent opaqueness and frequent evolution. Users may control data inputs and observe outputs but often struggle to explain the decision-making process or understand the data points involved. Additionally, the evolving nature of AI processes as systems learn over time which adds another layer of complexity to effective governance.

In this article, we explore the complex landscape of AI compliance, ethics, and standardisation. We delve into the current state of affairs, highlighting the challenges faced and emphasising the importance of establishing a comprehensive framework to guide the responsible development and deployment of AI technologies.

2. Ethics and AI

What preoccupies contemporaries concerning the ethics of AI adoption is its impact particularly in medicine. It is recognised that it is impossible to develop a code that covers all possibilities. Safety flaws in AI systems may endanger more patients than the possibility of misdiagnosis by a doctor, due to the fact that automated systems replicate errors (Macnish, 2012).

“First, Do No Harm,” an extrapolation of the Hippocratic oath, represents the first tenet of ethics. The principle of non-maleficence to sidestep causing harm or needless suffering forms the backbone of medical ethics. In the UK and in another sector, the Post Office, over 900 sub-postmasters and postmistresses were prosecuted for supposedly stealing money as a result of incorrect information generated by the Horizon, computer system (Peachey et al., 2024).

The swift progress of AI technology brings with it risks and challenges, supported by a consensus among experts that the ethical implications of these advancements require scrutiny (Guo, 2020). In attempts to portray their actions, products, and services as ethical, AI companies engage in what is often termed "Ethics Bluewashing" (Floridi, 2019). In essence, reality often falls short of the assurances given. Another strategy employed is the avoidance of direct ethical discussion, opting instead to focus on the concept of "trustworthiness". This approach allows the firm to frame trustworthiness as a gradable quality, suggesting that certain products or services are more trustworthy than others. In providing explanations as to why, Hagendorff (2020: 108) notes that the development and use of AI is “not primarily framed by value- or principle-based ethics, but obviously by an economic logic”.

Bias and fairness are primary ethical concerns in AI and revolve around the slant embedded in algorithms. AI systems trained on biased datasets can perpetuate and amplify societal prejudices. Addressing bias requires a multi-faceted approach, including diverse and representative training data, transparency in algorithmic decision-making, and continuous monitoring for unintended consequences.

Transparency and explainability are the other ethical concerns regarding AI systems. The opacity of many AI algorithms poses challenges in understanding and explaining their decision-making processes. Ethical AI demands transparency to build trust and accountability (Gebru et al., 2021). Developing explainable AI techniques is essential for providing users and stakeholders with insights into how AI systems arrive at specific outcomes.

The vast amount of data processed by AI systems raises concerns about individual privacy and data security. Striking a balance between extracting meaningful insights and protecting sensitive information is a further critical ethical consideration (Mittelstadt, 2019). Robust data anonymisation, encryption, and adherence to privacy regulations are essential components of ethical AI development.

Although accountability, privacy and fairness predominate, the present-day guidelines provide the minimal requirements for building and using “ethically sound” AI systems (Hagendorff, 2020).

3. AI Standardisation and Compliance

As AI technologies become increasingly pervasive, the absence of standardised practices poses challenges in ensuring consistency, interoperability, and ethical conduct. Standardisation is crucial for building a foundation that supports responsible AI development, deployment, and use across different sectors and regions.

Various international organisations are working towards establishing AI standards. Initiatives like the International Organization for Standardization (ISO) and the IEEE Standards Association are developing frameworks to address AI's technical, ethical, and societal aspects. These efforts aim to create a common ground for AI practitioners, researchers, and policymakers to align their approaches.

Further there are a growing number of government policies, ethical guidelines, and literature reviews addressing the current state of AI compliance. Almeida et al. (2021) conducted a systematic review of the literature on AI Regulation, identifying and analysing 21 unique models for policymaking, which aim to achieve gold-standard societal values, such as fairness, freedom, and long-term sustainability. Correa et al. (2023) undertook a meta-analysis of 200 governance policies and ethical guidelines for AI usage published by public bodies, academic institutions, private companies, and civil society organisations worldwide. They found 17 resonating principles are prevalent in policies and guidelines. The top five are accountability/liability, beneficence/non-maleficence, children's and adolescents' rights, dignity/human rights, and diversity/inclusion/pluralism/accessibility. Attard-Frost et al. (2023) reviewed 47 AI ethics guidelines using thematic analysis aimed at determining the extent to which the ethics of AI business practices are even considered. Attard-Frost et al. (2023: 389) found that AI ethics guidelines 'focus disproportionately on issues of algorithmic decision-making, while the fairness, accountability, sustainability, and transparency of the business decision-making contexts in which AI systems are situated remain seriously undermined by competitive and speculative norms, ethics washing, corporate secrecy, and other harmful business practices'. Moreover, the review suggests that AI business practices', political and economic implications are significantly underrepresented in AI ethics guidelines.

Similarly, expanding on the work of Morley et al. (2020), Prem (2023) undertook a systematic analysis of more than 100 frameworks, process models, and proposed remedies and tools for helping to make the necessary shift from AI principles to implementation. Prem (2023) concludes that explicability, fairness, privacy, and accountability are often addressed with proposals for software and algorithms. The literature suggests that there is an abundance of various frameworks and models, encompassing a breadth and variability of approaches and that the impact of AI demands a combination of ethical design, laws, and education. Yet, despite these insights little progress is made in terms of legislative frameworks.

The rapid evolution of AI has outpaced the development of comprehensive regulatory frameworks. Governments and international organisations are grappling with the task of creating laws that balance innovation with ethical considerations. As of 2022, China and the EU have taken significant strides in establishing AI guidelines, but a global consensus is yet to emerge.

In the absence of universal regulations, various industries and corporations are taking voluntary steps to ensure for AI compliance, whilst others are using the "free card" to advance their interests. Certain tech giants and AI developers have initiated ethical guidelines and best practices to address bias, transparency, and accountability concerns.

Collaboration between industry players and regulatory bodies is crucial to establishing a cohesive approach to AI compliance. Table 1 below summarises the approaches of leading AI countries to AI ethical regulation.

China has rolled out some of the world's first binding national regulations on AI. In so doing it is poised to implement some of the most stringent regulations on AI developers, driven by the need to strike a balance between controlling the information generated by AI models and maintaining competitiveness in the technology race, particularly with the United States (Sheehan, 2023).

Taking a proactive stance, China has advanced AI regulations beyond mere proposals. In March 2022, the country enacted a regulation governing the use of algorithms by companies in online recommendation systems. Although many analysts and policymakers in other countries dismiss China's regulations as irrelevant or political propaganda, the emergent regulation mandates that services must adhere to principles of morality, ethics, accountability, transparency, and the promotion of "positive energy" (Sheehan, 2023). These regulations target recommendation algorithms for disseminating content, synthetically generated images and video, and generative AI systems like OpenAI's ChatGPT. Companies must notify users when AI algorithms influence information presentation, allowing users to opt out of targeted interactions (Zhang, 2023). The regulation also prohibits using personal data in algorithms that result in different consumer prices. These principles are anticipated to influence the development of AI regulations globally.

Table 1 : Regulatory approaches by the leading AI economies

	EU	Israel	US	China
Regulation(s)	• General Data Protection Regulation (GDPR) Article 22. • Proposed Artificial Intelligence Act 2024 (Legislation Endorsed by Member States)	AI Policy (17/12/2023)	• No comprehensive federal AI regulation. Decentralised approach with various agencies addressing specific aspects of AI. • Executive Order on the Safe, Secure, and Trustworthy Development and Use of Artificial Intelligence, 30/10/2023	• 2021 regulation on recommendation algorithms (the algorithm registry), • the 2022 rules for deep synthesis (synthetically generated content), • the 2023 draft rules on generative AI. • New rules for synthetically generated images and chatbots in the mould of ChatGPT
Regulating Body	EU Global standard for AI regulation	Central Government	• A federal approach is to be developed. • State and local take the lead	• Central Government

	EU	Israel	US	China
Motivation	Consumer protection; fairness & safety	Innovative dynamism and safety	Self-regulation, pro-innovation	• State control; economic dynamism
Aim to	Set a common framework for AI use across member states, ensuring the responsible development and deployment of AI technologies. To regulate the development and use of AI by providing a framework of obligations for parties involved across the entire AI supply chain	Striking a balance between fostering innovation and ensuring ethical use whilst fostering technological advancements	Promote innovation and economic dynamism. Major IT companies act as a national state without any accountability.	• Information control, laying the groundwork for a capstone national AI law.
Approach	• Comprehensive umbrella laws • Horizontal	• "Soft" • Sector-specific regulation.	• Voluntary • Decentralised • Emergent	• Algorithms as a point of entry • Building regulatory tools and bureaucratic know-how • Vertical and iterative (for now)

	EU	Israel	US	China
Key features	• GDPR, Article 22 prohibits decisions based solely on automated processes unless the program gains the user's explicit consent or meets other requirements. • Conflicting Perspectives on AI Innovation • Fines (similar to the GDPR) of up to 7% of annual global turnover for certain offences.	• A common set of ethical AI principles based on the OECD AI Principles focuses on human-centric innovation, equality, transparency, reliability, accountability, and promoting sustainable development. • Forums for Regulators and Public Participation	• Varies across States and industries	• Firms must require a license to provide generative AI services to the public and submit a security assessment if public opinion attributes or social mobilisation capabilities are used in the model. • AI is an economic tool but must preserve social value.

Source: Based on European Council (2024); GDPR (2016); IMIST (2023); White House (2023); Sheehan (2023); Zhang (2023).

Both vertical and iterative elements characterise China's regulatory approach. Vertical regulations focus on specific applications or manifestations of technology, diverging from horizontal regulations like the European Union's AI Act, which seeks to comprehensively cover all applications of a given technology (Sheehan, 2023). While no regulation is entirely vertical or horizontal, most tend to lean toward one direction or the other. At the federal level, there is no AI-specific regulation.

Ethical considerations surrounding AI in the United States are typically handled on a case-by-case basis, with companies and institutions encouraged to voluntarily adopt ethical guidelines. However, in October 2023, the US President issued an executive order titled 'Safe, Secure, and Trustworthy Development and Use of Artificial Intelligence' (White House, 2023). This order underlines the need to maximize the benefits of AI while mitigating associated risks, and it envisions the development of federal standards.

There have also been a number of proposed, aspirational pieces of legislation to regulate the use of generative AI in political advertisements as well as monitoring employee activity in their hiring processes. However, as of now, no such regulations have been passed at the federal level.

Various federal agencies, including the Federal Trade Commission (FTC), the Equal Employment Opportunity Commission (EEOC), the Consumer Financial Protection Bureau (CFPB), and the Department of Justice (DOJ), have stated that existing legislation applies to AI systems, either because they are embodied in software or represent technological innovation which are within the scope of current laws. However, the effectiveness of applying these laws depends on the expertise of legal professionals.

Certain states, as Illinois, have taken steps to address AI ethics through specific legislation such as the AI Video Interview Act of 2022, which requires employers using AI systems in their hiring processes to inform applicants and obtain their consent. This raises questions, particularly regarding the ability of individuals desperate for employment to provide informed consent in such circumstances.

The lack of AI regulation in the country spearheading major AI developments and AI systems, the US, raises persist concerns regarding potential misuse through lack of accountability due to the absence of mandatory ethical standards.

4. Challenges in AI Compliance, Ethics, and Standardization

Turning principles into practice is one of the most pressing concerns for AI governance (Prunkl, 2022). The pace at which AI technologies evolve poses a significant challenge for regulators and standardisation bodies. Traditional regulatory approaches struggle to keep up with rapid advancements, creating a potential gap between technology development and ethical adoption. The distributed nature of AI development and deployment often leads to friction in assigning accountability. Determining responsibility for ethical lapses or compliance violations becomes intricate when multiple entities are involved in different stages of the AI lifecycle.

Diverse cultural, legal, and ethical norms across different regions complicate the establishment of global AI social and ethical practice standards. Achieving consensus on ethical principles and regulatory frameworks requires navigating these variations and fostering international collaboration.

The development of autonomous vehicles adds to the ethical challenges posed by AI. As self-driving cars become more prevalent, questions arise about their decision-making. Ethical considerations include determining how AI systems prioritise the safety of passengers, pedestrians, and other drivers and whether transparency in these decision processes is achievable. Currently, autonomous cars operate at level 2, where a driver is still in charge, but electronic chips control two or more elements, such as lane-keep assist and auto cruise control. Vehicles are now near to level 3, where humans are still hands-on at all times, but the car boasts safety-critical functions such as lane-change mode, self-parking features, driver monitoring, etc.

Level 4 driverless cars have the driver on standby and can be hands-off for periods of time. The car is fully autonomous in controlled areas based on next-gen sensors and algorithms. Laws for the level 5 fully autonomous or driverless cars with genuine hands-off driving where the driver is optional, are yet to come.

The use of AI in predictive policing has sparked ethical concerns related to bias and discrimination. Algorithms analysing historical crime data may perpetuate existing biases, leading to disproportionate targeting of specific communities (Reese, 2022). Striking a balance between effective crime prevention and avoiding discriminatory practices remains a significant challenge.

In healthcare, AI-driven diagnostic tools are gaining prominence. Ensuring the ethical use of these technologies involves addressing issues such as data privacy, informed consent, and the potential impact on doctor-patient relationships. Balancing the benefits of improved diagnostics with the ethical implications of handling sensitive health data requires careful consideration.

Today's data is known as the "new oil" due to its economic value (*The Economist*, 2021). For example, in 2020, a Chinese imaging AI was hacked, and its source code and training data were sold on the dark web for four bitcoins (about 210,000 RMB) (Zhang, 2020). Healthcare data has high research and business value, and data breaches occur frequently. In 2017, 15% of global data breaches came from the healthcare industry, second only to the financial sector.

As quantum computing advances, its intersection with AI introduces new challenges and ethical considerations (Brooks, 2023). The potential for exponential increases in computing power will impact the ethical dimensions of AI, particularly related to privacy, encryption, and the development of more powerful AI algorithms. Moreover, the convergence of AI with human augmentation technologies raises ethical questions about the boundaries between humans and machines (Cinel et al., 2019). Issues such as consent, autonomy and the potential for social inequality must be carefully considered as AI technologies become more integrated into the human experience. The ethical debate surrounding neuroscience, neuro-ergonomics, brain-to-brain communication, neural engineering, and their growth, is long overdue.

5. Compliance and Collaboration

Global collaboration is paramount to addressing AI compliance, ethics, and standardisation challenges. To date a variance of governance practice exists. China leads the way with US tech giants operating as 19-century "robber barons". Currently, certain major high tec companies act as a national state without any accountability. With such extremes of governance practices, continued self-regulation only harms the public interest. International efforts should be intensified to establish a harmonised set of standards that guide the responsible development and deployment of AI technologies across borders.

Governments play a pivotal role in shaping AI compliance and ethics. A great deal will depend on the direction provided by regulatory bodies to be ahead of technological advancements. There need to be considerable penalties for those who do not comply, and that needs to be higher than the EU-proposed Artificial Intelligence Act 2024, which imposes similar fines to GDPR of up to 7% of annual global turnover for certain offences. A more meaningful deterrent for unethical profiteering needs to be established.

Given the dynamic nature of AI, regulatory frameworks and standards need to be designed with flexibility and adaptability in mind. Regular updates and revisions should be facilitated to incorporate new knowledge, technological advancements, and evolving ethical considerations.

AI development requires input from various disciplines, including ethics, law, sociology, anthropology, and psychology. Only interdisciplinary collaboration can contribute to a more holistic raising of the governance standards of AI.

Bearing in mind the variance of practice, it is questionable whether tech companies will take a proactive role in fostering ethical practice. Transparency in algorithmic decision-making, responsible data management, and cooperation with regulatory bodies are crucial steps for industry leaders to contribute to a responsible and sustainable AI ecosystem.

But will they?

Burrell (2016) argues AI systems harbour three distinct opacities. Algorithms are trade secrets that companies intentionally hide. The low level of ability of lay people to understand programming and algorithmic techniques and the complex nature of the algorithms themselves, promotes a “black box” mindset. Inputs and outputs are visible and understandable, but the process from input to output often cannot be explained or even understood. (Burrell, 2016). The first two types of opacity can be improved by establishing better regulation and education. The third opacity, algorithms are black boxes due to the fact that machine learning is based on data rather than rules and imitates the multilayer structure of the human neural network.

Thus, engaging the public in AI compliance and ethics discussions is crucial for building a consensus on acceptable norms and values. Public awareness campaigns, educational initiatives, and forums for open dialogue can contribute to a more informed and engaged citizenry, influencing the direction of AI development and regulation. Public forums are the basis for the Israeli AI Policy (17/12/2023) which others should be adopted.

In parallel to campaigns for greater public awareness, embedding AI ethical considerations into education is vital for shaping the mindset of future developers, practitioners and users. Universities and training programs should have at their core the ethical implications of AI technologies, which foster a sense of responsibility and ethical awareness among those entering the field.

Academic institutions and research organisations play a key role in shaping the ethical landscape of AI. Research should focus not only on technological advancements but also on the societal implications of AI. Collaboration between academia, industry, and regulatory bodies can bridge the gap between theoretical ethical considerations and practical implementation.

Only governments can establish robust standards and ethical guidelines, so that advances can be made towards ensuring that AI contributes positively to society while minimising risk and preventing harm.

The challenges are complex in the dynamic landscape of AI compliance, ethics, and standardisation. The responsible development and deployment of AI technologies requires a concerted effort from governments and regulators to establish comprehensive standards which the private sector is likely to resist. The free-market argument is likely to be at the forefront with the firm camouflaging unacceptable practices.

Government must remain vigilant and committed to a collaborative and interdisciplinary approach. The challenge will be that of staying ahead of technological advancements, so that a future can be shaped to where AI enhances human well-being, respects diversity, and upholds the principles of transparency, fairness, and accountability. That is the desire. The path forward is likely to be that of no shared commitment to harnessing the potential of AI for the greater good while safeguarding the values that define us as a society.

In the years ahead, how government resists kidnap by the tec giants and the dollar loaded private equity interests behind them is the critical point of concern. The objective is to have organisations that utilise AI to document specific information about their systems totally in keeping with regulatory frameworks. To not do so must induce a punitive fine.

To secure compliance with emerging regulations and build trust in technology will require government to display independence from and resilience against powerful private interests. To date only the Chinese government displays such qualities with the US veering in the opposite direction.

Do not expect a fair for all society soon.

6. Conclusion

The regulation of AI in the four leading AI countries mirrors distinct approaches rooted in their unique philosophical, legal, cultural, and political contexts. Regardless of whether these regulations are mandatory or voluntary, a persistent challenge lies in ensuring that they remain adaptable to evolving technological advancements. Take, for instance, the establishment of standards for training AI systems with data. These standards lose their efficacy if they are based on outdated technology. Thus, the key lies in maintaining dynamic regulations that can keep pace with the rapid evolution of AI technology.

References

Almeida, P.G.R de, Santos, C.D. dos and Farias, J.S. (2021). Artificial Intelligence Regulation: A framework for governance. *Ethics and Information Technology*. 23: 505–525. https://doi.org/10.1007/s10676-021-09593-z.

Attard-Frost, B., Ríos, A.D.l. and·Walters, D.R. (2023). The ethics of AI business practices: A review of 47 AI ethics guidelines. *AI and Ethics*. 3: 389–406, https://doi.org/10.1007/s43681-022-00156-6

Bélisle-Pipon, J_C., Couture, V., Roy, Ganache,M-C., Goetghebeur, I.M. Cohen, I.G., (2021), What Makes Artificial Intelligence Exceptional in Health Technology Assessment? Frontiers in Artificial Intelligence, Vol. 4, doi: 10.3389/frai.2021.736697

Brooks, M. (2023). What's next for quantum computing, *MIT Technology Review*, 6 January, https://www.technologyreview.com/2023/01/06/1066317/whats-next-for-quantum-computing/

Burrell J. (2016). How the machine "thinks": Understanding opacity in machine learning algorithms. *Big Data and Society*. 3(1): https://doi.org/10.1177/2053951715622512.

Cinel, C., Valeriani, D., & Poli, R. (2019). Neurotechnologies for human cognitive augmentation: Current state of the art and future prospects. *Frontiers in Human Neuroscience*. 13, Article 13. https://doi.org/10.3389/fnhum.2019.00013

Collingridge D. (1980). *The social control of technology*. London: Frances Pinter.

Correa, N.K., Galvao, C., Santos, J.W., Galvao, L., Terem, E. and de Oliveira, N. (2023). Worldwide AI ethics: A review of 200 guidelines and recommendations for AI governance. *Patterns*. 4 (10), https://doi.org/10.1016/j.patter.2023.100857.

European Council (2024). Artificial intelligence act: Council and Parliament strike a deal on the first rules for AI in the world. *Press Release Update*, 2 February.

Floridi, L. (2019). Translating principles into practices of digital ethics: five risks of being unethical. *Philosophy & Technology*. 32(2):185–193.

GDPR (General Data Protection Regulation) (2016). Regulation (EU) 2016/679 of the European Parliament and of the Council. *Official Journal of the European Union*, L 119/1, 4.05.2015, https://eur-lex.europa.eu/legal-content/EN/TXT/PDF/?uri=CELEX:32016R0679

Gebru, T., Morgenstern, J., Vecchione, B., Vaughan, J. W., Wallach, H., Daumeé, III, H., Crawford, K. (2021). *Datasheets for Datasets*, arXiv:1803.09010v8 [cs. DB]. 1 December, pp. 1–17, https://arxiv.org/pdf/1803.09010v8.pdf.

Guo, R. (2020). The ethics and governance of artificial intelligence. Beijing. *Law Press*.

Hagendorff, T. (2020). The ethics of AI ethics: An evaluation of guidelines. *Minds and Machines*. 30, 99–120.

IMIST (Israeli Ministry of Innovation Science and Technology) (2023). *Responsible Innovation: Israel's Policy on Artificial Intelligence Regulation and Ethics*. https://www.gov.il/BlobFolder/policy/ai_2023/en/Israels%20AI%20Policy%202023.pdf

Macnish K. (2012). Unblinking eyes: the ethics of automating surveillance, *Ethics and Information Technology*. 14: 151–167.

Mason, R. O. (1986). Four Ethical Issues of the Information Age. *MIS Quarterly*. 10, 5-12, http://dx.doi.org/10.2307/248873

Ministry of Innovation, Science and Technology, (2023). Israel's Policy on Artificial Intelligence Regulation and Ethics, *Decisions*. No. 12, 17 December, https://www.gov.il/en/departments/policies/ai_2023

Mintz, Y., and Brodie, R. (2019). 'Introduction to artificial intelligence in medicine'. *Minimally Invasive Therapy & Allied Technologies*. 28, 73–81. doi: 10.1080/13645706.2019.1575882

Mittelstadt, B. (2019). Principles alone cannot guarantee ethical AI. *Nature Machine Intelligence*. 1(11), 501–507.

Morley, J., Floridi, L., Kinsey, L. and Elhalal, A. (2020). From what to how: an initial review of publicly available AI ethics tools, methods and research to translate principles into practices. *Science and Engineering Ethics*. 26: 2141–2168, https:// doi. org/ 10. 1007/ s11948- 019- 00165-5

Peachey, K., Race, M. and Sri-Pathma, V. (2024). 'Post Office scandal explained: What the Horizon saga is all about'. *BBC News*. 13 January, https://www.bbc.co.uk/news/business-56718036

Prem, E. (2023). From ethical AI frameworks to tools: a review of approaches. *AI and Ethics*. 3: 699–716. https://doi.org/10.1007/s43681-023-00258-9

Prunkil, C. (2022), Human autonomy in the age of artificial intelligence, Nature Machine Intelligence 4 (2), 99–101

Reese, H. (2022). What Happens When Police Use AI to Predict and Prevent Crime? *JSTOR Daily*. 23 February. https://daily.jstor.org/what-happens-when-police-use-ai-to-predict-and-prevent-crime/

Samuel, A.L. (1960). Some Moral and Technical Consequences of Automation—A Refutation, *Science*. 132(3429): 741–742. https://doi.org/10.1126/science.132.3429.741

Sheehan, M. (2023). China's AI Regulations and How They Get Made. Carnegie Endowment for International Peace, https://www.scirp.org/reference/referencespapers?referenceid=3962802

The Economist (2021). The World's Most Valuable Resource is No Longer Oil. *But Data*. https://www.economist.com/leaders/2017/05/06/the-worlds-most-valuable-resource-is-no-longer-oil-but-data.

Turing, A.M. (1950). Computing Machinery and Intelligence. *Mind New Series*. 59(236): 433-460.

White House, (2023). Executive Order on the Safe, Secure, and Trustworthy Development and Use of Artificial Intelligence. 30 October. https://www.whitehouse.gov/briefing-room/presidential-actions/2023/10/30/executive-order-on-the-safe-secure-and-trustworthy-development-and-use-of-artificial-intelligence/

Zhang F. (2020),. Chinese imaging AI firm hacked, coronavirus research sold online. 27 April. https://cntechpost.com/2020/04/27/chinese-imaging-ai-firm-hacked-coronavirus-research-sold-online/

Zhang, L. (2023). China: Provisions on Deep Synthesis Technology Enter into Effect. *Law Library of Congress*. 26 April. https://www.loc.gov/item/global-legal-monitor/2023-04-25/china-provisions-on-deep-synthesis-technology-enter-into-effect/.

The Use of AI in Compliance Management: A Practical Balancing Exercise

Simina Suciu[1]

1. Introduction

Artificial intelligence (AI) is not a novelty from a compliance perspective. The ever-evolving landscape of transformative technologies, including generative AI, however, has triggered extensive debate among legislators and compliance professionals regarding the extent to which AI can be leveraged to enhance compliance activities, on the one hand, and the risks it may trigger or entail, on the other hand.

This chapter delves, first, on how compliance functions can benefit from the recent advances in this field by shedding light on the difference between existing (and already implemented) solutions and the 'smarter', generative AI. The optimisation of processes, the analysis of large amounts of data, which may uncover non-compliant behaviour faster, and overall prevent the application of sanctions and fines, appear to be the asset of AI integration into compliance. Compliance officers can also benefit from reviewing extensive transactions and data, monitoring activities, reducing false positives and costs, addressing human error and minimizing compliance risks, and – ultimately – reducing the duration between regulatory requirements and institutional compliance.

Conversely, this chapter does not shy away from addressing the main point: AI being considered as a compliance risk itself. The author critically examines the challenges that compliance officers may face in balancing the benefits of AI, such as ethical and fairness implications, biases and the potential discrimination embedded in AI decisions. Some complexities encountered in data privacy and the upcoming EU AI Act are also discussed.

In conclusion, strategies for finding a balanced approach while navigating the AI-compliance landscape are set out. Whether the crux resides on accurate data, the appropriate training of the AI or a more comprehensive compliance approach, there is a need for responsible development and application of AI in compliance. While the ultimate destination of this AI-compliance journey remains uncertain at this stage, one thing is clear: abstaining from their interaction is not a viable solution.

Before diving into the exciting details of this chapter, let us first set the stage with the understanding of some fundamental AI concepts.

2. AI – related basic concepts

At the beginning of this week, you might have been suggested a new playlist based on the music you have been listening to lately. Or you may be bombarded currently with new ads for goods like the ones you have just bought on your usual go-to shopping platform? These recommendation platforms are examples of 'weak' or 'narrow' AI.[2] Similarly, the well-known voice assistants, medical diagnosis systems, chatbots, search engines, autocorrection for typing or translation tools and many others qualify under this category. 'Weak AI' is an AI technology aiming to simulate human cognitive functions with a specific purpose - this means that it reflects how a human being would act when accomplishing a certain, narrowly defined task or function.

In contrast, 'generative' or 'strong' AI (such as the well-known ChatGPT) goes beyond the pre-defined rules and boundaries characteristic for weak AI and creates generative and flexible content (in the shape of text, image, video, audio) which *'accommodates a wide-range of distinctive tasks'*[3] and resembles the human-created content. This type of AI is based on specialised machine learning models, which include - amongst others - foundation and specialised models trained on massive datasets, including publicly available information.[4] Therefore, strong AI has as a brain reference a corpus of information, could have the intelligence similar to humans and could teach itself, for instance, to solve problems.

These concepts, especially the weak AI technologies, have been applied for a while now in the day-today compliance management activities. The next section details the benefits of such applicability and highlights certain areas where there is space for smarter AI in compliance.

3. AI-fueled compliance management: benefits

The opportunities offered by the automation of activities in compliance have been tremendous. There is a myriad of tools available on the market that simplify vastly the life of a compliance officer. There are actually so diverse and in a high number that, sometimes, what is the best tool for a dedicated compliance activity becomes confusing. This section outlines, however, examples for compliance areas where the use of AI has already proven exquisite in (i) reducing greatly the amount of time and costs spent on compliance management, (ii) optimising extensive processes, (iii) offering a clearer picture of existing compliance risks and the necessary controls that support mitigation; and, (iv) overall, diminishing the exposure of an organisation towards behaviour that may affect an undisputed reputation and its reliability as a partner towards staff, suppliers, customers and other stakeholders. This section also sets out certain areas whereby strong AI could achieve more in compliance management.

3.1 Due Diligence (Know-Your-Customer)

A due diligence tool provides background checks for suppliers, customers and other stakeholders before an organisation enters a business relationship with a third party. These solutions check the identity of third parties, assess their risk level based on a variety of pre-determined criteria (e.g., behaviour of third party in line with regulatory requirements, scope and value of the envisaged agreement, sanctions exposure, pending or closed investigations, litigations). They also automate background checks and ensure a continuous monitoring of third parties, notify compliance red flags, can send out automatically due diligence questionnaires and inform about the expiry of validity of conducted due diligence. Given the extent of datasets underlying these tools, they are relied upon extensively in practice, for example, from a sanctions perspective. More specifically, they offer certain functionalities of notifying whether a third party or a linked entity part of the third party's group of companies has been captured by the overwhelming sanctions legislative packages worldwide – given their scope and geographical extent and rapid update, these have proved to be extremely difficult to navigate since the events in Ukraine.

In addition, these platforms are also semi- or fully- automated, which means that certain due diligence assessments can be automatically conducted and approved, based on the lack of red flags, without having Compliance intervening. Topics where generative AI could prove to be beneficial may include more in-depth compliance assessment of sanctions impact and the automated analysis of sources used as datasets for such tools from a reliability perspective.

3.2 Compliance policies and procedures

The establishment, review and distribution of compliance policies and procedures can be done through dedicated systems. These tools can track who are owners of such documents, when they have been issued and/or updated, can centralise comments from different departments and roll them out across an organisation.

There is a lot of discussion ongoing amongst compliance practitioners regarding the use of generative AI for automated drafting of company compliance policies and procedures from scratch in accordance with regulatory requirements and other relevant company documents. This would be welcome for ensuring consistency and thoroughness across a company, but does not excuse the necessity of human review.

3.3 Document and contract review management

Language Processing based/e-discovery tools can scan and analyse a very high number of documents and data in a much faster and cost-effective manner than a human document reviewer could do manually. They can be used for regulatory compliance, investigations, M&A, litigation, and they can highlight key terms, flag potential compliance issues, categorise, classify and label documents. Generative AI is showing to be promising for e-discovery:[5] (i) document-by-document review or a 'bottom-up approach', where documents are analysed one by one and there is a decision for each document and (ii) chatbot or a 'top-down approach', which looks at multiple documents simultaneously for addressing an instruction. Each option has its pros and cons and its suitability depends on the overall issue that needs to be addressed.

Contract management systems can establish template contracts, their review in line with legal and compliance standards and company policies, and ensure - for instance - that all required clauses are considered. Generative AI could generate different contracts templates reflecting legal compliance with different regulations across multiple jurisdictions, set out certain contractual risks based on the business relationship with or the market behaviour of the counter- party, automate the application of contractual controls to certain risks, conclude the way forward following the comments raised by multiple departments in an organisation. Template contracts would not need to be reviewed extensively individually.

3.4 Transaction assessment and monitoring

Anti-money laundering and fraud detection systems, especially in the finance/banking sector, assess large volumes of and monitor real-time transactions to identify suspicious activities, patterns and anomalies, which may indicate money laundering or fraud. Customer behaviour models and transactions could be developed with generative AI so that fraudulent behaviour is spotted easier and faster.

3.5 Training and awareness, including communication

There are multiple types of compliance trainings delivered in an organisation, e.g., live, online, general, deep dives, tailored, refreshers. Training platforms ensure that they are rolled out and are tracked, staff receives relevant up-to-date information and there is a centralised manner of monitoring how awareness is implemented. However, there is room for improvement through generative AI. More specifically, the way certain types of trainings interact on such platforms and whether the personnel require, at a certain point, a different type of training, is lacking. In addition, dashboards are not always clear or accurate. Based on the description of certain roles, the activities conducted by the personnel and their training background, automated trainings could directly tackle the compliance risks that personnel may be facing on a day-to-day basis in a more efficient manner. Furthermore, more interactive compliance scenarios and quizzes could be further tailored based on the organisation's activities and support the reinforcement the already conducted training.

Compliance communication, including reporting, may be extensive. Weak AI has been supportive in generating reports for regulatory authorities through the gathering and organization of data from various departments. Similarly to the policies and procedures point above, generative AI could assist with the initial drafting and formatting internal or external reports ensuring accurate and timely submissions. This would be of paramount importance given the sometimes stringent regulatory deadlines for submission/notification.

3.6 Risk and control management

Enterprise and compliance risk management systems centralise the risks linked to departmental activities, transactions, customers, and support companies to have a clear centralised visibility over the risks and the implemented controls throughout the organisation. Often, these risks and controls need to be individually and manually updated. Generative AI could ensure the automated update of risks and controls based on current data, the initial drafting of risks and controls and predict more accurate potential risk exposure, as well as patterns that may trigger non-compliance.

3.7 Legislative changes

The extent to which new regulation is internationally being enacted can be cumbersome to monitor. With the support of generative AI, lengthy pieces of legislation can be summarised concisely in seconds. The same goes for the identification of overlaps, differences and gaps in legislative requirements, the potential impact of new legislation on an organisation's activities, processes and policies and setting out the potential changes that may need to be implemented.

3.8 Case management

Case (including incident) management systems provide for the automation of compliance workflows associated with assessing, investigating and resolving compliance issues. They ensure the documentation and management of compliance workstreams in one dedicated place, the timely and effective resolution and the interaction of multiple stakeholders. These platforms can be built in-house or provided by external third parties, can be broad in scope or tailored to the compliance risk. Enhancing such tools with strong AI could support in gap assessments, identifying easier the root causes, especially in incidents, and offer suggested corrective actions based on market best practice and applicable legislation. It may also be easier to summarise or search into multiple incidents/assessed workflows for prevention, as well as create reports notifications/presentations.

4. Is AI a risk itself?

We have seen that there are clear advantages of having AI implemented in compliance management, and that generative AI could bring further opportunities. But what are the risks associated with it? Are they the same compliance risks as for those pertaining to any tool or system implemented in an organisation or we need to be extra cautious and look beyond those? Are there any specific AI challenges that need to be addressed?

'*While most AI systems pose limited to no risk and can contribute to solving many societal challenges, certain AI systems create risks that we must address to avoid undesirable outcomes.*'[6]

The main categories of AI risks referred to by compliance practitioners are: ethical use and harmful bias, transparency and privacy. At this incipient phase, it does not seem that the risks pertaining to the implementation of AI in compliance management would differ from general risks linked to AI implementation.

The potentially harmful biased nature of AI occurs in relation to the specific types of datasets and trainings fed into the AI. AI may be biased to the human beings that feed the data and train it. There is also the so-called 'black box effect' when decisions taken cannot be traced back, which may become dangerous as the AI changes continuously through its training – if manipulated, it could take the wrong decisions.[7] The most used example in this regard is a recruitment system that ends up preferring and suggesting the hiring of a certain group of individuals based on e.g., race, background, studies. This is just an example; the same outcome could be for other AI systems, including those used by Compliance.

Furthermore, AI systems need to be fully transparent about their functions and their purpose. Compliance of AI with data privacy is probably one of the most controversial risk area. This concern is triggered as the datasets may include personal data. There are multiple points starting to be investigated only now, and are pending to be addressed: How will personal data be processed fairly and transparently, by also giving the possibility to data subjects to opt out from data collection? How is personal data protected or erased after being inserted in the AI? What would be the legal basis for processing and how can data subjects exercise their rights?

Other guard rails related to AI considered are:[8] (i) intellectual property rights (IPRs) – AI systems could be based on worldwide web to generate an output, which may include copyrighted material and IPRs; (ii) if datasets fed into the AI are confidential, how is confidentiality maintained? (iii) cybersecurity – it appears to be predicted that IT crime will be more difficult to detect as AI can mimic physical appearance and voice of individuals and even teach itself about human personalities.

As depicted by the *AI Risk Management Framework*,[9] AI risks may differ from traditional software associated risks: (i) AI dependency on data for training combined with the complexity and volume of such data; (ii) changes during training impacts AI performance; (iii) interaction between the complex AI with more traditional software applications; (iv) higher degree of predicting failures; (iv) potential more frequent maintenance; (v) lack of visibility how AI software can be tested, just to name a few.

Finally, the accuracy and reliability of data embedded in the AI is concerning and challenging. There may be inaccuracies in the data, the AI may give boiler plate responses and the underlying corpus may not be updated as companies and their activities develop, or at least not in the same rhythm. Would such gaps become smaller as AI develops or as organisations catch-up with and understand AI more? In the current rush to adopt AI, a wait and see approach is not cautious enough for a compliance professional if there is business acumen to implement AI.[10] This means that the inherent AI risks need to be addressed, to the extent possible, now.

5. Finding the right balance between AI risks and controls

'[AI] technologies have significant potential to transform society and people's lives – from commerce and health to transportation and cybersecurity to the environment and our planet. AI technologies can drive inclusive economic growth and support scientific advancements that improve the conditions of our world. AI technologies, however, also pose risks that can negatively impact individuals, groups, organizations, communities, society, the environment, and the planet. Like risks for other types of technology, AI risks can emerge in a variety of ways […].'[11]

This is why AI needs to be trustworthy and requires to be built on inclusive growth, sustainable development and well-being; to respect the rule of law, human rights and democratic values, including fairness and privacy; to commit to transparency and explainability, accountability, robustness, security and safety.[12]

For achieving the 'trustworthy' qualification, a system of adequate controls managing the AI related risks – which ensure the AI's validity and reliability, safety, resiliency, accountability, transparency, explainability, interpretability, privacy-enhancement, and the management of harmful bias – would be implemented.[13] It may be difficult to ensure all these aspects in practice; therefore, certain trade-offs may be chosen vs. others depending on the overall purpose, company's strategy and AI model used. Setting up an AI risk management framework focused on the usual pillars is a good starting point: (i) GOVERN – the existence of a culture of risk management from a governance perspective, (ii) MAP – identification of risks, (iii) MEASURE – assessment and tracking of risks, (iv) MANAGE – risks prioritisation and action and continuous monitoring.[14]

Identifying the appropriate controls may be difficult given the novelty of generative AI. Companies (especially those that do not develop AI, but rather incorporate third-party AI in their organisation) may find some initial comfort through the regulation-based guiding path. The European Union (EU) has been at the forefront in this regard through the issuance of the EU AI Act (first ever legal framework on AI): *'[t]he AI Act is the first-ever comprehensive legal framework on AI worldwide. The aim of the new rules is to foster trustworthy AI in Europe and beyond, by ensuring that AI systems respect fundamental rights, safety, and ethical principles and by addressing risks of very powerful and impactful AI models.'*[15] The AI Act adopts a risk-based approach (minimal, limited, high and unacceptable risks) for AI systems based on multiple criteria and for high-risk AIs establishes a conformity assessment for compliance with AI requirements to be conducted. Transparency obligations and additional risk management obligations (e.g., self-assessment and mitigation of systemic risks, reporting of serious incidents, conducting test and model evaluations, cybersecurity requirements) have also been introduced. However, as in any first round of regulation, there is uncertainty in relation to its applicability (for instance how 'general purpose AI systems' and 'systemic risks' concepts are defined), how cumbersome the documentation and transparency requirements will prove to be,[16] and – overall - whether the legislation can catch-up in the future with the continuous technological development of generative AI. As other jurisdictions will follow the EU with enactment of regulation, it will be interesting to see to what extent these will interact, overlap, complement and/or duplicate each other. As in cryptocurrency, enforcement and complaints will be part of the AI development journey.[17]

Companies and compliance officers have already implemented controls for the implementation of weak AI. These include the due diligence of the third-party providing the system, contractual-related controls, checking the technical and organisational measures implemented by the third-party, implementing additional cybersecurity measures internally, conducting data privacy checks (where necessary). It could be difficult to determine what additional specific controls managing the risks triggered by generative AI need to be implemented.

A space to watch is which departments will manage the implementation and monitoring of AI related controls. This is an additional layer of control. Will it be Compliance or IT functions? Or the business itself? Or maybe they will be shared. Considering the novelty of generative AI, strong governance, including at Board and top management level, is essential.

In light of an unclear response based on the above, how could we all benefit from the advantages brought by AI but keeping in mind and tackling its shortages? Conducting a balancing exercise between a certain compliance risk and tailored controls may be the solution. A continuous update, testing and check of underlying datasets of an AI system, containing the confidentiality of data, strong and increased cyber and operational controls, as well as regulation where is needed, are of paramount importance. And on top of this, human compliance interference and experience is required throughout the AI implementation journey.

6. Conclusion

Having compliance professionals involved in the AI risk assessment and implementation of appropriate controls means that a compliance chatbot for addressing compliance related queries raised by personnel is not the solution.[18] Keeping human compliance experience throughout the AI implementation journey is fundamental. One of the inherent attributes of compliance officers is the human element, the ability to create bridges across an organisation and for staff to trust and feel comfortable to reach out to compliance experienced individuals. Think also about the deterrent and preventive effect that a compliance training has - staff is always more engaged and puts more attention to live/in-person compliance trainings rather than online/system-based trainings!

This chapter aimed to, first, highlight how generative AI can enhance various aspects of compliance management, improving efficiency, accuracy and adaptability in dealing with regulatory requirements. Second, given the number of specific risks that AI entails and triggers, AI could amount to a risk itself. Third, there are already tested controls that worked in practice for weak AI solutions, but these may not be enough. To what extent the use of AI regulation may prove to be helpful for ensuring the adherence to certain controls, while at the same time, without hindering the development of generative AI technologies remains to be seen.

The use of AI systems in compliance could be built up slowly with the automation of routine compliance tasks – not all of us are there yet! Streamlining document review, automating transactions assessment, due diligence or training tools, as well as having a centralised view of all compliance workflows is a good starting point. Narrower, known-compliance areas are better at inception. We can move afterwards to having summaries of legislation in seconds or obtaining a draft policy in one minute. This does not mean that it would not need to be reviewed though. There could be a gradual extension of compliance capabilities.

It is very difficult to estimate what impact AI solutions will have in compliance management. It is, absolutely, way too early to state that AI will reshape compliance. However, as we are currently merely scratching intensively the surface of AI technology, the future of compliance management could be surprising.

Notes

1 All views expressed in this chapter are personal and do not represent the position of any organisation.

2 The more general category of AI systems is defined as '*a machine-based system that, for explicit or implicit objectives, infers, from the input it receives, how to generate outputs such*

as predictions, content, recommendations, or decisions that can influence physical or virtual environments. Different AI systems vary in their levels of autonomy and adaptiveness after deployment' in OECD Recommendation on Artificial Intelligence, https://legalinstruments.oecd.org/en/instruments/oecd-legal-0449.

3 https://data.consilium.europa.eu/doc/document/PE-24-2024-INIT/en/pdf, para. 99.

4 European Data Protection Supervisor, 'Generative AI and the EUDPR. First EDPS Orientations for ensuring data protection compliance when using Generative AI systems', 3 June 2024, p.4, https://www.edps.europa.eu/system/files/2024-06/24-06-03_genai_orientations_en.pdf.

5 Chris Haley 'Document Review or Chatbot: Which Generative AI e-Discovery Solution Is Right for You?', Relativity Blog, 24 April 2024, https://www.relativity.com/blog/document-review-or-chatbot-which-generative-ai-e-discovery-solution-is-right-for-you/#:~:text=The%20bottom%2Dup%20approach%20leverages,thousands%20of%20documents%20to%20analyze.

6 European Commission, AI Act webpage, https://digital-strategy.ec.europa.eu/en/policies/regulatory-framework-ai.

7 Moritz Homann 'AI & Compliance: opportunity or challenge?', EQS, 19 February 2024.

8 Susan Divers 'Five essential 'guard rails' for using ChatGPT', The Compliance and Ethics Blog, 14 August 2023. Although the author refers to one particular AI (ChatGBPT), the principles set out therein could be applicable to other AI tools as well.

9 AI RMF 1.0 issued by NIST (the National Institute of Standards and Technology, U.S. Department of Commerce), January 2023 (hereinafter the 'U.S. Report').

10 The implementation of generative AI in organisations is still controversial. Certain companies (such as Google, Amazon, Samsung, Deutsche Bank) have set up guardrails on AI chatbots given the sensitivity of some data. In this regard, see for instance, Jeffrey Dastin and Anna Tong 'Focus: Google, one of AI's biggest backers, warns own staff about chatbots', Reuters, 15 June 2023, https://www.reuters.com/technology/google-one-ais-biggest-backers-warns-own-staff-about-chatbots-2023-06-15/. ChatGBT has been banned in Italy due to privacy concerns – see Shiona McCallum 'ChatGPT banned in Italy over privacy concerns', BBC, 1 April 2023, https://www.bbc.com/news/technology-65139406. Other EU jurisdictions, such as France, Ireland and Germany showed interest in liaising with the Italian Garante to potentially adopt a similar approach: '*We will coordinate with all EU data protection authorities in relation to this matter*' – see Supantha Mukherjee, Elvira Pollina and Rachel More 'Italy's ChatGPT ban attracts EU privacy regulators', 3 April, 2023, https://www.reuters.com/technology/germany-principle-could-block-chat-gpt-if-needed-data-protection-chief-2023-04-03/.

11 U.S. Report.

12 OECD, Recommendation of the Council on Artificial Intelligence, section 1.

13 U.S. Report.

14 Idem.

15 European Commission, AI Act webpage, AI Act | Shaping Europe's digital future (europa.eu).

16 Cleary Gottlieb 'Generative AI Will Stay Top of Mind in 2024', 17 January 2024 and Alexander Hendry, Paul Lugard & Parker Hancock, 'The EU AI Act: Uncharted Territory for General-Purpose AI', 8 April 2024.

17 For an overview of ongoing litigation in the U.S. see relevant section in Cleary Gottlieb 'Generative AI Will Stay Top of Mind in 2024', 17 January 2024.

18 For the necessity of human oversight in relation to AI, see Caitlin Andrews 'EU AI Act shines light on human oversight needs', IAPP, 12 June 2024.

Bibliography

Complianceandethics.org blog

Council of the EU, 'Artificial intelligence (AI) act: Council gives final green light to the first worldwide rules on AI', press release, 21 May 2024

Definitions:https://en.wikipedia.org/wiki/Weak_artificial_intelligence, https://www.techtarget.com/searchenterpriseai/definition/narrow-AI-weak-AI, https://www.eqs.com/compliance-blog/artificial-intelligence-and-compliance-management/, the EU AI Act

European Ethics and Compliance Conference

Giulio Coraggio 'AI Act finalised. Here is what has been agreed', DLA Piper and other articles published on Innovation Law Insights blog

Multiple articles under IAPP's AI Governance Centre, https://iapp.org/about/ai-governance-center/?mkt_tok=MTM4LUVaTS0wNDIAAAGTs-5Sz8oXaX1QSR4rDEbn5pL26yFgaz2bSvE16YeWhaJX6u1TOosKLp-5O8DZL1Y1PigE0VPyFg6_svnT5-eJaymaIh8EjYjbbTIv4jGDG9s1

Podcasts: Compliance & AI (The Compliance Podcast Network) by Thomas Fox, Compliance perspectives by SCCE, Compliance Clarified by Thomson Reuters

Regulation of the European Parliament and of the Council laying down harmonised rules on artificial intelligence and amending Regulations (EC) No 300/2008, (EU) No 167/2013, (EU) No 168/2013, (EU) 2018/858, (EU) 2018/1139 and (EU) 2019/2144 and Directives 2014/90/EU, (EU) 2016/797 and (EU) 2020/1828 (Artificial Intelligence Act), Brussels, 14 May 2024 (OR. en), 2021/0106(COD)

Revolutionizing Compliance Management: Integrating AI, Blockchain, and 100% Sampling for Robust Data-Driven Strategies

Rajeev Thykatt

Introduction

In the rapidly evolving landscape of compliance management, leveraging advanced technologies such as Artificial Intelligence (AI), Machine Learning (ML), and blockchain is becoming increasingly vital. These technologies offer transformative potential to enhance the robustness and defensibility of compliance systems, thereby serving as a crucial line of defense for organizations. This chapter explores the integration of these disruptive technologies in compliance management processes, providing compliance officers and Independent Directors (IDs) with more reliable tools to fulfill their oversight responsibilities effectively.

2. The Role of AI and ML in Compliance Management

Artificial Intelligence (AI) and Machine Learning (ML) are at the forefront of technological innovations that are transforming compliance management. These advanced technologies offer robust solutions for handling data, analyzing risks, and making informed decisions in real-time. They enhance the efficiency and effectiveness of compliance management by enabling automated, accurate, and proactive approaches. This section explores the transformative role of AI and ML in compliance management, focusing on enhanced risk assessment and management, automation of compliance processes, and improved decision-making.

2.1 Enhanced Risk Assessment and Management

Effective risk assessment and management are critical components of compliance management. AI and ML provide unparalleled capabilities to enhance these processes through proactive risk identification and predictive analytics.

2.1.1 Proactive Risk Identification:

AI and ML algorithms can analyze vast datasets from multiple sources, such as transactional data, communication logs, social media, and external databases, to identify potential compliance risks. These technologies excel at detecting anomalies and patterns that may be indicative of compliance issues. For example:

- **Transaction Monitoring:** AI systems can scrutinize financial transactions to detect unusual patterns that may indicate money laundering or fraud. By analyzing transaction amounts, frequencies, and destinations, AI can flag suspicious activities for further investigation.
- **Communication Analysis:** AI can analyze internal communications, such as emails and chat messages, to detect potential policy violations or unethical behavior. AI techniques can be used to identify keywords and phrases that might suggest misconduct.
- **External Data Integration:** By incorporating external data sources, such as news feeds and regulatory updates, AI can provide a comprehensive view of emerging risks that might affect the organization.

This proactive risk identification enables organizations to address potential issues before they escalate into significant problems, thereby enhancing overall compliance and reducing the likelihood of regulatory breaches.

2.1.2 Predictive Analytics:

Predictive analytics powered by ML can forecast potential compliance issues by analyzing historical data and identifying trends. This capability allows organizations to prepare for and mitigate risks more effectively. For instance:

- **Regulatory Impact Analysis:** ML models can simulate the impact of new regulations on the organization, helping compliance teams understand potential challenges and adjust their strategies accordingly.
- **Behavioral Predictions:** ML can analyze past behaviors of employees, customers, or third parties to predict future compliance risks. For example, if certain patterns of behavior have historically led to compliance

violations, ML can identify similar patterns in current data and alert compliance officers.

By leveraging predictive analytics, organizations can adopt a forward-looking approach to compliance management, allowing them to anticipate and mitigate risks before they materialize.

2.2 Automation of Compliance Processes

Compliance management involves numerous routine and repetitive tasks that can be efficiently automated using AI. Automation not only increases efficiency but also reduces the risk of human error, ensuring consistent and accurate compliance processes.

2.2.1 Routine Task Automation:

AI can automate various routine tasks associated with compliance management, such as data collection, aggregation, and initial analysis. Examples include:

- **Data Aggregation:** AI systems can automatically collect and aggregate data from various internal and external sources, ensuring that all relevant information is available for compliance analysis.
- **Regulatory Reporting:** AI can generate compliance reports by analyzing collected data and formatting it according to regulatory requirements. This automation speeds up the reporting process and ensures accuracy.

Automating these routine tasks frees up compliance officers to focus on more strategic activities, such as risk assessment, policy development, and strategic planning. Additionally, automation reduces the likelihood of errors that can occur during manual data handling, thereby enhancing the accuracy and reliability of compliance processes.

2.2.2 Continuous Monitoring and Real-Time Insights:

AI-driven compliance tools can continuously monitor financial transactions, operational processes, and other relevant activities, providing real-time insights and flagging suspicious activities for further investigation. This capability includes:

- **Transaction Monitoring:** AI systems can continuously analyze financial transactions to detect signs of fraud, money laundering, or other illicit activities. By comparing transaction patterns against known indicators of suspicious behavior, AI can flag transactions that require further review.
- **Operational Monitoring:** AI can monitor operational processes to ensure compliance with internal policies and regulatory requirements. For example, AI can track data access patterns to detect unauthorized access attempts or monitor supply chain activities to ensure compliance with ethical sourcing policies.

Continuous monitoring helps organizations maintain a high level of compliance by ensuring that potential issues are identified and addressed promptly. This proactive approach reduces the risk of regulatory breaches and associated penalties.

2.3 Improved Decision-Making

AI systems provide compliance officers with powerful tools for improved decision-making. By integrating data from various compliance systems and leveraging advanced analytics, AI can offer valuable insights that support more informed and effective decision-making.

2.3.1 Comprehensive Dashboards:

AI systems can provide compliance officers with comprehensive dashboards that integrate data from various compliance systems. These dashboards offer a holistic view of the organization's compliance status, presenting key metrics and insights in an easily digestible format. Features include:

- **Real-Time Compliance Status:** Dashboards can display real-time information on the organization's compliance performance, including metrics such as the number of compliance incidents, the status of ongoing investigations, and the overall risk level.
- **Key Performance Indicators (KPIs):** AI can track and visualize KPIs related to compliance, such as the percentage of employees trained on

compliance policies, the number of audits completed, and the rate of policy violations.

These comprehensive dashboards enable compliance officers to monitor the organization's compliance performance in real-time, identify areas of concern, and make informed decisions. By providing a centralized view of compliance data, AI dashboards help compliance teams stay on top of their responsibilities and ensure that all aspects of compliance are adequately addressed.

2.3.2 Document Analysis

AI technologies can assist compliance officers in reviewing extensive documentation by summarizing key points and highlighting areas of concern. AI algorithms can analyze large volumes of text, such as regulatory documents, policy manuals, and audit reports, to extract relevant information and identify potential issues. For example:

- **Regulatory Summarization:** AI can analyze new regulatory documents and generate summaries of key requirements and changes. This automation helps compliance officers quickly understand the implications of new regulations and adjust their strategies accordingly.
- **Policy Review:** AI can review internal policy documents to identify areas where the organization may be falling short of compliance requirements. For example, AI can flag outdated policies that need to be updated to comply with new regulations.

By automating the analysis of complex documents, AI helps compliance officers save time and ensure that they do not overlook critical information. This capability is particularly valuable in industries with complex and evolving regulatory environments, where staying informed about regulatory changes is crucial.

3. Blockchain: A Game Changer for Transparency and Accountability

Blockchain technology has emerged as a revolutionary tool in various sectors, offering unparalleled transparency, security, and accountability. In compliance management, blockchain holds the potential to transform how organizations handle data, verify transactions, and ensure adherence to regulations. This section explores the profound impact of blockchain on compliance management, focusing on secure and transparent record-keeping, enhanced data integrity, and facilitating regulatory compliance.

3.1 Secure and Transparent Record-Keeping

Blockchain's most significant contribution to compliance management lies in its ability to provide secure and transparent record-keeping. The technology's decentralized nature and cryptographic security features make it ideal for maintaining immutable records of transactions and activities.

3.1.1 Immutable Ledger:

A blockchain is essentially a distributed ledger that records all transactions across a network of computers. Each transaction is grouped into a block, and these blocks are linked together in chronological order, forming a chain. Once a block is added to the blockchain, it cannot be altered or deleted, ensuring the integrity and permanence of the recorded data. This immutability is crucial for compliance management as it guarantees that records are tamper-proof and verifiable.

For example, in the financial sector, blockchain can be used to record every financial transaction in a way that ensures no transaction can be altered retroactively. This feature is particularly beneficial for audit trails, where maintaining the integrity of financial records is paramount. Regulators and auditors can trust the accuracy of blockchain records, knowing that they reflect the true history of transactions.

3.1.2 Transparency and Accountability:

Blockchain's transparency is another key advantage for compliance management. Every participant in a blockchain network has access to the same version of the ledger, which means all transactions are visible to all authorized parties. This transparency enhances accountability by making it difficult for any single party to manipulate the data without detection.

In supply chain management, for instance, blockchain can track the movement of goods from origin to destination. Each step in the supply chain is recorded on the blockchain, providing a transparent and verifiable record of the product's journey. This transparency ensures that all parties, including suppliers, manufacturers, and regulators, can verify the authenticity and compliance of the products.

3.1.3 Smart Contracts:

Smart contracts are self-executing contracts with the terms of the agreement directly written into code. These contracts automatically execute and enforce the terms when predefined conditions are met. Blockchain technology underpins the functionality of smart contracts, offering significant advantages for compliance.

Smart contracts can automate compliance checks and regulatory reporting. For example, in the insurance industry, a smart contract can automatically verify claims against policy terms and process payments if the conditions are met. This automation reduces the need for manual intervention, speeds up processes, and ensures that all actions are compliant with the predefined rules.

3.2 Enhanced Data Integrity

Data integrity is a critical aspect of compliance management. Ensuring that data is accurate, consistent, and trustworthy is essential for making informed decisions and maintaining regulatory compliance. Blockchain technology enhances data integrity through its decentralized and cryptographic security features.

3.2.1 Decentralization:

In a traditional centralized database, data is stored in a single location, making it vulnerable to hacking, corruption, and unauthorized access. In contrast, blockchain's decentralized architecture distributes data across a network of nodes. Each node holds a copy of the entire blockchain, and consensus mechanisms ensure that all copies are identical and up-to-date.

This decentralization makes it extremely difficult for malicious actors to alter or delete data. To tamper with the blockchain, an attacker would need to gain control of a majority of the network's nodes simultaneously, which is practically impossible in a well-secured blockchain network.

For compliance management, this means that data stored on the blockchain is more secure and resilient against attacks. Organizations can rely on the integrity of the data, knowing that it has not been tampered with or compromised.

3.2.2 Cryptographic Security:

Blockchain uses advanced cryptographic techniques to secure data. Each block in the blockchain contains a cryptographic hash of the previous block, a timestamp, and transaction data. The hash functions as a unique digital fingerprint, ensuring the authenticity and integrity of the block's data.

If any data within a block is altered, the hash of that block changes, breaking the chain's continuity. This change is immediately detectable by the network, preventing unauthorized modifications. This cryptographic security ensures that all data recorded on the blockchain is authentic and has not been altered.

For example, in the healthcare industry, blockchain can be used to store patient records securely. Each record is encrypted and linked to the blockchain, ensuring that it cannot be altered or deleted without detection. This secure record-keeping ensures that patient data remains accurate and trustworthy, which is essential for regulatory compliance and effective healthcare delivery.

3.3 Facilitating Regulatory Compliance

Blockchain technology simplifies and enhances the regulatory compliance process by providing a transparent, secure, and verifiable record of all transactions and activities. This capability is particularly valuable in industries with stringent regulatory requirements, such as finance, healthcare, and supply chain management.

3.3.1 Regulatory Reporting:

Blockchain can streamline regulatory reporting by automating the collection and verification of compliance data. Regulators can access real-time data directly from the blockchain, eliminating the need for manual reporting and reducing the risk of errors.

For example, financial institutions can use blockchain to record all transactions in a way that is accessible to regulators. Smart contracts can automate the reporting process, ensuring that all relevant data is submitted accurately and on time. This automation reduces the administrative burden on organizations and ensures that regulatory requirements are consistently met.

3.3.2 Auditability:

Blockchain's immutable and transparent ledger provides a reliable audit trail that can be used to verify compliance with regulations. Auditors can access the blockchain to review transaction histories, verify data integrity, and ensure that all actions comply with regulatory requirements.

In the pharmaceutical industry, for instance, blockchain can be used to track the production and distribution of drugs. Regulators and auditors can review the blockchain to ensure that all products meet safety and quality standards and that they have been produced and distributed in compliance with regulations.

3.3.3 Cross-Border Compliance:

Globalization has increased the complexity of regulatory compliance, with organizations needing to comply with regulations in multiple jurisdictions. Blockchain's transparent and verifiable record-keeping simplifies cross-border compliance by providing a single source of truth that can be accessed by regulators in different countries.

For example, in international trade, blockchain can be used to record all transactions and movements of goods across borders. This transparent record allows customs authorities and regulatory bodies in different countries to verify that all transactions comply with relevant regulations, reducing the risk of delays and disputes.

4. 100% Sampling: A Novel Approach to Compliance

The traditional approach to compliance management often relies on sampling methods, where a subset of transactions or data points is analyzed to draw conclusions about the entire dataset. While this approach can be effective, it carries inherent risks such as missing critical anomalies or patterns due to the limited scope of the sample. The advent of Artificial Intelligence (AI) and Machine Learning (ML) has made it feasible to analyze entire datasets, paving the way for 100% sampling. This approach involves examining every transaction or data point, offering a comprehensive and robust strategy for compliance management. This section explores the concept of 100% sampling, its benefits, challenges, and implementation strategies.

4.1 Comprehensive Data Analysis

4.1.1 Unparalleled Coverage and Accuracy:

One of the primary advantages of 100% sampling is its ability to provide complete coverage of all transactions and data points within an organization. Unlike traditional sampling methods, which may overlook significant anomalies due to their limited scope, 100% sampling ensures that no transaction goes unchecked. This comprehensive approach enhances the accuracy and reliability of compliance management.

- **Detection of Anomalies:** By analyzing every transaction, AI and ML systems can identify even the smallest deviations from expected behavior. This capability is crucial for detecting fraud, money laundering, and other compliance violations that might otherwise go unnoticed.
- **Pattern Recognition:** ML algorithms can recognize patterns across the entire dataset, providing deeper insights into potential compliance risks. For example, patterns of behavior that indicate potential insider trading can be identified more effectively with 100% sampling.

4.1.2 Real-Time Data Processing:

The integration of AI and ML enables real-time processing of vast amounts of data. This capability ensures that compliance officers receive timely alerts and insights, allowing for immediate action.

- **Immediate Response:** Real-time analysis allows organizations to respond to compliance issues as they arise, rather than after the fact. This proactive approach minimizes the impact of potential violations and enhances overall compliance.
- **Continuous Monitoring:** Continuous monitoring through 100% sampling ensures that compliance is maintained at all times, rather than

being periodically checked. This ongoing vigilance is essential in dynamic regulatory environments.

4.2 Reduction of Compliance Risks and Fraud

4.2.1 Minimizing False Positives and Negatives:

Traditional sampling methods often result in false positives (incorrectly identifying compliant transactions as non-compliant) and false negatives (failing to identify non-compliant transactions). 100% sampling significantly reduces these risks by ensuring that every transaction is analyzed.

- **Enhanced Accuracy:** By examining the entire dataset, AI and ML systems can make more accurate determinations of compliance, reducing the likelihood of false alarms and missed violations.
- **Fraud Detection:** Comprehensive analysis improves the detection of fraudulent activities. For instance, in financial services, analyzing all transactions can uncover complex fraud schemes that span multiple accounts or transactions.

4.2.2 Enhanced Compliance with Regulatory Requirements:

Regulatory bodies increasingly demand comprehensive and transparent compliance practices. 100% sampling aligns with these expectations by providing a thorough and transparent approach to compliance management.

- **Regulatory Confidence:** Regulators are more likely to trust and approve compliance reports generated through 100% sampling, knowing that they reflect a complete analysis of all relevant data.
- **Audit Readiness:** Organizations that employ 100% sampling are better prepared for regulatory audits, as they can provide comprehensive documentation and evidence of their compliance efforts.

4.3 Increased Confidence in Decision-Making

4.3.1 Holistic View of Compliance:

100% sampling provides compliance officers and decision-makers with a holistic view of the organization's operations. By analyzing all transactions and data points, AI and ML systems can generate comprehensive reports that offer a complete picture of compliance status.

- **Integrated Insights:** Comprehensive data analysis integrates insights from various sources, providing a unified view of compliance. This integration helps identify correlations and interdependencies that might be missed with traditional sampling methods.
- **Strategic Decision-Making:** With access to complete and accurate data, compliance officers can make more informed and strategic decisions. This capability enhances the organization's ability to manage risks and maintain compliance.

4.3.2 Support for Risk-Based Approaches:

Regulators and industry standards increasingly advocate for risk-based approaches to compliance. 100% sampling supports these approaches by providing the data necessary to assess and prioritize risks accurately.

- **Risk Prioritization:** By analyzing the entire dataset, AI and ML can identify the most significant risks facing the organization. Compliance officers can then prioritize their efforts based on these insights, focusing on areas with the highest potential impact.
- **Resource Allocation:** Comprehensive data analysis enables more efficient allocation of resources. Compliance teams can direct their efforts towards the most critical areas, ensuring that resources are used effectively.

4.4 Implementation Strategies for 100% Sampling

4.4.1 Infrastructure and Technology:

Implementing 100% sampling requires robust technological infrastructure capable of handling large volumes of data. Organizations need to invest in high-performance computing systems and advanced analytics platforms.

- **Scalability:** The infrastructure must be scalable to accommodate growing data volumes. Cloud-based solutions offer the flexibility and scalability needed for effective 100% sampling.

- **Data Integration:** Effective 100% sampling requires the integration of data from multiple sources, including internal systems, external databases, and third-party services. Organizations need to establish seamless data integration processes.

4.4.2 AI and ML Capabilities:

Leveraging AI and ML is essential for the successful implementation of 100% sampling. These technologies provide the analytical power necessary to process and analyze vast datasets in real time.

- **Algorithm Development:** Developing and training AI and ML algorithms is a critical step. Organizations need to invest in data science expertise to create models tailored to their specific compliance requirements.
- **Continuous Improvement:** AI and ML models should be continuously refined and updated to reflect changing regulatory requirements and emerging compliance risks.

4.4.3 Compliance Culture:

Implementing 100% sampling requires a culture of compliance within the organization. Employees at all levels need to understand the importance of comprehensive compliance practices and be committed to maintaining them.

- **Training and Awareness:** Regular training programs can help employees understand the significance of 100% sampling and their role in supporting compliance efforts.
- **Leadership Support:** Strong support from leadership is essential for fostering a culture of compliance. Leaders should communicate the value of 100% sampling and ensure that necessary resources are allocated.

4.4.4 Ethical and Regulatory Considerations:

As with any advanced technology, implementing 100% sampling involves ethical and regulatory considerations. Organizations must ensure that their data practices comply with relevant regulations and respect ethical standards.

- **Data Privacy:** Ensuring data privacy is crucial. Organizations must implement measures to protect sensitive information and comply with data protection regulations such as GDPR.
- **Ethical Use of AI:** The ethical use of AI and ML is essential. Organizations should establish guidelines for the ethical use of these technologies and ensure transparency in their decision-making processes.

5. What Board, Top Management, and Independent Directors Can Expect

The adoption of AI, blockchain, and 100% sampling in compliance management brings significant benefits and strategic advantages to the Board, top management, and Independent Directors. This section outlines what these key stakeholders can expect from the integration of these advanced technologies.

5.1 Enhanced Oversight and Governance

5.1.1 Greater Transparency and Accountability:

The integration of AI and blockchain technologies provides an unprecedented level of transparency and accountability in compliance management. Board members and Independent Directors can expect:

- **Real-Time Access to Compliance Data:** AI-powered dashboards and blockchain records provide real-time visibility into compliance activities, allowing for immediate oversight and intervention when necessary.
- **Immutable Audit Trails:** Blockchain ensures that all compliance-related transactions and activities are recorded immutably, providing a verifiable audit trail that enhances accountability and trust.

5.1.2 Improved Risk Management:

AI and ML technologies offer advanced risk assessment and predictive analytics capabilities. Top management and Independent Directors can anticipate:

- **Proactive Risk Identification:** AI systems can identify potential compliance risks before they materialize, enabling proactive risk management and mitigation strategies.

- **Data-Driven Decision-Making:** Predictive analytics and comprehensive data analysis support informed decision-making, allowing the Board to prioritize and allocate resources effectively.

5.2 Increased Efficiency and Cost Savings

5.2.1 Streamlined Compliance Processes:

Automation of routine compliance tasks through AI reduces the manual workload and minimizes the risk of human error. Stakeholders can expect:

- **Operational Efficiency:** Automation streamlines compliance processes, reducing the time and effort required to meet regulatory requirements.
- **Cost Savings:** By automating labor-intensive tasks and improving process efficiency, organizations can achieve significant cost savings in compliance management.

5.2.2 Scalable Solutions:

The technological infrastructure required for AI, blockchain, and 100% sampling is scalable, accommodating growing data volumes and evolving regulatory landscapes. Top management can anticipate:

- **Future-Proof Compliance Management:** Scalable solutions ensure that compliance management systems can adapt to future regulatory changes and organizational growth.
- **Long-Term Investment:** Investing in these advanced technologies provides long-term benefits, reducing the need for frequent upgrades and system overhauls.

5.3 Strengthened Regulatory Relationships

5.3.1 Enhanced Compliance with Regulations:

100% sampling and blockchain technologies align with regulatory expectations for comprehensive and transparent compliance practices. Stakeholders can expect:

- **Regulatory Confidence:** Comprehensive data analysis and immutable records foster trust and confidence among regulators, facilitating smoother regulatory reviews and audits.
- **Improved Regulatory Reporting:** Automated reporting and real-time data access streamline the process of regulatory submissions, ensuring timely and accurate compliance reporting.

5.3.2 Proactive Compliance Strategies:

AI-driven insights enable organizations to anticipate and respond to regulatory changes proactively. Board members and top management can anticipate:

- **Regulatory Alignment:** Continuous monitoring and predictive analytics ensure that compliance strategies remain aligned with evolving regulatory requirements.
- **Reduced Risk of Penalties:** Proactive compliance management reduces the likelihood of regulatory breaches and associated penalties, safeguarding the organization's reputation.

5.4 Strategic Competitive Advantage

5.4.1 Enhanced Reputation and Trust:

Adopting cutting-edge technologies in compliance management positions the organization as a leader in transparency and ethical practices. Stakeholders can expect:

- **Strengthened Brand Reputation:** Demonstrating a commitment to robust compliance practices enhances the organization's reputation among customers, investors, and partners.
- **Increased Stakeholder Trust:** Transparent and accountable compliance management fosters trust among stakeholders, including shareholders, employees, and the wider community.

5.4.2 Competitive Differentiation:

Leveraging AI, blockchain, and 100% sampling provides a strategic competitive advantage. Top management can anticipate:

- **Innovation Leadership:** Being at the forefront of technology adoption in compliance management differentiates the organization from competitors.
- **Market Confidence:** Advanced compliance practices instill confidence in the market, attracting potential investors and partners who value strong governance and risk management.

5.4.3 Future Outlook

The integration of AI, blockchain, and 100% sampling represents a significant advancement in the field of compliance management. As these technologies continue to evolve, they will play an increasingly critical role in shaping the future of corporate compliance and risk management. Organizations that adopt these technologies will be better equipped to handle complex regulatory environments, enhance transparency, and make informed decisions.

By leveraging real-time data analytics, secure record-keeping, and comprehensive data analysis, organizations can achieve greater transparency, efficiency, and accountability. This proactive, transparent, and efficient approach to compliance will be essential for organizations to thrive in today's dynamic business landscape.

6. Conclusion

The integration of AI, ML, and blockchain technologies, combined with a 100% sampling strategy, represents a transformative approach to compliance management. These technologies enhance the ability of compliance officers and Independent Directors to satisfy themselves that the systems of risk management are robust and defensible. By leveraging real-time data analytics, secure record-keeping, and comprehensive data analysis, organizations can achieve greater transparency, efficiency, and accountability. As these technologies continue to evolve, they will play an increasingly critical role in shaping the future of corporate compliance and risk management.

New framework for compliance in late payments in commercial transactions

Ruben Bahamonde

Late payments significantly impact SMEs. One in four bankruptcies is due to invoices not being paid on time. One of the root causes of late payments is asymmetries in bargaining power between a large or more powerful client (debtor) and a smaller supplier (creditor). This often results in suppliers having to accept unfair payment terms and conditions, which make commercial transactions unsustainable in the long term.

To address this problem, the Commission proposes a new Regulation on combating late payments, revising the existing Directive 2011/7/EU. This revision aims to bring fairness to commercial transactions, increase the resilience of SMEs and supply chains and constitute a new challenge for compliance officers.

This paper will address the main changes in the legal framework of late payments and how they can foster commercial transactions, making them more ethical, fair and sustainable.

1. Introduction

The freedom of private initiative provided for in Article 61 CRP is one manifestation of the constitutional principle of freedom of private autonomy, namely in contractual freedom, which is more developed in Article 405 of the Portuguese Civil Code. At the European Union level, free private initiative is laid down in Article 16 of the Charter of Fundamental Rights of the European Union. In this context, companies are free, within the terms of the law, to draft the contracts they sign. In other words, the supplier/seller and buyer contractors may set the forms and payment periods they deem most convenient for the case.

Economic operators supply most goods and services in the European Union internal market to other economic operators and public entities under deferred payments, where the supplier gives the customer time to pay the invoice as agreed between the parties or according to the provisions described on the supplier's invoice. Small and Medium Enterprises (SMEs) play an essential role in the European market, and their ability to impose deadlines for payment of invoices issued for services rendered or goods sold clearly differs from those of large[1] companies. In fact, large companies are more able to impose more extended payment periods, usually 60 days, while the usual payment term for SMEs is 30 days. This asymmetry gives large enterprises a greater advantage, in operational terms, to the detriment of small enterprises, which bear, to a large extent, the costs of this[2] advantage.

In addition, in commercial transactions between economic operators or between economic operators and public entities, payments often occur later than agreed on in the contract or the general commercial conditions agreed on or applicable between the parties. Though goods are delivered or services provided, the corresponding invoices are paid long after the deadline has expired. These payment delays affect liquidity and complicate companies' financial management while undermining their competitiveness and viability. The creditor must resort to external financing and bear additional costs for recovering credit. At the same time, the debtors may finance themselves by not meeting their obligations, being very little penalized for their behaviour.

The first attempt by the European Union to combat late payments in commercial transactions was Directive 2000/35/[3] EC; twelve years later, Directive 2011/07/[4]EU reinforced the commitment to standardise the regulations in this area. However, the national rules for combating late payment have maintained several differences in the European context, which prevented the desired standardization of[5] rules. Twelve years after the entry into force of Directive 2011/07/EU (hereinafter Directive), the Commission proposed a new Regulation in September 2023 to further combat late payments in business transactions.[6] One of the main grounds for the proposal is the Directive's inadequacy, precisely because it lacks adequate preventive and deterrent measures, and the enforcement and compensation mechanisms have proven insufficient.

2. The state of late payments in transactions between operators

The Directive structures its standards considering five main points. **Firstly**, it lays down a thirty-day payment goal for the public sector to entrepreneurs for products or services. In certain circumstances, this limit may go up to 60[7] days. **Secondly**, contractual freedom is recognised in the relations among entrepreneurs. These invoices should be paid within 60 days unless the parties stipulate differently, and such stipulation is not a manifest abuse by the[8] creditor. **Thirdly**, entrepreneurs may claim interest payments and compensation for the costs of credit recovery[9]. **Fourthly,** a minimum compulsory interest rate of at least 8 % is laid down arising from late payments for all Union Member States on the interest rate the European Central Bank applied to its main recent refinancing operation[10]. **Fifthly and** finally, a procedure is described for collecting unchallenged debts, which provides 90 days for recovering debt starting from the date the procedure began[11].

Based on the evaluations and consultations carried out by the Commission before submitting the proposal for a Regulation and the experience in implementing the Directive, there seems to be an agreement as to introducing a contractual permitted ceiling for the settlement of invoices not exceeding 30 days for payments made by large companies to SMEs and the need to define better the circumstances in which 60 days on payments between companies can be exceeded. This entails a more precise definition of when more than 60 days constitutes a manifest abuse by the creditor.[12] Most interested parties consulted on this matter agreed to set a maximum payment limit for transactions among entrepreneurs, preferably 30 days. The consultation also found that interest and compensation resulting from late payments are rarely paid to creditors, thus the relevance of automatic interest payment.

3. The Commission's proposal and the Parliament's consideration

On 12.09.2023, the Commission presented its proposal for a Regulation to combat delays in payments of commercial transactions to combat late payments in commercial transactions to be applied to all transactions between companies or between companies and public entities[13]. Following the Directive, this text aims to improve the conditions for ensuring the proper functioning of the internal market by encouraging the competitiveness of enterprises, particularly SMEs. On 23.04.2024, the European Parliament modified specific provisions relevant to the present study through its legislative resolution and after the first reading of the proposed Regulation. We will discuss the main vectors of the regulation proposal and the main changes suggested by the European Parliament.

3.1 Laying down a 30-day payment deadline.

A maximum of 30 days is laid down for the settlement of invoices resulting from commercial transactions between companies and between companies and public entities. The Directive's regime remains which allows payment in installments and no more than 30 days between installments. Specific information should be considered regarding this proposal. Providing the obligation to pay invoices within 30 days in transactions between the State and individuals is especially relevant. First, it promotes a culture of timely payment in the economy, where the State can "lead by example." Secondly, the public sector plays a relevant economic role and develops it in partnership with private operators, so timely payment by this "important customer" within 30 days allows entrepreneurs access to a flow of liquidity, thus easing more significant financial constraints.[14] In this context, the obligation in public works contracts should also be mentioned. The contracting public authority must demand evidence from the contractor that they have paid their subcontractors the invoices due within the regulations' legally mandatory deadlines, i.e., 30 days.[15] The fact that contractors have better cash flow and liquidity does not automatically mean that they will pay their suppliers, who will also have better cash flow and liquidity. Therefore, this measure will allow us to monitor this compliance more closely since, with the request for each payment, the contractor will have to prove that they have settled the invoices of their subcontractors in due time.

Regarding the proposed Regulation establishing 30 days for payment of invoices between entrepreneurs and between the State and entrepreneurs, it is essential to note the statistical data for 2024 identify an average payment term for invoices by the public sector of 69 days; in most Member States the average duration for the payment of invoices among entrepreneurs is approximately 60[16]days. Thus, the proposed Regulation would halve the average settlement time of invoices, greatly benefiting affected creditors. On the other hand, this formal setting of maximum deadlines represents only some progress and an improvement of the deadlines already provided for in the Directive, whose effectiveness in practice is evidenced by the above-mentioned statistical data.

After the corresponding assessment at first reading, the European Parliament proposed a possible derogation from the 30 days in commercial transactions between companies, allowing that in these transactions, when expressly agreed in the contract, the payment period may be extended up to 60 calendar days. In commercial transactions between companies for purchasing low turnover or seasonal goods, the payment term may be extended up to 120 calendar days from the date the invoice was received or an equivalent payment notice by the debtor as long as the goods have been received. We believe this exception should not benefit all private operators, only SMEs; large companies should respect the most demanding period of 30 days. This proposal would align with the European Parliament's proposal on the unavailability of the right to interest and compensation, which we will discuss next.

3.2 Null and void contractual provisions.

In the Regulation proposal, the following provisions and practices should be considered null and void: a) Establishing a payment period over 30 days; (b) excluding or limiting the creditor's right to demand interest for the delay in payment or the right to obtain compensation for the costs incurred for the recovery of the credit; C) extending the duration of the verification and acceptance procedure period beyond 30 days and; d) intentionally delaying or preventing the time of invoice submission.

This provision's wording is new and replaces Article 7 of the Directive entitled Contractual Clauses and Abusive Practices, which is so difficult to apply. This new wording eliminates the concept of abusive practices and clarifies which contractual conditions will be considered null and void. As you will see later, the wording of this provision can hinder the success of implementing an alternative dispute resolution system.

The European Parliament has decided to ease the possibility of creditors surrendering their right to obtain interest on arrears for late payment or the corresponding compensation of the debtor, allowing this prerogative in cases where the debtor is neither a public entity nor a large enterprise. This measure seems appropriate in that it preserves a greater degree of private autonomy by creditors when there is a lesser discrepancy between the negotiating power of the parties involved and will allow greater willingness to join alternative ways of settling disputes. Parliament's proposal adds the nullity of clauses prohibiting, excluding or limiting the transfer of credits to a financial institution or third parties for access to financing services. This allows for greater ease in obtaining financing based on unsettled invoices.

4. Interest and compensation for credit recovery expenses

The proposal for a Regulation maintains a minimum compulsory interest rate arising from late payments for all Union Member States of at least 8 % on the interest rate applied by the European Central Bank, to be calculated daily and compensation. The fixed amount due by the debtor to the creditor as compensation for the costs incurred by the creditor with recovering the debt is increased from €40.00 to €50.00. Therefore, the debtor automatically incurs the obligation to pay the creditor a fixed amount of compensation for the costs of recovering the debt in a fixed amount of EUR 50 for each commercial transaction. Notably, automatic interest and automatic compensation do not exclude the possibility that the creditor can claim other compensatory amounts. Still, these will no longer be due automatically.

The automatic calculation of interest and compensation allows the creditor to rapidly issue an enforceable title that includes the outstanding amount, the principal amount, the interest on arrears, and compensation without further proof of what results from an invoice issued, expired and not paid on time.

The European Parliament has chosen to amend this regime by proposing a lump sum compensation for the costs incurred with debt collection, depending on debt amount, to provide higher protection for creditors and implement greater deterrence for debtors. A fixed amount of EUR 50 is proposed for each trade transaction of EUR 0 to EUR 1 500, EUR 100 for each trade transaction of EUR 1 501 to EUR 15 000 and EUR 150 for each trade transaction of more than EUR 15 000. In other words, automatic compensation is significantly increased, thus reducing creditors' losses in recovering their credit and allowing them to issue an enforceable title rapidly while maintaining the possibility of taking legal action to claim more significant damages if the economic relevance of those damages compensates for any costs.

5. Alternative dispute resolution

The proposal for a Regulation provides that-Member States should promote the voluntary use of an effective and independent alternative dispute settlement mechanism to resolve disputes between debtors and[17] creditors. The use of alternative dispute resolution mechanisms for disputes over off-term payments aims to encourage parties to seek a solution devised by themselves quickly and efficiently, thus maintaining the trust between the parties involved in the dispute.

The scope of this measure seems limited to us for two reasons mainly. Firstly, the system for combating late payments has, as one of its traditional pillars, the rapid issue of an enforceable title, and, in this context, the intervention of ADR does not seem to provide an even more rapid issue of an enforceable title. If the debtor does not comply voluntarily, the creditor will have the greatest interest in obtaining an enforceable title and proceed to enforce it as soon as possible. For example, in Portugal, in 2023, the average time for receiving debt through an enforceable credit was 45.9 months, i.e., almost four[18] years. Secondly, in those situations where there are impediments to obtaining the said enforceable title, the unavailability of rights (interest and compensation) will always be a limitation to the success of ADR since it limits the creditor's leeway and, consequently, the debtor's interest. Considering the null clauses regime as amended by Parliament, ADR will be of little interest to large companies and public entities, being more attractive to other economic agents, who can benefit from the withdrawal of interest or corresponding compensation by the creditor.

The European Parliament has chosen to amend this provision, which states that "notwithstanding Article 5(3), Article 8(3) and Article 9(1)(b) of this Regulation, the contracting parties may enter into negotiations to reach an amicable settlement on challenged debts." Thus, the idea is reinforced that no claims are possible resulting from late payments relating to interest payment for late payment (5.3) and the right to fixed compensation arising from late payment (8.3), any agreement or provision limiting these rights being null and void (9.1), whenever the debtor is either a large company or a public entity.

6. Conclusions

One of the Commission's main concerns in the proposed Regulation is the fear of unfair bargaining power that large companies and public bodies can have over SMEs. In this particular context, there is higher strictness in enforcing deadlines for settling invoices than in common practice because, as evidenced in studies, on average, companies in Europe settle invoices in sixty days, and public entities take even longer. However, we must not forget that most European companies are SMEs, and micro SMEs are very relevant. From the studies carried out, it follows that, within the private sector, SMEs are precisely those that most usually settle their invoices late, not necessarily the big companies. For this reason, considering the higher global relevance that small and medium-sized operators have in business, relaxing the deadline for payment of invoices among SMEs appears to be relevant, just as it seems fitting to us to impose a deadline of 30 days for both public entities and large companies. The proposed Regulation will contribute very little to boosting payments to small and medium-sized enterprises if the deadline for payment between companies, particularly from large enterprises to SMEs, does not enhance common daily practice, i.e., payments in approximately sixty days.

Notes

1 See. Di Bella, L., Katsinis, A., Lagüera-González, J., Odenthal, L., Hell, M., Lozar, B. Annual Report on European SMEs 2022/2023, Publications Office of the European Union, Luxemburg, 2023, doi:10.2760/028705. Specifically, on page 6, it states that SMEs (excluding those in the financial sector) accounted for 99.8 % of companies active in the 27 Member States.

2 As far as late payment is concerned, there is evidence that the type of companies that most usually pay off-term are SMEs. See Tim Miller, Sarongrat Wongsaroj, The Domino Effect: the impact of late payments, December 2017, pp. 12-14.

3 Directive 2000/35/EC of the European Parliament and of the Council of 29 June 2000 laying down measures to combat late payment in commercial transactions.

4 Directive 2011/17/EU of the European Parliament and of the Council of 16 February 2011 laying down measures to combat late payments in commercial transactions.

5 Léon Golden, Late Payment in Western Europe, Comparative Study, September 2014

6 COM (2023) 533 - Proposal for a regulation of the European Parliament and of the Council on combating late payment in commercial transactions.

7 Article 4.

8 Articles 3 and 7.

9 Article 6.

10 Paragraphs 6 and 7 of Article 2.

11 Article 10 .

12 The 2021 Opinion of the Fit for Future Platform, suggestion 7.

13 https://ec.europa.eu/info/law/better-regulation/have-your-say/initiatives/13665-Late-payments-update-of-EU-rules_pt.

14 Maurizio Conti, Leandro Elia, Antonella Rita Ferrara, Massimiliano Ferraresi, Goverment late paymentes and firms survival. Evidence from the EU, p. 29.

[15] Articles 3 and 4 of the proposal for a Regulation.
[16] European Payment Report 2024, The changing payments landscape: Optimism and opportunity ahead, Intrum, May 2024, p. 13.
[17] Article 16.
[18] See https://estatisticas.justica.gov.pt/sites/siej/pt-pt/Paginas/Temas/Duracao-dos-processos-findos.aspx, retrieved on 31.05.2024.

Combating Crypto Assets Money Laundering in Decentralized Finance (DeFi)

Ana Cristina Perdomo Gomez

1. Introduction

The rapid connectivity provided by internet access enables cross-border payments and funds transfer across multiple jurisdictions. Consequently, the number of VA business models or activities in the VA ecosystem have increased, such as coin offerings, cryptocurrencies, mixers and tumblers, decentralized platforms, exchanges, and privacy wallets. Concomitantly, money laundering, fraud, and market manipulation risks have intensified.

Strengthening collective endeavors from both public and private institutions, alongside global initiatives led by enforcement authorities, has been imperative in the ongoing battle against digital washing. Despite these concerted efforts, the challenge persists as criminals adeptly conceal their digital identities through sophisticated methods, which has been affecting fair and safe digital transactions.

According to the Europol´s report[1] (Decoding the EU's Most Threatening Criminal Networks, 2024) based on investigations of 821 criminal networks active in the EU, money laundering is a key part of criminal enterprises.

Those criminal networks have a strong leadership, the ability to deal with illicit transactions across the globe and a low probability of making amateurish mistakes. Moreover, when they cooperate, they do in partnerships, often under the crime as-a-service framework, to obtain specific on-the-ground support.

Furthermore, the EP and the Council of the European Union have adopted MiCA, which came into force on June 29, 2023, with the aim of reinforcing AML measures and countering the financing of terrorism, aligning the regulatory framework with the current complex international digital landscape, and enhancing harmonization in rules and supervision application. Nevertheless, such regulation omits DeFi platforms from its purview.

This article intends to focus on DeFi cryptocurrencies, digital assets that operate on smart contracts. Does regulation play a critical role in preventing and combating money laundering in relation to DeFi cryptocurrencies? Could the current framework provide sufficient tools to prevent and combat money laundering with DeFi cryptocurrencies?

Conversely, innovative online crimes using AI challenge the efficiency of current compliance methods for detection and prevention. Furthermore, the banking industry digitalization has rapidly increased the occurrence of cyber laundering with more sophisticated and innovative mechanisms, which has not always been accompanied with adequate and prompt responses from the private and public sectors.

Conversely, according to the Money Laundering National Risk Assessment Guidance issued by FATF (2024), a significant vulnerability in combating AML is the limited understanding of money laundering threats and risks with insufficient knowledge and expertise among national authorities. This undermines the effectiveness of supervision and enforcement mechanisms across different industries.

The authorities and the private sector have incorporated advanced cyber intelligence technology with the purpose of uncovering hidden e-commerce networks, facilitators, and other fraudulent activities. However, while major private sector players such as financial institutions and banks invest substantially in AML compliance, medium and small financial entities often invest only the minimum required.

In this context, regulations overlook digital aspects, hindering transaction laundering detection. Moreover, private, and public entities should integrate digital considerations into compliance programs to improve regulatory adherence and mitigate risks from illicit activities.

2. The Relationship between Crypto assets and Money Laundering

A crypto asset is a digital representation of value or rights, transferable and storable electronically via DLT. Recent publications by the IMF characterize crypto assets as digital representations of value that leverage both cryptography and and DLT for payment or investment purposes.[3]

The EC[4] has articulated the term crypto asset to denote a digital representation of value or rights, transferable and storable electronically, employing DLT or similar means.

For the sake of clarity within this article, the term "crypto asset" will be consistently utilized, adhering to the definition provided by the EC.

Within this context, it is crucial to establish a clear definition of blockchain technology. The UK Crypto Asset Task Force formed in October 2018[5] by the Treasury, FCA, and Bank of England, defines DLT, commonly known as "blockchain", as a groundbreaking technology facilitating secure and decentralized sharing and updating of encrypted data. It allows participants to authenticate and document modifications to a synchronized ledger distributed across a network.

Any alteration to the blockchain requires the establishment of a consensus mechanism to ensure accuracy and security. Additionally, blockchain transactions employ cryptography, utilizing a hash function akin to solving a puzzle for added security, confidentiality, and integrity. This process of validating and incorporating changes to the blockchain is commonly referred to as "mining"[6].

That being said, crypto assets come in various forms, such as digital currencies like Bitcoin, Litecoin, and equivalents, as well as digital representations of assets and NFTs. Unlike fiat currencies, they enable direct digital transfers without intermediaries.

As mentioned, MiCA introduces regulatory obligations for issuers of asset-referenced tokens, electronic money tokens, and crypto asset service providers. It also clarifies the powers of competent authorities, including cooperation and sanctions frameworks. MiCA is pivotal in combating money laundering, defined by EUROJUST as "the process through which criminals disguise the illicit origin of their property or income"[7],

In essence, money laundering involves engaging in transactions with the intent of establishing legitimate origins for illicitly obtained money and can be performed in three steps: placement, layering and insertion[8].

The placement phase is the entry of crime into the legitimate financial system. The layering is the most complex phase and consists of separating the illicit money from its source through a sophisticated process, with the purpose of destroying the connection with the original criminal activity. The insertion allows the illicit actors to integrate the money into the financial system and use it for legitimate purposes.

The scenario illustrates the dynamics of crypto assets. Money brokers open multiple accounts in the placement stage, utilizing money mules and falsified documents to acquire cryptocurrencies with cash or other coins. In the layering stage, "chain hopping" occurs, transferring cryptocurrency across jurisdictions with weaker AML regulatory frameworks, complicating traceability. This phase often involves the use of cryptocurrency mixers to sever the link between the original and final addresses via intermediary wallets.

Finally, in the integration phase, money mules open bank accounts for a short period of time, or criminals create online companies to accept payments in cryptocurrency and convert it into fiat currency.

Another form of illicit activity involving DeFi is the manipulation by using copious amounts of cryptocurrency to increase the trading volume of low-liquidity tokens on the target DeFi protocol, consequently creating significant price increases that are not reflected on the market. Those initial funds are subject to flash loans and then the attacker exchanges the artificially inflated holdings for other tokens with more liquidity and value or uses them to borrow assets which shall never be repaid.

Conversely, EUROPOL, the EU´s law enforcement agency tasked with aiding the Member States in combating international crime and terrorism, has acknowledged the intricate connection between money laundering, corruption, and various criminal activities. The 2023 report released by EUROPOL[9] underscores crucial aspects pivotal in the contemporary landscape of organized crime. It highlights the sophistication of laundering large illicit profits at scale, facilitated by a refined financial crime ecosystem, including digital banking without physical branches, increasingly adopted by consumers.

Furthermore, the digital landscape has brought complexities to AML investigations, with the integration of machine learning, AI, deepfake tech, and the metaverse, embraced by the financial sector. Moreover, illicit actors have expanded money laundering as-a-service activities, including crypto, for online and offline crimes, and fraud on dark web markets.

EUROPOL[10] highlights a need to scrutinize decentralized web platforms and P2P applications, rather than focus on centralized data hosting services. EUROPOL emphasized that 70% of criminal networks in the EU use basic money laundering techniques, while 60% employ corruptive methods to achieve their goals. This undermines both the rule of law and public trust in the justice system.

On the other hand, DeFi represents an innovative ecosystem of decentralized applications within the realm of financial services by using smart contracts, operating autonomously without central governing authority. It features an open, permissionless, and highly interoperable protocol, using public DLT to improve TradFi services.

DeFi cryptocurrencies are digital assets uniquely crafted for operation within blockchain-based systems, functioning via smart contracts to foster a genuinely decentralized financial environment. Katona (2021) compared the DeFi ecosystem to Money Lego, where individual protocols and applications can be assembled like Lego blocks, combining "to achieve optimal transaction outputs".

The term decentralize implies that the validation of power regarding the software code is publicly available for review and operation through a consensus power, which refers to the ability of individuals to write data to the blockchain, according to the protocol embodied in the software.

In line with this, the consensus power introduces another critical dimension to be addressed in DeFi regulation, namely competition. While competition is not a fundamental aspect of this analysis, the escalating concentration of mining pools poses a growing risk of collusion among miners, potentially leading to the centralization of network control.

Conversely, the decentralization of a blockchain warrants consideration if the open-source network system is genuinely decentralized and spread across autonomous entities. In reality, though, some block producers and core developers align themselves under a parent corporation or capital control, such as *Blockstream* (Bitcoin) or *ConsenSys* (Ethereum).

Hence, a deeper examination of DeFi protocol governance and its centralization implications is crucial. Moreover, due to the ambiguity regarding legal recourse in such transactions, it is uncertain which regulatory jurisdiction customers could appeal to for redress. A smart contract is a computerized protocol that autonomously executes instructions based on predefined conditions.

Furthermore, DeFi protocols rely on oracles for financial transactions, a feature absents in TradFi systems. This reliance renders DeFi vulnerable to exploitation through artificial price manipulation in digital asset markets, potentially harming investor trust. Conversely, DeFi's settlement layer integrates consensus protocols, empowering participants to resolve conflicts and establish unanimous agreement within the system.

Scholars[11] have highlighted certain technological facets within DeFi context. Among these considerations is algorithmic automation, emphasizing the transparency for all participants in financial transactions and their ability to manage and oversee their assets, and "DeFi compositions," which involves amalgamating various functionalities within DeFi protocols to create diverse financial products.

As highlighted by CCI[12], an effective DeFi framework necessitates decentralized protocols, predefined rules, and actions within the smart contract protocol. Moreover, it must utilize open-source technology, maintain autonomy, adhere to standardized practices, and ensure non-discriminatory access within the digital public infrastructure by guaranteeing neutrality, and independent financial control from the influence of any restricted group.

Within this context, ensuring transparency in on-chain transactions is paramount as it can effectively mitigate information asymmetries, diminish conflicts of interest, and alleviate risks associated with credit, liquidity, and concentration.

The Chainalysis crypto money laundering report[13] sheds light on key trends in 2023, offering intriguing insights into money laundering and DeFi. According to the report, cryptocurrency services decreased in 2023 compared to 2022, amounting to approximately a 10%-billion-dollar reduction. However, notably, the share of illicit funds channeled through DeFi protocols has seen a surge. One of the contributing factors to this rise is the absence of robust obfuscation methods for fund transfers. Furthermore, there has been an uptick in illicit funds flowing into gambling services and bridge protocols in 2023, typically linked with stolen funds and off-ramping services.

Interestingly, the report also highlights that money laundering is more concentrated in criminal activities related to CSAM and ransomware operations, underscoring the vulnerabilities in law enforcement due to the diffuse nature of the services involved.

Another notable trend is the increasing use of cross-chain bridges, driven by the lack of centralized oversight in fund custody. Additionally, hackers have exploited vulnerabilities in DeFi protocols, often due to protocol operators prioritizing growth over implementing robust security measures.

According to Shapiro (2023)[14], determining the applicability of regulations like securities laws to blockchain systems hinges on a comprehensive grasp of decentralization. Shapiro contends that, from a legal standpoint, validation power holds greater significance than consensus power. This is especially true when the system achieves a sufficient level of decentralization. In such cases, regulatory obligations and duties of disclosure and care should be directed towards miners and block producers who wield predominant control over the consensus power within a network, rendering the latter less critical in regulatory considerations.

In line with this, the blockchains must be free open-source software and the core developers cannot compel individuals to run or update nodes. Moreover, economic power may influence centralization and Shapiro suggests measuring as follows: "(...) it may be said that the broader and more diverse the base of users and the more power they have, the more likely a system is to be decentralized under the law (...)."

Shapiro's decentralization test can be summarized with two key criteria: i) no single entity should control any significant part of the Open Network System, and ii) if control exists over a component, other essential components must be structured to protect the rights and property of third parties within the system.

Finally, Shapiro concludes the test by introducing key presumptions about native token ownership and management of token-sale proceeds within an open network. These stipulate that ownership or control of token-sale proceeds should not exceed 20% of the market capitalization; exceeding this indicates control over the network's economic and consensus aspects. Another critical factor is dominance over a software client used by over 50% of validating nodes. Moreover, individuals or entities with "administrative" or "ownership" privileges for parameter changes, upgrades, and token minting are recognized as having control over the open network system.

Aramonte et al. (2021) consider DeFi "an illusion" or "used as a catch-all term that captures a wide spectrum of business models and technologies, some of which may not be decentralized across any meaningful dimension"[15].

As elucidated earlier, the DeFi mechanism exhibits centralized governance protocols and tends to utilize blockchain consensus mechanisms that can concentrate power. Consequently, it is imperative for policymakers to recognize it, when formulating an appropriate regulatory framework.

The examination of DeFi holds relevance in the formulation of improved regulations aimed at preventing criminal activities within the DeFi space. In line with this, Jeng (2024)[16], an advisor at CCI, emphasizes that DeFi should not be unfairly perceived as carrying more inherent risks than centralized finance.

Addressing concerns about cybersecurity, Jeng (2024) contends that the decentralized nature of DeFi, with its reliance on public permissionless blockchains, renders attacks more challenging. The multitude of nodes in DeFi systems acts as a formidable barrier, making it difficult for malicious actors to compromise the network. Contrary to allegations, Jeng (2024) underscores the robustness of DeFi against cyber threats.

In alignment with the recommendations of IOSCO, Jeng (2024) acknowledges the necessity for regulators to identify "responsible persons." However, she highlights a potential paradox wherein this identification implies a centralization tendency, akin to the structures observed in TradFi.

Furthermore, Jeng (2024) alludes to broader regulatory considerations beyond the financial realm, citing the impending Regulation 2023/2854[17]. This legislation mandates smart contracts to deactivate, necessitating a form of re-centralization under the control of intermediaries. This interplay between regulatory measures and DeFi presents a challenge that requires careful consideration to strike an optimal balance between security and decentralization.

3. The Relationship between DeFi and Money Laundering

Money laundering poses a significant threat to the integrity of global financial systems. Several regulations have been crafted to counteract money laundering, and to impose specific obligations on financial institutions, encompassing the reporting of transactions, detection of suspicious activities, and the implementation of robust customer due diligence procedures and international cooperation to combat cross-border money laundering.

Nevertheless, illicit actors might exploit DeFi protocols for money laundering operations and funnel illicit proceeds into the TradFi system. The vulnerability of DeFi systems to anonymity risks is particularly evident in decentralized setups like the Bitcoin protocol, where participant identification and verification are not mandatory, and historical transaction records can be challenging to link to real-world identities.

A report by Elliptic (2023)[18] provides practical insights into the primary risks associated with crypto assets and how to identify participants in these investments. According to the report, criminals operate pseudonymously or anonymously, often transferring illicit funds to jurisdictions with minimal AML/CTF regulations. These risks apply not only to non-compliant and unlicensed exchanges but also to legitimate exchanges and digital asset businesses, such as crypto asset brokerages.

Criminals also exploit legitimate exchanges by using fraudulent KYC documents, taking advantage of the lack of face-to-face interaction in the crypto industry. Along with this, crypto asset mixing services redistribute assets among users to break transaction traceability. Many VAs are self-custodied, often hosted within financial institutions or VASPs, raising vulnerability in the system.

Conversely, risks associated to unlicensed exchanges stem from inadequate KYC/CDD information, lacking or insufficient AML/CTF regulatory frameworks in their operating jurisdictions, discussions on the dark web, and the promotion of cash-to-crypto transactions, among other factors.

SEC and FinCEN have recognized the challenges in relation to decentralized risks, and the US Department of the Treasury[19] has released a compelling report addressing the risks inherent in DeFi.

Within this context, the BSA requires financial institutions to comply with AML obligations regardless of classification as a DeFi service. According to the US Department of the Treasury[20], in instances where a DeFi service falls outside the scope of the BSA, the obligation to identify and report suspicious activities to law enforcement and competent authorities persists. Hence, they argue that the existing AML/CFT regulatory framework in the US is adequate to manage risks associated with DeFi services within the country.

FATF[21] recently updated its guidance on risk-based approach standards for VAs and AML obligations. DeFi services, particularly, require enhancements due to challenges in identifying suspicious activity within blockchain data. FATF also acknowledges that relying solely on centralized VASPs to adhere to AML and sanctions obligations falls short of mitigating the risks of illicit finance associated with DeFi services.

In this realm, decentralized mixers are significant. Actors aim to obscure the source, destination, or amount of VA transactions by sending VAs into liquidity pools. They utilize techniques to offer VAs with reduced usage and traceability constraints, leveraging cross-chain bridges for inter-blockchain asset exchange, mixers for VA transactions, and liquidity pools as a layering mechanism.

Illicit actors might exploit DEXs for covert VA exchange, employing cross-chain bridges, mixers, or other DeFi services. Alternatively, they may use DEXs for swapping VAs with weaker illicit finance safeguards or less centralized oversight, as well as exchanging for assets with lower traceability.

With regards to mixers, criminals possess the capability to obfuscate the source by consolidating VAs from numerous wallets, individuals, or accounts into single or multiple transactions. It is prevalent to engage intermediaries with weak or absent AML controls, often situated in jurisdictions with insufficient AML standards for VAs.

To illustrate the relationship between money laundering and DeFi, the SEC filed charges against two individuals with a Cayman Islands-based company in 2021, in relation to an unregistered sale of more than $30 million in securities, using smart contracts and DeFi technology, as well as deceptive operations and profitability practices with investors.

In a nutshell, the SEC found that illicit actors used smart contracts and digital tokens to pay interest using specific digital assets. They also utilized a "governance token" with voting rights to profit from token resales in another market. This violated SEC antifraud provisions and KYC legal obligations. The wrongdoers admitted to the charges, agreeing to disgorge over $12 million and pay penalties of $125,000 for each individual respondent.

According to the US Department of the Treasury report[22] which gathered data from various sources, including the private sector, the common pain point lies in uncertainty of DeFi services definition and applicability of regulatory frameworks. Notwithstanding, the CFTC, FinCEN, and SEC defend the existence of guidance concerning enforcement actions targeting DeFi services that fail to adhere to regulatory obligations. They emphasized that technical functionalities do not exempt entities from their financial legal obligations.

Conversely, and from the practical perspective, the absence of a central server or service provider complicates law enforcement efforts, as there is no clarity among law enforcement agents when it comes to determining the specific entity to target for investigations or the implementation of asset seizure measures.

Regarding the previous aspects, divergent opinions persist on the efficacy of regulatory clarity in addressing AML concerns within the DeFi space. Advocates of this perspective contend that a well-defined regulatory framework, coupled with explicit AML legal obligations for DeFi entities, could serve as a viable solution to mitigate AML risks.

On the other hand, proponents like Jeng (2024) advocate for a deeper examination of DeFi's intricacies and MiCA. They argue that the regulatory disparity between digital and cash transactions might inadvertently incentivize illicit actors to choose cash transactions due to their lower traceability, potentially undermining AML safeguards.

Moreover, Jeng (2024) underscores a critical aspect tied to the centralization tendencies within blockchain networks, regarding entities such as *BigTechs* and TradFi which poses a dual threat by not only compromising decentralization principles but also jeopardizing privacy and competition protections.

Conversely, the Parliament and Council agreed to amend the sixth AML Directive and the EU "single rulebook" regulation[23], clarifying that physical cash and digital assets should adhere to identical regulatory limits. Furthermore, FIUs will receive increased authority to uncover instances of money laundering and identify suspicious transactions.

In line with the aforesaid, Paesano (203) pointed out in the 7th Global Conference on Criminal Finances and Cryptocurrencies[24] some challenges regarding money laundering investigations, such as the lack of professional experts and technical literacy among law enforcement and judicial officers who struggle to analyze and interpret digital wallets and blockchains to convict a suspect.

According to the Basel Institute of Governance, blockchain offers forensics benefits in investigations due to its immutability and inherent capability for traceability in financial transactions and streamlining them with fewer human resources.

Within this context, they propose recommendations to enhance AML investigations, integration of the crypto area within TradFi, in terms of supervision, enforcement and asset recovery, strengthen technical and information collaboration between private and public sectors, and enhance training to enforcement authorities.

As aforementioned, numerous countries have not incorporated FATF standards into their AML frameworks for VASPs. This creates a considerable challenge in allocating supervisory and enforcement resources to the VA sector.

On the other hand, it is indisputable that criminals will continually seek loopholes in potential solutions aimed at combating money laundering. Therefore, a key recommendation for the private sector is to carefully assess potential illicit risks before launching a new product.

4 The Current Legislative Framework

As previously discussed, regulatory frameworks impact the complexity of DeFi, influencing law enforcement dynamics regarding money laundering, which remains a subject of debate. In this context, Kremer & Werbach (2022)[25] elucidate that the need for law stems not from technological limitations but from inherent human limitations. They argue: "Where the software code is an inherently superior mechanism, law should gradually give way."

The efficacy of blockchain relies on the trust forged among parties committed to adhering to consensus rule updates. Werbach contends that relying solely on legal frameworks impedes blockchain's potential as a robust system for property rights transfer or tracking. This approach risks compromising key features like decentralization, immutability, and resistance—inherent to blockchain technology. Blockchain seeks to instill trust among peers, platforms, and products. While relationship and institution-based trust are crucial in adopting blockchain-based sharing economies, its technological aspects—immutability, transparency, and programmability—are paramount.

In line with this idea, Rashan Colbert[26] explained that decentralization has benefits and trade-offs related to policies and governance, since users must have an increased level of responsibility compared with traditional institutions.

Another facet concerning regulations pertains to the classification of a crypto asset as a financial instrument and transferable security, consequently making it subject to regulated markets and processes. Under this argument a product or service with comparable characteristics to an existing one should be regulated similarly.

In line with this, Alfredo Muñoz[27] reinforces that the regulation shall be "attractive" to incentivize investments rather than being used as a subterfuge for individuals to avoid complying with financial compliance regulatory frameworks.

4.1. Regulatory Oversight at an EU Level

The EU has updated its regulatory framework to combat money laundering and terrorist financing within regulated entities, aiming for a unified and standardized approach across the single market to safeguard financial system integrity. The EU AMLDs guiding these efforts are crafted by the EP and implemented by each Member State internally.

Firstly, the 5th AMLD[28] of 30 May 2018 aimed to enhance transparency within the EU, expanding its scope to encompass virtual currency exchanges. It introduced cryptocurrency controls like mandatory registration with authorities, stringent customer due diligence practices, and record management for FIUs.

Subsequently, the EU's 6th AMLD[29], imposed to regulated entities in 2021, aimed at strengthening AML controls, placing a greater emphasis on accountability for regulated entities in combating financial crime. This comprehensive approach also extended to addressing cybercrime as a prohibited activity associated with money laundering and pursues the EU´s aspiration to promote digitalization, harmonization, and consumer protection.

MiCA, effective from June 2023, represents a groundbreaking legal framework overseeing crypto assets globally, establishing a new EU AMLA. The EU AMLA serves as a central hub for coordinating national FIUs and information sharing. Compliance with privacy rules and the application of supervisory power to financial and non-financial entities can make this framework beneficial.

Furthermore, MiCA mandates prior authorization from the competent authority of each EU Member State for a range of activities, ensuring uniform application across the EU. These activities include custody, administration of crypto assets, operation of trading platforms, exchanges, and advisory services. MiCA stipulates that non-EU companies can only provide crypto asset services within the EU if they establish a company in an EU Member State and obtain authorization from the respective authorities.

CASPs must also exhibit internal controls and risk management mechanisms to ensure integrity and confidentiality. This includes measures such as preventing market manipulation and disclosing final beneficiaries to combat money laundering and terrorist financing.

As mentioned earlier, there is a lack of clarity regarding the legal or natural persons involved in providing services related to DeFi projects or representing third parties Maia & Vieira dos Santos (2021)[30] argue that these interfaces should fall under the scope of MiCA.

They also advise to ensure the safety, reputation, and adequacy of the protocol by verifying compliance with AML legislation and minimum standards set by the FATF[31], especially considering that MiCA is not obligatory for certain DeFi projects.

Another challenge arises regarding MiCA and DeFi. Decentralized services should not be controlled by individuals or legal entities but should rely on smart contracts. Therefore, it is crucial to confirm that decentralized protocols operate on a decentralized settlement layer, free from user asset control, and assess MiCA's applicability.

Some financial experts[32] consider MiCA a regulatory framework with positive aspects, in relation to legal certainty and promotion of trust in the industry, transparency, protection, and accountability for investors.

Nevertheless, crypto assets and service providers terminology should be interpreted comprehensively to consider all potential crypto assets under competent authorities monitoring. In this regard, any legislative initiative should be future-proof, and able to pursue innovation and technological developments and comply with AML/CTF rules of the Union.

4.2 DeFi and Application of Regulatory Frameworks: Path to Improvement

Certain authors, such as Jeng (2024), have contemplated the risks associated with TradFi, drawing parallels to those of DeFi. In this regard, regulatory efforts should be tailored to address the specific risks inherent in DeFi without applying the same regulatory measures as TradFi.

In 2021[33] academics and public sector figures convened at the World Economic Forum to explore potential regulatory approaches to DeFi. Building upon this discussion, Allen (2022) advocated for precautionary regulation to mitigate the potential societal harm posed by new financial products and services. Conversely, Durham (2023) emphasized the impracticality of blockchain regulation due to its decentralized nature, arguing that enforcement would be challenging given the essence of decentralization in blockchain operations.

One of the primary complexities inherent in DeFi regulation lies in striking a balance between trust and confidence in self-regulatory mechanisms versus the involvement of the state, particularly in the context of financial crises.

Many academics perceive DeFi as embodying a "techno-utopian vision of finance"[34] characterized by a lack of concentrated intermediaries and independence from states, governments, or regulators. This perspective stems from the belief that both TradFi and DeFi encounter comparable risks, a notion that warrants further exploration.

Technological advancements not only form the infrastructure of DeFi but also fuel its potential for disrupting and transforming the financial landscape. DeFi's globally distributed server capacity spans time zones and countries with lower operational and energy costs. Additionally, DeFi utilizes cost-saving mechanisms enabled by AI, the efficiency of smart contracts on distributed ledgers, and the decisive power of algorithmic data analysis within virtual cloud systems.

Notwithstanding, those elements undermine the rule of law, according to Zetzsche et al. (2020), because of the uncertainties surrounding risks and the state's role as both rule-maker and enforcer.

Within this framework, concerns arise regarding jurisdiction and governing law in DeFi. Legal concepts such as contracts, torts, joint ventures, antitrust law, and blockchain-specific legislation come under scrutiny.

Zetzsche et al. (2020) defend the prioritization of "law everywhere" over "law anywhere", and advocate for the application of decentralized governance mechanisms. This approach acknowledges the decentralized nature of DeFi participants while striving to establish a legal framework that operates universally rather than being tied to specific jurisdictions.

Cybersecurity is another concern. Ethereum's co-founder, Vitalik Buterin, formulated the "blockchain trilemma", a practical analysis concerning a trade-off among security, decentralization, and scalability. Zetzsche et al. (2020) recommend addressing cross border liability concerns through a reevaluation of compliance approaches.

With regards to jurisdiction and governing law, academics propose to regulators to apply "tech localization" by enforcing in accordance with infrastructure requirements and collaboration with stable tech supply networks which enable global supply chains management, particularly during times of crisis.

DeFi has the potential to diminish the concentration and control of data by the state and Big Tech. However, it is essential to determine which parts of the financial services chain should be centralized or decentralized to meet legal requirements and involve public stakeholders. Solutions like industry self-regulation in DeFi, using smart contracts for automated compliance, have been suggested. Regardless of the approach, regulators must stay agile and adaptable to the dynamic changes in the DeFi ecosystem.

In developed countries, where regulatory frameworks are often more robust, DeFi sectors may operate within clearer legal boundaries, benefiting from established guidelines that aim to safeguard consumer interests and maintain market integrity.

Conversely, in emerging market economies, the regulatory landscape for DeFi and crypto may be less defined, potentially exposing users to greater risks due to regulatory ambiguity and insufficient consumer protection measures.

Addressing these disparities requires a multifaceted approach that balances fostering innovation and engaging stakeholders across industries and jurisdictions to develop tailored regulatory frameworks that promote responsible innovation while mitigating risks associated with financial crime and consumer exploitation, for developed and emerging market jurisdictions.

5. Practical Cases: Oversight regarding Main AML Global Regulatory Frameworks

In the US, Judge Katherine Polk Failla of the U.S. District Court for the Southern District of New York presided over a significant case favoring

Uniswap. The ruling addressed the Group's liability for "scam tokens" traded on the decentralized exchange.

Essentially, Judge Failla concluded that "Due to the Protocol's decentralized nature, the identities of the Scam Token issuers are basically unknown and unknowable, leaving Plaintiffs with an identifiable injury but no identifiable defendant". Consequently, the current state of securities law did not support legal action against Uniswap.

Furthermore, the decision underscored that: "the Court declines to stretch the federal securities laws to cover the conduct alleged and concludes that Plaintiffs' concerns are better addressed to Congress than to this Court." However, the Tornado Cash case[35], not subject to securities law scrutiny, presents a paradox compared to the preceding case reviewed by the same judge. In this case, the Department of Justice alleges that Tornado Cash developer and co-founder Roman Storm used the platform to launder billions of dollars in stolen crypto funds.

In August 2022, OFAC imposed sanctions on Tornado Cash, alleging funds diversion to Lazarus Group, a North Korean entity. This led to a legal battle, with plaintiffs representing Tornado Cash participants suing the US Department of Treasury, alleging violations of constitutional rights, especially financial transaction privacy and freedom.

In the midst of legal turmoil, Tornado Cash co-founders were charged with money laundering. In August 2023, the Federal District Court for the Western District of Texas issued a landmark ruling. It found that Tornado Cash had a property interest in its immutable smart contract and ruled that benefits from smart contracts, like fees, were transferred to the DAO formed by its founders and participants. This decision highlighted a key interpretation: privacy rights in transactions through certain services may not be constitutionally protected.

In a parallel development, the court also ruled that Tornado Cash should be added to the OFAC Designated National and Blocked Persons List, aligning with the government's efforts to curb illicit financial activities. This decision reflects the growing intersection between DeFi platforms and regulatory scrutiny, highlighting the complexities surrounding privacy, financial regulation, and constitutional rights in the digital age.

The legal proceedings surrounding Tornado Cash serve as a pivotal case study, shaping the discourse on the regulation of DeFi services and the extent of constitutional protections in the realm of digital transactions. As the landscape continues to evolve, it underscores the imperative for policymakers, regulators, and industry stakeholders to navigate the delicate balance between innovation and compliance, ensuring the integrity of financial systems while upholding fundamental rights and freedoms.

On January 10, 2024, SEC made a significant move by approving spot Bitcoin exchange as a traded product. This decision marks a pivotal moment in the ongoing debate surrounding the classification of products and services subject to financial regulations in the US, a debate that has gained prominence in recent years.

The SEC's decision to greenlight spot Bitcoin exchange as a traded product has sparked both approval and dissent within the market. Proponents of the decision argue that it will provide increased protection and certainty to investors, bolstering confidence in the crypto market and facilitating its integration into traditional financial systems.

Conversely, critics of the decision contend that it runs counter to the fundamental principles of decentralization that underpin cryptocurrencies. They fear that subjecting spot Bitcoin exchange to regulatory oversight may stifle innovation and adversely impact investment in crypto assets by introducing burdensome compliance requirements and regulatory constraints.

As the crypto market continues to mature and evolve, striking the right balance between regulatory scrutiny and preserving the ethos of decentralization remains a key challenge for policymakers, regulators, and industry participants alike. The implications of the SEC's decision are likely to reverberate throughout the crypto ecosystem, shaping its trajectory in the years to come.

Viewing digital transactions through a positive lens reveals their potential to uncover illicit activities, as demonstrated by the case of "Welcome to Video" in 2019. In this case, the DOJ shut down one of the largest child pornography sites by volume of material stored and apprehended its operators. This operation was made possible through the tracking of bitcoin transactions on a public ledger.

Blockchain analytics firms have honed expertise in tracing illicit transactions laundered through DeFi protocols, striving to intercept funds before conversion into fiat currency.

In light of these advancements, scholars recommend a framework centered on redefining "independent control" over software systems. They suggest imposing regulatory obligations on entities with such control and on critical communications providers facilitating transaction communications.

In Hong Kong, financial regulators like the SFC, the HKMA, and the IA have taken proactive steps by issuing guidance on crypto assets, in order to provide clarity and establish regulatory expectations within the burgeoning crypto ecosystem.

Additionally, the FSTB VASP regime, effective from 2023, mandates providers to adhere to stringent AML requirements and maintain comprehensive records. Regulatory authorities are empowered to enforce actions against non-compliant entities. This framework also ensures that custodial services for crypto assets meet the same rigorous standards as TradFi institutions, enhancing investor protection and safeguarding against illicit activities.

In addition to the regulatory measures implemented by the HKMA, the SFC in Hong Kong has taken firm action against unauthorized operations in the crypto space. In 2023, the SFC issued a warning against JPEX for promoting its products and services without the necessary license as a VATP. Subsequently, the HKPF arrested six individuals following complaints of fraud totaling $128 million.

Furthermore, Hong Kong authorities uphold stringent requirements for compliance among fund managers, financial advisors, and distributors of financial products, irrespective of whether they involve digital assets not classified as securities or futures contracts.

Meanwhile, France has emerged as a hub for innovative regulatory approaches in the realm of digital assets. A 2023 report issued by the Banque De France[36] offers a pragmatic assessment of DeFi's technical framework, aimed at proposing regulatory solutions. The report identifies three main layers of DeFi: blockchain infrastructure, application layer, and user access systems.

The report's authors advocate for a regulatory approach that combines elements of TradFi regulation with frameworks from other economic sectors. This is motivated by the inherent challenges in applying *post facto* sanctions, which are central to TradFi regulation, to DeFi transactions, where the execution of smart contracts is triggered by the provision of information on a blockchain.

Moreover, while MiCA regulation does not encompass services provided in a decentralized manner, they argue for its extension to cover crypto assets linked to official currencies as reference points, thereby enhancing customer protection, and the use of specialized companies offering blockchain risk analysis.

Addressing fraud facilitated by anonymous techniques like mixers requires tailored regulatory frameworks that account for DeFi's unique characteristics, particularly smart contracts. The authors suggest implementing a certification system to verify the integrity of products before their distribution, thereby mitigating the risk of fraudulent activities within the DeFi space.

To achieve classification and ensure the safety of services offered to the public, establishing safety criteria and protocols is imperative, as outlined in the report. Additionally, attention must be paid to the concentration of validation capacities on public blockchains, which necessitates regulatory scrutiny. One proposed solution involves revealing the pseudonymity of capital holders through governance tokens.

In line with this, compliance monitoring of private blockchains should be governed by a specific supervisory framework within the EU, with reporting requirements imposed by blockchain administrators.

A contentious proposal in the report suggests conducting formal audits of the code behind smart contracts, followed by the release of a certified smart contracts list. However, the certification's time-limited validity and associated costs could hinder innovation.

Furthermore, the report recommends "recentralization" of sensitive services by placing governance token holders or protocol administrators under supervisory authority control. This contrasts with the existing regulation in France, where only centralized service providers fall under the PACTE framework.

Finally, the report underscores the importance of a common regulatory regime for DeFi services, a mandatory compliance with KYC procedures and MiFID II questionnaires to enhance investor protection and reduce the manipulation of customers.

On the other hand, the UK has emerged as a significant participant in discussions aimed at bolstering the regulatory framework concerning money laundering and crypto assets.

The HM Treasury[37] released a consultation on the regulatory framework for crypto assets, aiming to promote growth, innovation, and competition within the country. Additionally, it seeks to empower consumers to make informed decisions regarding the risks associated with crypto assets while safeguarding UK financial stability and market integrity.

The government adheres to the core principle of "Same risk, same regulatory outcome". Within this context, regulators should enforce regulations on individuals who hold substantial control or influence over a DeFi framework or protocol offering crypto asset services and activities, in the same manner as TradFi.

The government's regulatory aims to set a foundational level of essential information accessible to investors regarding crypto assets, ensure a balanced exchange of information between investors and issuers or trading venues, enforce accountability for illicit actors, and mandate a rigorous level of due diligence, including potentially detrimental marketing materials. Despite these measures, the government acknowledges the imperative for regulatory flexibility in DeFi international transactions.

Moreover, the AML/CTF registration regime has been operational since January 2020 for businesses engaging in crypto asset exchange or custody wallet services in the UK. The concept of crypto asset outlined in this regime is aligned with MiCA, and it also shares certain characteristics with FATF's recommendations.

6. Enhancing the Regulatory Environment

In addition to considerations of centralized governance and power concentration within DeFi, other aspects play a pivotal role in shaping future regulatory frameworks and can have far-reaching implications beyond combating money laundering.

A compelling study on money laundering investigations[38] reveals that a significant portion of transactions occur "off-chain", rather than on the DLT ledger, or through intricate protocols and smart contracts. In this landscape, pinpointing the concentration of crypto-asset holdings becomes challenging.

The study leveraged open-source investigative tools such as *Etherscan* and *Breadcrumbs*, uncovering various prevalent DeFi fraud trends. Primarily, money laundering schemes employed tactics focused on obfuscation, with scams frequently originating from centralized exchanges that have implemented KYC procedures.

Moreover, scholars have drawn attention to the emergence of "degen traders". The ongoing debate revolves around whether they should be considered "victims", given their prior involvement in gambling activities before engaging in these schemes.

Within this context, mixer services present a multifaceted challenge by using off-blockchain communications and varying mixing fees to obscure Bitcoin transaction trails, complicating law enforcement efforts. Regulators must consider deanonymization attacks, identification, and the shutdown of mixer services in response to money laundering.

In alignment with these considerations, a framework was proposed and the use of a methodology to assess the extent of money laundering within a Bitcoin mixing service by categorizing addresses mixing transactions and their objectives. Such methodology enables researchers to identify laundering activities within a mixing service.

Conversely, other sectors have been impacted by DeFi demanding regulatory framework review.

Within this context, contract law serves as an institution built on an *ex-post* basis, aiming to rectify situations *post facto*, for instance, compliance failure with terms and conditions in relation to incomplete wording *ex ante*.

Furthermore, smart contracts lack safeguards for more vulnerable customers and may cause irreversible harm not foreseen in their initial outcomes. Blockchain pseudonymity may be an obstacle to verify whether the code's developer benefits from any vulnerabilities, since they operate under different fiduciary standards.

However, while compliance with KYC and AML procedures by TradFi plays a crucial role in identifying criminal activities, in the context of DeFi, they may prove impractical and expensive.

Makarov & Schoar (2022)[39] recommend developing new standards for DeFi transactions, in furtherance of preserving an adequate level of transparency and accountability.

Another critical aspect in enforcing governance rules is the role of corporate agents, as punishment is not the primary incentive for compliance in DeFi. There's a tendency to avoid compliance and choose unregulated DeFi apps. Thus, embedding regulatory frameworks from the early stages of new solution development, security architectures, and smart contract design is recommended.

Christy Goldsmith Romero on CFTC's Digital Assets and Blockchain Technology issued a report[40] with recommendations to policymakers to address regulatory conundrums previously exposed and guide regulatory actors in the decision process to expand or adjust DeFi regulatory perimeter.

Policymakers should start by comprehensively understanding DeFi through mapping data points, resources, jurisdictions, and regulatory regimes to allocate responsibilities among DeFi actors. They can then utilize risk assessment to identify gaps, categorize risk levels, and devise a robust strategy for monitoring DeFi activities. Collaboration with industry stakeholders is essential to recalibrate risk approaches and drive innovation within the DeFi ecosystem. Regulators must also develop the technological and capacity skills to analyze "off-chain" transactions effectively.

Currently, reliance on centralized intermediaries for delivering financial products and services may lead policymakers to perceive these intermediaries as "too-big-to-fail". Such a perception not only contributes to concentration within the financial services industry but also hampers the development of alternative networks that are more resilient to financial and technological crises.

Within this context, CFTC advocates for collaboration with self-regulatory bodies and regulatory authorities, emphasizing the importance of sharing information to facilitate the harmonization of international regulatory frameworks and enforcement actions.

In alignment with this perspective, the Basel Institute of Governance and EUROPOL[41] advocate for a proactive approach regarding the DeFi framework and the risks associated with TradFi, summarized by the following principle: "Same Activity, Different Risks, Different Regulation BUT Same Regulatory Outcome' (NOT 'Same Activity, Same Regulatory Outcome') (…) But both TradFi and DeFi regulatory frameworks should achieve the same regulatory outcomes: safety and soundness of participants, financial stability, and consumer and investor protections".

While not directly within the scope of this study, a pertinent ongoing debate in the US surrounding DeFi refers to infringement upon the protections afforded by the First Amendment's right to freedom of expression. However, these arguments, while notable, are not sufficiently robust to undermine the primary objectives of DeFi regulation, which aim to safeguard investors, financial markets, consumers, and mitigate illicit activities.

7. Conclusion

The purpose of this article was to discuss the intricacies of money laundering in relation to crypto assets, specifically DeFi, and the need to have a clear regulatory framework which enables to prevent and effectively enforce money laundering in the DeFi ecosystem.

Notwithstanding the existence of certain similarities between TradFi and DeFi, in terms of money laundering operationalization, the risks associated with both differ, mainly, because of the highly technical nature and fast evolution of blockchain-based technologies.

Furthermore, law enforcement agencies worldwide encounter resource constraints and understanding capabilities regarding DeFi, posing challenges in identifying and addressing illicit activities.

Having said that, the development of comprehensive legislation that effectively regulates DeFi while also promoting innovation and safeguarding against illicit activities seems challenging.

Scholars have been debating DeFi regulatory frameworks. Some advocate for clear AML regulations integrated with TradFi, while others call for a comprehensive approach, including MiCA, to preserve DeFi's innovation and avoid discouraging investors.

Regardless of the aforesaid debates, policymakers must navigate through applicable legal and regulatory frameworks governing other digital infrastructures that either complement or replace TradFi policies and regulations. Moreover, any legislative initiative should be future-proof, and able to pursue innovation and technological developments and comply with AML/CTF rules.

To develop an effective AML regulatory framework for the DeFi ecosystem, it's crucial to understand the standards of various players, business operations, processes, and data flowing across different layers of DeFi, along with a thorough assessment of AML and KYC gaps worldwide. These efforts aid in harmonizing enforcement actions internationally and strengthen the collective ability to address emerging challenges in the DeFi landscape.

All in all, the coexistence of DeFi and TradFi in financial systems is undeniable, providing users with flexibility based on accessibility and functionalities. Hence, a comprehensive understanding of DeFi regulations is crucial to address associated risks related to investor protection, market integrity, and financial crime prevention. Compliance departments must acquaint themselves with the DeFi landscape and digital asset legislation to engage in discussions and implement regulatory improvements effectively.

Notes

1 *Decoding the EU's most threatening criminal networks.* (n.d.). Europol. Retrieved April 17, 2024, from https://www.europol.europa.eu/publication-events/main-reports/decoding-eus-most-threatening-criminal-networks#downloads

2 Kremer, B., & Werbach, K. (February 2022). *THE GLOBAL CHALLENGE OF DIGITAL ASSET REGULATION.* https://www.competitionpolicyinternational.com/wp-content/uploads/2022/02/2-The-Global-Challenge-of-Digital-Asset-Regulation-Bianca-Kremer-Kevin-Werbach.pdf

3 11th IMF Statistical Forum: Digitalization and New Forms of Money and Payments Systems. (November 15-16, 2023). IMF. Retrieved March 17, 2024, from https://www.imf.org/en/Videos/view?vid=6341315502112

4 Elliptic. (February 1, 2022). What is a crypto asset? | Blockchain Basics | Elliptic. www.elliptic.co. https://www.elliptic.co/blockchain-basics/what-is-a-cryptoasset

5 HM, TREASURY, FCA, BANK OF ENGLAND. (2018, October). *Crypto assets Taskforce: final report* [Review of *Crypto assets Taskforce: final report*]. https://assets.publishing.service.gov.uk/media/5bd6d6f0e5274a6e11247059/crypto%20assets_taskforce_final_report_final_web.pdf

6 *How Does Bitcoin Mining Work?* (March 09, 2024). Investopedia. https://www.investopedia.com/tech/how-does-bitcoin-mining-work/#toc-what-is-bitcoin-mining

7 *EUR-Lex - money_laundering - EN - EUR-Lex.* (n.d.). Eur-Lex.europa.eu. https://eur-lex.europa.eu/EN/legal-content/glossary/money-laundering.html

8 UNODC. (2019). *Organized Crime Module 4 Key Issues: Money-Laundering.* Unodc.org. https://www.unodc.org/e4j/en/organized-crime/module-4/key-issues/money-laundering.html

9 Europol, (2023). *The other side of the coin: an analysis of financial and economic crime,* Publications Office of the European Union. https://data.europa.eu/doi/10.2813/105613

10 Europol, (2023). *The other side of the coin: an analysis of financial and economic crime,* Publications Office of the European Union. https://data.europa.eu/doi/10.2813/105613

11 Auer, R., Haslhofer, B., Kitzler, S. *et al.* The technology of decentralized finance (DeFi). *Digit Finance* (2023). https://doi.org/10.1007/s42521-023-00088-8

12 Crypto Council For Innovation. (2023, October 5). *Key Elements of an Effective DeFi Framework* [Review of *Key Elements of an Effective DeFi Framework*]. Crypto Council for Innovation. https://ssrn.com/abstract=4594942

13 The Blockchain Data Platform. (February 2024). Chainalysis. Retrieved March 11, 2024, from https://go.chainalysis.com/rs/503-FAP-074/images/The%202024%20Crypto%20Crime%20Report.pdf?version=0

14 Shapiro, G. (2023, December 11). *Defining Decentralization for Law.* Medium. https://lex-node.medium.com/defining-decentralization-for-law-58ca54e18b2a

15 Aramonte, S., Huang, W., & Schrimpf, A. (2021). DeFi risks and the decentralisation illusion. *Www.bis.org.* https://www.bis.org/publ/qtrpdf/r_qt2112b.htm

16 Jeng, L. (2024, January 10). *The "Re-centralization" Trap: Global Regulation in 2024.* Forbes. Retrieved March 11, 2024, from https://www.forbes.com/sites/lindajeng/2024/01/10/blockchain-regulation-in-2024-the-re-centralization-trap/

17 *Regulation - EU - 2023/2854 - EN - EUR-Lex.* (2023). Europa.eu. https://eur-lex.europa.eu/legal-content/EN/TXT/?uri=CELEX%3A32023R2854&qid=1704709568425

18 Elliptic. (2023). *Typologies Report 2023 | Elliptic.* Www.elliptic.co. https://www.elliptic.co/resources/elliptic-typologies-report-2023

19 *Illicit Finance Risk Assessment of Decentralized Finance.* (April 2023). https://home.treasury.gov/system/files/136/DeFi-Risk-Full-Review.pdf

20 *Illicit Finance Risk Assessment of Decentralized Finance.* (April 2023). https://home.treasury.gov/system/files/136/DeFi-Risk-Full-Review.pdf

21 *Illicit Finance Risk Assessment of Decentralized Finance.* (April 2023). https://home.treasury.gov/system/files/136/DeFi-Risk-Full-Review.pdf

22 *Illicit Finance Risk Assessment of Decentralized Finance.* (April 2023). https://home.treasury.gov/system/files/136/DeFi-Risk-Full-Review.pdf

23 *Deal on a single rulebook against money laundering and terrorist financing | News | European Parliament.* (2024, January 18). Www.europarl.europa.eu. https://www.europarl.europa.eu/news/en/press-room/20240117IPR16880/deal-on-a-single-rulebook-against-money-laundering-and-terrorist-financing

24 Paesano, F. (2023, August 11). *Cryptocurrencies and money laundering investigations QUICK GUIDE SERIES.* https://baselgovernance.org/sites/default/files/2023-08/230822_quick_guide_update_en.pdf

25 Kremer, B., & Werbach, K. (February 2022). *THE GLOBAL CHALLENGE OF DIGITAL ASSET REGULATION.* https://www.competitionpolicyinternational.com/wp-content/uploads/2022/02/2-The-Global-Challenge-of-Digital-Asset-Regulation-Bianca-Kremer-Kevin-Werbach.pdf

26 *dYdX Interview - Decentralization & Policy.* (2023, November 3). Ckarchive.com. Retrieved March 12, 2024, from https://ckarchive.com/b/75u7h8hk3l7e7s6rgg7rlaq0q4o66

27 *Intervención de Alfredo Muñoz en el V Foro Blockchain & Activos digitales.* (2022). Www.youtube.com. Retrieved March 12, 2024, from https://www.youtube.com/watch?v=lc67SeqVRNU

28 *EUR-Lex - 32018L0843 - EN - EUR-Lex.* (2018, May 30). Eur-Lex.europa.eu. http://data.europa.eu/eli/dir/2018/843/oj

29 New EU measures against money laundering and terrorist financing | News | European Parliament. (2023, March 28). Www.europarl.europa.eu. https://www.europarl.europa.eu/news/en/press-room/20230327IPR78511/new-eu-measures-against-money-laundering-and-terrorist-financing

[30] Maia, G., & Vieira dos Santos, J. (2021). MiCA and DeFi ("Proposal for a Regulation on Market in Crypto-Assets" and "Decentralised Finance"). *SSRN Electronic Journal.* https://doi.org/10.2139/ssrn.3875355

[31] The FATF Recommendations. (2023). Www.fatf-Gafi.org. http://www.fatf-gafi.org/en/publications/Fatfrecommendations/Fatf-recommendations.html

[32] Moroney, C. (2023, September 15). *Digital Assets: MiCA Regulation - KPMG Ireland.* KPMG. https://kpmg.com/ie/en/home/insights/2023/08/digital-assets-mica-regulation-fs-asset-mgmt.html

[33] Aylin Elci, & World Economic Forum. (2021, August 6). *Issue Briefing: What's next for decentralized finance (DeFi)?* World Economic Forum. https://www.weforum.org/agenda/2021/08/issue-briefing-what-s-next-for-decentralized-finance-defi

[34] Zetzsche, D. A., Arner, D. W., & Buckley, R. P. (2020). Decentralized Finance. *Journal of Financial Regulation*, *6*(2), 172–203.

[35] Nandi, Ateesh and Bhargavi Nori, Siva. (2024, February 24). *Crypto and the Courts: A Global Case Law Analysis* [Review of *Crypto and the Courts: A Global Case Law Analysis*]. Coin DXC. https://coindcx.com/blog/wp-content/uploads/2024/02/Crypto-And-The-Courts.pdf

[36] *"Decentralised" or "disintermediated" finance: what regulatory response?*(2023). https://acpr.banque-france.fr/sites/default/files/medias/documents/20230403_decentralised_disintermediated_finance_en.pdf#page=4

[37] *Future financial services regulatory regime for cryptoassets.* (2023). GOV.UK. https://www.gov.uk/government/consultations/future-financial-services-regulatory-regime-for-cryptoassets

[38] *FSIDIIN | Forensic Science International: Digital Investigation | Journal | ScienceDirect.com by Elsevier.* (2024). Www.sciencedirect.com. https://www.sciencedirect.com/journal/forensic-science-international-digital-investigation

[39] Makarov, I., & Schoar, A. (2022). *Cryptocurrencies and Decentralized Finance (DeFi).* https://doi.org/10.3386/w30006. "Rules have to be set to facilitate coordination and provide incentives to adopt value increasing investments; and to prevent minority stakeholders from being expropriated by powerful insiders".

[40] *Statement of Commissioner Christy Goldsmith Romero on CFTC's Digital Assets and Blockchain Technology Subcommittee Release of Decentralized Finance Report | CFTC.* (n.d.). www.cftc.gov. Retrieved March 13, 2024, from https://www.cftc.gov/PressRoom/SpeechesTestimony/romerostatement010824b.

[41] *Seizing the opportunity: 5 recommendations for crypto assets-related crime and money laundering.* (2022, December 7). Basel Institute on Governance. https://baselgovernance.org/publications/seizing-opportunity-5-recommendations-crypto-assets-related-crime-and-money-laundering.

Bibliography

Alsaibai, H., Waheed, S., Alaali, F. and Wadi, R.A. "Online fraud and money laundering in ECommerce" (2020), ECCWS 2020 20th European Conference on Cyber Warfare and Security, Academic Conferences and publishing limited, p. 13.

Aravazhi, M.S. "Understanding cyber crime and cyber laundering: threat and solution" (2020), EPRA International Journal of Research and Development (IJRD), Vol. 5 No. 1, pp. 34-38.

Auer, R., Haslhofer, B., Kitzler, S., Saggese, P., & Victor, F. (2023). The Technology of Decentralized Finance (DeFi). Bank for International Settlements, Monetary and Economic Department. <https://repec.cepr.org/repec/cpr/ceprdp/DP18038.pdf> Accessed 07 January 2024.

Basel Institute Of Governance, "Combating virtual assets-based money laundering and crypto-enabled crime" (2022) <https://baselgovernance.org/sites/default/files/2022-01/2021%20Recommendations%20Crypto%20AML.pdf> Accessed 06 May 2023.

Basel Institute of Governance, "Seizing the opportunity: 5 recommendations for crypto assets-related crime and money laundering" (*EUROPOL*, 1 September 2022) <https://baselgovernance.org/publications/seizing-opportunity-5-recommendations-crypto-assets-related-crime-and-money-laundering>. Accessed 10 March 2024.

Beer, Kieran, "Around the Globe to Understand Crypto, With Zeke Faux" (*ACAMS*, 9 January 2024) <https://www.acamstoday.org/around-the-globe-to-understand-crypto-with-zeke-faux/>. Accessed 18 January 2024.

Berger, Pierre E. Boeve, Martijn and Kalokyris, Nicolas, "MiCA & TFR: the two new pillars of the EU crypto-assets regulatory framework"' (DLA PIPER, 20 June 2023) <https://www.dlapiper.com/en/insights/publications/2023/06/mica-tfr-the-two-new-pillars-of-the-eu-crypto assets-regulatory-framework>. Accessed 22 January 2024.

Benson, Vladlena and others, "Dark side of decentralised finance: a call for enhanced AML regulation based on use cases of illicit activities" [2024] Vol 32 No 1, 2024 (1358-1988) Journal of Financial Regulation and Compliance <https://www.emerald.com/insight/1358-1988.htm>. Accessed 26 January 2024.

Bok, Kenneth, "DeFi Regulation: New Approaches, Same Outcomes" (03 November 2023). <https://www.blockhead.co/2023/11/03/defi-regulation-approaches-same-outcomes/amp/>. Accessed 14 February 2024.

Bogardi, Etelka, "Cryptoasset regulation in Hong Kong" (*Norton Rose Fulbright*, July 2022) <https://www.nortonrosefulbright.com/en-gb/knowledge/publications/10fba6f7/crypto-asset-regulation-in-hong-kong> Accessed 24 February 2024.

Carlisle, David. *The Crypto Launderers: Crime and Cryptocurrencies from the Dark Web to DeFi and Beyond* (p. iii). Wiley. Kindle Edition.

Chainalysis, "The 2023 Crypto Crime Report'" (2023) <https://go.chainalysis.com/2023-crypto-crime-report.html>. Accessed 29 October 2023.

Chainalysis, "The 2024 Crypto Crime Report" (*Chainalysis*, February 2024) <https://go.chainalysis.com/rs/503-FAP-074/images/The%202024%20Crypto%20Crime%20Report.pdf?version=0>. Accessed 01 March 2024.

Chainalysis, "Global crypto adoption: Does regulation matter for growth?", (7 November 2023)<https://go.chainalysis.com/geography-of-crypto-webinar-thank-you.html?aliId=eyJpIjoiQ051UWdUWEJGem1MS1wvQksiLCJ0Ijoia1p1WmU1MkpLMDdtRHdDSUFPYlwvK3c9PSJ9>. Accessed 20 November 2023.

Clifford Chance, "Crypto Regulation: The Introduction of Mica into the eu Regulatory Landscape" (2022) Thought Leadership. https://www.europarl.europa.eu/RegData/etudes/BRIE/2022/739221/EPRS_BRI(2022)739221_EN.pdf. Accessed 12 November 2023.

Colbert, Rashan, "dYdX Interview: Decentralization & Policy" (03 November 2023), https://ckarchive.com/b/75u7h8hk3l7e7s6rgg7rlaq0q4o66. Accessed November 2023

Council of Europe Global Project on Cybercrime and MONEYVAL, "Criminal money flows on the Internet: methods, trends and multi-stakeholder counteraction" (2012) <http://www.coe.int/t/dghl/cooperation/economiccrime/cybercrime/documents/reportspresentations/MONEYVAL_2012_6_Reptyp_flows_en.pdf>. Accessed 27 April 2023.

Crypto Council For Innovation, "Key Elements of an Effective DeFi Framework" (Crypto Council for Innovation, October 5, 2023) <https://ssrn.com/abstract=4594942> Accessed January 13, 2024

Department of Justice. "Founder of Liberty Reserve Pleads Guilty to Laundering More than $250 Million through his Digital Currency Business" (January 29, 2016) <https://www.justice.gov/opa/pr/founder-liberty-reserve-pleads-guilty-laundering-more-250-million-through-his-digital>. Accessed 29 April 2023.

Deloitte, "The case for artificial intelligence in combating money laundering and terrorist financing Machine learning technology". <https://www2.deloitte.com/mm/en/pages/financial-advisory/articles/the-case-for

-artificial-intelligence-in-combating-money-laundering-and-terrorist-financing.html>. Accessed 03 July 2022.

Elliptic, "Risk Preventing Financial Crime in Crypto assets" (*Elliptic*, 2023) <https://www.elliptic.co/resources/elliptic-typologies-report-2023>. Accessed 26 February 2024.

Elliptic, "What is a Cryptoasset?" (*Elliptic*, 01 February 2022) <https://www.elliptic.co/blockchain-basics/what-is-a-cryptoasset>. Accessed 04 November 2023.

EUROJUST, "Money Laundering" (*EUROJUST*, 2024) <https://eur-lex.europa.eu/EN/legal-content/glossary/money-laundering.html>. Accessed 07 January 2024.

European Parliament, "Deal on a single rulebook against money laundering and terrorist financing" (*European Parliament*, 18 January 2024) <https://www.europarl.europa.eu/news/en/press-room/20240117IPR16880/deal-on-a-single-rulebook-against-money-laundering-and-terrorist-financing>. Accessed 19 January 2024.

European Data Protection Supervisor, "Opinion 12/2021 on the anti-money laundering and countering the financing of terrorism (AML/CFT) package of legislative proposals" (2021) <https://edps.europa.eu/system/files/2021-09/21-09-22_edps-opinion-aml_en.pdf>. Accessed 03 July 2022.

Europol and Basel Institute on Governance, "7th Global Conference on Criminal Finances and Cryptocurrencies" (EUROPOL 2021) <https://baselgovernance.org/node/2446>. Accessed 26 October 2023.

Europol, European Financial and Economic Crime Threat Assessment 2023 - "The Other Side of the Coin: An Analysis of Financial and Economic Crime, Publications Office of the European Union", (2023) Luxembourg <https://www.europol.europa.eu/cms/sites/default/files/documents/The%20Other%20Side%20of%20the%20Coin%20-%20Analysis%20of%20Financial%20and%20Economic%20Crime%20%28EN%29.pdf>. Accessed 20 January 2024.

European Commission Directorate-General for Financial Stability, Financial Services and Capital Markets Union European Commission, "Expert Group on Regulatory Obstacles to Financial Innovation (ROFIEG): 30 Recommendations on Regulation, Innovation and Finance - Final Report to the European Commission" (December 2019) 1049 Bruxelles/Brussel Belgium <https://europa.eu/!yu87Xf>. Accessed 13 January 2024.

FATF, "Opportunities and Challenges of New Technologies for AML/CFT, FATF, Paris, France" (FATF 2021) <https://www.fatf-gafi.org/publications/fatfrecommendations/documents/opportunities-challenges-newtechnologies-aml-cft.html>. Accessed 05 May 2023.

FATF, "Updated Guidance for a Risk-Based Approach to Virtual Assets and Virtual Asset Service Providers" (FATF 2021) <https://www.fatf-gafi.org/en/publications/Fatfrecommendations/Guidance-rba-virtual-assets-2021.html>. Accessed 05 May 2023.

FATF, "FATF REPORT Virtual Currencies Key Definitions and Potential AML/CFT Risks" (June 2014) <https://www.fatf-gafi.org/content/dam/fatf-gafi/reports/Virtual-currency-key-definitions-and-potential-aml-cft-risks.pdf>. Accessed 06 January 2024.

FATF (2012-2023), International Standards on Combating Money Laundering and the Financing of Terrorism & Proliferation, FATF, Paris, France, <www.fatf-gafi.org/en/publications/Fatfrecommendations/Fatf-recommendations.html>. Accessed 21 March 2024.

FATF (2024), Money Laundering National Risk Assessment Guidance, FATF, Paris, https://www.fatf-gafi.org/en/publications/Methodsandtrends/Money-Laundering-National-Risk-Assessment

Financial Intelligence Unit - The Netherlands, "What is money laundering?" (*FIU - The Netherlands*, 2024) <https://www.fiu-nederland.nl/en/home/what-is-money-laundering/>. Accessed 7 January 2024.

Handa, R. K., & Ansari, R. "Cyber-laundering: An Emerging Challenge for Law Enforcement". (2022) Journal of Victimology and Victim Justice, 5(1), 80–99. <https://doi.org/10.1177/25166069221115901>. Accessed 27 April 2023.

How, Euni; Brown, JeFredaR; Schmitt, Rohrs Kirsten. "How Does Bitcoin Mining Work?" (18 October 2023). Investopedia, <https://www.investopedia.com/tech/how-does-bitcoin-mining-work/#toc-what-is-bitcoin-mining>. Accessed 6 January 2024.

Hm, Treasury, Fca, Bank Of England, "Crypto assets Taskforce: final report"' (*The Open Government Licence*, October 2018) <https://assets.publishing.service.gov.uk/media/5bd6d6f0e5274a6e11247059/crypto assets_taskforce_final_report_final_web.pdf>. Accessed 17 December 2023

Hm Treasury, “Future financial services regulatory regime for crypto assets - Consultation and call for evidence” (*HM Treasury*, February 2023) <https://www.gov.uk/government/consultations/future-financial-services-regulatory-regime-for-cryptoassets>. Accessed 2 March 2024.

International Monetary Fund (IMF), “11th IMF Statistical Forum: Measuring Money in the Digital Age”. <https://www.imf.org/en/Videos/view?vid=6341315502112>. Accessed 15 November 2023.

Jeng, Linda, “The ‘Re-centralization’ Trap: Global Regulation in 2024” (10 January 2024). <https://www.forbes.com/sites/lindaJeng/2024/01/10/blockchain-regulation-in-2024-the-re-centralization-trap/>. Accessed 15 January 2024.

Katona, Tamás, “Decentralized Finance – The Possibilities of a Blockchain ‘Money Lego’ System”, 20 Fin. and Econ. Rev. 74, 86-89 (2021) (discussing replacement of central counterparties using DeFi) <https://en-hitelintezetiszemle.mnb.hu/letoltes/fer-20-1-st3-katona.pdf>. Accessed 20 January 2024.

Kim PhD, Seoyoung, DeFi *for dummies* (John Wiley & Sons, Inc 2023). P. 77

Kim, Seoyoung and Sarin, Atulya and Virdi, Daljeet, “Crypto-Assets Unencrypted”, (January 31, 2018). Journal of Investment Management, Forthcoming, Available at SSRN: <https://ssrn.com/abstract=3117859>. Accessed 17 January 2024.

Kirimhan, Destan, “Importance of anti-money laundering regulations among prosumers for a cybersecure decentralized finance”, Journal of Business Research, Volume 157, 2023, 113558, ISSN 0148-2963, <https://doi.org/10.1016/j.jbusres.2022.113558>. Accessed 20 January 2024.

KPMG, “Digital Assets: MiCA Regulation” (KPMG, 21 March 2024) <https://kpmg.com/ie/en/home/insights/2023/08/digital-assets-mica-regulation-fs-asset-mgmt.html>. Accessed 31 March 2024.

Kramer, JA., Blokland, A.A.J., Kleemans, E.R. et al. , “Money laundering as a service: Investigating business-like behavior in money laundering networks in the Netherlands. Trends Organ Crim” (Springer Link 2023) <https://doi.org/10.1007/s12117-022-09475-w>. Accessed 23 September 2023.

Kremer, Bianca & Werbach, Kevin, “The Global Challenge of Digital Asset Regulation” (2022)<https://www.competitionpolicyinternational.com

/wp-content/uploads/2022/02/2-The-Global-Challenge-of-Digital-Asset-Regulation-Bianca-Kremer-Kevin-Werbach.pdf>. Accessed 07 May 2023.

Karapatakis, A. "Virtual worlds and money laundering under E.U. Law: the inadequacy of the existing legal framework and the challenges of regulation" (2019), New Journal of European Criminal Law, Vol. 10 No. 2, pp. 128-150.

Leslie, D.A. "Introduction, money laundering and cyber crime" (2014), Legal Principles for Combatting Cyberlaundering, pp. 1-54, doi: 10.1007/978-3-319-06416-1_1.

Lim, Tung li, "How the JPEX saga has impacted Hong Kong's crypto ambitions" (*Elliptic*, 09 October 2023) <https://www.elliptic.co/blog/how-the-jpex-saga-has-impacted-hong-kongs-crypto-ambitions> Accessed 24 February 2024.

Liz Boison and Aleksandar Durik, "OFAC's Tornado Cash Action Leaves Open Questions" (Bloomberg 2022) <https://news.bloomberglaw.com/us-law-week/ofacs-tornado-cash-action-leaves-open-questions>. Accessed 27 April 2023.

London Stock Exchange Group (Lseg), "Eu Legislation - Anti-Money Laundering Directives" (22 January 2024) <https://www.lseg.com/en/risk-intelligence/financial-crime-risk-management/eu-anti-money-laundering-directive>. Accessed 22 January 2024.

Maia, Guilherme and Vieira dos Santos, João, MiCA and DeFi ('Proposal for a Regulation on Market in Crypto-Assets' and 'Decentralised Finance') (July 1, 2021). Forthcoming article in "Blockchain and the law: dynamics and dogmatism, current and future"; Eds: Francisco Pereira Coutinho, Martinho Lucas Pires and Bernardo Barradas, <SSRN: https://ssrn.com/abstract=3875355 or http://dx.doi.org/10.2139/ssrn.3875355>. Accessed 21 January 2024.

Mabunda, S. "Cyberlaundering and the future of corruption in America" (2018), JACL, Vol. 2, p. 214.

Makarov and Schoar, 2022 Makarov, I., & Schoar, A. (2022). *Cryptocurrencies and decentralized finance (DeFi)* (National Bureau of Economic Research Working Papers No. 30006). <https://doi.org/10.3386/w30006>. Accessed 08 March 2024.

Michael Schillig, "Lex Cryptographia, Cloud Crypto Land or What? – Blockchain Technology on the Legal Hype Cycle" (King's College London Law School Research Paper Forthcoming, 2021) <https://ssrn.com/abstract=3804197>. Accessed 05 October 2023.

Muñoz, Alfredo, "Intervención de Alfredo Muñoz en el V Foro Blockchain & Activos digitales" (Grant Thorton, 22 November 2022) <https://www.youtube.com/watch?v=lc67SeqVRNU>. Accessed 14 February 2024.

Nandi, Ateesh and Bhargavi Nori, Siva, "Crypto and the Courts: A Global Case Law Analysis" (*Coin DXC*, January 2024) <https://coindcx.com/blog/wp-content/uploads/2024/02/Crypto-And-The-Courts.pdf>. Accessed 24 February 2024.

NORTH HOUSE, "MiCA Regulation: Shaping the Landscape of Cryptoasset Markets" (2023) <https://www.northhouse.se/blog/mica-regulation-shaping-the-landscape-of-crypto-asset-markets>. Accessed 24 January 2024

Olivier fliche, Olivier; Uri, Julien; Vileyn, Mathieu Fintech-Innovation hub, "Decentralised" or "disintermediated" finance: what regulatory response? (*Banque De France*, April 2023) <https://acpr.banque-france.fr/sites/default/files/medias/documents/20230403_decentralised_disintermediated_finance_en.pdf#page=4>. Accessed 24 February 2024.

Payne, Daniel and Okoli, Ijeoma, "Crypto Experts Discuss the SEC's Approval of Bitcoin ETFs" (*New York University School of Law*, 15 January 2024) <https://wp.nyu.edu/compliance_enforcement/2024/01/22/crypto-exports-discuss-the-secs-approval-of-bitcoin-etfs/>. Accessed 22 January 2024.

Regulation (EU) 2023/1114 of the European Parliament and of the Council of 31 May 2023 on markets in crypto-assets and amending Regulations (EU) No 1093/2010 and (EU) No 1095/2010 and Directives 2013/36/EU and (EU) 2019/1937 [2023] OJ 2 150/40/01.

Regulation (EU) 2023/1114 of the European Parliament and of the Council of 31 May 2023 on markets in crypto-assets and amending Regulations (EU) No 1093/2010 and (EU) No 1095/2010 and Directives 2013/36/EU and (EU) 2019/1937 (Text with EEA relevance) <http://data.europa.eu/eli/reg/2023/1114/oj>. Accessed 23 January 2024.

Sienkiewicz, Stanley J., "Prepaid Cards: Vulnerable to Money Laundering?" (February 2007). Federal Reserve Bank of Philadelphia Payment Cards

Center Discussion Paper No. 07-02, <https://ssrn.com/abstract=969042> or <http://dx.doi.org/10.2139/ssrn.969042> Accessed 29 April 2023.

Paesano, Federico, "Cryptocurrencies and money laundering investigations" (Basel Institute of Governance, August 2023) <https://baselgovernance.org/sites/default/files/2023-08/230822_quick_guide_update_en.pdf>Accessed 18 January 2024.

Proposal for a Regulation of the European Parliament and of the Council on harmonised rules on fair access to and use of data (Data Act) COM/2022/68 final, <https://eur-lex.europa.eu/legal-content/EN/TXT/PDF/?uri=CELEX:52022PC0068> Accessed 16 January 2024.

Rettig, Rebecca and Mosier, Michael and Gilman, Katja, Genuine DeFi as Critical Infrastructure: A Conceptual Framework for Combating Illicit Finance Activity in Decentralized Finance (January 29, 2024). Available at SSRN: https://ssrn.com/abstract=4607332 or http://dx.doi.org/10.2139/ssrn.4607332. Accessed on 26 February 2024.

Shanique Smith. "You Think You Know, But You Have No Idea: Effective Oversight in the Era of Increasing Facelessness, is it Possible?". <https://www.acams.org/en/media/document/8231> Accessed 29 April 2023.

Sandali Handagama, "U.S. Court Calls ETH a Commodity While Tossing Investor Suit Against Uniswap." (Coindesk 2023) <https://www.coindesk.com/policy/2023/08/31/us-court-calls-eth-a-commodity-while-tossing-investor-suit-against-uniswap/?utm_source=Sailthru&utm_medium=email&utm_campaign=SoC%20090623&utm_term=State%20of%20Crypto>. Accessed 31 August 2023.

Schär, Fabian, "Decentralized Finance Could Support a New Financial Infrastructure if Challenges are Overcome, IMF: Finance & Development" (Sept. 2022), <https://www.imf.org/en/Publications/fandd/issues/2022/09/Defi-promise-and-pitfalls-Fabian-Schar>. Accessed 14 January 2024.

See, Kenneth, "The Satoshi laundromat: a review on the money laundering open door of Bitcoin mixers" (*Asian Institute of Digital Finance, National University of Singapore, Singapore, Singapore*, November 2022) <https://www.emerald.com/insight/1359-0790.htm>. Accessed 2 March 2024.

Shapiro, Gabriel, "Defining Decentralization for Law" (April 2020) Medium, <https://lex-node.medium.com/defining-decentralization-for-law-58ca54e18b2a>. Accessed 14 January 2024.

Tristam Hicks, “Re-thinking the war of “Dirty Money” (ACAMS 2023) <https://open.spotify.com/episode/4t4lNiyOZ88FQwxQoErGPk?si=bHP-L1-_TXaabd7J2_ijvQ&nd=1>. Accessed 23 September 2023.

Trace. Dr. Anastasia Kordoni, Dr. Joshua Hughes, Dr. Reinhard Kreissl, “Policy Brief on Improving Cross-Border Cooperation for Anti-Money Laundering Cases”' (May 2024) <https://trace-illicit-money-flows.eu/wp-content/uploads/2024/05/Policy-Brief-on-Improving-Cross-Border-Cooperation-for-Anti-Money-Laundering-Cases.pdf>. Accessed 15 May 2024.

United Nations, “Money-laundering” (United Nations Office on Drugs and Crime, April 2018)<https://www.unodc.org/e4j/en/organized-crime/module-4/key-issues/money-laundering.html>. Accessed 16 January 2024.

Yantis, B., Attia, M. and Lethouris, G., “Money laundering” (2018), American Criminal Law Review, Vol. 55, p. 1469.

Taverner, Marc, “Euroviews Are we trading Bitcoin's price for its centralisation?” (*Euroviews*, 15 January 2024) <https://www.euronews.com/next/2024/01/15/are-we-trading-bitcoins-price-for-its-centralisation> Accessed 22 January 2024.

Teichmann, F.M.J., Boticiu, S.R. and Sergi, B.S. (2023), "The EU MiCA Directive – chances and risks from a compliance perspective", *Journal of Money Laundering Control*, Vol. ahead-of-print No. ahead-of-print. <https://doi.org/10.1108/JMLC-02-2023-0030>Acessed 05 October 2023.

The Subcommittee on Digital Assets and Blockchain Technology, Technology Advisory Committee (TAC) of The US Commodity Futures Trading Commission, “Decentralized Finance” (Us Commodity Futures Trading Commission, *2024)* <https://www.cftc.gov/PressRoom/SpeechesTestimony/romerostatement010824b>. Accessed 8 March 2024.

Trozze, Arianna, Davies, Toby, Kleinberg Bennett, “Of degens and defrauders: Using open-source investigative tools to investigate decentralized finance frauds and money laundering” (*Elsevier - Forensic Science International: Digital Investigation 46 301575*, 2023) <https://www.sciencedirect.com/journal/forensic-science-international-digital-investigation> Accessed 2 March 2024.

Unchained, "What Is MiCA and What Does It Mean for Crypto Users in Europe?" (06 December 2023). <https://unchainedcrypto.com/what-is-mica/>. Accessed 22 January 2024.

UNODC. "Basic Manual on the Detection and Investigation of the Laundering of Crime Proceeds Using Virtual Currencies" (2014). <https://www.imolin.org/pdf/UNODC_VirtualCurrencies_final_EN_Print.pdf>. Accessed 7 May 2023.

Us Department of the Treasury, "Illicit Finance Risk Assessment of Decentralized Finance" (April 2023) <https://home.treasury.gov/system/files/136/DeFi-Risk-Full-Review.pdf>. Accessed 18 January 2024.

Wenqian Huang, and Andreas Schrimpf, "DeFi risks and the decentralisation illusion" (*BIS Quarterly Review*, 06 December 2021) <https://www.bis.org/publ/qtrpdf/r_qt2112b.htm>. Accessed 09 March 2024.

Whitehouse, Tammy, "Decentralized Finance May Transform How Money is Managed" (Deloitte, 21 July 2022) <https://deloitte.wsj.com/riskandcompliance/decentralized-finance-may-transform-how-money-is-managed-b443f30e?id=us:2sm:3li:4wsjsocial::6di:20240218190000::12649106909:5&utm_source=li&utm_campaign=wsjsocial&utm_content=di&utm_medium=social&linkId=322974973>. Accessed 20 February 2024.

Winter, Matthias, "How regulation is shaping the future of markets in digital assets" (Simmons&Simmons 2023) <https://www.simmons-simmons.com/en/publications/clm0o8xry01okth1sfiz55u1l/how-regulation-is-shaping-the-future-of-markets-in-digital-assets?utm_source=vuture&utm_medium=email&utm_campaign=the%20potential%20of%20digital%20innovation%3A%20a%20global%20journey-the%20potential%20of%20digital%20innovation%3A%20a%20global%20journey%20> Accessed 20 October 2023

World Economic Forum, "Issue Briefing: What's next for decentralized finance (DeFi)?" (CNBC, 21 July 2022) <https://www.weforum.org/agenda/2021/08/issue-briefing-what-s-next-for-decentralized-finance-defi/>. Accessed 06 August 2021

Wronka, Christoph. "Cyber-laundering: the change of money laundering in the digital age" (2022). <https://www.emerald.com/insight/content/

doi/10.1108/JMLC-04-2021-0035/full/html?skipTracking=true>. Accessed 29 April 2023

Wronka, C. (2023), "Financial crime in the decentralized finance ecosystem: new challenges for compliance", *Journal of Financial Crime*, Vol. 30 No. 1, pp. 97-113. <https://doi.org/10.1108/JFC-09-2021-0218>. Accessed 03 March 2024

Zerafa, A., Banks, J. and Waters, J., "The challenges of countering fraud in Malta's remote gaming industry" (2021), Journal of Financial Crime, ahead-of-print.

Zetzsche, Dirk A.; Arner, DouglasW.; Buckley, Ross P., "Decentralized Finance", *Journal of Financial Regulation*, 2020, 6, 172–203 Doi: 10.1093/jfr/fjaa010 Advance Access Publication Date: 30 September 2020. Accessed on 22 February 2024.

Table of Legislation

Directive (EU) 2015/849 of the European Parliament and of the Council of 20 May 2015 on the prevention of the use of the financial system for the purposes of money laundering or terrorist financing, amending Regulation (EU) No 648/2012 of the European Parliament and of the Council, and repealing Directive 2005/60/EC of the European Parliament and of the Council and Commission Directive 2006/70/EC (Text with EEA relevance).

Directive (EU) 2018/843 of the European Parliament and of the Council of 30 May 2018 amending Directive (EU) 2015/849 on the prevention of the use of the financial system for the purposes of money laundering or terrorist financing and amending Directives 2009/138/EC and 2013/36/EU (Text with EEA relevance).

Directive 2014/65/EU of the European Parliament and of the Council of 15 May 2014 on markets in financial instruments and amending Directive 2002/92/EC and Directive 2011/61/EU (recast) Text with EEA relevance (MiFID II).

Directive 2009/110/EC of the European Parliament and of the Council of 16 September 2009 on the taking up, pursuit and prudential supervision of the business of electronic money institutions amending Directives 2005/60/EC and 2006/48/EC and repealing Directive 2000/46/EC (Text with EEA relevance) (Electronic Money Directive II or EMD II).

Regulation (EU) 2023/2854 of the European Parliament and of the Council of 13 December 2023 on harmonised rules on fair access to and use of data and amending Regulation (EU) 2017/2394 and Directive (EU) 2020/1828 (Data Act).

Regulation (EU) 2023/1114 of the European Parliament and of the Council of 31 May 2023 on markets in crypto assets and amending Regulations (EU) No 1093/2010 and (EU) No 1095/2010 and Directives 2013/36/EU and (EU) 2019/1937 (Text with EEA relevance).

Regulation (EU) 2022/858 of the European Parliament and of the Council of 30 May 2022 on a pilot regime for market infrastructures based on distributed ledger technology and amending Regulations (EU) No 600/2014 and (EU) No 909/2014 and Directive 2014/65/EU (Text with EEA relevance).

Regulation (EU) 2022/2554 of the European Parliament and of the Council of 14 December 2022 on digital operational resilience for the financial sector and amending Regulations (EC) No 1060/2009, (EU) No 648/2012, (EU) No 600/2014, (EU) No 909/2014 and (EU) 2016/1011.

Chapter 5

Anti-Bribery Compliance

Strategic corruption: a lurking danger for our democracy

Mickaël Roumegoux Rouvelle

1. Corruption as a foreign policy tool

Democracy in Europe is facing major internal and external challenges. Russia's war of aggression against Ukraine has already entered its third year with no end in sight. Should Donald Trump return to power after the US elections in November 2024, it will probably be up to the European states alone to help Ukraine achieve victory. However, cracks in Europe's determination to support Ukraine are already appearing. The European elections of June 2024 have seen a surge in populist right-wing parties, with close ties to Russia.

There is no doubt that Russia will try to exploit this situation to undermine Western unity and resolve to support Ukraine. In recent years, Russia, China and other authoritarian states have been trying to strategically influence political decision-making in foreign countries, especially in the European Union. In addition to disinformation campaigns, cyberattacks and interference in elections, these authoritarian regimes have weaponized corrupt practices as a tenet of their foreign policy to capture political and economic decision-makers in other countries for their own geopolitical objectives.

This form of weaponized corruption is designed to exert strategic, long-term influence and can be seen as a component of the non-military arsenal of modern warfare, also called hybrid warfare. The focus lays not on the pursuit of private, often economic gain, but rather on achieving geopolitical objectives. The guiding principle behind the use of strategic corruption for autocratic regimes is to cement their grip on power, which is already underpinned by their extensive use of corruption domestically, allowing them to effectively control political institutions and hamper democratisation processes.

While the harm caused by strategic corruption and hybrid warfare is not as obvious as by conventional wars at first sight, this form of corruption is pernicious and hampers the ability of a state to make sovereign decisions. It poses a particular threat to our national security because it undermines citizens' trust in democracy and the rule of law in the long term. Alongside the USA and the European institutions, Germany is one of the main targets of this form of corruption, as it exerts considerable influence within the European Union and the G7 in particular.

2. Destabilising Western democracies

2.1 Russia's long shadow

Russia specifically aims at destabilising democracies. It relies heavily on proxies such as state-owned companies or oligarchs for its influence operations (Seely, 2021, p. 8). Their key advantage lies in the fact that they offer the Kremlin credible deniability, allowing it to deny involvement or responsibility for foreign interference operations. Russia relied in particular on the state-owned company Gazprom to build up an influence network of politicians, companies and non-governmental organisations (von Daniels, Joeres, & Richter, 2022) and make Germany dangerously dependent on Russian gas.

2.1.1 The use of proxies

Russia used Gazprom or companies in which Gazprom held a majority stake, such as Nord Stream AG, to award lucrative posts to former top politicians who then actively supported Russian interests. One of the most prominent cases of elite capture in Germany is that of former German Chancellor Gerhard Schröder, who was appointed to well-paid positions at Nord Stream AG and Rosneft (Bennhold, 2022). As a result, Schröder used his influence to lobby for the construction of the two controversial Nord Stream pipelines (Gathmann, et al., 2022). At the same time, as a former Chancellor, Gerhard Schröder continued to fulfil tasks related to his former office. Among other things, he was provided with a fully equipped office for this purpose, which was financed from the federal budget, i.e. with taxpayers' money (Tagesschau, 2022).

The Climate and Environment Protection Foundation in Mecklenburg-Western Pomerania also played a key role in the completion of the Nord Stream 2 pipeline. It was founded by the State of Mecklenburg-Western Pomerania at the initiative of Minister-President Manuela Schwesig from the socialist party in January 2021, and financed almost exclusively by a subsidiary of Gazprom. This organisation misused its legal form and primarily served as a mean to circumvent US sanctions to establish the Nord Stream 2 pipeline (Transparency International, 2022). Not only did the construction of the pipeline lead to disputes between Germany and the US, but it also sowed division among EU member states, thereby achieving one of Russia's key objectives. Reports seem to indicate that the foundation is not an isolated case and that other civil society actors in Germany and Europe were funded by the Russian government to influence the energy policy there (Bojanowski, 2022). Co-opting civil society actors is a key component of Russia's influence operations in Europe.

The role of some eminent players of the German private sector should also undergo critical scrutiny. With the mediation of Gerhard Schröder, the German meat magnate Clemens Tönnies enabled Gazprom to become the main sponsor of the soccer club Schalke 04, of which he was chairman of the supervisory board at the time. Schalke 04 subsequently played an important role in Russia's influence campaign (Merkur, 2023). In return, Tönnies' companies appear to have received preferential treatment for their business with Russia, receiving loans in the hundreds of millions euros from Russian state banks and subsidies from the Russian state (Hummel, Nikolskaya, Saito, Tsvetkova, & Zverev, 2023).

Oligarchs also play an important role. A prominent example of this is the case of the German journalist Hubert Seipel, which became public in November 2023. He allegedly received hundreds of thousands of euros via shell companies from an oligarch close to Putin, the long-standing major shareholder of the German travel company TUI, Alexei Mordashov, as part of a sponsorship agreement in order to write a book about the Russian president and his entourage (Amann, et al., 2023). With this publication, documentary films and a TV interview with Vladimir Putin, he helped shape a positive image of Russia and President Putin in Germany.

The importance of Russian oligarchs in the Kremlin's attempts to influence politics in Western countries is also evident in the case of the United Kingdom (Seely, 2021, p. 9). The country has been a target of choice for Russian oligarchs, because its investor's visa scheme, investment opportunities, lax regulations, and strong rule of law made it a safe haven for illicit funds. Oligarchs used this money to buy influence across the British establishment, including via generous political donations (Walker, 2022). The ties between the Russian elite and the United Kingdom are so deeply intertwined, that they cannot be entirely untangled (Intelligence and Security Committee of Parliament, 2020, p. 16).

2.1.2 The threat within: Far-right parties

The Kremlin maintains close links, some of them financial, with politicians from mainly far-right parties throughout Europe in order to use them to support its interests (Laine, Anesi, Bagnoli, & Tkachenko, 2023). For example, the former French Member of European Parliament (MEP) for the Rassemblement National, Jean-Luc Schaffhauser, received a commission of 140,000 euros (Sonne, 2018) to broker a loan of 9.4 million euros for his party with a private Russian bank with ties to the Kremlin (The Alliance for Securing Democracy; C4ADS, 2019, p. 1). This instance constitutes a direct financial interference of Russia in the political processes of another country via a private business surrogate. Had Marine Le Pen won the presidential elections in France in 2022, Moscow could have leveraged her party's debt to influence French politics. Parties such as the Rassemblement National, the Lega in Italy (Nardelli, 2019) and Fidesz in Hungary (Hegedűs, 2016, pp. 4-7) distinguish themselves as staunch supporters of the Kremlin's policies, partly due to such financial dependencies.

There are similar reports in relation to German parties. Investigative research has shed light on Russia's ties to right-wing populist Alternative für Deutschland (AfD, Alternative for Germany) politicians (Banholzer, Flade, Pittelkow, & Riedel, 2022). According to media reports, internal documents from the Kremlin prove that Markus Frohnmaier, a member of the German parliament from the AfD, received material and media support from Moscow during his 2017 parliamentary election campaign (Applebaum, 2019) and is allegedly "completely controlled by the Kremlin" (Gatehouse, 2019). Despite these worrying reports, no investigation appears to have been launched to date. Frohnmaier continues to defend the Kremlin's positions in the German Bundestag since his re-election in 2021.

Recent scandals show that Frohnmaier is not an isolated case within the AfD. A former parliamentary assistant to MP Eugen Schmidt, Wladimir Sergijenko, is suspected to have worked closely with the Russian secret services FSB to influence politics in Germany (Grozev, Dobrokhotov, Lehberger,

Schmid, & Wiedmann-Schmidt, 2024). He allegedly received money from the Kremlin and transferred it to the AfD or people close to the party. He travelled regularly to Russia and German customs discovered suspicious large sums of cash in Sergijenko's possession on two occasions after a trip to Russia. Each time the amount was slightly less than the 10,000-euro threshold above which a person must submit a cash declaration upon entering Germany from a non-EU country (Baumgärtner, et al., 2023).

The Czech government uncovered a large-scale Russian influence operation and placed the "Voice of Europe" platform and its operators – the pro-Russian Ukrainian oligarch Viktor Medvedchuk and the media manager Artyom Marchevskyi – on its national sanctions list. The aim of the influence operation was to undermine European support to Ukraine and influence the policies of European states in favour of the Kremlin. Politicians from six European countries are suspected to have received several hundred thousands of euros through "Voice of Europe" (Baumgärtner, et al., 2024). Among these politicians are Maximilian Krah and Petr Bystron, who were the lead AfD-candidates for the European elections. The Munich Public Prosecutor General's Office has already brought charges against Petr Bystron for bribery and money laundering. He allegedly received several tens of thousands of euros in cash for pro-Russian interviews.

These examples represent only the tip of the iceberg of Russia's use of strategic corruption in its foreign interference operations. The United States State Department disclosed in 2022 that Russia covertly spent over 300 million dollars since 2014 to influence politics in at least 24 countries (Wong, 2022). The dark figure could be even higher given estimates that Putin's entourage transferred some 300 billion dollars out of Russia since 2006 (Rudolph & Morley, 2020, p. 61).

2.2 Keeping an eye on China

China also uses corruption as a foreign policy tool to destabilise democratic states and influence political decision-making processes there. Alleged cases of strategic corruption from China have until recently been mostly reported in Taiwan (Davidson & Lin, 2024), Australia (Cave & Williams, 2017) and Canada (Yousif, 2023). In Australia for instance, former Senator Sam Dastyari from the Labour party received monetary and non-monetary gifts amounting to 1.5 million Australian dollars from Chinese entities in 2014 and has allegedly been a vocal supporter of China's interests in return (Rudolph & Morley, 2020, p. 74).

A series of revelations have rocked the European establishment and seem to indicate that China, like Russia, relies on far-right networks for its influence operations in Europe.

An operative of the Chinese secret services purportedly regularly paid the former Belgian parliamentarian Frank Creyelman from the far-right party Vlaams Belang (VB) to conduct influence operations in China's interests (Maik Baumgärtner, et al., 2023). One such operation involved the German Member of Parliament Stefan Keuter from the AfD. He submitted a parliamentary question (*Kleine Anfrage*) to the German government in 2021 to express concerns about refugees from Hong Kong being granted asylum in Germany, hinting at their potential affiliation to violent groups. As the asylum applications from Hong Kong totalled 8 between January 2016 and April 2021, the expressed concerns seem to have been part of a smear campaign against Hong Kong's independence movement. Manuel Ochsenreiter, who also worked as a parliamentary assistant of Markus Frohnmaier (see above), appears to have played an active role in this operation and allegedly received several thousands of euros in return (Maik Baumgärtner, et al., 2023).

The second major scandal to have surfaced in these past few months involves again the top candidate of the AfD for the European elections, Maximilian Krah. Not only is he suspected to have received money from Russian sources, but also from China. One of his closest parliamentary assistants, Jian G., was arrested on espionage charges, and is suspected to have worked for the Chinese secret services. Recent revelations seem to indicate that he might also have funnelled more than 50.000 euros from the Chinese secret services to his former boss (Diesteldorf, Preuß, Schmitt, & Wiegand, 2024). This may explain why Maximilian Krah has been a staunch and vocal supporter of China and has been pushing for a China-friendly course within his own party for years (Maik Baumgärtner, et al., 2023).

3. Reputation laundering

Other states such as Qatar, Morocco and Azerbaijan do not primarily use strategic corruption to destabilise European states, but rather to burnish their reputation and secure lucrative business opportunities. However, this does not alleviate the harm done to democracies, because it undermines people's trust in democratic institutions.

3.1 Caviar Diplomacy

Azerbaijan's ruling elite used a complex 2.5-billion-euro financial scheme and slush fund to launder money, buy luxury goods and make secret payments to European politicians (Harding, Barr, & Nagapetyants, 2017). For example, Azerbaijan managed to prevent a resolution on political prisoners from being passed in 2013 by lobbying leading members of the Parliamentary Assembly of the Council of Europe (PACE) (von Salzen, 2018). The system exploited loopholes in Western European countries by registering four shell companies in the UK, each of which had bank accounts at the Estonian branch of Danske Bank. The exact origin of the money is still unclear, although at least half of the money appears to have come from an account held by a shell company with links to the family of Azerbaijan's president, Ilham Aliyev (Ismayilova, Agha, & Biro, 2017). As this case and the previous case of journalist Hubert Seipel show, authoritarian states – just like organized crime – make extensive use of shell companies and offshore accounts to conceal their economic activities and the origin of the money they invest to covertly exert influence.

Among the recipients of funds funnelled through the Azerbaijani Laundromat were prominent German members of the Parliamentary Assembly of the Council of Europe (PACE). Eduard Lintner from the Christian Social Union (CSU), the Bavarian sister party of Germany's conservative Christian Democratic Union (CDU), is suspected to have received about four million euros from Azerbaijan (Der Spiegel, 2020). The former CDU member of parliament Karin Strenz, who died in 2021, reportedly received around 149,900 euros and her colleague Axel Fischer around 26,000 euros. At the end of 2023, the Munich Public Prosecutor General's Office brought charges against Lintner and Fischer for, among other things, bribery and corruption of elected officials and aiding and abetting the same. Further revelations show that the extent of Azerbaijan's influence in Germany's main conservative party might have run even deeper than previously known (Dachsel & Hofmann, 2021).

The use of strategic corruption helped Azerbaijan to deepen its business relations with the EU, also thanks to new gas supply agreements and the expansion of the Southern Gas Corridor, which was partly financed by EU funds. Domestically, President Aliyev was able to tighten his grip on power in his country and persecute members of the opposition without fear of repercussions.

3.2 Qatargate

Qatar (Braun, Volpicelli, & Wax, 2023) and Morocco (Braun & Moens, 2023) allegedly attempted to influence political decisions in the European Union in their favour by bribing MEPs. As part of the corruption investigation, several current and former MEPs, including the then Vice-President of the European Parliament, Eva Kaili, her partner, Francesco Giorgi, and former MEP Pier Antonio Panzeri, were arrested on December 9th, 2022. Panzeri is suspected to be the central figure in the influence network with his association "Fight Impunity" (Grytz, 2023). Investigators found large sums of cash in the suspects' possession, totalling 1.5 million euros. At the time, Qatar was negotiating an open skies agreement, from which the state-owned airline Qatar Airways would have benefited, as well as visa facilitation with the EU. Morocco wanted to deflect criticism of the kingdom's human rights record and solicit support for its claim to Western Sahara.

3.3 Frenenemies: allied states' use of strategic corruption

Some states considered strategic partners by Western governments also use corruption as a key instrument of their foreign policy. Turkey, an authoritarian state that is also part of NATO, offers a compelling example. The regime of President Recep Tayyip Erdoğan appears to have skilfully exploited opaque corporate structures to co-opt Western politicians into conducting smear campaigns against the regime's opposition. This is the case for Michael Flynn, the former national security adviser to ex-US President Donald Trump, who received $600,000 via a Dutch company whose beneficial owners are likely Turkish (Klasfeld, 2019) to write an opinion piece in *The Hill* comparing prominent Turkish opposition figure Fethullah Gülen to Osama Bin Laden (Flynn, 2016).

4. Countering Strategic Corruption

Our democracies are not defenceless against this form of illegitimate influence but need to be reformed from within. After all, autocratic states often make use of already known integrity deficits that are exploited by other actors.

In Germany, there still is a lack of sufficient knowledge about how, by what means and with what success Russia, China and other autocratic states influence political decision-making. Following the example of the United Kingdom or France, it would therefore be necessary to convene a parliamentary committee of inquiry to identify loopholes exploited by autocratic states and derive recommendations for action, particularly with regard to the fight against corruption.

Based on the findings of the report of the parliamentary committee of inquiry and in accordance with Art. 5 Para. 1 UNCAC, Germany should elaborate a comprehensive national strategy to combat corruption. This new strategy should identify and analyse corruption issues in all areas of society as well as relating to national security, and provide actionable policy recommendations to tackle them. Germany would thereby follow the example of the USA, which declared the fight against corruption as a core national security interest and released its Strategy on Countering Corruption in 2021.

4.1 Strengthening integrity in Politics

The German government can already introduce some fundamental reforms based on the examples of illegitimate foreign influence already known.

For example, the cooling-off period regulations for former members of the federal government should be tightened overall, with cooling-off periods extended to at least three years. In addition, an approval requirement should be introduced for former members of the Federal Government or state secretaries willing to take over management positions in companies, associations or foundations that are either majority-owned by non-EU state-owned companies or under the control of (former) national or regional government members from non-EU states. As a result, state-owned companies such as Gazprom should no longer be able to recruit former top politicians as lobbyists without the approval of the Federal Government. The approval requirement should also apply to former members of the Bundestag.

Also, the meetings of members of the Bundestag with lobbyists should be disclosed. The Parliament of the European Union has already introduced a similar regulation so that MEPs must publish all meetings with lobbyists – including diplomats from non-EU countries. This would make it possible to understand which lobbyists meet with members of the Bundestag, how often and on which topics. This regulation should also apply to members of the federal government and state secretaries, as recommended by the EU Council's anti-corruption body, the Group of States against Corruption (GRECO) (GRECO, 2023, pp. 6-8).

Members of the EU Commission and MEPs must declare their assets in accordance with EU rules in order to make potential conflicts of interest transparent. Of particular relevance are private business relationships, company shareholdings and liabilities relating to partners outside the EU. This declaration requirement should be introduced for members of the federal government, state secretaries, department heads and members of the Bundestag as well. They should submit a declaration of assets with details of their financial and business interests, including assets and liabilities. The declaration of assets should also include information on the assets and liabilities of family members. This measure is explicitly recommended by GRECO, which again criticised the lack of implementation in its report on the fifth evaluation round (GRECO, 2023, pp. 12-13).

4.2 Increasing transparency of lobbying activities

The European Union's ability to respond adequately to the threat posed by authoritarian countries depends on the ability of its weakest link to fend off foreign interference effectively. Hence, more harmonisation of laws and regulations in the European Union is needed, especially in the field of lobbying and anticorruption. The European Union should define minimum standards for the regulation of interest representation throughout the EU and push for the introduction of a mandatory lobby register in all EU member states. Similar to BORIS (Beneficial Ownership Registers Interconnection System), a database that enables the data search of beneficial owners in all EU transparency registers, the data from all EU lobby registers should be linked together. The interconnection of the commercial registers at the European level could also serve as a model in this respect. The directive should also provide for the establishment of an independent ethics authority to oversee the implementation of lobbying and transparency regulations in each Member State. These should be equipped with sufficient resources as well as investigative and sanctioning powers.

Authoritarian states co-opt civil society organisations to conduct foreign interference operations, as the examples of the Climate Foundation in Mecklenburg-Western Pomerania or the NGO "Fight Impunity" show. In order to prevent the risk of abuse of associations or foundations by autocratic states, these should be subject to disclosure obligations. In particular, an obligation to disclose annual financial statements should be introduced, similar to the obligations that apply to companies under commercial law (Sections 325 et seq. of the German Commercial Code). Also, organisations donating to political parties or engaging in lobbying activities should disclose the identity of the natural or legal persons from whom they receive funding when the amount per donor and per year exceeds a threshold of 10,000 euros, and provide information about the type of funding received (donation, loan, in-kind contribution, etc.).

4.3 Increasing the effectiveness of sanctions

Germany must step up its efforts to make beneficial ownership more transparent to ensure the integrity of its financial system. Currently, beneficial ownership information in the German transparency register is not verified unless a discrepancy is reported, which is why beneficial ownership data is not always accurate or up-to-date. This prevents authorities from tracing assets of sanctioned Russian oligarchs. Not only should Germany improve the tracing of assets, but it should also enable its law enforcement authorities to seize or even confiscate assets more easily. Hence, the introduction of an asset confiscation law would enable the state to search for suspicious assets ex officio and to seize or even confiscate them if there are sufficient indications that the assets originate from criminal offences or are intended to be used for criminal offences.

The introduction of a Magnitsky Act along the lines of the United States' Global Magnitsky Act would enable the German federal government to impose sanctions on foreign nationals and, in particular, foreign officials involved in human rights violations or serious corruption offences. Sanctions would include the freezing and confiscation of their assets. It should also include a procedure for drawing up proposals for the inclusion of entities on the EU sanctions list at the initiative of Germany. Other EU states such as the Czechia, Lithuania, Latvia and Estonia have already introduced similar laws.

The effectiveness of this type of law was shown by the prompt reaction of the Czech government in the wake of the "Voice of Europe" scandal.

At the end of 2020, the Council of the European Union introduced a global sanctions regime under the Common Foreign and Security Policy (CFSP) in relation to human rights, which allows the EU to impose sanctions on individuals and legal entities involved in serious human rights violations around the world. Following the example of the United States' Global Magnitsky Act, the EU Commission announced in May 2023, as part of the package to combat corruption in the EU and worldwide, that it intends to extend the EU sanctions regime to cases of serious corruption offences. However, this has not yet been decided. The German government should advocate for the prompt implementation of this measure.

5. Summary

The use of strategic corruption by authoritarian states against our democracies poses a direct threat to our national security. Authoritarian states have exploited Western countries' openness to foreign investment and financial secrecy to launder and hide their assets, which are then used to conduct a range of hostile activities, such as interfering in other countries' political systems by co-opting its elite or funding populist political parties. Strengthening our democracies' resilience against foreign interference requires overcoming integrity deficits in politics, the private sector and the civil society. The consistent fight against corruption and money laundering must be the guiding principle of democratic governments. Only then will we be able to regain citizens' trust in democratic institutions and the rule of law.

Bibliography

Amann, S., Baumann, S., Huppertz, C., Obermaier, F., Obermayer, B., & Schober, T. (2023, November 14). Preisgekrönter deutscher Journalist erhielt Hunderttausende Euro aus Russland. *Der Spiegel*. Retrieved June 8, 2024, from https://www.spiegel.de/wirtschaft/hubert-seipel-deutscher-reporter-erhielt-hunderttausende-euro-aus-russland-a-2c383028-2918-41ad-a8fd-26b1cf74369c

Applebaum, A. (2019, April 12). Russia is cultivating Germany's far right. Germans don't seem to care. *The Washington Post*. Retrieved June 8, 2024, from https://www.washingtonpost.com/opinions/global-opinions/russia-is-cultivating-germanys-far-right-germans-dont-seem-to-care/2019/04/12/ffa7b652-5d52-11e9-842d-7d3ed7eb3957_story.html

Banholzer, L., Flade, F., Pittelkow, S., & Riedel, K. (2022, December 16). Gemeinsam für Russland. *Tagesschau*. Retrieved June 8, 2024, from https://www.tagesschau.de/investigativ/ndr-wdr/russland-afd-oligarch-103.html

Baumgärtner, M., Chernyshev, A., Lehberger, R., Müller, A.-K., Höfner, R., & Wiedmann-Schmidt, W. (2023, July 13). Moskaus Mann im Bundestag. *Der Spiegel*. Retrieved June 15, 2024, from https://www.spiegel.de/politik/deutschland/aufregung-um-prorussischen-afd-mitarbeiter-moskaus-mann-im-bundestag-a-aad5cd99-f0c0-4a80-8304-0f5f54fab5c7

Baumgärtner, M., Höfner, R., Knobbe, M., Müller, A.-K., Rosenbach, M., Schmid, F., & Wiedmann-Schmidt, W. (2024, March 27). Europäische Politiker sollen Hunderttausende Euro aus Russland bekommen haben. *Der Spiegel*. Retrieved June 16, 2024, from https://www.spiegel.de/politik/deutschland/verdaechtiges-internetportal-voice-of-europe-westliche-geheimdienste-enttarnen-russische-desinformationskampagne-a-338f85ac-1714-4a05-b472-6e0ac3678675

Bennhold, K. (2022, April 23). The Former Chancellor Who Became Putin's Man in Germany. *The New York Times*. Retrieved June 8, 2024, from https://www.nytimes.com/2022/04/23/world/europe/schroder-germany-russia-gas-ukraine-war-energy.html

Bojanowski, A. (2022, März 24). Wie Putin Klimaschützer gegen den Westen einspannte. *Die WELT*. Retrieved June 8, 2024, from https://www.welt.de/politik/ausland/plus237519431/Energiekosten-Wie-Putin-Klimaschuetzer-gegen-den-Westen-einspannte.html?icid=search.product.onsitesearch

Braun, E., & Moens, B. (2023, November 28). Inside Morocco's efforts to corrupt the European Parliament. *Politico*. Retrieved June 9, 2024, from https://www.politico.eu/article/morocco-corrupt-european-parliament-union-qatargate-bribery-scandal-eu/

Braun, E., Volpicelli, G., & Wax, E. (2023, December 4). The Qatargate Files: Hundreds of leaked documents reveal scale of EU corruption scandal. *Politico*. Retrieved June 9, 2024, from https://www.politico.eu/article/european-parliament-qatargate-corruption-scandal-leaked-documents-pier-antonio-panzeri-francesco-giorgi-eva-kaili/

Cave, D., & Williams, J. (2017, June 6). Australian Politics Is Open to Foreign Cash, and China Has Much to Gain. *The New York Times*. Retrieved June 13, 2024, from https://www.nytimes.com/2017/06/06/world/australia/china-political-influence-campaign-finance.html?action=click&module=RelatedCoverage&pgtype=Article&region=Footer

Dachsel, F., & Hofmann, R. (2021, September 17). *Aserbaidschan-Affäre: Neue Geheimdokumente belasten Unionsabgeordnete*. Retrieved June 9, 2024, from VICE: https://www.vice.com/de/article/k78v53/aserbaidschan-affare-neue-geheimdokumente-belasten-unionsabgeordnete

Davidson, H., & Lin, C.-h. (2024, February 2). 'A race against time': Taiwan strives to root out China's spies. *The Guardian*. Retrieved June 24, 2024, from https://www.theguardian.com/world/2024/feb/02/taiwan-china-spies-beijing-espionage

Der Spiegel. (2020, January 30). Razzien gegen Unionspolitiker Strenz und Lintner. *Der Spiegel*. Retrieved June 9, 2024, from https://www.spiegel.de/politik/deutschland/aserbaidschan-affaere-razzien-gegen-unionspolitiker-strenz-und-lintner-a-21620f9e-93d7-4f29-9b68-476522e3af6b

Diesteldorf, J., Preuß, R., Schmitt, J., & Wiegand, R. (2024, May 16). Maximilian Krah und die Geldspur nach China. *Süddeutsche Zeitung*. Retrieved June 16, 2024, from https://www.sueddeutsche.de/politik/krah-afd-spionage-china-jiang-1.7252432?reduced=true

Flynn, M. T. (2016, November 8). Our ally Turkey is in crisis and needs our support. *The Hill*. Retrieved June 9, 2024, from https://thehill.com/blogs/pundits-blog/foreign-policy/305021-our-ally-turkey-is-in-crisis-and-needs-our-support/

Gatehouse, G. (2019, April 5). German far-right MP 'could be absolutely controlled by Russia'. *BBC*. Retrieved June 8, 2024, from https://www.bbc.com/news/world-europe-47822835

Gathmann, F., Großbongardt, A., Hagen, K., Hickmann, C., Hujer, M., Kollenbroich, P., . . . Teevs, C. (2022, February 11). Gerhard Schröder Casts a Dark Shadow over Berlin's Foreign Policy. *Der Spiegel*. Retrieved June 8, 2024, from https://www.spiegel.de/international/germany/gerhard-schroeder-casts-a-dark-shadow-over-berlin-s-foreign-policy-a-b1429dea-5db2-401e-b11d-71e22ee9d076

GRECO. (2023). *Fifth Evaluation Round: Preventing corruption and promoting integrity in central governments (top executive functions) and aw enforcement agencies, Compliance Report, Germany.* Retrieved June 23, 2024, from https://rm.coe.int/fifth-evaluation-round-preventing-corruption-and-promoting-integrity-i/1680aa89ee

Grozev, C., Dobrokhotov, R., Lehberger, R., Schmid, F., & Wiedmann-Schmidt, W. (2024, February 2). Mitarbeiter eines AfD-Abgeordneten soll Verbindung zu russischem FSB-Agenten haben. *Der Spiegel.* Retrieved June 15, 2024, from https://www.spiegel.de/politik/deutschland/wladimir-sergijenko-mitarbeiter-eines-afd-abgeordneten-soll-verbindung-zu-russischem-fsb-agenten-haben-a-0aa816aa-21f7-4144-9067-e7c00badeba4

Grytz, M. (2023, December 2). Ein Fall, der immer komplizierter wird. *Tagesschau.* Retrieved June 9, 2024, from https://www.tagesschau.de/ausland/europa/europaparlament-ein-jahr-katargate-100.html

Harding, L., Barr, C., & Nagapetyants, D. (2017, September 4). Everything you need to know about the Azerbaijani Laundromat. *The Guardian.* Retrieved June 8, 2024, from https://www.theguardian.com/world/2017/sep/04/everything-you-need-to-know-about-the-azerbaijani-laundromat

Hegedűs, D. (2016). *The Kremlin's Influence in Hungary: Are Russian Vested Interests Wearing Hungarian National Colors?* DGAPkompakt, DGAP. Retrieved from https://dgap.org/system/files/article_pdfs/2016-08-kompakt_5.pdf

Hummel, T., Nikolskaya, P., Saito, M., Tsvetkova, M., & Zverev, A. (2023, Mai 31). The meat magnate who pushed Putin's agenda in Germany. *Reuters.* Retrieved June 8, 2024, from https://www.reuters.com/investigates/special-report/ukraine-crisis-russia-germany-gazprom/

Intelligence and Security Committee of Parliament. (2020). *Russia.* Retrieved June 14, 2024, from https://isc.independent.gov.uk/wp-content/uploads/2021/03/CCS207_CCS0221966010-001_Russia-Report-v02-Web_Accessible.pdf

Ismayilova, K., Agha, I., & Biro, A. (2017, September 4). *The origin of the money.* Retrieved June 9, 2024, from OCCRP: https://www.occrp.org/en/azerbaijanilaundromat/the-origin-of-the-money

Klasfeld, A. (2019, October 31). *Boom Times for Turkey's Lobbyists in Trump's Washington.* Retrieved June 9, 2024, from Courthouse News Service: https://www.courthousenews.com/boom-times-for-turkeys-lobbyists-in-trumps-washington/

Laine, M., Anesi, C., Bagnoli, L., & Tkachenko, T. (2023, February 3). Kremlin-Linked Group Arranged Payments to European Politicians to Support Russia's Annexation of Crimea. *OCCRP.* Retrieved June 8, 2024, from https://www.occrp.org/en/investigations/kremlin-linked-group-arranged-payments-to-european-politicians-to-support-russias-annexation-of-crimea

Maik Baumgärtner, C. G., Höfner, R., Knobbe, M., Müller, A.-K., Rosenbach, M., Schult, C., . . . Wiedmann-Schmidt, W. (2023, December 15). Chinas Stasi, ein belgischer Handlanger und Spuren zur AfD. *Der Spiegel*(Der Spiegel 51/2023). Retrieved June 16, 2024, from https://www.spiegel.de/politik/deutschland/wie-chinas-stasi-einen-belgischen-politiker-anwarb-und-spuren-zur-afd-a-3ce67a4d-bbaa-4d39-baf3-7e2bb5b51b74

Merkur. (2023, June 1). *Eine besondere Verbindung: Wurstkönig Tönnies und Kreml-Machthaber Putin*. Retrieved June 6, 2024, from https://www.merkur.de/wirtschaft/toennies-putin-russland-schalke-gazprom-wurst-fleischproduzent-lobby-zr-92316405.html

Nardelli, A. (2019, July 19). Welcome To "Moscopoli": Here's Everything That's Happened Since BuzzFeed News Revealed The Proposed Secret Deal Between Italy's Far Right And Russia. *BuzzFeed News*. Retrieved June 8, 2024, from https://www.buzzfeednews.com/article/albertonardelli/welcome-to-moscopoli

Rudolph, J., & Morley, T. (2020). *Covert Foreign Money: Financial loopholes expolited by authoritarians to fund political interference in democracies.* The Alliance for Securing Democracy. Retrieved June 16, 2024, from https://securingdemocracy.gmfus.org/wp-content/uploads/2020/08/ASD-Covert-Foreign-Money.pdf

Seely, B. (2021). *Foreign Interference Unchecked: Models for a U.K. Foreign Lobbying Act.* London: The Henry Jackson Society. Retrieved June 8, 2024, from https://henryjacksonsociety.org/wp-content/uploads/2021/02/FINAL-FOLO-report.pdf

Sonne, P. (2018, December27). A Russian bank gave Marine Le Pen's party a loan. Then weird things began happening. *The New York Times*. Retrieved June 8, 2024, from https://www.washingtonpost.com/world/national-security/a-russian-bank-gave-marine-le-pens-party-a-loan-then-weird-things-began-happening/2018/12/27/960c7906-d320-11e8-a275-81c671a50422_story.html

Tagesschau. (2022, August 12). *Was ehemaligen Kanzlern zusteht*. Retrieved June 8, 2024, from https://www.tagesschau.de/inland/altkanzler-privilegien-101.html

The Alliance for Securing Democracy; C4ADS. (2019). *Illicit Influence Part 1 A Case study of the First Czech Russian Bank*. Retrieved from https://securingdemocracy.gmfus.org/wp-content/uploads/2018/12/Illicit-Influence-Part-One-First-Czech-Russian-Bank_web.pdf

Transparency International. (2022, February 22). *Germany: State Government conceals Gazprom's connection to its controversial environmental foundation*. Retrieved from https://www.transparency.org/en/press/germany-state-government-conceals-gazprom-connection-controversial-environmental-foundation-beneficial-ownership

von Daniels, J., Joeres, A., & Richter, F. (2022, September 20). Die Gazprom-Lobby. *Correctiv*. Retrieved June 8, 2024, from https://correctiv.org/aktuelles/russland-ukraine-2/2022/09/20/gas-gazprom-lobby-deutschland/

von Salzen, C. (2018, Januar 16). Der Europarat und Aserbaidschan: Ein Korruptionsskandal mit Folgen. *Tagesspiegel*. Retrieved June 9, 2024, from https://www.tagesspiegel.de/politik/ein-korruptionsskandal-mit-folgen-5923972.html

Walker, P. (2022, February 23). Party funding linked to Russia – how much have Tories benefited? *The Guardian*. Retrieved June 14, 2024, from https://www.theguardian.com/politics/2022/feb/23/oligarchs-funding-tories

Wong, E. (2022, September 13). Russia Secretly Gave $300 Million to Political Parties and Officials Worldwide, U.S. Says. *The New York Times*. Retrieved June 15, 2024, from https://www.nytimes.com/2022/09/13/us/politics/russia-election-interference.html

Yousif, N. (2023, May 23). What to know about Canada and China's foreign interference row. *BBC*. Retrieved June 13, 2024, from https://www.bbc.com/news/world-us-canada-64813182

Anti-Corruption in Times of Crisis and AI - New Chances and Challenges

Carlos Lelo Filipe

1. Introduction

This work cannot to be viewed as an academic or scientific approach to the topic but as a reflection centred on the practical side, based on the professional practice as Compliance Officer active in the financial sector, lawyer and citizen engaged in combatting corruption as a duty of citizenship.

Even if it is commonly known and accepted that the fight against Financial Crime and Corruption is a particularly challenging exercise that requires significant investment in terms of financial, human and technical resources, fact is that the main forces involved in such combat, either law enforcement, magistrates or Compliance Officers all agree that they are constantly "one step back" of the criminals.

This is a specially demanding struggle in terms of means, requiring appropriate budgets to assure continuous training, availability of adequate and up to date technical tools and sufficient human resources.

When the use of AI started to spread, being applied to different sectors with significant results in terms of problem solving at a speed never seen before, helping humans to cross barriers that had never been crossed, those involved in the combat against financial crime saw it as much more than a tool, as a real and effective weapon that could turn the "war" in their favour.

Per principle and having learned many lessons from past battles we must remain rational, curb the euphoria and take and realize that this "wonder weapon" can also be used by the criminals, can also be used to bring more complexity to this complex war.

This reflection intends to contribute to the awareness of such perils, of the risks of the (mis)use of AI by White Collar Criminals and also to propose some measures to make such (mis)use more difficult.

2. About the use of AI: ethical boundaries

When we realize what AI can represent for the future of mankind we cannot avoid making a travel back to early stages of the evolution of our species and think about the effect and impact caused by discoveries and findings in that continuous process until we reached our current point.

We dare to state that AI will represent the biggest step forward mankind has ever experienced, so vast is the potential of its use in every single part of our society, applicable to all types of situations.

If back on the XV century the Portuguese Sea Explorers claimed that the discovery of the ocean routes had given "new worlds to the world", and in 1962 the US President John Fitzgerald Kennedy used the same statement when referring to the country's Space Effort during a speech at Rice University, now we can state that AI will give a new dimension to mankind.

It seems too good and too marvellous to be real how algorithms, machine learning and all other aspects of AI can help us to solve extremely complex problems faster than blinking that we must consider a tendency or temptation to expand its use even to the most restricted areas of scientific investigation, raising several ethical questions.

The inappropriate use of AI can only be prevented by the establishment of strict ethical boundaries with the purpose of assuring permanent accountability, transparency and fairness.

3. Anti-Corruption and Fraud Prevention in Times of Crisis: Challenges

Stating that corruption and fraud are two of the main causes that undermines our societies with a severe and dramatic impact on economies, wellbeing of populations, social development and global performances of countries and companies may seem a Lapalice truth but must always be taken seriously and vigorously fought, especially in times of deep crisis like the ones we are currently facing.

Besides the impact on the economy and subsequently on the development and social conditions, corruption and fraud play also a significant role in the weakening of western democracies, nourishing populisms and extremist movements throughout Europe.

Without having this negative economic and political impacts taken into due account and being seriously considered we will not be able to succeed in this decisive fight even taking advantage of the potential of this amazing AI tool.

Several Southern and Eastern EU member states still suffering from economic, social and political vulnerabilities in consequence of decade long authoritarian political regimes, either communist or fascist ones, are excellent examples of the dangerous effects of corruption and fraud.

As a case study, let us take the case of Portugal, small southwestern european country which had the longest dictatorship in Europe, is EU member state since 1986 and has already been overpassed by almost all of the former Comecon member states that joined EU.

In 2022 a political party won the election with absolute majority and had all conditions to rule the country in a stable way in order to promote the reforms needed to diminish the gap between the country and the most developed partners in the EU. What happened between April 2022 and November 2023 was quite different, one corruption scandal after the other on a cadence that ended up with the resignation of the Prime Minister following another scandal with his Chief of Staff, a Minister and a Lawyer known to be his best friend all involved in a case of favouritism related to the approval of the of one of the biggest Data Centres in Europe, representing the most significant investment in the country since VW plant back in 1991.

This kind of behaviours caused not only serious distrust, placed the country democratic system in jeopardy but also represents a real danger and high-level risk in terms of the use of AI for corruption purposes.

The immediate result of that behaviour on the political sphere was the success of the local far right party, now the third political force in Portugal, having collected 1,1 million votes and elected 50 members of the Parliament.

When the ones that should be the „guardians« of the rule of law, that should give the tone for the society in terms of ethical and transparent behaviour act in such way and have the power to influence and control local scientific communities involved in the development and implementation of AI, it seems obvious that in such constellations the affected countries/ communities face an effective an serious risk of AI misuse for the gain/ profit of some groups.

4. AI and Anti-Corruption: Bright and Darker sides

Assuming that AI can play an important role in the combat against corruption, we must ask a previous question before proceeding: will it be an important tool, a new danger or both at the same time?

Using the wording of one the most successful Hollywood movie sagas "Star Wars", let us start with the "Bright Side" of AI, its positive impact as an instrument placed in service of the "good side of the Force".

4.1 Bright Side

Looking at the potential of AI and the most recent technologies developed with its help we would tend to be almost euphoric with the impact and results it can have both in general and also in particular for the domain of Compliance and the areas involved in the prevention and combat of corporate fraud, money laundering, terrorism financing, tax fraud and other illicit as well as criminal behaviours.

When we notice the offers currently available in the market in terms of tools designed for fraud detection, transaction monitoring or sanctions screening, just to mention some common examples, the way they are updated and upgraded, the speed of new releases to the market and we compare them with the tools used 5 – 10 years ago, the difference is almost so huge as the one between a floppy disk and a pen usb.

The use of AI by law enforcement forces, the judicial system and regulatory authorities on the public side and by compliance and internal audit departments on the private side should be seen as a significant opportunity to achieve higher levels of success in the fight against corruption and organized crime, representing significant gains in terms of efficiency, enhanced detection capabilities, increase of transparency and improvement of accountability.

Among the several domains positively impacted by the use of AI in the fight against corruption and financial criminality we can highlight the following ones:

1. **Prediction and Anticipation:** AI can analyse patterns and predict potential areas of corruption.
2. **Detection of Anomalies:** Machine Learning Algorithms can identify unusual transactions or behaviours which may indicate corrupt activities.

3. **Analysis of Supporting Documents:** Natural Language Processing can be used to analyse large volumes of text, like government reports and contracts, in order to detect discrepancies or potential frauds.

4.2. Dark Side

However we must be aware that AI is also available for the "Dark Side of the Force", criminal organizations are already using its potential for their illegal activities in the same way the use Internet.

A few decades "World Wide Web" changed human relations, contributed decisively to the globalization, deeply influenced trade and economic relations on a scale never seen before, reducing many complicated tasks to simple clicks.

We know how the so called "Dark Web" is used for money laundering, terrorism financing, drug, human and weapon trafficking among a myriad of other crimes.

Another example of the fast appropriation of the newest technologies by criminal organizations is use of blockchain technologies, crypto currencies and NFT's (non fungible tokens) with a significant number of cases already brought to justice in several countries. In this particular domain the time spent discussing the way this new digital currencies should be regulated, the way the International Organizations (IMF, FATF, ECB) were not able to join efforts to reach common standards of rules and regulations "opened the gates" and created great opportunities to the misuse of this technologies.

Diving more deeply into the "Dark Side of the Force" we must highlight several known scams of AI misuse for criminal purposes like the following ones:

a. **Automation of Illicit Transactions to introduce and move from funds generated by criminal activities without detection** through:

   i. Automated Trading Bots;
   ii. Cryptocurrency Mixing Services.

b. **Automation and precision improvement of fraudulent activities,** such as:

   i. Phishing and Spear Phishing;
   ii. Deepfakes.

c. **Evasion of Detection Systems** through the use of:

   i. Adversarial Machine Learning;
   ii. Synthetic Identity Fraud.

d. **Exploitation of the vulnerabilities in AI Systems**, by:

   i. Data Poisoning;
   ii. Model Inversion Attacks.

e. **Enhancement of Insider Attacks**, via:

   i. Insider Fraud Detection Avoidance;
   ii. Data Tampering;
   iii. Algorithmic Adjustements;
   iv. Automated Trading Manipulation;
   v. Financial Report Tampering.

4.3 Proposals and Future Directions

Once established the difference between the "Bright" and "Dark" sides of the "Force", having pointed and highlighted some of the most relevant opportunities, benefits, risks and dangers that should be always measured and balanced when dealing with AI, the next question concerns the future directions and some proposals destined to prevent and mitigate the misuse and ensure the prevail of the "Bright Side".

Proper and adequate use of AI can be achieved through the definition, adoption and implementation of measures covering three main domains or areas of intervention, namely Regulatory, Technical and Human.

4.3.1 Regulatory Domain

Starting by the Regulatory side, it is or at least should be, widely and peacefully accepted that AI should be regulated to assure its proper use. The definition of Ethical Principles for AI is essential and should include and properly cover the following points:

a. Respect for Human Autonomy.
b. Prevention of Harm and Misuse.
c. Assurance of Fairness and Justice.
d. Assurance of Accountability and Transparency.
e. Protection of Privacy and Personal Data.

Among the characteristics that AI Regulation should have, flexibility is perhaps the most relevant, in order to assure the fastest possible responses to the rapidly evolving nature of technologies.

The UK can be considered a pioneer on the establishment, adoption and promotion of ethical principles and good practices in this domain through the **Center for Data Ethics and Innovation (CDEI)**, providing guidance on ethical AI development and implementation in the Kingdom. CDEI works together with stakeholders to promote ethical best practices in AI, issues recommendations and also conducts research.

The recent approval of the European Artificial Intelligence Act on 21st May 2024 was not only a significant and decisive step forward towards the assurance of the proper use of AI but at the same time an important sign that, among others, the lessons learned with the misuse of blockchain technologies and crypto currencies have been taken seriously by the EU Institutions.

On the private sector side, several of the most relevant stakeholders have also adopted and implemented ethical AI rules and practices destined to assure fairness and mitigate biases. Industry giants like IBM, Google and Microsoft took the lead and gave the tone to the sector by the introduction of "AI Fairness 360 Toolkit", "Model Cards" and "Fair Learn".

4.3.2. Technical Domain

On the side of the Technical Domain we can point the following directions:

1. **Research and Development:** reinforced and continuous investment in research and development to overcome technical challenges.
2. **Global Cooperation:** implement collaborative approaches between Governments, Public Institutions, Private Sector and Civil Society with the goal of developing effective and ethical AI Systems.

4.3.3. Human Domain

The third and last domain/area of intervention is the human, covering and including the role played by scientists, programmers, politicians, other high level decision takers and users must be considered and also subject of adequate strategies and measures.

In this domain the future direction should start with the definition, adoption and implementation of Codes of Conduct, followed by training on ethics and ending by the reinforcement of whistleblowing protection.

5. Role of the latest technologies in the service of Compliance: corporate fraud prevention, asset tracing and recovery

Being aware that AI is not of exclusive use of the "Bright Side of the Force" but can is already being used by the "Dark Side", from a practical/field perspective we must point that the role of AI and in particular the latest technologies developed with support in AI is very important to support Compliance analysis and investigations throughout the different levels and the decision taking.

There are several relevant advantages of using the latest technologies in this decisive combat, like a more efficient and time reducing way to deal and manage the mass results/hits produced by the screening and monitoring tools, a different way to tune the algorithms used by the different tools through the incorporation of a wider range of fraud and potential fraud scenarios and/or the identification of uncommon transactional behaviours, for example.

Even knowing that the advantages of the use of AI are undeniable, defending that it can have/will have a significant impact in terms of gains of efficiency, freeing of human resources and a clear reflex in the balance sheets, we must point that at this level the problem or the major challenge remains on persuading top management to invest (not to spend) in the newest/most updated technologies when Compliance is still seen as cost for too many companies.

The Compliance Officer's struggle continues to be that of demonstrating the positive impact of Compliance in companies' balance sheets.

Compliance can only be successful in preventing financial crime and fighting corruption if provided with adequate resource, including the newest available AI tools, beautiful speeches and faith professions at Board levels without proper allocation of funds only contributes to the success of fraudsters and financial criminals.

6. Summary and Conclusions

From the „ground «perspective of a Compliance Officer, lawyer and citizen engaged in the fight against corruption, AI can be a very important tool to fight this type of criminality as long as the risks of its use and manipulation by corrupt forces are correctly identified, prevented and the adequate mitigation/remediation plans and measures are timely adopted and implemented.

The impact of AI on societies around the globe will continue to grow, while the rising capabilities of AI shift existing power structures. In a digital age, power resides with those who have the code and the algorithms – currently mostly large tech companies and governments.

As pointed throughout this reflection the "Dark Side of the Force" will try to remain one step forward of the "Bright Side" not hesitating to design, manipulate or applying AI systems for their criminal purposes. We should be aware and never forget that Corrupt AI is already occurring when power holders abuse this powerful tool/weapon for their private gains.

To respond to such misuse of AI, the "Bright Side of the Force" must engage all efforts in turning systems more resilient against corruption risks, which implies and requires new types of safeguards.

The success of the good side can only be achieved through the true engagement of the highest levels of decision, both political and scientific together with the civil society organizations. Therefore, we make an appeal to Governments and Policy-makers, Programmers, Private companies and also to Civil Society Organisations to address three main aspects:

1. **Develop innovative regulatory frameworks that support the ethical design and implementation of AI including model audits.**
2. **Assure the effectiveness of such audits by the adoption of transparent code and data and the interoperability of different programming languages.**
3. **Raise awareness of data scientists and programmers to AI ethics and anti-corruption, investing in trainings and implementing codes of conduct.**

On the specific field of the Compliance, in particular Anti-Money Laundering/Counter Terrorism Financing and Financial Crime sides, AI is already playing an important role in terms of the services/tasks related with the prevention of corporate fraud, money laundering and terrorism financing having relevant impact in terms of efficiency whether in managing alerts, detecting fraudulent, illicit and criminal behaviours or allocating human resources.

The "Bright Side of the Force" can and will overcome this fight once able to identify, prevent and mitigate the risks and dangers of the use of AI by organized crime and corrupt individuals, assuring the use of this revolutionary instrument in profit of the well being of mankind!

Bibliography and Sources

Aarvik, Per „*Artificial Intelligence- a promising anti-corruption tool in development settings?*", CMI Chr. Michelsen Institute, U4 Report 2019, https://www.u4.no/publications/artificial-intelligence-a-promising-anti-corruption-tool-in-development-settings/shortversion

Ambert, Bufford, „*AI & Financial Crimes*", August 2023, IBM Watson Books, USA

Bailey Sr, Cameron A, „ *AI Ethics and Legal Compliance, A Comprehensive Guide for Responsible AI Use*", 2024, Pillars Publishing Inc and Cameron A Bailey Sr, Amazon, France

Buolamwini, Joy, „*Unmasking AI*", October 2023, Random House, USA

Crawford, Kate, „*Atlas of AI: Power, Politics, and the Planetary Costs of Artificial Inteligence*", October 2022, Yale University Press, USA

Helmer, Laureen, „*The Europe's AI Act, How the Groundbreaking Regulation is Shaping Global AI Development and Its Implications in Various Sector* ", 2024, Amazon, France

Köbis, Nils, „*Bribes for Bias: can AI be corrupted?*", 27 February 2023, Transparency International , https://www.transparency.org/en/blog/bribes-for-bias-can-ai-be-corrupted

Köbis, Nils, Starke, Christopher & Edward-Gill, Jaselle, „*The promise and perils of using artificial intelligence to fight corruption*", 9 September 2022, Transparency International https://knowledgehub.transparency.org/product/the-corruption-risks-of-artificial-intelligence

Köbis, Nils, Starke, Christopher & Rahwan, Iyad, „*The promise and perils of using artificial intelligence to fight corruption*“, 23 May 2022, Springer Nature .com https://www.nature.com/articles/s42256-022-00489-1

Köbis, Nils, Starke, Christopher & Rahwan, Iyad, „*Artificial Intelligence as an Anti-Corruption Tool (AI-ACT) – Potentials and Pitfalls for Top-Down and Bottom-up approaches*“, February 2021, https://www.researchgate.net/publication/349546498_Artificial_Intelligence_as_an_Anti-Corruption_Tool_AI-ACT_--_Potentials_and_Pitfalls_for_Top-down_and_Bottom-up_Approaches

Komer, Sidney, „*Financial Crime & AI: Harnessing Technology for Improved Fraud Detection & Prevention*“, August 2023, IBM Watson, USA

Malan, Daniel; Heide, Marlan „*Why frontier technologies will drive the fight against corruption*“, World Economic Forum, 9 March 2023, https://www.weforum.org/agenda/2023/03/frontier-technologies-against-corruption/

Odilla, Fernanda, „*Bots against corruption: Exploring the benefits and limitations of AI based anti-corruption technology*“, 25 March 2023, Springer Nature.com https://link.springer.com/article/10.1007/s10611-023-10091-0

Various, „*EU Artificial Intelligence Act: The Essential Reference*“, February 2024, Lex Press, France

Zimiles, Helen, Mueller, Tim, „*How AI is transforming the fight against money laundering*”, World Economic Forum 17 January 2019, https://www.weforum.org/agenda/2019/01/how-ai-can-knock-the-starch-out-of-money-laundering/

European Union:

https://digital-strategy.ec.europa.eu/en/policies/european-approach-artificial-intelligence

https://commission.europa.eu/system/files/2020-02/commission-white-paper-artificial-intelligence-feb2020_en.pdf

https://eur-lex.europa.eu/legal-content/EN/TXT/PDF/?uri=CELEX:52020DC0064

Other:

Transparency International:

“Corruption Perception Index”

“Corruption in Crisis Situations”, 2019

World Bank:

"Governance and the Law", 2021

OECD:

"Using Artificial Intelligence in the Fight Against Corruption", 2021

United Nations:

"AI and Anti-Corruption", United Nations Office on Drugs and Crime (UNODC), 2021

Risks of Corruption and Anti-Corruption Compliance in Sport

Eduard Ivanov

1. Introduction

The problem of anti-corruption and compliance in sports becomes one of the priorities in the international anti-corruption agenda. In the UNGASS Political Declaration "Our common commitment to effectively addressing challenges and implementing measures to prevent and combat corruption and strengthen international cooperation", states declared safeguarding sport from corruption as one of the goals. The Conference of the States Parties to the United Nations Convention against Corruption adopted resolutions 7/8, entitled "Corruption in Sport" in its seventh session in 2017 and 8/4, entitled "Safeguarding Sport from Corruption" in the eighth session in 2019.

Corruption in sports has been acknowledged as an emerging risk area in the 2019-2021 G20 Anti-Corruption Working Group (ACWG) Action Plan. In 2020 - 2021, the Italian presidency in the G20 ACWG put this theme on the agenda. In 2021, G20 countries adopted High-Level Principles on Tackling Corruption in Sport.

Interpol established the Match-Fixing Task Force, which has around 100 members units, with more than 150 National Points of Contact worldwide (Interpol, 2023).

There are some interesting studies on corruption in sport. From a methodological point of view, the application of the TASP (Type, Activity, Sector, Place) tool developed by Graycar (Graycar, A., 2015) to corruption in sport, as suggested by Masters (Masters, A., 2015), looks very promising.

To establish a solid scientific background for a comprehensive anti-corruption framework in sport, further studies are required. The researchers mainly focused on specific corrupt practices in sports, such as match fixing and illegal betting, and on sports in which public scandals had happened, e.g., biathlon and soccer/football. However, corruption in sport is not limited to corruption offences and other misconduct directly related to sport competitions, such as manipulation of sport competition and the use of doping. It should not be forgotten that the organisation of major sport events often involves large-scale construction works, including those financed from states budgets, the involvement of sponsors, advertising, and broadcasting rights contracts. The selection of contractors and suppliers, price negotiation and contracts execution may be vulnerable for corrupt practices typical of business activities, e.g., violations in the procurement process, embezzlement of funds and trading in influence.

The complex nature of corruption in sport, its interconnection with corruption in the public service and business, organised crime and money laundering require the development of an effective anti-corruption framework both at the international and domestic levels. This framework is also important for governments, donors, advertisers, vendors, contractors, and other stakeholders in sport. One of the important elements of such a framework is the implementation of an anti-corruption compliance management system in international and national sports federations, professional leagues, and clubs.

In 2023, the International Anti-Corruption Academy (IACA) launched a research project "Integrity and Anti-Corruption Compliance in Sport" aimed at the analysis of typologies of corruption in sport, motivational factors that encourage or can prevent engagement in corruption, and the identification of best practices in designing, implementing, maintaining, monitoring, and evaluating integrity and compliance programmes in sports organizations in several summer and winter sports.

This article highlights forms of corruption in sport, provides an overview of the main corruption risks, and examines the role of ethics and anti-corruption compliance in safeguarding sport from corruption.

2. Forms of corruption in sport

Legal definitions of corruption and lists of criminal and administrative corruption offences vary from country to country. In this article, the author applies a broad concept of corruption in sport, which includes discrimination of athletes and harassment by managers and coaches.

Forms of corruption in sport can be divided into two categories: general and specific. General forms of corruption exist in sport, but are also widespread in the public, business, and non-profit sectors. Specific forms of corruption are typical only or primarily for sport.

General forms of corruption include bribery, extortion, violations in the process of election or appointment of officials of sports organisations, abuse of public office, violation of provisions on prevention and settlement of conflicts of interest, violation of procurement rules and procedures, embezzlement of funds of sports organisations using a person's official position, trading in influence, obstruction of justice in sports courts and arbitrations.

Less obvious general forms of corruption in sport include insider trading in countries where sports club securities are traded on the stock market and commercial espionage. Commercial espionage can be carried out for the benefit of competing sports teams or betting organisations. The purpose of commercial espionage is usually to illegally obtain information about team tactics, planned line-ups for specific games, training methods, health conditions, and injuries of athletes.

We also can consider as common forms of corruption in sport harassment, including sexual harassment (Armour, N., & Axon, R., 2017), and bullying of athletes by persons who have influence over them by virtue of their position.

Specific forms of corruption in sport include irregularities in the selection of host countries and cities for major sports events; manipulation of sports competitions, in particular the organisation and participation in match-fixing; illegal participation in betting activities; violations related to the use of doping; the use of transit clubs in the transfer of athletes to manipulate contract amounts and embezzlement of funds. It should be noted here that preventing corruption in the selection of host countries and cities is also essential for the organisers of artistic, musical and other cultural events.

The problem of match-fixing is one of the most discussed issues at international forums dedicated to the problem of corruption in sport. Several interesting comparative legal studies have been devoted to this topic (Steele, S. & Opie, H. (eds.), 2018). The Group of Copenhagen – the Network of National Platforms, established according to the Council of Europe Convention on the Manipulation of Sports Competitions (Macolin Convention) of 2014, published a comprehensive Resource Guide on typologies of sports manipulations (Council of Europe, 2023).

The development of modern information technologies makes it necessary to take a new look at both sports and corruption in sports competitions. Today, cybersport has become the leader in terms of attracted investments, surpassing traditional sports. The problem of using artificial intelligence in cybersports, as well as in chess, which has existed for over 1,500 years, is comparable to the problem of doping in traditional sports.

The use of modern information technologies in the process of refereeing sports competitions reduces the probability of refereeing mistakes, but at the same time creates new risks, including corruption risks and technical manipulation.

Corruption can facilitate the infiltration of organised crime into sport (Testa, A. & Sergi, A., 2017) and the use of sports organisations and competitions for money laundering purposes. The FATF report on the use of the football sector for money laundering provides a detailed analysis of existing typologies, in particular the investment of criminal proceeds in football clubs, player transfers and match fixing (FATF, 2009).

3. Risks of corruption in sport

In order to implement an effective and efficient anti-corruption compliance management system in sports organisations, it is crucial to determine which relationships in sport are most vulnerable to corruption and identify the main corruption risks.

For this purpose, the general governance framework in sport can be presented as a multi -level system consisting of the international level or the level of international sports organizations, the national level or the level of national sports organizations, the level of professional leagues such as the National Hockey League (NHL), the level of sports clubs and teams, and children's and youth sports.

At the international level, risks of corruption arise in election or appointment of officials and in the governance of international sports organisations, in the selection of host countries and cities for major international sports events (Conn D., 2017; Sudgen J. and Tomlinson A., 2017), distribution of broadcasting rights (U.S. Department of Justice, 2015), and in the process of organising and conducting such competitions. Most of these processes can also be affected by corrupt practices at the national level.

The governance systems of both international and national sports organisations are vulnerable to the risks of financial and business mismanagement, in particular to violations in the procurement process and misappropriation of funds. Such acts may be facilitated by the lack of transparent procurement procedures, effective third-party due diligence and risk management, monitoring, and auditing mechanisms in international sports organisations.

However, at the national level, the range of relations subject to corruption risks and their participants is much wider than at the international level. Special attention should be paid to the construction of sports facilities, including the selection of contractors, approval of prices, control over the implementation and timely completion of construction works. Corruption risks in this area include giving and receiving bribes, abuse of official position, irregularities in procurement, embezzlement of funds of sports organisations through overpricing of construction materials and works or failure of contractors to fulfil contracts. Thus, the Operation Panatenaico launched in 2015 by the Brazilian law enforcement authorities detected corruption and fraud in the construction project of the Mané Garrincha stadium in Brasília for the 2014 World Cup. In December 2022, two senior politicians – former governor Agnelo Queiroz and former vice governor Tadeu Filippelli were convicted of administrative impropriety by the Federal District and Territories Court of Justice and had their political rights suspended for ten years (Calgano, L., 2022).

At the level of sports clubs and teams, corruption risks exist in relations between athletes, sports agents, managers and coaches of sports clubs and teams. Such risks may include bribery, extortion, and harassment in the process of making decisions on admission to a team, participation in competitions or specific games, awarding of sports titles or qualifications, transfer to other sports clubs.

Consideration of these risks is equally important in youth and children's sports. Young athletes, and often also their parents, are the most vulnerable to corruption pressures. It is very difficult for young athletes to decide to report misconduct by a coach or manager.

The main corruption risks related to conducting sports competitions of various levels are the manipulation of sports competitions, illegal participation in betting activities and violations related to the use of doping.

The Macolin Convention of 2014 defined the manipulation of sports competitions as "an intentional arrangement, act or omission aimed at an improper alteration of the result or the course of a sports competition in order to remove all or part of the unpredictable nature of the aforementioned sports competition with a view to obtaining an undue advantage for oneself or for others". The manipulation of sports competitions may be aimed at achieving a certain result in a competition without the purpose of obtaining an economic benefit as a direct result of this manipulation, e.g. match-fixing. Much more often, the manipulation is connected with participation of its beneficiaries in illegal betting activities organized by criminal groups without licenses or illegal participation in betting activities.

The most popular sports attract the attention of criminal groups involved in illegal betting activities and are therefore more vulnerable to the manipulation. Thus, in 2023, the Brazilian law enforcement authorities carried out an operation in several Brazilian states against criminal groups, gamblers, and football players from the Brazilian top football's first and second divisions involved in match fixing and manipulating matches through specific actions, e.g., getting yellow cards (Globoesporte, 2023).

The issue of using doping by athletes is closely linked to corruption. Coaches, managers, athletes, and other persons involved use corruption to get access to prohibited substances, and to avoid detection, investigation, and prosecution. Corruption helps in falsifying or hiding results of doping probes, misleading or suppressing anti-doping investigations. The recent case of the former president of the International Biathlon Union (IBU) Anders Besseberg, sentenced in April 2024 in Norway, demonstrates that even senior officials of international sports organizations can be involved in corruption connected to the use of doping (Økokrim, 2023; Reuters, 2024).

4. The role of anti-corruption compliance in safeguarding sport from corruption

Implementation of integrity and anti-corruption compliance programmes in sports organizations at all levels and raising awareness of the risks and negative consequences of misconduct is an effective way to prevent corruption at the initial stage.

It is important to emphasise that sports organisations enjoy a certain degree of independence from states. According to the Olympic Charter, they have the rights and obligations of autonomy, which include freely establishing and controlling the rules of sport, determining the structure and governance of their organisations, enjoying the right of elections free from any outside influence and the responsibility for ensuring that principles of good governance be applied (International Olympic Committee, 2023).

As a rule, international sports federations have codes of ethics or similar documents with other titles. The codes of ethics are based on the fundamental principles of Olympism defined in the Olympic Charter (International Olympic Committee, 2023). The codes of ethics analysed by the author enshrine the principles of fair play, integrity, safeguarding the dignity of the individual, mutual respect, non-discrimination, and zero tolerance for corruption.

The International Basketball Federation (FIBA), the International Volleyball Federation (FIVB), the International Federation of Football Associations (FIFA), the International Biathlon Union (IBU) and the International Ice Hockey Federation (IIHF) representing mass sports have integrity and compliance programmes or at least policies on key elements of anti-corruption compliance.

Many international sports organizations established integrity or compliance units responsible for promoting integrity and preventing corruption. Thus, FIFA's Legal and Compliance Division is responsible for anti-corruption compliance function. FIFA also created the Integrity Department within the Legal and Compliance Division.

In addition to the prevention of misconduct, integrity units may receive and process whistleblower reports, conduct internal investigations, apply disciplinary sanctions, and cooperate with law enforcement authorities and other relevant stakeholders.

It should be noted that main stakeholders in esports pay a serious attention to anti-corruption and integrity. In 2016, they established the International Esports Integrity Commission (ESIC) responsible for prevention and investigation of all forms of cheating, including match manipulation and the use of doping. The Commission adopted four codes: Anti-Corruption Code, Anti-Doping Code, Code of Conduct, and Code of Ethics. The codes enshrine the main principles and values applicable to competitions and other activities in esports. The Commission cooperates with the International Betting Integrity Association and other stakeholders in the betting industry to prevent illegal betting and illegal participation in betting. The Commission's practice of creating a publicly accessible register of sanctions for individuals who have breached the ESIC Integrity Codes is noteworthy. The register contains information about all individuals who are or were previously banned by the ESIC.

An interesting experience of centralisation of certain anti-corruption functions at the international level exists in tennis. In 2021, the International Tennis Federation (ITF), the Association of Tennis Professionals (ATP), the Women's Tennis Association (WTA) and the federations organising Grand Slam tournaments (Australia, France, Great Britain, USA) established the International Tennis Integrity Agency (ITIA). The ITIA adopted the Tennis Anti-Corruption Programme and the Tennis Anti-Doping Programme applicable to all professional tennis events and to all governing bodies. The ITIA is authorized to conduct investigations and apply sanctions according to the procedures established in the Anti-Corruption Programme.

Knowledge of the typologies of corruption in sport, understanding the motivating factors, promoting ethical principles and values, complying with applicable laws and regulations, localising the compliance programme and using modern IT technologies can provide a solid foundation for an effective anti-corruption compliance programme in a sports organisation.

When developing anti-corruption compliance programmes, sports organisations usually take into account the provisions of international treaties, the Olympic Charter, national anti-corruption, sports, and other applicable legislations. National sports organisations usually consider codes of ethics, compliance programmes and policies and other relevant documents of international sports organisations in their sports.

The anti-corruption compliance programmes of sports organisations primarily focus on the interaction with government authorities and sponsors, anti-doping, prevention of manipulation of sports competitions, and violations related to participation in betting activities. Many sports organizations have policies on conflict of interest management, and gifts and hospitality.

At the same time, they may include general anti-corruption policies typical for compliance programmes of companies. These policies define a general framework of an anti-corruption compliance management system, regulate the application of an anti-corruption clause or a general compliance clause, anti-corruption procedures in recruitment and personnel management, third party due diligence and corruption risk management, anti-corruption procedures in procurement, the operation of a hotline and screening of reports, anti-corruption training and monitoring of the anti-corruption compliance programme.

In the author's opinion, general anti-corruption policies are no less important for sports organizations than specific ones. At the first stage, a manager of a sports organisation may be involved in corruption schemes that are not directly related to sports competitions, such as receiving a bribe to support the company in the procurement process or turning a blind eye to failure to meet contractual obligations within agreed timeframes. At the next stage, this manager, who is already involved in corrupt relations, may receive an offer to benefit from the match fixing and illegal betting. As we know, it can be easy to enter a corruption relationship, but very difficult to find a way out.

The FIFA compliance framework can be provided as an example of a very broad and detailed programme. The FIFA Code of Conduct and the Compliance Handbook cover all the main elements of anti-corruption compliance. The FIFA Code of Conduct for Third Parties establishes an obligation for all third parties to comply with all relevant anti-corruption laws and international standards, and to take measures to identify suspicious transactions potentially related to money laundering or other illegal activities (FIFA, 2020b).

Sports organizations usually take measures to avoid the misuse of gifts and hospitality for corruption purposes. According to the FIFA Compliance Handbook, gifts may be given or accepted if they pass the "FIT" (Frequency, Intent and Timing) test. The hospitality should be reasonable in expense (FIFA, 2020a).

The International Ice Hockey Federation (IIHF) adopted detailed Election Conduct Guidelines (IIHF, 2021). The Guidelines established obligations and restrictions for the IIHF staff and candidates to guarantee respect for the democratic voting and/or election process. Violations of the Guidelines should be reported to the IIHF Disciplinary Board which should promptly review reports and may open and manage a disciplinary case in accordance with Article 12.3 of the IIHF Disciplinary Regulations.

In designing and implementing general anti-corruption compliance policies, sports organizations can use the experience of the business sector, and international anti-corruption compliance standards and guidelines published by international organizations, NGOs and business associations (Ivanov, E., 2022).

Special attention should be paid to the organisation of whistleblowing hotlines for reporting violations in sport and to the procedures for screening and responding to reports. To support the implementation of hotlines by sports organisations, the UNODC published a practical guide containing key principles and recommendations (UNODC, 2019).

However, creating a hotline as such is not enough. It is very challenging for any athlete, especially a young athlete, to make the decision to report violations in their own team. The athlete should be informed not only about the reporting procedure, but also about the consequences. It is important for a potential whistleblower to assess the ethical aspects, possible risks, and existing protection mechanisms. Awareness raising campaigns and regular practically oriented anti-corruption trainings can have a positive impact on the building of anti-corruption and whistleblowing culture. The involvement of famous athletes as "anti-corruption ambassadors" in awareness campaigns can help young athletes to realise that competition should be based on fair-play rules and integrity and that reporting wrongdoing by a coach, or teammates is not a dishonest act.

Some sports organizations establish special educational programmes and projects to promote integrity in sport and reporting misconduct. Thus, the Kontinental Hockey League (KHL) launched an educational project "Know what's going on – Say NO – Tell us". The aim of the project is to educate all participants and prevent violations of the regulations concerning the salary cap, anti-doping measures and match-fixing or betting on games (KHL, 2024). The project answers the most sensitive questions that potential whistleblowers usually have, such as anonymity of the hot line, who have access to the information, confidentiality of the information, and how this information will be treated.

5. Summary

To summarise, several conclusions can be drawn.

Corruption in sport exists in general and specific forms. Relations in the management of sports organisations and the construction of large sports facilities are vulnerable to corruption risks associated with general forms of corruption. These risks include the appointment or election of officials of sports organisations at various levels, conflict of interest management, procurement, financial management, control over the performance of contracts by third parties, and data protection.

Corruption risks associated with specific forms of corruption in sport are primarily characteristic of relations arising in the process of organising and conducting sports competitions, such as the selection of countries and cities for sports competitions, the conclusion of agreements on broadcasting rights, and the determination of team compositions. Conducting of competitions is vulnerable to manipulating the process and results, the use of doping and illegal participation in betting activities.

Most of the corruption risks discussed are widespread in high-performance sport. At the same time, corruption risks also exist in children's and youth sports, when young athletes are just beginning their sporting journey. These include the risks of coaches and officials of sports organisations soliciting and accepting bribes for inclusion in a team, admission to competitions, and awarding sports qualifications.

The study, conducted by the author, identified the successful experience of a number of international and national sports organisations in developing and implementing codes of ethics, anti-corruption policies and regulations aimed primarily at ensuring integrity in sport competitions and preventing specific forms of corruption in sport. However, the documents reviewed do not always pay sufficient attention to the prevention of general forms of corruption.

An effective model of anti-corruption compliance in sports organizations should be aimed at the prevention of both general and specific forms of corruption in sports. It can consider best practices of international and national sports organizations, international standards and recommendations on anti-corruption compliance, the experience of corruption prevention in state and municipal services and the implementation of anti-corruption compliance in the business sector.

In order to support the implementation of anti-corruption compliance in sports organizations and clubs, and promote a culture of integrity, countries could develop general recommendations on the structure and content of a code of ethics and anti-corruption policies or regulations for sports organizations and clubs. The recommendations can be further detailed, considering the specifics of different sports and existing risks. It is important to mention that such recommendations should be used by sports organisations at various levels on a voluntary basis and should not create an excessive administrative and financial burden.

When implementing anti-corruption compliance programmes and possibly developing recommendations, it is crucial to take into account the possibilities of using emerging information technologies in the compliance system. The new technologies, including AI and big data analytics, can enhance the efficiency of conflict of interest management, third party due diligence and risk management, and internal investigations. At the same time, the new risks associated with the use of various information technologies and solutions should be considered, and the necessary preventive legal mechanisms and technical measures should be implemented.

References

Armour, N., & Axon, R. (2017). USA Gymnastics: Sexual assault investigation urges cultural change. USA TODAY. https://www.usatoday.com/story/sports/olympics/2017/06/27/sexual-assault-usa-gymnastics-olympics-usoc-larry-nassar-deborah-daniels-usa-gymnastics/431358001/

Calgano, L. (2022) Justiça condena Agnelo e Filippelli por desvios na construção do estádio Mané Garrincha. http://noticias.r7.com/brasilia/justica-condena-agnelo-e-filippelli-por-desvios-na-construcao-do-estadio-mane-garrincha-20122022

Conn, D. (2017). The Fall of the House of FIFA: The Multimillion-Dollar Corruption at the Heart of Global Soccer. New York: Nation Books, 328 p.

Council of Europe (2023). Typology of sports manipulations. Resource Guide. https://rm.coe.int/prems-051523-ex-160422-gbr-2581-working-group-typology-sports-a4-web/1680aacf39

FATF (2009). Money Laundering through the Football Sector. FATF Report. https://www.fatf-gafi.org/content/dam/fatf-gafi/reports/ML%20through%20the%20Football%20Sector.pdf.coredownload.pdf

FIFA (2020a). Compliance Handbook. https://digitalhub.fifa.com/m/4a1daee06e72f0c6/original/lp015yxfdqesvrleo6ii-pdf.pdf

FIFA (2020b). The FIFA Code of Conduct for Third Parties. https://digitalhub.fifa.com/m/6734cf98cbeaa070/original/i0mtve5d0zapbtzws1wt-pdf.pdf

Globoesporte (2023). Manipulação na Série A: tudo sobre o esquema que envolve jogadores e apostadores. https://ge.globo.com/futebol/noticia/2023/04/19/manipulacao-na-serie-a-tudo-sobre-o-esquema-que-envolve-jogadores-e-apostadores.ghtml

Graycar, A. (2015). Corruption: Classification and Analysis. Policy and Society. Volume 32, Issue 2. https://doi.org/10.1016/j.polsoc.2015.04.001

IIHF (2021). Election Conduct Guidelines. https://blob.iihf.com/iihf-media/iihfmvc/media/downloads/regulations/2024/2024_iihf_elections_conduct_guidelines.pdf

International Olympic Committee (2023). Olympic Charter. https://stillmed.olympics.com/media/Document%20Library/OlympicOrg/General/EN-Olympic-Charter.pdf

Interpol (2023). https://www.interpol.int/Crimes/Corruption/Corruption-in-sport

Ivanov, E. (2022). Overview of Anti-Corruption Compliance Standards and Guidelines. Second Revised Edition. Laxenburg: International Anti-Corruption Academy (IACA). https://www.iaca.int/media/attachments/2022/08/01/overview-of-anti-corruption-compliance-standards-and-guidelines-practical-tool-2nd-edition_with_covers.pdf

KHL (2024). https://en.khl.ru/integrity/

Masters, A. (2015) Corruption in Sport: From the Playing Field to the Field of Policy. Policy and Society. Volume 32, Issue 2. https://doi.org/10.1016/j.polsoc.2015.04.002

Økokrim (2023) Former president of the IBU (International Biathlon Union) indicted on charges of aggravated corruption. https://www.okokrim.no/former-president-of-the-ibu-international-biathlon-union-indicted-on-charges-of-aggravated-corruption.6592891-549344.html

Reuters (2024). Former IBU president sentenced to three years in prison on corruption charges. https://www.reuters.com/world/europe/former-ibu-president-sentenced-three-years-prison-corruption-charges-2024-04-12/

Steele, S. & Opie, H. (eds.) (2018). Match-Fixing in Sport: Comparative Studies from Australia, Japan, Korea and Beyond. New York: Routledge, 268 p.

Sugden J. and Tomlinson A. (2017) Football, Corruption and Lies: Revisiting 'Badfellas', the Book FIFA Tried to Ban. New York: Routledge, 290 p.

Testa, A. & Sergi, A. (2017). Corruption, Mafia Power and Italian Soccer. Abingdon: Routledge, 178 p.

UNODC (2019). Reporting Mechanisms in Sport: A Practical Guide for Development and Implementation [Online]. Vienna: UNODC. https://stillmed.olympic.org/media/Document%20Library/OlympicOrg/IOC/What-We-Do/Protecting Clean-Athletes/Competition-manipulation/IOC-UNODC-Reporting-Mechanisms-in-Sport-ebook.pdf

U.S. Department of Justice (2015). Jeffrey Webb et al Indictment. https://www.justice.gov/opa/file/450211/download

Foreign corruption at Swiss companies – new findings on risks and counter-strategies

Christian Hauser, Marc Herkenrath, Martin Hilti,
Jeanine Bretti Rainalter, Ramona Stampfli

1. Introduction and background to the study

Corruption is still widespread throughout the world and represents a continuing global problem. This is shown by Transparency International's CPI, which measures the perception of corruption in the public sector based on assessments by experts, with high values indicating a low level of corruption. In 2022, two thirds of all countries surveyed worldwide failed to achieve even half of the maximum possible 100 points (Transparency International, 2023). Corruption levels are particularly high in the two regions of Southern Africa (on average 32 points) and Eastern Europe/Central Asia (on average 35 points), with Eastern Europe/Central Asia in particular playing an important role as a target region for Swiss companies' foreign activities. However, corruption risks also remain high in other regions. Latin American and Caribbean countries, for example, only achieved an average of 41 points in the CPI 2022. Over the past decade, corruption has hardly decreased worldwide, but has tended to stagnate and has even increased in many countries. The CPI offers clear evidence of this, showing that between 2012 and 2022, the level of corruption remained unchanged or increased in 155 countries and only improved in 25 countries. There was a sharp deterioration in Cyprus, Hungary and Turkey, among others, as well as in Australia and Canada, but an improvement was seen in the Seychelles, Greece, Italy, Armenia and Asia-Pacific countries such as Vietnam, Laos, Nepal and South Korea (Transparency International, 2023).

Numerous countries with high economic growth potential also have a high risk of corruption; these include India and China, as well as Sub-Saharan Africa (Fontagné et al., 2022; Transparency International, 2023). For Swiss companies operating abroad, it is imperative to proactively tackle the issue of corruption. Swiss companies frequently face significant economic pressures, especially in international markets. Moreover, they must navigate foreign legal frameworks and unfamiliar political and cultural contexts. In such situations, corruption can appear lucrative as it supposedly enables companies to overcome bureaucratic obstacles or gain economic advantages.

Corruption can occur not only in dealings with government institutions (business to government, B2G), but also in business dealings between companies (business to business, B2B). However, there is little up-to-date and reliable international data on the global spread of corruption in the private sector, although previous studies have shown that Swiss companies abroad are confronted with corruption in both the public and private sectors (Becker et al., 2012; Isenring et al., 2016). As these studies show, a considerable number of Swiss companies also effectively complies with these corrupt demands. It is not uncommon for (local) third parties working for Swiss companies to be involved in corrupt behaviour. Furthermore, the results of the aforementioned studies reveal that there is still clear potential for improvement in corruption prevention measures.

Although it is primarily the corruption scandals of well-known large companies that attract media attention, foreign corruption does not only affect large companies. Some studies even suggest that small and medium-sized enterprises (SMEs) tend to be affected more frequently than larger companies (Goel et al., 2022; Martins et al., 2020). This is attributed to the fact that SMEs frequently have less negotiating power and legal influence than large companies. Furthermore, large companies usually have more human and financial resources to deal with corruption risks. However, other studies suggest that large companies are more susceptible to corruption compared to SMEs (PwC, 2022) or that there are no differences according to company size (Hauser/Kronthaler, 2013).

Until the turn of the millennium, there were few consequences in Switzerland for Swiss companies or authorised third parties who engaged in corruption in foreign countries. On the contrary, such payments were considered necessary for conducting business in specific countries and were eligible for tax deductions. However, over the past two decades there has been a significant paradigm shift. The fight against foreign corruption has been significantly strengthened, both in Switzerland and abroad. Corruption is now largely prohibited under criminal law. Individuals as well as companies and other organisations can be liable to prosecution. In particular, companies may be liable to prosecution if they are accused of failing to take all necessary and reasonable precautions to prevent serious offences such as corruption and money laundering committed in the course of their business activities (Art. 102 para 2 of the Swiss Criminal Code). Furthermore, companies can be held liable not only for the misconduct of their employees but also by third parties. Criminal liability is possible as soon as a third party carries out activities for the company that are related to the company's business activities. The company must therefore also take appropriate precautions to prevent serious criminal offences by third parties such as corruption and money laundering.

In addition to Swiss regulations, laws abroad are also decisive for companies operating internationally. These are initially the regulations in the countries in which the company operates. However, the laws of countries in which the company does not operate may also be applicable. In particular, the US and UK anti-corruption laws have an extremely broad scope of application. The US Foreign Corrupt Practices Act, for example, may already apply if a US server is used or a payment is made in US dollars (Transparency International Switzerland 2021a; 2022).

Moreover, bribery can result not only in criminal consequences for companies but also in potential exclusion from subsidies, as well as public and private contracts, and potentially lead to significant reputational harm. A single corruption scandal can quickly ruin a good reputation built up over many years. Moreover, a company that engages in corrupt practices exposes itself to blackmail and ultimately fosters a culture of corruption. This is because such actions cultivate an environment within the company where other offences are more likely to thrive (Staatssekretariat für Wirtschaft SECO, 2017). This underlines the imperative for Swiss companies, regardless of their size, to confront the corruption risks inherent in international business operations. In order to obtain information on the extent to which Swiss companies are affected by corruption and what measures they are taking to prevent it, this study seeks to answer the following research questions:

- How frequently are Swiss companies confronted with corrupt behaviour in other countries, and what proportion of their turnover do they spend on average on informal payments and gifts under the table?

- For which business activities are informal payments and gifts made under the table typically expected, and which company-specific factors influence the susceptibility to corrupt behaviour?
- What measures do Swiss companies that operate abroad take to prevent corruption?
- What conclusions do the survey results offer regarding the benefits and the challenges of corruption prevention? What are the challenges of corruption prevention for Swiss companies?

2. Methodology

2.1 Survey design, sample and response

To obtain information on the extent to which Swiss companies are affected by corruption and the measures they take to prevent it, a quantitative study among 539 internationally active Swiss companies of all sizes and sectors was conducted between March and April 2023. The response rate was 34 per cent. The online questionnaire was available in German, French and Italian. The respondents were members of management as well as employees from the export, distribution, sales, or other departments with regular contacts abroad. In addition to general socio-demographic questions, data were collected on business activities abroad, the prevailing governmental framework conditions and bureaucratic hurdles, the expectation of informal payments and gifts under the table and measures to prevent corruption. Participants were asked to report on a business relationship in a selected country about which they could best provide information on the prevailing bureaucracy and corruption within it.

The companies surveyed are active in all regions of the world. They most frequently maintain business relationships with countries in Central and Northern Europe. Business relationships with countries in Southern Europe and in Eastern Europe and Central Asia (former Eastern Bloc) are also common. Approximately half of the companies surveyed operate in North America (USA/Canada) and half in the other Asian countries (excluding Japan and Singapore). To obtain detailed information, the respondents were asked to name one main target country with which the company has business relations and about which they can provide good information. Most information was provided on Italy, China, India, Spain, Poland, Russia,

Brazil, Romania, Hong Kong and the United Arab Emirates. The companies are active in the target countries in different ways, e.g. through exports, own subsidiaries, via agents, intermediaries or local sales partnerships, or through licence or franchise agreements with companies. In 2022, the companies generated most of their turnover in the target country with private sector companies (B2B). The proportion of turnover generated directly with end consumers (B2C) and with state-owned companies or public authorities (B2G) was lower.

2.2 Data quality

Various measures were taken to ensure high data quality. For example, the questionnaire was reviewed and further developed with people with expertise in the areas of foreign trade and corruption. In addition, the questionnaire was analysed and validated as part of a preliminary study using computer-assisted telephone interviews (CATI). Furthermore, the design and programming of the questionnaire was tested for content, comprehensibility and user-friendliness, and the survey was started with a soft launch to recognise possible weaknesses at an early stage. Finally, the data were processed and analysed in detail with the assistance of an expert in statistics and econometrics.

Obtaining reliable information on the topic of corruption is challenging as corruption is a clandestine phenomenon and the people involved have little interest in disclosure. To address this problem, this study used a method developed by the World Bank and others to measure corruption at the company level. This made it possible to ask directly about the level of payments (Hauser/Hogenacker, 2014). In addition, the "Bayesian truth framework" was used, whereby the respondents were asked to give an assessment of the distribution of the level of payments of comparable companies in addition to their own answer, e.g. on the level of informal payments. These answers were used to calculate a factor that provides information on the extent of the respondents' socially desirable response behaviour. The responses were subsequently weighted so that the survey results could be adjusted for socially desirable response behaviour (Brandenberg/Fessler, 2012; Prelec, 2004).

The data were analysed using descriptive and multivariate statistical methods. Based on the sample, the results can be generalised to Swiss companies with international business activities that generate at least part of their sales outside of Central/Northern Europe, Australia, New Zealand, Japan, Singapore and North America (USA/Canada). The confidence interval is ±4.2 at a confidence level of 95 per cent.

3. Results

3.1 Nature and extent of corruption – at the companies

As part of the survey, the companies were asked to assess the bureaucratic framework conditions in the respective target country. Approximately two thirds of the companies surveyed stated that the legal system guarantees their contractual and property rights. Just over half of the companies also agreed with the statements that laws and regulations are clearly formulated, that information about laws and regulations affecting the company is easy to obtain, and that the legal system is impartial and not corrupt. Somewhat fewer (39%) agreed with the statement that organisational processes within government agencies are transparent (see Fig. 1).

Of particular interest was the question of the extent to which the companies surveyed are confronted with corruption abroad. The focus here is on whether companies are expected to make informal payments or gifts under the table when they do business in the respective country. Figure 2 shows that in 52 per cent of the companies surveyed, such payments were expected. Thirty-eight per cent stated that they are not confronted with such expectations. The remaining ten per cent of companies reported that

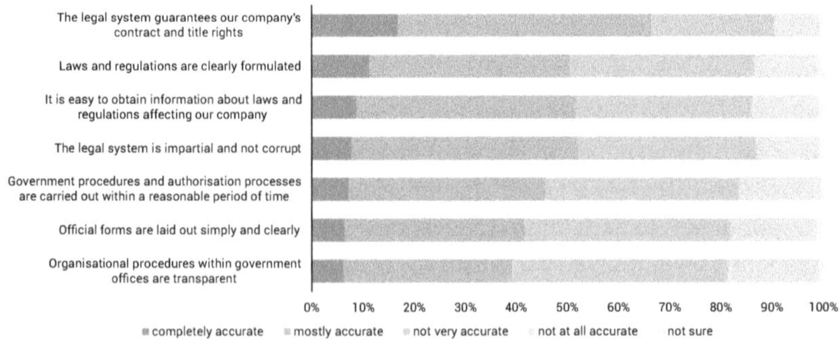

Figure 1: Bureaucratic framework conditions in target country

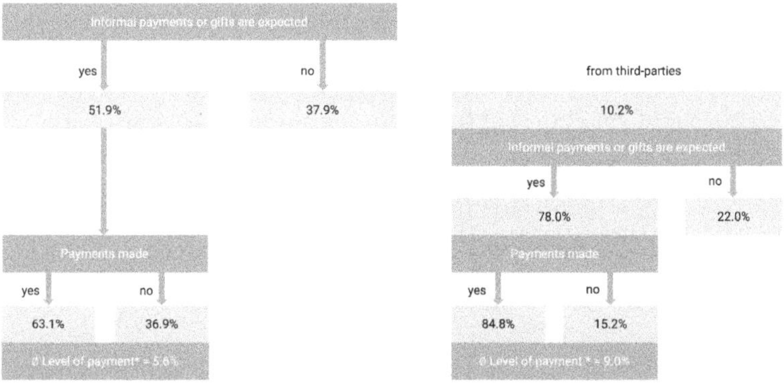

* Average share of the turnover generated in the target country that is spent annually on informal payments and gifts under the table.

Figure 2: Corruption claims and amount of payments

they work with third parties locally; for example, agents, intermediaries or sales partnerships.

The survey results also show that 63 per cent of the companies that are expected to make informal payments or gifts engage in such transactions. In contrast, 37 per cent of the companies stated that they refrain from making informal payments, despite the expectation to do so when doing business abroad. On average, the companies surveyed stated that they spend 5.6 per cent of the turnover generated in the target country on informal payments and gifts.

The survey findings indicate that companies are most frequently confronted with the expectation of informal payments or gifts under the table when contracts are awarded by private-sector companies (B2B). Seventy-one per cent of the companies surveyed stated that informal transactions are expected in this situation. In each case, approximately 60 per cent stated that such payments are required when awarding public contracts (government contracts, B2G) and when obtaining government licences.

The companies surveyed (56%) also confirmed that informal payments are expected during inspections by the police or other government agencies. Approximately half of the companies affirmed that they are expected to make informal payments when clearing goods at ports or airports and during

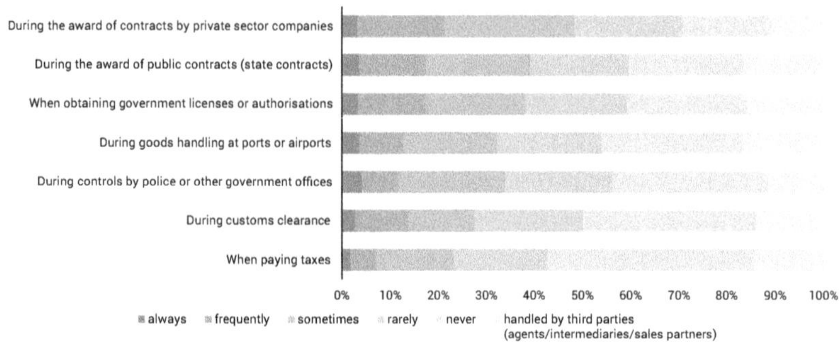

Figure 3: Situations in which Swiss companies are expected to make informal payments or gifts under the table

customs clearance. Finally, 43 per cent of the companies surveyed stated that informal payments are expected for tax payments (see Fig. 3).

A detailed analysis shows which companies are expected to make informal payments. On the one hand, informal payments are particularly expected from companies with stakes or joint ventures as well as from companies with their own sales or service branches in the respective country. On the other hand, companies that work with third parties locally and companies with management or consultancy agreements are also frequently confronted with corruption.

Furthermore, the probability of being confronted with corruption is higher if the companies perceive bureaucracy to be high and if corruption in the respective target country is high according to the CPI. Companies that generate a higher proportion of their turnover with the public sector and state-owned enterprises (B2G) are also more likely to be confronted with corrupt expectations. Companies from German-speaking Switzerland also more frequently reported being expected to make informal payments. In contrast, companies in the manufacturing sector as well as trading and service companies are less frequently affected by corruption.

Furthermore, the analyses show that companies with an ethical corporate culture are also less likely to face corrupt expectations. On the other hand, companies with a higher number of compliance measures are more frequently confronted with expectations of corruption. The size of the company has no significant influence on whether companies are expected to make informal payments. In other words, SMEs and large companies are equally confronted with the demand for informal payments.

The in-depth analyses also reveal that older companies, companies from the transport sector and companies with an ethical corporate culture are less likely to give in to demands for informal payments. If companies consider the bureaucratic effort to be high, they are also less likely to make informal payments. If the respondents stated that they were able to initiate or finalise orders through personal contacts, then they were also less likely to make informal payments.

Another focus of the study was to analyse the amounts companies spend on informal payments and gifts. The amount of the payments is understood as a percentage of the turnover generated by the company in the respective target country. The results show that companies with subsidiaries in the target country spend a higher proportion of their turnover in the target country on informal payments.

The same picture emerges for companies that are active in exports or have cooperation agreements. Companies from German-speaking Switzerland, on the other hand, spend a lower proportion of their respective turnover on informal payments. Regarding sectors, transport and service companies pay less.

Younger companies, on the other hand, spend a higher proportion of their turnover on informal payments. This may indicate that these companies feel they still have to assert themselves on the market, whereas older companies are more likely to already have an established market position. Once again, it is demonstrated that companies with a high ethical corporate culture spend a lower proportion of their turnover on informal payments.

Furthermore, it is evident that the size of the company has no significant influence on whether a company makes informal payments or on the amount of these payments. This means that both SMEs and large companies make informal payments, and their amount cannot be attributed to the size of the company.

3.2 Nature and extent of corruption – by third parties

Seventy-eight per cent of the Swiss companies that work with third parties in the target country assume that the third parties are expected to make informal payments or gifts under the table. Of these, 85 per cent assume that the authorised third parties make informal payments and gifts under the table if this is expected of them. In addition, the Swiss companies surveyed estimated that the third parties working for them in the target country spend an average of nine per cent of their turnover generated in the target country on informal transactions (see Fig. 2 above).

Regarding situations in which informal payments or gifts under the table are expected, a similar picture emerges for third parties as for the companies themselves. Swiss companies assume that informal payments are frequently expected from partner companies both when awarding public contracts (B2G) and when awarding contracts through private companies (B2B). Concerning customs clearance or tax payments, on the other hand, they are less likely to assume that informal payments are expected from the third parties working for them (see Fig. 4).

The detailed analysis shows that larger Swiss companies and those that consider the bureaucracy in the target country to be high are statistically significantly more likely to assume that informal payments are expected from the third parties working for them. In contrast, companies that are

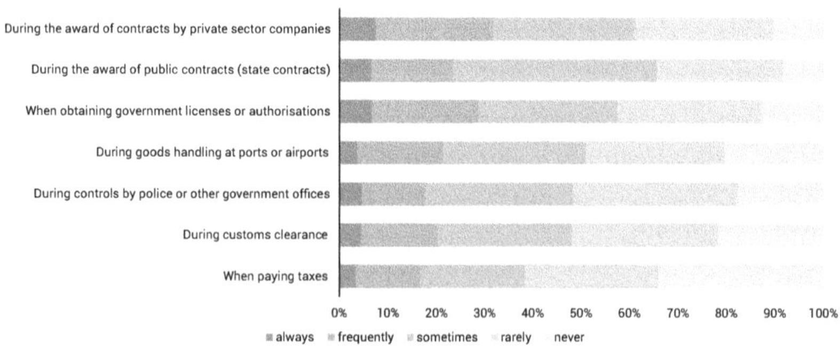

Figure 4: Situations in which third parties working for Swiss companies are expected to make informal payments or gifts under the table

family-run are less likely to assume that authorised third parties will be confronted with corruption.

Exporting companies and companies from German-speaking Switzerland more frequently stated that third parties working for them make informal payments if they are expected to do so. In contrast, companies with their own sales or service branches are less likely to assume that their partner companies make informal payments. Furthermore, companies with a more ethical corporate culture are less likely to assume that third parties working for them will make informal payments. Conversely, companies with a higher number of compliance measures more frequently stated that their partner companies make informal payments.

The findings also show that companies with their own sales or service branches in the respective country assume that the third parties they commission spend a lower proportion of their turnover on informal payments. This also applies to Swiss retail companies. Companies that generate a higher proportion of their turnover from government contracts (B2G), on the other hand, stated that their partner companies use a higher proportion of their turnover for informal payments. This also applies to companies that work with third parties in countries where corruption is high according to the CPI.

3.3 Affected by corruption of others

Just under a quarter of the companies surveyed assumed that the company had lost a contract from a public or private client in any country in the last two years to a competitor who the company assumes only obtained the contract through corrupt practices (see Fig. 5). The companies most frequently stated that this was the case in Italy, China, Russia and Germany. The respective competitors most frequently originate from China, Italy, Germany, France, and the United States.

The survey results also show that almost one in seven companies have refrained from entering a market in the last five years due to corruption risks. The companies surveyed most frequently stated that they have not entered the market in Russia, Iran, Belarus and Ukraine. In addition, one in eight companies has withdrawn from a market in the last five years due to corruption risks, and one in ten companies is currently considering withdrawing from a market. Companies most frequently withdrew from

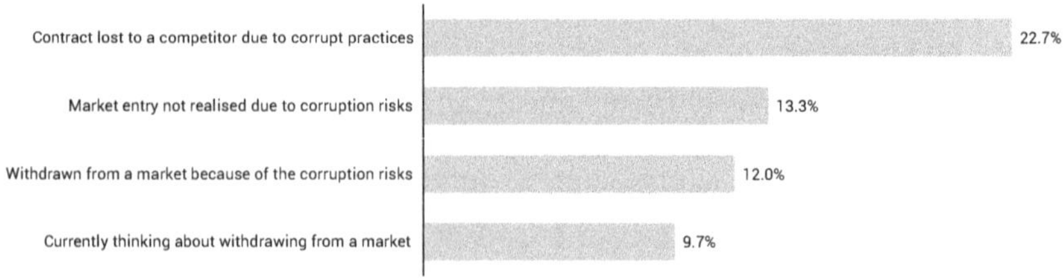

Figure 5: Corruption risk as an obstacle to Swiss foreign trade

Russia, Iran, Azerbaijan, Angola, and China. Furthermore, companies are currently most frequently considering withdrawing from Russia, Albania, Belarus, and Afghanistan.

3.4 Measures implemented to prevent corruption

The measures taken by the companies to prevent corruption were also included in the survey. The results clearly show that the majority of companies already use various measures to prevent corruption. The measure most frequently used by companies is the written documentation of all business transactions. Such documentation occurs in 79 per cent of the companies surveyed. Seventy-eight per cent of the companies stated that violations of legal, regulatory and internal provisions are consistently pursued and result in disciplinary and/or labour law consequences. The regular communication of ethics and integrity efforts is used as a measure by 76 per cent of companies. Three quarters of the companies surveyed reported that they require their agents, representatives and distribution partners to comply with legal and internal company regulations via a written agreement.

Almost as many companies (74%) have written business principles and a code of conduct that regulate the handling of corruption risks. In addition, companies frequently (71%) check third parties for their integrity before concluding contracts (due diligence).

In addition, the following measures are used to prevent corruption: contractual obligation of the company's employees to report concrete or suspected cases of corruption (70%); active and open addressing of the issue of corruption by the company management with the clear signal that informal payments or gifts will not be made under the table in any form (tone from the top, 70%); and the auditing of all areas of the company by an external auditing body (65%). Companies are less likely to implement systematic and planned staff rotation in companies at risk of corruption.

Just under half of the companies surveyed stated that there is an independent body (ombudsman, whistleblowing system) within the company to which employees, customers or suppliers can turn in confidence in the event of concrete or suspected cases of corruption (see Fig. 6).

The results also show that 3.5 per cent of companies do not use any of the prevention measures inquired about in the survey. Fifteen per cent of companies use between one and five compliance measures, whereas a further 15 per cent have implemented all of the measures inquired about in the survey (see Fig. 7).

In general, large companies are significantly more likely to use each of the anti-corruption measures and to have a higher number of these measures in place. Only the measure of regularly addressing the issue of ethics and integrity efforts by the company shows no statistically significant difference by company size.

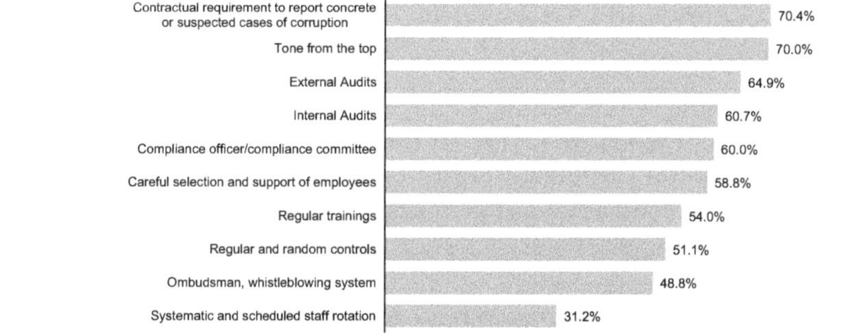

Figure 6: Measures to prevent corruption

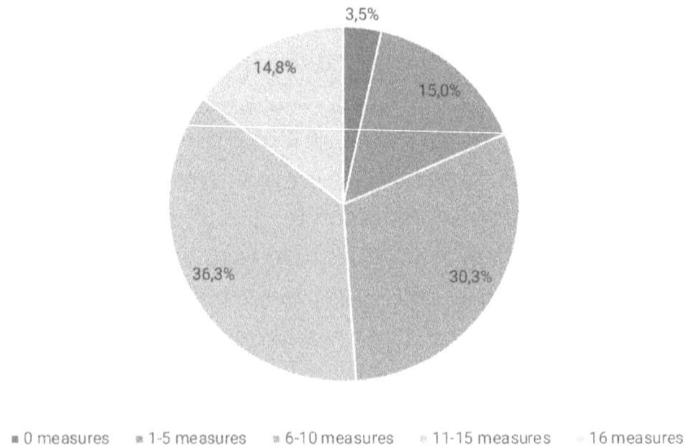

Figure 7: Number of compliance measures

In addition to compliance measures, the companies were also asked about their corporate culture regarding ethics and integrity. In most of the companies surveyed, it is common for participants to be able to express themselves freely in discussions about ethics and integrity. The majority of the companies surveyed also agreed that in discussions about ethics and integrity, it is clearly stated what should be done and that clear reasons are given as to why it should be done. In addition, the majority of the companies surveyed spoke positively about the company's stakeholder groups and reported taking their concerns into account.

In more than two thirds of the companies, the company's efforts to combat corruption are always or at least usually referred to in discussions about ethics and integrity. The results also show that external stakeholders are included in discussions about ethics and integrity in slightly less than half of the companies surveyed. This statement is the least frequently affirmed (see Fig. 8).

Regarding company size, there are no statistically significant differences concerning ethical corporate culture. This means that in SMEs, there is a corporate culture just as ethical as in large companies.

4. Discussion

The results of the study presented above show that Swiss companies operating abroad are exposed to considerable corruption risks. More than half of all

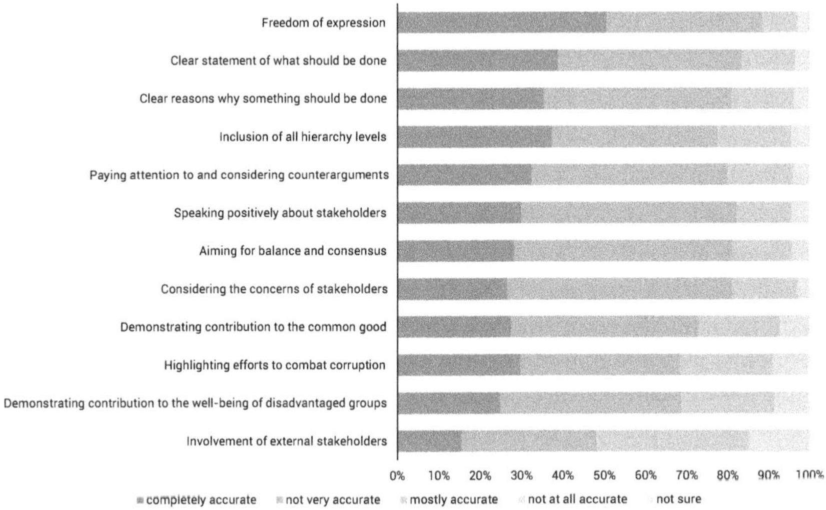

Figure 8: Elements of a corporate culture centered on ethics and integrity

companies surveyed are directly confronted with expectations of corruption in their foreign business activities, whereas a further eight per cent stated that they are indirectly exposed to such expectations via authorised third parties (agents, intermediaries, distribution partners). Overall, three-fifths (59.9%) of the Swiss companies surveyed perceive direct or indirect corruption pressure in their foreign business activities. This considerable figure reflects, on the one hand, that corruption is still widespread worldwide (Transparency International, 2023), and, on the other, that the highly internationalised Swiss economy is also active to a considerable extent in countries with a high level of corruption.

Also remarkable is the frequency with which Swiss companies give in to expectations of corruption in foreign business, i.e. actually engage in corrupt behaviour. As the findings of this study demonstrate, approximately two-fifths (39.5%) of all Swiss companies operating in high-risk foreign contexts are likely to commit acts of corruption, either themselves (32.7%) or through authorised third parties. The current results thus confirm the findings of earlier studies, which also found a considerable incidence of corruption regarding Swiss companies (Becker et al., 2012; Isenring et al., 2016).

Compared to the situation around ten years ago, the perceived pressure of corruption and the frequency of actual corrupt behaviour even appear to have increased. In the similarly designed study by Becker et al. (2012), just over two-fifths (43.2%) of the companies surveyed stated that they had been confronted with expectations of corruption either directly (40.3%) or via third parties (2.9%), and only approximately a quarter admitted to having committed acts of corruption in foreign business activities. Due to the different survey methods (telephone vs. online; use of new methods to reduce socially desirable response behaviour), however, the previous and current findings cannot be compared to each other without reservation. The further developed survey methodology on which the current study is based could imply a lower dark figure compared to the earlier study. Consequently, it is not possible to precisely determine the extent to which expectations of corruption in Swiss companies and their actual corrupt behaviour have actually increased over the past ten years. However, it can be stated with reasonable certainty that there has been no improvement in either respect.

Compared to the survey ten years ago, more companies now have measures in place to prevent and combat corruption. For example, approximately three quarters of the companies surveyed now have guidelines in place to prevent corruption (code of conduct), compared to only 39 per cent in the previous study (Becker et al., 2012). In the study by Isenring et al. (2016), such guidelines were even named as the most common measure, at 83 per cent. Regular spot checks in business areas exposed to corruption now occur in more than half of the companies, which also shows a significant increase compared to the situation ten years ago. At that time, only 28 per cent carried out regular spot checks (Becker et al., 2012).

Overall, increasing numbers of Swiss companies appear to have an anti-corruption system in place that is based on a diversified repertoire of different measures. In their 2016 study, Isenring et al. found that 39 per cent of the companies they investigated had invested up to five per cent of their annual turnover in the development and expansion of compliance measures in the years 2013–2015. This study shows that approximately four-fifths of companies use at least six different preventive measures. Numerous measures that were found in significantly less than half of the companies around ten years ago (Becker et al., 2012) are now found in the majority of the companies.

However, the measures analysed here to prevent and combat corruption in companies remain incomplete (see below).

Companies that act corruptly take considerable risks. As outlined above, they make themselves vulnerable to blackmail and expose themselves to the risk of criminal prosecution. If the case comes to light, they also suffer reputational damage and must expect to be excluded from contracts. Despite the growing spread of measures to prevent and combat corruption, the incidence of corruption in Swiss companies' foreign business activities remains high, if not rising, as demonstrated by the results of this study. The reasons for this finding were not explicitly investigated as part of the study. However, the following reasons are likely to play a role and may be more or less significant, depending on the company.

High risk appetite: It can be assumed that many companies continue to have a high risk appetite and a correspondingly lax approach to preventive measures. Evidence from practice shows that anti-corruption can enjoy a low strategic priority compared to short-term economic goals and is sometimes communicated ambivalently to employees or even contradicted by an opposing wage policy.

Little prosecution: As Transparency International Switzerland has shown in two recently published reports, very few companies involved in corruption and money laundering have been convicted of criminal offences in Switzerland to date (Transparency International Switzerland, 2021b; 2023). In the last twenty years, for example, only twelve companies have been finally convicted for failing to take all the necessary measures to prevent serious offences such as corruption and money laundering. However, the mere "drip-feed" prosecution of offending companies reduces the deterrent effect of criminal law and can further weaken an already insufficient prioritisation of anti-corruption at individual companies.

Insufficient sensitisation: Another reason for the high incidence of corruption among Swiss companies operating abroad is most likely that companies are frequently insufficiently sensitised to the risks and consequences of corruption or the lack of knowledge to deal with such risks appropriately. As Hauser and Hogenacker (2014) show, preventive measures are frequently only introduced after a case of corruption has actually occurred in the company.

Gaps in preventive measures: As this study shows, despite fundamental progress, there are still considerable gaps in the prevention of corruption in Swiss companies operating abroad. This is, of course, also likely to be a key reason for the high incidence of corruption. Approximately four per cent of all companies surveyed stated that they had not introduced any of the measures surveyed to prevent and combat corruption. An independent body (ombudsman, whistleblowing system) that can be informed confidentially about specific or suspected cases of corruption is only found in slightly less than half of all companies surveyed. Systematic and planned staff rotation in areas of the company at risk of corruption occurs in less than a third of the companies. Although regular spot checks in particularly high-risk business areas are, as mentioned above, more widespread than around ten years ago, they are still absent in almost half of companies.

By contrast, the measure most frequently mentioned in the survey, namely the written documentation of all business transactions, is only the minimum requirement for a functioning business organisation. However, only approximately four-fifths of all companies surveyed fulfil this requirement, meaning that the remaining fifth already lack this essential preventive measure. Relatedly, only three quarters of all companies surveyed appear to consistently pursue employees' violations of legal or internal company regulations. However, a consistent response to misconduct that has occurred is essential for the prevention of corruption as this is the only way to achieve a deterrent effect against future misconduct. Otherwise, the seriousness of the legal and internal company standards is questioned and the inhibition threshold for future misconduct is ultimately lowered.

Prevention measures not tailored to the company: The continued high susceptibility to corruption despite the fundamental expansion of preventive measures could also be because the preventive measures taken are not tailored to the specific corporate risks. Effective corruption prevention must be risk-based. In contrast, schematic measures from a standardised repertoire are likely to be less effective.

Inadequate implementation of preventive measures: Another important reason for the high incidence of corruption among Swiss companies operating abroad is most likely the inadequate implementation of existing preventive measures. A central prerequisite for the implementation of measures is the establishment of a corporate culture of zero tolerance towards corruption. Such a culture can only develop if top management actively demands it and sets an example. This study shows that this so-called "tone from the top" remains lacking in approximately a third of the companies surveyed. Furthermore, it is crucial for effective compliance that all employees know and understand the guidelines and procedures so that they can follow them correctly in their day-to-day work. Regular training is necessary for this. However, as this study shows, approximately half of all Swiss companies operating abroad still do not provide such regular training.

5. Summary

The results of the study show that 52 per cent of the Swiss companies surveyed are confronted with demands for informal payments in other countries. Of the companies concerned, 63 per cent make such payments. On average, they spend 5.6 per cent of their turnover in the respective target country on informal payments and gifts under the table. SMEs are confronted with demands for informal payments to the same extent as large companies. The size of the company also has no significant influence on whether and to what extent a company makes such payments.

Companies with production facilities, joint ventures or equity investments tend to make informal payments in the respective country. This also applies to companies with management and consultancy contracts in the respective country as well as companies that fulfil contracts for state-owned companies or government authorities. In contrast, companies with an ethical corporate culture are less likely to make informal payments.

Demands for informal payments are frequently made in connection with sales activities. More than 70 per cent of the companies concerned stated that they are expected to make informal payments under the table when contracts are awarded by private-sector companies. 60 per cent of respondents confirmed this for the award of public or state contracts.

Approximately a quarter of the companies surveyed assumed that they have lost a contract from a public or private client in the last two years to a competitor who only won the contract due to corrupt behaviour. Thirteen per cent of the companies surveyed stated that they have refrained from entering a market in a particular country in the last five years due to corruption risks. A further twelve per cent reported that they have withdrawn from a market in the last five years due to corruption risks.

The companies surveyed already use various measures to prevent corruption. The most frequently cited measures were the written documentation of all business transactions; disciplinary and/or labour law consequences for violations of statutory, regulatory and internal provisions; the regular discussion of efforts to promote ethics and integrity; and the written obligation of contracted third parties to comply with statutory and internal company provisions. Many aspects of an ethical corporate culture are also already considered in the companies analysed. For example, it is common practice in the vast majority of companies for participants to be able to express themselves freely in discussions about ethics and integrity. Furthermore, a majority of the companies surveyed stated that they clearly indicate what needs to be done and that this is justified.

Although Swiss companies operating abroad have expanded their measures to prevent corruption in recent years, they currently appear to commit acts of corruption just as frequently or even more frequently than around ten years ago. However, comparisons with earlier studies are only possible with reservations, for methodological reasons.

Depending on the case, the main reasons for the continued high incidence of corrupt behaviour among Swiss companies operating abroad are likely to include insufficient awareness, gaps in the preventive measures, and deficiencies in the implementation of these measures in addition to an overly large appetite for risk. The latter is likely to be further fuelled by the limited frequency of prosecution of offending companies.

There remains considerable potential for improvement in the prevention of corruption by Swiss companies operating abroad. For example, approximately a quarter lack basic measures, such as binding behavioural guidelines or due diligence checks of contracted third parties. Regular employee training on corruption prevention and an independent reporting centre to which employees can turn in the event of suspected cases are only found in half of all companies surveyed. Finally, in approximately a third of the companies surveyed, there is even a lack of commitment from top management to a zero-tolerance approach to corruption.

Acknowledgements

This chapter presents research conducted within the project “Foreign Corruption and Swiss Companies” funded by the KBA-NotaSys Integrity Fund under grant number 2021_28. It is an adapted version of a German publication by Hauser et al. (2024).

Bibliography

Becker, K., Hauser, C., & Kronthaler, F. (2012). *Korruptionsrisiken erfolgreich begegnen: Strategien für international tätige Unternehmen*. Chur. https://www.fhgr.ch/fileadmin/fhgr/unternehmerisches_handeln/SIFE/publikationen/corporate_responsibility/publikation-leitfaden-korruptionsrisiken-erfolgreich-begegnen.pdf

Brandenberg, A. & Fessler, P. (2012), Ein Wahrheitsserum für die Preisforschung. *Planung & Analyse*, 2012(3), 31-34.

Fontagné, L., Perego, E., & Santoni, G. (2022). MaGE 3.1: Long-term macroeconomic projections of the World economy. *International Economics*, *172*, 168-189. https://doi.org/10.1016/j.inteco.2022.08.002

Goel, R. K., Mazhar, U. & Ram, R. (2022). Dimensions of size and corruption perceptions versus corruption experiences by firms in emerging economies. *Journal of Economics and Finance*, 46(2), 374–396. https://doi.org/10.1007/s12197-022-09571-1

Hauser, C., Herkenrath, M., Hilti, M., Stampfli, R., Bretti-Rainalter, J. (2024). *Auslandkorruption bei Schweizer Unternehmen – neue Erkenntnisse zu Risiken und Gegenstrategien*. FHGR Verlag/Transparency International Schweiz, Chur/Bern, ISBN 978-3-907247-26-6

Hauser, C. & Hogenacker, J. (2014). Do Firms Proactively Take Measures to Prevent Corruption in Their International Operations? *European Management Review*, 11(3-4), 223–237. https://doi.org/10.1111/emre.12035

Hauser, C. & Kronthaler, F. (2013): Neue Märkte, neue Risiken – Empirische Evidenz zum Korruptionsrisiko für den international aktiven Mittelstand. *Zeitschrift für Betriebswirtschaft (ZfB)*, SI 4/2013, 37–60.

Isenring, G. L., Mugellini, G. & Killias, M. (2016). *Assessing the areas of vulnerability for Swiss firms in international business activities: The Swiss International Corruption Survey (SICS)*. St. Gallen.

Martins, L., Cerdeira, J. & Teixeira, A. A. (2020). Does corruption boost or harm firms' performance in developing and emerging economies? A firm-level study. *The World Economy*, 43(8), 2119–2152. https://doi.org/10.1111/twec.12966

Prelec, D. (2004). *A Bayesian Truth Serum for Subjective Data*. Cambridge MA

PwC. (2022). *PwC's Global Economic Crime an Fraud Survey 2022: Protecting the perimeter: The rise of external fraud*. https://www.pwc.com/fraudsurvey

Staatssekretariat für Wirtschaft SECO. (2017). *Korruption vermeiden: Hinweise für im Ausland tätige Schweizer Unternehmen*. Bern. https://www.seco.admin.ch/seco/de/home/Publikationen_Dienstleistungen/Publikationen_und_Formulare/Aussenwirtschafts/broschueren/korruption_vermeiden.html

Transparency International. (2023). *Corruption Perceptions Index 2022*. Berlin. https://www.transparency.org/en/cpi/2022

Transparency International Switzerland. (2021a). *Korruptionsprävention und -bekämpfung: Ein Ratgeber für Schweizer KMU*. Bern. https://transparency.ch/wp-content/uploads/2021/09/Ratgeber-KMU.pdf

Transparency International Switzerland. (2021b). *Strafbarkeit des Unternehmens: lückenhafte Regelung, mangelhafter Vollzug, erhebliche Transparenzdefizite*. Bern. https://transparency.ch/wp-content/uploads/2021/02/Strafbarkeit_des_Unternehmens.pdf

Transparency International Switzerland. (2022). *Korruptionsprävention und -bekämpfung in KMU: Geschäftspartnerrisiken*. Bern. https://transparency.ch/wp-content/uploads/2022/09/Geschaeftspartnerrisiken.pdf

Transparency International Switzerland. (2023). *Strafverfolgung des Unternehmens: Wie der Vollzug der Strafbarkeit des Unternehmens zu verbessern ist*. Bern. https://transparency.ch/wp-content/uploads/2023/01/Bericht_Strafverfolgung_Unternehmen.pdf

Chapter 6

Foreign Trade Compliance - Focus on Supply Chains and Sanctions

Compliance with the CS3D: A New Era of Corporate Responsibility

Antonio Giuseppe Di Pietro, Andrejs Klisans

1. Introduction to sustainable procurement and the CS3D

Procurement practices have evolved significantly over time. While for decades the focus of good procurement procedures has been aimed at the sourcing and management of materials, during the first half of the 20th century the emphasis remained on cost-cutting and efficiency in liability distribution across the supply chain.

In the latter half, following the globalization of supplier and vendor relationships, a new focus on quality and standardization was established as companies opened up to more diverse competition in the eyes of the consumers. The regulations that we have been witnessing in the past twenty years call for a new change in procurement: targeted control and regulation of the process is required for the public good, where ethical sourcing, responsible material use, and minimizing environmental impact take priority.

This recent shift has seen the integration of environmental and social considerations into the entire procurement lifecycle, giving birth to sustainable procurement (Preuss, 2009). This approach includes selecting suppliers with strong environmental practices, reducing resource consumption, and prioritizing ethical sourcing and fair labor practices (Beske & Seuring, 2014). Companies adopting sustainable procurement benefit from enhanced brand reputation, improved risk management, and operational efficiency (Carter et al., 2020). Moreover, these practices contribute to reduced pollution and resource depletion while promoting fair labor practices globally.

It is crucial to understand how the rise of sustainable procurement has surely come from regulators, but that happened in response to a call for transparency and ethical practices made by more informed and more concerned consumers, leading companies to adopt sustainable procurement (Fontenot et al., 2018). The urgency of action required by consumers has also pushed governments into enforcing stricter environmental and social responsibility regulations, making sustainable procurement a legal requirement in different shapes and forms (Carter et al., 2020). As sustainability has concrete market value both in terms of legal risk and commercial opportunity, investors are also increasingly considering a company's sustainability profile, further pushing the adoption of these practices (Beske, 2010).

The premise of this chapter is therefore that sustainable procurement has become essential for modern business. It offers numerous benefits for companies and society, driven by consumer, regulatory, and investor pressures, and it is here to stay and shape a new approach to the supply chain that, to the eyes of the authors, will radically change the work of legal practitioners and best practices themselves.

2. The European Corporate Sustainability Due Diligence Directive *

The European Union has implemented the Corporate Sustainability Due Diligence Directive (CS3D, or the Directive), imposing due diligence obligations for companies operating within the EU and abroad to address environmental and human rights risks in global supply chains, ultimately promoting responsible business practices.

The CS3D requires companies to map their supply chains and address "known unknowns" about their partners and suppliers, by transparently reporting on their due diligence efforts. This transparency allows stakeholders

* Please note that, at the time of this writing, the final text of the CS3D has been adopted by the EU Parliament, on 24 April 2024, and it has been given final approval by the EU Council of Ministers on 24 May 2024. After being signed by the President of the European Parliament and the President of the Council, the directive will be published in the Official Journal of the European Union and will enter into force on the twentieth day following its publication.
Member States will have two years to implement the regulations and administrative procedures to comply with this legal text.
For the sake of this paper, since the legislative process is essentially complete and Member States are solely awaiting publication in the Official Journal of the European, we will address the content and merit of the CS3D as if it has already been published, referencing it - as customary - as Directive 2024/XXX/EU.

to hold companies accountable for the actions they take to mitigate identified risks, improve sourcing practices or working conditions (Article 6 of Directive 2024/XXX/EU).

It will later be shown in detail how companies need to develop a practical roadmap not only to comply with the new norm but in most cases revolutionize their supply chain and identify new suppliers in the global scene. A robust due diligence policy outlines how companies will identify, assess, and address risks, integrating due diligence into corporate governance structures, allowing for measurability and monitoring as – in the course of time - they monitor and report on their due diligence efforts (Article 8 of Directive 2024/XXX/EU).

2.1 Historical overview of corporate sustainability initiatives in Europe

The EU's sustainability journey began in the early 1970s with a focus on environmental regulations aimed at pollution control (Jordan et al., 2003). This focus on environmental protection continued with key milestones like the Single European Act (1987), which integrated environmental considerations, and the Rio Earth Summit (1992) where the EU played a leading role in shaping international sustainability principles (Mol, Sonnenfeld & Spaargaren, 2005).

The turn of the millennium witnessed a growing emphasis on corporate social responsibility (CSR), as the Lisbon Strategy (2000) set ambitious goals for sustainable development and economic growth (European Commission, 2000), and the 2001 European Commission's Green Paper on CSR (COM(2001) 0366) highlighted the role of businesses in promoting social justice and environmental protection.

The reader should not forget that, at that time, the effort was global and unified, at least in the West. Supra-national efforts landed the UN Global Compact (2000) – a voluntary initiative encouraging businesses to align with ten universally accepted principles in human rights, labor, environment, and anti-corruption – which received strong EU support and still represents a major global initiative to this day (UN Global Compact, 2024). The European Union incorporated it into the more specific EU Strategy for Sustainable

Development (2001) (COM(2001) 264) by outlining a comprehensive framework that put businesses at the core of this change.

2.2 Existing regulations and directives related to sustainability and due diligence

The way to CS3D was paved by numerous regulations, promoted and issued with business transparency and accountability at the core, even if only for a number of industries or activities at first, prioritized in terms of risk and urgency.

First and foremost, the Non-Financial Reporting Directive (NFRD) (Directive 2014/95/EU), adopted in 2014 mandates large companies operating in the EU to disclose information on environmental, social, and governance (ESG) factors (European Commission, 2024a). The impact of the NFRD in the corporate and financial sectors has already been noteworthy, as investment funds - especially - led the change by openly ranking their portfolios in terms of ESG. This disclosure requirement has significantly influenced corporate sustainability reporting practices and awareness among stakeholders (Flammer et al., 2019).

Other regulations are more sectorial but, if the reader were to carefully examine their requisites, they would find that they all influenced the approach of the CS3D.

One such example is the Ecodesign Directive (2009/125/EC) as it sets requirements for the design of energy-using products to make them more efficient, its focus on sustainability at the product level complements the CS3D's emphasis on responsible sourcing (European Commission. (2024b)).

Similarly, the Conflict Minerals Regulation (Regulation (EU) 2017/821) tackles the trade in minerals mined in conflict zones, which can fund violence and human rights abuses (European Commission. (2024c)). Its regulation influenced the CS3D's focus on human rights due diligence.

Another example can be found in the Timber Regulation (Regulation (EU) No 995/2010), requiring businesses placing timber products on the EU market to conduct due diligence to ensure the wood comes from legal sources and avoids contributing to deforestation (European Commission. (2024d)). This approach is extended to the CS3D, which coherently mandates responsible sourcing practices for a wide range of materials and products.

At the global level, the UN Guiding Principles on Business and Human Rights (UNGPs) (2011) also played a vital role. While not legally binding, the UNGPs provide a framework for preventing, addressing, and remedying corporate-related human rights abuses, and its principles can be openly found in the working papers of the CS3D, highlighting their importance in establishing this not-so-new global standard.

These regulations demonstrate that the European Union has been active for decades in regulating business practices to ensure sustainable and ethical business practices, laying the foundations for necessary controls: while the NFRD focuses on transparency, the UNGPs and sectoral regulations address specific areas for due diligence.

2.3 The legislative process leading to the adoption of the CS3D

In 2020, the European Commission proposed a draft regulation for corporate sustainability due diligence (COM(2020) 183). Over the next two years (2021-2022), the European Parliament and the Council of the European Union engaged in extensive discussions and negotiations to refine it, raising numerous concerns and triggering extensive pushbacks from industry representatives.

The controversy around the added burden on businesses to comply with the initial proposed requirements created fertile ground for extensive stakeholder consultation and several key revisions. The European Commission conducted a public consultation from October 2020 to February 2021, gathering input from over 473,000 respondents, including NGOs, businesses, and public authorities (European Commission, 2024e). The consultation revealed varying - although not surprising - perspectives among stakeholders: NGOs supported a holistic approach to corporate governance and mandatory due diligence, emphasizing the importance of environmental and social criteria; businesses and business associations expressed concerns about increased administrative costs, competitive disadvantages, and the complexity of compliance, vouching for lighter requirements for small and medium-sized enterprises; Public Authorities highlighted the need for harmonization to avoid regulatory fragmentation within the EU.

The insights from this consultation informed the impact assessment, guiding the final directive to promote sustainability and human rights while addressing practical implementation challenges. After revisions and negotiations, in April 2024 the CS3D was formally adopted and in May 2024 it received formalization by the EU Council of Ministers.

With the directive now adopted, the focus shifts to implementation. Member States will have a two-year transposition period to integrate the directive's provisions into national legislation and companies will need to adapt their operations and supply chain management practices to comply with the new requirements.

3. Scope and requirements of the CS3D

3.1 Scope of companies affected

The CS3D targets large companies formed under the legislation of a Member State or a third country, provided they meet specific criteria regarding employee count and financial performance. According to Article 2 of the Directive, it applies to:

(i) EU companies with over 1000 employees and a net worldwide turnover exceeding EUR 450 million.
(ii) Ultimate parent companies of groups generating a net turnover of more than EUR 450 million within the EU or meeting equivalent group-level thresholds.
(iii) EU-based companies with over 1000 employees engaged in franchising or licensing within the EU, generating more than EUR 22.5 million in royalties and having a net worldwide turnover of over EUR 80 million. Non-EU companies fall under the Directive's scope if they generate a net worldwide turnover exceeding EUR 80 million and royalties of more than EUR 22.5 million within the EU, regardless of the employee count.

These thresholds are relevant only if a company satisfies them for two consecutive financial years (Article 2(3a)). Thus, the Directive seeks to eliminate the inclusion of companies on grounds of temporary changes instead preferring sustained performance.

In cases where a company falls within the scope of the Directive, the whole compliance duty falls on the parent undertaking. Nonetheless, if the ultimate parent company is primarily a holding company and does not participate in the management, financial or operational decision-making in respect of the group or individual subsidiaries within it, these responsibilities may be delegated to an entrusted subsidiary (Article 2(2a)). This subsidiary will then be required to comply with due diligence requirements on behalf of the parent company.

Small and medium-sized enterprises (SMEs) are not directly covered by the CS3D. However, they may come under its provisions indirectly if they work as contractors or subcontractors for companies operating within the scope of this Directive. In order to avoid placing a heavy economic and administrative burden upon SMEs, Member States should consider setting up user-friendly platforms through which information and support can be provided for this purpose. This might include dedicated websites/portals/other interactive forums that offer resources as well as guidance services to such firms.

Extension of financial support and capacity development programs to SMEs and upstream economic actors in third countries should be considered. The firms that work with small-scale organizations are advised to aid these partners in meeting the requirement for due process through fair, reasonable, non-discriminatory and proportionate measures.

This model makes sure that while the major obligations fall on larger entities, SMEs are helped in their indirect roles without suffering from unnecessary burdens especially considering the current global economic difficulties. This well-considered approach helps integrate smaller enterprises within a wider framework of sustainable and responsible business conduct thereby ensuring comprehensiveness of achievement of objectives envisaged by the Directive.

3.2 Scope of activities

The CS3D provides that all EU and non-EU companies that fall within the scope of the Directive must conduct due diligence throughout their value chains. The requirement extends to its own business operations, upstream activities and specific downstream operations (Article 3(1g)).

Companies are required to conduct due diligence on all upstream activities related to the production of goods or provision of services. This includes activities related to the production of goods or the provision of services by the company, including the design, extraction, sourcing, manufacture, transport, storage and supply of raw materials, products or parts of the products and development of the product or the service.

The Directive also stresses the importance for companies to institute mechanisms to ensure that they exercise due diligence on their own operations. It covers any activity carried out directly by a company or one of its subsidiaries.

There is also reference in the Directive regarding certain downstream activities which firms ought to keep an eye on. Such activities are related to the distribution, transport and storage of a company's product.

However, it should be recognized that this requirement does not cover downstream activities relating to the disposal of products including decommissioning, recycling, composting or land filling and consumer disposal as well as activities subject to export control regulations. Of note, service providers and companies providing financial services not have due diligence obligations as regards to downstream activities as established in this Directive.

3.3 Implementation

The Directive will enter into force after twenty days of its publication in the Official Journal of the European Union. Once it takes effect, the rules will be applied in phases. This begins with a two-year period for Member States to integrate the CS3D into their national laws. This means that countries with existing due diligence laws are not required to come up with novel legislation but rather adjust and strengthen them according to the CS3D.

The implementation of CS3D will be phased based on company size and turnover starting from three years following the time the Direct came into force. For EU companies employing more than 5000 workers on average worldwide and having an annual turnover exceeding EUR 1500 million, these provisions shall become effective three years after entry into force as provided by Article 2 (1)(a) and (b). The same timeframe is being set for third country companies within the EU which generate an annual net turnover above EUR 1500 million according to Article 2 (2)(a) and (b).

Companies with average staff of over 3000 in the EU and a worldwide turnover of over EUR 900 million are required to comply with the Directive within four years of its entry into force (Article 2(1)(a) and (b)). The third-country companies generating over EUR 900 million net revenues within the EU shall also be included in this phase (Article 2(2)(a) and (b)).

Within five years after the Directive's entry into force, all other companies stipulated in Article 2(1)(a) and (b), Article 2(2)(a) and (b) will fall under the scope of the Directive. These encompass franchising or licensing operations carried out by companies in the EU as outlined in Article 2(1)(ba) and Article 2(2)(ba). Their turnover should be more than EUR 80 million while royalties should exceed EUR 22.5 million.

From the date of its entry into force, Member States have 24 months to transpose the Directive within their national legislation (Article 30).

The EU Commission is responsible for determining whether there are any extra due diligence obligations that should be placed on financial companies offering services such as investment activities as per the Directive. The findings of the research are expected to be published by May 2026, which could mean new regulations tailored for the financial industry.

3.5 Risk assessments

Comprehensive methodologies of risk identification and assessment must be adopted by companies in line with globally recognized standards such as the OECD Guidelines for Multinational Enterprises and the UN Guiding Principles on Business and Human Rights.

Additionally, established best practices may be built upon through existing frameworks like the Task Force on Climate-related Financial Disclosures (TCFD), Global Reporting Initiative (GRI), and Sustainability Accounting Standards Board (SASB).

Also valuable are EBA Guidelines on the management of ESG risks (EBA/CP/2024/02). These guidelines emphasize integrating ESG risks into the existing risk management model; conducting regular assessments of materiality of ESG risks; use exposure analysis, portfolio analysis or scenario analysis. They also require robust systems for collection and analysis of ESG risk data, incorporation of these risks into ongoing risk management processes and formulation of transitional plans towards sustainable operations.

3.6 Due diligence

The CS3D outlines a comprehensive framework for companies to integrate due diligence processes into their operations and management systems. The key obligations and provisions, along with their legislative references, are detailed in the following sections.

3.6.1 Integrating due diligence into policies and risk management systems (Article 5)

All applicable policies and risk management frameworks within organizations must include due diligence as a requirement. According to Article 5(1) of the CS3D, Member States should mandate the formulation of due diligence policy based on risk. A prior consultation with a company's employees and/or their representatives should be done before drawing up this policy, according to Article 5(1a). The policy ought to have details about the company's approach in relation to due diligence, a code of conduct, as well as processes for integrating and verifying compliance with it (Article 5(1a)(a)-(c)).

3.6.2 Identifying and assessing actual and potential adverse impacts (Article 6)

Companies are required to take appropriate measures to identify as well as assess both actual and potential adverse impacts arising from their operations, subsidiaries, and business partners in accordance with Article 6(1). This includes mapping its operation to discover areas where adverse impacts are most likely and severe, followed by carrying out detailed assessments on those areas (Article 6(1a)(a)-(b)). In making these assessments, companies should utilize relevant sources of internal and external information that include third party reports and stakeholder inputs (Article 6(4)). When necessary, companies should prioritize obtaining information directly from business partners where adverse impacts are most likely to occur (Article 6(4b)).

3.6.3 Preventing and mitigating potential adverse impacts and addressing actual adverse impacts (Articles 7 & 8)

To prevent and mitigate potential adverse impacts, companies must take appropriate measures such as developing prevention action plans, seeking contractual assurances from business partners, making necessary investments and adjustments, and providing support to SMEs where necessary, as outlined in Article 7(1)-(2). If adverse impacts cannot be prevented, companies must develop corrective action plans and take steps to minimize the extent of these impacts (Article 8(1)). This includes measures to neutralize or minimize adverse impacts, seek contractual assurances, make necessary investments, and provide targeted support to SMEs (Article 8(3)(a)-(e)). If necessary, companies may need to terminate business relationships as a last resort if severe impacts cannot be mitigated (Article 8(6)).

3.6.4 Establishing a notification mechanism and complaints procedure (Article 9)

Companies are required to provide a mechanism for stakeholders to submit complaints (also known as grievances) regarding actual or potential adverse impacts. According to Article 9(1), Member States must ensure that complaints can be made by natural or legal persons affected by an adverse impact, trade unions, and civil society organizations. Companies must establish a fair, transparent, and accessible procedure for handling these complaints (Article 9(3)). The procedure must protect the confidentiality of complainants to prevent retaliation and ensure that well-founded complaints are addressed in line with Articles 7, 8, and 8c (Article 9(3) & (4)). Additionally, companies must provide follow-up on complaints and offer the opportunity for complainants to meet with company representatives (Article 9(4)).

3.6.5 Monitoring the effectiveness of due diligence policies and measures (Article 10)

Companies must carry out regular assessments of their operations, subsidiaries, and business partners to monitor the implementation and effectiveness of their due diligence processes. As specified in Article 10, these assessments should be conducted without undue delay after significant changes and at least every 12 months. The assessments should use both qualitative and quantitative indicators to ensure the identification, prevention, mitigation, and minimization of adverse impacts. The results of these assessments should inform updates to the due diligence policies and measures.

3.6.6 Publicly communicating on due diligence (Article 11)

Member States must ensure that companies publish an annual statement on their website detailing their due diligence efforts, as required by Article 11(1). This statement must be available in at least one official language of the EU and a language customary in international business. The statement should be published no later than 12 months after the end of the financial year or in line with the publication of annual financial statements (Article 11(1)(b)). Companies subject to sustainability reporting requirements under Directive 2013/34/EU are exempt from this requirement (Article 11(2)). The Commission is tasked with adopting delegated acts to specify the content and criteria for this reporting by 31 March 2027 (Article 11(3)).

3.6.7 Combatting climate change (Article 15)

Companies must adopt and implement a transition plan for climate change mitigation, ensuring compatibility with the Paris Agreement and the EU's climate neutrality goals. Article 15(1) mandates that this plan includes time-bound targets for 2030 and in five-year increments up to 2050, based on scientific evidence. The plan should detail decarbonization strategies, key actions, investments, and the role of administrative bodies in achieving these targets (Article 15(1)(a)-(d)). Companies reporting under Directive 2013/34/EU are deemed to comply with this requirement (Article 15(3)). The transition plan must be updated annually, including a progress report on achieving the targets (Article 15(3a)).

3.6.8 Enforcement mechanisms

Each Member State must designate one or more supervisory authorities to oversee compliance with the Directive, as specified in Article 17, which can be either an existing or a new one. The role of these authorities is quite extensive, as they are responsible not only for receiving claims and concerns from individuals and organizations about companies' non-compliance with the Directive, but also for autonomously investigating and responding in a timely fashion, as outlined in Article 19.

These authorities are required to operate independently, free from external influence, and maintain both legal and functional independence. They are empowered to demand information from companies, conduct thorough investigations, and impose necessary penalties (Article 18), ensuring that companies adhere to the CS3D's requirements.

The actual powers of investigation and enforcement of these authorities will necessarily vary across different jurisdictions depending on how the Directive is nationalized by respective Member States.

However, as a pre-established threshold, Article 20 mandates that Member States must establish rules on penalties that are effective, proportionate, and dissuasive. CS3D sets the maximum penalty for non-compliance at a minimum of 5% of the company's net worldwide turnover in the previous financial year.

3.7 Civil liability under the CS3D

Although Member States will find it difficult to harmonize civil liability, the CS3D sets out certain minimum requirements. The Directive enables individuals, trade unions and civil society organizations to submit civil liability claims for at least five years to seek compensation for damages if adversely affected by companies' failure to comply, although the claimant must provide full details of the infringement and the identity of the infringer in order to avoid generalized class actions and unsubstantiated claims (Article 22(2a)(a)).

Victims have the right to full compensation for the damages caused, ensuring that the compensation is proportionate to the harm suffered and does not result in overcompensation through punitive or multiple damages, whenever a company causes harm to a natural or legal person's legal interests by intentionally or negligently failing to comply under obligations regarding the prevention, mitigation and response to adverse impacts of its supply chain (obligations under Articles 7 and 8, as previously showcased).

Of note, a company cannot be held liable if the damage was caused solely by its business partners (Article 22(1)). It should be highlighted that companies that have participated in industry or multi-stakeholder initiatives or used third-party verification or contractual clauses to support their due diligence obligations can still be held liable (Article 22(2b)). Thus, compliance with this Directive cannot be characterized by a mere tick-the-box exercise.

4. Practical guidance for compliance

4.1 Conduct a comprehensive supply chain audit

For complete CS3D compliance, a comprehensive supply chain audit is essential. The extent of this audit depends on the complexity of operations, and organizations without proper contract management may struggle with supply chain mapping. This process involves tracing raw materials from their source to the finished product, ensuring each supply chain entity provides operational assurance.

Initial mapping is just the start. A full picture of suppliers, subcontractors, and partners is needed, along with an assessment of potential environmental and human rights risks. Factors like industry sector and geographic location are crucial. For instance, risks differ between a cobalt mine in the Democratic Republic of Congo and a local organic farm. This audit should also examine suppliers' current practices, including environmental management, labor standards, and human rights policies through document reviews, factory visits, and employee interviews. Understanding their sustainability approaches allows for collaboration and improvement.

Collecting and analyzing relevant data, such as through environmental impact assessments and labor certifications, provides valuable insights. Combined with risk assessments and supplier evaluations, this data offers a holistic view of your company's sustainability performance.

Investing in a comprehensive audit has significant benefits, including early identification of potential problems, informed decision-making in procurement, and prioritizing sustainable practices. It establishes a baseline for tracking progress and demonstrating commitment to responsible sourcing and ethical practices. The CS3D aims to ensure businesses contribute to a sustainable, ethical future, with the supply chain audit providing the necessary roadmap.

4.2 Implementing effective risk assessments

4.2.1 Conducting detailed risk assessments in supply chains

To determine possible risks to a company's productivity, public image and sustainability, it is of paramount importance for companies to conduct detailed risk assessments within their supply chains. Some of the activities involved in this process are systematic data collection, stakeholder engagement, risk evaluation and development of effective assessment tools.

The first step involves collecting extensive information about suppliers that encompasses geographical locations, production processes, labor practices, environmental impacts and regulatory compliance. This may expose managers to hazards but it is necessary for understanding supplier risks. For example, data reliability can be assured through internal audits (such as those performed by internal audit departments or teams), self-assessments by suppliers and third-party audits where internal audits oversee while third-party auditors provide unbiased evaluations.

The second step is stakeholder engagement, which is crucial in getting an overall view of supply chain risks. This entails consulting employees, local communities, NGOs, and industry experts so as to acquire diverse views on the field that cannot be found in quantitative data alone. By building strong relationships with suppliers, transparency and cooperation can be fostered thus making effective risk management possible.

After data gathering, analysis and application are necessary. Some of the critical factors to be checked include risk assessment in terms of environmental, social and governance (ESG) criteria, which can concentrate on human rights abuses, environmental degradation, and ethical misconduct. The risk assessment process is structured by employing tried frameworks like the United Nations' Guiding Principles for Business and Human Rights or the Organization for Economic Co-operation and Development's Guidelines for Multinational Enterprises. A simplified way of managing risks can be achieved through developing a risk matrix whereby prioritization of risks is done using either risk matrices or heat maps while scoring systems offer a basis for comparison as well as decision making.

4.2.2 Identifying and prioritizing high-risk areas

Identifying and prioritizing high-risk areas within supply chains is crucial for effective risk management. By categorizing risks, focusing on high-risk sectors and regions, and conducting in-depth analyses, organizations can allocate resources efficiently and address the most pressing issues.

- **Categorize risks** - Categorize identified risks according to their potential impact and likelihood, breaking them into high-, medium-, and low-levels. Areas of high risk are usually characterized by gross human rights violations, extensive environmental degradation or major ethical problems. A risk matrix should be used as a tool for visualizing and prioritizing risks, which involves mapping severity against probability in order to show the most urgent areas requiring attention.

- **Focus on high-risk sectors and regions** - Certain industries and regions inherently carry higher risks due to their nature and context. Look at such sectors as mining, agriculture and manufacturing that have complex and nuanced labor practices, ecological concerns as well as ethics-related issues. Additionally, consider regions having loose regulations, human rights abuses or political instability as these present great threats to supply chain reliability and reputation. Industry specific risk reports and databases provide useful information on risk trends for prioritization.
- **Conduct in-depth analysis of high-risk areas** - Once high-risk areas have been establish their root causes through comprehensive examinations with possible consequences afterwards. On spot inspections may also help understand particular hazards with reference to interviews conducted by the affected stakeholders within the internal environment inclusive of extensive documentation reviews being done. Involving local NGOs and experts adds valuable perspectives on how accurate/facilitate more accurate assessment of risk effectiveness.

4.3 Setting sustainability criteria for supplier selection

The incorporation of the CS3D requirements into supplier contracts would mean that such should include some specific clauses, which stipulate the necessity to abide by sustainability standards, specify criteria, reporting obligations and penalties for non-compliance. This is a way of integrating supplier selection for sustainability that goes beyond price and quality.

Key issues are examining whether suppliers have an environmental management system (EMS) in line with international standards like ISO 14001:2015, showcasing the willingness to abide by renowned environmental performance. It is important to evaluate ethical labor practices focusing on living wages, occupational safety and health conditions as well as adherence to labor laws evidenced by certifications from organizations like Fair Labor Association.

Transparency within supply chain is critical. Ensuring that suppliers can trace back raw materials sources allows identification and mitigation of environmental as well as human rights risks. Moreover, it is essential to scrutinize supplier commitment towards improving their environmental and social performance such as through adoption of better technologies, training for ethical sourcing or taking part in sustainability initiatives.

Compliance with these criteria supports the CS3D and fosters relationships with companies that share the same environmental values, build responsible supply chains, and contribute to sustainable development. According to research, responsible sourcing leads to positive results such as improved reputation of brands and better supply chain performance (Eltantawy et al, 2009). By setting explicit requirements for suppliers concerning sustainability, purchasing decisions can be harmonized with sustainability goals thus creating a more conscientious business environment.

4.4 Developing and maintaining grievance mechanisms

4.4.1 Setting up accessible grievance mechanisms

It is essential to establish effective grievance mechanisms for addressing and resolving issues within supply chains. These mechanisms should be inclusive, transparent, confidential and well-resourced to enable all stakeholders to report their grievances safely and effectively.

- **Design inclusive mechanisms** - It is important that mechanisms for lodging complaints are developed in a manner that considers the needs of all concerned. One way to promote the use of effective grievance handling processes is by giving an opportunity for all complainants irrespective of their geographical location or any other factor that may limit them from accessing technology, thus using multiple channels. Such efforts include having hotlines, web-based systems as well as traditional complaint boxes situated within the firm's premises.
- **Ensure confidentiality and protection** - Protecting the confidentiality and safety of those who raise complaints is key. In order to prevent reprisals, confidentiality measures should be operationalized that include the possibility of anonymity and discreet handling of all reports. Additionally, it is necessary to institute measures that would safeguard whistleblowers and other complainants from any form of retaliation or adverse consequences thus encouraging the stakeholders to report issues free from fear of retribution.
- **Allocate adequate resources** - There needs to be adequate resources for effective management of grievance mechanisms. This will ensure that enough resources including personnel with skills, financial support and

technological infrastructure are provided to make sure the grievance mechanism operates smoothly. In addition, it is vital for grievance handlers to undergo training on human rights, conflict resolution as well as familiarizing themselves with specific requirements contained in the Corporate Sustainability Reporting Directive (CSRD) so that they can expertly handle grievances in a sensitive manner.

4.4.2 Handling and resolving grievances effectively

Effectively handling and resolving grievances within supply chains requires a structured and responsive approach. This ensures that issues are addressed promptly and fairly, fostering trust and accountability.

- **Timely acknowledgment and response** - When a complaint is lodged, it should be acknowledged as soon as possible and then a timeline for further action should be provided. By doing this, an organization demonstrates a commitment to addressing concerns and builds stakeholder trust. In addition, complainants must be kept informed about the process through regular updates on the status of their case, and its outcomes. Regular communication guarantees transparency while also reassuring stakeholders that their issues are being taken seriously.
- **Impartial and thorough investigation** - Fair dispute resolution requires impartiality in conducting exhaustive investigations. Furthermore, avoid any conflicts of interest by employing independent officers to conduct the investigations who have no direct links with the matter at hand so as to ensure a legitimate process. Next, collect all important details, interview the parties involved and review documents so as to have an overall comprehension about what caused the problem. A comprehensive investigation will take into account all aspects of the complaint.
- **Develop and implement corrective actions** - Addressing grievances requires an effective implementation of corrective measures. Establish appropriate remedial actions based on the investigation results, which may consist of policy modifications, disciplinary steps, compensation or any other relief measures that relate to the specific problem. Make sure that these measures are implemented adequately and timely, as well as

investigating their effect in order to establish whether the underlying issue has been resolved and prevent its recurrence.

4.5 Regular monitoring and reporting

Procurement decisions and sourcing policies are merely the start of a sustainable supply chain journey. The CS3D emphasizes continuous improvement and monitoring, which entails following up supplier performance in relation to diverse sustainability indices as well as promoting the culture of continual progress.

These strategies include developing KPIs for key areas such as energy usage, waste generation, water consumption, workplace security and inclusivity, in line with your company's activities. This ensures that these KPIs match with industrial best practices or sustainability benchmarks thereby enabling thorough appraisal of supplier performance. For instance, regular performance reviews are vital because they evaluate how far supplier have come toward these KPIs; also, they can be used by companies to encourage open communication within such processes since they celebrate successes and identify areas requiring improvements.

Capacity building and knowledge sharing are also vital components. Offering training programs and workshops will enable suppliers to create strong sustainability practices by borrowing a leaf from other best industry practices or success stories.

In this way, companies promote shared accountability and continuous improvement in their supply chains, which leads to higher standards for suppliers, who then improve transparency and efficiency in the supply chain in addition to brand reputation. Ultimately, investing in these mechanisms ensures that the supply chain remains resilient and responsible, effectively adapting to changing sustainability regulations and consumer demands.

5. Conclusion

The Corporate Sustainability Due Diligence Directive (CS3D) represents a major leap forward in driving sustainable and ethical business practices across the European Union. It requires companies to integrate due diligence into their operations to ensure that environmental and human rights are considered when dealing with supply chains. This Directive argues for a risk-based approach that takes cognizance of international standards such as OECD Guidelines for Multinational Enterprises and UN Guiding Principles on Business and Human Rights. Its objective is to encourage transparency, stakeholder involvement, and continual improvement through the promotion of sustainability and ethical governance within corporate structures.

As a result, EU companies will have to introduce strong sustainability criteria into their purchasing practices, especially in procurement and supplier selection. Companies should do comprehensive audits of their supply chains, put in place complaint mechanisms along with constantly monitoring and improving on all aspects to do with sustainability. This rule builds up transparency and accountability thereby making sure that companies give more importance to sustainability than they would normally do given traditional parameters only. In doing so, it aims at an environmentally friendly market where human rights are respected creating value for businesses and society at large.

A variety of benefits are available for a company to enjoy if it wholeheartedly embraces the concepts provided by the CS3D. By incorporating sustainability criteria into their product development processes, firms can enhance brand reputation and gain competitive advantage, which attract consumers with a conscience and investors, who value corporate social responsibility. Proactive risk identification and mitigation is essential in increasing operational efficiency as well as reducing long-term costs. Suppliers that are environmentally friendly may drive innovation and result in new eco-products or services. The adherence to the stipulations set out under the CS3D program is instrumental in building more robust supply chains for businesses better positioned to cope with future regulatory changes.

However, compliance with the CS3D presents various challenges. Implementing due diligence procedures is resource-intensive and complex, particularly for large companies. Smaller organizations might face significant administrative and financial burdens associated with these compliance measures. Gathering and analyzing accurate data from numerous suppliers across different regions will surely present challenges, and resistance from suppliers in regions with weaker regulations may hinder environmental initiatives. Non-compliance can result in loss of stakeholder trust, legal consequences, and reputational damage. Overcoming these roadblocks requires substantial investment in resources, training, technology, and an inclusive approach that involves all stakeholders.

Bibliography

Beske, F. (2010). Corporate social responsibility and investor relations in a stakeholder society. Edward Elgar Publishing.

Beske, P. (2010). Corporate social responsibility and investor relations in a stakeholder society. Corporate Governance: An International Journal, 10(4), 321-331.

Beske, P., & Seuring, S. (2014). Putting the cart before the horse? How social responsibility in purchasing can drive environmental performance. Journal of Business Ethics, 121(2), 265-280.

Carter, C. R., Ellinor, A. R., & Krishnan, V. V. (2020). Procurement and supply chain management for sustainability: A handbook for practitioners and students. Business Expert Press.

Carter, C. R., Ellram, L. M., & Kaufmann, P. (2020). Sustainable procurement practices: Their impact on organizational performance. Business Horizons, 63(3), 353-362.

Eltantawy, R. A., Fox, G. L., & Giunipero, L. (2009). Supply chain management. Supply Chain Management, 14(2), 99-108.

European Commission. (2001). Communication from the Commission A Sustainable Europe for a Better World: A European Union Strategy for Sustainable Development (Commission's proposal to the Gothenburg European Council). [COM/2001/0264]. ec.europa.eu

European Commission. (2001). Green paper - Promoting a European framework for corporate social responsibility. [COM/2001/0366 final *]. ec.europa.eu

European Commission. (2010). Lisbon Strategy Evaluation Document by Commission Staff. Brussels: European Commission.

European Commission. (2020). Proposal for a Directive on corporate sustainability due diligence. https://commission.europa.eu/business-economy-euro/doing-business-eu/corporate-sustainability-due-diligence_en

European Commission. (2020, April 22). Proposal for a Regulation of the European Parliament and of the Council on corporate sustainability due diligence and amending Regulation (EU) 2019/1020 [COM(2020) 183 final]. ec.europa.eu

European Commission. (2024a). Non-financial reporting directive. https://www.europarl.europa.eu/RegData/etudes/BRIE/2021/654213/EPRS_BRI%282021%29654213_EN.pdf

European Commission. (2024b). Ecodesign directive (2009/125/EC). https://eur-lex.europa.eu/legal-content/EN/ALL/?uri=celex%3A32009L0125

European Commission. (2024c). Regulation (EU) 2017/821 on conflict minerals. https://eur-lex.europa.eu/eli/reg/2017/821/oj

European Commission. (2024d). Timber regulation (EU) No 995/2010. https://eur-lex.europa.eu/legal-content/EN/TXT/?uri=celex%3A32010R0995

European Commission. (2024e). Corporate sustainability due diligence directive. https://commission.europa.eu/business-economy-euro/doing-business-eu/corporate-sustainability-due-diligence_en (to be updated with the final directive reference upon publication)

European Council. (2000). 'Lisbon European Council - Presidency Conclusions'. http://www.consilium.europa.eu/uedocs/cms_data/docs/pressdata/en/ec/00100-r1.en0.htm

European Investment Bank, (2021). Task force on climate-related financial disclosures (TCFD) report 2020, European Investment Bank. https://data.europa.eu/doi/10.2867/234525

Financial Accounting Standards Board (FASB). (2009). Accounting Standards Codification (ASC 605-50-45-1). https://asc.fasb.org/section&trid=2197430

Flammer, C., Luo, L., & Zhao, H. (2019). The influence of the non-financial reporting directive on corporate sustainability reporting: A stakeholder perspective. Sustainability Accounting, Management and Policy Journal, 10(2), 316-344.

Fontenot, M. J., Hahn, T., & Kunstmann, S. (2018). Does sustainable procurement enhance brand reputation? A stakeholder theory perspective. Journal of Business Ethics, 153(1), 71-84.

Geffen, C., & Rothenberg, S. (2000). Suppliers and environmental management: An analysis of the automobile industry. Journal of Cleaner Production, 8(6), 347-357.

GRI Standards (2016). Consolidated Set of GRI Sustainability Reporting Standards. Global Sustainability Standards Board. http://www.ekvilib.org/wp-content/uploads/2018/03/GRI-standardi-2016.pdf

International Organization for Standardization. (2015). ISO 14001:2015 - Environmental management systems - Requirements with guidance for use (ISO standard). [invalid URL removed]

Jordan, A., Wurzel, R., Zürn, M. (2003). A tale of two texts: European integration and environmental policy. Journal of European Public Policy, 10(1), 14-38.

Mol, A. P., Sonnenfeld, D. A., & Spaargaren, G. (2005). The ecological modernization of production systems in the Netherlands: The case of the automobile industry. Environmental Politics, 14(2), 201-221.

OECD (2023), OECD Guidelines for Multinational Enterprises on Responsible Business Conduct, OECD Publishing, Paris, https://doi.org/10.1787/81f92357-en

Preuss, L. (2009). Addressing sustainable development through public procurement: The case of local government. Supply Chain Manag. Int. J, 14, 213–223.

Ruggie, John G. (2011). Guiding principles on business and human rights: Implementing the United Nations "Protect, Respect and Remedy" Framework. United Nations Office of the High Commissioner for Human Rights.

UN Global Compact. (2024). https://unglobalcompact.org/

UN Human Rights Council. (2011). Guiding principles on business and human rights: Implementing the United Nations “Protect, Respect and Remedy” framework (A/HRC/17/31). New York, NY: United Nations.

Trustful relationships with the Global South for effective supply chain due diligence

Susanne Friedrich

1. Introduction

> Two people are talking about climate change.
> The first says: "Eating beef, driving a car and
> heating are the biggest private climate killers."
> Says the second: "Yes, I know and I'm giving up all three!"
> "Wow, all three?"
> "Yes, I don't eat beef in the morning, I don't drive at lunchtime, and I switch off the heating in summer." (source unknown)

It was not so long ago that heavy rainfall in many parts of Germany, which is partly due to the warming of the oceans, has once again shown us how the consequences of climate change are increasingly jeopardising people's lives and our prosperity. What we are experiencing in Germany is being felt much more drastically by people in other parts of the world (IPCC, 2023). The consequences for people there are often dramatic, especially where social security systems are lacking, and institutions are weak. In the Anthropocene, the age in which humans have become the dominant influencing factor on the earth and its ecosystems, we are threatening our livelihoods in both, the Global North and the Global South. The global challenges require all social actors to assume responsibility far beyond the usual level. This is the only way we can maintain our room for manoeuvre in the future and not drift from one "flood of the century" to the next, at ever shorter intervals and with ever-increasing costs. The pressure to act is growing. Larger and faster steps are needed, broadly effective and scaling contributions in the important areas, for a genuine transformation to an economic system within planetary boundaries.

2. The international framework

The United Nations' Agenda 2023 with the goal of economic, ecological, and socially just change and the Paris Climate Agreement to achieve the 1.5°C target, to which almost all countries in the world have committed, form the global orientation framework and define the common path for transformation. The European Union has developed the European Green Deal as a key policy framework for its area of responsibility to shape the transition to a modern, resource-efficient and competitive economy with the aim of achieving climate neutrality by 2050 and secure Europe's future. The G7 countries also want to become greenhouse gas neutral by 2050, Germany even by 2045.

The latest EU regulations on corporate due diligence and sustainability reporting, together with some EU standards that have been in place for some time, such as the Conflict Minerals Regulation contribute to this. Even if the EU Commission's so-called Omnibus Initiatives extend the implementation and application of these regulations in part and lower the requirements, the objectives of the Green Deal remain valid. The major damage caused by climate disruption is already placing a financial burden on the economy and will increase in the future.

3. Supply chains at the centre of attention

Supply and value chains are thus increasingly taking centre stage. Unfortunately, the conflicts between the major economic areas and the US tariff disputes with the EU and China are exerting considerable pressure on companies' cost structures. They must reduce their end-to-end costs and at the same time develop strategic resilience. Supply chains need to be restructured and diversified. This is precisely why long-term, clear legal requirements are important for companies. A zigzag course is not in their interest.

4. Good for business

The social-ecological transformation and the associated application of corporate due diligence create opportunities. The German Council of Economic Experts speaks of "climate protection as an industrial policy opportunity" (Sachverständigenrat der Deutschen Wirtschaft, 2020/21). "The necessary sector coupling,", the interlinking of electricity, heat, industry and transport to reduce CO_2 emissions, "and the diversity of the sectors involved are significantly changing the value chains. German industry has a great deal of expertise in many relevant fields of technology, enabling it to assume a position as a leading provider of climate-neutral applications and products in Germany and abroad (ibid)." Climate protection goes hand in hand with innovation and increases competitiveness. At the same time, risk management strategies that integrate environmental, economic and social impacts into their supply chains make companies more resilient. They enable them to counter the risks of climate change, reduce the risk of supply disruptions, and create advantages in terms of access to capital, insurance and customer loyalty.

Another positive effect is the fact that corporate due diligence obligations are promoting digitalisation. Cloud technologies, data analytics, blockchain, digital tracking and sustainability tools or artificial intelligence: digital solutions contribute to the implementation of due diligence obligations and accelerate digitalisation - the second major challenge alongside sustainability - in companies. One example: artificial intelligence is now being used in the USA to increase transparency in the textile industry and enable the traceability of cotton from forced labour-free cultivation. DNA technology enables cotton to be tracked at fibre level throughout the entire supply chain and distribution process. Cotton products that use molecular labelling can be traced back to the farm where the cotton was grown. (New York Times, 2023)

5. The foreshortened view from the North

All of this is widely known. Numerous advisory services are now available to support companies in implementing their due diligence obligations[1]. Good practices and case studies are widely documented[2], extensive guidelines and handouts have been published and are generally available. In all high-risk industries such as textiles, food and mining, there are numerous industry initiatives, trade union agreements and multi-stakeholder initiatives[3] that have developed strategies or codes of conduct for their members. Many companies in Europe are already making very valuable contributions and have explicitly supported the adaptation of the CSDDD (IDVO, n.d).

Nevertheless, the impression remains that compliance with due diligence obligations in Germany often still revolves very much around the formal fulfilment of legal requirements, sustainability clauses in contracts and supplier audits. Business processes are geared towards minimising the risks of civil liability or the imposition of fines, penalties and other sanctions: due diligence as a technical process.

This is not enough to generate acceptance for the measures in the supply chain. Lasting change can only succeed if companies are prepared to engage with the perspective of the Global South. There are also players there who are interested in socially responsible and climate-friendly production processes, either to fulfil the legal requirements of their customers in the global North or because they have set their own sustainability goals[4]. For whatever reason, these stakeholders - suppliers, workers, local communities - certainly understand much better than companies in the North where the greatest risks lie, how they can best be prevented and how they can be remedied if necessary.

6. Understanding the challenges on the ground

Until now, the relationships between companies and their suppliers have been characterized by contractual relationships, but the complexity of the requirements requires a new perspective on global supply chains: A deeper understanding of local conditions, the distribution of social resources such as influence and legitimacy, the capacities and interests of the various stakeholder groups are necessary to manage risks and implement measures appropriately.

One example is the issue of child labour. In many countries, the risk of child labour exists in agriculture. However, a ban does not solve the problem. Families are often dependent on the income of their children. Banning it then simply means that child labour shifts to other economic sectors and activities. In addition to a ban child labour in supply contracts, it is therefore necessary to get involved directly at the farm level. There are numerous companies that take action to combat child labour with a differentiated approach. As an example, different awareness-raising measures can be carried out depending on the target group. These can include, for example, printing appropriate messages on the seed packaging or personal discussions with the farmers. Concrete measures to strengthen the productivity of farmers help to increase harvest productivity and thus also increase the profitability of seed production. This in turn reduces financial dependence on income from child labour and enables parents to raise money for their children's education. The UN Global Compact Network Germany has documented a series of cases. (UNGC Network Germany, n.d.)

Further measures can include child-sensitive complaint mechanisms. They provide companies with valuable information about the impact of their business activities on children's rights and can therefore help to implement systemic, structural measures that better protect and promote children's rights (BMAS, 2022).

7. Information from the Global South

Companies still often rely on information from actors in their own environment. However, it is often difficult from the Global North to assess what is happening in the Global South and what the perspective of the local actors is. Companies from the Global North can benefit from communicating directly with local actors. Not only do they gain a better insight into the risks that exist and how they can be managed, they also benefit from the acceptance of local partners and create trusting relationships.

The actors in the Global South are also thinking about the due diligence approaches of their customers from the Global North and are classifying them. For example, in a major daily newspaper (Daily Star, 2024) in Bangladesh, a trade union representative elaborates on the opportunities and difficulties that could arise for his country from the supply chain laws.

The implications and opportunities of the due diligence approach, however, are far from being discussed everywhere. In some cases, the new legislation is perceived as a unilaterally imposed trade restriction or non-tariff trade barrier. This is precisely why it is important to listen carefully on site, build trust and act together.

8. Implementation in partnership

Even if the individual company does not release itself from its responsibility to identify, prevent and reduce damage, cooperation to identify risks and implement measures to fulfil the due diligence obligations can have many advantages, whether at industry level or across industries, for example when raw materials are sourced from several sectors, such as the raw material coltan, which is used in the automotive industry, mechanical engineering and the electronics industry (UBA, 2022, p.120). In supply chains in which the exact production sites or locations of raw material extraction are not known, but with a likelihood that the company is located in a high-risk water catchment area or if a company alone has too little influence on its own suppliers and the general reduction of risk, it makes sense to participate in a water stewardship initiative for the responsible use of the water resource (UBA, 2022, p. 120 ff).

The partnership approach is also a key factor in the establishment of grievance mechanisms. An example of a quite sophisticated mechanism is the cross-company grievance mechanism of some representatives of the German automotive industry in Mexico. Mexican civil society, which was involved in the development of the mechanism, also draws a positive conclusion from the process so far. After an intensive dialogue between companies, trade unions, governments, national human rights organizations and civil society, first in Germany and then with Mexican actors, the mechanism has been in operation since May 2024. It covers the entire supply chain of German automotive companies in Mexico up to final assembly and is aimed at all types of potentially affected actors. Complaints are examined by independent experts (Germanwatch, 2024). What is needed now is the participation of more companies.

9. Interactions between environmental and social due diligence obligations

In principle, all approaches should ideally include local actors, who are well aware of the obstacles on the ground and ask them what the best starting points are for strengthening human rights and improving environmental protection. This is particularly true if there are interactions or even conflicting objectives in implementation.

For example, the activities of companies and their impact on the environment can lead to negative impacts on human rights, directly or indirectly. Air, water and soil pollution can threaten the livelihoods of the local population. If a company, for example, uses excessive amounts of water or pollutes water bodies in a region that is already suffering from water shortages, this can lead to the local population not having enough clean drinking water or being unable to irrigate their fields. Likewise, improper handling of hazardous waste can lead to human rights violations if the waste contaminates the environment and thus poses a risk to human health. (BMAS, 2022, p. 11)

Misguided climate measures can also have a negative impact on employees, local companies and local communities. Not only climate change, but also adaptation measures can themselves violate human rights. Examples include the increased cultivation of biofuels, which can endanger food security in some countries, and the production of renewable energies when the construction of hydropower dams or the large-scale creation of wind farms lead to displacement of human settlements due to its enormous land use (German Institute for Human Rights, 2021). It therefore makes sense to apply corporate due diligence to the issue of human rights along the entire value chain and to consider both with each other and in their interactions.

10. Conclusion

Adequate due diligence measures in the supply chain must be guided by a real interest in understanding the perspective of the Global South. The information and experience provided by the local actors must be a corner stone of the approach. While due to the interrelation between climate measures and human rights these two areas should be observed in parallel, collaboration with the local actors is key. Only collaboration schemes allow for the necessary trust as the fundament of sustainable measures.

In all supply chain approaches, however, it must not be lost sight of the fact that it is not just about delivery, but about own value creation in the Global South. If sustainability is not considered in its economic dimension, the people there will not go along with it. They have a legitimate interest in development and prosperity. We must therefore involve local partners, define common goals and handle differing opinions so that value creation in the countries of the Global South increases significantly. Only this way, we will achieve the social-ecological transformation.

Notes

1 The Agency for Business and Economic Development (AWE in German) for instance, runs a Helpdesk on Business and Human Rights. A list of further support activities is provided on the csr-in-deutschland website.

2 The UN Global Compact Network Germany offers, among others, a wide range of case studies.

3 An overview of multi-stakeholder initiatives supported by the German government can be found on the website of csr-in-deutschland.

4 For example India: At COP26, India's 2030 decarbonization target was announced. The highly ambitious goal includes decarbonizing energy to 50% and achieving 500 GW of fossil fuel-free generating capacity by 2030 (Energy Transitions Commission, August 2022)

Bibliography

CSR-in-Deutschland (n.d.) Information and advice. Information and advice - CSR (csr-in-deutschland.de). Accessed 4 June 2024.

Energy Transitions Commission (August 2022). Roadmap to India's 2030 Descarbonization Target. Roadmap to India's 2030 Decarbonization Target - ETC (energy-transitions.org). Accessed 10 June 2024.

Federal Ministry of Labour and Social Affairs (BMAS). (June, 2022). Automotive Industry Dialogue - Guidelines for the Core Element Grievance Mechanism. Grievance mechanism (bmas.de)

German Institute for Human Rights (May 2021). Stellungnahme Menschenrechte und Klimakrise, Öffentliche Anhörung des Bundestagsauschusses für Menschenrechte und humanitäre Hilfe am 19.05.2021. file:///C:/Users/friedrich/Downloads/Stellungnahme_Menschenrechte_und_Klimakrise %20(2).pdf.

Germanwatch (7 May 2024). Launch of grievance mechanism of the German automotive industry in Mexico. Launch of grievance mechanism of the German automotive industry in Mexico | Germanwatch e.V. Accessed 31 May 2024.

Initiative for Sustainable & Responsible Business Conduct (IDVO). (n.d.). Broad support for the CSDDD. Broad support for the CSDDD (we-support -the-csddd.eu). Accessed 17 June 2024.

Intergovernmental Panel on Climate Change (IPCC). (2023). Climate Change 2023: Synthesis Report. IPCC_AR6_SYR_FullVolume.pdf,

Kashyap, Aruna. Daily Star. (31 May 2024). What does the EU Due Diligence Directive mean for Bangladesh? Impact of EU Due Diligence Directive on Bangladesh | What does the EU due diligence directive mean for Bangladesh? (thedailystar.net). Accessed 2 June 2024.

Milano, Johnny. New York Times (20.03.2023). How A.I. and DNA are unlocking the Mysteries of Global Supply Chains. How AI and DNA Are Unlocking the Mysteries of Global Supply Chains - The New York Times (nytimes.com). Accessed 16 June 2024.

Sachverständigenrat der Deutschen Wirtschaft (2022). Jahresgutachten 2020/21: Corona-Krise gemeinsam bewältigen, Resilienz und Wachstum stärken. Chapter 4: Klimaschutz als industriepolitische Chance. Kapitel 4 - Klimaschutz als industriepolitische Chance (sachverstaendigenrat -wirtschaft.de)

Umweltbundesamt (UBA). (2022). Umweltrisiken und -auswirkungen in globalen Lieferketten deutscher Unternehmen – Branchenstudie Automobilindustrie. Umweltrisiken und - auswirkungen in globalen Lieferketten deutscher Unternehmen – Branchenstudie Automobilindustrie (umweltbundesamt.de)

United Nations. (2011). Guiding Principles on Business and Human Rights. GuidingPrinciplesBusinessHR_EN.pdf (ohchr.org)

UN Global Compact (August 2023). Just Transition in Supply Chains – A Business Brief. Just_Transition_in_Supply_Chains_Business_Brief.pdf (globalcompact.de)

UN Global Compact Network Germany (n.d.). Case Studies. Bayer nimmt Ursachen von Kinderarbeit in den Blick. UN Global Compact Netzwerk Deutschland: Bayer nimmt die Ursachen von Kinderarbeit in den Blick. Accessed 10 June 2024.

Human Rights Impact Assessment in the energy sector and the CSDDD Directive

Adam Domagała, Anna Tomiczek

1. Introduction

This study aims to explain what Human rights impact assessment is (hria) and for what purposes and in which cases companies should assess the impact of their activities on human rights as part of their operational activities. This issue is particularly important due to the requirements arising from Directive (EU) 2019/1937 on corporate due diligence for sustainable development (CSDDD) adopted by the EU Council on May 24, 2024 [1]. CSDDD assumes the introduction of an obligation of duc diligence for specific groups of enterprises in order to counteract the negative effects of business activities in the field of human rights and the environment. In the light of the new legal requirements, the issue of conducting hria, appropriate methodology, its scope, and situationswhere it should be applied have been particularly significant. The article also aims to explain the differences between Human rights impact assessment (hria), and Human Rights Impact Assessment (HRIA), as well as the Human Rights process Due Diligence (HRDD). The analysis of the new legal requirements was carried out with reference to the hria and HRDD solutions already implemented by international energy companies. The article takes into account the specificity and role of the above-mentioned issues in the energy sector.

2. CSDDD

The CSDDD introduces a legal framework requiring companies to demonstrate the actions they are taking to protect the environment and human rights. Due diligence should be exercised not only in relation to one's own practices, but also to the activities of the subsidiaries and other entities in value chains with which enterprises have direct and indirect business relations.

The adoption of the CSDDD directive culminated a nearly four-year process of developing regulations. At the last stage of the legislative work on the Directive 2019/1937, significant changes were introduced regarding the applicable thresholds of the directive, which resulted in a reduction in the number of enterprises subject to the obligations arising from it.

As for the subjective scope, the CSDDD Directive will apply to enterprises from the EU countries, but also to enterprises from outside the EU. Pursuant to Art. 2 CSDDD, entities established in accordance with the law of an EU Member State that will be covered by regulation can be divided into the following groups:

1. enterprises that, in the last financial year for which annual financial statements have been or should be prepared, employed on average more than 1,000 employees and their net sales revenues worldwide exceeded EUR 450 million;
2. companies that did not themselves meet the thresholds indicated above but were the ultimate parent company ('ultimate parent company") in the group that achieved these thresholds;
3. enterprises that have themselves entered into, or are the ultimate parent company of, a group that has entered into franchise or licensing agreements in the EU with independent third-party companies in exchange for royalties amounting to more than EUR 22.5 million, where these agreements ensure a common identity, a common business concept and the application of uniform methods of doing business.

For non-EU companies, the criterion for being subject to the directive is not based on the number of employees. However, it is related to the generated net turnover in the EU and similarly applies to parent companies, franchise and license agreements.

The new provisions will be applied gradually (Article 30 on transposition). First, the regulations will apply, 3 years after the entry into force of the directive, to the largest EU enterprises that employ over 5,000 employees and recorded a global net turnover of over EUR 1,500 million in the last financial year. For non-EU companies, a net turnover generated in the EU of over EUR 1,500 million will apply. Four years after the entry into force of the directive, the thresholds for EU companies covered by the directive will be 3,000 employees and EUR 900 million of global net turnover. After 5 years, the provisions of the directive will cover enterprises with the lowest thresholds indicated in Art. 2 CSDDD.

In 2025, the European Commission proposed the so-called "Omnibus Simplification Package." The EU's "Stop the Clock" proposal includes a postponement of reporting deadlines. On 17 April 2025, the Directive (UE) 2025/794 of the Parlament and of the Council of 14 April 2025 entered into force, amending Directive (EU) 2022/2464 (CSRD) and Directive (EU) 2024/1760 (CSDDD) as regards the dates from which Member States are to apply certain sustainability reporting requirements and certain corporate sustainability due diligence obligations. This directive introduces a one-year postponement of corporate due diligence obligations under the CSDDD – shifting the application from 2026 to 2027. The mandatory transposition into national legal systems should take place by 31 December 2025.

Small and medium-sized enterprises will not be directly covered by the provisions of the directive, but the entry into force of the CSDDD will also have an indirect impact on the SME sector. The most important obligations arising from the CSDDD directive include, among others:

- incorporating due diligence into corporate policy and risk management (Article 5),
- identification, assessment and prioritization of actual and potential negative impacts (Articles 6 and 6a),
- preventing potential negative effects (Article 7),
- suspending actual negative effects (Article 8) and taking corrective actions (Article 8c),
- meaningful stakeholder engagement in the due diligence process (Article 8d),
- implementation of complaint procedures enabling the submission of complaints in the event of justified concerns about actual or potential negative effects on the activities of enterprises (Article 9),
- monitoring the effectiveness and adequacy of due diligence activities undertaken (Article 10),

- publishing an annual report on matters covered by the Directive on the company's website (Article 11),
- adoption and implementation of a transformation plan to mitigate climate change (Article 15).

It cannot be ruled out that the ongoing EU-level work on the so-called large Omnibus package may lead to changes in the scope of obligations under the CSDDD, potentially aiming to reduce or limit those requirements.

Taking into account the above obligations, it seems that the desired effect of the EU legislator is for enterprises to have the knowledge, insights and perspectives that enable them to incorporate responsibility for human rights into their management systems. Such activities should include understanding how the company can prevent, mitigate or eliminate adverse human rights impacts and develop a human rights strategy designed to exert an appropriate level of impact on any adverse human rights impacts.

The CSDDD aims to harmonize due diligence requirements across EU Member States. It should be noted that detailed regulations relating to due diligence are already in force, e.g. in France or Germany (Duty of Vigilance Act in France, Supply Chain Due Diligence Act in Germany). The implementation of the CSDDD directive in Poland will be a novelty. The CSDDD Directive introduces requirements for companies to identify, prevent, eliminate or mitigate the actual and potential environmental and human rights impacts of their activities. Given the above information, the question arises: how to organize this process in the company?

3. Human Rights Due Diligence (HRDD)

In the context of running a business, the term *due dilligence* is often used. Most people associate it with a comprehensive examination of the company's condition, which is usually commissioned by an external investor interested in aquringthe company. During such a review, the financial, commercial, tax or legal condition of the audited entity may be analyzed. Such verification may also include the issue of the company's compliance with human rights. This issue seems important in terms of risk mapping, as enterprises can affect the entire spectrum of generally recognized human rights, and their responsibility applies to all of these rights. It should also be emphasized that violations of human rights by companies may pose a business, legal, financial or reputational risk to an organization .

It should be noted here that in the content of the Guidelines on Business and Human Rights: Implementation of the UN Framework Document "Protect, Respect and Remediate" [2], companies should, as a minimum, respect the rights included in the International Bill of Human Rights (which consists of the Universal Declaration of Human Rights Human Rights and the International Covenant on Civil and Political Rights and the International Covenant on Economic, Social and Cultural Rights) and the rights set out in the International Labor Organization's Declaration on Fundamental Principles and Rights at Work. The above regulations do not prevent enterprises from applying additional standards, depending on the specific nature of their business. Entities in the energy industry should take into account in particular labor rights and the rights of indigenous peoples. Of course, the responsibility of companies to respect human rights is a different issue than that resulting from the responsibility provided for by generally applicable law, which remains the domain of national regulations.

3.1. Human rights due diligence process

In accordance with the OECD Guidelines on Due Diligence for Responsible Business Conduct [3], the human rights due diligence process includes six main stages, as illustrated in the graphic below, i.e. 1) incorporating the principles of due diligence into policies and management systems; 2) identification and assessment of adverse effects on human rights and the environment; 3) preventing and stopping or minimizing actual and potential adverse effects on human rights and the environment; 4) assessment of the effectiveness of the measures; 5) communication; 6) providing remedial measures. Additionally, the due diligence process under the CSDDD should include the six steps outlined above.

The OECD Guidelines cited above encourage companies to identify, prevent, monitor, take remedial action and report on how they address impacts on human rights. Human Rights Process Due Diligence (HRDD) is mainly intended to identify and assess the impact of a company's own activities or business relations on human rights.

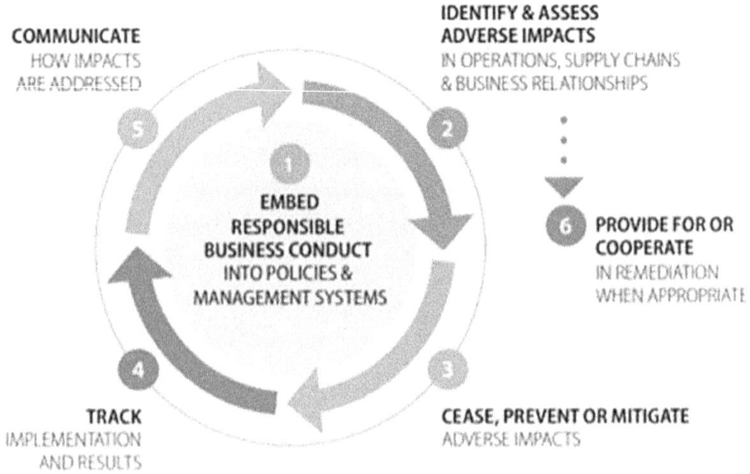

Figure 1: Source: OECD Due Diligence Guidance for Responsible Business Conduct (2018), p. 21, link: OECD-Due-Diligence-Guidance-for-Responsi ble-Business-Conduct.pdf (access: 06/06/2024)

It is important that enterprises cooperate with stakeholders when implementing each individual stage. Only thanks to such cooperation, HRDD will reflect the actual situation and render it possible to take effective remedial measures.

When discussing the above process, reference should be made to several of the most important stages. The first one is to analyze and assess the actual and potential effects (impact) on human rights of the so-called Human rights impact assessment (hria). Enterprises should not limit themselves only to their activities, but should take into account their business relationships with contractors. In this respect, it is important to use the knowledge of people within the organization, as well as independent external experts, which should also include consultations with groups potentially affected by the negative impact generated by the company in the field of human rights. It should be emphasized here that HRIA written in capital letters does not mean the same as HRIA written in lowercase letters. It is assumed that HRIA means carrying out an analysis and assessment of actual and potential effects (impact) on human rights, while HRIA refers to the methodology adopted in preparing this assessment, e.g. proposed by BSR or the Danish Institute of Human Rights [4].

The second stage involves taking appropriate action and incorporating the findings from the impact assessment into the relevant company processes. These actions will be conditional on establishing direct or indirect impacts on human rights. After carrying out the above, the company should track the reactions and effectiveness of the measures taken on these activities. Monitoring in this area is necessary to test its effectiveness, and in accordance with the UN Guidelines, [5]it should be based on qualitative and quantitative indicators. Ultimately, the above process should end with communication within the company about what actions are being taken to prevent or minimize the negative impact on human rights generated by the company.

All of the above activities are intended to identify the negative impact on human rights in order to prevent it, mitigate its effects and account for the company's activities. It is expected that this process will vary depending on the size of the enterprise and its scale or scope of activity. In this regard, companies should take into account the OECD Guidelines for Multinational Enterprises on Responsible Business Conduct [6]. In chapter IV point 5 of the above-mentioned the guidelines indicate that the human rights due diligence process should be carried out in accordance with the size, nature and context of the business and the importance of the risks of negative effects on human rights [7].

Regardless of the above, it should be emphasized that the HRDD process is continuous and should take into account the fact that risks related to human rights may constantly change along with changes in the enterprise. It is therefore worth considering incorporating the human rights due diligence process into the enterprise's risk management system.

3.2. The impact of the human rights due diligence process

The human rights due diligence process, in particular by companies that pose a risk of a serious negative impact on human rights, should be completed with an appropriate report.

This report should include data and information on the most important issues related to human rights occurring in the course of business activities. Moreover, the issues presented in the report should include, among others: assessment of the impact of the company's activities on human rights and identification of risks related to their compliance, information on the undertaken mitigating actions, as well as an action plan for respect for human rights. Such disclosure is an important instrument through which the obligation to respect human rights in our operational activities is implemented in practice.

The final result of this process should also take into account the fact that due diligence is intended to help enterprises anticipate, prevent and mitigate negative effects. A reliable HRDD may also make it easier for the company to decide whether to continue or discontinue activities, or even withdraw from business relationships due to the risk of negative consequences being too high or the mitigation measures being ineffective.

It is worth emphasizing that if there are no funds to conduct HRDD, the company can integrate it with other functions in the company. Regardless, reliance solely on audits and certificates should be avoided, as they may be expensive and will not allow the company to demonstrate due diligence in respecting human rights.

4. Human Rights Due Diligence (HRDD) and Human rights impact assessment (hria)

Contrary to popular belief, Human rights impact assessment is not the same as Human Rights Due Diligence. HRIA is an evidence-based analysis of how companies influence, for example, the local community, employees and consumers. It may reveal less obvious situations relating to the human rights impact a company may have had [8]. It should be emphasized that HRD is an element of HRDD - a continuous practice that applies to all levels of activity [9]. Only after conducting HRDD will the company gain knowledge in what situations HRIA should be carried out. Therefore, hria is a narrower concept than HRDD, and it is an element of the sound business process that enterprises will be obliged to perform under Art. 6 of the CSDDD Directive. Bearing the above in mind, companies should now carry out HRI at the early stages of implementing their new products or services, or when entering new

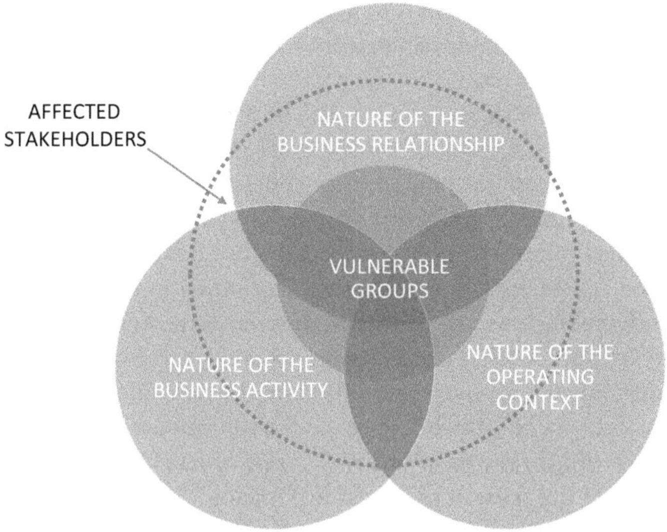

Figure 2: Source: Shift , Human Rights Due Diligence in High Risk Circumstances: Practical Strategies for Businesses (March 2015), Human Rights Due Diligence in High Risk Circumstances : Practical Strategies for Businesses (Shift , 2015) - Resources (securityhumanrightshub.org)

foreign markets. It should be recalled that the difference in the meaning of HRIA and HRIA was explained in subsection 3.1 of this study.

The performance of Human Rights Impact The assessment must be preceded by providing an answer to the question why we want to carry out such an assessment.

It is worth emphasizing here that the main reasons for assessing the impact on human rights in the energy industry is the energy transformation, which has consequences for local and global supply chains, the need to adapt to new regulations, as well as the digitization of operational activities and relations with the end user.

As an example, we can point to local communities that are at risk of negative impact during the construction of wind and photovoltaic farms. This risk may be related to the transport of materials, equipment and elements needed for the construction of wind and photovoltaic farms, which may cause inconvenience to residents in the form of night transport, noise, vibration and dust. Another example may be a potential violation of employees' right to health by allowing employees to work without the required qualifications or medical examinations.

A vivid example in this respect can also be the forced labor of the Uighurs. As reported by Politico in 2021, almost every photovoltaic panel sold in the European Union contains components manufactured in the Xinjiang autonomous region in China. Meanwhile, this region is known for the persecution of the Muslim minority - primarily the Uyghur people. One form of this persecution is detention in labor camps. According to media information, up to a million Muslims may be held in these facilities. According to reports, prisoners of Chinese labor camps can be used not only for tasks such as cotton picking, but also for more specialized production - including: to prepare polycrystalline silicon, which is then used in the production of photovoltaic panels. According to media information, approximately 95% of panels available on the market contain silicon from Xinjiang [10].

Once we answer the question why we needto conduct HRIA [once we determine the purpose of the implementaton of HRIA], it is worth using specialized HRIA methodologies developed by e.g. BSR or the Danish Institute of Human Rights, which will help us go through the entire process step by step [11].

Therefore, when preparing the hria, the company should examine whether it has a broad impact on human rights. In the case of energy companies, this impact seems to be large, especially when the company owns coal deposits. This decision should be made on the basis of severity and likelihood of impact [12]. The mere exercise of hria should not serve the sole purpose of fulfilling an upcoming legal obligation. Enterprises should see it as part of a process, an opportunity to improve organizational culture and their image on the market. Therefore, companies should continuously cooperate with stakeholders in this regard.

It should be emphasized that simply having a code of conduct for suppliers or an audit report is not sufficient to demonstrate a human rights impact assessment. Audits have limitations in the form of examining a specific period of time, they involve a high risk of irregularities resulting from poor qualifications of the auditor and difficulties resulting from auditing social issues. The best example here is the construction disaster of April 24, 2013 in Szabhara (Rana Plaza), which resulted in the death of 1,127 people. The audit of this facility did not reveal any irregularities, and the audit itself did not prevent the eight-story building from collapsing [13].

Please remember that hria is a continuous process that needs to be constantly updated. Enterprises that start this process should carry it out where they pose the greatest risk as a result of their activities. The best solution would be to act on information obtained from affected recipients. Therefore, it is not worth using ready-made and publicly available hria prepared by other entities as this process is individual. At an early stage, the hria does not have to be prepared for all suppliers or investments. The focus should be on the most serious risks and impacts, and then on suppliers closely related to them.

Bearing in mind that work on human rights should be subject to continuous improvement within the framework of Human Rights impact assessment, it is worth considering consulting now with groups potentially affected by human rights violations, including workers and other relevant stakeholders, to gather information on actual or potential adverse impacts.

All these activities should lead to the preparation of long-term remedial plans and analysis of possible gaps in the application of human rights, which are defined, among others in the OECD Guidelines for Multinational Enterprises.

Moreover, in order to maintain independence and transparency, it is worth considering the participation of an external entity in assessing the company's impact on human rights. When carrying out an impact assessment, remember to also identify all the positive human rights impacts that the company has. All those measureswill allow us to gain approval in the eyes of our stakeholders, shareholders and rating agencies.

5. HRIA and HRDD in the energy sector

For the purposes of this article, a review of the HRDD and HRIA processes implemented in selected leading foreign and Polish energy companies was performed, based on publicly available information contained on the websites or in the non-financial/ESG reports of these entities.

5.1 Vattenfall

Vattenfall is one of the largest producers and sellers of electricity and heat in Europe. The parent company, Vattenfall AB, is 100% owned by the Swedish state and is headquartered in Sweden. The main markets are Sweden, Germany, the Netherlands, Denmark and the United Kingdom. The group employs approximately 21,000 employees.

The Company provides extensive information on respect for human rights on its website, emphasizing that it has an obligation to identify, prevent, mitigate and remedy potential and actual negative impacts on human rights throughout our value chain.

Vattenfall points out that its activities are based on the UN Global Compact (UNGC), the core conventions of the International Labor Organization (ILO), the OECD Guidelines for Multinational Enterprises, the UN Guiding Principles on Business and Human Rights and the International Charter of Human Rights. Its commitment to respecting human rights is set out in its Code of Conduct and Integrity, Code of Conduct for Suppliers and Partners, Statement on Slavery and Human Trafficking (under the UK Modern Slavery Act) and Human Rights Policy.

The company publishes a number of documents related to human rights issues on its website:

1. Human Rights Policy [14]- this document contains the company's commitment to respect human rights and to regularly identify, assess and manage risks related to human rights.
2. Vattenfall's human rights action plan [15]- this document contains reflections on the company's action plan "11 steps to 2022"
3. Summary of Vattenfall's Human Rights Assessment by BSR [16], which describes why the company assessed its impact on human rights. When preparing the HRIA impact assessment, the company used the BSR methodology.
4. Vattenfall's human rights progress report [17]- this document refers to the fifth level of due diligence indicated in the OECD, i.e. communication, and contains an update on Vattenfall's progress in priority areas.
5. Vattenfall's statement on slavery and trafficking [18]- this document contains a statement in which the company opposes slavery and human trafficking and issues related to examining these areas in the supply chain.

5.2 Iberdrola

Iberdola is an international energy company based in , Spain. Iberdrola employs approximately 41,000 staff and serves approximately 34.3 million customers (2023). Subsidiaries include Iberdrola España (Spain), SAU, ScottishPower (United Kingdom), Avangrid (United States), Neoenergia , SA (Brazil), Iberdrola Mexico, SA de CV (Mexico), Iberdrola Energía Internacional, SAU (international activities).

Iberdrola is the largest producer of wind energy and the world's second largest energy company in terms of market capitalization. As of 2023, the company had a capacity of 62,045 MW, of which 41,246 MW came from renewable sources worldwide.

Iberdola Group is strongly committed to the defense of human rights and has a set of tools that ensure and promote protection and respect for people in order to prevent, mitigate and remedy any possible human rights impacts.

The company declares on its website that its practices are compliant with the main international standards [19]:

- The principles underlying the United Nations Global Compact.
- United Nations Guiding Principles on Business and Human Rights (UNGPs).
- OECD Guidelines for Multinational Enterprises.
- Tripartite Declaration of Principles on Multinational Enterprises.
- Social policy of the International Labor Organization (including the 169th convention).
- Sustainable Development Goals adopted by the United Nations.

In addition, Iberdola has a human rights due diligence system based on its Governance and Sustainability System as well as a three-line-of-defense audit model, which is a continuous process.

The company publishes a number of documents related to human rights issues on its website:

1. Human Rights Policy [20]- this document rejects child labor, forced or compulsory labor or any other form of modern slavery and seeks to respect freedom of association and collective bargaining as well as

non-discrimination, the right to free movement within any country and takes into account the rights of minorities ethnic and indigenous peoples in places where Iberdola operates.

2. Human Rights Report 2022 [21]- the document presents step by step how Iberdola carried out HRDD and HRA in its organization.

5.3 EDP

EDP (Energias de Portugal, formerly Electricidade de Portugal) is a Portuguese energy company based in Lisbon. It was established in 1976. Currently, it is an international, vertically integrated energy company. The EDP Group is present in 29 markets and on 3 continents. With over 13,000 employees, it is present throughout the entire electricity value chain.

EDP promotes a culture of sharing and mutual respect, consistent with a strict ethics and compliance policy that encourages the highest ethical standards and prevents and combats illegal activities. A reflection of this commitment is the creation of the Ethics and Compliance Department at EDP, promoting a culture of ethical behavior and compliance with laws and regulations in force in all countries where EDP operates, in accordance with international best practices.

The EDP Group Human Rights Policy implements a due diligence management system in accordance with UN guidelines, OECD frameworks and ILO conventions. The company publishes a number of documents related to human rights issues on its website:

Human and labor [22]rights policy - this document aims to ensure respect for human and labor rights in the sphere of activity of the EDP Group, to implement the obligations set out in its policies, to define international reference treaties and standards and to establish procedures to ensure their compliance. It is worth pointing out that this policy applies to all EDP Group companies and employees, business relationships and activities in all geographical locations, regardless of local practices or level of social and economic development.

2. Human and Labor Rights Report 2022 [23]- This report assesses the impact of the activity EDP on human rights and risk identification related to their compliance, information on the undertaken mitigating actions, and an action plan for respect for human rights in EDP.

5.4 RWE

RWE AG (until 1990 Rheinisch-Westfälisches Elektrizitätswerk AG (German: "Rhenish-Westphalia Energy Plant") is a German energy concern. The RWE Group was present in Poland primarily through , which sold electricity to the residents of Warsaw. Currently, the RWE Group has 125 years of history and is a leading supplier of renewable energy sources in the world. The RWE Group operates in countries such as the USA, Australia, China, France, Ireland, Spain, Turkey, Japan, Poland, Scandinavian countries and Great Britain.

The entity's website states that for RWE, respect of human rights is a fundamental element of responsible business management. The goal of the capital group is to respect human rights in all companies and supply chains. Therefore, RWE has developed a systematic approach to respecting human rights and has implemented the Human Rights Risk Management System (IIRRMS).

The company publishes a number of documents related to human rights issues on its website:

1. Policy Statement on RWE's Human Rights Strategy [24]– this policy constitutes the basis for the implementation of human rights standards at RWE and complements the Code of Conduct for Suppliers and constitutes an annex to the Agreement for Suppliers regarding respect for human rights. This document indicates the basic rights that are respected by the group and suppliers are also obliged to respect.
2. Human Rights Regulations [25]- This document includes information on the complaints procedure, which is an integral part of the Human Rights Risk Management System (HRRMS).

5.5 TAURON

The Tauron Group is one of the largest business entities in Poland and one of the largest energy holdings. Tauron Polska Energia SA is the parent company of the TAURON capital group .

According to TAURON representatives, the Human Rights Respect Policy is in force, under which every employee, contractor and business partner is obliged to respect and promote compliance with human rights and ensure their protection, refuse to participate in any events that may constitute a violation of human rights, mobbing and discrimination, as well as unequal treatment.

Respecting human rights is an important element of the TAURON Group's activities. Taking into account the importance of these rights for its stakeholders, in particular the employees, a "Report on respect for human rights in the TAURON Group" has been developed. It contains data and information on the most significant issues related to human rights occurring in the course of business activities. The issues presented include, among others: assessment of the impact of the TAURON Group's activities on human rights and identification of risks related to their compliance. The report also contains information on the undertaken mitigating actions, as well as an action plan for respect for human rights in the TAURON Group. These activities implement the goals indicated in the TAURON Group Strategy under ESG.

The company publishes documents related to human rights issues on its website, including:

1. Policy of Respect for Human Rights in the TAURON Group, [26] which defines the principles of activities and behaviors related to human rights in the TAURON Group, dedicated to all stakeholders of the TAURON Group, in particular Employees, contractors and business partners.
2. Report on respect for human rights in the TAURON Group, [27] the issues of which include, among others: assessment of the impact of the TAURON Group's activities on human rights and identification of risks related to their compliance. The report also contains information on the undertaken mitigating actions, as well as an action plan for respect for human rights in the TAURON Group.

6. Summary

The upcoming CSDDD Directive imposes a number of obligations on entrepreneurs, including counteracting the negative effects of business activities in the field of human rights and the environment. To do this, companies should now identify and assess the actual or potential negative effects of the company's activities on human rights. In this respect, it will be necessary to determine whose and which human rights the company may violate, as well as on whose or which human rights the company may have a negative impact. In particular, these issues should be taken into account by the energy sector, which provides services of strategic importance to respective country. The most important issue that should always be remembered is thatt is the people who constitute that attention and focus should always be on people, and that the greatest threats usually result from unidentified risk.

Notes

1 Directive of the European Parliament and of the Council on corporate due diligence in the field of sustainable development and amending Directive (EU) 2019/1937, link: EUR-Lex - 52022PC0071 - EN - EUR-Lex (europa.eu) (accessed: 05/06/2024)

2 Report of the Special Representative of the UN Secretary-General for Human Rights and Transnational Corporations and other Business Entities, John Ruggie , link: gui dingprinciplesbusinesshr_en.pdf (ohchr.org) (accessed: 05/06/2024)

3 OECD Due Diligence Guidelines for Responsible Business Conduct, link: OECD-Due -Diligence-Guidance-for-Responsible-Business-Conduct.pdf , (accessed: 05/06/2024)

4 Human Rights Assessment , December 2021, link: BSR Human Rights Assessment Brief v4 MB

Human rights impact assessment guidance and toolbox , link: Human rights impact assessment guidance and toolbox | The Danish Institute for Human Rights , (accessed: 05/06/2024)

5 Report of the Special Representative of the UN Secretary-General for Human Rights and Transnational Corporations and other Business Entities, John Ruggie , link: gui dingprinciplesbusinesshr_en.pdf (ohchr.org) , (accessed: 05/06/2024)

6 OECD Guidelines for Multinational Enterprises on Responsible Business Conduct , link: OECD Guidelines for Multinational Enterprises on Responsible Business Conduct (oecd-ilibrary.org) , (accessed: 05/06/2024)

7 OECD Guidelines for Multinational Enterprises on Responsible Business Conduct , link: OECD Guidelines for Multinational Enterprises on Responsible Business Conduct (oecd-ilibrary.org) , (accessed: 05/06/2024)

8 B-Tech, "UN Guiding Principles in the Age of Technology" (September 2020), link: introduction-ungp-age-technology.pdf (ohchr.org) (accessed June 5, 2024)

9 Danish Institute for Human Rights, "Guidelines for assessing the impact of digital technologies on human rights Activities: Introduction", 2020, p.18.

10 The EU may hit the import of photovoltaics from China. The reason is forced labor of Uyghurs | Energetyka24 Is the UK solar industry powered by Uyghur forced labor ? (freedomunited.org) New Report: Uyghur Forced Labor Increased in 2023 (bitterwinter .org) (accessed 05/06/2024)

11 Human Rights Assessment , December 2021, link: BSR Human Rights Assessment Brief v4 MB

Human rights impact assessment guidance and toolbox , link: Human rights impact assessment guidance and toolbox | The Danish Institute for Human Rights , (accessed: 05/06/2024)

12 Danish Institute for Human Rights, "Human Rights Impact Assessment and Legal Advice: Frequently Asked Questions", 2017, p. 28.

13 10 years after Rana Plaza, is Bangladesh's garment industry any safer ? | CNN , (accessed: 05/06/2024)

14 https://group.vattenfall.com/siteassets/corporate/who-we-are/sustainability/doc/human-rights-policy-2024.pdf

15 human-rights-action-plan-vattenfall.pdf

16 https://group.vattenfall.com/siteassets/corporate/who-we are / sustainability / doc / human_rights_assessment_summary.pdf

17 https://group.vattenfall.com/siteassets/corporate/who-we-are/sustainability/doc/vattenfall-human-rights-progress-report-2023.pdf

18 https://group.vattenfall.com/siteassets/corporate/who-we-are/sustainability/doc/vattenfall-modern-slavery-statement-2023.pdf

19 Human rights - Iberdrola (accessed: 05/06/2024)

20 Policy of respect for human rights - Iberdrola (accessed: 05/06/2024)

21 Human Rights Report 2022 - Iberdrola (accessed: 05/06/2024)

22 Human rights | edp.com (access: June 5, 2024)

23 Human and Labor Rights Report 2022 | edp.com (access: June 5, 2024)

24 RWE (access: 05/06/2024)

25 Human Rights Rules of Procedure https://www.rwe.com/-/media/RWE/documents/09-verantwortung-nachhaltigkeit/menschenrechtliche-sorgfaltspflicht/human-rights-rules-of-procedure/human-rights-rules-of-procedure-en.pdf(rwe.com) (accessed: 05/06/2024)

26 Compliance in the TAURON Group | TAURON (access: 05/06/2024)

27 https://www.tauron.pl/-/media/offer-documents/tauron/compliance/report-on-respect-for-human-rights-in-tauron-group.ashx (accessed: June 5, 2024)

From Guidelines to Reality: (Re-)Insurer's Journey through Russian Oil Sanctions

Alexander Leonhardt

1. Short Overview

This paper examines compliance challenges of the (re)insurance industry in the context of international sanctions against Russian crude oil in maritime transportation. The G7 oil price cap on maritime export of Russian crude oil and petroleum products along with the associated ban on offering (re) insurance for the transportation of such oil above the price cap has posed major challenges to (re)insurers. (Re)insurers are supposed to be the actors that contribute significantly to the enforcement of the imposed sanctions, but on the other hand, they are confronted with a considerable lack of information and thus a major compliance risk when (re)insuring maritime transportation of Russian oil.

This paper guides through the requirements of the various sanctions regulations, the published guidelines of the competent authorities such as US Office of Foreign Assets Control (OFAC), UK Office of Financial Sanctions Implementation (OFSI) as well as the European Commission, the challenges of appropriate due diligence and the inherent reputational risks that the (re) insurance industry must navigate. A brief review of recent developments will lead into an examination of the compliance impact of these sanctions on the (re)insurance industry and will result in a practical approach to minimizing risk and meeting compliance requirements, without losing permitted business through over-compliance and de-risking.

This paper is intended to provide a general overview of the main points of consideration for international operators in view of their due-diligence work and to support their compliance efforts.

2. Brief review of recent developments

2.1 Introduction

Immediately after the illegal invasion of Ukraine by the Russian Federation in February 2022, the G7 imposed sanctions against Russian individuals and companies as well as embargoes on certain goods and economic sectors in order to bring about a rethinking of Russia's war of aggression. In particular, pressure was to be exerted on sectors of the economy that generated significant revenues for Russia and therefore served to finance the war. One of these economic sectors was the Russian oil export industry.

In the first six months after the attack on Ukraine, Russia generated revenues of around 158 billion euro from the export of fossil fuels despite falling export volumes. These revenues were exceeding the war costs which are estimated of 100 billion euros in these six months (Myllyvirta, 2022). While Russia was earning over $100 per barrel on its oil sales before the war, prices were rising higher than $140 per barrel in spring of 2022 (U.S. Department of the Treasury's Office of Foreign Assets Control (OFAC), 2023b). Around two thirds of this revenue were coming from oil exports and around half of its total oil exports was going to the EU. The EU has been the main buyer at 85 billion euros, significantly ahead of China with 35 billion euros (Myllyvirta, 2022).

2.2 Import ban and transport ban to third countries

The western industrialized countries USA, Canada, UK and EU, as well as Australia, wanted to cut Russia off from these profits and reduce their dependence on Russian energy, including gradually phasing out of the use of Russian oil. The ban on all imports of Russian seaborne crude oil should deprive Russia of billions of dollars in revenues and thus make it more difficult to finance the war in the Ukraine. The United States of America, the United Kingdom and the European Union announced on 8 March 2022 to transit away from Russian oil and oil products. The USA imposed an immediate and full ban of all imports of Russian Oil whilst the UK and the EU intended to phase out seaborne crude oil by the end of the year 2022. US President Biden said:

> We're moving forward this ban understanding that many of our European allies and partners may not be in a position to join us. But we're working closely with Europe and our partners to develop a long-term strategy to reduce their dependence on Russian energy as well[1].

In June 2022, the Council of the European Union followed up its pledge with action and adopted after lengthy discussion the so-called sixth sanctions package. This included a ban on the direct or indirect purchase, import or transfer into Member States of seaborne crude oil and certain petroleum products originating in or exported from Russia (Regulation (EU) 833/2014, Article 3m) along with a ban on (re)insurance for said purchase, import or transfer. The import ban did cover about 90% of all Russian oil imports into the European Union as up to this point the vast majority has entered the Union by ship (Council of the European Union, 2024). The phase-out of Russian oil was to last 6 months for crude oil (5 December 2022) and 8 months for other refined petroleum products (5 February 2023).

At the same time an additional ban was introduced on maritime transport to third countries and related provision of insurance or reinsurance (Article 3n). To be precise, it should be noted that it is prohibited to provide "finance or financial assistance", which includes all types of insurance and reinsurance (Art. 1 lit. o) Reg. (EU) 833/2014).

2.3 Oil Price Cap

After several analysts predicted that an absolute ban on maritime transport of Russian oil to third countries, and the ban on related services such as (re) insurance, could lead to skyrocketing global oil prices and intensify global inflationary pressure, a coalition consisting of Australia, Canada, the EU, Japan, the UK, and the US, jointly decided in September 2022 to undertake counteracting measures to mitigate these consequences: The so-called Oil Price Cap.

Analysts at Barclays say that disrupting Russia's seaborne crude exports could push oil prices above $200 a barrel. The insurance ban "would have further-reaching consequences for the oil market than the EU oil embargo," Commerzbank analyst Carsten Fritsch told the AFP wire service[2].

The oil price cap is an exception to the previously stated ban on the maritime transportation of crude oil and petroleum products with Russian origin to third countries. The prohibition shall not apply if the traded products were purchased at a price below the price cap previously set by the so-called Price Cap Coalition.

At first glance, the oil price cap is intended to serve two seemingly opposing goals:

The exemption shall limit Russia's oil revenues and therefore prevent Russia from financing its war in Ukraine. At the same time, the Cap is intended to ensure that the global market continues to be supplied with oil and that energy prices remain stable. Not only does this ensure to keep energy costs down for consumers and businesses around the world, but also to allow economically weaker nations to build up pressure in price negotiations with Russia and thus ensure continued access to oil (OFAC, 2023b).

3. Why and how is enforcement possible?

Historically, the world's most important players in the marine insurance market are based in the countries of the Oil Price Coalition. European and British companies alone handle 85 to 90 % of the financing, insurance, and reinsurance of maritime transportation of Russian crude oil (Wessel, 2022).

Companies based in Coalition countries have historically accounted for around 90 percent of the market for relevant maritime insurance products and reinsurance. Traders, brokers, and importers depend on these services to trade, and vessel owners rely on insurance to protect their ships. Moreover, almost all ports and major canals require ships to carry protection and indemnity (P&I) insurance[3].

That enforcement of the oil price cap can work by non-granting insurance cover was evident when the oil price cap came into force in December 2022, as continuously oil tankers piled up on the Bosporus because the Turkish authorities blocked the passage through Turkish waters for ships without appropriate insurance cover (Wilson, 2022). In the context of international sanctions, Turkey had tightened its requirements for transit through its waters in order to mitigate environmental and safety risks and requested proof of valid and appropriate maritime insurance cover. The same does also apply to other waterways that are important for the global economy, such as the Suez Canal, which does not allow uninsured ships to transit the Canal.

Insurance is one of the key services that enables the movement of oil by sea, particularly protection and indemnity (P&I) insurance which relates to third-party liability claims – the UK is a global leader in the provision of P&I cover, writing 60% of the global cover written by the International Group of the P&I clubs[4].

The insurance industry is therefore one of the most important levers for the implementation and enforcement of the oil price cap.

4. Area of conflict – Disparity in information

Although (re)insurers are supposed to contribute significantly to the enforcement of the imposed sanctions, they are confronted with a considerable lack of information and thus a major compliance risk when (re)insuring the supposedly permissible maritime transportation of Russian oil. OFAC, OFSI and the EU Commission have been extremely open to dialog with all economic operators involved in order to understand the individual problems and uncertainties as well as to support them in achieving appropriate compliance. All three sanctions authorities thus offer some sort of exculpation. The OFAC tries to tackle the challenging situation of certain market actors such as (re-)insurers by providing clearer framework and offering a so called "safe harbour". Actors following certain conditions and processes will not be prosecuted. The EU follows this approach and EU operators will not be considered as in breach of the price cap when certain conditions have been met[5].

All three authorities are in line that they do not take enforcement action against market actors in case of falsified attestation (provided that the conditions set have been met) and that they intend to go after market actors acting in bad faith and with intent. OFAC made clear throughout its guidance documents that the absolute focus will be on providers knowingly violating or evading the oil price cap and that actors that comply in good faith with the laid down requirements and inadvertently violate for instance due to falsified or erroneous records by illicit actors will not be subject to a sanctions enforcement action by OFAC (OFAC, 2023a). The EU Commission has also emphasized the same.

In cases when an EU operator without direct access to price information reasonably relies on an attestation, after performing appropriate due diligence, and such an attestation was falsified or provided by illegitimate actors, the EU operator would not be considered in breach of the price cap provided it acted in good faith[6].

However, it should be noted that while OFAC provides both guidance and enforcement from a single source, in the EU there is at least the possibility of different implementation and interpretation of the regulation between the guidance of the EU Commission as non-binding soft law and the implementation of the sanctions provisions in the individual member states.

The three sanctions authorities provide opportunities for exculpation but focus on the individual case and on ambiguous wording such as "reasonable cause". In addition, they do request that the market participants have undertaken appropriate due diligence in each individual case (Office of Financial Sanctions Implementation HM Treasury (OFSI), 2024). The European Commission states that "EU operators should exercise appropriate due diligence in assessing the origin of the oil and should rely on documentation at their disposal to determine the origin of the oil, which may include certificates of origin" (European Commission, 2023b, question 2).

The wording "at their disposal" makes it apparent that different market participants have different levels of knowledge and different ways of accessing information. The three major competent authorities have identified that prerequisites can differ significantly between individual market participants. A so-called tier system was therefore introduced in September 2022 by the OFAC (adopted later by the UK and EU) to do justice to this disparity in information among the participants. The expected level of conducted due diligence should henceforth be determined on the basis of a three-tier classification, which is based on the respective access of each participant to the actual price information.

Insurers and reinsurers were jointly categorized as tier three actors which were defined as actors who do not regularly have direct access to price information in the ordinary course of business. No differentiation was made between insurer and reinsurer, and both were expected to receive attestation from tier one or tier two actors regarding compliance with the price cap. The attestation could be in form of a signed attestation stating compliance with the oil price cap or as contractual obligation in the reviewed insurance policy. The attestation could be valid for multiple instances of supply or delivery.

OFAC stated in its November 2022 Guidance Update that the sufficient documentation required for the safe harbor could be in form of a sanctions exclusion clause written into the (re-)insurance contracts or through the use of clauses that exclude coverage for activities related to the maritime transport of Russian oil purchased above the price cap. The most recent Industry Guidance of OFSI (OFSI, 2024) refer to Lloyds Market Association 3100, LMA3100A or LMA3200 as examples of sufficient sanctions clauses:

LMA3100A

No (re)insurer shall be deemed to provide cover and no (re)insurer shall be liable to pay any claim or provide any benefit hereunder to the extent that the provision of such cover, payment of such claim or provision of such benefit would expose that (re)insurer to any sanction, prohibition or restriction under United Nations resolutions or the trade or economic sanctions, laws or regulations of the European Union, United Kingdom or United States of America.

The different roles of insurers and reinsurers were subsequently taken into account and a distinction was introduced. Whilst the OFAC kept their joint classification as tier three but introduced different expectations regarding documentation, did the EU and UK opt for a more visual differentiation by establishing tier 3A and tier 3B in February 2024. Insurers and P&I Clubs were amongst other tier 3A actors whilst reinsurers were moved to tier 3B. The reliance on only a sanction exclusion clause is henceforth only sufficient for reinsurers. Insurers on the other hand require either an attestation or a contractual clause excluding coverage for activities related to the maritime transport of Russian oil or petroleum products purchased above the price cap. At the same time, the guidance was amended to the effect that attestations have to be provided on a per-voyage basis and that an annual attestation no longer will be seen as sufficient.

5. Requirements regarding "appropriate" Due Diligence

Over time, the Price Cap Coalition and several sanctions authorities have jointly issued a series of Advisories, Guidances and FAQs related to the export ban and the oil price cap to an unprecedented level of coordination among each other. The coalition tries by publishing guidance documents to promote responsible practices enabling industry stakeholders to reduce risks whilst disrupting sanctioned trade and ensuring safe flow of oil.

5.1 Customized Sanctions Compliance Programme (SCP)

EU operators are required to customize due diligence and to develop and implement a sanctions compliance programme based on the individual business model, business sector, geographic areas of operations and specificities and related risk-assessment of the own business and the related risk exposure regarding customers, business partners and staff (European Commission, 2023a). The EU Commission did recommend in the Q&A on due diligence for business with Iran from 2020 a risk-based approach in terms of due diligence (European Commission, 2020). The OFAC did also propose a risk-based Sanctions Compliance Programme (SCP) already in 2019 in its "Framework for OFAC Compliance Commitments":

While each risk-based SCP will vary depending on a variety of factors – including the company's size and sophistication, products and services, customers and counterparties, geographic locations – each program should be predicated on and incorporate at least five essential components of compliance: (1) management commitment; (2) risk assessment; (3) internal controls; (4) testing and auditing; and (5) training[7].

5.2 Due Diligence Measures

The Price Cap Coalition has jointly published an advisory in October 2023 outlining best practices for the maritime oil industry. Insurers and reinsurers are identified among others as actors in this sector. The advisory recommends undertaking "appropriate" due diligence in order to support enhanced compliance with the oil price cap (Price Cap Coalition, 2023).

There is no one-size-fits-all model of due diligence. It may depend – and be calibrated accordingly – on the business specificities and the related risk exposure. It is for each operator to develop, implement, and routinely update an EU sanctions compliance programme that reflects their individual business models, geographic and sectoral areas of operations and related risk assessment[8].

In order to do so operators have to identify, assess and understand the possible risks of sanctions exposure that are most relevant for the own business activity and operational model (1 - **risk assessment**).

A fundamental element of a sound SCP is the assessment of specific clients, products, services, and geographic locations in order to determine potential

OFAC sanctions risk. The purpose of a risk assessment is to identify inherent risks in order to inform risk-based decisions and controls[9].

Besides mapping out threats and vulnerabilities, it is recommended to design and implement mitigating measures in order to reduce the risks inherent with the own relationships and business activities (2 - **mitigating measures**).

Furthermore, staff training, sanctions awareness amongst the staff and involvement of senior management (tone from the top) has to be ensured (3 - **training and awareness**). Legal frameworks and guidance documents are constantly being updated. Legal monitoring is therefore a general due diligence obligation to ensure knowledge and awareness of sanctions programmes. Controls shall be implemented to test the effective functioning of the sanctions compliance programme. The internal risk management procedures, risk analysis, mitigating measures and training shall regularly be updated in line with the latest sanctions developments and most recent sanctions legislation (4 - **testing and updating**).

An integral component of each sanction compliance program is the analysis of the involved parties in your business such as customer, supplier or intermediaries. It is necessary to know your new and existing counterparties (5 - **know your counterparties**). Besides identification and verification of the involved parties, one shall (6) **screen against sanction lists** and check the beneficial ownership and control structure (7 - **check ownership and control**) and stay alert for suspicious indicators such as recent mergers, complex corporate or trust structures as well as the reduction and change of beneficial ownership. In addition, one shall take into account the type, purpose and anticipated activity, the nature and duration of the relationship with the partner and the supervisory regime of the jurisdiction in which the partner is licensed.

It is advisable to (8) **obtain a sanctions statement** by the business partner stating sanctions compliance and how compliance is ensured. A sanctions statement can also be incorporated in the underlying contract alongside a sanction clause (see LMA3100A above). Additional (9) **contractual safeguards** could be clauses with third-country business partners prohibiting further re-exports or the introduction of provisions destined to ensure that any imported or exported goods are not covered by the sanctions restrictions (European Union, 2022).

Another crucial part of required due diligence is (10) **transaction monitoring:** Scrutinize transactions for irregular payment methods, amounts, or frequencies that could indicate circumvention attempts as well as the flow of money.

Operators are required to be (11) **vigilant for red flags** regarding circumvention such as:

- ships that have undergone numerous administrative changes
- dealing with intermediary companies (e.g. management companies, traders, brokerages, etc.) that conceal their beneficial ownership or otherwise engage in unusually opaque practices
- the use of "circumvention hubs" or irregular routes
- business partners that are founded after the start of the Russian war of aggression or after the announcement of the oil sanctions
- business partners in the supply chain that deny access to further information in the context of the implementation of the price cap
- market assessments indicating that Russian oil prices exceed the price cap

(12) **Adverse media investigation** is seen as another element to due diligence. Adverse media investigations refer to searches on the internet and news (media investigations) to find evidence that a contractual counterpart, even if not designated (so it passes the screening against the sanctions list), is actually controlled by a designated person[10].

6. Additional Areas of conflict

The principles of appropriate due diligence, albeit scattered, have been established for a number of years and the sanctions authorities grant exculpation if due diligence is sufficiently complied with. Nevertheless, this does not mean that insurers and reinsurers do not expose themselves to liability risks if they just include the necessary clauses and obtain information. International oil sanctions are highly complex and constantly changing.

6.1 Growing Dark Fleet

Western insurance companies are increasingly concerned that the price cap on Russian oil is not working. The measure appears to be increasingly difficult to enforce, according to an industry statement by the International Group of P&I Clubs on questions from the UK parliament on the effectiveness of the oil price cap. The International Group's statement carries particular weight as it is an insurance association comprising those twelve ship liability insurers that offer ship liability insurance to shipowners of around 87% of global maritime tonnage. The Insurance Association is concerned that not only the current oil price cap (OPC) is not working, but that its current design creates incentives to evade a G7 nexus, effectively undermining the oil price cap.

This growth in so-called parallel markets is a direct consequence of the introduction of a regime that imposes severe restrictions and compliance obligations on entities that operate within the G7 while allowing entities outside the G7 the freedom to operate legitimately, provided there is no G7 nexus. The OPC, therefore, appears increasingly unenforceable as more ships and associated services move into this parallel trade. […] The International Group is concerned that increasing responsibility and obligations on companies in the G7 coalition will result in a further migration of trade activities and ancillary services outside of the G7. We estimate around 800 tankers have already left the International Group Clubs as a direct result of the introduction of the OPC. This will in effect limit the enforcement and effectiveness of the OPC[11].

The parallel fleet or also called dark or shadow fleet consists of old, questionably maintained tankers which are often underinsured or even uninsured. The Kyev School of Economics (KSE) has determined that the volume share of Russian crude oil exports transported by shadow fleet vessels increased from 56% in 2023 to 71% in Q4 2024. At the same time, the volume share of Russian seaborne crude oil exports transported by International Group P&I insurance decreased from 41% in 2023 to 27% in Q4 2024. (Hilgenstock, 2024)

As the purchase and operation of a dark fleet is associated with significant costs, at least this is seen as a partial success by the Price Cap Coalition, as it reduces the revenue that can be used for the war in Ukraine. Nonetheless, the sanctions authorities will consider new or enhanced measures to keep the enforcement level high by extending the effectiveness of the sanctions to other participants and will try to demotivate tankers from moving away from western (re-)insurance and therefore out of an oil price cap nexus.

6.2 Falsified Attestations

The Price Cap Coalition established that market assessments indicating that Russian oil prices exceed the price cap are seen as possible red flag. When taking for instance a closer look at the Eastern Siberia-Pacific Ocean oil (ESPO) blend crude price exported from Russian pacific port of Kozmino, the price cap and its enforcement has to be marked with question marks. While the average price of Urals grade oil fell significantly below the set price cap of 60 USD in the weeks immediately after the cap came into force in December 2022, ESPO, however, continued to be sold above the price cap (Kennedy, 2023, chapter 5, para 2). After a temporary decline of ships with western insurance in Kozmino, the first ships with Western insurance were already taking on Russian oil in December, as they were assured that the cargo was not priced above the price cap. In addition to the switch from conventional tankers with western insurance to an increasing shadow fleet, one conceivable reason for conspicuously high prices is "attestation fraud" meaning the provision of falsified price attestations in order to enable the use of western insurance.

There has been an overreliance on the attestation process. The attestation is a flawed regime which potentially exposes both the P&I Club and a shipowner, operator, charterer to a breach of the OPC. The so-called Tier 1 attestation is merely a self-declaration signed by traders that the sale price of oil or oil products comply with the price cap. Our concern has always been that the G7 coalition partners have failed to direct sufficient attention on Tier 1 traders[12].

However, a high price of Urals (leaving Russian ports in the Baltic Sea and Black Sea) is also likely to cause the sanctions authorities more and more discomfort. As the US news portal Bloomberg reports, Russia's oil revenues more than doubled in April 2024 compared to the previous year. Bloomberg calculated an average price of USD 75 for Urals, which is USD 15 above the set price cap (Nightingale and Julian, 2024). Fluctuating Urals and ESPO crudes rates have induced the European Commission to issue a Compliance

Alert in May 2024 reminding EU operators to adjust due diligence requirements as necessary to take into account the fluctuation of global oil prices and developing deceptive practices (European Commission, 2024b).

It seems that the "carte blanche" that the competent sanctions authorities have given through their guidelines (i.e. safe harbor provided by OFAC) could be in contradiction to the obvious nature of sanction violations (persistently too high price level). Against this backdrop, a seemingly easy achievable exculpation might not be a viable model for the future, and exculpation might inevitably has to be tightened up or even discontinued especially for tier 1 and tier 2 actors.

While appropriate due diligence shall prevent liability in case of a sanctions breach, it might not prevent reputational damage. Tankers shipping Russian oil with a price cap attestation and later are identified as in breach of the oil price cap might leave oily stains on the otherwise white vest of (re-)insurers.

7. Closing Remarks

As stated, the oil price cap is intended to serve two seemingly opposing goals: Hinder Russia significantly from generating revenues out of oil exports and thus prevent Russia from financing its war in Ukraine while ensuring a steady global energy supply especially for weaker nations.

Average oil prices above the price cap over a longer period of time can represent a red flag, which can be an indicator of circumvention patterns and that price cap compliance is limited or even that the price cap mechanism itself is insufficient and failing. If the effectiveness of the sanction measures remains questionable, it can be assumed that responsibility for monitoring and enforcing sanctions will increase along the supply chain. The expected level of vigilance and commitment from market participants involved in the transportation of oil will be noticeably increased. It can be assumed that the members of the Oil Price Coalition will gradually sharpen their focus and thus also increase the requirements for insurance and reinsurance.

This will have to be followed by measures to tackle the growing dark fleet, such as tightening and extending insurance requirements for tankers even just for driving through G7 and EU territorial waters. Denmark for instance did already urge the EU Commission to target Russian oil tankers without western insurance in general (Reuters, 2023).

At this point in time, compliance with appropriate due diligence, in accordance with the requirements that have existed and should been practiced by all market participants for years, should be absolutely sufficient. For insurers and reinsurers, this means that they can rely on their contractual clauses. However, every market participant must be aware that appropriate due diligence cannot be limited to a simple attestation or contractual clause. The same basic idea applies here as in the Ownership and Control check: it is not sufficient to simply add up shares and check whether the total share is above 50%, but market participants are expected to look beyond the end of their noses in order to identify suspicious contexts.

General recommendations are to stay vigilant, request self-declarations along the supply chain, re-evaluate the own Sanctions Compliance Programme and strengthen the own due diligence efforts. One should join roundtables, attend conferences, do network and exchange with colleagues from the sector as well as try to follow each update by any relevant sanction authority. Contractual partners who urge to continue doing business with the transportation of Russian oil should be critically scrutinized. This does not mean a general de-risking, over-compliance or exclusion of this kind of business. As oil transportation can be legally permissible (provided the price cap is observed), this would be merely a business policy decision that could be driven, for example, by a potential reputational risk. Nevertheless, the respective contractual partner should be checked. Is it a European company or a company from countries that are increasingly suspected of circumventing sanctions, such as Kazakhstan, the UAE or Turkey? Or are they contractual partners from countries that have an openly critical attitude towards international sanctions, such as China?

Taking into consideration that there are efforts in the EU to sanction soon Russian Liquefied Natural Gas (LNG), it is especially important to have a solid sanctions compliance programme in place.

OFAC, OFSI and the EU Commission are united in their efforts to strengthen enforcement and avoid circumvention. Accordingly, a relaxation is not to be expected in the near future, which is why affected economic actors should now prepare themselves for a tightening sanctions situation in order to be able to react quickly and appropriately. An alternative oil sanctions strategy might be more disruptive for all.

Notes

1 (U.S. President Biden, 2022)
2 (Wessel, 2022)
3 (OFAC, 2023b, para 3)
4 (Henty, 2023, para 4)
5 Actions by natural or legal persons, entities or bodies shall not give rise to liability of any kind on their part, if they did not know, and had no reasonable cause to suspect, that their actions would infringe the measures set out in this Regulation, art. 10 Council Regulation (EU) No 833/2014.
6 (European Commission, 2024a, question 35a)
7 (OFAC, 2019, p. 1)
8 (European Commission, 2023a, question 4)
9 (OFAC, 2019, p. 4)
10 (European Commission, 2023a, question 2)
11 (International Group of P&I Clubs (IG), 2024, question 1)
12 (IG, 2023)

Bibliography

Council of the European Union. (2024, May 27). *EU sanctions against Russia explained.* https://www.consilium.europa.eu/en/policies/sanctions/restrictive-measures-against-russia-over-ukraine/sanctions-against-russia-explained/

European Commission. (2020, January). *Q&A Due Diligence on Restrictive Measures*

For Eu Businesses Dealing with Iran. https://finance.ec.europa.eu/system/files/2020-01/faqs-restrictive-measures-iran_en.pdf

European Commission. (2023a, June 30). *Frequently asked questions on circumvention and due diligence concerning sanctions adopted following Russia's military aggression against Ukraine and Belarus' involvement in it.* https://finance.ec.europa.eu/publications/circumvention-and-due-diligence_en

European Commission. (2023b, August 2). *Frequently asked questions on oil imports concerning sanctions adopted following Russia's military aggression against Ukraine.* https://finance.ec.europa.eu/publications/oil-imports_en

European Commission. (2024a, January 26). *Guidance on oil price cap.* https://finance.ec.europa.eu/publications/oil-price-cap_en

European Commission. (2024b, May 17). *Russian Oil Price Cap (OPC) Compliance Alert.* https://finance.ec.europa.eu/document/download/29691a23-6f42-4c52-bc11-f3dd7e7d712b_en?filename=240517-alert-compliance-oil-price-caps_en.pdf

European Union. (2022, April 1). *Notice to economic operators, importers and exporters (2022/C 145 I/01).* https://eur-lex.europa.eu/legal-content/EN/TXT/HTML/?uri=CELEX:52022XC0401(04)

Henty, P. (2023, February). *Sanctions Update: EU and UK Price Caps to hit Insurers and other Sectors.* Beale&Co. https://beale-law.com/article/sanctions-update-eu-and-uk-price-caps-to-hit-insurers-and-other-sectors/

Hilgenstock, B. (2024, April 18). *Effectiveness of Energy Sanctions & Questions of Corporate Responsibility.* [unpublished conference presentation] Sanctions in Insurance, London, United Kingdom.

International Group of P&I Clubs. (2024, March). *Written evidence submitted by International Group of P&I Clubs.* https://committees.parliament.uk/writtenevidence/129266/html/

Kennedy, C. (2023, August 23). Measuring the Shadows - Moscow's Strategies for Evading Oil Sanctions and How to Stop them from Succeeding. *Navigating Russia. https://navigatingrussia.substack.com/p/measuring-the-shadows#%C2%A7chapter-the-kozmino-mystery-how-did-mainstream-compliant-fleet-tankers-end-up-transporting-russian-oil-priced-above-the-cap*

Myllyvirta, L. (2022, September 6). *Financing Putin's war: Fossil fuel exports from Russia in the first six months of the invasion of Ukraine.* Centre for Research on Energy and Clean Air. https://energyandcleanair.org/wp/wp-content/uploads/2022/09/Final_-Financing-Putins-war_-Fossil-fuel-exports-from-Russia-in-the-first-six-months-of-the-invasion-of-Ukraine.pdf

Nightingale, A., & Lee, Julian. (2024, April 10). Russian Oil Is Once Again Trading Far Above the G-7's Price Cap Everywhere. *Bloomberg.* https://www.bloomberg.com/news/articles/2024-04-10/russian-oil-is-once-again-trading-far-above-the-g-7-s-price-cap-everywhere

Office of Financial Sanctions Implementation HM Treasury. (2024, May 24). *UK Maritime Services Band and Oil Price Cap – Industry Guidance.* https://assets.publishing.service.gov.uk/media/66507f5a2eb55b89628fc4b1/OFSI_OPC_Guidance_-_24_May_2024.pdf

Price Cap Coalition. (2023, October 12). *Price Cap Coalition Advisory for the Maritime Oil Industry and Related Sectors - Best Practices in Response to Recent Developments in the Maritime Oil Trade. https://ofac.treasury.gov/media/932201/download?inline*

Reuters. (2023, November 15). Russian oil tankers not targeted in EU sanctions proposal -EU diplomats. *Reuters.* https://www.reuters.com/markets/commodities/denmark-could-block-russian-oil-tankers-reaching-markets-ft-2023-11-15/

U.S. Department of the Treasury's Office of Foreign Assets Control. (2019, May 2). *A Framework for OFAC Compliance Commitments.* https://ofac.treasury.gov/media/16331/download?inline

U.S. Department of the Treasury's Office of Foreign Assets Control. (2023a, February 3). *OFAC Guidance on Implementation of the Price Cap Policy for Crude Oil and Petroleum Products of Russian Federation Origin.* https://ofac.treasury.gov/media/931036/download?inline

U.S. Department of the Treasury's Office of Foreign Assets Control. (2023b, May 18). *The Price Cap on Russian Oil: A Progress Report.* https://home.treasury.gov/news/featured-stories/the-price-cap-on-russian-oil-a-progress-report

U.S. President Biden, J. (2022, March 8). *Remarks by President Biden Announcing U.S. Ban on Imports of Russian Oil, Liquefied Natural Gas, and Coal.* https://it.usembassy.gov/remarks-by-president-biden-announcing-u-s-ban-on-imports-of-russian-oil-liquefied-natural-gas-and-coal/

Wessel, D. (2022, July 5). The story behind the proposed price cap on Russian oil. *Brookings Institution.* https://www.brookings.edu/articles/the-story-behind-the-proposed-price-cap-on-russian-oil/

Wilson, T. (2022, December 6). How the G7's oil price cap blocked the Bosphorus. *Financial Times.* https://www.ft.com/content/dc40a88f-7d20-4a17-a37c-332f35b65942

Chapter 7

Whistleblowing and Internal Investigations

The Role of Whistleblowing in Integrated Governance

Andrew Samuels

1. Introduction

In 2024 whistleblowing remains one of the most misunderstood, contentious, and underutilised tools for enabling and protecting organisations to operate efficiently and effectively.

This article looks at the role that whistleblowing plays within an integrated governance framework. Both integrated governance and whistleblowing in an integrated governance model could both have lengthy books written about them. In this article I will give readers an introduction to both based on my work on the International Standards Organisation (ISO) work I have been involved in for nearly 8 years via ISO TC309[1] along with my commercial experience globally in this field for well over a decade.

The 2023 Yearbook for Global Ethics, Compliance & Integrity provides good introductions and information on both ISO37000 Governance of Organisations and ISO37002 Whistleblowing Management Systems, ISO standards which I will reference in this article as a part of ISO TC309, so rather than repeat in detail what has been so well written previously, I will focus on the operational aspects integrated governance and the specific role of whistleblowing within this model, outlining the benefits, opportunities and challenges associated with this approach, whilst looking at the current environment in the EU and abroad to bring context to the reasons and benefits of this approach.

2. Integrated Governance

Governance, in the context of ISO TC309, refers to the systems and processes that ensure the overall direction, control, and accountability of an organisation. Effective governance involves establishing policies, practices, and procedures that guide an organisation towards achieving its objectives while maintaining ethical standards and compliance with laws and regulations.

Integrated governance implies that these elements are not managed in isolation but are interwoven into the fabric of the organisation's strategic and operational activities.

The ISOTC309 Strategic Plan outlines that "Integrated governance systems include the use of integrated governance frameworks that enable the governing groups the management functions and systems necessary for governance (e.g. risk, compliance) are enabled to work effectively together" and "Effective governance frameworks include effective compliance, whistleblowing, anti-bribery, risk management systems, amongst others"[2].

2.1 Benefits of Integrated Governance

2.1.1 Enhanced Risk Management

By aligning compliance activities with governance frameworks, organisations can better identify and mitigate risks. This proactive approach to risk management ensures that potential issues are addressed before they escalate.[3]

2.1.2 Improved Efficiency

Integrated systems reduce duplication of efforts and streamline processes. This leads to more efficient use of resources and better alignment of activities with organisational goals.

2.1.3 Strengthened Organisational Culture

An integrated approach fosters a culture of accountability, transparency, and ethical behaviour. It promotes a shared understanding of the importance of compliance and governance across all levels of the organisation.

2.1.4 Regulatory Confidence

Organisations with robust integrated governance and compliance systems are more likely to meet regulatory expectations. This builds confidence among regulators, stakeholders, and the public.[4]

2.1.5 Improved Management Information Insights:

A more aligned collation and utilisation of internal and external data can provide early threat detection to mitigate risks and provide trend analysis and market insights that can deliver insights on opportunities.[5]

2.2 High Level Integrated Governance Framework

The four key areas that I focus on when building integrated solutions are 1) Policy Frameworks, 2) Technology and Data, 3) Capability and Capacity, 4) Insights and Continual Improvement

In line with ISO37000, purpose remains at the core of this model (See below model). By understanding an organisation's purpose and objectives, aligning these with key performance indicators (KPI's) and operations performance indicators (OPI's), standard and streamlined processes can be developed. Simplified processes remove vulnerability and make it easier to focus on and strengthen controls.

2.2.1 Policy Frameworks

Aligning and integrating a policy framework provides a cohesive system designed to streamline decision-making, policy implementation, and management across various levels and sectors of organisations. This approach enables the harmonisation of policies, processes, and practices to ensure consistency, efficiency, and transparency. From a governance perspective, an integrated policy framework facilitates better coordination amongst organisational entities, reducing redundancies and improving resource allocation.

Aligning organisational policies leads to coherence that makes engagement by stakeholders simpler and more effective through consistent use of language, format, access, style. It also provides an opportunity to ensure ongoing alignment to an organisations purpose and objectives.

Moreover, a unified framework supports accountability and transparency. With standardised procedures and clear lines of responsibility, it becomes easier to track and monitor progress, measure outcomes, measure the performance of individuals and functions against like for like objectives.

These frameworks promote inclusivity and stakeholder engagement. By creating a structured environment for participation, organisations can involve diverse groups in the decision-making process, ensuring that policies reflect the needs and aspirations of all stakeholders.

2.2.2 Technology and Data

Integrating systems and data supports simplified processes, reduces the costs of running, maintaining and upgrading systems, and reduces the volume of controls required to protect the integrity of data and systems.

From a user perspective and based on clearly defined roles within systems, employees and other stakeholders have easier access to policies, information and training. This also ensures via the right controls and document management that redundant or out of date materials aren't available or accessible which keeps all users up to date with the latest details.

Taking a less is more approach, from a data perspective utilising common approved sources of internal and external data make comparable like for like reporting easier to achieve which in turn makes reporting against objectives more straight forward. Insights into risk and opportunities are quicker to identify and are more relevant to the context of the organisation.

The use of standard reports with a regular cadence rather than many ad hoc reports at varying times helps to maintain a focus on performance from an historic perspective, and to gain insights into opportunities based on trend analysis over time, and via use of external data sources that are relevant to the organisation's context. Ad hoc reports can be utilised where there is a need for deeper insights as an example and the capability remains important, however many organisations struggle with too much data which can impact decision making.[6]

2.2.3 Capability and Capacity

Simplified processes and controls require less capacity to manage, maintain and update. This in turn is supports the ability to better define capability requirements for both people and systems to support the organisation's purpose and objectives.

Clearly defined roles and responsibilities that are aligned to purpose and objectives supported by KPI's and OPI's enable a better and stronger balance of resources required to lead, manage, and operate with the organisations integrated governance framework.

Supported by a technology ecosystem with clearly defined and implemented user roles, data that is consistent, like for like, and timely, and with policies supported by controls and processes that have commonality in application of language, style, and objectives, human resources, especially in smaller organisations, can cover multiple functions

2.2.4 Insights and Continuous Improvement

Data and insights, though interconnected, differ significantly in their nature and utility. Data represents raw, unprocessed facts and figures. It is the foundational material collected from various sources like sensors, surveys, transactions, or digital interactions. Insights, on the other hand, emerge from the synthesis of data with human experience, context, and analytical thinking. They are the meaningful understandings or actionable knowledge derived from analysing data. Insights provide deeper comprehension and foresight, enabling informed decision-making.

3. The Role of Whistleblowing in Integrated Governance

Whistleblowing has become an increasingly important mechanism in organisational governance frameworks, particularly in enhancing transparency, accountability, and ethical behaviour. Within an integrated governance framework, whistleblowing serves critical roles in governance, risk management,

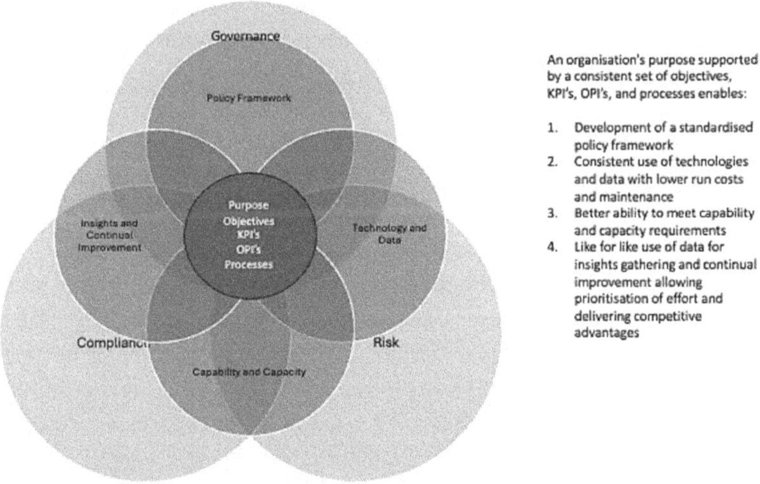

Figure 1 Organisation of Integrated Governance

and compliance (GRC). This essay explores the distinct and interconnected roles whistleblowing plays in these three areas, emphasising its contribution to a robust and ethical organisational environment.

3.1 Whistleblowing and Governance

Governance in any organisation refers to the structures and processes designed to ensure accountability, transparency, responsiveness, rule of law, stability, equity, and inclusiveness. Whistleblowing plays a pivotal role in enhancing these governance attributes by providing a channel for uncovering and addressing unethical or illegal activities that may otherwise remain hidden.

Whistleblowing mechanisms are essential in fostering accountability and transparency within organisations. By enabling employees and other stakeholders to report misconduct anonymously, organisations can uncover issues such as fraud, corruption, and other unethical practices that might otherwise be concealed. The presence of a whistleblowing system signals to employees that the organisation values integrity and is committed to addressing wrongdoing, thus promoting a culture of accountability.

When employees believe they can report issues without fear of retaliation, they are more likely to come forward with information that can be critical for decision-makers. This, in turn, enhances the transparency of operations, as stakeholders, including regulators and shareholders, gain insights into potential issues and the steps taken to resolve them. Consequently, the organisation's governance framework is strengthened, as transparency and accountability are key pillars of good governance.

Furthermore, the effective handling of whistleblower reports can reinforce the organisation's commitment to ethical practices. When whistleblowers see that their concerns are taken seriously and addressed appropriately, it reinforces their trust in the organisation's governance structures. Over time, this can lead to a more ethically conscious workforce, where employees feel empowered to speak up and take responsibility for upholding the organisation's values.

3.2 Strengthening Governance Structures

The integration of whistleblowing into governance frameworks also necessitates the establishment of robust procedures and protections for whistleblowers. This includes clear policies outlining how reports are handled, assurances of confidentiality, and protections against retaliation. These structures not only support whistleblowers but also enhance the overall governance framework by ensuring that there are systematic approaches to dealing with misconduct.

By embedding whistleblowing procedures into governance frameworks, organisations can ensure that they are prepared to respond to issues effectively and transparently. This proactive approach can prevent minor issues from escalating into major scandals, thereby protecting the organisation's reputation and ensuring its long-term sustainability.

3.3 Whistleblowing and Risk Management

Risk management involves identifying, assessing, and prioritising risks followed by coordinated efforts to minimise, monitor, and control the probability or impact of unfortunate events. Whistleblowing plays a crucial role in the risk management processes of an organisation by acting as an early warning system and contributing to risk mitigation strategies.

3.3.1 Early Detection of Risks

One of the primary roles of whistleblowing in risk management is the early detection of risks. Whistleblowers often have access to information that is not readily available to external auditors or senior management. By reporting issues such as financial discrepancies, safety violations, or regulatory breaches, whistleblowers provide critical information that can prevent potential risks from escalating.

Early detection allows organisations to address problems before they become significant threats. For example, identifying and addressing financial mismanagement early can prevent substantial financial losses. Similarly, reporting safety violations can avert accidents and protect the well-being of employees and customers. Thus, whistleblowing is an integral part of an organisation's risk management strategy, helping to identify and mitigate risks promptly.

3.3.2 Enhancing Risk Assessment Processes

Whistleblowing also enhances the effectiveness of risk assessment processes. By providing firsthand accounts of potential risks and issues, whistleblowers contribute valuable insights that can be incorporated into risk assessments.

This ensures that risk assessments are based on comprehensive and accurate information, leading to more effective risk management strategies.

Furthermore, the existence of a whistleblowing mechanism can influence the organisation's risk culture. When employees know that they can report concerns safely and that their reports will be taken seriously, they are more likely to be vigilant and proactive in identifying potential risks. This collective vigilance can improve the overall risk profile of the organisation.

3.3.3 Supporting a Risk-Aware Culture

Whistleblowing supports the development of a risk-aware culture within an organisation. By encouraging employees to report risks and issues, organisations can foster an environment where risk management is everyone's responsibility. This collective approach to risk management ensures that potential issues are identified and addressed at all levels of the organisation.

A risk-aware culture also involves regular training and communication about the importance of risk management and the role of whistleblowing. When employees are aware of the risks associated with their roles and the channels available for reporting concerns, they are more likely to act in ways that mitigate risks. This proactive approach to risk management can lead to a more resilient organisation capable of navigating challenges effectively.

3.4 Whistleblowing and Compliance

Compliance refers to adhering to laws, regulations, standards, and ethical practices relevant to an organisation's operations. Whistleblowing is a critical component of compliance frameworks, as it helps ensure that organisations adhere to legal and regulatory requirements and maintain ethical standards.

3.4.1 Ensuring Legal and Regulatory Compliance

Whistleblowing mechanisms are essential for ensuring that organisations comply with legal and regulatory requirements. Employees who are aware of non-compliance issues, such as violations of labour laws, environmental regulations, or financial reporting standards, can report these concerns through whistleblowing channels. This enables organisations to address non-compliance issues before they result in legal penalties or reputational damage.

By providing a means for employees to report non-compliance confidentially, organisations can gain insights into potential legal and regulatory breaches that might not be visible through regular audits or inspections. Addressing these issues promptly ensures that the organisation remains in good standing with regulators and avoids the consequences of non-compliance.

3.4.2 Enhancing Internal Controls

Whistleblowing also contributes to the enhancement of internal controls within an organisation. Internal controls are processes designed to provide reasonable assurance regarding the achievement of objectives in the areas of operations, reporting, and compliance. Whistleblowing mechanisms can identify weaknesses or failures in these controls, enabling organisations to address gaps and strengthen their compliance frameworks.

For example, if a whistleblower reports issues related to financial misreporting or fraud, this information can prompt a review of internal financial controls and lead to improvements. Similarly, reports of safety violations can result in the enhancement of health and safety protocols. By continuously improving internal controls based on whistleblower reports, organisations can maintain robust compliance frameworks that effectively mitigate risks.

3.4.3 Promoting Ethical Compliance

In addition to legal and regulatory compliance, whistleblowing promotes ethical compliance within organisations. Ethical compliance involves adhering to the organisation's code of conduct and ethical standards, which may extend beyond legal requirements. Whistleblowers often report issues related to ethical misconduct, such as discrimination, harassment, or conflicts of interest.

Addressing these ethical concerns is crucial for maintaining a positive organisational culture and reputation. When organisations take whistleblower reports seriously and act on them, they demonstrate their commitment to ethical conduct. This not only supports compliance with ethical standards but also enhances employee morale and trust in the organisation's leadership.

By bringing concerns via multiple channels into a single assessment or triage process that is built in alignment with an organisations risk framework, decisions on next steps become more objective. The consolidation of concern based data into a central database allows for more accurate insights based

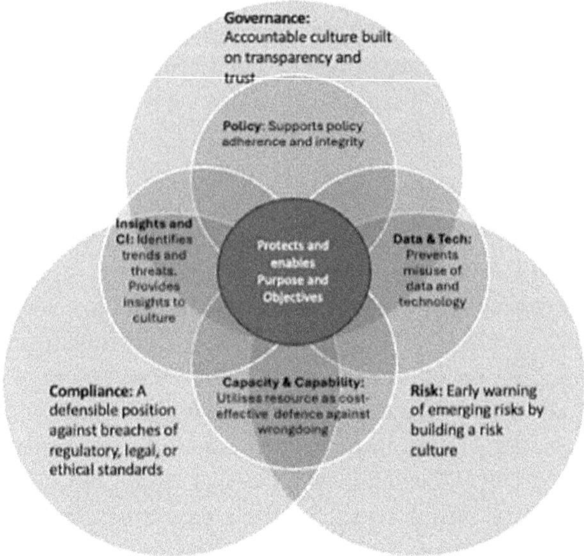

Figure 2 Alignment of Whistleblowing Systems to Integrated Governance, Risk and Compliance (source: A. Samuels)

on joined up and consistent information which in turn allows for better decision making, management information, and lessons learnt which can be prioritised within a continuous learning framework.

4. Sticks and Carrots – Reasons to Implement Whistleblowing

For the last 10 years I have used the analogy of children and carrot cake to make the point about whistleblowing. I tell my daughters that eating vegetables will help them grow to be big and strong. Healthy to take advantages of the opportunities that come their way, better protected against illness and bad health. They say yes Dad and go straight for the cake. I've found the same to be true with organisations. Many great conversations about the ethical, economic and reputational benefits of whistleblowing met with enthusiasm and acknowledgment, only for a tick box approach or worse, no approach at all to be take.

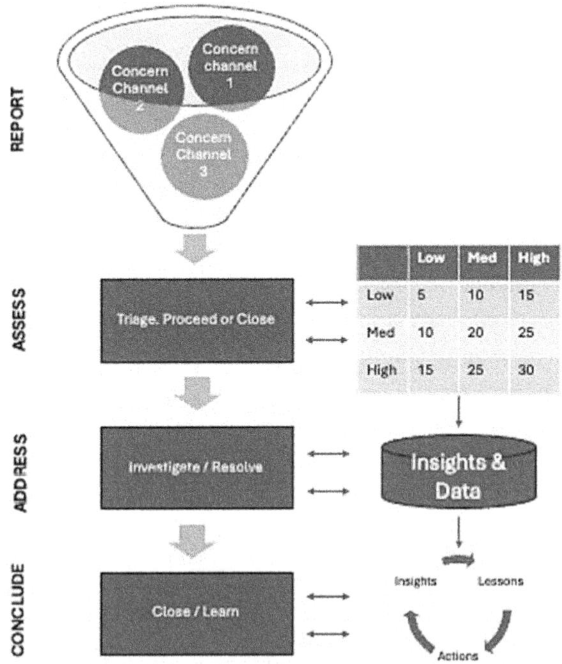

Figure 3 Single integrated whistleblowing model (source: A. Samuels)

So now I make carrot cake for my daughters who I know are getting the benefits of vegetables, whilst they get the enjoyment of cake (not made by me for full disclosure!)

And the same is true for whistleblowing. By integrating whistleblowing systems directly into GRC systems, I now help organisations not just defend themselves against wrongdoing and the associated negative impacts, but to support and enhance their purpose and objectives. All by saving costs, reducing complexity, better utilising resources, and making better use of data.

4.1 The current State of the EU Whistleblowing Directive

The EU Whistleblowing Directive[7] was met with little enthusiasm and in many cases ambivalence. As at the time of writing, all 27 member states have now transposed the laws, however their remain inconsistences and in some cases legal action.[8]

4.1.1 Delays in Implementation

Germany experienced notable delays in transposing the directive due to political disagreements and legislative bottlenecks. The transposition was only finalised in mid-2022. The delay prompted the European Commission to issue a formal notice, followed by a reasoned opinion in the infringement procedure, urging Germany to comply with its obligations under the directive. Eventually, Germany adopted comprehensive whistleblower protection measures, although the initial delay highlighted challenges within its legislative process.

Spain missed the December 2021 deadline and faced delays primarily due to prolonged legislative procedures and political negotiations. The European Commission initiated infringement proceedings against Spain, which included a formal notice and a subsequent reasoned opinion. Spain's legislation was finally enacted in late 2022, incorporating the directive's requirements into national law. The delay reflected the complexities of achieving consensus on whistleblower protection in the Spanish political landscape.

Italy's transposition process was delayed until early 2023, hindered by bureaucratic hurdles and the need for extensive consultations among stakeholders. The European Commission's infringement procedure against Italy involved a formal notice and a reasoned opinion, pressuring the country to expedite its legislative process. Italy eventually adopted the necessary measures, but the delays underscored the challenges of navigating its intricate legislative framework.

Portugal also missed the transposition deadline, completing the process only by mid-2023. Legislative delays and a crowded parliamentary agenda contributed to the protracted timeline. The European Commission took legal action against Portugal, issuing a formal notice and a reasoned opinion. In response, Portugal accelerated its efforts to comply with the directive, ultimately enacting comprehensive whistleblower protection laws.

France's transposition of the directive was delayed until early 2023 due to legislative and procedural complexities. The European Commission initiated infringement proceedings, including a formal notice and a reasoned opinion, to prompt France to meet its obligations. France eventually incorporated the directive's provisions into national law, ensuring robust protection for whistleblowers. The delay highlighted the need for streamlined legislative processes to meet EU deadlines.

Luxembourg faced delays in transposing the directive, completing the process only in early 2023. The European Commission's legal action involved a formal notice and a reasoned opinion, urging Luxembourg to expedite its legislative efforts. The delay was attributed to the small country's limited legislative capacity and the need for thorough consultations. Luxembourg eventually adopted comprehensive whistleblower protection measures, aligning with the directive's requirements.

Austria missed the transposition deadline, finalising its legislation in mid-2023. The European Commission issued a formal notice and a reasoned opinion as part of the infringement procedure, pressing Austria to comply with the directive. The delay was due to legislative backlogs and the need for detailed stakeholder consultations. Austria's eventual compliance demonstrated its commitment to enhancing whistleblower protections.

4.1.2 EU Legal Actions

Hungary's implementation of the directive has been criticised for its limited scope and lack of comprehensive protections. The European Commission issued a formal notice and a reasoned opinion, highlighting the deficiencies in Hungary's legislation. Despite these actions, Hungary's transposition remains incomplete, with significant gaps in protections and coverage. The ongoing legal action underscores the EU's commitment to ensuring member states fully comply with the directive.

Poland faced legal action from the European Commission due to delays and inadequate whistleblower protections. The formal notice and reasoned opinion addressed issues such as limited coverage and insufficient protection against retaliation. Poland's transposition process has been slow, with ongoing efforts to align its legislation with the directive's requirements. The EU's legal action emphasises the need for comprehensive and effective whistleblower protections.

Greece encountered delays in transposing the directive, leading to a formal notice and reasoned opinion from the European Commission. The deficiencies in Greece's legislation included inadequate confidentiality provisions and weak protection mechanisms. The transposition was eventually completed in late 2023, but the delay highlighted the challenges of aligning national laws with EU standards. The legal action reinforced the importance of timely and robust legislative measures.

Bulgaria's implementation of the directive faced criticism for being insufficiently detailed and lacking clear procedures for reporting. The European Commission's legal action, including a formal notice and reasoned opinion, pressured Bulgaria to enhance its whistleblower protections. The delay was due to legislative backlogs and the need for thorough consultations. Bulgaria eventually complied, but the process underscored the challenges of achieving comprehensive whistleblower protections.

Slovenia experienced delays in transposing the directive, with significant gaps in the scope of its legislation. The European Commission initiated legal action, issuing a formal notice and reasoned opinion to prompt Slovenia to comply. The delay highlighted issues such as limited protections for private sector whistleblowers and public procurement issues. Slovenia's eventual compliance demonstrated the EU's commitment to enforcing uniform whistleblower protections across member states.

4.2 Sticks

4.2.1 EU Laws

Below is a selection of EU laws with provisions for allowing the reporting of breaches with protection for those raising the concerns. Not a complete list, this demonstrates that the need for whistleblowing channels goes beyond the EU Whistleblowing Directive.

The burden to organisations that are subject to more than 1 of these laws increases with each regulation. Taking an integrated approach to managing concerns against legal requirements is one way to mitigate cost and complexity.

- **Market Abuse Regulation (MAR) (Regulation (EU) No 596/2014):** The MAR establishes a robust framework to prevent market abuse, including insider trading and market manipulation. Article 32 of the MAR specifically addresses the need for effective mechanisms to report breaches. It requires Member States to implement procedures for reporting actual or potential infringements, ensuring the protection of whistleblowers and maintaining their confidentiality. Companies must also establish internal reporting channels for employees to report misconduct anonymously.[9]

- **Anti-Money Laundering (AML) Directive (Directive (EU) 2015/849):** The AML Directive aims to combat money laundering and terrorist financing. Article 61 emphasises the importance of whistleblower protection. It mandates that Member States establish secure channels for reporting breaches of the directive. These channels must protect the identity of whistleblowers and provide them with protection against retaliation. The directive also requires financial institutions to implement internal procedures for employees to report suspicious activities.[10]
- **Capital Requirements Directive (CRD IV) (Directive 2013/36/EU):** The CRD IV focuses on the prudential supervision of credit institutions and investment firms. Article 71 requires institutions to have effective mechanisms for reporting breaches. This includes establishing independent and autonomous channels for employees to report regulatory violations confidentially. The directive also mandates protection against retaliation for those who report misconduct.[11]
- **Accounting Directive (Directive 2013/34/EU):** The Accounting Directive sets the framework for financial reporting within the EU. Article 22 emphasises the importance of transparency and the need for whistleblower protections. It requires Member States to ensure that companies have procedures in place for reporting breaches of accounting rules. These procedures must protect the confidentiality of the whistleblower and provide safeguards against retaliation.[12]
- **Public Procurement Directive (Directive 2014/24/EU):** The Public Procurement Directive aims to ensure fair competition and transparency in public procurement processes. Article 83 mandates Member States to establish effective and confidential channels for reporting breaches related to public procurement. It also emphasises the protection of whistleblowers from retaliation, ensuring that those who report misconduct can do so without fear of adverse consequences.[13]
- **Environmental Liability Directive (Directive 2004/35/EC):** The Environmental Liability Directive focuses on preventing and remedying

environmental damage. Article 14 requires Member States to establish procedures for reporting environmental damage. These procedures must protect the confidentiality of whistleblowers and provide them with protection against retaliation. The directive encourages public participation in environmental protection and ensures that those who report environmental violations are safeguarded.[14]

- **Industrial Emissions Directive (Directive 2010/75/EU):** The Industrial Emissions Directive aims to prevent and control industrial pollution. Article 24 requires Member States to ensure that operators provide channels for reporting breaches of the directive. These channels must protect the identity of whistleblowers and ensure that they are not subject to retaliation. The directive also mandates public access to information about industrial emissions and encourages the public to report violations.[15]
- **General Product Safety Directive (Directive 2001/95/EC):** The General Product Safety Directive ensures that products placed on the EU market are safe. Article 5 requires Member States to establish procedures for reporting unsafe products. These procedures must protect the confidentiality of the whistleblower and provide them with protection against retaliation. The directive also mandates that manufacturers and distributors implement internal procedures for reporting product safety concerns.[16]
- **Medical Devices Regulation (Regulation (EU) 2017/745):** The Medical Devices Regulation aims to ensure the safety and performance of medical devices within the EU. Article 92 requires Member States to establish systems for reporting serious incidents and non-compliance. These systems must include provisions for protecting the confidentiality of whistleblowers and providing them with safeguards against retaliation. The regulation also mandates that manufacturers establish procedures for reporting and investigating safety concerns.[17]
- **Directive on Antitrust Damages Actions (Directive 2014/104/EU):** The Directive on Antitrust Damages Actions aims to facilitate compensation for victims of antitrust violations. Article 20 emphasises the importance of whistleblower protection. It requires Member States to establish mechanisms for reporting antitrust violations and ensures that whistleblowers

are protected from retaliation. The directive also mandates confidentiality for those who report breaches of competition law.[18]

- **General Data Protection Regulation (GDPR) (Regulation (EU) 2016/679):** The GDPR sets the framework for data protection and privacy within the EU. Article 33 requires data controllers to report personal data breaches to supervisory authorities. It also mandates the establishment of procedures for reporting data breaches internally. Article 34 emphasises the importance of protecting whistleblowers who report data breaches, ensuring their confidentiality and protection against retaliation.[19]

4.2.2 US Laws

US whistleblowing laws have the potential to significantly impact European organisations, affecting their compliance and operational strategies. The intersection of US and European whistleblowing regulations can create a complex environment for multinational corporations.

The Sarbanes-Oxley Act (SOX) (21), enacted in 2002 in response to major corporate and accounting scandals such as Enron and WorldCom, aims to enhance corporate governance, improve the accuracy of financial reporting, and protect investors from fraudulent financial practices.

Whistleblowing Requirements: SOX provides specific protections for whistleblowers to encourage the reporting of corporate fraud and misconduct. Key whistleblowing provisions include:

- Anti-Retaliation Protections (Section 806): Employees who report fraudulent activities or violations of securities laws are protected from retaliation by their employers. This includes protection against termination, demotion, suspension, harassment, and other forms of discrimination.
- Confidential Reporting Mechanisms (Section 301): Public companies must establish procedures for the confidential and anonymous submission of concerns regarding questionable accounting or auditing matters.
- Incentive Schemes:
- While SOX primarily focuses on protections rather than direct financial incentives, its anti-retaliation measures create a safer environment for employees to report misconduct, indirectly encouraging whistleblowing.

The Dodd-Frank Act[20] enacted in 2010 in response to the 2008 financial crisis, aims to reduce risks in the financial system, increase transparency, and protect consumers from abusive financial practices.

Key whistleblowing Provisions include:

- SEC Whistleblower Program (Section 922): The SEC is authorised to provide monetary rewards to whistleblowers who provide original information leading to successful enforcement actions with sanctions exceeding $1 million.
- CFTC Whistleblower Program (Section 748): Like the SEC program, the Commodity Futures Trading Commission (CFTC) can reward whistleblowers for information that leads to successful enforcement actions.
- Anti-Retaliation Protections: Whistleblowers are protected from retaliation by their employers, and they can bring private lawsuits against employers who retaliate.

The Dodd-Frank Act includes robust incentive schemes to encourage whistleblowing:

- Financial Rewards: Whistleblowers can receive between 10% and 30% of the monetary sanctions collected because of their information. This substantial financial incentive aims to motivate individuals to come forward with critical information.
- Anonymity: Whistleblowers can report anonymously through an attorney, ensuring their identity is protected.

The Foreign Corrupt Practices Act (FCPA)[21], enacted in 1977, aims to prevent bribery of foreign officials to obtain or retain business and ensure accurate accounting records by companies. It seeks to combat corruption and promote ethical business practices globally.

Key Provisions: Prohibits US companies, foreign companies listed on US stock exchanges, and individuals from bribing foreign officials to gain a business advantage and requires publicly traded companies to maintain accurate books and records and to implement internal controls to prevent bribery and corruption.

Whistleblowing Requirements: The FCPA relies heavily on whistleblower reports to uncover violations. While it does not have its own dedicated whistleblower program, whistleblowers reporting FCPA violations can benefit from the provisions under the Dodd-Frank Act, as FCPA violations fall within the scope of securities laws. Whistleblowers can report suspected FCPA violations to the SEC, which can investigate and impose sanctions and can receive financial rewards and protections through the Dodd-Frank Act's whistleblower program.

The False Claims Act (FCA)[22], originally enacted during the Civil War, is designed to combat fraud against the federal government. It includes a "qui tam" provision, allowing private individuals to file lawsuits on behalf of the government and share in any recovered funds. It allows whistleblowers, known as relators, to sue on behalf of the government if they have knowledge of false claims made to obtain government funds. The FCA encourages whistleblowing by providing a legal framework for individuals to report fraud against the government and participate in legal actions to recover funds. If the government decides to intervene and the lawsuit is successful, the whistleblower can receive 15% to 30% of the recovered amount, This substantial reward aims to incentivise individuals to report fraud. Whistleblowers are protected from retaliation, with provisions for reinstatement, double back pay, and compensation for any special damages.

4.2.3 Examples of European Organisations Fined Under US Laws

- **Deutsche Bank:** In 2022, Deutsche Bank agreed to pay over $130 million to resolve investigations into violations of the FCPA. The allegations included the bribery of foreign officials and falsification of records. Whistleblower reports were pivotal in uncovering these practices, triggering both SEC and Department of Justice (DOJ) investigations.[23]

- **Novartis AG:** Novartis AG was fined $345 million in 2020 for FCPA violations. The company was accused of engaging in corrupt practices to win business in Greece, Vietnam, and South Korea. Whistleblowers within the company provided crucial information that led to the enforcement action.[24]
- **Airbus:** In a landmark case, Airbus SE, the European aerospace corporation, settled for a record $3.9 billion in 2020 with US, UK, and French authorities over bribery and corruption allegations. The settlement included $294 million paid to US authorities. The investigation was significantly advanced by whistleblower disclosures that revealed extensive bribery practices.[25]

With ever increasing regulation, growing focus on ESG from investor groups, supply chain risk and disruption, and inflationary pressure, the perceived burden of governance continues to rise. A 2024 survey by Business Europe found that over half of member federations (54%) believe that the regulatory burden for companies operating in the EU increased in 2023.[26]

If the sticks aren't enough of a worry or call to action, read on – the carrots should make the case.

4.3 The Carrots

For most organisations there's the need to have and nice to have. In tough economic climates as many have seen over these last 4-5 years, it's more important than ever to be able to build the business case for what is needed rather than what is wanted.

The 2020 paper, Evidence on the Use and Efficacy of Internal Whistleblowing Systems[27] remains one of the most comprehensive studies on the effectiveness of whistleblowing systems. It found that organisations that actively use whistleblowing systems tend to be more profitable as measured by return on assets (ROI). It goes on to identify that there are on average 6.9% fewer material lawsuits, a 20.4% reduction in settlements and 46% fewer negative news stories.

The Association of Certified Fraud Examiners Annual Report to The Nations[28] continues to demonstrate the value that internal whistleblowing brings. In the 2024 report it found that 43% of internal fraud is identified by whistleblowers. This is three times higher than the next most common way which was identified by auditors. The average fraud schemes were identified sooner (12 months) than non-active forms of review such as audit. It is estimated that organisations lose on average 5% of revenue to fraud each year with a mean average loss per case of USD$145,000.

Strong and visible whistleblowing programmes act as a deterrent to would be fraudsters and other wrong-doers and as evidenced above, has the capability to protect revenue and minimise losses to help deliver return on investment within the governance framework.

5. Conclusion

Integrated Governance offers organisations opportunities to strengthen their governance, risk, and compliance culture by simplifying and aligning the processes, controls and systems. Whistleblowing systems are a key component in enabling and protecting this culture of integrated governance and should be at the core of supporting an organisation's purpose and objectives.

Often the ethical argument, though understood and agreed with, is not a strong enough call to action for organisations to set up effective programmes. With the growing acknowledgement in regulations and legislation that reporting channels play (sticks), combined with the reputational and economic benefits that are demonstratably delivered (carrots), whistleblowing should be embraced and integrated directly into GRC programmes to ensure that all benefits are met and protected.

Notes

1 https://www.iso.org/committee/6266703.html.

2 file:///Users/admin/Downloads/ISO-TC%20309%20-Governance%20of%20organizations-.pdf.

3 https://kpmg.com/us/en/articles/2022/ten-key-regulatory-challenges-2023-risk-governance.html.

4 https://www.emerald.com/insight/content/doi/10.1108/JFC-12-2021-0275/full/html#sec008.

5 https://integratedreporting.ifrs.org/wp-content/uploads/2021/01/InternationalIntegratedReportingFramework.pdf#:~:text=URL%3A%20https%3A%2F%2Fintegratedreporting.ifrs.org%2Fwp.

6 https://www.mckinsey.com/capabilities/people-and-organizational-performance/our-insights/decision-making-in-the-age-of-urgency; https://www.mckinsey.com/

capabilities/people-and-organizational-performance/our-insights/untangling-your-organizations-decision-making.

7 https://eur-lex.europa.eu/legal-content/en/TXT/?uri=CELEX%3A32019L1937.
8 https://www.whistleblowingmonitor.eu/.
9 https://eur-lex.europa.eu/legal-content/EN/TXT/?uri=CELEX:32014R0596.
10 https://eur-lex.europa.eu/legal-content/EN/TXT/?uri=CELEX%3A32015L0849.
11 https://eur-lex.europa.eu/legal-content/EN/TXT/?uri=CELEX%3A32013L0036.
12 https://eur-lex.europa.eu/legal-content/EN/TXT/?uri=CELEX%3A32013L0034.
13 https://eur-lex.europa.eu/legal-content/EN/TXT/?uri=CELEX%3A32014L0024.
14 https://eur-lex.europa.eu/legal-content/EN/TXT/?uri=CELEX%3A32004L0035.
15 https://eur-lex.europa.eu/legal-content/EN/TXT/?uri=CELEX%3A32010L0075.
16 https://eur-lex.europa.eu/legal-content/EN/TXT/?uri=CELEX%3A32001L0095.
17 https://eur-lex.europa.eu/legal-content/EN/TXT/?uri=CELEX%3A32017R0745.
18 https://eur-lex.europa.eu/legal-content/EN/TXT/?uri=CELEX%3A32014L0104.
19 https://eur-lex.europa.eu/legal-content/EN/TXT/?uri=CELEX%3A32016R0679.
20 https://www.congress.gov/bill/111th-congress/house-bill/4173/text.
21 https://www.justice.gov/criminal/criminal-fraud/foreign-corrupt-practices-act.
22 https://www.justice.gov/sites/default/files/civil/legacy/2011/04/22/C-FRAUDS_FCA_Primer.pdf.
23 https://www.justice.gov/usao-edny/pr/deutsche-bank-agrees-pay-over-130-million-resolve-foreign-corrupt-practices-act-and#:~:text=BROOKLYN%2C%20NY%20%E2%80%93%20Deutsche%20Bank%20Aktiengesellschaft,into%20a%20commodities%20fraud%20scheme .
24 https://www.justice.gov/usao-nj/pr/novartis-ag-and-subsidiaries-pay-345-million-resolve-foreign-corrupt-practices-act-cases#:~:text=The%20resolutions%20arise%20out%20of,record%20improper%20payments%20in%20Vietnam.
25 https://www.justice.gov/opa/pr/airbus-agrees-pay-over-39-billion-global-penalties-resolve-foreign-bribery-and-itar-case#:~:text=Airbus%20SE%20(Airbus%20or%20the,Company's%20scheme%20to%20use%20third%2D.
26 https://www.businesseurope.eu/policies/economy-and-finance/structural-reforms-and-economic-governance.
27 https://papers.ssrn.com/sol3/papers.cfm?abstract_id=3273589.
28 https://legacy.acfe.com/report-to-the-nations/2024/.

The whistleblowing system in Portugal, two years after its regulation

Alex Sander Pires

1. Introduction

In modern times, democratic values are increasingly being discussed, so that, directly or indirectly, individuals are encouraged, and sometimes challenged, to participate in solutions to social problems, in all their dimensions and manifestations, with the economic, political and legal perspectives being the most visible.

From private life to the public environment, people are urged to get involved, both in order to really feel that they form part of the state and in order to learn about the challenges that surround life in politically constituted and legally guaranteed societies. Among many phenomena, this perception makes it possible to study living in society from an ethical perspective, centred on reflecting on how individuals should behave socially, beyond voting and paying taxes. In short, the individual must behave as the essential centre of the people and, from then on, participate in public life by contributing to the solution of problems and accessing primary social goods, thus recovering the unity of the state.

In this context, the purpose of this text is to present the transposition of Directive (EU) 2019/1937 of the European Parliament and of the Council of 23 October 2019[1] in the light of the political-governmental programme of the Portuguese Republic to address the issue of the protection and guarantee of whistleblowers beyond the broad system of EU Law.

Specifically, the Directive was politically and legally integrated into the National Anti-Corruption Strategy 2020-2024, an initiative of the XXII Constitutional Government of the Portuguese Republic, which, from the outset, makes it possible to demarcate the importance of whistleblowing as an element of greater popular participation of a moral nature in the direction of the ethically conceived State, for the purposes of curbing and combating fraud and corruption, which are, therefore, the most elementary foundations for the processing of Law n.º 93/2021, of 20 December, which regulated the issue, taking care of transposition, almost two years ago.

2. The treatment of the issue within the National Anti-Corruption Strategy 2020-2024

The issue of the protection of whistleblowers in Portugal, dealing with Directive (EU) 2019/1937 of the European Parliament and of the Council of 23 October 2019, was incorporated into the "National Anti-Corruption Strategy 2020-2024", facilitating and adapting the transposition to Portuguese domestic law, as provided by the XXII Constitutional Government as a way to combat corruption and fraud, whose objectives are to regain confidence in institutions, strengthen the economy with an emphasis on protecting state finances and reducing social inequalities[2].

The document recognises the importance of protecting those who comply with the law from retaliation, justifying the need to create "whistleblowing channels" as a tool for preventing and detecting corruption risks in public action, alongside other instruments such as the adoption of public compliance programmes, risk analysis and risk prevention or management plans, the implementation of a Code of Ethics or Code of Conduct, and the determination of the person responsible for the compliance programme.

Since then, whistleblowing channels have had to be set up taking into account, on the one hand, adequate protection for whistleblowers, always respecting transparency and integrity; and, on the other hand, the need to disrupt the "pacts of silence" in which whistleblowing had been recognised as an important autonomous instrument of criminal policy put at the service of the fight against corruption, especially in the field of corporate crime.

This provision fulfils the orientation of Article 33 on the protection of whistleblowers (in normative terms, "reporting persons") under the United Nations Convention against Corruption, both in terms of the duty of each state to provide protection against unjustified treatment of those who, in good faith and upon reasonable suspicion, provide information to public authorities about the crimes set out in the Convention, and the commitment to transpose the provisions into domestic law[3].

In addition to strengthening protection for whistleblowers by encouraging the creation of a specific legal statute, the aim was to bring together legal provisions that had previously existed in the Portuguese legal system, systematising and making them compatible, for example:

a) Regulation of the "application of measures for the protection of witnesses in criminal proceedings when their life, physical or psychological integrity, freedom or property of considerably high value are endangered because of their contribution to the proof of the facts that are the subject of the proceedings" (Law no. 93/99, of 14 July, Article 1, (1))[4];
b) Regulation of whistleblowers in the fight against corruption, recognising that "employees of the Public Administration and of companies in the state corporate sector who report the perpetration of offences of which they become aware in the course of their duties or because of them may not, in any form whatsoever, including non-voluntary transfer, be disadvantaged" (Law no. 19/2008, of 21 April, Article 4(1))[5];
c) Provision for whistleblowing in the fight against money laundering and terrorism, where "any person who has knowledge of violations or indications of violations of this law and the respective sectoral implementing regulations may make a complaint to the relevant sectoral authority" (Law no. 83/2017, 18 August, Article 108(1))[6], whereby "the protection of the personal data of the whistleblower and the data subject is guaranteed, in accordance with Regulation (EU) 2016/679 of the European Parliament and of the Council of 27 April 2016 and other data protection legislation' (Law no. 83/2017, of 18 August, Article 108(2))[7].

   In addition, "confidentiality about the identity of the whistleblower is also guaranteed at all times or until such time as this information is required to safeguard the rights of defence of those affected by the complaint, within the scope of the investigations to which it gives rise or subsequent legal proceedings" (Law no. 83/2017, of 18 August, Article 108(3))[8];
d) Wide-ranging treatment by the Securities Market Commission (*Comissão do Mercado de Valores Mobiliários* — CMVM), from the filing of criminal reports (Decree-Law no. 486/99, of 13 November, Article 382(1))[9] to the regulation of the provision of information and the production of evidence (Decree-Law no. 486/99, of 13 November, Article 368);

e) Similarly, the General Regime for Financial Institutions and Companies gave direct and broad treatment to the protection of whistleblowers, both for the purposes of internal reporting of irregularities (Decree-Law no. 298/92, of 31 December, Article 115-X)[10] and for reporting to the Bank of Portugal (Decree-Law no. 298/92, of 31 December, Article 116); and,
f) For reference, the document on the "National Anti-Corruption Strategy 2020-2024" also mentions provisions of the General Regime for Collective Investment Undertakings, the legal order of which was amended by Decree-Law no. 27/2023, of 23 April, with the following wording of Article 7(1): "management entities of collective investment undertakings and collective investment undertakings covered by the General Regime for Collective Investment Undertakings, approved in annex to Law no. 16/2015, of 24 February, in its current wording (RGOIC), and by the Legal Regime for Venture Capital, Social Entrepreneurship and Specialised Investment, approved in annex to Law no. 18/2015, in its current wording (RGOIC). º 16/2015, of 24 February, in its current wording (RGOIC), and the Legal Framework for Venture Capital, Social Entrepreneurship and Specialised Investment, approved in annex to Law no. 18/2015, of 4 March, in its current wording (RJCRESIE), have a period of 180 days after the date of entry into force of this decree-law to adapt to the provisions of the RGA"[11].

As a public institutional initiative, the "National Anti-Corruption Strategy 2020-2024" presented the digital portal created on the website of the Attorney General's Office (PGR), dedicated to receiving reports of corruption and fraud offences, called "Corruption: report it here" [12]. On that occasion, the statistics for 2019 were revealed, which show that of the 1966 electronic complaints, 249 led to enquiries, 31 to preventive investigations, 787 were forwarded to other entities and 896 were archived[13].

Also presented was the reporting platform created in March 2017 as a joint initiative of the Portuguese Football Federation (FPF) and the Professional Football Players' Union (SJPF), with the support of the Portuguese Judicial Police (PJ). In recognition of the need to maintain the integrity of competitions, the initiative aims to encourage the denunciation of practices that go against the uncertainty of the result that characterises sports competitions, whose manipulation undermines the good faith of disputes, through irregular influences, tending to be corrupt, for their own benefit or that of third parties, with the vitiation of sports results (match fixing)[14].

3. Transposition of the Directive into Portuguese domestic law

With the approval of the National Anti-Corruption Strategy 2020-2024, by Resolution of the Council of Minister[15]s no. 37/2021, of 06 April, the Body, in a Communication of 29 April 2021, informed the guidelines of the government's anti-corruption policy, with a view to the commitment to improve the quality of legislation and the transparency of procedures.

Among the numerous pieces of legislation, approval was given to sending a bill to Parliament to transpose into national law "Directive (EU) 2019/1937 on the protection of persons who report breaches of EU law". The aim of this proposal is to ensure an effective and balanced level of protection for whistleblowers who report breaches of EU law by establishing channels for reporting, prohibiting any form of retaliation and enshrining measures to protect and support whistleblowers"[16].

The next step, on June 9, 2021, was the publication of Draft Law no. 866/XIV/2.a, on the Creation of the Whistleblower Protection Regime, recognising, on the one hand, that the fight against corruption and highly organised crime is one of the biggest and most problematic challenges facing Portuguese justice, largely due to the silence, fear and close relationship between those involved that mark the protection network for this conduct; and, on the other hand, the lack of human and technical resources to ensure an effective criminal investigation, capable of proving the facts.

Once the problem and its causes were known, one could think of the whistleblower[17] protection scheme as an effective instrument for breaking the protection network. However, it was necessary to overcome the concrete obstacle based on the fear of reprisals (especially professional persecution, which can lead to disciplinary proceedings that damage professional careers) characterised by the risk of the whistleblower being discovered.

The need was therefore recognised to: "a) create appropriate communication channels and procedures to follow up on complaints in conditions of confidentiality, both internally (within the organisation where you work) and externally (with the competent authorities), guaranteeing that the complaint can be made confidentially"[18]; and, "b) introduce labour protection schemes that prevent, in particular, negative discrimination against the whistleblower, such as obstacles to career progression or disguised disciplinary proceedings"[19] (DAR no. 149, 2021, p. 2).

After going through the legislative process[20], from the admissibility note[21] to the publication of Assembly of the Republic Decree no. 212/XIV, which establishes the General Regime for the Protection of Whistleblowers, transposing Directive (EU) 2019/1937 of the European Parliament and of the Council of 23 October 2019 on the protection of persons who report breaches of Union law[22]; Bill no. 866/XIV/2.a was approved, and then converted into Law no. 93/2021, of 20 December, following approval on 26 November 2021, promulgation on 9 December 2021, and a referendum on 13 December 2021.

4. The treatment of whistleblowing under Law 93/2021 of 20 December

Law 93/2021 of 20 December is based on a normative foundation taking in the political-legal sphere; on the one hand, it is based on Directive (EU) 2019/1937 of the European Parliament and of the Council of 23 October 2019 on the protection of persons who report breaches of Union law; and, on the other hand, on the National Anti-Corruption Strategy 2020-2024. These are the limits to be considered for the purposes of framing the issue.

4.1 Regulatory structure of Law 93/2021 of 20 December

Law no. 93/2021, of 20 December, consists of thirty-one articles distributed as follows:

> Chapter I. General Provisions: Object (Article 1), Scope (Article 2), Articulation with other regimes (Article 3), Object and content of the complaint or public disclosure (Article 4), Complainant (Article 5), and Conditions of protection (Article 6).
>
> Chapter II (Means of Whistleblowing and Public Disclosure) is divided into four sections, whose Section I, entitled "Precedence between means of whistleblowing and public disclosure", containing Article 7 (Precedence between means of whistleblowing and public disclosure).

Section II is called "Internal Whistleblowing", bringing together Article 8 (Obligation to establish internal whistleblowing channels), Article 9 (Characteristics of internal whistleblowing channels), Article 10 (Form and admissibility of internal whistleblowing), and Article 11 (Follow-up to internal whistleblowing).

Section III, named "External Whistleblowing", brings together Article 12 (Competent authorities), Article 13 (Characteristics of external whistleblowing channels), Article 14 (Form and admissibility of external whistleblowing), Article 15 (Follow-up to external whistleblowing), Article 16 (Information obligation), and Article 17 (Annual reports).

Section IV, entitled "Provisions applicable to internal and external complaints", brings together Article 18 (Confidentiality), Article 19 (Processing of personal data), and Article 20 (Retention of complaints).

Chapter III. Protection Measures: Prohibition of retaliation (Article 21), and Support Measures (Article 22).

Chapter IV. Jurisdictional Protection: divided into Section I (General Provisions), dealing with Articles 23 (Effective Jurisdictional Protection), 24 (Responsibility of the Complainant), 25 (Protection of the Person Concerned), and 26 (Unavailability of Rights). Section II (administrative offences) deals with Articles 27 (administrative offences and fines), 28 (concurrent offences), 29 (jurisdiction to process and impose fines) and 30 (subsidiary rules).

Chapter V. Final Provision, according to Article 31 (Entry into Force).

4.2 Forms of whistleblowing

Law no. 93/2021, of 20 December, provides for three means or forms of whistleblowing: an internal whistleblowing channel, an external whistleblowing channel and public disclosure (Law no. 93/2021, Article 7(1)).

Considering that legal persons with fifty or more employees, including the State and others legal persons governed by public law, as well as entities within the scope of the European Union referred to in Directive (EU) 2019/1937 of the European Parliament and of the Council, have a legal duty to set up internal whistleblowing channels, it was determined that this means would be the most suitable for whistleblowing, which leads it to be considered a general rule (Law no. 93/2021, Article 8(1)).

Therefore, access to the external whistleblowing channel is only possible if at least one of the following hypotheses occurs: a) there is no internal whistleblowing channel; b) "The internal whistleblowing channel only accepts complaints from employees, and the whistleblower is not the whistleblower";

c) "The whistleblower has reasonable grounds to believe that the offence cannot be effectively investigated or resolved internally or that there is a risk of retaliation"; d) "The whistleblower initially lodged an internal complaint without being informed of the measures envisaged or adopted following the complaint within the time limits provided for in Article 11; and, e) "The offence constitutes a crime or an administrative offence punishable by a fine of more than €50,000"[23] (Law no.93/2021, Article 7(2)).

Furthermore, public disclosure of the offence is only permitted in two cases: firstly, if the whistleblower has "reasonable grounds to believe that the offence may constitute an imminent or manifest danger to the public interest, that the offence cannot be effectively known or resolved by the competent authorities, taking into account the specific circumstances of the case, or that there is a risk of retaliation even in the event of an external complaint"[24] (Law no. 93/2021, Article 7(3)(a)); or, secondly, "has lodged an internal complaint and an external complaint, or directly an external complaint under the terms of this law, without appropriate measures having been taken within the time limits provided for in Articles 11 and 15"[25] (Law no. 93/2021, Article 7(3)(b)).

4.3 Framework of Decree-Law no. 109-E/2021, of 9 December

Decree-Law no. 109-E/2021, of 9 December, creates the National Anti-Corruption Mechanism and establishes the general regime for the prevention of corruption.[26] It is clear that the law is a consequence of Council of Ministers Resolution 37/2021, of 6 April, which approved the National Anti-Corruption Strategy 2020-2024, which it intends to regulate, along with the prerogatives of the whistleblower statute.

From the outset, the General Regime for the Prevention of Corruption (GRPC), regulated in the Annex to the Decree-Law, promises to make instruments to combat these criminal practices effective and normative, including the creation of whistleblowing channels as a preventive measure (RGPC, Article 5(1)), following the provisions of the legislation transposing Directive (EU) 2019/1937 of the European Parliament and of the Council of 23 October 2019, namely Law no. 93/2021, of 20 December (RGRPC, Article 8(1)).

The RGPC "applies to legal persons with registered offices in Portugal that employ 50 or more workers and to branches in Portugal of legal persons with registered offices abroad that employ 50 or more workers"[27] (RGPC,

Article 1, no. 1). The regime also applies to "services and legal persons of the direct and indirect administration of the state, autonomous regions, local authorities and the public business sector that employ 50 or more workers, as well as independent administrative entities with functions of regulating economic activity in the private, public and cooperative sectors and the Bank of Portugal[28]"[29] (RGPC, Article 1, (2)).

5. Some relevant whistleblowing channels

Almost two years on from its entry into force after the 180-day *vacatio legis*, on 18 June 2022, there have been several initiatives in Portugal to implement whistleblowing channels in line with the values, procedures and guarantees regulated in Law no. 93/2021, of 20 December, and, why not mention it, expanding the initiative of the portals "Corruption: report it here" ("Corrupção: denuncie aqui" — MP/PGR/DCIAP) and "Whistleblower Portal: Integrity" ("Portal de Denúncia: Integridade" — FPF/SJPF/PJ).

Also considering Decree-Law 109-E/2021 of 9 December, namely the duty to comply with the rules immanent to the whistleblower statute, specifically the duty to create whistleblowing channels in compliance with all legal guidelines, at the risk of charging the persons concerned with administrative offences, five initiatives are mentioned under these provisions.

5.1 National Security Office (NSO)

The National Security Office[30] (NSO) "is a central service of the direct administration of the State, endowed with administrative autonomy, dependent on the Prime Minister or the member of the Government to whom he delegates"[31] (Decree-Law no. 3/2012, of 16 January, Article 1 (1))[32], and is headed by the National Security Authority[33] (NSA), which has exclusivity in the protection, control and safeguarding of classified information (Decree-Law no. 3/2012, of 16 January, Article 1 (2)).

In these terms, the NSO's mission is to "guarantee the security of classified information at national level and that of international organisations to which Portugal is a party, and to act as an accreditation authority for natural or legal persons to access and handle classified information, as well as the accreditation and supervisory authority of entities operating within the scope of the State Electronic Certification System - Public Key Infrastructure (SCEE) and the accreditation entity under the provisions of the law governing the provision and use of electronic public procurement platforms"[34] (Decree-Law no. 3/2012, of 16 January, Article 2 (1)); as well as taking care of the National Cybersecurity Centre (Decree-Law no. 3/2012, of 16 January, Article 2 (2)).

In practical terms, the NSO provides access to the complaints channel on its website via the link https://www.gns.gov.pt/pt/canal-de-denuncias/#enq, as well as a manual with the main information on the procedure and guidelines[35].

5.2 Bank of Portugal

Under the terms of its Organic Law as amended by Law no. 5/98 of 31 January, the Bank of Portugal, according to Article 3, is the central bank of the Portuguese Republic, participating in the European System of Central Banks (ESCB), to whose statutes it submits, as well as acting in accordance with the guidelines of the European Central Bank (ECB). As for its legal nature, it is a legal person governed by public law, with its own assets and administrative and financial autonomy (Annex to Law no. 5/98 of 31 January).

Specifically on the issue of whistleblowing, Banco de Portugal has approved some relevant legislation, such as the Regulation of Conduct[36], which shows interest in preventing and repressing harassment and discrimination, especially with the creation of a whistleblowing channel for this purpose (Article 39, point 'd' in systematic interpretation with Articles 40 to 43), the grounds for which have been elevated to the level of adjudicatory principles[37], and ethical duty[38].

On a more specific note, within the scope of the specific legislation on the whistleblower statute and the National Anti-Corruption Strategy, it created its internal whistleblowing channel in writing, via post or email (gabinete.compliance@bportugal.pt), to be accessed by persons whose activities are linked to the activities of the Bank of Portugal, interested in reporting offences based on information obtained in the course of their duties, namely: employees of Banco de Portugal; members of Banco de Portugal's bodies; service providers, contractors, subcontractors and suppliers of Banco de Portugal, as well as any persons acting under their supervision or direction; volunteers and trainees of Banco de Portugal, paid or unpaid; and, recipients of Banco de Portugal's activities.

5.3 Council of Ministers

Within the Council of Ministers, the General Secretariat of the Presidency of the Council of Ministers[39] (GSPCM) is responsible for providing internal whistleblowing channels, as well as guaranteeing the application of specific measures based on confidentiality, responsible processing of personal data and the preservation of complaints, as well as protecting and supporting whistleblowers, especially against possible retaliation.

In terms of form, the whistleblowing can be written or verbal, the main details of which can be found in the Complaints Manual[40]. If it is written, it can be submitted by e-mail (auditoria@sg.pcm.gov.pt) or by traditional post, the specific details of which can be found on the institutional website[41]; on the other hand, if it is verbal, it can be made by telephone (+351) 21 392 7920, or in a face-to-face meeting, if requested by the complainant and by prior appointment.

5.4 Superior Council of the Judiciary

Constitutionally constituted, the Superior Council of the Judiciary[42] (SCJ), as a collegiate and autonomous body, is responsible for both appointing, placing, transferring and promoting judges of the Judicial Courts, as well as handling disciplinary actions and guaranteeing the institutional prerogatives and independence of judges.

In view of its institutional role, the SCJ has set up a complaints channel to comply with Law no. 93/2021, of 20 December, in a digital environment for related matters, such as citizen complaints that fall within the remit of the disciplinary functions. Complaints should therefore preferably be submitted in writing, by accessing the specific link for this purpose[43].

In addition to the specific link, other forms are allowed, namely: e-mail with the indication that it is a 'confidential' matter; postal mail, with the instruction 'do not open', and to the 'attention' of the Team dedicated to receiving and processing complaints; telephone, with immediate reliable transcription by a member of the Team for receiving complaints; or in person, by prior appointment, with recording or writing of the respective minutes.

5.5 Ministry of Internal Administration

The mission of the Ministry of Internal Administration[44] (MIA) "is to formulate, coordinate, execute and evaluate policies on internal security, border control, protection and assistance, road safety and electoral administration"[45] (Decree-Law 126-B/2022, Article 1). The whistleblowing channel is presented in the "citizen's area" of the institutional website, followed by frequently asked questions on the subject.

6. Summary

Considering the proposal to present descriptively the normative foundations that led to the creation of the whistleblowing system according to the political and legal values of the XXII Constitutional Government of the Portuguese Republic, especially the "National Anti-Corruption Strategy 2020-2024", having as a parliamentary interest the transposition of Directive (EU) 2019/1937 of the European Parliament and of the Council of October 23, 2019, it seems evident that one cannot speak of a conclusion, but of summary, with the following arguments:

1. In Portuguese domestic law, the whistleblowing system referred to in Directive (EU) 2019/1937 of the European Parliament and of the Council of 23 October 2019 has been integrated into the National Anti-Corruption Strategy 2020-2024, recognizing it as an important element of criminal policy regarding the evidence's system against crimes of fraud and corruption.
2. In Portuguese law there were already some public initiatives prior to the current regulation of the whistleblowing system, including: "corruption: report it here", proposed by the Attorney General's Office, established in 2010; and the "reporting platform - integrity", as a joint act of the Portuguese Football Federation and the Union of Professional Football Players, with the institutional support of the Portuguese Judiciary Police.
3. Following Council of Ministers Resolution no. 37/2021, of April 6, in accordance with the Communication of April 29, 2021, which set in motion the National Anti-Corruption Strategy 2020-2024, Bill no. 866/XIV/2.a was presented to the Assembly of the Republic which, after

parliamentary proceedings, culminated in its: approval on November 26, 2021, promulgation on December 9, 2021, and referendum on December 13, 2021.

4. Formally, Law no. 93/2021, of December 20, is made up of thirty-one articles, divided into five chapters, which provide the rules for the creation of whistleblowing channels for legal persons of a public and private nature, whose forms of whistleblowing provided for in the law are the internal whistleblowing channel, the external whistleblowing channel, and public disclosure.
5. Law no. 93/2021, of December 20, forms a regulatory microsystem with Decree-Law no. 109-E/2021, of December 9, which created the National Anti-Corruption Mechanism, establishing the general prevention regime for this purpose.
6. Given the duty to create internal whistleblowing channels for public bodies, under the terms of Law no. 93/2021, of December 20, and the methodological rules restricting space for the presentation of this text, five whistleblowing systems have been briefly mentioned under the new legal regulations: the National Security Office, the Bank of Portugal, the Council of Ministers, the Superior Council of the Judiciary, and the Ministry of Internal Administration.
7. The short time that Law no. 93/2021, of December 20, has been in force, let alone the creation of internal whistleblowing channels by the bodies obliged to do so, has made any qualitative or quantitative analysis of complaints difficult (perhaps it would be more appropriate to say impossible), both in terms of receipt and treatment.

Finally, it is hoped that the political and legal spirit of the National Anti-Corruption Strategy 2020-2024 will be respected, both by the external elements (initiative of the European Union and the United Nations) and by the political initiative of the XXI Constitutional Government of the Portuguese Republic. Furthermore, it is hoped that the whistleblowing systems will be operated in accordance with the principles of transparency and democratic ethics, allowing the whistleblowing system in Portugal to be observed and considered in a more substantial and critical way.

Notes

1 Parlamento Europeu. Conselho da União Europeia. DIRETIVA (UE) 2019/1937 DO PARLAMENTO EUROPEU E DO CONSELHO, de 23 de outubro de 2019, relativa à proteção das pessoas que denunciam violações do direito da União. Jornal Oficial da União Europeia (JO) L 305, 26.11.2019, pp. 17-56. Disponível em: https://eur -lex .europa .eu /eli /dir /2019 /1937 /oj; último acesso: 24.05.2024..

2 Presidência do Conselho de Ministros. Resolução do Conselho de Ministros nº 37/2021. Aprova a Estratégia Nacional Anticorrupção 2020-2024. Diário da República (DR), 1ª série, nº 66, 06 de abril de 2021; pp. 8-49. Available at: https://files.dre.pt/1s/2021/04 /06600/0000800049.pdf; last access: 17.05.2024.

3 "United Nations Convention Against Corruption, Article 33. (Protection of reporting persons). Each State Party shall consider incorporating into its domestic legal system appropriate measures to provide protection against any unjustified treatment for any person who reports in good faith and on reasonable grounds to the competent authorities any facts concerning offences established in accordance with this Convention".

4 In attention of the original text as proposed: "aplicação de medidas para protecção de testemunhas em processo penal quando a sua vida, integridade física ou psíquica, liberdade ou bens patrimoniais de valor consideravelmente elevado sejam postos em perigo por causa do seu contributo para a prova dos factos que constituem objecto do processo" (Lei n.º 93/99, de 14 de Julho, Artigo 1º, n.º 1).

5 In attention of the original text as proposed: "os trabalhadores da Administração Pública e de empresas do sector empresarial do Estado que denunciem o cometimento de infracções de que tiverem conhecimento no exercício das suas funções ou por causa delas não podem, sob qualquer forma, incluindo a transferência não voluntária, ser prejudicados" (Lei n.º 19/2008, de 21 de Abril, Artigo 4º, n.º 1).

6 In attention fo the original text as proposed: "qualquer pessoa que tenha conhecimento de violações ou de indícios de violações à presente lei e aos respetivos diplomas regulamentares de aplicação setorial pode fazer uma denúncia à autoridade setorial relevante (Lei n.º 83/2017, de 18 de Agosto, Artigo 108.º, n.º 1).

7 The original texto: "garantida a proteção dos dados pessoais do denunciante e do visado, nos termos do Regulamento (UE) 2016/679 do Parlamento Europeu e do Conselho, de 27 de abril de 2016, e demais legislação de proteção de dados" (Lei n.º 83/2017, de 18 de Agosto, Artigo 108.º, n.º 2).

8 The original texto: "igualmente garantida a confidencialidade sobre a identidade do denunciante a todo o tempo ou até ao momento em que essa informação seja exigida para salvaguarda dos direitos de defesa dos visados pela denúncia, no âmbito das investigações a que a mesma dê lugar ou de processos judiciais subsequentes" (Lei n.º 83/2017, de 18 de Agosto, Artigo 108.º, n.º 3).

9 Governo de Portugal, Ministério das Finanças. Decreto-Lei n.º 486/99, de 13 de Novembro. Aprova o novo Código dos Valores Mobiliários. Diário da República (DR), n.º 265/1999, Série I-A, 13.11.1999, pp. 7968-8040. Disponível em: https://diariodarepublica .pt /dr /detalhe /decreto -lei /486 -1999 -682983; último acesso: 23.05.2024.

10 Governo de Portugal, Ministério das Finanças. Decreto-Lei n.º 298/92, de31 de Dezembro. Aprova o Regime Geral das Instituições de Créditoe Sociedades Financeiras. Diário da República (DR), n.º 301/1992, 6ºSuplemento, Série I-A, 31.12.1992, pp. 24-51. Disponível em: https://diariodarepublica.pt/dr/legislacao-consolidada/decreto-lei/1992-70072322; último acesso: 23.05.2024.

11 Original text: "as entidades gestoras de organismos de investimento coletivo e os organismos de investimento coletivo abrangidos pelo Regime Geral dos Organismos de Investimento Coletivo, aprovado em anexo à Lei n.º 16/2015, de 24 de fevereiro, na sua redação atual (RGOIC), e pelo Regime Jurídico do Capital de Risco, Empreendedorismo Social e Investimento Especializado, aprovado em anexo à Lei n.º 18/2015, de 4 de março, na sua redação atual (RJCRESIE), dispõem de um prazo de 180 dias após a data da entrada em vigor do presente decreto-lei para se adaptar ao disposto no RGA".

12 Available at: https://simp.pgr.pt/dciap/denuncias/index2.php; last access: 23.05.2024.

13 In 2023, the first eleven months show that the portal received 1,748 electronic complaints, the preliminary analysis of which, taking into account data from the previous year (2022) that has not been finalised, indicates the opening of 137 enquiries, 1 preventive investigation, 587 complaints referred to other entities, and 1,428 filings, according to the report on 'Statistical data - corruption and related crimes/2023', available at: https://www.ministeriopublico.pt/sites/default/files/documentos/pdf/corrupcao_e_crimes_conexos_2023.pdf; last access: 23.05.2024.

14 Whistleblowing platform - integrity. Available at: https://integridade.fpf.pt/; last access: 23.05.2024.

15 The Council of Ministers, according to Article 184 of the Constitution of the Portuguese Republic of 1976 (CRP/1976), is made up of the Prime Minister, Deputy Prime Ministers (if any), and Ministers; the Secretaries and Undersecretaries of State may attend meetings when called upon to do so. Furthermore, the decisions taken by the body are binding on the members of the government (CRP/1976, Article 189), which is exactly what is happening with the National Anti-Corruption Strategy 2020-2024, as a general line of government policy to be implemented in accordance with the approved action plan (CRP/1976, Article 200(1a)).

16 Comunicado do Conselho de Ministros de 29 de abril de 2021. Available at: https://www.portugal.gov.pt/pt/gc22/governo/comunicado-de-conselho-de-ministros?i=416; last access: 23.05.2024.

17 According to the draft law (DAR no. 149, 2021, p. 2), whistleblowers are "people who work for or are in contact with organisations that engage in illegal practices as part of their professional activity, particularly with regard to corruption and organised crime - such as money laundering, tax fraud, public procurement or product and transport safety, to give just a few examples - and are therefore in the best position to report and prove these illegal practices"; personal translation of "as pessoas que trabalham ou que estão em contacto com organizações que no âmbito da sua atividade profissional tenham práticas ilícitas, designadamente no que toca à corrupção e à criminalidade organizada – como branqueamento de capitais, fraude fiscal, contratação pública ou segurança dos produtos e dos transportes, para dar apenas alguns exemplos –, são quem,

por isso mesmo, está em melhores condições de denunciar, e provar, estas mesmas práticas ilícitas".

18 Original text: "a) criar canais e procedimentos de comunicação adequados para dar seguimento às denúncias em condições de confidencialidade, quer seja a nível interno (dentro da organização onde trabalha) quer externo (junto das autoridades competentes), garantindo que a denúncia pode ser feita confidencialmente"

19 Original text: "b) introduzir regimes de proteção ao nível laboral que impeçam, nomeadamente, discriminações negativas ao denunciante, como os entraves à progressão na carreira ou processos disciplinares encapotados"

20 The stages of the legislative process on the parliamentary initiative can be consulted at: https://www.parlamento.pt/ActividadeParlamentar/Paginas/DetalheIniciativa.aspx?BID=120906; last accessed on: 24.05.2024.

21 Available at: Disponível em: https://app.parlamento.pt/webutils/docs/doc.pdf?path=6148523063484d364c793968636d356c6443397a6158526c63793959535565a4d5a5763765247396a6457316c626e527663306c7561574e7059585270646d45764d7a63324e446c684e7a6b744e445a6b4e7930305a5449344c5467335a5449744d6a5a6a4d544534597a67314f5751794c6d52765933673d&fich=37649a79-46d7-4e28-87e2-26c118c859d2.docx&Inline=true; last access: 24.05.2024.

22 Available at: https://debates.parlamento.pt/catalogo/r3/dar/s2a/14/03/049/2021-12-02/6?pgs=6-19&org=PLC; last access: 24.05.2024.

23 Original text: b) "O canal de denúncia interna admita apenas a apresentação de denúncias por trabalhadores, não o sendo o denunciante"; c) "Tenha motivos razoáveis para crer que a infração não pode ser eficazmente conhecida ou resolvida a nível interno ou que existe risco de retaliação"; d) "Tenha inicialmente apresentado uma denúncia interna sem que lhe tenham sido comunicadas as medidas previstas ou adotadas na sequência da denúncia nos prazos previstos no artigo 11.º"; e, e) "A infração constitua crime ou contraordenação punível com coima superior a 50 000 €"

24 Original text: "motivos razoáveis para crer que a infração pode constituir um perigo iminente ou manifesto para o interesse público, que a infração não pode ser eficazmente conhecida ou resolvida pelas autoridades competentes, atendendo às circunstâncias especificas do caso, ou que existe um risco de retaliação inclusivamente em caso de denúncia externa".

25 Original text: "tenha apresentado uma denúncia interna e uma denúncia externa, ou diretamente uma denúncia externa nos termos previstos na presente lei, sem que tenham sido adotadas medidas adequadas nos prazos previstos nos artigos 11.º e 15.º".

26 Presidência do Conselho de Ministros, Ministério da Justiça. Decreto-Lei n.º 109-E/2021, de 9 de dezembro. Cria o Mecanismo Nacional Anticorrupção e estabelece o regime geral de prevenção da corrupção. Diário da República (DR), n.º 237/2021, 1º Suplemento, Série I, 09.12.2021, pp. 19-42. Disponível em: https://diariodarepublica.pt /dr /detalhe /decreto -lei /109-e -2021 -175659840; último acesso: 23.05.2024

27 Original text: O RGPC "é aplicável às pessoas coletivas com sede em Portugal que empreguem 50 ou mais trabalhadores e às sucursais em território nacional de pessoas coletivas com sede no estrangeiro que empreguem 50 ou mais trabalhadores".

[28] With regard to the Bank of Portugal, it is important to note that 'it is not subject to the provisions of the present regime with regard to matters concerning its participation in the performance of the tasks entrusted to the European System of Central Banks' (RGPC, Article 1 (4)).

[29] Original text: "aos serviços e às pessoas coletivas da administração direta e indireta do Estado, das regiões autónomas, das autarquias locais e do setor público empresarial que empreguem 50 ou mais trabalhadores, e ainda às entidades administrativas independentes com funções de regulação da atividade económica dos setores privado, público e cooperativo e ao Banco de Portugal".

[30] In Portuguese, Gabinete Nacional de Segurança (GNS).

[31] Original text: "é um serviço central da administração directa do Estado, dotado de autonomia administrativa, na dependência do Primeiro-Ministro ou do membro do Governo em quem aquele delegar".

[32] Presidência do Conselho de Ministros. Decreto-Lei n.º 3/2012, de 16 dejaneiro. Aprova a orgânica do Gabinete Nacional de Segurança. Diário daRepública (DR), n.º 11/2012, Série I, 16.01.2012, pp. 174-177. Disponívelem: https://diariodarepublica .pt /dr /legislacao -consolidada /decreto -lei /2012-114157278; último acesso: 23.05.2024.

[33] In Portuguese; Autoridade Nacional de Segurança (ANS).

[34] Original text: "garantir a segurança da informação classificada no âmbito nacional e das organizações internacionais de que Portugal é parte, e exercer a função de autoridade de credenciação de pessoas singulares ou coletivas para o acesso e manuseamento de informação classificada, bem como a de autoridade credenciadora e de fiscalização de entidades que atuem no âmbito do Sistema de Certificação Eletrónica do Estado — Infraestrutura de Chaves Públicas (SCEE) e de entidade credenciadora por força do disposto na lei que regula a disponibilização e a utilização das plataformas eletrónicas de contratação pública".

[35] Available at: https://www.gns.gov.pt/docs/manual-canal-denuncias.pdf; last access: 24.05.2024.

[36] Available at: https://www.bportugal.pt/sites/default/files/anexos/documentos-relacionados/regulamento_conduta.pdf; last access: 24.05.2024.

[37] Treatment given under the "General Framework of Principles for Bank of Portugal Contractors". Available at: https://www.bportugal.pt/sites/default/files/anexos/documentos-relacionados/quadro_geral_de_principios_dos_adjudicatarios_do_banco_de_portugal.pdf; last access: 25.05.2024.

[38] Both for employees, as can be seen in Provision 3.1 of the Code of Conduct for Employees of Banco de Portugal (https://www.bportugal.pt/sites/default/files/anexos/documentos-relacionados/codigo_de_conduta_trabalhadores_bdp.pdf), and for the Members of the Board of Directors in Provision 4.1 (https://www.bportugal.pt/sites/default/files/anexos/documentos-relacionados/codigodecondutaca.pdf).

[39] In Portuguese, Secretaria-Geral da Presidência do Conselho de Ministros (SGPCM).

[40] Available at: https://www.sg.pcm.gov.pt/media/5m5pod4x/regime-geral-de-protecao-de-denunciantes-de-infracoes.pdf; last access: 24.05.2024.

[41] Available at: https://www.sg.pcm.gov.pt/a-sgpcm/canal-de-denuncias/; last access: 24.05.2024.

[42] In Portuguese, Conselho Superior da Magistratura (CSM).
[43] Available at: https://denuncias.csm.org.pt/#/; last access: 27.06.2024.
[44] In Portuguese, Ministério da Administração Interna (MAI).
[45] Original texto, "tem por missão a formulação, coordenação, execução e avaliação das políticas de segurança interna, do controlo de fronteiras, de protecção e socorro, de segurança rodoviária e de administração eleitoral".

Bibliography

Digital References

Banco de Portugal. "Quadro Geral de Princípios dos Adjudicatários do Banco de Portugal". Disponível em: https://www.bportugal.pt/sites/default/files/anexos/documentos-relacionados/quadro_geral_de_principios_dos_adjudicatarios_do_banco_de_portugal.pdf; último acesso: 25.05.2024.

Banco de Portugal. "Código de Conduta dos Trabalhadores do Banco de Portugal". Disponível em: https://www.bportugal.pt/sites/default/files/anexos/documentos-relacionados/codigo_de_conduta_trabalhadores_bdp.pdf; último acesso: 25.05.2024.

Banco de Portugal. "Código de Conduta dos Membros do Conselho de Administração do Banco de Portugal". Disponível em: https://www.bportugal.pt/sites/default/files/anexos/documentos-relacionados/codigodecondutaca.pdf; último acesso: 25.05.2024.

Banco de Portugal. "Regulamento de Conduta do Banco de Portugal". Disponível em: https://www.bportugal.pt/sites/default/files/anexos/documentos-relacionados/regulamento_conduta.pdf; último acesso: 24.05.2024.

Federação Portuguesa de Futebol (FPF). "Portal de denúncia: Integridade". Disponível em: https://integridade.fpf.pt/; último acesso: 23.05.2024.

Gabinete Nacional de Segurança (GNS). "GNS: canal de denúncias". Disponível em: https://www.gns.gov.pt/pt/canal-de-denuncias/#enq; último acesso: 24.05.2024.

Gabinete Nacional de Segurança (GNS). "Manual de Procedimentos: canal de denúncias". Disponível em: https://www.gns.gov.pt/docs/manual-canal-denuncias.pdf; último acesso: 24.05.2024.

Ministério da Administração Interna (MAI). "Canal de denúncia". Disponível em: https://www.sg.mai.gov.pt/EspacoCidadao/CanalDenuncia/Paginas/default.aspx; último acesso: 25.05.2024.

Procuradoria Geral da República (PGR). "Corrupção: denuncie aqui". Disponível em: https://simp.pgr.pt/dciap/denuncias/index2.php; último acesso: 23.05.2024.

Secretaria-Geral da Presidência do Conselho de Ministros (SGPCM). "Canal de Denúncia Interna". Disponível em: https://www.sg.pcm.gov.pt/a-sgpcm/canal-de-denuncias/; último acesso: 24.05.2024.

Documentary References

Conselho de Ministros. Comunicado do Conselho de Ministros de 29 de abril de 2021. Disponível em: https://www.portugal.gov.pt/pt/gc22/governo/comunicado-de-conselho-de-ministros?i=416; último acesso: 23.05.2024.

Presidência do Conselho de Ministros (2021). Resolução do Conselho de Ministros nº 37/2021. Aprova a Estratégia Nacional Anticorrupção 2020-2024. Diário da República (DR), 1ª série, nº 66, 06 de abril de 2021; pp. 8-49. Disponível em: https://files.dre.pt/1s/2021/04/06600/0000800049.pdf; último acesso: 17.05.2024.

United Nations Office on Drugs and Crime (2004). *United Nations Convention Against Corruption*. United Nations. Disponível em: https://www.unodc.org/documents/brussels/UN_Convention_Against_Corruption.pdf; último acesso: 17.05.2024.

Procuradoria Geral da República (PGR), Ministério Público de Portugal. Dados estatísticos — corrupção e crimes conexos/2023. disponível em: https://www.ministeriopublico.pt/sites/default/files/documentos/pdf/corrupcao_e_crimes_conexos_2023.pdf; último acesso: 23.05.2024.

Normative References

Assembleia da República. Lei n.º 93/99, de 14 de Julho. Regula a aplicação de medidas para protecção de testemunhas em processo penal. Diário da República (DR), n.º 162/1999, Série I-A, 14.07.1999, pp. 4386-4391. Disponível em: https://diariodarepublica.pt/dr/legislacao-consolidada/lei/1999-71049723; último acesso: 23.05.2024.

Assembleia da República. Lei n.º 19/2008, de 21 de Abril. Aprova medidas de combate à corrupção e procede à primeira alteração à Lei n.º 5/2002, de 11 de Janeiro, à décima sétima alteração à lei geral tributária e à terceira alteração à Lei n.º 4/83, de 2 de Abril. Diário da República (DR), n.º 78/2008,

Série I, 21.04.2008, pp. 2288-2289. Disponível em: https://diariodarepublica.pt/dr/legislacao-consolidada/lei/2008-34457875; último acesso: 23.05.2024.

Assembleia da República. Lei n.º 83/2017, de 18 de agosto. Estabelece medidas de combate ao branqueamento de capitais e ao financiamento do terrorismo, transpõe parcialmente as Diretivas 2015/849/UE, do Parlamento Europeu e do Conselho, de 20 de maio de 2015, e 2016/2258/UE, do Conselho, de 6 de dezembro de 2016, altera o Código Penal e o Código da Propriedade Industrial e revoga a Lei n.º 25/2008, de 5 de junho, e o Decreto-Lei n.º 125/2008, de 21 de julho. Diário da República (DR), n.º 159/2017, Série I, 18.08.2017, pp. 4784 - 4848. Disponível em: https://diariodarepublica.pt/dr/legislacao-consolidada/lei/2017-108024643; último acesso: 23.05.2024.

Assembleia da República. Projeto de Lei n.º 866/XIV/2.a, Criação do Regime de Proteção do Denunciante. Diário da Assembleia da República (DAR), n.º 149/2021, II Série A, 09.06.2021, pp. 2-7.

Assembleia da República. Lei n.º 93/2021, de 20 de dezembro, Estabelece o regime geral de proteção de denunciantes de infrações, transpondo a Diretiva (UE) 2019/1937 do Parlamento Europeu e do Conselho, de 23 de outubro de 2019, relativa à proteção das pessoas que denunciam violações do direito da União. Diário da República (DR), n.º 244/2021, Série I, 20.12.2021, pp. 3-15.

Assembleia da República. Lei n.º 5/1998, de 31 de janeiro, altera a Lei Orgânica do Banco de Portugal, tendo em vista a sua integração no Sistema Europeu de bancos Centrais. Diário da República (DR), n.º 26/1998, Série I-A, 31.01.1998, pp. 405-415.

Governo de Portugal, Ministério da Justiça. Decreto-Lei n.º 190/2003, de 22 de Agosto. Regula a aplicação de medidas para protecção de testemunhas em processo penal. Diário da República (DR), n.º 193/2003, Série I-A, 22.08.2003, pp. 5411 -5415. Disponível em: https://diariodarepublica.pt/dr/legislacao-consolidada/decreto-lei/2003-71058477; último acesso: 23.05.2024.

Governo de Portugal, Ministério das Finanças. Decreto-Lei n.º 486/99, de 13 de Novembro. Aprova o novo Código dos Valores Mobiliários. Diário da República (DR), n.º 265/1999, Série I-A, 13.11.1999, pp. 7968-8040. Disponível em: https://diariodarepublica.pt/dr/detalhe/decreto-lei/486-1999-682983; último acesso: 23.05.2024.

Governo de Portugal, Ministério das Finanças. Decreto-Lei n.º 298/92, de 31 de Dezembro. Aprova o Regime Geral das Instituições de Crédito e Sociedades Financeiras. Diário da República (DR), n.º 301/1992, 6º Suplemento, Série I-A, 31.12.1992, pp. 24-51. Disponível em: https://diariodarepublica.pt/dr/legislacao-consolidada/decreto-lei/1992-70072322; último acesso: 23.05.2024.

Parlamento Europeu. Conselho da União Europeia. DIRETIVA (UE) 2019/1937 DO PARLAMENTO EUROPEU E DO CONSELHO, de 23 de outubro de 2019, relativa à proteção das pessoas que denunciam violações do direito da União. Jornal Oficial da União Europeia (JO) L 305, 26.11.2019, pp. 17-56. Disponível em: https://eur-lex.europa.eu/eli/dir/2019/1937/oj; último acesso: 24.05.2024.

Presidência do Conselho de Ministros, Ministério da Justiça. Decreto-Lei n.º 109-E/2021, de 9 de dezembro. Cria o Mecanismo Nacional Anticorrupção e estabelece o regime geral de prevenção da corrupção. Diário da República (DR), n.º 237/2021, 1º Suplemento, Série I, 09.12.2021, pp. 19-42. Disponível em: https://diariodarepublica.pt/dr/detalhe/decreto-lei/109-e-2021-175659840; último acesso: 23.05.2024.

Presidência do Conselho de Ministros, Ministério das Finanças. Decreto-Lei n.º 27/2023, de 23 de Abril. Aprova o Regime da Gestão de Ativos. Diário da República (DR), n.º 83/2023, Série I, 28.04.2023, pp. 2-184. Disponível em: https://diariodarepublica.pt/dr/detalhe/decreto-lei/27-2023-212379454; último acesso: 23.05.2024.

Presidência do Conselho de Ministros. Decreto-Lei n.º 3/2012, de 16 de janeiro. Aprova a orgânica do Gabinete Nacional de Segurança. Diário da República (DR), n.º 11/2012, Série I, 16.01.2012, pp. 174-177. Disponível em: https://diariodarepublica.pt/dr/legislacao-consolidada/decreto-lei/2012-114157278; último acesso: 23.05.2024.

It is here to stay - Artificial Intelligence in internal investigations

Christian Miege

1. Introduction

In our rapidly changing world, AI is the EVERYWHERE buzzword, it is THE dominating subject matter leading to groundbreaking developments in almost all fields: from everyday applications to complex scientific research, AI shapes and changes our professional as well as our private lives.

The compliance world is of course no exception to this: Technology support in internal investigations is not a new phenomenon. But with the rise of Artificial Intelligence (AI) supported systems being increasingly employed in internal investigations we see substantial changes at a rapid speed. The article will explore the use of AI in compliance-driven internal investigations. It will delve into how AI algorithms can even more efficiently analyze large volumes of data, identifying patterns and anomalies indicative of misconduct, but also how to review information in contexts not just for search terms.

However, the new tools come with some flip side. This article will thus consider not only potential benefits but also challenges the use of AI presents. For instance, the integration of AI into internal investigations can raise data protection and criminal law considerations. The article will discuss how to manage sensitive data and uphold individual privacy rights. Furthermore, it will investigate potential criminal liability and the complex nature of prosecuting AI-derived evidence.

2. AI and internal investigations

When there is suspicion of misconduct, whether through internal reports, regulatory actions, or external allegations, a swift, thorough internal investigation is necessary. As globalization and digitization advance and as the regulatory frameworks become ever more demanding, the requirements for internal investigators increase in complexity, in particular in international organizations. In an era in which data is produced at an unprecedented rate, also internal investigators (internal sources as well as external consultants) face significant challenges in managing, analyzing, and reviewing information during investigations. Furthermore, the incident numbers increase due to rising levels of awareness while in parallel they tend to become multidimensional and more challenging, be it around greenwashing allegations, product compliance or #metoo cases.

This is where AI tools comes into play. They change or are going to change end-to-end all aspects of internal investigations. However, the most prevalent and promising use case for AI support is probably around eDiscovery.

3. eDiscovery

AI tools can already transform more traditional methods of eDiscovery. As AI technology advances, its application in eDiscovery offers enhanced efficiency and accuracy, making it an essential tool for modern internal investigations.

3.1. Understanding eDiscovery

eDiscovery is the process of identifying, collecting, preserving, reviewing, and exchanging electronically stored information (ESI) in the context of internal investigations. This can include a wide range of data types such as emails, documents, databases, audio and video files, social media posts, and any other digital content that may be relevant to the fact finding.

eDiscovery as such is a 'traditional' investigation tool established for at least over two decades, crucial in the digital age as it provides a systematic approach to handle the vast amounts of electronic data that are potentially needed to collect facts, to understand patterns or that finally might be used as evidence in legal and compliance matters. eDiscovery helps internal investigators navigate the complexities of digital information in a way that is efficient, cost- and time-effective.

3.2. More 'traditional' vs. more modern approaches

There are various challenges around data and subsequently around the eDiscovery:

i. Data Volume: The sheer amount of ESI has grown exponentially with the rise of digital communication and storage. Managing and reviewing vast quantities of data is challenging, can be overwhelming and is usually very resource intensive, time consuming, and therefore costly.

ii. Data Complexity (technical): Data comes in various formats, from simple text documents to complex databases, and includes unstructured data like emails, social media, and multimedia files. The various data types requires different tools and methods for effective eDiscovery.

iii. Data Relevance (content): Determining the relevance of documents can be challenging, especially when dealing with large datasets and complex issues. Irrelevant data can increase review time and costs.

iv. Data Governance: Organizations often lack proper information governance policies, which can lead to challenges in preserving, collecting, and managing ESI effectively during eDiscovery.

v. Review Consistency: Ensuring consistent judgments on document relevance and privilege across different reviewers can be challenging, especially in large-scale reviews.

vi. Data Privacy and Compliance: With strict privacy regulations like the General Data Protection Regulation (GDPR) in the EU or the California Consumer Privacy Act (CCPA) in the United States, eDiscovery must be conducted in a way that respects privacy laws, which can complicate the collection and review of data across jurisdictions.

vii. Data Security: Protecting sensitive and confidential information during the eDiscovery process is critical. There is a constant risk of data breaches and unauthorized access, which can have legal and reputational consequences.

viii. Costs: eDiscovery can be very expensive, especially when large volumes of data are involved. Costs include software, hardware and service providers.

ix. Time Constraints: Legal proceedings often operate under strict deadlines. The time-sensitive nature of eDiscovery can add pressure to investigation teams to work quickly.

x. Preservation: Properly preserving ESI to prevent spoliation (destruction or alteration of evidence) is a critical challenge, as failure to do so can lead to legal consequences.

As mentioned, using advanced technological tools is not new in internal investigations, at least not in eDiscovery. Still, it makes sense to contrast more 'traditional' methods of document review with modern AI-assisted techniques. See in the below table a comparison between these two:

Process step	**Traditional Approach**	**More modern Approach**
Review Process	Manual review of each document.	Technology-assisted review (TAR) and predictive coding.
Review Order	Strict linear review from first to last document.	Prioritized review focusing on most likely relevant documents.
Search Methodology	Basic keyword searches	Advanced analytics, including concept searches and contextual analysis.
Data Organization	Limited organization, often leading to redundant reviews.	Advanced analytics for email threading, deduplication, and clustering.
Consistency	Potential for inconsistency due to manual processes.	Increased consistency with standardized, automated processes.
Accuracy	Depending on experience of reviewer	Definitely also not 100% safe, but as precise as a well experienced senior reviewer, but much faster.
Time	Manual review of probably not more than 700-800 documents per day per reviewer (first level review)	The machine does not get tired, it works on and on and on – time saved is likely one of the most relevant aspects of AI in internal investigations
Cost	High costs due to manual labor and time.	Direct cost efficiency through reduced manual review, indirect (cost) benefits through faster processes (e.g. for leniency applications).

The Role of AI in eDiscovery

AI has become a game-changer in the field of eDiscovery by enhancing the ability to process and analyze vast amounts of digital data. Traditional eDiscovery methods are often labor-intensive and time-consuming, but AI technologies, such as machine learning and natural language processing, can automate these tasks, significantly improving efficiency. AI can quickly sift through large datasets to identify relevant information, predict outcomes based on patterns, and even uncover hidden connections that might be missed by human investigators. For example, AI tools can retrieve company information very effectively and allow for network displays potentially revealing relationships that otherwise would have gone unnoticed. There are several technologies commonly used in eDiscovery (e.g., machine learning, natural language processing (NLP)), which become even more powerful when boosted with the latest AI capabilities:

- Predictive Coding (Technology-Assisted Review - TAR): In eDiscovery, AI predicts which documents are relevant based on sample data using a process called predictive coding or Technology-Assisted Review (TAR). The AI system is first 'trained' by having human reviewers manually tag a representative set of documents as relevant or irrelevant. The AI then analyzes these tagged samples to identify patterns, keywords, and concepts that distinguish relevant from irrelevant documents. This concept is not new but becomes much better with better AI tools applied. Using machine learning algorithms, the AI applies this understanding to the larger dataset, predicting the relevance of each document with a degree of confidence. As the AI encounters more reviewed documents, it refines its predictions, becoming increasingly accurate in identifying relevant documents.
- Data Processing and Analysis: The role of AI in sorting and analyzing large datasets. AI significantly enhances data processing and analysis in eDiscovery by swiftly organizing, categorizing, and indexing large datasets. It employs text analytics, pattern recognition, and clustering algorithms to sort through vast amounts of information, identifying and grouping related documents. In analyzing large datasets, AI's role is to filter out noise, prioritize relevant data, and uncover hidden patterns, relationships, and trends that might not be immediately apparent to human reviewers, thereby facilitating a more focused and efficient review process.
- Document Review and Redaction: Use of AI to automate the review process and ensure sensitive information is redacted. It employs algorithms to understand context and content, automating the identification and redaction of privileged information or personal data that requires redaction. For redaction, AI can automatically detect and obscure sensitive information like social security numbers, financial details (personally identifiable information (PII)), or confidential business information, ensuring compliance

with privacy regulations before data is shared or analyzed. This reduces the manual effort typically associated with this meticulous task and helps mitigate the risk of data breaches and unauthorized access.

- Email Threading: Identifying and grouping together email threads, which helps reviewers to understand the context of conversations and reduces the need to review redundant information.
- Near-Duplicate Detection: Finding and grouping documents that are nearly identical but may have minor differences, ensuring that similar documents are reviewed consistently.
- Sentiment Analysis: By analyzing the sentiment expressed in communications, AI can help identify documents that may be more likely to be relevant to certain legal matters, such as disputes or investigations involving emotional content (e.g. discrimination, harassment, #metoo).
- Audio and Video Analysis: With the increasing relevance of multimedia content in legal cases, AI technologies can transcribe audio and video files and make them searchable, expanding the scope of eDiscovery beyond text-based documents.
- Chat and Instant Message Analysis: Organizing and analyzing data from chat and instant messaging platforms, which often have unique formats and metadata.
- Language Translation: AI-powered translation tools can automatically translate documents in foreign languages, making it easier to review documents in cross border investigation.
- Data Visualization: AI-driven data visualization tools can represent data in graphical formats, making it easier to identify patterns, relationships, and trends within the ESI.
- Anomaly Detection: AI can identify outliers or anomalies in data sets that may indicate important or unusual activity, which could be particularly relevant in investigations.

3.3. Data Identification and Collection: How AI helps in identifying relevant data quickly.

Data identification and collection are critical steps in the data analysis process to be able to focus on relevant issues. This is particularly important to reduce costs of reviews which might be priced either on the amount of data or number of documents reviewed. In either way, the smaller and focused the data set, less efforts in terms of money and time are required for review. Also from a data protection perspective a cautious approach is required, data protection rules demand, as a principle, data minimization.

AI can significantly enhance these steps in several ways: AI can automatically classify and categorize data based on predefined criteria, making it easier to organize and retrieve relevant datasets when needed. It can process and identify relevant data in real-time, which can be crucial for applications that require immediate insights, such as fraud detection. Overall, AI can accelerate the data identification and collection process, reduces the potential for human error, and enables more efficient and effective use of data.

3.4. Benefits of AI in eDiscovery: Efficiency, accuracy, cost-effectiveness, and speed.

As described above, AI in eDiscovery offers numerous benefits, including increased efficiency by automating the identification and categorization of relevant documents, which significantly reduces the time and labor involved in manual review. AI, thus, can help to lower costs by streamlining the eDiscovery process and reducing the volume of data that requires human review. The cost factor is dependent on the amount of data or number of documents processed. Although costs are expected to decrease, a decisive factor so as not to balance the decrease in costs with an increase in the amount of data analysed, will be to focus on the relevant data. Furthermore, in critical investigations, most often time is of the essence. Imagine a situation in which a company wants to apply for leniency to a competition authority; or a case involving a member of the executive board when almost instantly at least indicative results are expected to judge whether an in-depth analysis is required or whether the allegations seem to have no basis. Furthermore, AI supported reviews enhance accuracy by minimizing human error and ensuring consistent application of review criteria across large datasets. In a test it was established that AI tools were as good as an experienced senior reviewer, but of course at an incomparable pace.

4. Ethical and Legal Considerations

4.1. Data Privacy and Security: How AI tools ensure data privacy and security during eDiscovery.

Data protection is a critical concern in eDiscovery, especially given the stringent regulations governing the handling of personal data. Strict data protection rules like the EU-GDPR and the CCPA in the United States set high standards for data privacy and protection. Thus, AI tools need to be designed to comply with such legal and regulatory standards. They also must ensure data security during eDiscovery by implementing strict access controls, ensuring only authorized users can access sensitive data. The use of encryption protocols to protect data both at rest and in transit is mandatory. Monitoring systems should be implemented to detect and respond to any security breaches promptly.

Still, as described above, one important question will be the amount of data to be processed. Only such data where a legitimate reason for processing exists can become subject of an eDiscovery at all. It remains a probably growing challenge to managing excessively large volumes of data and maintaining the security of AI systems themselves.

4.2. Bias and Fairness: Addressing concerns about AI bias in investigation contexts.

AI in investigation contexts involves ensuring transparency in AI 'decision-making processes', maintaining rigorous validation and testing of AI tools to establish their reliability, and adhering to ethical standards. It is also crucial to keep human oversight integral to AI tools in investigation work to interpret results correctly and make final judgments.

The use of AI in eDiscovery also raises important ethical considerations. One major concern is the potential for bias in AI algorithms, which can lead to unfair outcomes. Bias can be introduced at various stages, from data selection to algorithm design, and can perpetuate existing inequalities. Ensuring transparency in AI decision-making processes is essential to address these concerns. Investigation professionals and technologists must work together to develop ethical guidelines and frameworks that promote fairness and accountability in AI applications. Additionally, the human factor is crucial, that means the users of AI tools must be on guard for these challenges and trained and enabled to detect biased outcomes.

There is need for ongoing education and training to equip investigation professionals (inhouse as well as external consultants) with the skills to work alongside AI technologies with the aim to further mitigate concerns of AI in investigations and legal contexts.

5. Interaction with whistleblowers

AI tools can be extremely helpful to support dealings with whistleblowers. First, they can provide support to hand in the hint, e.g. with a supporting chat bot solution guiding the whistleblower through the process to collect as much information as possible. Second, a tool could be used to transform (including translations if need be) incoming messages into a predefined format, providing meaningful summaries of the message and/or attached documentation allowing for a quick understanding of its merits. This could also help to level message to a uniform format, eliminating e.g. improper use of language or grammar. While on the one hand this attaches some inclusive elements to the process as the 'value' of the message is no longer dependent on the whistleblower's language or storytelling qualities, on the other experienced investigators usually will like to have an 'uncensored' view and own impression of the original message.

Further on, AI tools can support the internal investigator to set up an investigation plan based on the information received. After such analysis, the tool can help to prepare a response to the whistleblower, to confirm receipt and to request further information if need be.

Whether the application of such tools is proportionate and of significant help to the investigation team depends on the sheer number of incoming messages, their variety (geographies, languages) and complexity as well as the capabilities of the system to justify attached costs or the training efforts.

6. Interviews

AI can also be useful for all aspects around interviews: preparation, conducting it, its documentation and the conclusions derived from it. Based on the information available, AI can support to compile a questionnaire specifically addressing the key issues of the investigation and the interviewee. However, the human factor remains important, as AI thus far will not provide for any guidance how to practically run the interview, e.g. when to ask critical questions or to confront the interviewee with certain documents. Not to forget specific interrogation techniques like the PEACE interview approach[1] that only human investigators can bring to the table.

A real practical benefit lies in transcription as well as translation of interviews. AI systems already easily transcribe speech to text in real-time, enabling an immediate written record of the conversation. The interviewees (it is usually a team of at least two conducting interviews) can fully focus on the progress and the content of the conversation, and do not need to bother producing interview notes interrupting the flow of the interview. The focus of the internal investigators can then lie more on interrogation qualities than on being good notetakers. For informational interviews (in contrast to confrontational interviews) we even might see increased pressure to conduct them with only one interviewer. However, in many jurisdictions for recording interviews (transcription is likely to be considered as some form of temporary recording) the confirmation of the interviewee is required. In some parts of the world this is no big deal, in central Europe people might not be that used to that yet.

It is technically possible, that even non-textual cues can be captured, e.g. the tone of the voice, the talking speed or pauses in relation to certain questions and last not least, when it is a video interview, the physical behavior of people, e.g. overall 'body language', eye movements, use of the hands. Such analyses could support to determine the interviewee's mental state, for example, anxious, angry, or nervous, providing additional insights into the interviewee's statement behavior. This is in general technically already possible. However, there are severe ethical and legal issues. First, the accuracy of such analyses should not be overstated, given that individuals behave very differently and unpredictable in an uncomfortable situation like a forensic interview. Second, from a data protection or overall legal perspective, such an application is highly questionable.

There is a permanent debate what sort of interview notes is preferable. With this technology word protocols (maybe eliminating filler words or hesitation sounds) likely will become dominant, as the AI tool can produce an abstract with different detail levels of the content focusing on the merits of the case. International interviews can also become easier to handle, as the tools even provide for simultaneous translation, at least for some major languages. It is possible however likely in very critical cases not recommendable that the interview partners use transcription tools simultaneously translating the conversation into different languages. There is a risk of decisive information being missed.

The interview notes can be used by AI tools under the critical surveillance of an experienced internal investigator to e.g. derive new questions for other interviews, further clues for other investigative steps, or the form of the final report.

7. Data analyses

By analyzing historical data and using machine learning, AI can identify patterns and trends to either run further in-depth analyses as part of the investigation or to predict possible violations or future risks. AI tools can analyse financial data of companies like balance sheets, inventory lists, bank statements etc. to detect anomalies or red flags to be further reviewed.

In the context of background research, artificial intelligence can also be used to semi-automatically search publicly available sources and display relationships between individuals and companies.

8. Investigation Reporting

AI tools can be used to support the report writing. That means the tools feed relevant data into more or less defined documents to save the internal investigator the pain of compiling or retrieving all this relevant data from the bunch of information collected and produced during the investigation. This support will likely focus on the facts of the case. However, it is feasible that tools also can support in legal analysis, be it upon internal company rules, regulations and process descriptions, or be it on official laws and regulations. This raises the question whether any assessment competence or even decision-making authority will be handed to an algorithm or an AI tool. Given, that the decision-making paths of AI are often difficult to understand – a phenomenon known as the "Black Box" problem of AI - the lack of transparency and traceability can make it difficult to review decisions and present the results of the investigation in a audit proof or court-admissible manner. In addition, also for mere internal decisions, the ultimate responsibility must be borne by humans; mere AI based decisions should not be accepted.[2]

9. Challenges around AI-based investigation actions

The use of specialized AI, regardless of its advanced processing and analysis capabilities, remains very complex. Crucial is always the underlying data and how these are introduced into the applications, as well as the formulation of the text inputs ("prompts"). If the data or the "questions" are faulty or inaccurate, this leads to misleading results ("Garbage in, garbage out"). Moreover, AI is only as good as the prompt it is dealing with to make use of its ability to capture contextual nuances and human judgments, which are often crucial in forensic investigations, for example, to identify coded agreements between participants in a crime. A detailed description of the prompts is always necessary, which in turn requires specialized knowledge for the operational operation and interpretation of the results. One should also not fall into the mistaken belief that AI makes the investigator's thinking work, especially in the conceptual area, superfluous – the more unstructured and complex the facts, the more the human is still in demand.

As mentioned before, further challenges lie around data protection and legal requirements. When analyzing large data sets, there is always the risk of violating personal rights if sensitive data is handled improperly. It is therefore essential to ensure the protection of private information of the affected individuals and to comply with the legally required level of data protection. Moreover, despite a European standard, data protection regulations vary from country to country, which further complicates the use of AI, especially in cross-border investigations (particularly in connection with third countries). Overall, the technology of artificial intelligence is developing at a breakneck pace – legislation can hardly keep up. Since internal investigations still mostly lack a specific legal basis, there are also (still) no clear framework conditions, standards, or best practices for many aspects of the use of AI in forensic investigations.[3]

10. The future: AI developments

10.1. The Future of AI in eDiscovery

The landscape of eDiscovery is rapidly evolving with the integration of even further advanced AI technologies which promise to transform eDiscovery by enabling more sophisticated data interrogation and document generation.

The future of AI in eDiscovery is poised for continued growth and innovation, with several emerging trends and developments shaping the landscape:

- Advanced Predictive Coding: As machine learning algorithms become more sophisticated, predictive coding will evolve to provide even more accurate document classification, reducing the need for human review.
- Greater Integration of AI: AI will become more seamlessly integrated into all stages of the eDiscovery process, from identification and collection to review and production, creating a more unified and efficient workflow.
- AI for Multilingual eDiscovery: AI tools will further improve in handling and analyzing documents in multiple languages, making cross-border eDiscovery easier and more efficient.
- Voice and Video Analysis: AI will get better at transcribing and analyzing voice and video content, which is increasingly important as these types of data become more relevant.
- Regulatory Compliance Tools: AI will increasingly be used to ensure that eDiscovery practices comply with evolving data privacy laws and regulations.

10.2. Other aspects of Internal Investigations

AI tools will be capable of not only guiding the whistleblowers, but also provide guidance whether a reported matter can be considered critical based on the information provided or which further information would be needed for such conclusion. However, this leads to the same ethical and legal questions just discussed above.

Future generative AI systems will be able to identify complex patterns and relationships within data even more accurately and make more precise predictions about future events. Advances in natural language processing could lead to AI being able to identify suspicious conversations or decrypt the meaning of encrypted or coded messages – at a level far beyond what exists today, provided a legal basis for its use is there.

It is also conceivable that machines will conduct audiovisual interviews and compare statements from interviewees in real-time with findings from data analyses or email reviews. In addition, this could allow to redefine interview strategies on the spot, the system recognizing human anomalies and making assessments about the truthfulness of statements might be further developed. Still, solid ethical concerns remain.

Reporting will also be simplified as AI assists the investigator in writing concise reports in a comparable stable quality, especially in presenting repetitive processes (such as multiple fraud or theft offenses with the same modus operandi). Also here, questions of legal admissibility remain open to date.

We will likely see a vast increase in what can be called 'smaller eDiscoveries', provided that a) legal implications, in particular data protection considerations, can be managed, b) costs will decrease (which is to be expected) for decent amounts of data to be processed and c) results are sufficiently accurate to form the basis of further internal investigations or even the legal analysis. We are going to see that AI based results – sufficiently scrutinized and transparent (as far as this is possible)- will more and more be accepted by authorities and courts.

At least in the mid-term, there will even be more and more sophisticated, dedicated AI systems, probably even for specific types of compliance misbehavior (e.g. more data driven vs. more context based). But this is a separate story.

11. Conclusion

The potential of AI to continually enhance eDiscovery and internal investigations is undoubtedly there and it is manifest. In conclusion, AI has a profound impact on eDiscovery, offering significant benefits in terms of (time) efficiency, accuracy, and cost-effectiveness. For this reason, all internal investigation professionals are encouraged to embrace AI tools. They don't need to be afraid to get redundant. It is quite the opposite, they will have much more time to do the fun stuff, for which the empathetic human analysis is required, instead of 'clicking' through thousands of mails, day after day.

As described above, the integration of AI in legal investigations also raises important considerations related to fundamental ethical questions, but also legal topics like data protection or data security. Addressing ethical challenges, ensuring compliance with data protection regulations, a thorough understanding of national and international laws and regulations, and facilitating secure cross-border data transfers are crucial for the responsible use of AI in international internal investigations.

AI will have an impact on the future of internal investigations, thus, as AI technologies continuously evolve, it is - although it sometimes seems impossible – eminent for internal investigation professionals to stay informed and adapt to these changes to maximize the benefits. But no doubt the challenge in parallel will be to mitigate potential risks, finding the right balance between leveraging the capabilities of AI technologies while maintaining high ethical and legal standards. The future of AI in eDiscovery holds great promise, and ongoing evaluation and adaptation will be key to harnessing its full potential.

Notes

1 PEACE is a five-stage process of investigative interviewing: the acronym stands for: 1) Planning and Preparation, 2) Engage and Explain, 3) Account, Clarify and Challenge, 4) Closure, and 5) Evaluation.

2 See the debate about AI tools already used by US authorities for sentencing or bail decisions, e.g. https://www.bu.edu/articles/2023/do-algorithms-reduce-bias-in-criminal-justice/

3 ISO norm 37008 does not cover this topic.

A roadmap to Certification of Association of Corporate Investigators ("ACI")

Patrick Wellens

1. Background

The Association of Corporate Investigators ("ACI") is a global not-for-profit association founded by corporate investigators to meet the needs of the corporation investigation community in its widest sense, from entrants to seasoned professionals, across all sectors. ACI provide platforms for sharing thought leadership, cross-industry insights, networking opportunities and centralized resources. We are developing the gold standard in corporate investigations training, drawing from leading industry experts in our community.

In the last years the ACi has developed an Investigators Handbook [1], created the principles for effective investigations[2], good practice guidance[3] and actively contributed to by taking a leading role in the creation of the ISO37008 standard on "corporation investigations".

To pursue professional excellence and establish "the gold standard in corporate investigations", it is needed for the ACI to develop a certification for investigators. This abstract describes the research undertaken to identify the content and best method of delivery for a corporate investigator accredited qualification.

2. The various stages of ACI Certified Corporate Investigator (CCI) accreditation.

As can be seen on Figure 1 the ACI went through various project stages for almost 2 years to develop and launch the CCI credential to its members all over the globe.

2.1 Project stage – member survey

To obtain input on what its members believe should be part of a certification, the ACI conducted a survey among its members in April-May 2022. 125 members responded to the survey.

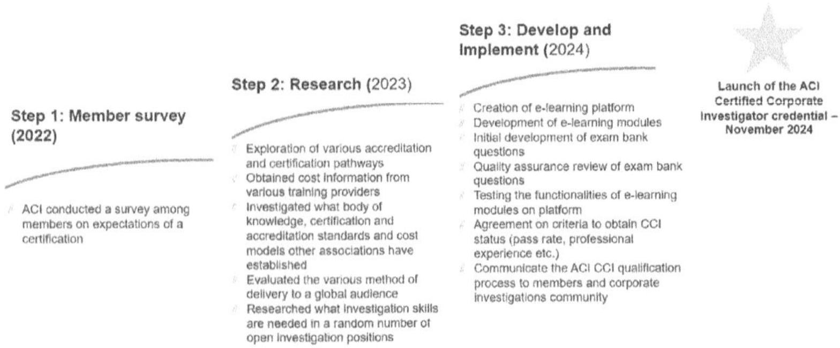

Figure 1: Project stages of the Certified Corporate Investigator credential

Respondents were asked:

- Would you be in interested in being recognized as an accredited investigator (results: see Figure 3)
- Which type of certification do you think that ACI should offer? (Figure 4)
- What relevant professional experience should be required to obtain the ACI certification? (Figure 5)
- Should professional references be required to obtain the certification? (Figure 6)
- Should a test/exam be needed to obtain the certification? (Figure 7)
- Should there be a mandatory course as pre-requisite to obtain the certification (Figure 8)
- What knowledge/skillset is needed to obtain a certification (Figure 9)
- Should other professional certifications be considered? (Figure 10)

The profile of the respondents is shown in Figure 2.

When asking ACI members whether they would be interested in a professional certification the overwhelming part (99 out of 119 or 83%) said yes, as can be seen on Figure 3.

As can be seen on Figure 4, 71% of respondents would be in favor of a general accreditation and slightly over 50% would be in favor of an advanced level or specialist level accreditation/certification.

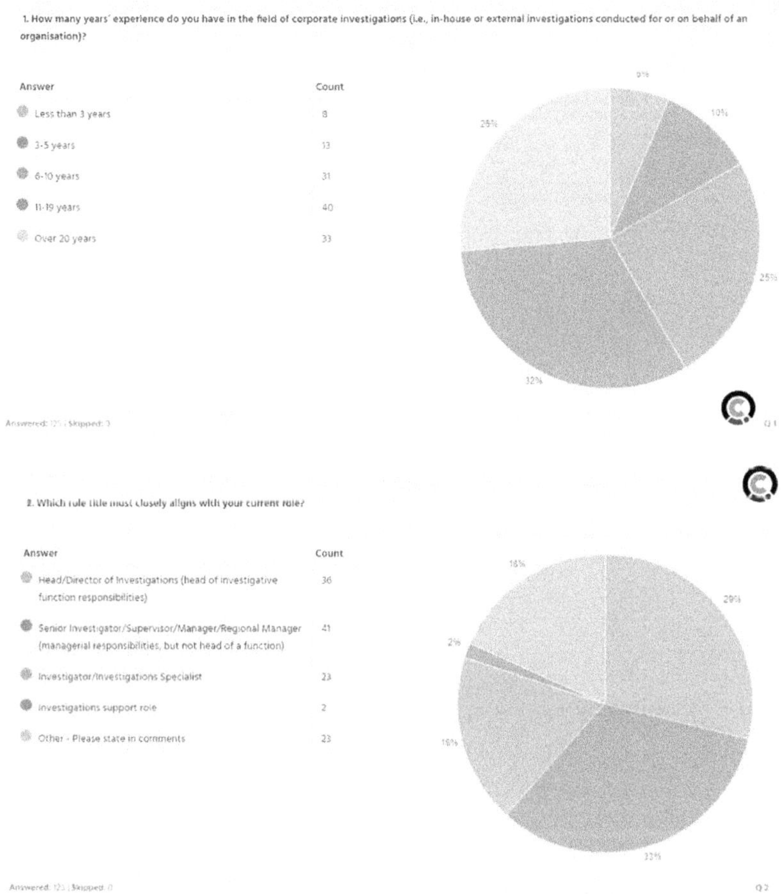

Figure 2: Profile of those participating in certification survey by number of years investigation experience and by job title

Survey respondents did not provide a clear answer on how many years professional experience is needed to obtain a certification. Whereas 16% of respondents say that more than 5 years professional experience is needed, 22% of respondents say that 5 years professional experience is needed, 25% of respondents say that 3 years professional experience is needed, 23% of

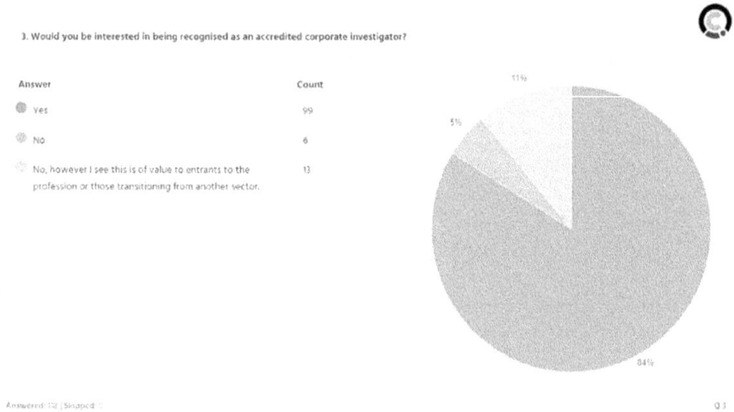

Figure 3: interest in professional ACI certification

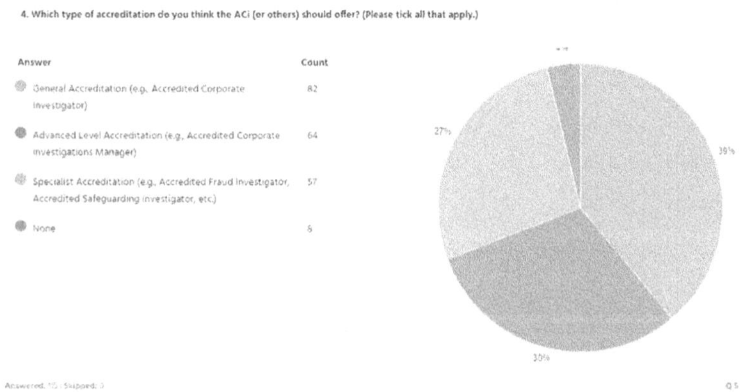

Figure 4: what kind of certification would be interested to ACI members?

respondents say that 2 years professional experience is needed and 11% of respondents even believe that no professional experience whatsoever is needed.

Survey respondents overwhelmingly believe that professional references should be verified, as can be seen on Figure 6.

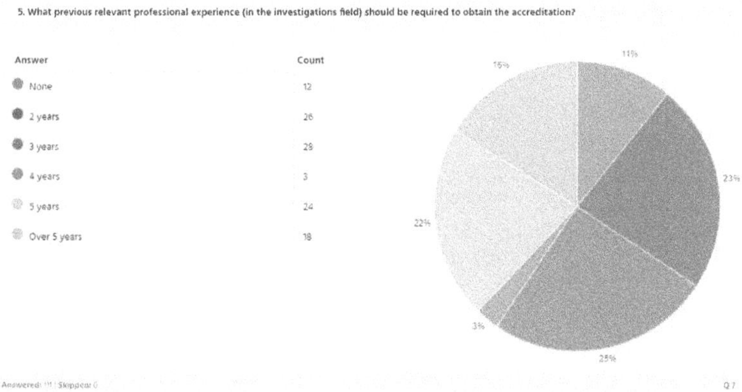

Figure 5: what professional experience would be required to obtain the certification?

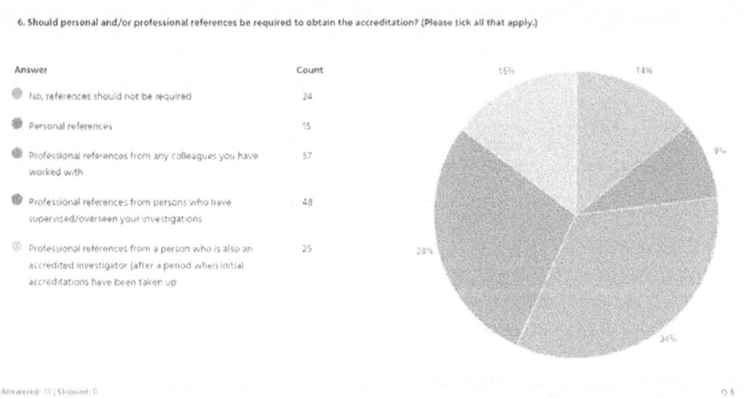

Figure 6: Should professional references be required to obtain the certification?

33% of respondents are in favor of an exam consisting of a combination of multiple choice and written responses; 20% believes the forementioned written exam with multiple choice and open response questions should be combined with an oral exam; and 19% believes that only a multiple- choice exam should suffice.

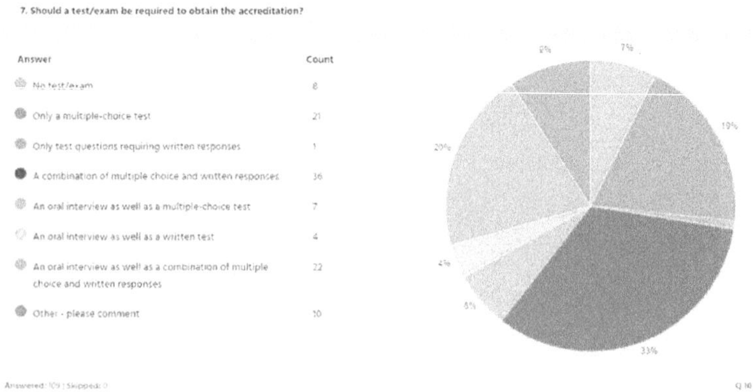

Figure 7: Should a test/exam be needed to obtain the certification?

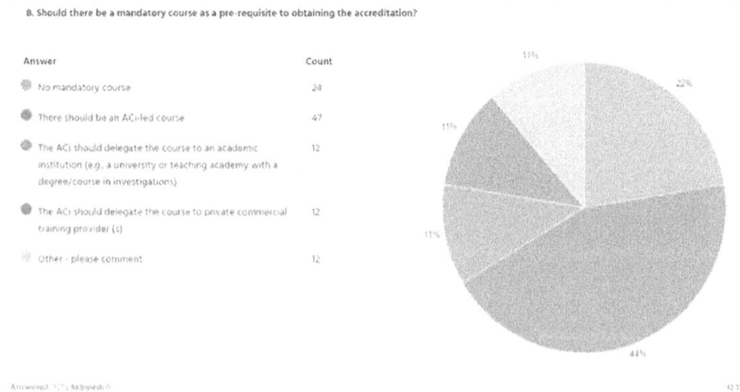

Figure 8: Should there be a mandatory course as pre-requisite to obtain the certification?

44% of survey respondents are of the opinion that there should be an ACI led course; 12% of respondents believe that the ACI should delegate such course to a private training provider and another 12% believe that ACI should delegate the course to an academic institution. Overall, 70% are in favor of a course whereas 22% believe no course is needed.

As can be seen on Figure 9, in decreasing order of importance, respondents feel that the following skillset would be needed as part of ACI certification:

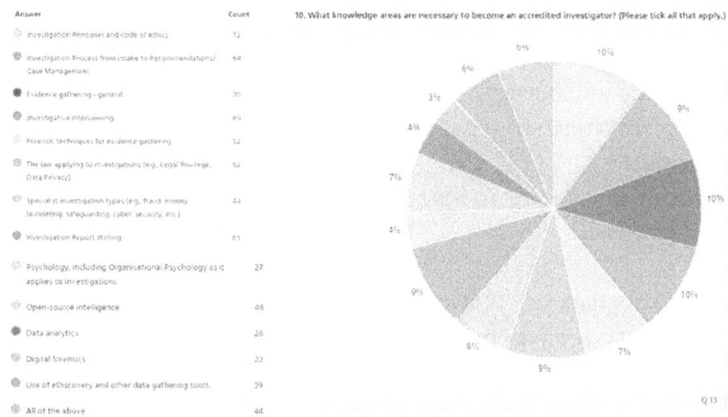

Figure 9: What knowledge/which skillset is needed to obtain the certification?

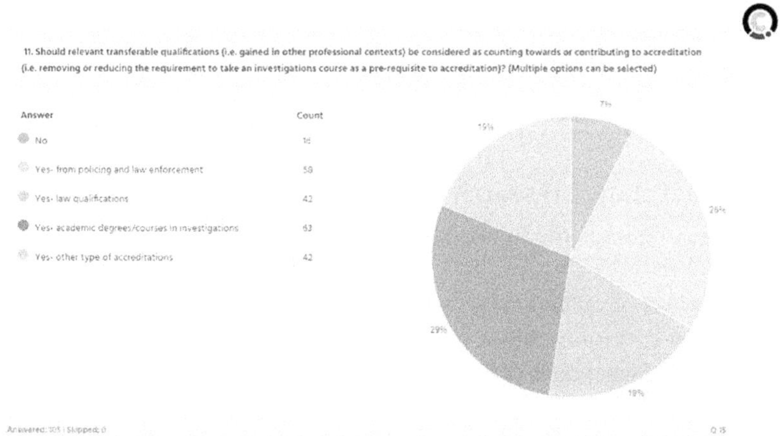

Figure 10: should other professional certifications be considered?

- Investigation principles and code of ethics
- Evidence gathering
- Investigative Interviewing skills
- Investigation report writing
- Investigation process from report intake to report writing/case management.
- Forensic techniques for evidence gathering.
- Law applying to investigations (legal privilege, data privacy)
- Open-source intelligence
- Specialist investigation types (fraud, money laundering etc.)
- Data analytics
- Psychology as it applies to investigation
- Digital forensics

Comments also suggested that knowledge requirements would be dependent on the level of accreditation, either general, advanced or specialist.

Most survey respondents believe that professional certifications and academic degrees /courses should be considered in obtaining the ACI certification. Opinions however are different as to what type of certifications/courses should be considered:

- Academic degree/courses in investigations (29%)
- Police/law enforcement (26%)
- Degree in Law (19%)
- Other certifications (19%)

2.2 Project stage – research

In the research stage the following activities happened:

- Exploration of various accreditation and certification pathways
- Obtained cost information from various training providers.
- Investigated what body of knowledge, certification and accreditation standards and cost models other associations have established
- Evaluated the various methods of delivery to a global audience.
- Researched what investigation skills are needed (in a random number of open investigation positions)

2.2.1 Exploration of various accreditation and certification pathways

The ACI explored creating a certification for its members and getting an accreditation. Accreditation involves the assessment of the competence and impartiality of an organisation and the compliance of their work to nationally and internationally recognised standards or schemes. Accreditation is very specific to the activities it covers under the relevant standard.

In the UK the Accreditation body is Ofqual. It administers the Regulated Qualifications Framework (RQF), and this Framework is mapped against international Frameworks. Note especially the Awarding Organization must have the systems, processes and resources, and the financial resources and facilities, to enable it to undertake, in accordance with its Conditions of Recognition, the development, delivery and award of any qualification which it may make available as a recognised awarding organisation. Another option for accreditation is working with UKAS- the body in the UK responsible for accreditation of certification bodies (ANAB or ASCB in the US).

If ACi were to become an Ofqual Awarding Organisation we would then need to accredit centres to deliver our qualifications. To be able to operate internationally and offer an RQF qualification, ACi would need a network of approved training providers or centres. As this comes with certain financial challenges, the ACI opted to go for a certification.

2.2.2 Comparison with other associations

The ACI investigated the required body of knowledge, membership criteria and cost models applied by numerous associations, e.g., The Association of Certified Fraud Examiners, The Association of Security Professionals (ASIS), The Institute of Internal Auditors, The Association of International Certified Public Accountants, The Association of Certified Anti-money laundering specialists and the Society for Corporate Compliance and Ethics.

Association	Area of expertise / specialism	Notes
Association of Certified Anti-Money Laundering Specialists (ACAMS)	Financial crime with specialism in anti-money laundering	Over 100,000 members are offering Associate, Specialist and Advanced certifications in a range of specialisms, e.g., anti-money laundering, financial crime investigations, KYC and sanctions. Other certifications include Audit and risk management. There are regional chapters. Webinars and conferences (global and regional) offer continued learning and ACAMS credits.
Association of Certified Fraud Examiners (ACFE)	Fraud	Over 90,000 members worldwide and over 190 ACFE chapters. ACFE provides an accreditation exam and offers webinars and (global and regional) conferences to attain Continuing Professional Education points. Also offers a Corporate Alliance for corporate group members.
Association of Financial Crime Specialists (ACFCS)	Financial crime	Full membership not public but 33,000 plus followers on LinkedIn and 20 plus global chapters. Certifications in financial crime; and crypto currency investigations. Webinars and conferences offer learning and CPE points.
Society of Corporate Compliance and Ethics (SCCE)	Compliance and Ethics	7,000 plus members with 45 plus global and local conferences. Webinars offer learning and Continued Education Units.
The Global Institute of Internal Auditors	The body of knowledge contains a minor section on Fraud	245,000 members offering Certification in Internal Auditing and Certification in Risk Management Assurance. It has local chapters in most countries and have a wide offering of global and regional trainings and webinars.
American Society for Industrial Security (ASIS)	Security investigations and practice	34,000 members globally. A range of certifications covering security matters (protective, physical, corporate). Global conferences and webinars offered in addition to the certifications.

Contrary to some of the other associations that are primarily for profit, the ACI is a non-for-profit organization therefore the aim is not to charge a high cost for the exam fee/certification and/or high annual fees for continuous professional education. The ACI is of the opinion that exam fees need to consider "equality of opportunity" modeling exam fees towards members from "developing countries" that do not have the same financial resources as USA or Western Europe.

Important for the ACI is that the exam can be accessible anywhere around the world. Therefore, we investigated the option to enter in a contract with providers of global testing centers offering remote testing with proctor option and in person testing at a testing center. The financial commitments towards such testing center providers, the lack of flexibility to change providers (if it wanted to) and constraints on format and type of exam content in a manner that is suitable for the IT equipment of such testing centers, the ACI decided not to pursue this option.

The ACI also considered with working with external training providers. However, the requirement to offer the exam globally in combination with consistent quality assurance standards around the world, made the ACI give up this option. Therefore, it was decided that the ACI would deliver itself the required training materials, exams, and certification.

2.2.3 Evaluation of various methods of delivery to a global audience

When considering the effectiveness of training delivery to support ACi certification and accreditation within a global membership base, the ACi is no different to many other organizations who have wrestled with this over the years.

Whilst on the face of it this may seem to be a daunting task for the ACi given the number of considerations which include budget, size, membership type (and desire), location, time frame, and goals, we also must add the complexity of multiple training delivery options available today which makes our decision-making easier said than done.

Many training professionals often evaluate delivery methods based on their association's overall learning objectives. Most will use multiple delivery methods, as single options do not necessarily deliver everything "well." So with this in mind the ACi have considered adopting a number of options, which – within a blended learning environment – should meet the vast majority of our membership needs.

2.2.3.1 Instructor- led training.

Instructor-led training (e.g., classroom training) is the most traditional form of training, best leveraged for creating an overall understanding of the ACi and the topics to be delivered. This is the mode which is most preferred by learners[4], with well over 55% of learners reporting a preference for this method.

The ACi note that this is most effective when you need to provide a large group of learners with a relatively small amount of information and in a short period, but with an important value-add being the background and credibility of the instructor, and their training skills. The ACi are fortunate to be very well connected in this respect.

Another key advantage of face-to-face training is the obvious interactivity, as those participating can ask questions and receive instant responses. It remains an excellent option for the ACi, does not require a dedicated training venue (and is therefore scalable) where member interactivity is vital and key to the learning experience.

Our members would participate in training sessions led by instructors who typically utilize PowerPoint or Whiteboard presentations, with sessions and courses often divided into shorter segments or abbreviated with short activities. This style of training delivery still holds great importance in the investigative community because certain topics, such as advanced investigative interview or technical skills, make more sense to teach in person. Instructor-led training encourages our ACi members to build relationships with one another and improve the experience by providing more opportunities for collaboration.

2.2.3.2. Virtual classrooms

Advancements in technology have significantly developed the use of virtual classrooms, or virtual instructor-led training. Virtual classrooms allow the ACi to deliver training in the form of text, video, and documents in real time, can be delivered from anywhere, and learners can attend the session from wherever they are located, saving valuable time and money on logistics and venues. Again, the ACi are fortunate to have excellent virtual trainers who are still able to offer a "human touch," although one drawback is the "retention of concentration" during lengthier training sessions, and individual ability to focus on key aspects when not in a face-to-face environment.

Virtual classroom learning can happen synchronously, where all learners receive their lessons simultaneously, or asynchronously where learners take classes at their own pace. Virtual instructor-led training is most effective when the ACi are called on to train a larger group, and when geographically difficult or impossible to bring everyone together at one venue. It is also only truly effective when excellent technical support is available to the trainer and those joining.

2.2.3.3 *eLearning*

eLearning is one of the most popular forms of training delivery available today, with research suggesting that the global e-Learning market is set to reach over £250 billion in value by 2025[5]. Online learning uses a mix of text audio and video, discussion forums and / or interactive assessments.

eLearning remains a good option for the ACi should we want to offer flexible learning opportunities in a short time frame to a global member audience, by delivering interactive and engaging training programs.

2.2.3.4 *Mobile Learning*

It is well known that many learners now use available spare time to use their mobile device to access training content, with nearly 90% of smartphone users download apps for learning or productivity. One specific use which is now more prevalent than ever is to use bitesize learning using Podcasts and Webinars, of which the ACi are using already or launching in 2023.

Although a relatively new training delivery method, it is increasingly offered by leading associations and organizations because of the numerous benefits it offers, including the ability to deliver training anytime, anywhere and on any device and in the form of microlearning[6], short "how-to" videos, social learning[7] and other engaging formats.

Microlearning involves separating course information into shorter sections or topics that can be easily delivered and completed asynchronously. Smaller learning sessions offer the appropriate amount of information necessary for our ACi members to achieve a specific training objective, making microlearning valuable in many investigative workplace contexts. It is also effective because learners apply the skills they have acquired before losing attention, thus improving knowledge retention. This is also referred to as "real-time" learning. It works well when incorporated into a Digital Adoption Platform[8], which dividing the course content into smaller chunks and integrating it into any software ACi members use whilst they are learning.

While best suited to the needs of the "on-the-go" ACi member, mobile learning is also popular where the nature of the industry they work in involves work at locations where there are no internet connections, which makes an offline mobile learning app or platform the go-to solution with "saved content" available 24/7/365.

2.2.3.5 Blended Learning

The ACi consider blended learning[9] to be crucial in the 21st Century, as something which – for our members – allows us to leverage a combination of approaches, ensuring that every member can retain the information we offer. A blended learning approach is perfect for the ACi in that we have diverse training requirements and complex learning objectives.

This allows us to neatly bring together all training methods with advancements in technology, and when moving towards a recognized qualification, the opportunity to provide the learning in multiple options and environments. Another advantage to blended learning is that whilst learning and development has typically been through synchronously (e.g. all at once) delivery, the advent of blended learning has made it possible to blend synchronous and asynchronous learning. together, combining the best of two training environments: Face to Face and eLearning. It is often useful for engaging all types of ACi members, both those who learn better in a traditional classroom environment as well as those who work best with semi-autonomous training (such as computer-based). The key to this is the identification and use of a suitable Learning Management System (LMS).

2.2.3.6 Spaced Learning

Spaced learning is another form or learning, based on the concept that learning is enhanced when knowledge is repeated after certain intervals. Spaced learning breaks down long ACi training programs or elements into several sessions or modules of shorter durations, with spaced intervals in between.

Parts of these sessions are reintroduced multiple times over the course of the next few days or weeks for members to recall information, driving long-term knowledge retention. This assists our members with avoiding information overload and improving the overall ACi learning experience.

2.2.3.7 Collaborative training

Collaborative training is a methodology where members can share their knowledge and expertise, teaching and learning from one another at the same time. Whilst not replacing other more prescribed forms of training, this technique helps to enhance the overall (blended) training experience for our members by capitalizing on their experience, skills, ideas, and knowledge. It helps members to enhance their understanding as a group more so than they do as individuals by listening to other viewpoints, reframing ideas, and articulating their points. This makes collaborative training an effective enhanced technique for ACi member training.

2.2.3.8 Mentorship and Coaching

A key deliverable for the ACi to focus on in the medium to longer term is where the ACi relies on building relationships that serve the purpose of ACi L&D initiatives throughout a member's journey. Mentors are experienced ACi advisors who are invested in the success of the member. Mentorship training can be used to provide continuous, informal training, but this approach absolutely necessitates a good operational relationship with the member, otherwise it runs into risks of over-dependence and potentially creating an overwhelming burden for the mentor.

Whilst coaching is somewhat like mentorship, this involves trained ACi individuals to serve in a mentor-like role for a period of time. Whist this training method can increase learning efficiency, it does not hold all the benefits of relationship building.

This research project undertakes not only the research to identify the content and best method of delivery for a corporate investigator accredited qualification, but also how the ACI will deliver an internationally recognized accredited qualification to its members.

- **Developing delivery methods to the aim of the certification, and therefore training required**

  We will choose our appropriate training delivery methods based on the aim of training. Some areas will be simpler than others, and where we are focused on learning intricate and vital skills, this would be commensurate with a face-to-face approach. Simpler learning can be a combination of eLearning and multiple-choice examination style segments. The value of having face to face sessions places greater emphasis on the value associated with the accreditation / certification.
- **The ACI have their membership in mind.**

  Also, important to consider when choosing training delivery methods is the ACi audience – what are the individual session needs?
- can this be delivered in bite-size segments? and
- what is the logistics involved in gathering delegates together?
- **Timelines associated with accreditation and certification.**

  The urgency of training objectives plays a significant role when determining how the blended learning method is established. The ACi would need to consider how quickly students are required to learn information, and in what order of importance the training segments are delivered. Different training delivery methods will be suited for these differing needs, and the needs identified from the program content.

The ACI Executive Committee are interested in developing a Certification Scheme suitable and affordable for their members throughout the world. They are considering a range of ideas, formats, and approaches. The delivery infrastructure and the cost would largely depend on the format, the types of materials to be distributed, instruction costs and ACi infrastructure support for any of the options.

2.2.4 Research on required investigation skills.

In January 2023 the job market was screened on Linkedin for open positions by applying the keywords "investigation/investigations manager/director of investigations/head of investigations".

We evaluated the job descriptions based on required competencies, qualifications, number of years' experience, degrees etc.

Title	Company	Degree	Certification required	Experience	Investigations Experience	Interview Skills	Report writing	Forensic review tools	data analytics
Fraud Investigator	Philips	Minimum Bachelor's degree	none	2-3 years of proven experience in a similar	X	X	X	X	x
Investigations Nordic	Greenpeace	educational relevant degree	none	significant experience in research and investigations	X				
Investigations Manager	Worldline	University degree in relevant field	none	3-5 years of relevant experience in CDD, KYC	X				
Senior Corporate Investigator	Ericsson	not mentioned	none	10 years' experience in investigations	X			X	x
Senior Investigator	Shell	A Bachelor's degree in a relevant discipline such as accounting,	none	substantial experience in the field of corporate investigations	X	x	x		x
Regional Investigations and Monitoring Lead EMEA/APAC	Sanofi	University degree	CFE, CPA, CIA, CCEP	7 yrs. + experience of conducting corporate investigations	X	x	x	x	x
Senior Auditor Special Investigations	Continental	Bachelor/Master in business administration or	CFE considered helpful	at least three years of audit related experience ; compliance and /or	X		X		
External Fraud Investigator	Allianz	University degree in a relevant discipline	none	Minimum of 3 years of relevant experience	X				
compliance investigator	ZF group	undergraduate degree	CIA, CFE or equivalent	3-5 years minimum experience in one of the following fields: investigations, forensic,	X				
Manager AML Investiagtions	American Ex	Bachelors/University degree.	CAMS	6+ years of work experience in Financial	X				
Security Intelligence Investigator	Tesla	not mentioned	none	Several years experience as an investigator with international/national law enforcement or intelligence community	X			X	
EMEA sanctions investigations team leader	citi	Bachelor's/University	none	2-5 years of experience in a related role					
senior manager investigations	gavi	Under-graduate degr	professionall	A minimum of 8 years professional investigation	x				
Manager	Barclays	degree level qualifica	Financial Crir	not mentioned	x				
Head of Investigations	PepsiCo	Bachelor's degree/Di	Certified Frau	Minimum 5-8 years' experience in SAPS/Law Enforcement ; 3+ years of experience conducting	x	x			x
Senior Investigator	International Rescue Committee	Bachelor's degree	CFE/CFF/CPA	7+ years of progressively responsible experience in the field of investigations	X	X			x
Investigations Manager	Motion Pictu	not mentioned	not mentione	At least 2 years of relevant work experience	X		X		
Compliance Investigation Lead	Energy com	not mentioned	ACA / ACCA	not mentioned					
Fraud Investigation manager	signify	accounting, cybersecurity, data analytics or Legal	not mentione	At least 5 years of forensic investigation experience	X	X	X		
head of Investigations &MLRO	standard chartered bank	not mentioned	ICA/ACAMS	Previous experience as a MLRO; significant and complex financial crime investigations in a	X				
head investigations	Mercury	not mentioned	not mentione	extensive experience managing teams at financial services	X				
Head of sanctions investigations	Society Gen	not mentioned	not mentioned						
Lead Monitoring & Investigations	Takeda	bachelor degree	not mentione	7+ years of legal, compliance or	x				
Sr Compliance Manager Investigations	Otsuka Phar	Bachelor's degree /m	not mentione	3+ years of experience in compliance in pharmaceutical industry					
Sr Compliance Investigations Consultant	Parkland He	Bachelor's degree /m	certifications a plus, CCEP/CHC	six years' experience in healthcare compliance and investigations	X				

Figure 11: table with investigation skill-set

As can be seen on Figure 11

- 90% of all job descriptions requested job applicants to have investigations experience and knowledge of investigation processes and standards.
- 44% of job descriptions requested a professional certification (CFE, CIA, CCEP, CPA)
- 30% of job descriptions mentioned no formal educational requirements. In the remaining 70% typically minimum bachelor's degree but preferred master's degree was mentioned in job description.
- Only 25% of job descriptions mention necessary experience in "interviewing".
- Only 25% of job descriptions mention necessary experience in "report writing".
- Only 20% of job descriptions mention necessary experience in "data analytics".
- Only 16% of job descriptions mention specifically experience in "e-discovery and forensic review tools"
- In terms of years of investigations experience
- 25% of job descriptions required at least 3 years professional experience.
- 12% of job descriptions required at least 7 years professional experience.
- 8% of job descriptions required at least 2 years professional experience.
- 8% of job descriptions required at least 5+ years professional experience.
- 8% of job descriptions required at least 6 years professional experience.
- 5% of job descriptions required at least 10 years professional experience.
- 35% of job descriptions mentioned significant experience without specifying how many years would be considered "significant experience".
- Depending on industry required skills asked for where money laundering/sanctions (financial services industry); knowledge of pharmaceutical laws and regulations (life science industry), copyright enforcement knowledge (movie industry)

2.3 Project stage – Develop and implement

In Q4 2023 members of the ACI Executive Committee and its general manager worked on describing the key functionalities needed of a learning management system which will be the foundation of the CCI Certification.

Some of the required functionalities that can be mentioned are:

- Training /learning modules offered on the platform are of superior quality.
- Training/learning modules allow for maximum flexibility in the format they are delivered (presentations, videos, texts, case studies etc.)
- The platform must be user friendly and provide for excellent customer experience in the eyes of (prospective) ACi members.
- The platform allows to track with of the on-line learning modules have been taken.
- The administrative handling of learning experience (registration, certifications etc.) is seamlessly integrated with the other modules (member database, accounting /invoicing) ensuring maximal efficiency.
- The platform allows candidates to upload evidence (e.g., CV, endorsement letters etc.) confirming that they fulfill the requirements to sit for the examination.
- The platform allows to store a huge bank with exam questions.
- The platform has the functionality to evaluate the exam results with maximum efficiency
- The platform should have the possibility for several user access roles with different functionalities linked to each role.
- The platform should have state of the art "security management" (e.g., maximum length password, user authentication, blocking of users after numerous false password attempts)
    - The platform must allow for compliance with data privacy laws:
    - A data privacy statement (content details will be provided by ACi)
    - Functionality to track cookies.
    - Offer the possibility to users to "Opt-in" or "opt-out" of certain functionalities.
    - The platform is ideally hosted in the EU.
    - The necessary technical and organizational measures to prevent ACi member personal data be lost, stolen, edited etc.
    - Able to respond in a timely fashion to any data privacy requests from users.
    - System documentation (in case asked for by data privacy authorities)

Based on the above mentioned minimum needed functionalities, various learning platforms were evaluated and one learning module system was selected.

Starting Q1 2024 the ACI head of learning, supported by members of ACI Executive Committee, started to develop the content of e-learning modules and the creation of exam questions.

The expected content of the modules is as follows:

- ACi code of conduct good practice guidance, and the uniform principles of investigations.
- The International Standards Organization (ISO) standards for internal investigations.
- Assessing, scoping, and devising investigation plans.
- Use of technology and case management systems.
- Managing investigations.
- Data collection and privacy.
- Data searching and mining.
- Information and data presentation.
- Investigation records and documenting actions.
- Open-source research.
- Investigative interviewing part 1.
- Investigative interviewing part 2.
- Legal privilege.
- Cross border investigations.
- Whistleblowing investigations.
- Investigation reports.
- Evidence giving.
- Cyber investigations.
- Working with external consultants, lawyers, forensic accountants, and other experts.
- Working with internal stakeholders.

3. Conclusions and outlook

During Q2/Q3 2024 extensive quality assurance testing will be done – not only on the IT infrastructure to ensure the registration for training, training modules and examination questions are working as desired but additionally independent review will be conducted to ensure that exam questions are well formulated, easily understandable and have an acceptable pass rate for each of the modules.

By November 2024 we are aiming to celebrate the launch of our Certified Corporate Investigator (CCI) exam, another milestone in our mission to professionalize the investigations community. Our work however does not stop there. After the CCI certification, the plan is to come up with a more "advanced" certification for those who have many years of professional experience in corporate investigations.

Notes

1 Association of Corporate Investigators – Created by investigators for investigators (my -aci.com)
2 ACi Investigation Principles – Association of Corporate Investigators (my-aci.com)
3 Good Practice Guidance – Association of Corporate Investigators (my-aci.com)
4 Research conducted by Training Industry, Inc.
5 Global Market Insights Report
6 https://trainingindustry.com/glossary/microlearning
7 Htpps://trainingindustry.com/glossary/social-learning
8 Digital adoption platform - Wikipedia
9 https://trainingindustry.com/glossary/blended-learning/

Author Biographies

Kalapurakkal Suresh Aravind

K.S. Aravind is a BA.LLB graduate from Symbiosis Law School, Hyderabad, where he actively participated in moot court and client counseling activities. He has experience in contract drafting, environmental law, IT law, employment law, and litigation. Aravind has a keen interest in ESG development and has published various articles on ESG topics, with a specific focus on law. Currently, he works as an Assistant Manager Legal at Re Sustainability Limited in Hyderabad, where he continues to pursue his interest in ESG and environmental law development. His hobbies include drawing, traveling, and reading.

Prof. Dr. Ruben Bahamonde

PhD in Law from the University of A Coruña, Spain. Associate Professor at the Autónoma University of Lisbon, Sub-Director of the Law Department at the Autónoma University of Lisbon, Visiting Professor at the Africa Business School (ABS), Mohammed VI Polytechnic University, Morocco and at the Universidad de San Carlos de Guatemala. Researcher at the Justice and Governance Research Center of the University of Minho, and member of CERGI - Centro de estudios de la empresa: Responsabilidad social y competencia, Universidad de Santiago de Compostela. Coordinator of the research project "Autotutela e realização do direito Privado" at the Ratio Legis Research Centre. Lawyer, arbitrator and legal expert.

CS Shujath Bin Ali

CS Shujath Bin Ali is the Global General Counsel & Chief Compliance Officer at Re Sustainability Limited, backed by global private equity firm KKR &Co. He leads the Global Legal & Compliance, Corporate Governance & Secretarial, Ethics, and Risk Management functions. Shujath is also a member of the ESG Committee, Risk Management Committee, and DEI Council. Previously, Shujath served as Senior Director- Legal, Risk Management & Company Secretary and India Compliance Officer at PAREXEL International – India. He also held roles as Senior Legal Counsel & Corporate Secretary for

International Paper-India and Associate Vice President-Legal & Corporate Secretary for Deloitte US-India offices. With 23 years of experience, he has expertise in Governance, Compliance, Risk Management, Corporate & Commercial Laws, Employment laws, and Litigation across industries like Pharma, IT, Professional Services, and Manufacturing. Shujath is a Commerce and Law graduate, a Fellow Member of the Institute of Company Secretaries of India, and has attended executive education programs at Harvard University, Indian School of Business, Hyderabad, and National Law School, Bengaluru. He holds a Masters in Law in Alternate Dispute Resolution & International Commercial Arbitration. Recognized for his legal and compliance leadership in the areas of GRC and ESG, Shujath has been named among "India's Finest In-House Counsels" and "Top 100 General Counsels" by various organizations. He is a frequent speaker at national and international conferences, presenting on topics such as Integrity, Ethics, Compliance, ESG, Sustainability, Governance, Risk & Compliance Management, and Legal Technology. Passionate about community involvement, Diversity & Inclusion, and mentorship activities, Shujath enjoys teaching, traveling, and reading on health, fitness, and spirituality.

Dr. Meric Bloch

Meric Bloch is the Principal of Winter Investigations, a consulting firm specializing in workplace investigations design and implementation. Meric has designed, implemented, and managed workplace-investigations processes for multinational public companies. He has trained thousands of HR and compliance professionals to conduct workplace investigations. Meric has personally conducted over eight hundred internal investigations of fraud and serious workplace misconduct globally. Meric is an adjunct professor at Fordham University School of Law. He was an instructor for the Society of Corporate Compliance and Ethics Academy for ten years, where he taught the module on workplace investigations. Meric holds Bachelor of Arts and Juris Doctor degrees from New York University. He is a Certified Fraud Examiner, a Professional Certified Investigator, a Certified Financial Crime Specialist, a Certified Information Privacy Professional, and has the Corporate Compliance and Ethics Professional – Fellow designation. Meric is the author of four books on investigations: *The Art of Investigations; In the Arena; Workplace Investigations: Techniques and Strategies for Investigators and Compliance Officers; Investigative Interviewing,* and *The First Information Is Wrong.* He also wrote chapters in the *Bribery and Corruption Casebook* and *The Complete Compliance and Ethics Manual.*

Piotr Chmiel

Piotr Chmiel – Compliance Officer, Compliance Management Department Director at T-Mobile Polska S.A. (part of Deutsche Telekom Group). Currently responsible for the Compliance function and Risk Management, started his work at T-Mobile Polska in 2009, being one of the first employees building the Compliance Management System and maintaining it. Before moving to the telecommunication industry was working for „Big 4" consulting companies, analyzing, evaluating and designing control systems and activities in business and IT processes. Experience and skills confined by international certificates: CFE (Certified Fraud Examiner), CIA (Certified Internal Auditor), CISA (Certified Information Systems Auditor), Certified Compliance Manager International, (Frankfurt School of Finance and Management). Actively involved in activities of Polish UN Global Compact, with focus on „Standard of Business Ethics" and related programs. Co-author of „Ethical Standard" guidance for organizations. Teaches compliance topics on post graduate studies. Finished Master of Science and engineering degree at the Academy of Mining and Metallurgy, Nuclear Physics Faculty in Cracow, Poland. Specialized in Medical Physics and Dosimetry.

Ana Lúcia de Melo Custódio

Ana Lúcia de Melo Custódio is a Deputy Director at the Ethos Institute, overseeing research activities, development of tools and methodologies, consulting, and training in the fields of Responsible Management for Sustainability, Sustainable Value Chains, Human Rights, Diversity, and Integrity. She earned a Bachelor's degree in Letters from the University of São Paulo, specializing in Brazilian Economy from the Foundation Institute of Economic Research (FIPE), and holds an MBA in Business Management from Fundação Getulio Vargas (FGV).

Meriem Debbih

Meriem Debbih combines a background in Mathematics and Computer Science with legal expertise as a JD candidate at the University of Washington School of Law. Before law school, she worked as a patent agent, drafting and prosecuting patent applications across various technical fields. Her experience bridging technical and legal domains has shaped her approach to technology law. After graduation, she will join a leading law firm in Seattle where she will focus on technology transactions and privacy law. She maintains an active interest in Environmental, Social, and Governance (ESG) issues and their intersection with emerging technologies.

Antonio Giuseppe Di Pietro

Antonio Giuseppe is an Italian corporate lawyer and founder with a robust background in law, technology and compliance. He leads Di Pietro Studio Legale, where he specializes in M&A, business law, and white-collar crime investigations. Antonio co-founded 36Brains, a corporate intelligence and investigations firm later acquired by RSM, integrating advanced technologies like AI and data analytics to enhance operations. His professional journey includes roles at Kroll and contributions as a research assistant at The American University in Cairo. Antonio holds a Master's degree in Global Affairs and International Security from The American University in Cairo and a law degree from Università degli Studi di Milano. He is actively engaged in social and academic endeavours, including numerous speaking engagements and publications on compliance and forensic investigations.

Adam Domagała

Adam Domagała – legal counsel , specializing in labor law. He works as a compliance officer in an energy company. Professionally, he deals with issues related to whistleblowing and human rights. He completed postgraduate studies at the Jagiellonian University in Kraków in the field of labor law and a course at the Collegium Civitas in Warsaw on human rights.

Yasmine Farag

Yasmine is an experienced legal and compliance professional with an unwavering commitment to ethics, governance, and accountability. With over two decades in leading financial institutions and a strong foundation as a lawyer, she has excelled in navigating complex legal and regulatory frameworks at the intersection of ethics, corporate governance, and risk management. Her expertise includes designing and embedding robust compliance programs, ethical standards, and policies that uphold transparency and responsibility. A seasoned professional, Yasmine has managed and mentored diverse teams in dynamic environments, ensuring alignment with the highest ethical standards. Her contributions span developing comprehensive compliance, financial crime, conduct and governance programs, controls and training, overseeing anticorruption and whistleblower protection frameworks and guiding organizations through intricate regulatory landscapes. Teaching law is central to Yasmine's professional identity. She strongly believes in the importance of shaping future generations and embraces the critical role of transmission in today's world. By sharing her expertise and embedding ethical awareness, she empowers the leaders of tomorrow to uphold values of integrity and accountability in their pursuits. With a passion for fostering integrity, Yasmine specializes in conflict-of-interest management, anti-corruption practices, and adherence to international regulatory standards. Her ability to manage change and lead transformation projects has consistently strengthened organizational resilience and trust. Fluent in English, French, and Arabic, Yasmine brings an international perspective to her work, bridging cross-cultural gaps to drive ethical leadership and regulatory excellence.

Carlos Lelo Filipe

Carlos Lelo Filipe (*21.06.1964) is Compliance Officer of Leonteq Securities Europe GmbH - Sucursal em Portugal and Lawyer, Post-Graduated in European Studies, member of the Board of Transparency International Portugal Chapter, President of the Disciplinary Counsel of the Portuguese Basketball Federation. Author of several articles about Compliance.

Susanne Friedrich

Susanne Friedrich is an organizational developer with large experience in capacity building and multi-stakeholder management at the German development cooperation. She started her professional career at the Chilean Export Promotion Bureau and worked as an advisor for public-private partnerships in development cooperation for several years. Since 2009 she has been working in various projects in Latin America and Germany, in fields such as inclusive business, export promotion for SMEs and quality infrastructure. Until 2023 she headed the "Alliance for Integrity", a global business-driven, multi-stakeholder initiative seeking to promote transparency and integrity in the economic system. Since July 2024 she has headed the Agency for Business and Economic Development. She is a member of the Advisory Board of Transparency International Germany.

Maria Eugenia Gil

Maria Eugenia Gil is Manager in Forensic and Compliance & Risk Analytics practice for PwC in Argentina, Paraguay and Uruguay, and has more than 15 years of experience in the prevention and investigation of fraud and corruption and the development of integrity programs. She is a lawyer graduated from the National University of Córdoba in 2004, in Argentina. She is specialized in Economic Criminal Law and holds the LPEC Leadership Professional in Ethics & Compliance certification. She is also a selected researcher of Universidad Austral (OCEDIC) and Universidad Empresarial Siglo 21, both in Argentina. Throughout her professional and work career she has specialized in the analysis of documentation, in investigations related to fraud, bribery and corruption in Argentina and different Latin American countries; as well as in the development, evaluation and monitoring and audit of Integrity Programs for a diverse group of clients, both public and private, and in different industries (e.g., energy, pharmaceutical, entertainment and technology). She also specializes in compliance due diligence in M&A procedures and in auditing integrity programs. Se was selected as a member to attend the International Summer Academy Program from IACA - International Anti Corruption Academy, in Brazil in 2023. She has participated in different academic events in the compliance area both as a guest and as an organizer. As a lawyer, she has participated in major corruption cases in Brazil, such as Mensalão, etc.

Ana Cristina Perdomo Gomez

Ana Cristina Perdomo is an International Counsel with 15+ years of in-house experience, specializing in legal, compliance, and privacy management for leading multinational corporations across diverse industries. She earned her

LLM in Business Law from FGV in Brazil and further an LLM in Digital Economy and Transnational Law from Católica Global School of Law in Portugal. She earned a professional certificate in Innovation, Management and Entrepreneurship Executive Program at Stanford Business School. She is also a Certified Information Privacy Manager (CIPM) accredited by the International Association of Privacy Professionals (IAPP).

Prof. Marcela Greggo

Marcela Greggo, Coordinator of Integrity, Transparency, and Anti-corruption projects at the Ethos Institute and university professor. She holds a law degree (PUC/SP), a master's degree in Global Governance and International Policy Formulation (PUC/SP) and specializes in economic criminal law (FGV/SP). Responsible for coordinating and supporting sectoral and multisectoral projects such as the Movement for Integrity in the Engineering and Construction Sector (MISEC), a collective action currently involving more than 40 companies, and the Integrity Working Group for companies associated with the Ethos Institute, which currently has over 100 participating companies. She is also responsible for coordinating the Business Pact for Integrity and Against Corruption, which currently has 1687 signatory companies. She serves as a full member of the Pro-Ethics Council of the Brazilian Office of the Comptroller General (CGU), an initiative aimed at promoting the voluntary adoption of integrity measures by companies, through the public recognition of those that, regardless of size and sector, are committed to implementing measures focused on preventing, detecting, and remediating acts of corruption and fraud.

Prof. Dr. Christian Hauser

Dr. Christian Hauser is Professor of Business Economics and International Management at the University of Applied Sciences of the Grisons and a visiting scholar at the Digital Society Initiative of the University of Zurich, Switzerland. He is a member of the topical platform Ethics of the Swiss Academy of Engineering Sciences (SATW), chair of the United Nations Principles for Responsible Management Education (PRME) Working Group on Anti-Corruption and head of the first PRME Business Integrity Action Centre in Europe. His research interests include international entrepreneurship,

SME and private sector development, corporate responsibility and business integrity.

Dr. Marc Herkenrath

Dr. Marc Herkenrath is the Deputy Executive Director of Transparency International Switzerland. In 2017, he was awarded the title of Adjunct Professor of Sociology by the University of Zurich, at which he has had recurrent teaching assignments in the areas of development studies, economic sociology, political sociology, and social movement studies. From 2015 to 2021 he was the Director of Alliance Sud, the Swiss Coalition of Development Organizations. From 2008 to 2015 he worked for Alliance Sud as a Senior Policy Officer in the area of international financial markets and tax policy.

Dr. Martin Hilti

Dr. Martin Hilti is a lawyer by profession and has been Executive Director of Transparency International Switzerland since 2015. Prior to that, he worked as a lawyer for the Federal Office of Justice and the Federal Office of Culture and served as a legal lecturer at the Bern Education Center for Nursing and the University of Basel.

Ph.D. Anna Hlebicka-Józefowicz

Head of the Regulatory Affairs, Legislation and Compliance Practice at DZP, advocate, PhD in constitutional law, lecturer at the Warsaw School of Economics and University of Warsaw. Advises clients on regulatory issues including sensitive products sector (tobacco, alcohol, gambling) and compliance. Expert in constitutional law representing clients' interests in the legislative process. Member of the Working Group on Ethics and Standards for Responsible Business Conduct under the Polish Ministry of Development (2017-2018). Named a Rising Star Lawyer – Leader of Tomorrow by Wolters Kluwer Poland for outstanding work in support of the rule of law and society, and for creativity and the use of new technologies in her professional work.

Prof. Dr. Eduard Ivanov

Prof. Dr. Eduard Ivanov is senior researcher at the IACA and member of the SIGA Permanent Committee on Anti-Corruption in Sport. He has a solid academic and practical experience in compliance, preventing of and combating corruption, money-laundering, and terrorist financing. Eduard Ivanov lectured at DIREITO GV (Sao Paulo, Brazil), the University of Nice (France), the University of Muenster (Germany), the Ca' Foscary University of Venice (Italy), and the National Research University Higher School of Economics (Moscow, Russia). In 2013 - 2016 he was a chair of the Law Schools Global League's Study Group on Combating Corruption, and a member of the International Law Association's Study group on Cybersecurity, Terrorism and International Law. From 2005 – 2008, he served as co-chair of the Working Group on Typologies in the Eurasian Group on Combating Money Laundering and Financing of Terrorism and was a member of the FATF Working Group on Typologies.

Dr. Bethany Jackson

Senior Research Fellow in Modern Slavery and Sustainable Ecosystems, Rights Lab University of Nottingham. Dr Jackson's research focuses on the co-occurrence and monitoring of environmentally degrading sectors/activities associated with exploitative working conditions. Her expertise has led to extensive research on the impacts of climate change on communities in Bangladesh and India, workers at risk of multiple economic and environmental stressors in the India brick manufacturing sector, and the risks of forced labour within the food supply. She was previously the Rights Lab lead during COP26 Glasgow and has worked on encouraging collaborative action between the anti-slavery and environmental sectors.

Dr Piotr Janecki, LL.M.

Manager, trainer and implementer. Head of Compliance and DP Poland and SCA for Eastern Europe at International company. Before he cultivated team implementing SSC processes. He organized both implementation and matching compliance Projects to ensure required compliance level both in merged and newly established entities. Valued trainer for professionals and business. A long-time lecturer of post-graduate studies. PhD in law an author of publications, huge fan of the interdisciplinary approach. Honored as the Compliance Officer of the year 2019 –Compliance Awards 2019. His motto is: create and drive secure and efficient processes, or poor-quality processes will drive you.

Prof. Andrew Kakabadse

Professor of Governance and Leadership. Andrew joined Henley Business School in July 2013 after 34 years at Cranfield School of Management, Cranfield University, where he finished as Professor of International Management Development in December 2012 and was awarded the honour of Emeritus Professor. Andrew has been ACT Visiting Professor at the Australian National University, Canberra, was Visiting Professor at Hangzhou University, China, was Visiting Fellow at Babson College, Boston, USA, was Honorary Professorial Fellow, Curtin University of Technology, Perth, Australia, was the H. Smith Richardson Visiting Fellow at the Centre for Creative Leadership, North Carolina, USA. Visiting Scholar in Residence at Thunderbird, School of Global Management, USA. Visiting Professor at the University of Ulster; He is a Fellow of the International Academy of Management, Fellow of the British Psychology Society and Fellow of the British Academy of Management. On behalf of the Cabinet Office, Andrew submitted the biggest survey ever since 1854 on the functioning of the British Government entitled 'Is Government fit for purpose; The Kakabadse Report'. He has consulted and lectured in the UK, Europe, USA, SE Asia, China, Japan, Russia, Georgia, the Gulf States, India and Australia. His current areas of interest focus on improving the performance of top executives, top executive/ teams and boards, leadership, corporate governance, conflict resolution and international relations. His study of the strategic skills of top teams has now extended into Japan, China, Hong Kong and the USA. Andrew is currently embarked on a major world study of boardroom effectiveness and governance practice. Andrew is one of the very few to be elected lifelong member of the Thinkers 50 Hall of Fame 2015; a list of distinguished thinkers throughout the world whose contributions to management thinking have made it what it is today. Andrew has published 47 books, over 100 book chapters, over 250 articles and 18 monographs.

Prof. Nada K. Kakabadse

Nada K. Kakabadse, Professor of Policy, Governance and Ethics, Henley Business School, University of Reading. She is elected Member of the European Academy of Sciences and Arts and their representative in the UK and Brussels. She has also contributed over 96 chapters to international volumes and has published over 200 scholarly articles. She has co-authored 23 books. Her work in the area of global governance has spawned critical publications around the nature of the global board, how to lead boards and the challenges corporations face in realising sustainable success in highly dynamic markets. Similarly, she has extensively examined the nature of corporate social responsibility and CSR implementation. Nada has worked for international organisations in Scandinavia, the Middle East and North Africa as well as the Canadian and Australian Federal Governments. Her clients have included Citigroup, Microsoft, Motorola, Vodafone Australia, Severstal, and in the public sector a number of UK, Australian and Omani government departments. She is a member of the Governing Council of the Empress Theophano Foundation. Previously, she held the position of Professor in Management and Business Research at the University of Northampton, Business School (UK) and was Senior Fellow, Cranfield School of Management. Nada and her co-authors won the William E. Mosher and Frederick C. Mosher Award for the best article written by an academic in the journal *Public Administration Review* (PAR) in 2003 as well as best paper of the year in the *Journal of Managerial Psychology* (JMP) in 1998. She has co-authored 21 books including *Entrepreneurship and Global Cities: Diversity, Opportunity and Cosmopolitanism* (2019) and *Bilderberg People* (2011) and published over 200 scholarly articles.

Andrejs Klisans

Andrejs is a Senior Manager at RSM. With a multi-jurisdictional background in law, Andrejs coordinates investigations with private equity firms, law firms, and corporations, primarily on due diligence and reputation audit assignments, supply chain investigations, internal investigations, and regulatory compliance matters. He initially completed a Dual LL.B. comprising both Spanish and English qualifying law degrees and worked for a renowned arbitration boutique in Madrid. Having lived in six countries spanning four continents and capable of speaking four languages, understanding how cultural subtleties influence behavior is his trade. Prior to joining RSM, he worked in the Business Intelligence & Investigations team of Kroll. In this time, Andrejs amassed comprehensive knowledge in multijurisdictional information-gathering and investigations. Andrejs has operated globally with an emphasis in Germany and most Southern European countries, including Spain, Portugal, Italy, Greece, Gibraltar, and Malta.

Prof. Dr. Claus Köhler, LL.M

Prof. Dr. Claus Köhler, LL.M. (Georgetown University) is a certified specialist in commercial and corporate law and an attorney-at-law (New York, US Supreme Ct.). Claus Köhler is a founding partner of the law firm Meister Rechtsanwälte in Munich and a professor at Kozminski University in Warsaw.

Jeannine Lemker

Jeannine Lemker is a Managing Director in Major, Lindsey & Africa's In-House and Board Services practices. Prior to joining MLA, Jeannine was Director & AGC in Meta Platforms Legal, leading a team who designed and landed the global compliance program and ESG work, and helped drive the ERM, Privacy and regulatory compliance strategy. Prior to Meta, Jeannine was a senior leader in Microsoft Corporate, External & Legal Affairs, with responsibility for the global business ethics program. In her first 10 years of practice, Jeannine was a regulatory and litigation counsel at Cadwalader, Wickersham & Taft LLP. Jeannine counseled Boards on risk management, ethics and compliance, regulatory investigations, corporate governance, and ESG. Jeannine is an adjunct professor at UW Law and a co-director for the Global Business Law Institute. She co-leads MLA's parent ERG, is a 4x non-profit Board member and dedicated community volunteer and PKD Foundation fundraiser.

Alexander Leonhardt

Alexander Leonhardt holds a law degree from the University of Mannheim (Germany) paired with studies abroad at the University of Antwerp (Belgium). He then gained valuable experience in the field of European Law and dispute resolution in the legal department of an European airline. After finishing his Business Law and Compliance LL.M. degree, he decided to pursue a career in Compliance. In 2022, right before Russia's war of aggression against Ukraine, he started at R+V Re, an international reinsurance company. Since then, he spent his time passionately in the fast-pacing and fast-changing global sanctions world, always vigilant and on the edge. He has been fortunate to be invited to pass on his knowledge to current students in lectures at his former university and to employees within the company on a yearly basis.

Mariola Lisewska

Mariola is Assistant Director of Academic Success, University of Washington School of Law. She recently transitioned to a full-time role at the University of Washington School of Law as Assistant Director of Academic Success, where she is dedicated to supporting students in their academic and professional development. Additionally, she serves as Associate Director at the Global Business Law Institute at the University of Washington. Prior to joining UW School of Law, Mariola was an attorney at Coopersmith Law + Strategy, advising clients on complex compliance, legal and business issues. Before that, she served as General Counsel for a multinational manufacturer and distributor based in Germany, where she was responsible for building and leading the company's compliance and legal department, overseeing all corporate, contractual, and regulatory matters, and securing multimillion-dollar investments. Mariola also spearheaded the company's data protection program and mentored teams on compliance implementation and enforcement. Mariola's legal career began at Deloitte's office in Poland, where she advised on corporate, transactional, and regulatory issues. She has authored numerous publications and lectured at international conferences on legal and compliance matters. Mariola is passionate about advancing international legal education.

Prof. Dr. Bartosz Makowicz

Prof. Makowicz is university professor at the Faculty of Law, European-University Viadrina in Frankfurt (O.), Germany. He is the founder and director of Viadrina Compliance Center which is an interdisciplinary research center and a compliance think-tank. He is a member of Academic Advisory Council of many compliance associations and journals like German Institute for Compliance (DICO) or Transparency International Germany. Furthermore, Bartosz is author of numerous publications on compliance and editor in chief of the German journal "COMPLY." He gave more than 100 speeches on different compliance issues at national and international conferences and congresses in the past five years. He has been chief of German delegation to ISO committees on ISO 37301, ISO 37000, ISO 37002 and ISO 37001. He advised German Federal Ministry of Defense on implementing CMS. Author of more than 100 scientific texts and editor of the annual "Yearbook for Global Ethics, Compliance & Integrity" with yearly over 40 authors from all over the world.

Akif Mert

Akif Mert is a German lawyer specialized in Compliance and white-collar crime with more than 14 years of international experience in managing legal, corporate compliance and data privacy matters in both emerging and highly regulated markets. After 2 years with KPMG, Akif joined the Group Compliance function of Allianz SE in Munich in 2012. From 2016 to 2019, he was located in Singapore as the Regional Head of Compliance and DPO of Allianz Asia Pacific before moving to Switzerland in 2020 to assume the role of the Chief Compliance Officer of Allianz Switzerland. Since November 2022, Akif is the Head of Compliance of Allianz Partners Australia. Akif is an active member of the German Institute for Compliance and a regular author of publications about regulatory trends in Compliance.

Joan Meyer

Joan has more than 30 years' experience handling complex criminal and civil litigation, primarily domestic and international white collar defense for companies involving anti-corruption, financial frauds, government contracting, false claims, securities and commodities violations, and trade compliance matters. She has tried scores of cases at the state and federal levels and handled more than 40 appeals in state and federal appeals courts. Joan also conducts domestic and international internal investigations for corporate clients to determine if legal andregulatory violations were committed and defends companies and individuals in negotiation and litigation with U.S. government agencies.

Christian Miege

Christian Miege is lawyer in Duesseldorf, Germany. Before that, until 2024 he was Partner in the Forensic & Integrity Team of EY, where he specialized in conducting internal investigations into suspected incidents, including antitrust violations, corruption, fraud, and embezzlement, often in conjunction with official inquiries and routine audits of compliance management systems. With a 15-year tenure in the legal and compliance fields, Christian has built a substantial career. From 2015 to 2022, he served as the head of the Internal Investigations department at German industrial conglomerate thyssenkrupp. In this capacity, he oversaw intricate compliance investigations and audits across the thyssenkrupp Group globally, with a particular emphasis on antitrust and corruption issues. His experience is extensive, including the development and management of whistleblower reporting systems. He has also contributed to the discourse on the proposed whistleblower protection legislation in Germany. Prior to his engagement at thyssenkrupp in 2012, Miege was a senior associate at Clifford Chance law firm, where he honed his expertise in antitrust proceedings and internal investigations, provided antitrust compliance training, managed global merger control proceedings, and offered counsel on distribution antitrust law. Additionally, he co-chairs the 'Internal Investigations & Whistleblowing Systems' working group at the German Institute for Compliance (DICO).

Juan Nazar de Boulin

Juan Nazar de Boulin is a Forensic´s Manager within the Compliance & Risk Analytics at PwC Argentina, Uruguay & Paraguay. Juan has 20+ years' experience as corporate lawyer in multinational Legal & Compliance areas as director/general counsel, as well as in technologically supported risk models development, fraud prevention and investigations, both in the private and federal public sector. He has drafted and implemented policies and processes on Integrity Programs on several industries (energy, pharma, financial sector). Juan worked as executive federal liaison between ministries, Anti-bribery federal Agency and Argentina's OECD membership application. He has working legal experience on local and regional investigations under the FCPA and UKBA rules, as well as M&A, due diligences processes, FINCEN/UIF reporting and CIADI and SEC arbitral proceedings. Juan holds several diplomas and magister degrees, an LLM, MPP (with a "Transparency International" training module), MBA and currently attends a PHD on constitutional rights. He's a Compliance and Risk trainer, writes and speaks fluently on English,

French and Portuguese, intermediate in German and Italian. Juan's a Spanish native speaker.

Prof. Dr. Alex Sander Xavier Pires

Alex Sander Xavier Pires (Alex Sander Pires), in terms of qualifications, holds a PhD in Legal and Social Sciences from Argentina (2009), whose title was recognised in Portugal by the Universidade Nova de Lisboa, with the mention of "distinction and value", as a PhD in Law (2017); in further research, he completed post-doctoral studies in European constitutional justice from the Portuguese reality at the Faculty of Law of the Universidade Nova de Lisboa (2014) and in human rights at the Universidad de Salamanca (2023). He also has a second doctorate in Political Science from the Universidade Cândido Mendes (2015). He also holds a Master's degree in Law (2015), a specialist in Legal Teaching (2022), a specialist in Contemporary Philosophy (2013), a specialist in Civil Law and Civil Procedure (2004), a specialist in State and Administrative Law (2003), and a Bachelor's degree in Law (2001). As a lecturer, he has been teaching for over twenty years. He currently works as associate professor in the Department of Law at the Universidade Autónoma de Lisboa - Luís de Camões. In terms of research, he is a doctoral researcher at the Justice and Governance Research Centre (Jusgov) at the Universidade do Minho (UMinho), a doctoral researcher and coordinator of the Research Project on Culture of Peace and Democracy at the Ratio Legis Legal Sciences Research Centre at the Universidade Autónoma de Lisboa, and a collaborator at the Nova School of Law Research Centre (CEDIS). To internationalise his academic and scientific experience, he is Chair-elect of Research Committee on Human Rights from International Political Science Association (IPSA RC#26), observer in Portugal of The Eurowhistle.eu Project portal at Viadrina Compliance Center at the European University Viadrina, Secretary-General from Ethical and Compliance International Institute (ECII), and Member of International Association of Constitutional Law (IACL). He is a lawyer registered with the Brazilian Bar Association.

Anita Punwani

Anita is an independent facilitator, adviser, trainer and educator with experience across the public, not-for-profit and private sectors including public-private partnerships for UK government. Her work for an international charity followed research on humanitarian response as part of her MSc in Global Governance & Ethics from University College London (UCL). She also holds degrees in engineering, management and economics from Imperial College and UCL. Anita represents the UK at ISO in the development of international standards. She is the founder of the IRM ESG Group and appeared on the BBC and CNBC to raise public awareness of risk management during the global health crisis. Anita is a member of Royal Institute of International Affairs as well as the UN Association-UK and is committed to supporting achievement of the UN Sustainable Development Goals.

Jeanine Bretti Rainalter

Jeanine Bretti Rainalter is a research associate at the Swiss Institute for Entrepreneurship (SIFE) at the University of Applied Sciences of the Grisons in Chur, Switzerland. Prior to that she worked as a Finance & Controlling Advisor for SOS Children's Villages International. She holds a degree in international business management. Her research interests include corporate responsibility, internationalisation, business integrity and supply chain management.

Matthew Ridings

Matthew Ridings is a partner at Benesch Friedlander Coplan and Aronoff, where he focuses his practice on international compliance and internal investigations. As a Certified Compliance & Ethics Professional, Matt advises companies of all sizes on risk management, organizational ethics, and the creation and management of compliance programs. He regularly evaluates and audits compliance programs and counsels companies on risk management and the creation of a culture of compliance within the organization. Matt has spearheaded multinational internal investigations all over the world, focusing on antitrust and anticorruption issues, particularly in the oil and gas, telecom, chemical, and automotive industries.

Mickaël Roumegoux Rouvelle

Mickaël Roumegoux Rouvelle is a policy analyst at Transparency International Deutschland e.V. He works on strategic corruption, illicit financial flows, business integrity and corruption in the defence sector. He studied business administration in Nancy, Nuremberg, Münster, Bologna and Moscow.

Andrew Samuels

Andrew Samuels is a recognised expert in whistleblowing operations, governance and compliance. For well over the last decade, Andrew has been involved in helping organisations across the globe remediate and improve their governance and compliance systems, often in response to high profile breaches and government fines and interventions on both sides of the Atlantic. In this time Andrew has seen the key role that whistleblowing systems play in protecting the integrity of governance and compliance programmes and in doing so has innovated and developed systems and controls that enable organisations to operate with integrity and in a defensible fashion. Since 2017, Andrew has been a Subject Matter Expert and former Head of the U.K. delegation to ISO Technical Committee 309 for the Governance of Organisations working on standards for governance, compliance and whistleblowing amongst others. As the Founder and CEO of WislPort Compliance (www.wislportcompliance.com), Andrew has led the development of truly integrated governance and compliance solutions that utilise open-source and AI technologies that align to ISO standards. This provides organisations with simple, effective compliance. And at the heart of this best practice remains safe, impartial, and trustworthy reporting mechanisms.

Ramona Stampfli

Ramona Stampfli is a research associate at the Swiss Institute for Entrepreneurship (SIFE) at the University of Applied Sciences of the Grisons in Chur, Switzerland. She graduated with a Master's degree in business administration with a specialisation in 'New Business'. Her current research fields include foreign corruption, ethical decision-making, and compliance training.

Stanisław Strejmer

The author is an attorney-at-law, compliance officer, lecturer, trainer and public speaker with more than a decade of experience in advising organization's and educating professionals on matters related to compliance, business ethics and risk management.

Simina Suciu

Simina is an international lawyer with more than 15 years of cross knitting experience covering ethics & compliance, business ethics and governance, data privacy, as well as energy regulation, competition and international trade law, sanctions. Her diverse expertise combines private practice for more than a decade spent in Brussels, London and Bucharest, and in-house experience in Switzerland. She is currently leading the compliance activities of a large energy European infrastructure company. She is also a passionate speaker and writer on effective compliance management, EU energy regulation and antitrust law.

Prof. Ph.D. Pedro Gonçalo Tavares Trovão Do Rosário

PhD in Law (Constitutional Law – Political Law), he began teaching in higher education in September 1991, initially as a Law graduate, and since 2008 with a scientific Doctorate in Law (PhD) from UNED - Madrid. He has been a university lecturer without interruption since 1991, currently an Associate Professor, always in the area of Law. Thus, he has taught and continues to teach in Bachelor's, Master's and Doctorate courses at Portuguese, Spanish and Brazilian Universities, as well as at the Portuguese Bar Association and also in higher education institutions in postgraduate and MBA courses. He is currently Director of the Law Department of the Universidade Autónoma de Lisboa - UAL, President of ECII – Ethical & Compliance International Institute, President of the Study Group on Training and Interdisciplinary Relations (GEFRI) of the CRE of the Portuguese Bar Association. He was Vice-President of the Fundación Universitária Internacional, based in Madrid. He holds an Honorary Doctorate from ULAC – Latin American and Caribbean University, based in Caracas, Venezuela; Member of IACL/AIDC – International Association of Constitutional Law/ Association Internationale de Droit Constitutionnel; Honorary Member of the Institute of Brazilian Lawyers – IAB; International Member of the Right to Education Committee of the Rio de Janeiro State Section of the Brazilian Bar Association; Emeritus Member of the Committee for Comparative Law Studies of the Brazilian Bar Association (Rio de Janeiro - 57th subsection) and Member of the Permanent

Forum for Law in the Lusophone Region of the School of Magistracy of the State of Rio de Janeiro (EMERJ). He is a supervisor of Doctoral Theses and Master's Dissertations, having participated as a Member (President, Arguer or Member) in several Master's and Doctoral Juries in Law, in European Universities. He has several publications in the area of Law, in Portugal, Spain, Brazil and Venezuela. Researcher registered with the Foundation for Science and Technology (FCT) since 25 January 2010, having been Director of "Ratio Legis" – Centre for Research and Development in Legal Sciences at UAL until 2015. Integrated Researcher at JUSGOV/UMinho – Centre for Research in Justice and Governance (GLOB – Research Group: globalisation, democracy and power) and Researcher and Co-coordinator of the Research Group: Culture of Peace and Democracy of Ratio Legis/UAL – Centre for Research and Development in Legal Sciences. He has been a lawyer in continuous practice since 1993 (he began his internship at the Portuguese Bar Association in 1991) and currently works at "Trovão do Rosário & Associados – Sociedade de Advogados, SP, RL"

Rajeev Thykatt

Mr. Rajeev Thykatt is the Convenor of ISO/TC 306/WG6 - Governance Maturity Model and ISO/TC 292/WG8 - Supply Chain Security. He is a Risk Management professional with more than 24 years of experience in handling Standards, Contractual, Regulatory, Compliance, Business Continuity, Risk, Resilience, Supplier/Vendor/Partner Risk and Information/cyber Security issues. He started his career as a practicing Advocate at the Hon'ble High Court of Karnataka, at Bangalore, India.

Anna Tomiczek

Anna Tomiczek – lawyer, Chef Compliance Officer in one of the largest energy companies in Poland. Specializes in public economic law and compliance. Speaker at conferences, seminars and trainings in the field of energy law and compliance. She graduated in law from the University of Silesia in Katowice and The School of Chinese Law and Culture.

Nicole Vossius

Nicole Vossius is an attorney-at-law at the law firm Meister Rechtsanwälte in Munich.

Nick John Weir

Nick John Weir is the founding member of the security program at Redox, Inc., and has led the company's Compliance and Risk Management team for eight years. He's developed wide-ranging policies and processes impacting nearly all facets of business at Redox. Prior to joining Redox, Nick served as the head of integration implementation at Epic for 11 years, and as the head of partner success at BrightMD. Nick graduated with honors studying computer science and mathematics at Purdue University and carries a CISSP certification through ISC(2). Outside of work you'll find Nick backpacking in the mountains or performing contemporary circus arts in beautiful, sunny Portland, Oregon.

Patrick Wellens

Patrick Wellens brings 20+ years' experience in conducting investigations and 30+ years' experience in Governance, Risk and Compliance. He is currently working as Global Compliance business partner for a division of a multinational life science company, based in Zurich, Switzerland where he oversaw the implementation of a compliance management system. Previously he has worked as a Senior Manager Forensic services within Big4, Corporate Internal Audit Manager of a pharma company, as Regional Finance Manager and Country CFO. Patrick has managed large investigation teams in numerous countries, worked with prosecutors, numerous law firms and testified in court. Patrick is the Chief Compliance Officer of the Association of Corporate Investigators, Vice- Chair of Ethics and Compliance Switzerland and a member of the editorial board of the Society for Corporate Compliance and Ethics. He has published extensively in numerous compliance journals and contributed to ACI Corporate Investigator's Handbook. He is a Certified Fraud Examiner (CFE), Certified Internal Auditor (CIA), Certified Risk Manager Assurance (CRMA) and Certified Compliance and Ethics Professional (CCEP-I).

Gniewomir Wycichowski-Kuchta

PhD candidate in Law at the Doctoral School of Social Sciences, University of Warsaw. He teaches criminal law at the Faculty of Law and Administration of the University of Warsaw. He is also a research associate of the Institute of Legal Sciences of the Polish Academy of Sciences and a member of the European Law Institute in Vienna. He completed a legislative apprenticeship and has experience in government administration. He is the author of numerous scientific publications on compliance, criminal law and EU law.

www.ingramcontent.com/pod-product-compliance
Ingram Content Group UK Ltd.
Pitfield, Milton Keynes, MK11 3LW, UK
UKHW021830100926
8556IPUK00004B/250

9 783631 937532